'Throwing Down White Man'

'Throwing Down White Man'

Cape Rule and Misrule in Colonial Lesotho, 1871-1884

Peter Sanders

MERLIN PRESS

© Peter Sanders 2010

First published in 2010 by Morija Museum & Archives
PO Box 12, Morija 190, Lesotho

First published in the UK in 2011 by
The Merlin Press Ltd.
6 Crane Street Chambers
Crane Street
Pontypool
NP4 6ND
Wales

ISBN. 978-0-85036-654-9

British Library Cataloguing in Publication Data
is available from the British Library

All rights reserved. No part of the publication may be reproduced, stored in a retrieval system, or transmitted, in any form or by any means, electronic, mechanical, photocopying, recording or otherwise, without the prior permission of the publisher.

Printed in the UK by Imprint Digital, Exeter

CONTENTS

List of maps... iv
Note on illustrations... iv
Preface... v
Note on names, orthography and pronunciation... vii
Abbreviations... vii
Selective genealogy... viii

INTRODUCTION 1
    The Gun War 1
    Causes and consequences: the key questions... 3
    The title and the praise poems: 'Throwing down White Man' 6

PART I   MAGISTRATES AND CHIEFS 9

1 Moshoeshoe the Wise and Victoria the Good 11
    1868: the imperial annexation 11
    1871: annexation to the Cape 16

2 Moshoeshoe's chiefdom, Letsie's inheritance 18
    Basutoland 18
    Moshoeshoe's chiefdom 18
    Letsie's inheritance 20

3 The Cape government 30
    The policy 30
    The magistrates 31
    Peace and prosperity 35

4 The attack on the chiefs 39
    The land 39
    The courts 44
    Stray stock and Sesotho custom 49

5 'Success' and fear 52
    A record of 'success' 52
    The first alarms 54
    Further alarms 59

6 The Moorosi War 64
    Moorosi's chiefdom and the Quthing magistracy 64
    The first crisis 65
    The second crisis 66
    The third crisis 66
    The fourth crisis 68
    The outbreak of war 70

6	**The Moorosi War (cont.)**	73
	The first attack on Mount Moorosi	73
	The second attack	75
	Negotiations	77
	The third attack	78
7	**Conspiracy and confederation**	82
	An African conspiracy?	82
	Confederation, 'vigour' and disarmament	83
8	**Disarmament and the confiscation of Quthing**	92
	Sprigg's mission	92
	The order to disarm	94
	The confiscation of Quthing	96
	The Peace Preservation Act	97
9	**The descent to war**	104
	Divisions among the Basotho and the intimidation of the loyalists	104
	Colonial delays	107
	Letsie's initiative	111
	Sprigg's final mission	113
10	**Guns, chieftainship, land and drought**	117
	PART II THE GUN WAR	123
11	**Predictions and prophecies**	125
	Fears and expectations	125
	Organisation, resources, strategy and leadership: the Basotho	128
	Organisation, resources, strategy and leadership: the Cape	134
12	**The first phase of the war**	142
	Introduction	142
	The war in the south	142
	The war in the centre	146
	The war in the north	150
13	**The second phase of the war**	153
	The war in the south	153
	The war in the centre	165
	The war in the north	166
	Overtures for peace	174
14	**The third phase of the war**	176
	Negotiations for peace	176
	The resumption of fighting	181
	Sir Hercules Robinson's award	184

PART III THE COLLAPSE OF CAPE RULE.. 189

15 The mission of J.W. Sauer.. 191
J.W. Sauer.. 191
The talks at Morija.. 192
The fine, 'disarmament' and compensation... 193
Masupha's 'submission'... 198

16 Joseph Millerd Orpen... 200
Orpen and his magistrates... 200
Trying to get justice for the *Mateketoa*... 202
The attempt to coerce Masupha.. 209

17 From 'ultimatum' to 'expectation'.. 215
'Ultimatum'.. 215
The campaign against Orpen... 218
The policy of 'expectation'... 220

18 General Gordon... 223
Gordon's appointment... 223
Gordon's policy.. 224
Gordon goes to Basutoland... 226
Gordon's departure.. 233
The making of a myth... 235

19 Retreat and despair.. 238
Picking up the threads.. 238
Civil war in the house of Molapo: Jonathan and Joel (1)...................... 239
A further retreat.. 242
Civil war in the house of Molapo: Jonathan and Joel (2)...................... 247
Preparing for the last retreat.. 250

20 The final retreat.. 251
Merriman's mission to London... 251
Marking time in Basutoland... 252
The Basotho are called upon to decide... 254
The final decision.. 255
The end of colonial rule.. 257

21 Imperial rule and the triumph of the chiefs.................................. 258
More of the same.. 258
The submission of Masupha... 262
The consolidation of imperial rule and the paramountcy.................... 264

22 Conclusion.. 266

Sources... 272
Index.. 291

LIST OF MAPS

Basutoland, 1880 – page x
Map to illustrate the Gun War in the south – page 141
Sketch map to illustrate the Gun War in Maseru – page 147
Map to illustrate the Gun War in the north – page 151

These maps are attributed in section G of the Sources.

NOTE ON ILLUSTRATIONS

The illustrations between pages 178 and 179 are attributed in section H of the Sources.

PREFACE

This book has an unusual provenance. I wanted to write a history of the Gun War of 1880-81, a war provoked by the determination of the Cape Colony to disarm the Basotho. It was not a big war, and in the popular imagination outside Lesotho it has been eclipsed by the almost contemporaneous Zulu War. On the Cape side it was fought largely by colonial, not imperial troops, and over a period of six months' fighting fewer than 200 whites were killed.[1] The number of Basotho killed, though impossible to assess with any confidence, probably did not amount to more than 700-800. But in one all-important respect the Gun War was different, not just from the Zulu War, but from all the other wars that were fought out in southern Africa at that time: the whites were humiliatingly defeated, or at least they were decisively held at bay. For this reason alone it called out for close enquiry.

I soon came to realise, however, that the Gun War was only the most dramatic expression of Basotho resistance throughout the period of Cape rule, that is from 1871, when the Colony had taken over Basutoland (as Lesotho was then known) from the imperial government, to 1884, when, despairing of imposing its authority again, it persuaded the imperial government to resume control. Indeed the issues underlying this resistance were finally resolved only with the defeat of Masupha, the most intransigent of the Basotho chiefs, in 1898. For a proper understanding of this struggle the whole period of Cape rule had to be examined, as well as the early years of renewed imperial rule.

I knew that in 1965-66 Tony Atmore had conducted research into the period of Cape rule but for various reasons had not written it up. It would have been impossible to replicate his work. The archives of the Lesotho Government were no longer usable, having been scandalously dumped in an unoccupied house in Maseru in no order and with no organised access, and the Basotho informants whom Tony had interviewed almost forty years ago were now dead. I suggested to Tony that we should work together. He readily agreed, and brought down from his loft a large collection of meticulously kept files. These he dusted off and handed over to me, and for the official records, especially those of the Cape Archives and the Lesotho National Archives, they provided most of the evidence which I needed. After a while we agreed that I should write the book alone, though at every stage I sent Tony draft chapters and benefited from his penetrating comments and suggestions. Without him it would have been impossible for this book to have been written.

Other scholars have studied the period of Cape rule, notably Major Geoffrey Tylden, the military historian, Edna Bradlow, J.M. Mohapeloa, and above all Sandra Burman. I have not sought to challenge their findings, but rather to tell the story anew, drawing on a wider range of sources, probing more deeply into the internal dynamics of the Basotho chiefdom, and asking what are in part new questions, as set out in the Introduction below. None of these scholars, not even Tylden, examined the Gun War in any depth or described its vivid and unexpected course in any detail.

---

[1] In his 'Roll of Honour' drawn up many years later Tylden listed the names of 173 men who had been killed or had died of wounds or disease. Thirty of these were Africans: Tylden (December 1969). The official figures for the 'Colonial Forces' were 77 men killed and 141 wounded: G.5-'83, p. 42, Appendix E to Gordon's 'Report: Colonial Regular Forces', enclosed with Gordon to Colonial Secretary, 6 June 1882. According to *The Journal*, 22 June 1882, 'Monument at Mafeteng', 124 men were commemorated on a monument at Mafeteng, and of these seven were Africans.

Apart from Tony Atmore, my greatest personal debts are to David Ambrose, who, as always, responded generously to every request for information, provided much more besides, and finally read through the text with meticulous care and insight; and to Colin Murray, who also read through the text and challenged various aspects of my approach with his usual sharp analysis. My son, Richard Sanders, made helpful comments from the perspective of the more general reader. I am grateful to Andy Garnett and Sir Toby Clarke for helping me to track down a photograph of their grandfather, Sir Charles Mansfield Clarke, to Kate Wood, who checked several references for me in the Cape Archives and the South African Public Library in Cape Town, and to Craig Hincks for the very clear and helpful maps that he has produced on pages x, 141 and 151. All the staff at the public libraries which I consulted – the Public Archives at Kew, the Library of the School of Oriental and African Studies, the Army Museum, Rhodes House Library at Oxford, and the British Library and the Newspaper Library at Colindale – were unfailingly courteous and helpful, but I would like to pay special thanks to Claire-Lise Lombard of what used to be known as the Archives of the Paris Evangelical Missionary Society in Paris, but is now the Bibliothèque protestante d'histoire de la mission et de missiologie.

Finally I would have wanted to thank Anita Jackson, my constant friend and adviser, whose suggestions and support were all the more encouraging following, as they did, her initial reservations. She died in June 2006, and this book is dedicated to her memory.

NOTE ON NAMES, ORTHOGRAPHY AND PRONUNCIATION

Africans who live in Lesotho generally refer to themselves as Basotho. The singular is Mosotho. The language, culture and way of life are referred to as Sesotho. In the colonial period the usages Basuto or Basutos were common, but are here used only in direct quotation. The country was then officially known as Basutoland.

The Sesotho language has two orthographies, one used in Lesotho, the other in South Africa. I use the Lesotho orthography. It has several peculiarities. (1) A double consonant, as in *ho lla* (to cry), is a prolongation of the single consonant. The double *Mm* in the prefix of a woman's name is written *'M*, as in 'Masenate. (2) When placed before another vowel *e* is often pronounced as *y*. (3) An *l* before an *i* or a *u* is pronounced as *d*. So Lerotholi is pronounced as Lerothodi. (4) When placed before another vowel *o* is often pronounced as *w*. So Moshoeshoe is pronounced as Moshweshwe. (5) *ph* represents as aspirated p; *th* an aspirated *t*; and *tš* an aspirated *ts*.

ABBREVIATIONS

AA	Anthony Atmore
APS	Aborigines Protection Society
BR	*Basutoland Records*
CA	Cape Archives
CMR	Cape Mounted Rifles
FS	Orange Free State Archives
JME	*Journal des Missions Évangéliques*
LNA	Lesotho National Archives
PEMS	Paris Evangelical Missionary Society
PRO	Public Records Office, Kew [now National Archives]
SNA	Secretary for Native Affairs
SOAS	School of Oriental and African Studies, London

SELECTIVE GENEALOGY

The names of Paramount Chiefs are in capital letters.

Sons of Mokhachane

In his first house:
    MOSHOESHOE
    Makhabane (father of Ramanella[1], aka Lesaoana, and grandfather of Peete)
    Posholi (father of Leluma and Mapeshoane)

In his second house
    Mohale (father of Molomo)

In his third house
    Mopeli

In his fourth house
    Lelosa (Jobo)
    Tšiame (Gideon)

Sons of MOSHOESHOE

In his first house:
    LETSIE
    Molapo
    Masupha[2]
    Majara

In his third house:
    Sekhonyana (Nehemiah)

In his fourth house:
    Ntsane

In his fifth house:
    Tlali (George)

In his sixth house:
    Pii (Sofonia)
    Tsekelo

---

[1] The correct form is Ramane'ella, but the usual spelling is Ramanella.
[2] The correct form is Masopha, but the usual spelling is Masupha.

Selective Genealogy

Sons and daughter of LETSIE

In his first house:
    Senate (daughter)

In his second house:
    LEROTHOLI
    Bereng
    Theko

In his fourth house:
    Maama
    Seeiso

In his fifth house:
    Mpiti
    Nkuebe[3]

In his sixth house:
    Mojela

Sons of Molapo

In his first house:
    Josefa (father of Motšoene)
    Jonathan

In his second house:
    Joel

In other houses:
    Khethisa
    Hlasoa
    Moliboea

Sons of Masupha

    Lepoqo
    Senekane
    Thebe
    Moiketsi

Son of Majara

    Leshoboro

---

[3] The correct form is Nkoebe, but the usual spelling is Nkuebe.

Map 1: Basutoland in 1880

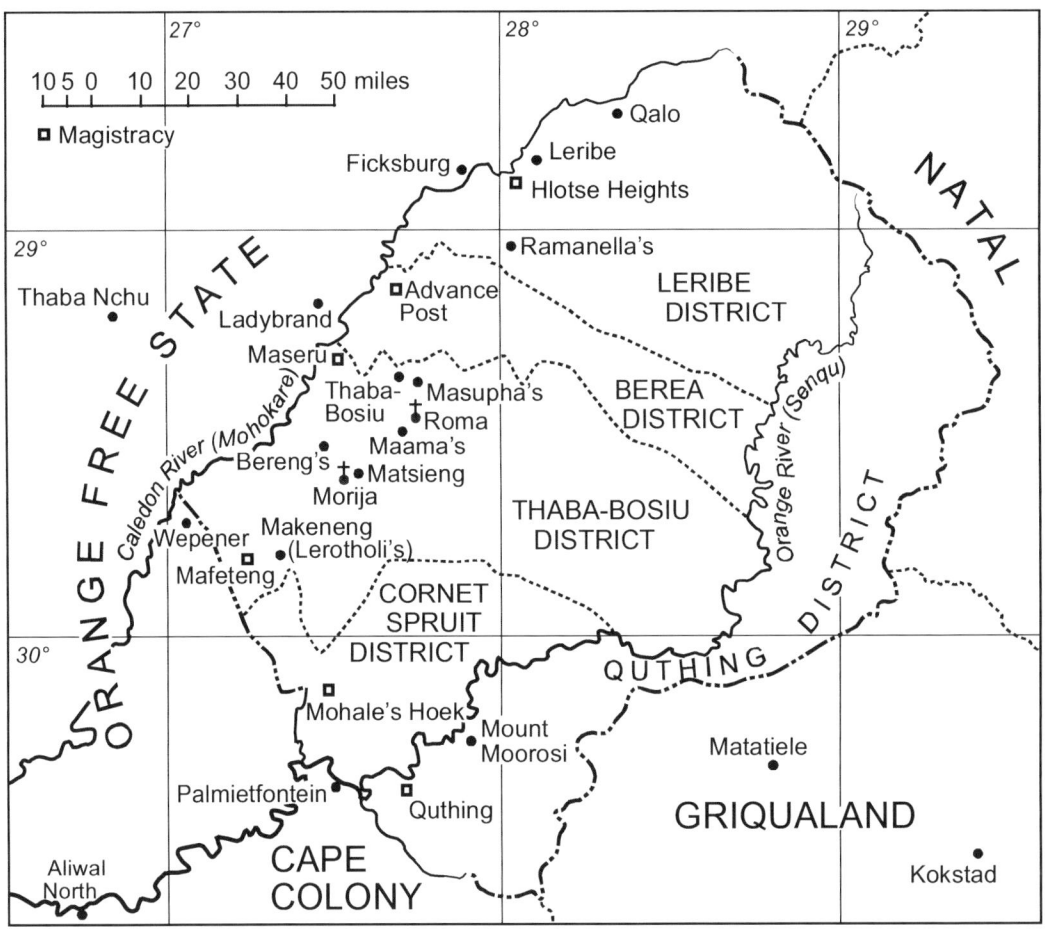

INTRODUCTION

The Gun War

> Lekena's the father of unending debts:
> He's just refused that the guns should go,
> That the guns be loaded up and taken to the Cape.
> Lekena's the father of unending debts:
> In the end they'll be paid by those who sired him,
> By his parents, the Frog and Mokhachane.
>
> Praise poems of Lerotholi.[1]

On 8 July 1880, Letsie, the ageing paramount chief of the Basotho, gave orders that nine of his guns should be loaded onto a cart and taken to Maseru, the administrative headquarters of Basutoland, there to be handed over to the Governor's Agent, Charles Griffith. He was doing this to comply with the Peace Preservation Act of 1878, which had been put into force in Basutoland by a Proclamation requiring the surrender of all arms and ammunition by 21 May, a deadline that had been extended to 12 July. In spite of all their protests and petitions, the Basotho were to be disarmed.

The cart trundled out of Letsie's village at noon under the charge of two of his councillors, Kuili and Nthoana. It had gone only a hundred metres when some of Letsie's sons jumped onto it, seized three of the guns and ran off with them. Letsie then went himself to the cart. He drove it on a few metres, but then came back to his village and brought out two more guns. The cart set off again, this time with eight guns, and with Letsie's brother, Nehemiah, now in charge as well as Kuili and Nthoana.

After the cart had gone about a thousand metres some of Letsie's sons came down from a nearby hill and followed it, and they were joined by another group of young men who came down from another hill. One of them rushed at Kuili, who was driving, and threw him to the ground. The other young men jumped onto the cart, seized the guns and carried them off.

Letsie at once sent a messenger to Maseru to tell Griffith what had happened, and to assure him that he was still determined to surrender his guns and that he still hoped to persuade his sons to do the same.[2] He did in fact send in a few, but his sons continued to defy his instructions.

Fighting in the Gun War did not break out until 13 September, two months later, when a detachment of Cape Mounted Riflemen entered Basutoland and was attacked by an armed force led by Lerotholi, Letsie's senior son. For many Basotho, however, it was the seizure of Letsie's guns that came to be seen as the immediate cause of the war. Although Lerotholi was not present, the young men who seized the guns – 'mere boys' Letsie called them – were acting under his directions and under the directions of his brother Bereng.[3]

---

[1] Damane and Sanders (1974: 149). Translation slightly altered.
[2] C.2755, pp. 50-51, Statement of 'Motemekoane Nchela', 8 July 1880.
[3] C.2755, p. 157, interview between Sprigg and Letsie, 26 August 1880, and G.26-'82, p. 26, 'Report of proceedings of Meeting ... 22 June 1881', reconvened on 23 June; C. 2755, p. 160, interview between Sprigg and George Moshoeshoe, 30 August 1880; CA, Griffith Papers, Surmon to Griffith, 11 July 1880. In Basotho tradition it is commonly held that Lerotholi seized the guns himself: AA's interviews with Mosebi Damane, 17 November 1965, and Stephen Pinda, 7 October 1965.

It was this incident that inspired the praises of Lerotholi set out at the beginning of this Introduction. He is given his praise-name of Lekena, the Enterer, the warrior who goes right in among the enemy. But the poet, while admiring Lerotholi's audacity, is worried about what might follow. Debts have been incurred, debts so great that in the end they will have to be paid by the whole of the Basotho people, personified by two of Lerotholi's ancestors, his grandfather Moshoeshoe (the Frog) and his great-grandfather Mokhachane. So the praises are ambivalent. Underlying the eulogy there is a profound anxiety, perhaps even an implied criticism.

Lerotholi's decision to resist the Cape authorities was supported and shared by most of the Basotho, especially by his junior brothers, Bereng, Maama and Seeiso, and by his powerful and formidable uncle, Masupha. But it was a decision that overturned the policy that had been laid down by Moshoeshoe, the first Paramount Chief of the Basotho, and faithfully followed by the second, Moshoeshoe's son Letsie. Confronted by the emigrant Boers, and then by the increasing power of the Orange Free State, Moshoeshoe had consistently sought British protection, and in 1868, after a devastating three-year war, when the Basotho were on the verge of extinction as a united chiefdom, they were saved by the intervention of Sir Philip Wodehouse, the British Governor and High Commissioner of the Cape. Wodehouse formally declared the Basotho to be British subjects and their territory British territory and brought them under direct imperial rule. In the Convention of Aliwal North, however, as the price that he had to pay for peace, he was forced to concede much of the Basotho's most fertile land to the Free State, the area still known as the Conquered Territory. In 1871, after Wodehouse's departure, Basutoland was transferred to the Cape Colony, and this was followed by almost a decade of undisturbed peace and increasing prosperity. The Basotho, together with the Cape Mfengu (or Fingoes), were commonly described as the most progressive and promising native race in southern Africa. If they defied the Cape all this would be jeopardised. They might well be deprived of yet more of their land, and if Cape rule were withdrawn they would be exposed once again to the threat of war with the Free State. Moshoeshoe had impressed on his people that he had found a refuge for them in the cave of Queen Victoria, where at last they would be safe from their enemies. Letsie urged them never to leave the cave that Moshoeshoe had found for them. Now Lerotholi, Masupha and their allies seemed determined to abandon it.

But they were not only destroying Moshoeshoe's carefully constructed alliance with the British against the Boers. They were also trying to reverse, or at least check, what seemed to many at the time to be the inevitable march of history. Ever since the arrival of the whites in South Africa the blacks had been driven back or brought under control on all fronts. The process had been slow and intermittent, with long periods of uneasy peace, but in almost every encounter white arms had ultimately triumphed. Towards the end of the 1870s the white advance took on a new momentum and the surviving African chiefdoms came under increasing pressure. In 1877 and 1878 the Griqua, Tswana and Khoikhoi around the Diamond Fields in Griqualand West were defeated with heavy loss of life. In the same years fighting broke out in the Transkei, and the Xhosa chiefdoms of the Gcaleka and the Ngqika were crushed by a combination of colonial and imperial troops. In 1879, in the most dramatic intervention of all, British troops invaded Zululand and, after the initial disaster of Isandhlwana, shattered Cetshwayo's Zulu army, the most powerful African military force in southern Africa. Later in the year British forces again, this time with the help of the Swazi, defeated the powerful Pedi chiefdom of Sekhukhune in the Transvaal. Also in 1879, Moorosi, one of Letsie's vassals, but acting independently of Letsie, defied his magistrate and rose in rebellion. After an eight-month siege his mountain fortress was captured by colonial troops, his people scattered, and he himself killed. In spite of the Zulu's temporary triumph at Isandhlwana, and in spite of Moorosi's dogged resistance, the whites seemed invincible and irresistible. It was madness for the Basotho to stand in their way. So Griffith told them. So their missionaries told them. Yet that was precisely what the rebels resolved to do.

The apprehensions expressed by Lerotholi's poet, however, ran deep, and the Basotho's response to the proposed disarmament was far from united. Many, but for their fear of the chiefs, would have surrendered their weapons, though with great reluctance, and when fighting actually broke out several chiefs threw in their lot with the Cape, notably Jonathan Molapo, the leading chief in the north of Basutoland, and several of Letsie's younger brothers, such as George, Sofonia and Tsekelo. Their motives varied, but one of the most powerful considerations was their assessment of who was likely to come out on top. George Moshoeshoe, who was often their leading spokesman, was surely right when he said that the Basotho in general 'had always looked upon the British Government as invincible and as far superior in strength to all the native races of South Africa combined'.[4] These people, Loyalists to the Cape administration, were contemptuously called *Maketetoa*, the Ticketees, by the rebels because they were given tickets when they handed in their guns. The rebels were known either as *Marebele* or as *Mabelete*, the Wild Ones, a word derived from the Afrikaans *wild*. It suggested a fierce and obstinate resistance that defied all rational argument. Letsie himself professed loyalty to the Cape government and took no direct part in the fighting, but he was never labelled a Ticketee and never suffered in his prestige with the Basotho because of the stand that he took, or failed to take. Among the whites he was widely suspected of playing a double game – of pretending to be loyal in his communications with the Cape authorities but secretly encouraging the rebels. It was suspected that he had sent in his guns knowing full well that they would be intercepted.[5]

But the Basotho's determination to resist, though fraught with danger, was not as irrational as it seemed at the time. They had been defeated by the Free State mainly because they had been poorly armed. In the intervening period thousands had gone to work on the newly discovered Diamond Fields in Griqualand West and on the railways being constructed in the Cape, and with their hard-earned wages they had bought and brought back a vast quantity of guns, many of them of the latest make. They also knew that, unlike the Gcaleka, the Ngqika, the Zulu and the Pedi, they would not have to face the might of the imperial army, since the imperial government had made it clear that if the Cape authorities went ahead with disarmament and provoked a rebellion they would have to deal with it on their own.

The Basotho had no great military reputation, and the Cape government was confident that it needed no help. Gordon Sprigg, the Prime Minister, and his colleagues, backed up by the Governor and High Commissioner, Sir Bartle Frere, were sure either that the Basotho would submit and give up their arms, or that if they rebelled they would be put down in a matter of months, perhaps even weeks. But most of the Basotho refused to submit, and when war came they more than held their own. After seven months of inconclusive fighting it was the Cape that had to back down and make concessions. Uniquely among the African chiefdoms at this time the Basotho were unsubdued and to that extent victorious.

Causes and consequences: the key questions

The Gun War was a conflict of compelling interest and great consequence. The Basotho, contrary to general expectation, emerged undefeated; they did this by the use of horses and guns, fighting more

---

[4] George Moshoeshoe's speech, 25 August 1881, Tylden (1950A: 176-7), from a report in the *Eastern Star*, n.d. The speech was also reported at length in *The Journal*, 9 September 1881, 'The Pitso of the Sons and Grandsons of Moshesh', which took it from *The [Kaffrarian] Watchman*.

[5] Barkly, (1893: 142); Mosebi Damane, interview with AA, 17 November 1965.

like Boer commandos than Zulu regiments; and their successful defiance was the first of many hammerblows that brought down two Cape ministries and would ultimately destroy the Cape's authority, leading to the reluctant reassertion of imperial authority in the very heart of southern Africa.

On the face of it the primary cause of the war was simple. Alarmed by the build-up of guns, the Cape wanted to disarm the Africans under its rule, and the Basotho refused to be disarmed. But disarmament must be seen in context. Since 1871 the Cape had been intent on undermining the chiefs and replacing their authority with magisterial control. Gordon Sprigg, who became Prime Minister in 1878, wanted to go further and faster, with more 'vigour' and determination than before. 'Our intention', he announced, 'is to recognise no chief whatsoever in the Colony ... Our object will therefore be to break up all the tribes ...'[6] The destruction of the old order was essential if white South Africa was to carry out its civilizing mission. Disarmament, he believed, was essential to this process. And following the overthrow of Moorosi the Cape resolved to annex his land, the district of Quthing, contrary to all the assurances the Basotho had been given by Wodehouse that their land would be preserved to them for ever. Next, they feared, would be the dismemberment of the whole of Basutoland.

So much was openly stated. But the Gun War was only one of a series of wars that flared up at this time, and we need to consider whether all these conflicts, or at least some of them, had their origins in the imperial policy of confederation, initiated by Lord Carnarvon as Secretary of State, and spearheaded in South Africa by Sir Bartle Frere with the full support of Gordon Sprigg. This policy was developed in response to the burgeoning of the South African economy following the discovery of diamonds in Griqualand West,[7] and its aim was to persuade the two British colonies and the two Boer republics to come together in a confederation so that they would be able to confront their African subjects and neighbours from a position of unity and strength and deal with them in a consistent and coherent way. Was disarmament, in Sandra Burman's phrase, 'an offshoot' of this initiative?[8]

On the Basotho side too there were broader issues. Without disarmament there would have been no rebellion. But opposition to Cape rule neither began nor ended with the Gun War. The Cape's imposition of magisterial control had won remarkable popular support, but the chiefs had resisted it from the start and in the end had acquiesced only because they could do nothing else. But the proposed disarmament had shocked the whole country, and there were many who believed that, in going to war, the *Mabelete* chiefs had seized on this popular reaction not just to resist disarmament, but to throw off the restraints of Cape rule, to unite the people once again behind them and to recover their old powers and privileges.

Sprigg was a powerful advocate of this argument. 'The outbreak has nothing to do with disarmament', he said, '... but is a struggle for independence'.[9] And when the Opposition accused him of needlessly provoking a loyal people into rebellion, he protested that it was not the Cape that had forced on hostilities, but the rebel chiefs, who had 'eaten up' those of their followers who had had the temerity to hand in their guns. For how could the Cape stand by and allow its loyal subjects to suffer merely for obeying the directives of their lawful government? The question was not whether the

---

[6] *Cape Argus*, 14 March 1878.
[7] Atmore and Marks (1974: 120-7).
[8] Burman (1981: 3).
[9] C.2755, p. 183, Sprigg to Administrator, 20 September 1880.

Basotho should be disarmed, but who ruled the country. Masupha, the most intransigent of the rebel chiefs, said much the same. He went to war, he said, 'in order to test the power of the Chiefs to punish and eat up their own people'.[10]

After the war the Basotho were allowed to retain their guns. Letsie, Lerotholi and most of the other chiefs were prepared to settle down once more under the Cape, though it seems unlikely that they would ever have submitted to the full reimposition of magisterial authority. But Masupha would not tolerate Cape oversight in any shape or form, and he enjoyed great support throughout the country. A new ministry in the Cape, under Thomas Scanlen, tried to enlist the other chiefs to coerce him into submission, but in the final confrontation they backed down. General Gordon was called in – Chinese Gordon, as he was already known – in the hope that his charismatic power would overawe Masupha, but this initiative ended in farce and failure. The government made one concession after another. The chiefs would have all their old powers, the magistrates would be withdrawn, the functions of the colonial administration would be reduced to a minimum. But Masupha would settle for nothing less than the total withdrawal of colonial authority. Defeated and humiliated, the Cape government saw only one way out, to hand Basutoland back to direct imperial rule. In March 1884, after long negotiations, the imperial government reluctantly assumed control again.

The return of imperial rule was one of the great turning points in Basotho history, and yet the continuities were just as important as the changes. For almost two years Masupha refused to recognise the authority of the imperial government, and even after he had made his formal submission he continued to be fractious and difficult to control. Finally, in 1898, he was crushed by his nephew, Lerotholi, now Paramount Chief, and it was only at this stage that the conflicts that had bedevilled Cape rule were resolved.

For the Basotho chiefs, therefore, and for their supporters, disarmament was not the only issue. The Gun War was part of a much longer resistance. Was it also part of a much wider resistance? Were the wars throughout southern Africa at this time, as many whites believed, part of some dark pan-African conspiracy to drive the whites into the sea, a conspiracy carried on through messengers travelling secretly between chiefdom and chiefdom? At the least, it was argued, one African war might have set off another. Moorosi, for example, might have been encouraged to rebel by the reports of the Zulu's victory at Isandhlwana.

For the historian C.W. de Kiewiet there was another underlying cause of all the wars at this time – competition for land exacerbated by the prevalence of drought. 'It was the want of land', he wrote, 'that Basutoland found most oppressive.' Deprived of the Conquered Territory, the Basotho were pressed up together and there was no longer sufficient land for their cattle. And then fell 'the scourge of drought, that laid the land in dust, and the plague of cattle disease that decimated the herds. The decision of the Cape Government to disarm the Basuto affected a people shaken by an economic revolution and whipped by intemperate seasons. Disarmament was a provocation; the causes of war were deeper.' So 'the hard times that helped to provoke or exasperate conflict on the Eastern Frontier, in Zululand and the Eastern Transvaal, played their part in Basutoland as well.' Elizabeth Eldredge agreed that 'the timing of overt conflicts' between white and black, among them the Gun

---

[10] LNA, S9/1/2/2, Orpen to Sauer, 13 September 1882.

War, was 'determined' by drought, but she did not go on to identify a wider South African pattern.[11]

The consequences of the Gun War and of Masupha's continued resistance were profound. The most obvious was the emergence of Basutoland as a British colony in the heart of South Africa, to be followed later by the Bechuanaland Protectorate and Swaziland, the three making up the High Commission Territories. Without this development Basutoland's history would probably have been similar to that of the Transkei. A great deal is implied in this. The chiefs, for good or ill, retained much of their old power. The Basotho kept their land intact, and they escaped the direct imposition of apartheid.

But there is one final question to be asked. In the face of constant pressure from the Union of South Africa for Basutoland and the other High Commission territories to be transferred to its control, chiefs and imperial administrators alike adduced the Basotho's unhappy experience of Cape rule as a reason for keeping the country separate. In this way the failed attempt at disarmament completely obscured the earlier successes of Griffith and his magistrates in their policy of undermining the chiefs and establishing magisterial control. More important, disarmament was represented as the natural culmination of this policy, and both were therefore discredited. In this way the imperial authorities sought to justify their policy of ruling through the chiefs, highly questionable though that policy was. So was disarmament the crowning folly of a foolish policy, or an appalling error of judgement which undid all the good work that had been done before?

The title and the praise poems: 'Throwing down White Man'

A word of explanation is needed for the title – 'Throwing down White Man'. It is inspired by the praise poems of Chief Maama Letsie, Lerotholi's younger brother:

> I struck White Man, I threw him down:
> He fell before the face of my horse,
> He fell before the face of my horse, Koloboi.[12]

White Man is a translation of *Lekhooa*, a term which had originally been free from any taint, but which had come to be used as a term of contempt. Dr. Henry Taylor, who was based in Hlotse Heights, observed that as the country moved towards war 'people passed us without saluting and with averted faces, or would greet us contemptuously with '*Dumela Lekho[o]a*' ('Good day, white man') – the equivalent of saying to a native, 'Good day, you nigger.'[13]

A further word of explanation is needed for the praise poems, the *lithoko*, which provide a poetic commentary on the war. When a Mosotho chief came home from battle he or some of his gifted followers would compose praise poems in his honour, and these poems would then be recited at public meetings and on many other occasions. In 1921 Z.D. Mangoaela published a collection of poems that he and others had recorded. In 1974 Mosebi Damane and I published an annotated translation of some of these poems, several of them relating to the Gun War.

As a source of evidence the praise poems are unique. There are many documents that are of Basotho origin or that report what the Basotho said, but in almost every case they have been

---

[11] C.W. de Kiewiet (1937: 263-5); Eldredge (1993: 80).
[12] Damane and Sanders (1974: 156).
[13] Taylor (1972: 57-8). See also *JME* 1884, p. 383, F.H. Kruger, '*Suite de la Leçon de Geographie ou quelques jours dans le bas-Lessouto*', n.d.: Kruger says that for the Basotho *Makhooa* was the equivalent of 'kaffirs' for Anglo-Saxons in the Cape or 'niggers' in the United States.

produced with white susceptibilities in mind. Letters have been written to white recipients, speeches made in their presence. Care has been taken not to give offence, and white pride has been duly deferred to. But the praise poems were composed for a Basotho audience alone, which gives them a certain authority and authenticity. In reading them the white historian enjoys the rare privilege of being a hidden observer, of listening, unseen, to the Basotho talking among themselves.

In the Basotho's historical consciousness the Gun War has taken an honoured place as part of their heroic past, alongside their struggles during the *lifaqane* in the 1820s and 1830s,[14] their victories over the Batlokoa and others during the period of the Orange River Sovereignty, the Battle of the Berea in 1852, when they resisted the British forces of High Commissioner Cathcart, and the wars against the Orange Free State in the 1850s and 1860s. The praise poems are the most powerful expression of this consciousness. They are still vividly remembered and passionately recited. People are still moved to tears when they hear them. And on the centenary of the Gun War in 1980-81 the government of Lesotho issued commemorative stamps on one of which, in the tactful obscurity of the original Sesotho, were quoted the praises of Maama Letsie that have been used for the title of this book.

---

[14] The origins, nature and scope of the *lifaqane* (*mfecane* in the Nguni form) have become the subject of fierce scholarly debate. Strictly speaking, the term refers only to the wars of wandering peoples, as distinct from wars between fighting men, but it has been commonly and conveniently used to refer also to the disturbances on the highveld which immediately followed these wars.

'Throwing Down White Man'

PART I

MAGISTRATES AND CHIEFS

'The cow of our alliance with Maseru'[1]

---

[1] Damane and Sanders (1974: 153), Lerotholi's praise poems.

CHAPTER 1: MOSHOESHOE THE WISE AND VICTORIA THE GOOD

1868: the imperial annexation

At the beginning of 1868, after almost three years of war with the Orange Free State, the Basotho were on the verge of collapse. Moshoeshoe, over 80 years of age, was still holding out on his mountain fortress of Thaba-Bosiu, the embodiment of their defiance and resistance. But their other strongholds were all lost or about to be lost. In the north Mopeli and Molapo, Moshoeshoe's brother and son, had made separate terms and been accepted as Free State subjects, Mopeli being given a location in Witzieshoek and Molapo being allowed to stay at his home in Leribe, though with much less land than before. In the south Moshoeshoe's son and heir Letsie had also entered into a separate peace, but had been left with so little land that he had no option but to take up arms again.

Denied legal access to guns and ammunition, the Basotho were unable to hold their own in the field. Lerotholi's praise poet likened the Free State commandos to a fearsome hailstorm induced by witchcraft.

> The hail sent by sorcerers from afar is strong:
> We tried, but we couldn't scare it off.
> It drummed down, it swept the soil from the fields.[1]

Many of the Basotho's herds and flocks fell into enemy hands. Vast stores of grain were carried off. Ploughs and wagons were captured or destroyed. Almost every village was burnt to the ground. Many people fled the country and went to the Cape Colony or joined Molapo and Mopeli in the north. Many of those who stayed were reduced to penury and starvation. Emaciated and dressed only in frayed and torn skins, they sought shelter in caves or in the rugged fastnesses of the Maloti. It seemed only a matter of time before Thaba-Bosiu was taken.

Yet, in spite of President Brand's pretensions, the Free State was never able to clear the territory that had been formally ceded to it, and the farmers to whom the land had been allocated were not able to take possession of their new homes. The Basotho clung on, and when they were attacked they often put up a spirited resistance. And all the time Moshoeshoe pressed on with the policy he had pursued for more than 20 years, seeking the protection of the British government. At last, in January 1868, the long-awaited letter arrived telling him that the Queen had been 'graciously pleased' to receive him and his people as 'subjects of the British Throne'.[2]

> 'I have not words enough', he wrote to High Commissioner Wodehouse, 'to tell Your Excellency how exceedingly welcome has been the good news which Your Excellency has favoured me with. The whole of my tribe, all the Chiefs of Basutoland, and myself more than any one, we are all glad. ...I am become old; therefore I am glad that my people should have been allowed to rest and to lie under the large folds of the flag of England before I am no more.'[3]

On 12 March 1868 the Basotho were formally declared to be British subjects, and two weeks later, on 26 March, Walter Currie arrived at Thaba-Bosiu as High Commissioner's Agent with a small detachment of the Frontier Armed and Mounted Police. For the time being the commandos

---

[1] Damane and Sanders (1974: 141). Translation slightly altered.
[2] *Basutoland Records* [hereafter *BR*] III.840, Wodehouse to Moshoeshoe, 13 January 1868.
[3] *BR* III.843, Moshoeshoe to Wodehouse, 26 January 1868.

maintained their positions, but from now on the war was no more than occasional raids and sorties on both sides. The threat to Thaba-Bosiu fell away. Moshoeshoe's chiefdom was safe.

After this it was an established part of the colonial narrative, the foundation story of British rule, that Queen Victoria the Good, in response to the pleas of Chief Moshoeshoe the Wise, had saved the Basotho from the Boers, and that for this act of magnanimity the Basotho should be eternally grateful, obedient and loyal.[4] Charles Griffith, the first Governor's Agent under Cape rule, hammered home this lesson at a *pitso* (meeting) in 1873:

> Remember, and let me again remind you, as I have often done before, that Government did not take this country under its wing for any gain or profit or convenience ... It did so simply to protect the Basuto people and nation from being utterly eaten up, and your country from being entirely confiscated by enemies whom you were quite powerless to resist. ... in pure compassion ... it has taken you under its protection.[5]

Although the Free State would have found it difficult to clear the ceded territory and to establish a lasting peace, there can be doubt that British intervention saved the Basotho from even greater hardships. Moshoeshoe acknowledged that his people were facing 'total ruin'.[6] 'Take the country,' he told Wodehouse, 'and do what you like with it; we are all dead.'[7] But the Queen's magnanimity was overstated. The imperial government had been reluctant to intervene. It did not want to be embroiled any further in the troublesome and costly affairs of South Africa's interior, and it allowed Wodehouse to intervene only on condition that a boundary settlement was reached with the Free State, that Basutoland was to be incorporated into Natal, and that no expenditure should fall on the British taxpayer. It was Wodehouse, the man on the spot, who pressed the case for annexation, and who, to the alarm of the government in London, declared the Basotho to be British subjects before reaching a settlement with the Free State or getting the consent of the Natal legislature to take it over. He was moved by the Basotho's sufferings and infuriated by President Brand's rejection of his earlier offer of mediation, but the factors that weighed most with him were the damage being inflicted by the war on the commercial activities of the Cape Colony and Natal, his doubts about the Free State's ability to impose a peaceful settlement on the region, and his anxieties about further disruption if the Basotho broke up completely and sought refuge among the Zulu and the Africans on the Cape's eastern frontier. He was also worried that the Free State would be encouraged by acquiring Basutoland to press on to gain an outlet to the Indian Ocean. Humanitarian considerations weighed strongly with him, but on their own they would never have prevailed.[8]

As well as exaggerating British magnanimity, the foundation story also overlooked everything that had happened before the imperial annexation. It was as if white memories went back only as far as 1868. The Basotho, by contrast, looked back with anguish to an earlier time when Moshoeshoe's

---

[4] Wodehouse, letter from Smithfield, 21 April 1868, in *The Friend*, 24 April 1868; BR IV.89, Wodehouse to the Duke of Buckingham, 2 May 1868.

[5] CA, NA 272, 'Minutes of Meeting held at Maseru on the 20th August 1873'.

[6] BR IV.219, Moshoeshoe to Wodehouse, 21 April 1868.

[7] BR VI.50, evidence of J.H. Bowker to the Select Committee on Basutoland Annexation Bill 7 July 1871. See also CA, NA 272, 'Minutes of Meeting held at Maseru on the 20th August 1873', speeches of Tsekelo and Nathanael Makotoko.

[8] Benyon (1975: 89-97). See also Sanders (1975: 293, 317-8); Thompson (1975: 296-302); Lelimo (1998: 200-202); Campbell (1959: 70-76).

country had been much more extensive, and when much of it had been lost through disputes and conflicts with the Boers and through British mediations and interventions for which they had no reason to feel grateful at all.

The foundation story also ignored why it was that the Basotho regiments were no match for the Free State commandos in the open field. Under the Sand River Convention of 1852 and the Bloemfontein Convention of 1854 the British government was bound to prohibit trade in arms and ammunition with Africans north and south of the Vaal and at the same time to allow such trade with the newly created Orange Free State. By 1865, when the final war broke out, the Free State commandos were better armed and supplied with ammunition than the Basotho regiments, and it was the British regulation of the arms trade that was mainly responsible for this. 'If Mr. Brand says that my people have not been able to cope with his burghers in the field', Moshoeshoe pointed out, 'no wonder, since they have the best rifles, the best powder, and cannons'.[9] Moshoeshoe's own home on Thaba-Bosiu had been struck five times by the Free State artillery, and the war became known as the *Ntoa ea Seqiti*, the Seqiti or Cannon-boom War.

In welcoming Wodehouse's intervention Moshoeshoe had expected to recover most if not all of the territory which the Basotho had held before the war. Wodehouse in fact assured him as much. But President Brand was outraged by the British annexation. After a long and costly struggle the prize was about to fall into his hands. He was determined that it should not be snatched away. Wodehouse knew that it was out of the question to embark on war with the Free State. When at last Brand agreed to enter into negotiations Wodehouse was forced to make major concessions. In 1869, in the Convention of Aliwal North, all of the Basotho's territory north and west of the Caledon river was given up. Moshoeshoe was shocked and distressed. 'I have been covered with shame,' he wrote '– and I feel great grief ... affairs have been settled in quite a different way to what we had been led to expect.'[10]

In response to the resultant protests to London Wodehouse called into play the card that was to be used repeatedly in imperial and colonial dealings with the Basotho – the threat of abandonment. Moshoeshoe was cowed into disowning the protesters, at least ostensibly, but even so it was only in 1870, after a year's delay, that the Convention was finally ratified.

The other main question to be settled was whether Basutoland was to be incorporated into Natal or the Cape or placed under the direct rule of the High Commissioner. Because Wodehouse had been obliged to reject Moshoeshoe's earlier requests for protection, the old chief had made an approach to Natal, which was why the home government had made its agreement to annexation subject to incorporation into that colony. In his determination to achieve annexation Wodehouse made use of Moshoeshoe's approach to Natal, but he was also determined that in the eventual outcome Basutoland should not be annexed to that colony. Natal's 'native policy' was to rule through the chiefs, and the overriding aim was to keep law and order. The Cape's policy was gradually to supplant the chiefs with magistrates, and the aim was to 'civilize' the Africans – to turn them from 'barbarian' enemies into fellow citizens with common interests. Wodehouse was an ardent supporter of the Cape's policy of magisterial rule: Natal's perpetuation of 'tribalism' was anathema to him.

---

[9] *BR* IV.6, Moshoeshoe to Burnet, 19 March 1868.
[10] *BR* V.77, Moshoeshoe to Buchanan, 16 March 1869.

On one issue at least Moshoeshoe might have been expected to favour Natal over the Cape. In his appeal for British protection in 1862 he had declared that if the government sent magistrates the Basotho would not understand. It would be 'like a stone which is too heavy for them to carry'.[11] Later, when it was clear that magistrates would be sent, he was anxious to keep their number to a minimum.[12] In secret dealings with the old chief, however, Wodehouse urged him to resist annexation to Natal and to ask instead for annexation to the Cape, and Moshoeshoe, according to his missionary adviser, Adolphe Mabille, was 'only too pleased to do so'.[13] The reasons which he professed mirrored Wodehouse's own: that the Basotho had little to do with Natal, from which they were largely cut off by the mountains, whereas they were familiar with the Cape, where many of them had gone to work and with which they had close trading relations; that all Moshoeshoe's political dealings had been with the successive High Commissioners at the Cape and not with the Lieutenant-Governors of Natal; and that he wanted his people to 'advance in civilisation, under the fostering care of the Queen'. But he then went further, perhaps once again at Wodehouse's prompting. Ideally, he wrote, he wanted the Basotho 'to depend from the High Commissioner alone', and he explained that the Cape Parliament, 'being partly, perhaps mostly, composed of Boers', might sometimes act contrary to the Basotho's interests.[14]

It is difficult to judge how far these sentiments were Moshoeshoe's own or were put into his mouth by Wodehouse's agents. He was not always consistent. He responded in different ways to different pressures, and so did the other Basotho chiefs. But his preference for direct rule by the High Commissioner was unwavering and well grounded. Many colonists had volunteered to help the Free State in the Seqiti War, and the Cape might well, at some later date, want to get hold of his land. The High Commissioner, the Queen's personal representative, was more likely to protect the Basotho's interests.

As for the preference for the Cape over Natal, the reasons put forward by Moshoeshoe were valid considerations, but there was apparently another factor which weighed heavily with him. Unlike the Cape, Natal did not allow Africans to own guns. Eleven years later, when threatened with disarmament, the Basotho chiefs and their councillors repeatedly adduced this as the main reason for Moshoeshoe's rejection of Natal.[15]

There is no mention of this factor in the contemporary documents, which is not surprising, since neither Wodehouse nor the chiefs would have wanted to give it any prominence. Looking back, G.St.V. Cripps, one of the officials who went up to Basutoland with Wodehouse in April 1868, was 'convinced that at that time there was no such ground of objection on the part of the Basutos'. He believed that the argument was introduced at a later stage in order to put pressure on the Cape – 'an ingenious reason', as he described it, 'fabricated to suit the occasion'.[16]

---

[11] *BR* III.143, 'Minutes of Conferences held at Thaba Bosigo, from the 11th February, 1862, to the 21st ....'
[12] *BR* IV.77, Moshoeshoe to Buchanan, 16 March 1869.
[13] Rhodes House Library, Oxford, Anti-Slavery Papers, MSS Brit. Emp. S.18, C140/212, Mabille to Chesson, 11 August 1880.
[14] *BR* IV.78-9, Moshoeshoe to Wodehouse, 21 April 1868. The best account of Wodehouse's intrigues is in Benyon (1980: 93-100).
[15] G.33-'79, pp. 32, 34, report of *pitso*, 24 October 1878, speeches of Ntho and George Moshoeshoe; C.2482, pp. 495, 503, 'Official Report of ... Pitso ... held at Maseru, on ...the 16th and 17th October 1879', speeches of 'Mathlelebe' and Sofonia; FS, G.S. 1172, Masupha to Brand, 23 November 1880; G.26-'82, p. 11, 'Report of proceedings of Meeting in school-room of the Morija Mission Station on the 22nd June, 1881'.
[16] Cripps (1882: 687).

As early as 1873, however, Tšita Mofoka, one of the speakers at the national *pitso* that year, declared that the Basotho had chosen the Cape because they had heard that the Cape, unlike Natal, allowed its African subjects to possess arms.[17] And in June 1880 Thomas Fuller, speaking in the House of Assembly, read out a letter from Richard Southey, Wodehouse's Colonial Secretary at the time, to the effect that he was 'quite certain that Moshesh objected to be annexed to Natal because of their gun laws'. He had evidently been present at the large *pitso* at Korokoro when Wodehouse had come up to take over the country, and he could state perfectly well from his own recollection that this point was held out to the Basotho in making their choice and 'that they were told they would not be deprived of their arms'. He had also been told that Wodehouse wrote to the Wesleyan missionary, John Daniel, that Moshoeshoe wanted the Cape 'because Natal takes arms away from natives'.[18] In December 1880 the Paris Evangelical Society asserted that when Wodehouse gave the Basotho their option they chose the Cape Colony over Natal, 'giving as their motive that, by the laws of that Colony they would be able to keep their arms. This was distinctly expressed by them when the annexation took place. No written document of this transaction between Moshesh and the High Commissioner was preserved, but there are many witnesses to this fact.'[19]

From all this it seems most likely that arms control was one of the considerations put forward by Wodehouse and his advisers to induce the Basotho to opt against Natal, but that at the time it was merely one factor among others and that it was given more prominence only when the Basotho were threatened with disarmament.

According to the missionaries, Wodehouse also assured the chiefs 'that the land would be kept for the Basutos, their children and children's children, and no white man, not even a magistrate, would be allowed to possess any portion of it'.[20] Again there was no written record of this, but Griffith later freely acknowledged that the Government was 'keeping the country for the Basutos to whom it rightfully belongs. That is what Moshesh wanted and that is what the Government is now doing.'[21] When the matter was called into dispute Wodehouse himself assured the imperial government that 'Basutoland for the Basutos' was 'the very thing to the attainment of which all my efforts were directed.'[22]

In the end the imperial government accepted Wodehouse's advice that the Basotho should be placed under the control of the High Commissioner, but only as a temporary measure. It was still driven by the need for economy, and it was determined that the Cape Colony should be given responsible government and take on the burdens of 'native' and frontier policies. In the long run it was resolved to withdraw imperial troops from South Africa except those that were needed for the defence of its vital shipping routes. It failed to recognise, or refused to acknowledge, that in handing over the Basotho to the Cape it was 'negating its own powers of trusteeship'.[23]

---

[17] CA, NA 272, 'Minutes of Meeting held at Maseru on the 20th August 1873'.
[18] C. 2755, p. 353, Fuller's speech to House of Assembly, 1 June 1880.
[19] C. 2821, p. 71, Paris Evangelical Society to Colonial Office, 9 December 1880. See also Rhodes House Library, Oxford, Anti-Slavery Papers, MSS Brit. Emp. S.18, C140/212, Mabille to Chesson, 21 August 1880, and C. 2821, p. 82, Mabille to the Earl of Kimberley, 27 December 1880.
[20] C. 2821, p. 71, Paris Evangelical Society to Colonial Office, 9 December 1880.
[21] CA, NA 272, 'Minutes of Meeting held at Maseru on the 20th August 1873'.
[22] PRO, CO 48/494, memorandum by Wodehouse, c. 15 March 1880. See also Smith (1939: 201).
[23] Schreuder (2009:24).

1871: annexation to the Cape

The Cape was not keen to take on more Africans, but it was won over by the prospect of a wider market for its goods and a more assured source of grain and labour for its slowly expanding economy.[24] Under pressure from Wodehouse's successor, Sir Henry Barkly, the Cape Parliament passed the Basutoland Annexation Bill in August 1871, and this was confirmed by an Order-in-Council in November that year. Basutoland was to be treated as a special case. Unlike the Cape's other African territories, it was not to be subject to colonial law but would continue to be ruled by Barkly as Governor and High Commissioner. He was empowered to pass regulations, which had to be laid before the Cape Parliament but would remain in force unless they were altered, and no Act of the Cape Parliament applied to Basutoland unless this was expressly stated in the Act itself or unless it was extended by a Proclamation by the Governor.

In the following year, 1872, the Cape was given responsible government, and as part of its new arrangements it established a Department of Native Affairs headed by a Secretary for Native Affairs. From this time onwards Barkly would act only on the advice of the Cape Ministers.

The overall effect of annexation and responsible government was that Barkly now administered Basutoland not in his capacity as High Commissioner (with imperial responsibilities for affairs beyond the Cape frontier), but in his capacity as Governor of the Cape; that his Agent in Basutoland was now the Governor's Agent and not the High Commissioner's Agent; and that control had passed to the Ministers of the Cape government who were ultimately responsible to the Cape Parliament.[25]

There had been no lack of warnings about the dangers of this transfer of power. Wodehouse had advised strongly against it because of the potential clash of interests between the Basotho and the colonists.[26] Barkly's own Attorney-General had pointed out that the Basotho had asked to be brought under the Queen's government, not under a colonial ministry, and that the change 'would excite great dissatisfaction ... and would not improbably be the cause of future native wars'. Other members of Barkly's Executive Council pointed out the injustice of imposing the change on the Basotho and the danger of subjecting policy to 'incessant fluctuations' depending on parliamentary majorities.[27]

Barkly's new Agent, however, Charles Griffith, who arrived in the territory in August 1871, was instructed to tell the Basotho that annexation to the Cape made no difference to their position, and that his relations with the Basotho would continue on exactly the same footing as those of the High Commissioner's Agents before him. As for the change to responsible government, when he was asked by Tsekelo Moshoeshoe in 1874 whether the Basotho were still under the Queen or were now under the Cape, he replied: 'you are still under the Queen. There is no change in your Government since Responsible Government was established in the Colony'.[28]

For the present the Basotho noticed no change. The shift in title from the High Commissioner's Agent to the Governor's Agent made no impression on them: they were still governed by Sir Henry

---

[24] BR VI.37-73, Report of the Select Committee appointed by the Legislative Council to consider the provisions of the Basutoland Annexation Bill, July 1871; BR VI.75-82 and 82-6, debates on the report in the Legislative Council and the House of Assembly, August 1871. See also Benyon (1980: 118-20).

[25] Benyon (1980: 118-20, 128-9); Burman (1981: 47-9). For a later explanation of these arrangements, see C.2755, pp. 70-3, Bright to Griffith, 26 February 1880.

[26] PRO, CO 48/449, Wodehouse to Granville, 17 January 1870.

[27] PRO, CO 48/455, undated minute by Attorney-General, and undated minute by Colonial Secretary, Treasurer-General, Auditor General and Collector of Customs.

[28] G.21-'75, p. 24, 'Minutes of the Annual Public Meeting held at Maseru on 2nd October, 1874'.

Barkly's Agent. The fact that Barkly, as Governor of the Cape, was now bound to act on the advice of his Ministers was not disclosed to them.

They were misled, however, not just by Griffith's assurances that nothing had changed. The colonial authorities encouraged them to think in very personal terms of the Queen as the source of all power and authority and of the Governor and High Commissioner as her eye and ear in South Africa. It was all part of a highly conscious policy of building up the monarchical mystique. Through Sir Philip Wodehouse, Queen Victoria's personal representative, the Basotho had placed themselves under the Queen herself. The Queen, they were told, though far away, took a deep personal interest in them as her subjects. She rejoiced in their loyalty, and she wanted them to enjoy the blessings of peace and to advance in civilisation.[29]

This expression of political relationships in highly personal terms was readily understood and accepted by the Basotho. It was consistent with their own highly personalised chieftainship. It was only in 1880, when they were confronted by the prospect of disarmament and wanted to appeal to the Governor and the Queen, that they were told at last that it was all a myth: the Governor was no longer in command and he and the Queen were powerless to help them.

---

[29] E.g., Griffith's speeches at the annual *pitsos* in 1874 (*The Little Light of Basutoland*, November 1874) and 1876 (G.12-'77, p. 12, 'Notes of the Annual Meeting ("Pitso") held at Maseru on the 12th October, 1876'). At the *pitso* held on 16 October 1879 the Cape Premier, Gordon Sprigg, was introduced 'as the ears and the mouth-piece of the Queen': G.13-'80, p. 38. For a more general discussion of this subject, see Ranger (1983: 211-62, especially 231-2).

CHAPTER 2. MOSHOESHOE'S CHIEFDOM, LETSIE'S INHERITANCE

Basutoland

The much reduced territory of Basutoland, as defined in the Convention of Aliwal North, was about the size of Wales, but more than three quarters of it was covered by the Maloti, the great basalt mountains that rose to more than 3,000 metres in parts. Even the so-called lowlands all stood above 1,350 metres and were dominated by sandstone hills and plateaux. The valleys were still among the most fertile parts of South Africa, yielding abundant crops of millet, maize and wheat, which was why they had been coveted so eagerly by the Free State. But already the land was being scarred by sheet erosion and scored by dongas, a process that was hastened not just by the increasing pressure of population but also by the breaking up of new ploughed land, at the expense of pasture, stimulated by the demand for grain from the Diamond Fields. Up to this time the Maloti had been used solely for grazing in the summer months and for the occasional hunt, but towards the end of the 1870s people began to establish their villages there, a movement which gathered momentum during the Gun War, when thousands took refuge there during the summer of 1880/81 and did not all return to the lowlands. By the early 1880s there were literally hundreds of such villages. The growing season in the Maloti was too short for millet and maize, but summer wheat could be grown with some success.

Moshoeshoe's chiefdom

Moshoeshoe had been deeply embittered by the loss of so much of his territory. But he had other worries about his political legacy. On 18 January 1870, just two months before his death, aged about 84 and utterly worn out by the cares of his chieftainship, he formally surrendered his paramountcy to his eldest and senior son, Letsie. He urged his other sons to be loyal to their new chief, and at the same time, looking ahead to the next generation, he announced an extraordinary and unprecedented arrangement for the succession to Letsie. Letsie had no sons by his senior wife, 'Masenate, and in the normal course of events the next paramount would have been his eldest son in his second house, Lerotholi. Instead Moshoeshoe announced that it would be Motšoene, the son of Letsie's daughter Senate by Molapo's son Josefa. For this purpose Senate was to be regarded as a man and Josefa as her wife, and Motšoene was to be regarded as 'Masenate's son, so taking precedence over Lerotholi.[1]

This arrangement was flatly contrary to Sesotho custom and was never widely accepted among the Basotho, especially as Lerotholi was very popular while Josefa became subject to fits of madness and Motšoene himself was unstable.[2] It was designed to reconcile Molapo to Letsie's paramountcy, and it reveals the depth of Moshoeshoe's anxiety that after his death the chiefdom would fall apart, and in particular that Molapo would break away from Letsie. On his death-bed he was urging his children 'at all costs' to 'strive and pull together'.[3]

Basotho chieftainship tended to fragmentation. Before Moshoeshoe there had been no great chief, only a host of little chiefs, each with his own village or cluster of villages.[4] Ambitious chiefs

---

[1] C.3717, pp. 154-5, Orpen to Sauer, 12 January 1883, annual report for 1882; LNA, S3/5/13/9, Jonathan Molapo to Buxton, January 1916; Sanders (1975: 207, 310); Thompson (1975: 316); Machobane (2000).
[2] LNA, L2/1/4, Bailie to Acting Governor's Agent, 20 February 1884; Machobane (2000); AA's interview with Motsarapane J. Molapo, May 1966.
[3] LNA, S3/5/13/9, Jonathan Molapo to Buxton, January 1916.
[4] The only exception, it seems, was Mohlomi, chief of the Bamonaheng, but his chiefdom never reached the later size of Moshoeshoe's and it did not survive his death c.1816.

tried to keep their younger brothers and sons under their control, while ambitious younger brothers and sons tried to break away to establish independent chiefdoms of their own. Conditions favoured the junior relatives. Because of the steady growth of population, the availability of land and the sparseness of the grazing, new villages and new chiefdoms were constantly being established and spawning yet more villages and chiefdoms.

Moshoeshoe had been able to build up a large following because of the pressures of the *lifaqane*, the dozen or so years of turmoil, conflict and widespread starvation that followed the invasion of the highveld by people fleeing from the wars below the Drakensberg in 1822. He retreated to the mountain fortress of Thaba-Bosiu, where he was able to maintain and even increase his herds. Other chiefs joined him, giving up their independence in order to escape destitution or destruction. By the end of the *lifaqane* his following numbered about 25,000. Once survival was assured the old centrifugal tendencies threatened to reassert themselves, but then came the emigrant Boers who occupied much of the surrounding land and steadily encroached on Moshoeshoe's territory. Paradoxically, the very forces that threatened the existence of Moshoeshoe's chiefdom at the same time hemmed it in and made it more cohesive.[5] By the time of the last war with the Free State his followers numbered at least 150,000.

Moshoeshoe did not make any radical institutional changes in order to hold his people together. In the main his chiefdom was the old pre-*lifaqane* chiefdom writ large. By loaning out his cattle under the *mafisa* system, whereby he retained ownership while they enjoyed the use of them, he was able to bind many of his impoverished subjects to him by ties of economic dependence. He also used polygamy and intermarriage on an unprecedented scale in order to build up a network of kinship connections between the various branches of his family and with his many subordinate chiefs. He himself had more than 150 wives, and the three surviving sons of his senior house, Letsie, Molapo and Masupha, about 50 each. (Majara, the fourth son, died young.) The scope for dynastic alliances was wide. The 'marriage' between Senate and Josefa was only one such union. Among others Lerotholi, the eldest son in Letsie's second house, married a daughter of Molapo; Jonathan, the second son in Molapo's first house, married a daughter of Masupha and also a daughter of Ramanella, the son of Moshoeshoe's brother Makhabane; Joel, the first son in Molapo's second house, married a daughter of Letsie.

To control the many chiefs who had come under his rule Moshoeshoe first placed his brothers over them and then the sons of his senior house. These close relatives were the rope, it was said, by which he held them in check.[6] Some chiefs complained about this loss of power, and his brothers were aggrieved when they in turn came under the domination of his sons.[7] Moshoeshoe's missionary, Eugène Casalis, noted that difficulties were 'constantly arising', and the chiefdom was 'only held together by means of a system of concessions and acts of rigour, skilfully combined ....'[8]

So long as Moshoeshoe was alive he was the focus of his followers' loyalty. In a very real sense the Basotho were his people. Their identity as a chiefdom was defined, not by their being Basotho, but by their recognition of him as their chief. He alone among all the Sesotho-speaking chiefs had become known as the *Morena oa Basotho*, the Chief of the Basotho, but there were many Sesotho-speakers who did not come under his rule and there were many among his followers who were not

---

[5] Sanders (1975: 71-2).
[6] Sekese, '*Taba tse ling tsa khale*', *Leselinyana*, 21 July 1914.
[7] Sanders (1975: 206).
[8] Casalis (1861: 212).

Sesotho-speakers. As the man who had ridden out the storms of the *lifaqane*, who had welcomed refugees and sustained them with his cattle, who had resisted the commandos of the Orange Free State and had at last brought his people under Queen Victoria, his reputation for wisdom and statesmanship was unparalleled among the chiefs of southern Africa.

Letsie's inheritance

As Moshoeshoe grew old his authority weakened, and with his death in 1870 the last vestiges of his unifying influence were removed. Letsie was the undisputed successor but his control over his brothers, especially Molapo and Masupha, was tenuous at best. They consulted together on matters affecting the Basotho as a whole, such as how they should respond to the policies and initiatives of the colonial authorities. But if his brothers disagreed with him Letsie could not, or would not, command obedience. With his base at Matsieng he ruled directly over the southern part of the country, but in the north and in the centre Molapo and Masupha, in the tradition of countless junior sons in the days before the *lifaqane*, conducted themselves as if they were independent. Moshoeshoe had placed his sons over his brothers. Letsie could never place his sons over Molapo and Masupha, or even give them land in his brothers' wards.

The colonial government undermined Letsie's authority still further by dividing the country into districts. Wodehouse had initially established three, and Barkly increased them to four – Leribe, Berea, Thaba-Bosiu and Cornet Spruit. Legally they defined the magistrates' areas of jurisdiction, but Barkly believed that the first three could also be 'described as comprising exactly the patrimonial estates of the great sons of Moshesh, Molapo, Masupha and Letsie', while the fourth was inhabited by several 'minor Chieftains', including Moletsane of the Bataung and Moorosi of the Baphuthi, 'who owed Moshesh scarcely more than nominal allegiance'.[9] The colonial authorities soon discovered that the boundaries of the magistrates' districts differed significantly from those of the chiefs' wards and had to assure the chiefs that they were not intended to define their areas of authority. But the effect of establishing districts based, however roughly, on the chiefs' wards was to encourage Molapo and Masupha in their pretensions to independence. Leribe and Berea came to be regarded as 'their' districts, especially as they were rewarded with 10% of the hut tax collected there.[10] Letsie protested against this from the beginning, and after the Gun War, when challenged to say if he was paramount chief and whether Masupha was subordinate to him, he replied that trouble had come

> because the country was divided by the Government, so that it was said that Letsie was chief in this part of the country, and that Masupha and Molapo were chiefs in their own districts; and the proof that it was so is the percentage which was paid to them. ... therefore I was told I had nothing to do in the other districts.[11]

The Basotho were now held together, not so much by their allegiance to Letsie, as by their subjection to the colonial state within clearly defined boundaries.

---

[9] BR VI.106, Barkly to Secretary of State, 30 August 1871. It was later recognised that Letsie exercised authority, 'more or less complete', over both the Thaba-Bosiu and the Cornet Spruit districts: LNA, S9/2/1/1, Griffith to Colonial Secretary, 11 March 1873.

[10] As well as his percentage for the Thaba-Bosiu district, Letsie was paid a fixed sum for the Cornet Spruit district and nominal amounts in respect of Leribe and Berea: LNA, S2/1/1, Griffith to Colonial Secretary, 11 March and 16 April 1873.

[11] C.3708, p. 89, report of meeting held at Morija on 26 March 1883. See also LNA, S9/1/2/2, Orpen to Sauer, 16 January 1881; C.3708, p. 95, report of meeting held at Morija on 27 March 1883.

Letsie was about 59 when he succeeded to the paramountcy, and about 69 at the beginning of the Gun War. He had been blinded in one eye in his youth and wounded in the right hand by an exploding gun. Though tall and strongly built in his prime, he became 'very stout and unwieldy' with age and was badly afflicted with gout.[12] Because of his poor health he was often unable to go to meetings, and by the time of the Gun War he rarely left his village.[13]

He suffered in constant comparison with Moshoeshoe. He had no great reputation as a warrior,[14] and on occasion could be cruel and oppressive to his followers. Adèle Mabille, his missionary's wife, described him as lacking his father's 'distinction',[15] and he himself declared that, although he was Moshoeshoe's 'son and successor', he was 'ignorant' and did not have his wisdom.[16] Colonial officials complained repeatedly of his weakness, vacillation and duplicity.[17]

But Letsie was more able than the comparisons with his father suggest, and his protestations of ignorance were not to be taken at their face value. Moshoeshoe had the great advantage of being in effect the founder of the Basotho chiefdom. 'Moshoeshoe ruled alone ...', Letsie said, 'But now division is made.'[18] Looking back, however, both black and white tended to idealise Moshoeshoe's rule, ascribing to him a firmness of purpose and control that were not generally observed and commented on at the time. In fact the weaknesses for which Letsie was criticised were the same as those for which Moshoeshoe had been criticised, and they are indicative more of the conflicting pressures on the paramount than of the personality of any particular individual.

Letsie resented the seepage of power from the chiefs to the magistrates. Like his father, he would have preferred protection to control.[19] At times he worked surreptitiously to thwart the government. Faced with unwelcome demands, he promised one thing but did another. But he believed that outright defiance would be dangerous. He was timid and cautious, and the Governor's Agent, Charles Griffith, described him as 'a weak-minded, ignorant man, easily led by others'.[20] At times, bewildered by new pressures and demands, he became pathetically dependent on Griffith himself. But his influence was considerable, especially before the Gun War, and especially in his own ward,[21] and that influence was exercised in the interests of peace. In 1878 Emile Rolland, a missionary turned government official, described him as 'timorous', 'indolent', 'mild', and 'suspicious', but he was also 'peaceably inclined'.[22]

As a young man he had opposed Moshoeshoe's policy of seeking an alliance with the British, but by the end of the Seqiti War he was persuaded that his father was right. For all his weakness and vacillation, he never wavered in his conviction that it was essential for the Basotho to remain on good

---

[12] CA, NA 275, Rolland to SNA, 19 July 1878.
[13] C.2755, p. 94, H.L. Davies to Griffith, 23 April 1880.
[14] Damane and Sanders (1974: 107).
[15] Smith (1939: 186).
[16] *BR* VI.11, Minutes of Meeting between Barkly and Letsie, 16 March 1871. See also *The Journal*, 12 December 1883, 'Basutoland': Letsie described himself as 'a coward', 'stupid' and 'deformed'.
[17] See, e.g., LNA, S9/1/1/2, Griffith to Colonial Secretary, 29 August 1872, and LNA, MF2/1/1, Rolland to Griffith, 30 December 1872.
[18] *Leselinyana*, November 1874: speech at *pitso*, 2 October 1874.
[19] C.3708, p. 50, report of meeting at Maseru, 19 March 1883, evidence of Sofonia Moshoeshoe.
[20] G.27-'73, p. 2, Griffith to Colonial Secretary, 15 March 1873.
[21] C. 3708, p. 56, report of meeting held at Maseru on 20 March 1883, evidence of Tlali (George) Moshoeshoe; CA, NA 276, Arthur Barkly to Griffith, 15 February 1879.
[22] CA, NA 275, Rolland to SNA, 19 July 1878.

terms with the colonial authorities. 'He is a great gross animal', Wodehouse wrote in 1868, 'but he has sense and determination and influence, and is I think thoroughly disposed to stick to us.'[23] Looking back after the Gun War, Masupha declared that Letsie was always 'loyal'.[24] His leading advisers were also 'loyal' – Ntho Mokeke, Setha Matete and Ramabilikoe Matete. Ntho and his like were reviled in Lerotholi's praise poems as 'those who flatter for sugar among the Whites'.[25]

Letsie was unresponsive to his missionaries' teaching, and we have a description of him in his old age, while Adolphe Mabille was passionately appealing to his listeners to repent and to turn to God, sitting quietly and counting out on his fingers how many cattle he was going to give to one of his chiefly allies.[26] Mabille believed that he was not blind to the truths of Christianity, but that he was tied to his old beliefs by his polygamy and other 'pagan' practices.[27] He would not have a school in his village, and his adoption of European ways was half-hearted. An official visitor in 1874 found him 'dressed in a suit of corduroy' and was received in 'a square-built stone cottage resembling the meanest of the Boers' farmhouses'. In the yard was a wagon which must have cost at least £150, but which was 'utterly neglected, and from exposure and want of care was being allowed rapidly to fall to pieces ....'[28] He was pictured at a *pitso* in 1879 riding in at the head of ten thousand armed men holding his stirrups with his big toes and using rope for a bridle.[29] He was pleased, however, to send several of his sons to the Cape to be educated, and he relied heavily on his educated brothers, as well as on Mabille, for help and advice.

Molapo, the second son in Moshoeshoe's senior house, was widely regarded as more able and ambitious than Letsie, and the rivalry between them was notorious. As a young man he had distinguished himself as a warrior and won popularity by generously distributing the stock which he captured. He had then been converted to Christianity, and had been one of the first Basotho in the country to learn how to read. Later, however, he turned against the missionaries and became one of their fiercest opponents.[30] François Coillard, his missionary, denounced him as a servant of Satan.[31]

In the 1850s he had established his village at Leribe, in the north of the country. Because he made an early peace in the Seqiti War, accepting Free State rule, he was able to retain much of his stock and to cultivate his crops undisturbed. The Convention of Aliwal North, however, hit him hard, taking away all his land north of the Caledon, and he was heavily involved in the protest against the Convention and in the negotiations with Natal. He was anxious to rid himself of Free State control, and probably the outcome he most wanted was for himself to come under Natal while the rest of the country came under the Cape. In this way he would have been completely independent of Letsie.[32] Wodehouse, however, was determined that he and his followers should rejoin the rest of the Basotho, and the formal arrangements for this were at last completed in April 1870.

Although he was criticised for his defection during the war, it does not seem to have weakened

---

[23] BR IV.335, Wodehouse to Bowker, 16 June 1868.
[24] G.26-'82, p. 21: report of meeting held at Morija on 23 June 1881.
[25] Damane and Sanders (1974: 153).
[26] PEMS Archives, Morija, anonymous note dated 15 November 1885.
[27] PEMS Archives, Paris, Mabille to Casalis, 16 January 1880.
[28] Cunynghame (1879: 91).
[29] Kilpin (1912: 243).
[30] Sanders (1975: 117-8).
[31] Favre (1946: 121).
[32] BR IV.121-2: Bowker to Wodehouse, 2 June 1868; BR VI.27-8, Barkly to Secretary of State for the Colonies, 23 May 1871.

his position. A white observer at the *pitso* with Wodehouse in 1868 noted that 'Molapo in general bearing and manner appeared to great advantage among the other Chiefs, and his word appeared to be law'.[33] In 1872 Griffith described him as having 'the most independent manner and bearing' of all the ruling chiefs in Basutoland. By placing themselves under the Free State, he explained, 'he and his people escaped the rude severities of war, and in so doing failed to receive many of the valuable lessons which the other chiefs learnt in the school of adversity and misfortune.'[34]

He was prodigiously wealthy. Vast areas of land were under his direct control, great herds of cattle were loaned out to his subjects, and he also possessed 'large sums' of money.[35] He had two expensive houses built in European style. According to the local doctor, Henry Taylor, 'One seemed to be used as a sort of dining-place for his wives'. The other was kept for the reception of white visitors. Taylor described it as 'furnished in European style, with chairs and tables, curtains to the windows, a Brussels carpet on the floor, and oleographs hanging on the walls.'[36]

He prided himself on his European clothes, and he could often be seen strolling round his property, wearing a waistcoat and trousers of European cut.[37] On other occasions he received white visitors dressed *ka Sesotho*, with a magnificent cloak of silver jackal skins over his shoulders and the rest of his body 'glistening with oil and red ochre': 'his wrists were loaded with bracelets and his knuckles with rings'.[38] When the Anglican John Widdicombe first visited him in 1876 what struck him most was Molapo's stoutness, and the stoutness of his many wives and children. 'Fat men are said to be good-natured', he wrote, 'and Molapo did not belie the truth of the saying. He received us with the utmost cordiality ....'[39]

His magistrate, Major Bell, described him as capricious, arbitrary and jealous of his prerogatives.[40] His missionary, François Coillard, condemned him as a tyrant who did not tolerate any opposition.[41] But Bell was criticising him for his initial resistance to the Cape government, and Coillard for his rejection of Christianity and his 'persecution' of the church. Their judgements do not accord with Basotho tradition. All sources are agreed that Molapo was popular with his followers, and one of his Christian subjects, Azariel Sekese, later wrote admiringly in the mission newspaper, *Leselinyana*, that he was intelligent, farsighted and impartial in his judgements. He respected his people and was in turn respected and obeyed.[42]

It was a cardinal principle of Molapo's policy to maintain his independence of Letsie. He and his followers regarded the Leribe district as their own and even claimed that it did not belong to the rest of the Basotho. It was Molapo who had preserved it during the Seqiti War and it therefore belonged to him.[43] But Rolland was probably going too far when he wrote of the 'very strong jealousy and

---

[33] *The Friend*, 25 February 1869, in BR V.71.
[34] BR VI.148, Griffith to Colonial Secretary, 27 February 1872.
[35] Taylor (1972: 44).
[36] Taylor (1972: 39).
[37] Roche (1951: 269).
[38] Widdicombe (1895: 91); Roche (1951: 269); Taylor (1972: 39).
[39] Widdicombe (1895: 91).
[40] BR VI.143, Bell to Griffith, 17 February 1872.
[41] *JME* 1880, Coillard, letter of 5 July 1880. See also Favre (1931: 328-32).
[42] *Leselinyana*, 15 August 1893.
[43] CA, NA 272, statement of Jan Makhatlane, 17 October 1873, enclosed with Griffith to Colonial Secretary, 28

hatred' between Letsie and Molapo.⁴⁴ As young men they had clashed badly, but there is no record of any disagreement between them during the period of Cape rule. At first Molapo was more determined than Letsie to resist any encroachment by the magistrates on his power, but later he and his elder brother were resolutely united in keeping on good terms with the colonial authorities. According to Sekese, Molapo was trusted by Letsie, just as he had been trusted by Moshoeshoe, and his illness, and then his death in 1879, were a great setback to Letsie's hopes of avoiding hostilities. After the Gun War Letsie cried loudly and sobbed bitterly for the loss of Molapo: 'Nobody will stand with me now my brother Molapo is dead.'⁴⁵ His chief adviser, Nathanael Makotoko, like Letsie's chief advisers, was a staunch supporter of the government, and also a leading member of the church.

Masupha, the third surviving son in the senior house, was perhaps the most popular chief in the country. As a young man he had established himself as one of the bravest of the Basotho leaders in war. One of his praise-names was *Pulumo*, the Wildebeest, because of the wildness and ferocity of his attacks – a name which strikingly anticipated his role as one of the leading *Mabelete*.⁴⁶ It added to his prestige that he alone of the great chiefs had stayed by his father at Thaba-Bosiu throughout the Seqiti War.⁴⁷ He was admired as the great champion of Basotho resistance and independence, a role he would play again, and with more success, during the Gun War and the period following. When General Cunynghame, the commander of the Cape forces, visited him in 1874, Masupha greeted him with an escort of 300 mounted men, many of them in slouch hats and blue uniforms.

He was an impassioned defender of Sesotho. As a young man he had been won over to Christianity and had been baptized with the name of David, and he had spent a year under missionary tutelage in the Cape, learning English and being impressed with the wonders of Christianity and European civilization.⁴⁸ Like Molapo, however, he had turned against the church, and in the 1870s he was dismaying the missionaries by vigorously promoting initiation schools.⁴⁹ A few days before the outbreak of the Gun War the exasperated High Commissioner, Sir Bartle Frere, described him, in the terms of those who knew him best, as representing, 'in a singular degree, the untamed spirit of the old savage race. He affects to despise all the efforts made by Moshesh to bring the tribe into accord with European civilization, and systematically opposes all European ways ....'⁵⁰ He regretted the passing of Basotho independence, and often argued that blacks and whites were so different that they should be kept apart, like cattle and goats in separate kraals.⁵¹ Like Letsie, however, he made use of his more educated brothers as advisers, and he sent at least one of his sons to the Cape to be educated.

Shortly before the Gun War his magistrate gave another reason for his popularity.

> Masupha, who is so different from his two brothers Letsea and Molapo, is still active, and energetic, constantly riding amongst his people, holding meetings, attending weddings,

---

October 1873; Sekese, '*Buka ea taba tsa Basotho*', *Leselinyana*, 1 February 1904.
⁴⁴ LNA, S9/1/3/3, Rolland to Frere, 12 February 1878.
⁴⁵ G.8-'84, p. 44, continuation of *pitso* at Hlotse Heights, 23 May 1883. See C. 3855, p. 52, report on *pitso*, 29 November 1883.
⁴⁶ Damane and Sanders (1974: 120, 122, etc.). See also Tylden (1950A: 199).
⁴⁷ LNA, S9/1/1/1, Griffith to Barkly, 8 August 1871.
⁴⁸ Sanders (1975: 129).
⁴⁹ *Leselinyana*, May 1874; G.21-75, p. 9, Surmon to Griffith, 18 January 1875; *The Little Light of Basutoland*, February 1877; LNA, MF2/1/1, Surmon to Griffith, 7 January 1878.
⁵⁰ C.2755, p. 115, Frere to Kimberley, 24 August 1880.
⁵¹ G.8-'83 (Appendix), p.134, statement of 'Lithlomo', 27 June 1883.

circumcision feasts, and other festive gatherings, and in this manner keeping up the old love and respect for the chief, so inherent in a native.[52]

According to a local trader he was 'by far the most active and independent of the three great chiefs … active and clear-headed, sensible of his rights and determined to maintain them.'[53]

At times he was suspected of aiming to supplant Letsie as paramount. After the Seqiti War he established his village close to the foot of Thaba-Bosiu, a move which Molapo interpreted as a threat to turn Letsie out and 'sit on Moshesh's throne'.[54] He was also opposed to Moshoeshoe's arrangement for Molapo's son, Motšoene, to succeed when Letsie died.[55] But he never mounted a bid for Letsie's position and it seems clear that the realistic limit of his ambitions was to maintain himself, like Molapo, as an independent chief in his own ward with as little interference as possible from Letsie or anyone else. In one respect, however, he was always at a disadvantage, since he had much less land than Letsie and Molapo.[56] Within the constricted boundaries of Basutoland all three had problems in 'placing' their many sons, in giving them villages and areas large enough to satisfy their needs and ambitions. For Masupha these problems were especially severe.

These three sons of the senior house – Letsie, Molapo and Masupha – were now the great chiefs of Basutoland. The ward of the fourth son, Majara, who had died young, was much smaller, and Majara's son and successor, Leshoboro, was never a great force in the land. According to Joseph Orpen, Griffith's successor as Governor's Agent, he was a timid man, very much under Masupha's thumb.[57]

The houses of Moshoeshoe's brothers were eclipsed by those of his three sons. His two full brothers, Makhabane and Posholi, were dead, and so too was Mohale, the most senior of his half-brothers. Makhabane's son, the troublesome Ramanella (also known as Lesaoana), had lost all his land in the Convention of Aliwal North, and was placed in the north in the area of Mapoteng, where, squeezed between Molapo and Masupha, he was embroiled in boundary disputes with both. In the south the sons of Posholi and Mohale fell directly under Letsie. The next senior brother, Mopeli, who like Ramanella had lost all his land, decided to remain under Free State rule at Witzieshoek, where at least he could have his own chiefdom free from the irksome control of his nephews.

In the other houses of Moshoeshoe the most influential surviving sons were Nehemiah (Sekhonyana), George (Tlali), Sofonia (Pii) and Tsekelo. All four had been educated in the Cape and were fluent in English. All had their own villages and would have wanted to be great chiefs, but were frustrated by the dominance of their more senior brothers. For the colonial authorities they were natural allies.

Nehemiah used to say that chieftainship dwelt on a mountain, and as he was climbing up the pass, being so near to the summit that he could hear the people talking and the dogs barking and chickens cackling, he was sent back and was told that he had no share in it. So he squatted down on the slopes of that mountain, and was unable to go any further.[58] At times he had acted as his father's secretary and adviser, but in the end his way of shaking off his senior brothers was to seek land below

---

[52] G.33-'79, p. 12, Charles Bell to Griffith, 31 December 1878.
[53] *Cape Argus*, 4 March 1880, 'The Truth about Masupha. Letter from an Old Trader'.
[54] G.8-'83 (Appendix), pp. 130-1, Blyth to SNA, 22 June 1883.
[55] PEMS Archives, Morija, Dyke to Sprigg, 27 August 1880.
[56] C.3708, p. 47, report of meeting held at Maseru on 19 March 1883, Nehemiah Moshoeshoe's speech.
[57] G.89-'82, p. 184, Orpen to SNA, 18 January 1882.
[58] Sekese, *'Taba tse ling tsa khalè'*, *Leselinyana*, 21 July 1914; Ellenberger, 'Chief Nehemiah S. Moshoeshoe', *Leselinyana*, 15 May 1906.

the Drakensberg in what was then called Nomansland, later Matatiele, outside the borders of Basutoland, where he had lived for some time before, and where Wodehouse gave him land in the post-war settlement. The Basotho claimed this area by virtue of a cession to Moshoeshoe by the Mpondo chief Faku, but this claim was not recognised by the colonial authorities. Nehemiah was never able to achieve the position he wanted. He was 'very unpopular' with the Basotho, 'not a wise chief',[59] and he was constantly involved in conflicts with his neighbours.

The other three – George, Tsekelo and Sofonia – sought power and influence as tax collectors, police officers and advisers in the service of the colonial administration. New opportunities presented themselves and they were quick to take advantage of them. As early as April 1868 George and Tsekelo wrote to Wodehouse, telling him that they had always urged their father to look to the Queen and not to make terms with the Free State, assuring him that he could therefore trust them, 'not looking to the colour of our skin, but believing that we are real Englishmen at heart', and offering their services in support of the government.[60]

After his education in Cape Town George had at first flaunted his imagined superiority, for which Moshoeshoe had quickly cut him down to size.[61] In 1866 he was described by one white visitor as 'a swell, with a black hat, drab suit of clothes, and shiny japanned gaiters, with boots you could see to shave in'.[62] By 1871 he was working as a tax collector for the government, and in the same year he was appointed as a sub-inspector of police, later being promoted to inspector.[63] He carried out his duties well, winning the confidence of the colonial authorities, and in the Gun War he emerged as the *Mateketoa*'s leading spokesman. After the war, in 1883, he was described as 'a fine-looking man. He ... was dressed like an English country gentleman, in cord riding-breeches and a rough coat, wore spurs, and carried a hunting crop. Burly and strong in figure, his manners had ... something about them quite polished and dignified.'[64] His village was south of Maseru, uncomfortably close to his nephew Bereng.[65]

Sofonia too became an inspector of police, and remained faithful to the Cape government throughout. His 'magnificiently built stone house', close to the territory controlled by Masupha, was a sight pointed out to visiting whites.[66]

Tsekelo was evidently a man of great charm and plausibility. He had been educated with George at the Cape, but had been sent home in disgrace after being found with his arm round the waist of a serving-maid. He had angered some of his brothers by seducing their wives, and had excused himself on the ground that he was so attractive that women could not keep away from him. Moshoeshoe had used him as an adviser and messenger, but he had proved to be unreliable, even enlisting with the Free State police.[67] He had been involved in the agitation against the Convention of Aliwal North, and had accompanied the French missionary, Daumas, and the Natal journalist, Buchanan, to France in an

---

[59] A.6-'79, Report of the Select Committee Appointed to Consider and Report on Hostilities in Basutoland, p. 85, evidence of E. Rolland, 27 August 1879; Ellenberger, 'Chief Nehemiah S. Moshoeshoe', *Leselinyana*, 15 May 1906.
[60] *BR* IV.73-5, Tsekelo and George Moshesh to Wodehouse, 19 April 1868.
[61] Sanders (1975: 274).
[62] *The Friend*, 27 April 1866, account by 'a burgher of the late Free State force'.
[63] *BR* VI.131, Griffith to Colonial Secretary, 15 January 1871; LNA, S9/2/1/1, Griffith to Colonial Secretary, 15 September 1873.
[64] Kilpin (1912: 244).
[65] C. 2755, p. 158, interview between Sprigg and George Moshoeshoe, 30 August 1880.
[66] J.W. Matthews (1887: 374).
[67] Sanders (1975: 279-80).

attempt to get it nullified. There too he had exercised his charms. He spoke French 'like a sworn interpreter', it was said, and on one occasion 'led off a ball …with his arm around the waist of a fascinating princess'.[68] He was at the heart of countless intrigues and machinations, and yet he was immediately employed by the colonial authorities as a tax collector and sub-inspector of police. He was later dismissed for being absent without leave; was imprisoned for three months for being an accessory to stock theft and complained when he left gaol that there should be separate facilities for educated prisoners like himself; and yet, in 1880, was reappointed to the police.[69] He was a fine orator, on one occasion speaking to such effect that even Gordon Sprigg, the Cape Premier, needed time to overcome his emotion.[70] Among the Basotho he enjoyed great influence and prestige and he often acted as an adviser to his senior brothers,[71] though he was regarded as too clever and devious to be trusted.[72] On occasion his brothers found it useful to blame him when things went wrong. It was convenient to have someone like Tsekelo as a scapegoat.[73]

Outside Moshoeshoe's family only three chiefdoms retained any kind of autonomy, in the sense that they reported direct to the Paramount Chief and no other chief could be placed over them. These were the Makhoakhoa of Matela[74] in the far north of the country; the Bataung of Moletsane, who had lost their land north of the Caledon and migrated south to the Cornet Spruit District; and the Baphuthi of Moorosi, who in 1879 would be the first to rise in rebellion against the Cape. In the Seqiti War Moorosi had fled up the Orange valley and made his headquarters on the mountain fortress where he lived for the rest of his life.

Most people in Basutoland spoke Sesotho in one form or another, but there had long been a substantial minority of Nguni-speakers. There were many Hlubi, mainly in the north of the country, where they had settled during the *lifaqane*.[75] They were generally referred to by the whites as Fingoes or Zulu and by the Basotho as Matebele. In the Leribe District it was reckoned that about one fifth of the population was 'Zulu' and the magistrate needed a Zulu as well as a Sesotho interpreter.[76] In the south the Baphuthi's language was a form of Nguni, and in the Quthing area there were about a thousand Xhosa-speaking Thembu.[77]

Moshoeshoe had made great efforts to integrate these Nguni-speakers into his chiefdom and to get them accepted by his followers, and in many instances there were good relations between them. Ntho,

---

[68] *Cape Argus*, 22 November 1879, 'Occasional Notes'.
[69] LNA, S9/2/1/1, Griffith to Colonial Secretary, 23 February 1876; LNA S9/1/2/1, Rolland to SNA, 19 November 1877; *Leselinyana*, December 1877, report of *pitso* held on 1 November 1877; LNA, S9/1/3/4, Griffith to Tsekelo, 14 September 1880.
[70] *Cape Argus*, 14 September 1880, Editorial. See also *Cape Argus*, 4 November 1879 and 15 September 1880.
[71] CA, NA 174, A. Barkly to Rolland, 16 November 1877.
[72] Stephen Pinda, interview with AA, 7 October 1965.
[73] For a later, colourful account of Tsekelo – huge, jovial, always proud to speak French, always ready to talk for as long as the listener was prepared to listen, see *JME*, 1886, p. 223, Dieterlen, 16 March 1886.
[74] Joel claimed that Matela was placed under Molapo, but this was disputed by the Makhoakhoa and by Jonathan. In 1890 Lagden gave judgement in favour of the Makhoakhoa: LNA, S7/3/1, record of *pitso* held at Qalo, 3 October 1890.
[75] LNA, S9/2/1/1, Griffith to Colonial Secretary, 7 January 1874.
[76] G.27-'73, p. 6, Bell to Griffith, 14 January 1873; LNA, L2/1/1, Bell to Griffith, 21 December 1873; S9/1/3/2, Griffith to Bell, 25 February 1874.
[77] CA, NA 274, Rolland to SNA, 18 December 1877.

Letsie's chief councillor, was a Hlubi.[78] But suspicions and jealousies persisted. According to Rolland, the Basotho looked down on the 'Kafir-speaking peoples' as inferior to themselves in intelligence, industry and morality, and there were 'strong natural antipathies between the Basuto and the Kafer speaking tribes' outside Basutoland.[79] Mokone (Nguni) and Letebele were sometimes used as terms of abuse. On the other hand, according to an Anglican source, the Fingoes, 'or more correctly ... the Amahlubis', looked down on the Basotho and there was 'much jealousy between them'.[80] Their loyalty to the Basotho chiefs was questionable, and like the 'loyal Fingoes' on the Cape's eastern frontier many of them were more inclined to look to the British authorities for guidance and leadership. One of them, the 'loyal' Tokonya (the Sesotho form of Ndugunya), a Hlubi headman under Masupha, was later to play a significant role in the events leading up to the Gun War. In the north, at the time when Molapo was forbidding his men to join the police, the only people who would enlist at first were 'Zulu'.[81]

Other groups whose loyalty to the chiefs was doubtful were the congregations of the Paris Evangelical Missionary Society, which had been active in the country since 1833 and which now had a dozen stations in the country, each headed by a European missionary, supported by an extensive system of annexes, each headed by a Mosotho catechist. The number of church members was not high, though it almost trebled from 1,831 in 1871 to 4,277 in 1880,[82] but the number of people attending church was much higher – at the end of 1877 it was estimated at 17-20,000 – while the number of children attending school in that year was well over 2,000.[83] These people were frequently in conflict with their chiefs on such issues as working on the lands of junior wives and the rights of Christian widows, and they looked to the government to support and protect them. Shortly before the Gun War Rolland described them as the chiefs' 'natural enemies', and confidently predicted that in any outbreak they would be on the government side 'to a man'.[84]

Rolland was also confident that the missionaries would back the government. The dominant spirit among them was Adolphe Mabille, who was stationed at the mission's headquarters at Morija, a few kilometres from Letsie's home at Matsieng. His wife, Adèle, was the daughter of Eugène Casalis, Moshoeshoe's missionary and adviser. Mabille in turn became Letsie's adviser. Like his colleagues, he believed that the Basotho's best hope of progress was to live peacefully under colonial or imperial rule, and that if they rebelled they would be destroyed as a united chiefdom and the work of the mission would be broken up. He was a hard-working, tireless, uncompromising evangelical, a ferocious assailant not only of heathenism but of any form of Christianity, such as Roman Catholicism or 'Ritualism', as he habitually called High Church Anglicanism, which in his view fell short of the true gospel.[85] Shortly before the Gun War he was ordered to return to Europe for rest and recuperation, and his departure at this critical time, soon to be followed by the death of Molapo, deprived Letsie of a great force for peace.

---

[78] Mosebi Damane, interview with AA, 14 February 1965; Bereng and Lehloenya (1991: 88).
[79] CA, NA 274, Rolland to SNA, 18 December 1877; NA 275, Rolland to SNA, 19 July 1878.
[80] *Mission Field*, 1877, p. 454, E.W. Stenson, letter, n.d. See also *JME* 1878, p. 291, Report of Missionary Conference, 21 May 1878: The '*Cafres*' who lived around Morija did not attend the Basotho's services because of '*des préjugés de race*'.
[81] LNA, L2/1/1, Bell to Griffith, 25 March 1873.
[82] V. Ellenberger (1938: 163, 180).
[83] CA, N.A. 274, Report of Acting Governor's Agent to SNA, 28 December 1877, reprinted in Burman (1976A: 71).
[84] CA, NA 174, Report of Acting Governor's Agent to SNA, 28 December 1877, quoted in Burman (1976A: 73).
[85] For a joint biography of Adolphe and Adèle Mabille, see Smith (1939).

The Roman Catholics had started work at Roma in 1862, thirteen kilometres to the south of Thaba-Bosiu, and from small beginnings were starting to build up their strength and influence. Eventually they would outnumber the French Protestants, but as yet they were too small to be of any great account.

The same was true of the Anglicans, who in 1876 established stations at two of the district headquarters – Mohale's Hoek in the Cornet Spruit District and Hlotse Heights in the Leribe District. In 1878 another station was established at Sekubu, in the far north-east, but from the start the church of the Queen was closely identified with the government of the Queen.[86]

Over the years following the Seqiti War many Basotho who had fled to the Cape Colony and the Free State returned to Basutoland, but, partly because of the shortage of land, there were many who remained and who still regarded themselves, at least to some extent, as belonging to the Basotho chiefdom. A speaker at the annual *pitso* in 1874 believed that there were more Basotho in the Free State than in Basutoland.[87] He was exaggerating, since he was arguing that there was not enough room for them to return and that the country's boundaries should be extended. Even so the numbers involved were considerable. In the Colony they worked mainly as labourers and servants. In the Free State, especially in the Conquered Territory, many of them, while staying close to their old homes, came to terms with the new owners of the land, not just providing labour but running stock and growing cereals as well. Share-cropping arrangements, or 'farming-on-the-half', were common.[88] It was even reported in 1876 that many new villages were being established.[89]

Letsie's chiefdom, then, was far from united. In 1868, in the last years of Moshoeshoe's rule, Emile Rolland, then a missionary, noted that of late the lesser chiefs had been doing all they could to render themselves independent and to acknowledge merely the nominal supremacy of the Paramount.[90] Ten years later, as a government official, he gave very much the same account. Letsie commanded 'great personal influence, being looked up to as the head of the Tribe', but among their own people each of the lesser chiefs commanded more influence than Letsie himself. In the Leribe district, where 'Molapo is supreme, and does not obey Letsie', the Paramount's authority was 'merely nominal'; the same was true in the Berea district, where Masupha was 'quasi-independent'; in the south Moletsane, the chief of the Bataung, and Moorosi, the chief of the Baphuthi, were 'more or less practically independent'; and there were also several minor chiefs 'who would be glad to be independent' if they could. 'The mutual jealousies which are so characteristic of the Basutos', he concluded, 'and which exist between all the chiefs, render any combination of the whole tribe in the highest degree improbable. No such combination could be formed or carried out except through gross mismanagement on our part ....'[91]

---

[86] For the early history of the Anglican church in Basutoland, see Dove (1975).

[87] G.21-'75, p. 20, 'Minutes of the Annual Public Meeting held at Maseru on 2nd October 1874', speech of Headman Maphathe. In 1871 Molapo said that many of his people were still living in the Free State: *BR* VI.21, Barkly to Secretary of State for the Colonies, 18 May 1871.

[88] De Kok (1904: 151, 180); Eldredge (1993: 178).

[89] *The Little Light of Basutoland*, March 1876.

[90] *BR* IV.43, Rolland, 'Notes on the Political and Social Position of the Basuto Tribe', 30 March 1868.

[91] CA, NA 275, Rolland to SNA, 19 July 1878.

CHAPTER 3: THE CAPE GOVERNMENT

The policy

Colonel Charles Duncan Griffith, the first Governor's Agent under the Cape, arrived in Basutoland in August 1871. As Sir Henry Barkly's representative he claimed to be different from other colonial officials in that he received his instructions from the Governor direct.[1] The policy he followed, however, was the policy laid down and directed by the colonial government, initially under the premiership of John Molteno, and in particular by the Department of Native Affairs, which was set up in December 1872 under Charles Brownlee. Griffith was to keep law and order and to work towards the replacement of chiefly rule by magisterial authority. He was to help the Basotho to advance in 'civilization', and he was to raise a hut tax to cover the costs of the administration.

This policy, which had been initiated by Sir George Grey in the 1850s on the Cape's Eastern Frontier, was a continuation and development of Wodehouse's policy in the period of direct rule by the High Commissioner. James Bowker, Wodehouse's agent in Basutoland, was quite clear that 'our policy has been to break up the power of the Native chiefs'.[2] Very little had been done to implement this policy before Griffith's arrival. It was more than three years since Wodehouse had declared the Basotho to be British subjects and Basutoland British territory, but for the first year the Free State had refused to recognise the legality of his annexation, and for the second the ratification of the Convention of Aliwal North had been held up by the Basotho's campaign for a more generous boundary. It was only after the Convention was finally ratified on 10 March 1870, a day before Moshoeshoe's death, that Wodehouse was able to turn his attention to the government of the country.

Wodehouse's regulations,[3] which were read out to the Basotho at a *pitso* towards the end of 1870, aroused some opposition because they superimposed magisterial authority on that of the chiefs, who felt they were being 'put aside'.[4] Letsie however declared that Moshoeshoe had called in the British government and he would stick by it,[5] and since Bowker, the High Commissioner's Agent, was supported by only one other magistrate the regulations in effect remained 'a dead letter', as Griffith described them later.[6] In the brief period that remained Bowker and, for the last few months, William Surmon, who replaced him, were heavily preoccupied with keeping the peace, resettling the country's inhabitants, and beginning the collection of an annual hut tax of ten shillings. For these purposes they had the support of a small force of Frontier Armed and Mounted Police, at first 100 strong, later reduced to 36. For the most part the chiefs went on ruling in much the same way as before.

There were some, Griffith among them, who regarded this hiatus as a lost opportunity. In 1868 the country was prostrate and the chiefs discredited, since people blamed them for their sufferings at the hands of the Free State. If the government had been able to intervene decisively, it was argued, it could have abolished those customs which were 'the greatest barriers to civilization and progress' and gone a long way towards destroying the chiefs' power. As it was the Basotho had recovered econo-

---

[1] CA, NA 279, memorandum by J. Rose-Innes, 23 May 1881.
[2] BR VI.47, 'Minutes of Evidence taken by the Select Committee on Basutoland Annexation Bill', 7 July 1871.
[3] BR V.291-5, Government Notice, 13 May 1870.
[4] BR V.306-7, 'Basuto Chiefs' to Bowker, 22 December 1870.
[5] BR VI.5-6, Austen to Bowker, 26 January 1871.
[6] G.27-'74, p. 22, Griffith to SNA, 31 January 1874.

mically and the chiefs had resumed their old position.[7]

The magistrates

With only one significant break, in 1877-1878, Griffith was to remain in office until 1881, until after the end of the Gun War. Born in Grahamstown in 1830, he had become an officer in the Frontier Armed and Mounted Police, and had served as a magistrate over a period of 19 years. He was a man of impressive appearance, with a huge beard that had once been in fashion but which he kept long after it had gone out of fashion.[8] His manner was generally 'placid and quiet', and according to the missionaries all the more effective for that.[9] Although he had a reputation as a firm disciplinarian, he was also 'of a very kindly nature'.[10] Without exception, he enjoyed the confidence of his superiors and the respect, even devotion, of his colleagues and subordinates.[11] He was deeply admired by the French Protestant missionaries, an admiration that survived several sharp clashes, especially in the run-up to the Gun War,[12] and above all he won the trust of the Basotho people and the chiefs. He was watched carefully at first, but by 1875 George Moshoeshoe was able to declare publicly that all the Basotho thought well of him: 'You have been here four years. We haven't a spot to point out in your conduct. All hearts are happy when they speak of you ....'[13] Letsie came to depend heavily on his advice and guidance, and was badly shaken when he was temporarily removed from the country.[14] His previous experience, reinforced by his success in Basutoland, gave him immense authority. For the most part he was left to run the country as he thought fit, and when he was thwarted he did not hesitate to invoke his past record and even to threaten resignation.

Like most colonial administrators at the time, he was a strict paternalist. He did not question the wisdom of drawing the Basotho away from their own culture and into the ways of 'civilization', and he believed that they had to be treated like children – praised and rewarded when they behaved well and scolded and punished when they behaved badly. But he developed a genuine affection for them, and on several occasions stood up strongly for their interests against the government in Cape Town.

He was heavily overworked, since as well as being the Governor's Agent he was also Chief Magistrate, hearing appeals from other magistrates, and until 1877 he was the magistrate of the Thaba-Bosiu District and the Accounting Officer as well. He conducted his administration in a very 'economical … manner',[15] and by 1878 had built up a reserve of £24,462. He spent so little on roads that after seven years of his administration there was not 'a mile of artificial road in good repair in the whole of Basutoland',[16] and the government of the country was carried out 'in the most inconvenient

---

[7] G.27-'74, pp. 21-2, Griffith to SNA, 31 January 1874.
[8] Hook (1906: 83).
[9] *The Little Light of Basutoland*, November 1874, 'The National Gathering of 1874'.
[10] Taylor (1972: 22). See also LNA, S9/1/2/1, Rolland to SNA, 28 January 1878.
[11] E.g. CA, Griffith Papers, Merriman to Griffith, 6 February 1878; Taylor (1972: 22-3).
[12] E.g., *The Little Light of Basutoland*, October 1877; Malan (1878: 116-7); CA, Griffith Papers, E. Casalis to Griffith, 29 September 1881, and H. Moore Dyke to Griffith, 29 September 1881.
[13] G.16-'76, p. 14, 'Minutes of the Annual Meeting ("Pitso") held at Maseru, on the 4th of November 1875'.
[14] CA, NA 274, Rolland to SNA, 22 September 1877, and Letsie to Frere, 10 September 1877, printed in Burman (1976A: 68-9 and 69-70 respectively). (See also C.1961, pp. 124-6.)
[15] LNA, S9/1/2/1, Rolland to SNA, 20 March 1878.
[16] A.6-'79, Report of the Select Committee appointed to consider and report on hostilities in Basutoland, p. 56, Bowker's evidence, 7 August 1879.

and dilapidated buildings possible'.[17] His own offices, which he had taken over from a trader in the first year of his administration, were described by another officer in 1878 as 'very small and stuffy, and very inadequate, – hot in summer and icy cold in winter'. Overall the premises were 'quite unworthy of being the head offices of Government ... shabby and paltry beyond description'.[18] Griffith himself described his court room as 'more fit for a stable than a judicial chamber'.[19]

In his duties as Magistrate of the Thaba-Bosiu District Griffith was helped by an Assistant Magistrate, Emile Rolland, the son of the missionary Samuel Rolland and himself a missionary until he resigned in 1871, at the age of 33, to take up his official duties. He had been recommended for his post by Bowker, who described him as 'a first rate man and well liked by the Basutos'.[20]

Even before his appointment as a magistrate Rolland was in sympathy with the administration's aims and aspirations. In a memorandum written in March 1868 he had argued that the main obstacle to the Basotho's acceptance of British law would be the power of the chiefs and that everything possible should be done to strike at the roots of that power.[21] As well as being well educated – he had studied theology in Edinburgh and Paris – he was fluent in Sesotho, and with his profound knowledge of the country he became Griffith's right-hand man and sometimes acted for him in his absence. He was also the brother-in-law of Joseph Orpen, who was later to succeed Griffith as Governor's Agent.

In the north, in the Leribe District, Major Charles Harland Bell – Majorobelo to the Basotho – assumed duty as Magistrate in May 1871. He was about 46, and was a retired officer from the British army who had served in India and South Africa.[22] The qualities that seem to have impressed others most were those of the English 'gentleman'. Barkly referred to him as 'late of the Cape Mounted Rifles, a gentleman of much experience in dealing with the Kaffer Tribes of the Eastern Frontier',[23] and later the doctor in the Leribe District, Henry Taylor, described him as 'a thorough gentleman, and a type of the old-time British officer, very dignified, but of a most kindly and generous disposition'. According to Taylor he 'was held in the highest respect, alike by the officials who served under him, and by chiefs and natives'.[24] Pressing the case for his son to be appointed as his clerk, Bell argued that both magistrates and clerks should be drawn from 'gentlemen', since the Basotho would be impressed by their superior qualities.[25] With his military background he was acutely conscious of the weakness of the resources at his immediate disposal and the vulnerability of his position at Leribe, and in 1876 he moved his headquarters a few kilometres southwards to the more defensible Hlotse Heights, where he built a small fort, part of which is still standing and still known as Major Bell's Tower. Griffith regarded him as an officer of no ordinary ability,[26] but Bell was 'mortified' when Rolland, a much younger officer, was appointed to act as Governor's Agent when Griffith was away.[27]

---

[17] LNA, S9/1/2/1, Rolland to SNA, 20 March 1878.
[18] LNA, S9/1/2/1, Bowker to SNA, 18 March 1878.
[19] LNA, S9/1/2/1, Griffith to SNA, n.d.
[20] BR V.301, Bowker to Colonial Secretary, 10 November 1870.
[21] BR IV.43-50, E.S. Rolland, 'Notes on the Political and Social Position of the Basuto Tribe', 39 March 1868.
[22] For Bell's background, see Tylden (1939).
[23] BR VI.20, Barkly to Secretary of State, 18 May 1871.
[24] Taylor (1972: 91). See also *JME*, 1881, p. 178, Dormoy to Director, 28 January 1881; Widdicombe, (1895: 204-5).
[25] CA, Southey Papers, Vol. 45, Bell to Southey, 30 July and 16 August 1871.
[26] LNA, S9/1/2/2, Griffith to SNA, 19 July 1881.
[27] LNA, L2/1/1, Bell to Colonial Secretary, 21 August 1875.

William ('Billy') Henry Surmon, who had acted as the High Commissioner's Agent after Bowker's departure, was appointed as Magistrate in the Berea District, which lay between Leribe and Thaba-Bosiu, and set up his headquarters at Advance Post. He had previously been an officer in the Frontier Armed and Mounted Police, but Bowker referred to him as 'Young Surmon' and he was described as 'quite a colt' in 1868.[28] He had some knowledge of surveying, which was useful later in defining the country's precise borders, and he spoke Dutch, which was helpful in resolving disputes with the Free State farmers. He remained in the territory throughout the period of Cape rule, winning the respect of successive Governor's Agents, and stayed on under imperial rule. 'He is an upright officer in whom I have complete confidence,' wrote Marshal Clarke, the first Resident Commissioner in 1885, 'and is much respected by the natives.'[29]

In the Cornet Spruit District in the south John Austen had his headquarters at Mohale's Hoek. As a young man he had worked for the Wesleyan mission for ten years, and he had then spent 19 years in the Cape's Border Department, most of them as the Superintendent of the Wittebergen Native Reserve on Basutoland's southern borders, where he had administered a strange mixture of African and colonial law, conducting himself more like a chief than a magistrate, handing out very rough and ready justice and attempting to supplement his meagre salary by engaging, together with his family, in trade, a venture which ended in bankruptcy. In face of mounting criticism Wodehouse realised that Austen's methods could no longer stand up to scrutiny, but he recognised his toughness and effectiveness and appointed him as a magistrate in March 1870 to control the disparate population in the south, among them the sons of Moshoeshoe's brothers, Posholi and Mohale, Moletsane's Bataung, Moorosi's Baphuthi and various Thembu chiefdoms.[30]

With his limited education, and with his Wesleyan background and trading activities, Austen was unlikely to have satisfied Bell's requirements of a gentleman, and one French missionary commented belittlingly that he was a great talker.[31] But he might have had difficulties on another score as well. In the praises of the Batlokoa chief, Lelingoana Maketekete, he was mocked as *Leqhea*, which is defined in the dictionary as 'Bushman; half-caste person' in the Tlokoa 'dialect'.[32] Two of the French missionaries described him as '*un mulâtre*', while another referred to him as '*un homme de couleur*', and Burman has perceptively suggested that 'in a race-conscious country' this 'may explain his touchy, defensive attitude throughout his term as a magistrate in Basutoland'.[33] He was not popular with his fellow magistrates,[34] and shortly before the Gun War he complained bitterly about Griffith's lack of

---

[28] *BR* V.301, Bowker to Colonial Secretary, 10 November 1870; Hook (1906: 73).
[29] CA, NA 274, Rolland to SNA, 18 December 1877; PRO, CO 417/5, Clarke to Robinson, 7 May 1885.
[30] *BR* V.237-8, 266-7 and 270, Wodehouse to Bowker, 4 January 1870; Wodehouse to Austen, 28 February 1870; Austen to Wodehouse, 12 March 1870.
[31] PEMS Archives, Morija, Ellenberger Papers, Ellenberger to Director, 27 May 1880.
[32] Mangoaela, (1957: 84). Stephen Pinda was 'definite' that Austen was 'a half-caste, a Coloured', interview with AA, 22 November 1965.
[33] PEMS Archives, Morija, Ellenberger Papers, Ellenberger to Director, 27 May 1880; *JME* 1875, p.286, Hermann Dieterlen, '*Voyage à Matatiele*'; Burman (1981: 54).
[34] A.6-'79, Report of the Select Committee appointed to consider and report on hostilities in Basutoland, p.60, Bowker's evidence, 7 August 1879; *Cape Argus*, 29 May 1879, letter from Sauer, 18 May 1879, reprinted from *Northern Post*. For the hostility between Austen and Rolland, see *Cape Argus*, 16 October 1879, Editorial, and G.13-'80, p. 36, Austen to Griffith, 24 December 1879.

confidence in him and the contemptuous rejection of his opinions and suggestions.[35] Until the outbreak of the Moorosi War, however, there were no doubts about his general competence.[36]

Among the Basotho his appointment was viewed with apprehension, even fear. His hostility towards them was notorious. His son had fought for the Free State in the Seqiti War, and so had many Mfengu from his Reserve. He was also known to have given advice to the commandos on how to conduct their campaign.[37] Even after the Basotho had been declared British subjects his actions as the Reserve Superintendent gave a strong impression of bias against them.[38] By 1879 much of the hostility against him had died down. It was reported that he was 'not so unpopular as he was' and even that he was 'liked by the people of his own district'.[39] Ellenberger, however, the missionary who knew him best, described him a year later as 'our sworn enemy'.[40]

Austen was closer to colonial susceptibilities than the other magistrates, and it was typical of him that throughout his magistracy he was convinced that the chiefs were involved in a wider African conspiracy against the whites and were always looking out for an opportunity to break out and regain their independence.

It is a striking testimony to the stability and success of the administration that all these men – Griffith, Rolland, Bell, Surmon and Austen – were in post, though not all in the same posts, at the outbreak of the Gun War. In the course of the 1870s the administration slowly expanded. In 1874 the district of Thaba-Bosiu was divided into two sub-districts: Maseru, where Griffith remained in direct control, and Mafeteng, where Rolland took charge. In 1877 Griffith was at last relieved of his magisterial duties in Maseru by the appointment of Henry Lee Davies, who had been a clerk there for several years, and at Mafeteng William Surmon replaced Emile Rolland, who became a superintendent of schools.[41] While Surmon was now Resident Magistrate of the Thaba-Bosiu District based at Mafeteng, Davies was the Assistant Resident Magistrate based at Maseru.

Surmon's old post as magistrate of the Berea District was taken by Arthur Barkly, the son of the High Commissioner, Sir Henry Barkly, who by that time had been replaced by Sir Bartle Frere. Masupha, whose ward included the Magistracy, expressed his gratitude that he had been given the son of the great Ramabekebeke, or 'Glitter' as the Basotho called Sir Henry Barkly because of his glittering uniform and decorations. Arthur Barkly himself became known as Mabekebeke.[42]

---

[35] CA, NA 276, Austen to Ayliff, 5 August 1879.
[36] A.6-'79, Report of the Select Committee appointed to consider and report on hostilities in Basutoland, p. 15, Orpen's evidence, 15 July 1879, and p. 47, Bright's evidence, 23 July 1879.
[37] E.g., PEMS Archives, Morija, Dyke to Cochet, 6 June 1879; A.6-'79, Report of the Select Committee appointed to consider and report on hostilities in Basutoland, pp. 15-6, Orpen's evidence, 15 July 1879, and pp. 15-6, Rolland's evidence, 26 August 1879, pp. 80, 91; C. 2821, p. 9, Mabille to Frere, 17 February 1880.
[38] BR IV.183-4, Bowker to Austen, 22 October 1868, and BR IV.197, Bowker to Wodehouse, 16 November 1868.
[39] A.6-'79, Report of the Select Committee appointed to consider and report on hostilities in Basutoland, p. 91, Rolland's evidence, 27 August 1879.
[40] PEMS Archives, Morija, Ellenberger Papers, Ellenberger to Director, 27 May 1880. Translated from the French. See also *Cape Argus*, 29 May 1879, For missionary hostility generally, see *Cape Argus*, 29 May 1879, letter from Sauer, 18 May 1879, reprinted from *Northern Post*.
[41] His post was variously described as Head of the Education Department and Director of Model Schools: LNA, S9/1/3/3, Griffith to the Proprietors of *Northern Post*, Aliwal North, 19 July 1877; LNA, S9/2/3/1, Davies to Acting Governor's Agent, 1 January 1878.
[42] *Leselinyana*, December 1877, account of the annual *pitso* held on 1 November 1877; G.17-'78, p. 24, 'Minutes of the Annual Meeting or "Pitso" held at Maseru, Basutoland, on the 1st November, 1877'. The primary meaning of Rama-

It was also in 1877 that the new district of Quthing, south of the Orange, was separated from the Cornet Spruit District. The impetuous young Hamilton Hope was put in charge, but he ran into difficulties with the Baphuthi chief, Moorosi, and in 1878 he was moved to a post outside Basutoland and Austen took up his position at Quthing. Surmon replaced Austen at Mohale's Hoek, Barkly replaced Surmon at Mafeteng, and Charlie Bell, Major Bell's son, replaced Surmon in the Berea district.

These then were the dispositions of staff, from north to south, at the outbreak of the Gun War.

District/Sub-District	Headquarters	Magistrate
Leribe	Hlotse Heights	Major Bell
Berea	Advance Post	Charles Bell
Thaba-Bosiu/Maseru	Maseru	Henry Davies (Assistant)
Thaba-Bosiu/Mafeteng	Mafeteng	Arthur Barkly
Cornet Spruit	Mohale's Hoek	William Surmon
Quthing	Quthing	John Austen

Each magistrate was assisted by a clerk, and was supported by a contingent of the Basutoland Native Police Force, which was established in October 1872 after the withdrawal of the Frontier Armed and Mounted Police (FAMP). Until the Gun War its overall complement was never more than a hundred men. It consisted entirely of Africans, and for the most part it was officered by junior sons of Moshoeshoe, notably George, Tsekelo, Sofonia and later Ntsane. As a military force it was negligible. Uniforms were provided and guns, but the men had to provide their own horses, and at least one constable had to resign from the force when his mare came into foal.[43]

Just beyond the Basutoland border a small force of FAMP was stationed at Palmietfontein, on the Tele river, but in 1879 this was only 76 men strong and of no practical military strength.[44] No doubt the Basotho were conscious of more distant forces – the rest of the FAMP, with its headquarters at King William's Town, and the imperial regiments based at Cape Town. In an early confrontation with Molapo Major Bell told the chief and his followers that, although they could see only three or four police constables, 'the whole of the Forces of the Queen' were at his back.[45] He commented wryly that 'this was true in theory but unfortunately not practically', but the possibility that more troops might be summoned must always have been present to the Basotho's minds. The common description of the government as an exercise in moral force alone was misleading.

Peace and prosperity
Given the resources available in the country, the Cape's attack on the chiefs was astonishingly bold and ambitious. Chieftainship, *borena*, was the only form of government the Basotho had known. For as far back as the collective memory went chieftainship was there, a fact of life, unquestioned. No other form of government was ever envisaged. It was the chiefs who pointed out where people could build their homes, who allocated their arable fields and set aside the areas for winter pasture. It was the

---

bekebeke is 'Father of Mabekebeke', and so Arthur Barkly was called Mabekebeke. See also Fanny Barkly (1893: 31).
[43] LNA, L2/1/1, Bell to Griffith, 16 October 1873 and 29 January 1874.
[44] CA, NA 274, Rolland to SNA, 18 December 1877.
[45] CA, NA 272, Bell to Griffith, 19 October 1873, printed in Burman (1976A: 59-60).

chiefs who settled disputes and who decided cases of every kind, who could summon their subjects to court and exact fines. It was the chiefs who summoned the men to battle, or sent them out on errands and messages. They were not despots. They acted with the advice of their senior men, and if they alienated their people they were likely to find their support draining away. But in every matter affecting the community as a whole the power of decision rested finally with them. The only formal check on junior chiefs and headmen was the right of appeal to more senior chiefs. The chief was the centre of all lawful authority, and the Basotho's profound reverence for the chieftainship, if not for every individual chief, was bound up with their respect for lawful authority and with the need for law and order in general.

The Cape recognised that it would be unwise, as well as impossible, to sweep away the chieftainship. With only a handful of magistrates it depended on the chiefs for the collection of hut tax and the orderly functioning of the country. In 1871 Sir Henry Barkly assured Letsie that after annexation his Agent would rule Basutoland as before 'with due respect for the power of the Chiefs',[46] and a year later Griffith impressed upon the chiefs that they would always be supported in the exercise of their just authority.[47] But the long-term aim was clear – gradually to win over the people, and in this way to undermine the power of the chiefs and to establish the government and its magistrates as the primary focus of authority and loyalty in the country.

There were many in the Colony who were apprehensive about this policy, and who warned the government that if it tried to supersede the power of the chiefs it would bring 'a hornet's nest' about its ears.[48] But from the start there were vital factors which favoured the administration. The greatest benefit of colonial rule was the removal of any serious danger from the Free State. Stock theft virtually came to an end, and the few cattle that were stolen were soon recovered. The Free State authorities could no longer brand the Basotho as a nation of thieves and use stock theft either as a reason or as a pretext for war.[49] There were still rumours and alarms, and if the Basotho had still been independent some of these might have given rise to hostilities. But with a British presence, as Moshoeshoe had foreseen, there was no longer any danger of a Free State attack, and for this there were repeated expressions of appreciation and gratitude from commoners and chiefs alike. When Sir Henry Barkly was about to leave South Africa Letsie and his 'principal men' sent him a letter of farewell in which they likened him to 'one who chases away the birds, while we have been the cornfield'. The 'birds', as Griffith explained to Barkly, were 'Brand and the Free State Boers'.[50]

Peace brought a rapid renewal of prosperity. The Basotho had lost a wide area of land, and they repeatedly complained of their need for more, but even before Cape rule was established observers were marvelling at their swift recovery. The opening of the Diamond Fields in Griqualand West created new markets for their grain and labour. Prices soared. More and more land was brought under cultivation, hoes gave way increasingly to ploughs, and transport operators from the Free State and elsewhere conveyed hundreds of wagons of grain to Kimberley as well as to the Basotho's old markets in the Free State and the Cape Colony. In 1879 exports of 200- 400,000 muids of all cereals

---

[46] *BR* VI.10, Minutes of Meeting between Barkly and Letsie, 16 March 1871.
[47] LNA, S9/2/1/1, Griffith to Colonial Secretary, 27 August 1872.
[48] *The Little Light of Basutoland*, October 1877.
[49] E.g., *BR* VI.24, Barkly to Kimberley, 18 May 1871; *BR* VI.176, Griffith to Colonial Secretary, 26 August 1872; G.27-'74, p. 23, Griffith to SNA, 31 January 1874; *The Little Light of Basutoland*, August 1874;
[50] CA, NA 274, Letsie to Barkly, 12 February 1877, enclosed with Griffith to Barkly, 14 February 1877.

were officially recorded, as well as £75,000 worth of wool and other produce.⁵¹

It was already a common practice for Basotho to take on domestic or farm work in the Free State and the Cape. Now thousands of them flocked to the Diamond Fields, usually under contracts of three to six months, and later, from the mid-70s onwards, to railway construction and other public works in the Cape. Wages rose dramatically, so much so that it was difficult for the Free State farmers to attract Basotho labour. In his report for 1875 Rolland estimated that of the adult male population of 25,000 at least 15,000 went out to work each year.⁵²

The cash that flowed into the country led to the monetarisation of the economy and a rapid extension of trade. In 1871 most of the hut tax was paid in kind; in 1872 it was paid entirely in cash.⁵³ In 1871 there were about 20 fixed trading stations in the country, by 1873 about 50, and by 1877 about 70.⁵⁴ The Basotho were buying blankets, ready-made clothing, handkerchiefs, beads, copper wire, tobacco, sugar, rice, soap, salt, ploughs, spades, axes and hoes.⁵⁵ By 1879, according to one trader, it was rare to find a man who was not in European dress.⁵⁶ Throughout the country stone houses were replacing the traditional Basotho *mehlongoafatše*.⁵⁷ At first only wagons were in short supply, since most had been seized or destroyed in the Seqiti War and they were so much in demand at the Diamond Fields, but this deficiency was soon partly made up.⁵⁸

Not everyone benefited. There were still men so poor that they found it difficult to find ten shillings each year for the hut tax,⁵⁹ and in 1876 there was a period of depression when wages at the Diamond Fields were reduced and thousands of labourers returned home.⁶⁰ More serious still, with the increasing pressure of population and the constant breaking up of new land there was a shortage of pasture in the lowlands and an inexorable increase in the ravages of soil erosion.

But overall most Basotho rejoiced in their prosperity, and it was linked in their eyes with peace and Cape colonial rule. In the annual *pitso* in 1875 one speaker spoke of his joy that because of peace 'Our horses increase. Our children are begotten in the house. Our cattle milked in the kraals. A man going on a journey leaves his children at home without anxiety. We are confident and happy. We all are well dressed.' Joel Molapo expressed these views more succinctly: 'The Basutos are happy and thankful because of their prosperity.'⁶¹

At the end of the decade a visitor to the country recorded his impressions in an article in *The Grahamstown Journal*:

---

[51] Kimble (1978: 200). A muid was about three bushels.
[52] G.16-'76, p. 8, Rolland to Griffith, 31 December 1875.
[53] LNA, S9/2/1/1, Griffith to Colonial Secretary, 15 March 1873.
[54] G.27-'73, p. 1, Griffith to Colonial Secretary, 15 March 1873; G.27-'74, p. 23, Griffith to SNA, 31 January 1874; CA, NA 274, Rolland to SNA, 18 December 1877.
[55] BR VI.176, Griffith to Colonial Secretary, 26 August 1872.
[56] *Cape Argus*, 28 October 1879, 'Basutoland'.
[57] *JME* 1877, p. 329, Jousse, letter of 8 July 1877. *Mohlongoafatše*, pl. *mehlongoafatše*, was a hemispherical hut made from a framework of flexible branches planted in a circle in the ground.
[58] *The Little Light of Basotholand*, January 1872, p. 4, 'State of Basotholand'; *JME* 1872, pp. 83-4, 'Nouvelles Générales. Afrique du Sud'; G.21-'75, p. 4, Griffith to SNA, 10 February 1875.
[59] G.12-'77, p. 13, 'Notes of the Annual Meeting ("Pitso") held at Maseru on the 12th October, 1876', speeches of Ntsane Nchaku and Ramohapi.
[60] Kimble (1978: 230).
[61] G.16-'76, p. 17, 'Minutes of the Annual Meeting ("Pitso") held at Maseru, on the 4th of November 1875'.

Even the most casual observer would not fail to remark in traversing it, that it is a prosperous and peaceful country. The valleys and the slopes of the hills are black with cattle; in every direction fields of maize and wheat extend as far as the eye can reach. The inhabitants, more especially the men, are nearly all dressed in the European fashion, and the whole country is studded with villages. Here and there a trader's store is encountered along the route; in the far distance the white buildings of a mission station stand out against the green of the trees which surround it. Transport wagons advance in single file along the roads and testify by their numbers to the extension which both the import and the export trade has assumed. A glance at the interior of the shops, which are often vast, is enough to convince one of the progress which civilization has made among the Basuto. But the most remarkable thing is the atmosphere of quiet security which prevails everywhere among natives and Europeans alike. This peace is largely due to the very wise rule of the magistrates and particularly to the confidence which Mr. Griffith, the Government agent, universally inspires ....[62]

In one way the chiefs benefited from this economic advance. With their large land-holdings they stood to gain from the profitable sale of surplus wheat and other cereals. But in another way they lost out. The more wealth their subjects obtained the less they depended on the chiefs and the more independent they became. As early as 1872 Rolland reported that because of this the chiefs were losing 'one of the main sources of their influence'.[63] 'Men who used to live and be dependent on their chiefs' cattle,' he wrote five years later, 'now acquire cattle of their own and emancipate themselves from their chiefs.'[64] The empowerment of the individual was as important in breaking down the power of the chiefs as the imposition of magistrates.

The Cape authorities were convinced that, in seeking to undermine the power of the chiefs, they had strong popular support. The common people, they believed, had not only lost confidence in the chiefs because of their sufferings in the recent war, but were tired of their oppressions and would no longer submit to them. Even if the chiefs recovered their power, said Bowker, they would have to be submissive, for 'the common people are now all on our side'; Richard Southey was sure that, although the chiefs were recovering their power after the Seqiti War, there was 'a feeling growing up among the people not to submit to that'; and John Merriman believed that there was a growing disposition among the people to welcome anything that would take them away from the power of the chiefs.[65] This growing spirit of opposition to the chiefs was particularly strong among the Christians in the country.

Lastly, the government had the support of the missionaries, who believed that the power of the chiefs would have to be broken if the Sesotho way of life, with its initiation ceremonies, cattle-marriage and polygamy, was to be replaced by the Christian faith.[66]

'The cow of our alliance with Maseru': Lerotholi's praise poet had good reason to use this term. For the Mosotho cattle were the great symbol of wealth, a source of pride and of a sense of well-being. In a similar way, or so it seemed, Cape rule had brought great benefits to Basutoland. There was all the more reason to remain obedient and loyal.

---

[62] Quoted in Germond (1967: 328). For a similar article see *Cape Argus*, 24 February 1880, 'British Basutoland'.
[63] G.27-'73, p. 12, Rolland to Griffith, 31 December 1873.
[64] CA, NA 274, Rolland to SNA, 18 December 1877.
[65] *BR* VI.54, 63, 66, *Minutes of Evidence taken by the Select Committee on Basutoland Annexation Bill*, evidence of Bowker, Southey and Merriman respectively.
[66] *BR* IV.43, Rolland, 'Notes on the Political and Social Position of the Basuto Tribe', 30 March 1868.

CHAPTER 4: THE ATTACK ON THE CHIEFS

The land

It was an underlying principle of colonial rule that Moshoeshoe had given the country to the Queen and that the right of assigning land was now vested in the High Commissioner and Governor and, through him, his Agent and his magistrates. This principle was spelt out in Wodehouse's regulations of 1870 and repeated in Barkly's regulations of 1871 and 1877.[1] These gave the administration the final say in every territorial issue from the allocation of wards to the chiefs, including the determination of the boundaries between them, to the allocation of lands to individual commoners. The chiefs were consulted and given delegated powers, but they were no longer in overall control.

This transfer of territorial authority was something entirely new to the chiefs, and Moshoeshoe in particular seemed incapable of grasping its implications. When Bowker moved his headquarters to Maseru the old chief complained that he had not been consulted. Bowker told him bluntly that the land had been won by the High Commissioner from the Free State and he did not have to thank the Basotho for it.[2] After the Convention of Aliwal North the most pressing and difficult business was to resettle those chiefs and their followers whose lands now fell in the Free State. Moshoeshoe criticised his subordinates for applying to the British for land: Wodehouse might be the Governor, he argued, but it was for him, Moshoeshoe, to point out to his followers their gardens.[3] His objections were swept aside.

By the time Griffith and his magistrates took office the task of resettlement was complete, but as the amount of land available to the Basotho was now less than before, as the population was rapidly increasing, and as each young chief demanded his own holding as soon as he came of age, disputes constantly arose, some of them erupting into armed confrontations. It had not been Moshoeshoe's usual practice to define boundaries when placing a chief – so much land had been available that he could simply indicate where the chief was to establish his village – but as the country became more crowded the chiefs' claims to the intervening land began to overlap.[4] In 1875 Griffith toured the country defining the limits between villages,[5] and both before and after this initiative the administration was frequently called on to intervene in response to real or threatened hostilities.

It was impossible for the government to attend to every detail of land allocation, especially to individual commoners, and for this purpose the Regulations provided for the country to be divided into wards and for a chief or headman to be appointed to 'superintend' each ward. If anyone, chief or commoner, believed that he or she had been treated unjustly they could appeal to Griffith or the local magistrate.[6] It seems that the three principal chiefs were made 'wardmasters' of the four districts, with

---

[1] *Basutoland: High Commissioner's Proclamations and Notices to June 30 1901* (Cape Town, n.d.), p.41, Wodehouse's Regulations, 13 May 1870; p. 51, Barkly's Regulations, 6 November 1871; p. 61, Barkly's Regulations, 29 March 1877.
[2] BR V.90, Bowker to Wodehouse, 28 March 1869.
[3] Sanders (1975: 308).
[4] G.33-'79, p. 13, Charles Bell to Griffith, 31 December 1878; LNA, L2/1/1, Major Bell to Griffith, 1 January 1879; Memorandum of statement of Basuto deputation to J M Orpen, MLA, 1880, LNA, file not noted. This is a copy of a document that was apparently sent to Orpen in January 1880 before the outbreak of the Gun War. But there were apparently some cases in which Moshoeshoe laid down a boundary: see p. 41 below.
[5] *The Little Light of Basutoland*, February and March 1875, p. 12.
[6] *Basutoland: High Commissioners' Proclamations and Notices to June 30th 1901* (Cape Town, n.d.), p. 41, Wodehouse's

Letsie being responsible for Thaba-Bosiu and Cornet Spruit, and that they in turn delegated powers to their subordinate chiefs, who were designated as wardmasters in their own areas. The appointment of wardmasters was subject to colonial control, which in effect gave the magistrates the right to appoint chiefs. For the most part they followed the wishes of the greater chiefs, but there were exceptions. In 1875, for example, Surmon angered Masupha by recognising the Hlubi chief Tokonya as wardmaster instead of Masupha's nominee.[7] In another case Rolland, after consulting the local people, appointed Daniel Letsosa as a wardmaster, the eldest son of the 'late petty chief and wardmaster Letsosa', without consulting Letsie.[8]

Griffith was quick to assert his authority. When the chiefs complained about the number and extent of the reserves set aside for the magistracies, they were told – or so Masupha said later – 'that they had no more to say' about the Basotho's country.[9] In 1871, when a junior chief complained that Masupha was trying to make him move, Griffith asked for an immediate explanation: 'it is only the High Commissioner', he wrote, 'who has the right of allotting land, and no addition or alteration can be made except with my approval'.[10] In 1874, when Letsie ordered one of his subordinates to move, Rolland told him not to mind 'Letsie's nonsense';[11] and when Letsie's son and heir, Lerotholi, began allocating land on his own authority Rolland declared that he had no right to make or alter boundaries unless his changes were referred to and approved by government.[12] In the same year, at the annual *pitso*, the chiefs were informed that all wood, reeds and grass for thatching, rope-making, basket-making etc., which they had previously controlled, now belonged to the Queen. They would be allowed to administer them on her behalf, but they would be deprived of this power if they abused it.[13] The chiefs were also worried about the extent of land granted for trading stations, though they were usually consulted and their views taken into account.

In the north there were repeated conflicts between Molapo, Masupha and Ramanella. One of the main sources of disturbance was a valuable reed-bed which was shared between Ramanella's and Molapo's followers. Dr. Henry Taylor, who arrived at Hlotse Heights, in the Leribe District, in 1877, gave the following account of a court case which, though he did not name them, clearly arose because of a boundary dispute between Molapo and Ramanella:

> guns were brought out and some sharp fighting took place. Colonel Griffith at once sent to the chiefs, ordering them to cease fighting and to meet him at Thlotsi [Hlotse Heights]..... On the appointed day the Colonel rode up from Maseru, about sixty miles from Thlotsi, and the rival chiefs, with thousands of their people, came to meet him. In a flood of oratory the speakers made

---

Regulations, 13 May 1870; p. 51, Barkly's Regulations, 6 November 1871; p. 61, Barkly's Regulations, 29 March 1877. Each chief or headman in charge of a particular area was required to submit to the Governor's Agent a list of persons to whom he proposed to allocate land, but in practice this was not done: G.33-'79, p. 36, report on *pitso*, 24 October 1878, speech by Griffith.

[7] LNA, S9/1/3/2, Griffith to Masupha, 8 December 1875.

[8] LNA, MF 2/1/1, Rolland to Griffith, 8 June 1874. See also LNA, S9/1/2/1, Rolland to SNA, 15 and 25 February 1878.

[9] G.26-'82, p. 21, account of meeting held on 23 June 1881.

[10] LNA, S9/1/3/1, Griffith to Masupha, 9 September 1871. See also LNA, S9/1/3/2, Griffith to Masupha, 10 May 1873.

[11] LNA, MF 2/1/1, Rolland to Griffith, 19 October and 10 November 1874.

[12] LNA, MF 2/1/1, Hope to Rolland, 30 July 1874, and S9/1/3/2, Rolland to Hope, 5 August 1874.

[13] G.21-'75, p. 25, 'Minutes of the Annual Public Meeting held at Maseru on 2nd October, 1874'.

frequent reference to their former great Chief Moshesh, and the boundary lines which he had made, evidently considering that everything he had done was sacred for ever after. Colonel Griffith sat quite still, and spoke no word till the last orator had exhausted himself. Then he rose and delivered himself of a few short sentences, as follows:

'Moshesh is dead, and his boundary lines are dead too, and thus I rub them out.' Here he drew his foot rapidly along the ground several times, as if effacing a mark. 'Now, I am going to make a boundary, and let any man try to rub it out at his peril.'[14]

In the south there were constant disputes among the chiefs under Letsie's command. There is evidence in 1872, for example, of Rolland determining a land dispute between two of Letsie's subordinates, with Letsie being shuffling and 'duplicitous'.[15] And in the following year Rolland and Austen made recommendations to Griffith about a dispute between Lerotholi and Moletsane's Bataung.[16] Practice seems to have varied from case to case, but invariably the colonial authorities insisted on having final control.

The most important, and the most dangerous, of these territorial disputes arose from Masupha's refusal to leave the area of Thaba-Bosiu. After the Seqiti War he had settled at Qiloane, close to the foot of his father's mountain. Letsie was disturbed, partly because Masupha was living within the Thaba-Bosiu District, which he regarded as his personal ward, but also because Masupha would gain prestige from living near his father's mountain. Bowker ordered Masupha to move, and when Sir Henry Barkly visited the country in 1871 he warned him, apparently under the impression that Masupha was living on the summit of Thaba-Bosiu,[17] that if he did not move he would no longer be recognised as a chief. Letsie too ordered Masupha to move, but he refused and said he would maintain his position by force if necessary.

This was the situation which faced Griffith when he arrived in Basutoland in August. His own view was that it was a pity that Bowker had ordered Masupha to move, especially as Masupha was not actually living on the mountain. But Barkly insisted that Masupha had to go. He conceded that it would be impossible not to recognise Masupha as a chief, but gave directions that he should not be paid the percentage of the hut tax which was now being allocated to the senior chiefs. Masupha retaliated by ordering his people not to pay the tax.

In October 1871 Griffith gave the first of several orders that Masupha should move into the Berea District. Masupha ignored him. Letsie renewed his orders to move, and Masupha fobbed him off. Griffith became increasingly anxious. In November 1873 he demanded 'clear and definite instructions how to act'. He was 'daily more and more impressed with the importance' of this affair: 'whichever way the decision may be, the result cannot but prove hereafter of the most vital importance to the prestige of British Authority in this Territory.'[18]

Both the government and Letsie were reluctant to use force. An excuse to back down was desperately needed. At this point Letsie indicated that he was willing to ask the government for the

---

[14] Taylor (1972: 23). See also LNA, S3/5/3/1A: Memorandum showing the boundary of the ward of Chief Lesaoana [Ramanella], in the District of Leribe, as defined by Griffith, 28 November 1878.
[15] LNA, MF 2/1/1, Rolland to Griffith, 30 December 1872.
[16] CA, NA 272, Rolland to Griffith, 23 June 1873.
[17] *BR* VI.111, Barkly to Griffith, 2 September 1871; CA, NA 840, Brownlee to Griffith, 10 January 1874; *Leselinyana*, June 1874.
[18] LNA, S9/1/2/1, Griffith to SNA, 21 November 1873.

district boundary to be altered so that Masupha's village would fall within the Berea District. (It was apparently only a few kilometres on the Thaba-Bosiu side of the border.) Barkly seized on this and said that, if Letsie made this request, he would be willing for Masupha to stay where he was.[19]

He had another reason, or excuse, for clemency. At the end of 1873 the Hlubi chief, Langalibalele, fled with his followers from Natal into Basutoland after refusing to give up his guns to the Natal authorities and killing several men in a skirmish. This gave rise to disproportionate alarm, and it was feared that the Basotho would join forces with the Hlubi. Instead Molapo and his sons tricked Langalibalele into surrender. The government, relieved, was effusive in its expressions of appreciation of the Basotho's loyalty. Although Masupha himself had not taken part Brownlee suggested that his being allowed to stay should be presented as a reward for the Basotho's conduct at this time.[20]

Before Griffith could convey this message to the chiefs, however, Masupha, quite fortuitously it seems, let it be known that he was at last willing to move,[21] and by May 1874 Griffith could report that he had ploughed up land in his 'new place'. Even so the plan to alter the boundary was proceeded with, and at a large *pitso* at Thaba-Bosiu Griffith went with Letsie to point out the new boundary to Masupha, which included his 'present residence'. So although Masupha ploughed up new land he was apparently allowed to stay at Qiloane in his existing village.[22]

All parties declared that they were satisfied, and Masupha's percentage of the hut tax was restored to him. But the confrontation had exposed the government's weakness and foreshadowed many similar confrontations in later years when Masupha defied both the government and Letsie with impunity.

A few years later, in 1877, the Cape authorities were similarly helpless when several chiefs in the south, descendants of Moshoeshoe's brothers, Posholi and Mohale, moved with their people into the Maloti without authority. Austen suspected that they were trying to avoid the hut tax, but shortage of land was a more probable cause. It was one of the first Basotho migrations into the mountains, and apart from insisting that they still had to pay their tax Griffith felt there was little he could do.[23]

For the most part, however, the government's authority was welcomed by the smaller chiefs and accepted, at least grudgingly, by the principal chiefs. In 1879 one of Molapo's subordinates, Selebalo Moshoeshoe, fled with all his followers to Major Bell's magistracy because he believed that Molapo intended to attack him, and he was then reinstated on Bell's insistence. 'I mention this circumstance', Bell reported, 'as shewing the confidence there is in the Government as a protection from tyranny.'[24]

The common people had even more cause to welcome the protection afforded by the government. It was one of the administration's repeated boasts that it maintained every man in possession of his own,[25] and as early as September 1871, only a month after his arrival in the country, Griffith was reprimanding Nehemiah for turning a man off his fields at Mokhokhung:

---

[19] CA, NA 272, Barkly, memorandum, 8 January 1874. For the position of Masupha's village, see *The Journal*, 29 October 1880, 'Round About Basutoland. Thaba Bosigo', and Ambrose (1972).
[20] CA, NA 840, Brownlee to Griffith, 10 January 1874.
[21] LNA, S9/1/2/1, Griffith to Brownlee, 30 January 1874.
[22] LNA, S9/1/2/1, Griffith to Brownlee, 14 May 1874; *Leselinyana*, June 1874; Ambrose (1972).
[23] CA, NA 274, Austen to Griffith, 9 July 1877; LNA, S9/1/2/1, Griffith to SNA, 19 July 1877; CA, NA 274, Brownlee's undated memorandum; LNA, S9/1/3/3, Griffith to Austen, 12 September 1877.
[24] LNA, L2/1/1, Bell to Molapo, 8 April 1878, and G.33-'79, p. 6, Bell to Griffith, 1 January 1879.
[25] *BR* VI.176, Griffith to Colonial Secretary, 26 August 1872.

> You must know that you have no authority to turn people away from their own places .... Recollect that you are under the Queen's Government where the least of Her Subjects are entitled to the same justice as the Highest.[26]

Other chiefs known to have been checked in this way were Ramanella, Jonathan Molapo and Sofonia Moshoeshoe,[27] and there must have been many others too. It was impossible for the government to prevent every injustice: in 1874 Griffith complained that the chiefs were oppressing people who were not their favourites in the allocation of reeds,[28] and in 1878 he warned them that if they continued to turn people off land to make way for their friends and relatives the government would have to carry out a 'land survey to give each man his portion'.[29] In 1878 Rolland reported that 'They [the people] look upon the Government as their protector against the chiefs and would be glad to see the power of the chiefs still more restrained and their individual rights more definitely recognised, especially in the direction of land rights.'[30]

At the time there was surprisingly little protest from the chiefs about the loss of their territorial powers. In 1877, however, Griffith was transferred from Basutoland (temporarily as it turned out) to take charge of the Cape's military operations on its eastern frontier, and Rolland, as Acting Governor's Agent, asked the Basotho, if they had any serious grievances, to submit these in writing to him. In the petition that was subsequently drawn up one of the main 'causes of dissatisfaction' expressed was the chiefs' loss of power over the allocation of land. Some people were ploughing land without permission, and when challenged were retorting that under the Cape government all men were now equal.[31]

Two months later, in September 1878, what Rolland described as 'a very noisy and tumultuous meeting' was held in the Thaba-Bosiu District at the village of a headman who had been placed there by Griffith. Nehemiah Moshoeshoe claimed the land for himself and denied Griffith's right to allocate it to anyone else, and he was backed up by Maama, Letsie's son.[32] Letsie disowned them, but at the annual *pitso* in the following month, at which the July petition was discussed, his councillor, Ntho, speaking on his behalf, said that Letsie 'had a grievance about the land; that he saw that he was no longer a master or allotter'. The pasturage was being ploughed up. Masupha too declared that he wanted the authority of the chiefs to be respected with regard to the allocation of land.[33]

After the war, when the Basotho were asked what form of government they wanted, Ntho again spoke out strongly. Having protested about the extent of land that had been taken for the government reserves, he went on to complain about 'a second matter' which was serious and gave rise to anxiety, that

---

[26] LNA, S9/1/3/1, Griffith to Nehemiah Moshoeshoe, 9 September 1871.
[27] LNA, L2/1/1, Bell to Ramanella, 13 June 1877, and Bell to Jonathan, 23 September 1878; C. 3708, p. 52, report of meeting held at Maseru on 19 March 1883.
[28] G.21-'75, pp. 25-66, Griffith to SNA, 'Minutes of the Annual Public Meeting held at Maseru on 2nd October, 1874'.
[29] G.33-'79, p. 36, minutes of *pitso*, 24 October 1878.
[30] CA, NA 275, Rolland to SNA, 19 July 1878.
[31] CA, NA 275, 'Petition of the Chiefs and People of Basutoland ...', enclosed with Letsie and Tsekelo to Rolland, 3 July 1878.
[32] LNA, S 9/1/2/1, Rolland to SNA, 17 September 1878.
[33] G.33-'79, p. 33, minutes of *pitso*, 24 October 1878.

the magistrates said that no chief in Basutoland had any right to place a man without the leave of the magistrate, and the chiefs said to the magistrates, well, if we have no right to place anybody without your consent what right have we left to us of our chieftainship?

Ntho described a dispute between two headmen in which, he said, Letsie was 'almost crying with pain' because the magistrate had overturned Moshoeshoe's arrangements. And he went on to tell of another case, in which the local magistrate had told Lerotholi that his village at Likhoele would never be 'firm' because he had been placed there by Moshoeshoe, not by the government. Letsie had protested that the magistrates were ignoring Moshoeshoe's arrangements and making their own, 'setting the chiefs completely aside'.[34]

Even a chief who was as closely identified with the government as Sofonia felt he had reason to complain. 'One thing we didn't like', he said after the war, 'was that if one of my people under me was disobedient to me, and I ordered him away, he complained to the Government that I had ordered him to go away, and the Government kept him there. The ward is mine all the same ....'[35]

In the increasingly crowded area available there was bound to be pressure by the senior chiefs to provide wards for their sons at the expense of their subordinates. Griffith and his magistrates believed that, in exercising territorial control, they were protecting the rights of lesser chiefs and commoners against the oppressions of the senior chiefs. On the other hand the senior chiefs regarded the government's intervention as an unwarranted interference, and indeed an injustice, especially when it set aside long-standing arrangements. For them the people who appealed to the magistrates were not victims of oppression, but malcontents who were exploiting the opportunity to appeal to a new centre of authority, to play off the magistrates against them.

The courts

This assumption of territorial control was closely connected with the second great assault on the powers of the chiefs – the establishment of the magistrates' courts. The chiefs' courts were not mentioned in the colonial regulations. They were not part of the official judicial framework. There was nothing to stop the chiefs holding their courts, but they were deprived of their power to summon their subjects and they could no longer punish them by fines. A magistrate's court was established in each district and people had the right to go to these courts whether or not the case had first been heard by their chief. They could even take their own chief to court, a possibility that had never been open to them before. Crimes that were punishable by the death penalty – murder and arson with intent to kill – could no longer be heard by the chiefs, but had to be taken before a combined court consisting of at least three magistrates.

Under these regulations the chiefs stood to lose a major source of income through the fines they had imposed in their courts. They also stood to lose a major source of control over their subjects. In cases of extreme disobedience, they lost the power of 'eating them up', that is of punishing them by seizing all their goods and livestock and burning down their home. It was common among whites to condemn 'eating up' as an abuse of power in itself. It was certainly a power that was often abused. Covetous or capricious chiefs arranged for wealthy commoners, or men who had incurred their displeasure, to be 'smelt out' on spurious charges of witchcraft and then 'eaten up' by way of punish-

---

[34] C.3708, pp. 78-9, report of meeting held at Morija on 26 March 1883. See also CA, NA 272, minutes of meeting held at Maseru on 20 August 1873.

[35] C.3708, pp. 52-3, report of meeting held at Maseru on 19 March 1883.

ment – a practice, of course, which deterred men from building up their wealth or offending their chief.[36] But 'eating up' in itself was no more than the Basotho's most extreme form of punishment, and the loss of this form of control was resented. 'What greater cruelty and oppression can there be than this', wrote Ramanella, 'that Government should prevent chiefs from eating up their own people?'[37] Later Masupha was to declare that he had entered on the Gun War 'in order to test the power of the Chiefs to punish and eat up their own people'.[38]

The introduction of a police force, however small and weak, was another intrusion on the chiefs' powers, and in the early years there were reports of people being afraid to join the police and of policemen being hindered in carrying out their duties.

It was an essential part of the government's programme to draw cases away from the chiefs to the magistrates, and they inevitably ran into determined, though often covert, opposition, especially from the three great sons of Moshoeshoe. In the south Letsie listened sympathetically to those who lost their cases in the courts and complained repeatedly to Rolland on their behalf. He protested that a magistrate had no right to entertain a case unless it was sent to him by a chief. At the same time Rolland found it difficult to get men to enrol in the police.[39] In the north Molapo was even better placed to hinder the work of the courts. His village was only a few hundred metres from Bell's headquarters and people were afraid that they would be punished if they were seen going to the magistrate's court.[40] Molapo also forbade his men to join the police, and in March 1873 Bell reported that he had been able to recruit only four men, all of them 'Zulu'.[41] Later in the year the police complained that the chiefs were interfering with the execution of their duties, that they had poisoned the minds of the people against them, and that it was not safe for them to go about alone.[42] In the Berea District Masupha discouraged his people from taking their cases to the magistrates and ordered them to resist the police.[43] In his report for 1874 Surmon complained that Masupha was doing everything that he could to hinder him.[44] Tsekelo Moshoeshoe, now ingratiating himself with the colonial authorities, told Griffith that Letsie, Molapo and Masupha were condemning people who took their cases to the magistrates as enemies and renegades, and that they comforted those against whom judgement was given by telling them that they had been 'killed' without cause.[45]

In spite of this opposition more and more people took their cases to the magistrates. In August 1872, reporting on his first year in office, Griffith claimed that both the common people and the minor chiefs were contented with colonial rule because it protected them from the 'oppression' of the

---

[36] See, e.g., G.27-'73, p. 8, Rolland to Griffith, Report for Year Ending 31 December 1872.

[37] CA, ACC 302, Orpen Papers, loose undated pages, evidently from a letter. See also LNA, S9/1/2/1, Rolland to SNA, 17 September 1878. For similar resentment among the chiefs on the Cape's Eastern Frontier, see MacQuarrie (1958: 103).

[38] LNA, S9/1/2/2, Orpen to Sauer, 13 September 1882.

[39] LNA, S9/2/1/2, Rolland to Griffith, Mafeteng, 7 April and 5 May 1873; G.20-'81, p. 14, Austen to Griffith, 31 December 1880.

[40] G.27-'73, p. 6, Bell to Griffith, 14 January 1873.

[41] LNA, L2/1/1, Bell to Griffith, 25 March 1873.

[42] LNA, S9/1/3/2, Griffith to Bell, 28 October 1873, and L2/1/1, Bell to Griffith, 2 November 1873.

[43] G.27-'73, p.7, Surmon to Griffith, 28 January 1873.

[44] G.21-'75, p. 9, Surmon to Griffith, 18 January 1875.

[45] CA, NA 272, Tsekelo to Griffith, 30 August 1873, reprinted in Burman (1976A: 55-6).

principal chiefs and maintained every man in the possession of his own.[46] In his annual report for 1873 he amplified this account:

> At first very few Basutos brought their cases before the magistrates, most of them being deterred by fear of the chiefs, who did all in their power, short of open opposition, to prevent them. Strong prejudices also existed in the minds of the people against the magistrates, and these were fostered by the chiefs, who foresaw the loss of their power. The people were taught to believe that the magistrates had come to subvert all their cherished laws and customs. ....
>
> Gradually, however, ... the magistrates succeeded in winning the confidence of the common people. These began to find out that the Government was their true friend and protector against the arbitrary and unjust acts of their chiefs. Every case which was decided by the magistrates was duly canvassed, and increased the prestige of the Government. Prejudices began to disappear, and many people openly supported the Government; those who did so prominently being jeered at by the chiefs as 'rebels and turncoats'.[47]

Over the next few years Griffith and his magistrates claimed increasing success, and their annual reports, recording one encouraging advance after another, were like a triumphal procession.

In the south Letsie's opposition was soon swept aside. From Mafeteng, in his report for 1874, Rolland declared that the influence of the government had steadily increased, that much of the former 'diffidence and mistrust' had disappeared, and that the government's authority was recognised everywhere and was 'more and more superseding that of the native chiefs'. The people seemed 'content and happy'.[48] At Mohale's Hoek, in his report for the same year, John Austen stated that 'The Basutos flock now daily in large numbers to the magistrate's office with all their complaints, ask advice, and will seldom accept the decisions of their own chiefs and headmen in their disputes. The fear of the chief has completely broken down, and there appears the fullest confidence in British administration of justice.'[49]

Letsie accepted the position, but only because he was powerless to do anything else. In 1875 he complained about being deprived of the power to summon his own subjects and to decide cases himself, but Griffith told him 'that this would never do as the Chiefs would favour some and be against others. The Magistrates are the proper persons to issue summonses and decide cases. In the Colony it is exactly the same, even the Governor cannot summons people.'[50] Commenting later, Letsie's councillor, Ntho, said that Letsie was so angry with this reply 'that he refused to go and eat the Governor's Agent's steak'.[51]

In the north, in the Leribe District, there was a complete transformation as Molapo swung round to support the government. He and his sons had played a leading part in the suppression of the so-called Langalibalele rebellion at the end of 1873, and they were rewarded with some of the Hlubi's cattle. Major Bell, who had constantly agonised about the absence of any visible support for the administration, believed that it was the firm action taken against Langalibalele, and in particular the

---

[46] *BR* VI.176, Griffith to Colonial Secretary, 26 August 1872.
[47] G.27-'74, p. 22, Griffith to SNA, 31 January 1874.
[48] G.21-'75, p.9, Rolland, 'Annual Report on the Sub-District of Thaba Bosigo for the year 1874', January 1875.
[49] G.21-'75, p. 6, Austen to Griffith, 21 January 1875.
[50] G.16-'76, p. 17, 'Minutes of the Annual Meeting ("Pitso") held at Maseru on the 4th day of November 1875'.
[51] C.3708, p. 78, report on meeting held at Morija on 26 March 1883.

intervention of the Frontier Armed and Mounted Police, that had led to Molapo's change of mind.[52] Writing in February 1874, Molapo acknowledged that when Bell had first been appointed he had been full of 'reluctance and misgiving', but he asked the government to forgive his stupidity. 'Today it is I, Molapo, who praise Major Bell, ...'[53] Molapo was also pleasantly surprised by the amount of cash he received from his percentage of the hut tax, and told Bell that 'formerly he used to look to Moshesh as his father but now he looked to the Government'.[54] In his report for 1874 Bell wrote: 'The feeling of the chiefs and people towards the British Government appears satisfactory. More cases are brought to my court as one year succeeds another. The greater part of them have been previously reported to Molapo, with whose sanction they are brought to me.'[55] Bell did not say whether Molapo ever refused to give his sanction, but we hear no more of opposition from the chief. In his report for 1876 Bell recorded that he had moved his magistracy from Leribe to Hlotse Heights and that the number of cases referred to his court had 'much increased'. 'The Chiefs appear to be, and the people undoubtedly are, contented.'[56]

In the Berea District even Masupha's opposition was gradually overcome. At the annual *pitso* in 1875 he protested, like Letsie, that he should have the power to summon his people and to punish and correct them. He also wanted the right to hear cases first, before they were referred to the magistrates. 'We are of no use as chiefs', he concluded. 'We have no more power. The people despise us.'[57] In his report for 1878 the newly appointed magistrate, Charles Bell, recorded a great improvement on previous years. There had been an increase in the number of cases brought to the magistrate's office, and Masupha himself was occasionally 'a suitor in the Court'.

> Chief Masupha, ... one of the most arbitrary and capricious chiefs in Basutoland, is gradually becoming aware of the fact that his efforts to throw off [the government's] yoke, and retain his gradually waning power, are unavailing, and fruitless.
>
> Appeals against his judgement are of frequent occurrence; and in fact, were it not for the cattle and horses the people possess, belonging to him, giving him a certain hold upon them, his power would soon wane ....[58]

In his report for 1877 the new magistrate at Maseru, Henry Davies, recorded an increase in the number of cases over the previous year, so that it was difficult for him to keep pace with all the work. There was a growing confidence in the government, he wrote, and many people came to his office to have their cases settled or to seek advice.[59]

The French missionaries confirmed these reports. Looking back at the end of 1880, their Director in Paris, Eugène Casalis, testified that the Basotho 'were gradually getting accustomed to English law and administration. The courts of the Native chiefs were being deserted.'[60]

---

[52] CA, NA 272, Bell to Griffith, 3 January 1874.
[53] CA, NA 272, Molapo to Brownlee, 17 February 1874.
[54] LNA, L2/1/1, Bell to Griffith, 21 September 1873.
[55] G.21-'75, p. 8, Bell to Griffith, 16 January 1875.
[56] G.12-'77, p. 7, Bell to Griffith, 3 January 1877.
[57] G.16-'76, p. 17, 'Minutes of the Annual Meeting ("Pitso") held at Maseru on 4th November 1875'.
[58] G.33-'79, p. 12, Charles Bell to Griffith, 31 December 1878.
[59] LNA, S9/2/3/1, Davies to Acting Governor's Agent, 1 January 1878.
[60] C.2821, p. 71, Casalis and others to Colonial Office, 9 December 1880.

Throughout the country the opposition to the police fell away. After 1873 difficulties in recruitment were no longer reported. Griffith had been given authority to enlist 100 police. By July 1873 he had enlisted 69 and received 'numerous' applications for the remaining posts, but was then told to cut back to 50.[61] There was still a disproportionate number of 'Zulu' and Hlubi in the force, but its loyalty was now assured.[62] Armed with Sniders and with smart uniforms, it was a force to command respect. And it helped good relations that the chiefs were often called upon to carry out police duties, being asked to arrest criminals, for example, and to help in the suppression of stock theft.

It was a great shock to the chiefs, however, that they themselves could now be taken to court.[63] Nor was this just a matter of form. Griffith insisted repeatedly that the law was no respecter of persons, and many chiefs were indeed taken to court, both in criminal and in civil cases. In the early years the most striking prosecution was that of Chief Sekake Molomo, a descendant of Moshoeshoe's brother Mohale, who was convicted of murder in 1873.[64] In 1875 Letsie himself was taken to court in a dispute over cattle, and although he won the case it demonstrated that even the greatest chief in the land could be brought to account.[65] And in 1877 Tsekelo Moshoeshoe was convicted of being an accessory to the theft of two oxen and of receiving stolen property.[66] There were compromises. Great play had been made of the introduction of the death penalty for murder: it was a mark of high civilization, it was said, showing that human life was sacred and that murder was a serious crime to be severely punished, not a civil wrong to be remedied by compensation to the victim's family. Yet Sekake was not hanged, but sentenced to two years in prison, which was later commuted to a fine of £75.[67] And though Tsekelo was sentenced to three months in prison and 25 lashes, Griffith remitted the lashes.[68] But overall the message was clear: the chiefs were no longer above the law.

If they wanted to take action against their own subjects they had to apply to the court. As early as 1872 Rolland was claiming that the old practice of the chiefs 'eating up' their subjects had now fallen away. Commoners could now better themselves without the fear of being struck down.[69] In 1878, Henry Davies, the magistrate in Maseru, reported that, whereas in the past the chiefs 'were continually "smelling out" and "eating up" those of their subjects who had the misfortune to have accumulated property', 'now-a-days ... this power is daily waning and such oppression is no longer heard of; so that every one feels secure under the protecting wing of the Government'.[70] In 1880 a certain Filibert Makosholo, writing in the mission newspaper, *Leselinyana*, thanked the government that it had put a stop to 'eating up' for no apparent reason.[71] No doubt the government exaggerated the injustices per-

---

[61] LNA, S9/2/1/2, Griffith to Colonial Secretary, 15 July 1873.
[62] E.g., *Mission Field*, 1877, pp. 89-90, Widdicombe's letter of 30 December 1876.
[63] E.g., CA, NA 272, Tsekelo to Griffith, 30 August 1873, enclosed with Griffith to Colonial Secretary, 11 September 1873; C.3708, p. 52, report on meeting held at Maseru on 19 March 1883, evidence of Sofonia Moshoeshoe, and p. 56, report on meeting held at Maseru on 20 March 1883, evidence of George Moshoeshoe.
[64] *The Little Light of Basutholand*, October 1873, p. 32.
[65] *The Little Light of Basutoland*, February and March 1875, p.12; *The Cape Argus*, 23 March 1875, quoted in Bradlow (1968: 132).
[66] LNA, S9/1/3/3, Griffith to Letsie, 1 February 1877.
[67] LNA, S9/1/3/2, Griffith to Letsie, 30 January 1874.
[68] LNA, S9/1/3/3, Griffith to Letsie, 1 February 1877.
[69] G.27-'73, p. 8, Rolland to Griffith, Report for the Year Ending 31 December 1872.
[70] LNA, S9/2/3/1, Davies to Acting Governor's Agent, 1 January 1878.
[71] *Leselinyana*, January 1880.

Stray stock and Sesotho custom

petrated by the chiefs, but the mere fact that so many people deserted their courts for the magistrates' speaks for itself.

Stray stock and Sesotho custom

The government also tried to put an end to the chiefs' arrogation of stray stock to themselves by stipulating in 1871 that anyone acting in this way would be guilty of theft and by establishing a government pound at Maseru.[72] Letsie was opposed to this measure, and in 1874 it was noted that many strays were not being sent to the pound, but were being kept at the chiefs' villages, partly because they were a source of revenue for them, and partly for fear of offending Letsie.[73] In the petition drawn up by Tsekelo for the chiefs in 1878 one of the main sources of grievance was the law about stray stock.[74]

Much more serious was Griffith's attempt to restrict the chiefs' right to call on the free labour of their subjects, since this would strike at their capacity to profit from their extensive land-holdings – a capacity that was all the more important as the price of grain rocketed during the 1870s. In 1872 he imposed a fine on Masupha for punishing one of his followers who had refused to take part in a communal work-party, a *letsema*. He had good reason for taking this step. A chief had the right to call out his subjects to supply free labour on his public fields, *masimo a lira*, and on the fields of his senior wife, since the produce from these fields was put to public use – to feed travellers, or people who appeared before the chief's court, or those who were in need.[75] But the leading chiefs were abusing this right by getting their people to work on the fields of all their wives, not just the senior, and by punishing them if they refused to attend.

Once again Griffith was intervening on behalf of the commoner against the chief, and he was fully supported by the missionaries, who regarded endorsing free labour for junior wives as tantamount to endorsing polygamy. But he had not consulted the chiefs, and he ran into a storm of opposition. Striking a blow at *matsema* was a step too far at this stage, especially as his interpretation of the custom was too narrow: he believed that it related to 'one garden' alone, that of the senior wife[76] Surprisingly, Masupha paid the fine demanded, but both Letsie and Molapo objected strongly. Griffith referred the matter to Cape Town, and was rebuked for acting 'somewhat precipitately in endeavouring to set aside suddenly and without reference to the several native chiefs, a custom of long standing in the country ....'[77] With no support from his masters, Griffith had to back down.[78]

In its dealings with Sesotho custom in general the administration was careful and circumspect. In 1872 Griffith and his four magistrates (Austen, Bell, Rolland and Surmon) were appointed as a Commission 'to inquire into the Native Laws and Customs of the Basutos'. The French missionaries called for the abolition of the three practices which they found most offensive – initiation, polygamy and marriage by cattle. The Commissioners disagreed. They disapproved of 'these heathenish and

---

[72] LNA, S9/1/3/1, Griffith's circular to his magistrates, 7 September 1871, and circular to senior chiefs.
[73] LNA, MF2/1/1, Rolland to Griffith, 7 December 1874.
[74] CA, NA 275, 'Petition ....' enclosed with Letsie and Tsekelo to Rolland, 3 July 1878. See also C.3708, p. 79, report of meeting held at Morija on 26 March 1883, Ntho's statement.
[75] There is a wealth of literature on *matsema*, and practice changed over time. This account is based mainly on articles in *Leselinyana*, February and March 1873.
[76] BR VI.147-8, Griffith to Southey, 27 February 1872.
[77] BR VI.156, Southey to Griffith, 16 March 1872.
[78] For detailed discussions of this issue, see Burman (1981: 76-7) and Mohapeloa (1971: 15-6).

barbarous customs' and 'would gladly see them abolished', but people could not be made Christians by legislation, only by conviction.[79] The hut tax acted as a disincentive to polygamy, and under the Governor's regulations it was unlawful to force a boy to be initiated against his or his parents' wishes or to force a woman to be married against her will, and widows were allowed to remarry. But such mitigating measures were as far as the government was prepared to go. Had it tried to enforce the sweeping changes advocated by the missionaries it would have played into the hands of those chiefs who tried to frighten the people by telling them that 'the magistrates had come to subvert all their cherished laws and customs'.[80] It would have jeopardised the popular support that it needed for its attack on the chiefs.

As it was there were complaints that, as a result of the government's regulations, women were becoming 'independent and insubordinate'.[81] And from time to time there were reports of 'pagan' reactions against Christianity and 'civilization'. According to the missionaries in 1876, polygamy and marriage by cattle flourished 'quite as much as ever'.[82] Initiation ceremonies, so far from dying away, were vigorously encouraged, especially in Masupha's area.[83]

In 1873 certain 'prophets' claimed to have received messages from the ancestors, above all Moshoeshoe, who was said to have condemned his children for allowing the white men to make a plaything of his people. His ultimate aim was to regain their independence, and in the meantime they 'must only enter into the Queen's government with one foot'. Letsie and Molapo were said to be sacrificing oxen at Moshoeshoe's grave.[84] In 1875 and 1876 there was a more widespread movement, a crusade against Christianity the missionaries called it, led this time by women and girls, who declared that the whites' God did not exist and who called on the Basotho to destroy everything of European origin – merino sheep, Angora goats, horses, ploughs, pots, pipes, woollen and cotton blankets and European clothing.[85]

In the event there was little response: only a few pipes were broken, according to the missionaries. The government by and large ignored the movement;[86] and by the end of 1876 it appeared to have lost momentum. The missionaries suspected that the prophets had been put up by the chiefs, who, they alleged, wanted to destroy Christianity which they saw as conflicting with their chieftainship and their polygamy.[87] It seems more likely that it was a spontaneous movement, and that the chiefs were responding to it rather than instigating it.[88]

---

[79] *BR* VI.192, Report of the Special Commission.
[80] G.27-'74, p. 22, Griffith to SNA, 31 January 1874.
[81] G.16-'76, p, 14, 'Minutes of the Annual Meeting ("Pitso") held at Maseru on the 4th day of November 1875', speech of Tšita Mofoka; G.20-81, p. 12, Austen to Griffith, 31 December 1880. See also CA, NA 272, Tsekelo to Griffith, 30 August 1873, enclosed with Griffith to Colonial Secretary, 11 September 1873 [reprinted in Burman, (1976A: 54)]; *Leselinyana*, August 1901, article by D.F. Ellenberger.
[82] *The Little Light of Basutoland*, January 1876, p. 2.
[83] *Leselinyana*, May 1874, August 1874, March 1880; *The Little Light of Basutoland*, February 1877.
[84] CA, NA 272, Tsekelo to Griffith, 30 August 1873, reprinted in Burman (1976A: 57).
[85] *The Little Light of Basutoland*, October - December 1875, pp. 46-7, and April-May 1876, p. 17.
[86] CA, NA 274, Barkly's farewell letter to the Basotho, March 1877.
[87] *The Little Light of Basutoland*, October - December 1875, p. 47, and January 1876, p. 2
[88] For Masupha being influenced by prophets, see C.2755, p. 158, evidence of George Moshoeshoe, 30 August 1880, and *JME*, 1882, p. 57, H. Dieterlen, '*La Situation Politique au Lessouto*'. For a detailed discussion of the movement, see Burman (1981: 100-7). Burman speculates that it might have been particularly strong in 1876 because Nehemiah and Tsekelo were stirring up trouble in Matatiele at that time.

There were other ways in which the government diminished the prestige and influence of the chiefs. Embassies from other chiefs were required to report to the administration. Invitations to meetings and notices about new laws were sent direct to subordinate chiefs, and not through the principal chiefs. The hut tax was collected from the people direct, not through the chiefs, though the chiefs assisted. All this gave rise to discontent.[89] Against this, at least for the three senior chiefs, there was the great compensation that they each received 10% of the hut tax collected in their districts, and smaller, discretionary payments were made to many of the other chiefs. Even Masupha, once it had been agreed that his percentage should be granted, gave every encouragement to his people to pay.

---

[89] E.g., CA, NA 272, Tsekelo's statement of 3 November 1873, enclosed with Surmon to Griffith, 10 November 1873; G.21-'75, pp. 16, 19, 'Minutes of the Annual Public Meeting held at Maseru on 2nd October, 1874'.

CHAPTER 5: 'SUCCESS' AND FEAR

A record of 'success'

By 1877 the Cape administration was revelling in its achievements. It was 'with the greatest satisfaction' that Griffith sent in his annual report for 1876: 'the system which now obtains in this territory,' he wrote, '... has thus far succeeded beyond the most sanguine expectation.'[1] A year later, in his report for 1877, Rolland declared that 'The Basutoland system of Government may be deemed to have been hitherto a success.'[2]

The Paris missionaries agreed: in spite of the initial misgivings in many quarters, the 'experiment' of transferring power from the chiefs to the magistrates had 'become a success'.[3] The veteran François Maeder expressed his hope, indeed his confidence, that war was now a thing of the past: the government was 'firm, respected and active', and the Basotho felt 'protected, cared for, loved'.[4]

It may seem surprising that there was so much support among the people for alien magistrates against their own chiefs, but the popular satisfaction with the administration was attested to by Basotho as well as colonial and missionary sources. A Mosotho correspondent in the mission newspaper, *Leselinyana*, stressed how grateful the Basotho were,[5] and after the war, when the best form of government was being considered, several of the *Maketetoa*'s spokesmen openly declared that the common people were terrified of being abandoned to the mercy of the chiefs. 'They see the Government protects them', said Sofonia. 'Before the rebellion ... the people themselves were satisfied .... They had no complaints. ... each one could do what he liked with his own.' 'They like to be treated justly,' said 'Tlaele' Moshoeshoe, 'and they look to be relieved from their chiefs .... They love the Government; they had already tasted what the Government was before the rebellion.'[6] Many years later Azariel Sekese, a Christian who was about 30 years old when the Gun War broke out, wrote that in the period of Cape rule:

> The Basotho were governed by laws which they respected. These laws were very uplifting and protected each person's property. No chief was allowed to take or steal from his subjects. The Basotho and the mission stations were progressing very favourably. There was peace and plenty all over the country. The people were indeed happy under the protection of Her Majesty's flag where Moshoeshoe left them when he died.[7]

At the time there was only one serious voice of dissent. After Griffith was posted to the Cape's Eastern Frontier in 1877 James Bowker, who had been Wodehouse's Agent in Basutoland, was appointed to take his place. He had been away from the country for about seven years, and he spent only a few months in office before retiring because of ill health. Giving his impressions in April 1878, a month after his arrival, he wrote:

> There is one point upon which I think the public have formed an erroneous opinion, and that is that the Basuto chiefs have lost their power and influence. It is true that our plan works well, and the

---

[1] G.12-'77, pp. 2-3, Griffith to SNA, 10 January 1877.
[2] G.17-'78, p. 4, Rolland to SNA, 28 January 1878.
[3] *The Little Light of Basutoland*, October 1877, p. 2.
[4] PEMS Archives, Paris, Maeder to '*Messieurs et honorés Directeurs*', 20 August 1877. Translated from the French.
[5] Filibert Makosholo, *Leselinyana*, January 1880.
[6] C.3708, pp. 52, 68, report of meeting at Maseru, 19-20 March 1883.
[7] '*History ea Ba-Sotho*', *Leselinyana*, 1 February 1905. Translated from the Sesotho.

chiefs do not discourage the introduction of law, or their people resorting to the magistrates' courts, as it releases them from a large amount of work, and the percentage paid them out of the hut-tax is equivalent in money. But in every other way their attachment to the chiefs is quite as strong as when I took over the country from Moshesh in 1868. ... consequently the introduction of any new system must be most cautiously done, and every preparation for a united opposition seen to.[8]

Bowker was right to sound a note of caution. There was a limit to which a mere four magistrates and their clerks could penetrate and influence every corner of such a rugged and mountainous country. The Basotho were still deeply attached to their chiefs, and all the old structures were still in place. The chiefs' courts were still the main focus, the main public space in every village. The chiefs still settled their followers' disputes, though some went instead to the magistrates, and, though under colonial control, they still carried out the allocation of land with little colonial interference. In short, they were indispensable. The colonial government was not. If the magistrates were withdrawn everything would fall back into place.

Nevertheless the chiefs' loss of control was more significant than Bowker recognised. In the early years of Cape rule they had vigorously opposed the referral of cases to the magistrates' courts, but they had been forced to give way. Speaking after the Gun War George Moshoeshoe put the matter quite simply. The senior chiefs, he said, 'wanted to have the same power as they had before in eating people up and punishing them: ... they were dissatisfied with the people coming to the magistrates to lay complaints before them.' But in the end 'they gave in'. And according to Tsekelo the two most intransigent of the chiefs, Masupha and Ramanella, were never well disposed towards the government, and 'it was only the weight of the country that dragged them along'.[9]

The senior chiefs, of course, were unhappy about their changed condition. Rolland 'never blinked the fact' that they would not always be content with their state of subjection and would sometimes regret their loss of independence; and he acknowledged that they had 'at least one tangible grievance … the loss of the power of "eating up" those of their subjects who have offended them.'[10] At the height of the Gun War Major Bell noted that 'To the ambitious chiefs our sway was very impalatable. They were jealous of the magistrates, who were gradually usurping their powers.'[11]

In the case of Letsie the lethargy of old age had no doubt played a part, and Molapo, also an old man, had perhaps been more ready to acquiesce in the change. But Masupha still resented his loss of power, and after the war he expressed his feelings openly: 'the magistrates have taken away all our power, and they tell us that when we have once given ourselves to the Queen's Government we have nothing whatever to say ....'[12] Many of the younger chiefs were also resentful. In 1879 Bowker noted that at present the government had 'a great advantage.... We have all the old broken down chiefs, Letsea, Molappo, and others.' If they were out of the way their sons would take a more active line.[13]

---

[8] A.49-'79, pp. 30-1, Bowker to Ayliff, 18 April 1878.
[9] C.3708, pp. 56, 61, report on meeting held at Maseru on 20 March 1883.
[10] LNA, S9/1/2/1/1, Rolland to SNA, 17 September 1878.
[11] C.3112, p. 113, Bell to Griffith, 10 January 1881.
[12] G.26-'82, Report of the Hon'ble the Secretary for Native Affairs on his Visit to Basutoland in June, 1881, p. 22, report of meeting held on 23 June 1881 at Morija.
[13] A.6-'79, Report of the Select Committee appointed to consider and report on hostilities in Basutoland, p. 53, Bowker's evidence, 7 August 1879.

The French missionaries agreed, and listed Lerotholi among the leading malcontents.[14]

The first alarms

Aware of this powerful undercurrent of discontent, Griffith and his magistrates were always on the lookout for signs of disaffection that might lead to rebellion. The possibility of revolt was always present to their minds. It came naturally to them to speculate what would happen if the chiefs turned against them and tried to overthrow their rule. And beyond the Basutoland borders, on the farms and in the towns of the Cape and the Free State, and in the often fevered columns of the colonial press, there were constant reports that the Basotho were restive, that they were planning rebellion or an attack on the Free State, that they were neglecting their fields and fortifying their mountains. More generally, there were recurrent fears of a pan-African uprising throughout southern Africa, especially in the late 1870s when wars broke out on the Cape's Eastern Frontier and in the Transvaal.

For the most part Griffith and his colleagues, with the lofty disdain of the men on the spot who 'knew the natives', dismissed these reports as groundless rumours put around either by panicky farmers and over-excited journalists or by more sinister parties trying to provoke war. But at times they themselves were seriously worried, and the development that most disturbed them was the Basotho's acquisition of firearms and ammunition.

From 1870 onwards the opening up of the Diamond Fields in Griqualand West gave rise to a voracious demand for African labour, and it was soon found that this could be obtained only if firearms were made freely available. By the early 1870s it was reckoned that 50,000 men went to work each year in Kimberley from almost every part of southern Africa. In 1872 about 3,000 of these were Basotho, and within a few years there were about twice as many.[15] The wages paid by the diggers were much higher than those offered by the Free State farmers, but for the Basotho, and many other Africans as well, the great attraction was the opportunity to buy guns.[16] Under Cape law an African could buy a gun only if he had a permit from a magistrate, who had to be satisfied of his good character, but because of the need for African labour such permits were freely granted. The Cape authorities were alarmed, but they took no action because they did not want to dry up the diggers' sources of labour. To get back to their homes the Basotho labourers had to pass through the Free State, and under Free State law an African was not allowed to possess a gun except with the authority of his white employer. Some Basotho were intercepted and had their guns confiscated, and a few were killed when they resisted. To avoid this many of them travelled by night and hid during the day, but these difficulties did not deter them from buying and bringing back their guns.

Griffith sounded the alarm as early as March 1873:

> It is with great regret that I observe the open traffic in firearms which has lately sprung up at the Diamond Fields. I am aware that the weapons in question are of inferior construction and imperfect finish, but it is not so much their use that I refer to as their abuse. .... Essentially warlike and turbulent by disposition and character, as soon as [these people] are well supplied with firearms they invariably ... become restless, agitative, and insolent. The desire for a struggle, whether against

---

[14] PEMS Archives, Paris, Dieterlen to Casalis, 2 April 1878; C.2821, p. 71, Casalis and others to the Colonial Office, 9 December 1880.

[15] Worger (1987: 71, 75, 82); Kimble (1978: 251).

[16] Worger (1987: 73 and following) draws attention to the many reasons for migrant labour, but there can be no doubt from Basutoland sources that for the Basotho guns were the major attraction.

each other, or against the white man, becomes irresistible to them ... years of progress can be pulled down in a few months.[17]

He repeated his warning four months later, but this time with the modification that the firearms being brought into the country were 'not all of an inferior description, as is generally supposed,' but included several makes of breech-loading rifles. Hundreds of these weapons were 'being constantly brought into this Territory', and 'large numbers of Basutos, from all the Districts of the Territory, are now proceeding almost daily to the Diamond Fields for the sole purpose of procuring firearms'.[18]

Tsekelo Moshoeshoe gave a similar warning. The people 'loved' the new government, he told Griffith, but the difficulty lay with Letsie, Molapo and Masupha who longed for their lost independence. People were going to work for guns, not by their own spontaneous wish, but by order of the chiefs. He begged the government to ban the purchase of guns and their introduction into Basutoland: 'these guns will beget insubordination, disputes, arrogance, and refusal to conform to the laws ... they will beget a desire to get rid of this Government ....'[19]

Tsekelo had reasons of his own for wanting to throw suspicion on his senior brothers and to ingratiate himself with the government, but nonetheless Griffith was impressed by his warnings. At the same time he was getting similar reports from Major Bell in Leribe. Like Tsekelo, Bell believed that it was at the chiefs' instigation that men were going to the Diamond Fields to get guns, and he had been told that they wanted their men well armed in case the government should try to arrest them. There would soon be scarcely an able-bodied man in the district without an Enfield rifle.[20]

The Cape government was unresponsive. Brownlee pointed out that since the diggers needed African labour it was impossible to stop the trade in arms, and it would be much too dangerous to try to disarm men as they returned to Basutoland. So he merely asked Griffith to warn the chiefs that the government was concerned that this acquisition of guns might well bring about their ruin.[21]

Griffith gave out this message at the annual *pitso* in August 1873, and at the same time he urged the Basotho to shift their labour from the Diamond Fields to the railway construction that was now under way in the Cape. Although other issues were discussed as well, it was the question of guns that provoked the greatest comment, and in many ways the debate at this *pitso* anticipated the debate several years later when the Cape government decided to disarm the Basotho.

Griffith had been obliged to report to the High Commissioner, he said, that the Basotho were going to the Diamond Fields solely in order to get guns and 'principally if not entirely at the instigation of their chiefs'. The government had no fear for itself. It was much too powerful for that. But it was afraid for the people of Basutoland, whom it had taken under its protection out of the goodness of its heart. It wanted them to be safe, to be free from danger to themselves and free from bringing other people into danger. But how could that be when every man had a gun in his hand? They did not need guns, since no one would attack them now that they were the Queen's subjects. Nor was there any game in their country. The great danger was that, thinking themselves strong in the possession of guns, they would bring ruin on themselves. They should remember their old troubles

---

[17] CA, NA 272, Griffith to Colonial Secretary, 12 March 1873.
[18] LNA, S9/2/1/1, Griffith to Colonial Secretary, 8 July 1873.
[19] CA, NA 272, Tsekelo to Griffith, 27 June 1873.
[20] LNA, L2/1/1, Bell to Griffith, 9 and 14 February, 14 and 28 June 1873.
[21] CA, NA 840, Brownlee to Griffith, 31 July 1873.

with the Free State: their new troubles would be even worse, for they would certainly entail the loss of their country, their 'last refuge'. Finally he advised them to go to work, not on the Diamond Fields, but on the railways, where the pay was just as good and the work less dangerous; and not to waste their money on guns, but to spend it on useful objects like ploughs and wagons.

In the debate that followed there were several speakers who supported Griffith. These were men who would later be *Mateketoa* in the Gun War – Nathanael Makotoko, Molapo's chief councillor; Tšita Mofoka; Tsekelo Moshoeshoe; Nehemiah Moshoeshoe and Moshoeshoe's brother, Jobo. George Moshoeshoe said he was not worried about the Basotho's acquiring guns: it was merely a passing fashion, like eloping with girls. But the most interesting intervention came from Sofonia, who said, in effect, that if the chiefs had fully understood and trusted the government 'these guns would never have entered the country'. The government was here to stay. It would never leave the Basotho to confront the Free State again.

From the other speakers there were three main responses. First, there were denials that the chiefs were sending their men to the Diamond Fields. They were going of their own volition. Second, there were vehement protestations that these guns would never be turned against the Queen, who had been so kind and merciful to the Basotho. Third, several speakers explained why the Basotho wanted guns. 'Guns are men's teeth!', Letsie said. 'Their weapons of defence.' Jonathan Molapo echoed this argument. Every animal had its weapons of defence, whether they were teeth, claws or horns. Should man be the only animal without such weapons? And then he explained why he had gone to the mines.

> I went to the Diamondfields of my own accord. Nobody sent me. I saw guns there, and I wanted one – that's all! When I was a boy I went about with a kerrie. When I grew a little older and had been circumcised I had assegais given to me; and when I felt myself a fully grown man I wished for a gun.

Lerotholi said the same:

> I have lately come back from the Diamond fields. Feeling myself to be now a full-grown man, and seeing guns, I wanted to possess one, of my own. I went to the Fields without Letsie's consent.... When I bought a gun, it was for my manhood. I had no special object in buying one. Beyond the wish to show myself a man, with the arms of a man.

The two chiefs had explained, in simple and direct terms, why so many had gone to work for guns at the Diamond Fields. Like the knobkerrie and the assegai, the gun had become a symbol of manhood.[22]

Griffith professed himself satisfied with this meeting: it had been attended by 'a vast concourse of Basutos' and 'everything passed off with the greatest harmony'.[23] Yet he must have realised that, although more Basotho might now be going to the railway works, they would not stop getting guns. Indeed it soon became clear that the only way to ensure a good supply of Basotho labour on the railways was to make guns freely available there. Only two months later, in October 1873, Molapo was reported to be instructing his people to go to the railway works for guns,[24] and within a year there

---

[22] CA, NA 272, 'Minutes of Meeting held at Maseru on the 20th August 1873'. Rolland later referred to the 'traditional wish with every young Basuto to possess a horse and gun, without which he does not consider himself "a man" and is liable to be jeered at by his more fortunate fellows': G.21-'75, p. 10, Rolland to Griffith, January 1875.
[23] LNA, S9/2/1/1, Griffith to Colonial Secretary, 27 August 1873.
[24] CA, NA 272, Bell to Griffith, 19 October 1873, reprinted in Burman (1976A: 59).

were complaints that the Basotho were able to purchase guns there almost as easily as at the Diamond Fields.[25]

The fears of an uprising reached a new pitch. In August Tsekelo raised the alarm again. The three great chiefs were plotting against the government, their 'hunting expedition' was resolved upon, they were simply waiting for the opportunity to strike.[26] Rolland, at Mafeteng, was sure that there was some 'deep-rooted scheme' afoot among the chiefs, or at least the germ of such a scheme, 'having for its purpose a general rising ....'[27] Austen, looking back in 1880, asserted that this 'deep-laid plan' extended to the neighbouring chiefs as well.[28] At Hlotse Heights Major Bell felt dangerously threatened when some of Molapo's men assaulted the Chief Constable of his police and Molapo turned up at the resulting court proceedings with 150 armed followers.[29]

Griffith did not share the conspiracy theories, but in spite of the assurances given at the *pitso* he continued to believe that the rush to get guns was being instigated by the chiefs. Whether or not this would lead to open defiance he was not sure. His uncertainty was understandable. Some chiefs, especially Molapo, were certainly encouraging their followers to work at the Diamond Fields or on the railways for guns. They were disturbed by the Cape's assault on their powers, and they might well have believed that the magistrates would be more careful if the Basotho were well armed. Molapo's implicit challenge to Bell might well have been the kind of confrontation that they had in mind. But they also wanted to be able to defend themselves if necessary. As Sofonia had pointed out at the *pitso*, they did not trust the Cape to defend their interests against the Free State. The British government had assumed responsibility for the area between the Orange and the Vaal before, in 1848, when Sir Harry Smith had proclaimed the Orange River Sovereignty, and the Basotho remembered only too well that in 1854 it had abandoned the Sovereignty and left them to confront the newly created Free State on their own. What guarantee could there be that the Cape government would not abandon them in the same way?[30]

But the main impetus for the migration came from the migrants themselves. If the chiefs were giving orders they were readily obeyed. There is no evidence of any compulsion being used. And there must have been many thousands who went entirely of their own volition, without any encouragement from the chiefs at all. As Lerotholi and Jonathan Molapo had explained, the main reason why so many Basotho flocked to the Fields was their own craving to be possessed of a gun and in this way to assert their manhood.[31]

---

[25] Cunynghame (1879: xi).

[26] CA, NA 272, Tsekelo to Griffith, 30 August 1873, enclosed with Griffith to Colonial Secretary, 11 September 1873: reprinted in Burman (1976A: 53-8).

[27] CA, CO 3232, Rolland to Griffith, 5 January 1874.

[28] G.20-'81, p. 12, Austen to Griffith, 31 December 1880.

[29] For an account of this incident and its consequences, see Burman (1976A: 58-62).

[30] E.g., C.2482, p. 8, Dyke to President of Conference, 20 February 1879. See also A.6-'79, Report of the Select Committee appointed to consider and report on hostilities in Basutoland, p. 93, Rolland's evidence, 27 August 1879.

[31] Judith Kimble (1978) exaggerates the role of the chiefs: see Eldredge (1993: 169-70, 183), and Worger (1987: 83). Compare the experience of the Pedi, described by Peter Delius (1983: 77-8). Delius concludes that, although chiefs had been sending their men to get guns, no great coercion was needed, and by the 1870s labour migration was the accepted norm. 'Indeed, it seems that by this decade, the acquisition of a gun had become incorporated as an essential part of the transition from being a 'youth' to being an adult male ....' Kimble (1978: 57, 130, 279) also exaggerates the extent to which guns were owned by the chiefs and lent out to their subjects. By the time of the Gun War most guns were privately owned: see, e.g., G.13-'80, pp. 46-7, Report of Pitso held on 16 October

The colonial authorities were in a painful dilemma. They could not ban the sale of guns because they needed the Basotho's labour, and confiscation of guns was out of the question. As Griffith pointed out, there was no force in the country to back up such a measure and in any event it would be profoundly unjust for the same government to allow the Basotho to purchase guns at the Diamond Fields and then to take them away in Basutoland.[32]

Then, at the end of 1873, the Hlubi chief Langalibalele and his followers, after defying the Natal government, took refuge in Basutoland, where they were pursued by forces from the Cape and Natal and finally captured through the deceit and treachery of Molapo and his son Jonathan. Whether or not the Basotho chiefs had been planning an armed uprising, Griffith believed that the crushing of the Langalibalele rebellion in their own territory and before their very eyes persuaded them of the futility of any resistance. 'A lesson not less severe than salutary was thus taught them', he recorded, 'which will have a most beneficial effect in the future ... This event has done more to place the Government in a firm and commanding position than years of careful administration.'[33]

Griffith's magistrates agreed that Langalibalele's defeat was an event of major significance. Austen believed that the Hlubi chief's resistance had been nothing less than 'the first outburst' of a widespread conspiracy against the whites, and that the situation had been saved only by the administration's prompt action.[34] Rolland declared that it was only through the crushing of Langalibalele that a widespread conspiracy had been quashed.[35] Bell, the magistrate on the spot, expressed no views about an alleged conspiracy, but believed that the defeat and capture of Langalibalele brought about a great change for the better in the manner of the chiefs and the people in his district.[36] It was after this that Molapo professed a change of heart towards his magistrate and gave no more serious trouble.

There was a strange irony in this turn of events. The immediate cause of Langalibalele's defiance was the attempt by the Natal authorities to disarm some of his men who had returned with firearms from the Diamond Fields.[37] The very issue on which the Basotho were later to go to war was the issue on which they collaborated with the government against Langalibalele, and they then adduced their loyalty in this collaboration as a reason why they themselves should not be disarmed.

So far from being in league with Langalibalele, Molapo had helped to bring about his capture, and his 'loyalty' to the government was condemned as profound 'disloyalty' by his fellow Africans, such as Cetshwayo, chief of the Zulu ('how is it that Molapo had caught a black man like himself?')[38] and Lobengula, chief of the Matebele (Molapo's followers smelt, they were not worthy to be called

---

1879, George Moshoeshoe's speech; C.2755, p. 161, *Cape Times*, 9 September 1880; C.2821, p. 6, Coillard to Frere, 12 January 1880; Sekese, articles in *Leselinyana*, 15 August and 15 September 1893, 15 September 1907.

[32] LNA, S9/2/1/1, Griffith to SNA, 30 August 1873.

[33] G.27-'74, p. 23 Griffith to SNA, 31 January 1874. The defeat of the Hlubi had a similar effect below the Drakensberg in Nomansland: Campbell (1959: 132).

[34] G.20-'81, p. 12, Austen to Griffith, 31 December 1880.

[35] CA, CO 3232 (also LNA, MF 2/1/1), Rolland to Griffith, 5 January 1874.

[36] CA, NA 272, Bell to Griffith, 3 January 1874.

[37] The Hlubi refused to register their guns because they were afraid that they would be taken away. According to Norman Etherington (1978: 17-19), however, there were other, perhaps more significant, factors underlying the initiative taken against the Hlubi by the Natal authorities.

[38] CA, CO 3232, Griffith to Colonial Secretary, 15 September 1874, enclosing statement of 'Kukami', Molapo's messenger to Cetshwayo, 6 September 1874.

people).³⁹ Even among the Basotho there were many who reproached him for his role in Langalibalele's capture.⁴⁰

In spite of their 'loyalty' at this time the rumours that the Basotho were plotting rebellion persisted, so much so that Letsie called a *pitso* at Thaba-Bosiu in January 1874 to protest his innocence. In Griffith's presence he denied emphatically that either he or his people intended to rebel, but on the contrary 'they were living happily under the Government which his father Moshesh had called in to take care of them'. Other chiefs and headmen, among them Masupha and Lerotholi, said the same.⁴¹

Further alarms

There was no relaxation in the Basotho's determination to get guns and ammunition. From Mafeteng Rolland reported in 1874 that they were 'flocking' to the Diamond Fields, and that after working there for six months they were returning with good Enfield rifles;⁴² and in the following year he observed that every man not fully occupied at home had gone or was going to the Fields.⁴³ In 1876 the Paris missionaries referred to what 'everyone living amongst the natives knows', that 'the ease of obtaining guns at the Diamond Fields has created among all the natives of S. Africa a gun fever.'⁴⁴ The government of Natal complained about the 'indiscriminate sale of arms to natives', but as Richard Southey, the Lieutenant-Governor of Griqualand West, pointed out, the law did not allow discrimination between blacks and whites. And he urged that Africans should not be regarded as 'the natural enemy of the white man', but rather as potential friends and loyal subjects.⁴⁵

There was also a continuing crescendo of concern about the ease with which the Basotho were acquiring guns and ammunition after labouring on public works in the eastern Cape. Most of these men went from the south of Basutoland, from the district of Cornet Spruit, where Austen wrote of the easy availability of guns giving rise to 'a sort of mania to be possessed of a gun and ammunition'. His anger was focused on Chalmers, the magistrate at Cradock, who, he alleged, was providing certificates to Basotho passing through his district, certifying that they were fit and proper persons to have guns, even though they were perfect strangers to him. Austen condemned this as 'a most pernicious practice, fraught with extreme danger'.⁴⁶

For Chalmers, echoing Southey, the central issue was race. If a British Mosotho had worked well and honestly for the money he used to buy a gun, and had not committed any crime or offence, why

---

³⁹ *Leselinyana*, June 1878, letter from Coillard. See also *JME* 1878, pp. 174-6, Coillard to '*Messieurs et chers frères*', 5 March 1878.
⁴⁰ G.33-'79, p. 33, report of *pitso* held on 24 October 1878, speech of Jonathan Molapo. See also Mackintosh (1907: 207). In an interview with AA, 11 February 1965, Damane said that Molapo and Jonathan were unpopular to that day because of their role in the capture of Langalibalele.
⁴¹ LNA, S9/2/1/1, Griffith to Colonial Secretary, 4 February 1874; *Leselinyana*, February 1874.
⁴² LNA, S9/1/3/2, Rolland to J. Gardner, Secretary to the Directors of the Port Alfred Landing and Shipping Company, 13 July 1874; G.21-'75, p. 10, Rolland, 'Annual Report on the Sub-District of Thaba-Bosigo for the year 1874', January 1875.
⁴³ LNA, S9/1/3/2, Rolland to Labour Agent, King William's Town, 4 October 1875.
⁴⁴ *The Little Light of Basutoland*, April-May 1876, p. 22.
⁴⁵ For this correspondence, see A.68-'81.
⁴⁶ G.21-'75, p. 7, Austen to Griffith, 21 January 1875. See also CA, NA 273, Austen to Griffith, 5 July and 9 November 1875, and Scully (1913: 58).

should he not be regarded as a fit and proper person? Was it because he was black? If so a law must be passed to justify refusal for such a reason.

> ... I am firmly convinced that if we display such extreme anxiety not to allow the natives who are under our rule to have guns, we will ... only give them the idea ... that we look upon them as enemies .... It is already a matter which ... causes much dissatisfaction amongst them, why, if they are really British subjects, we should be so anxious that they should not possess guns. They become suspicious of us, and ... they will ultimately come to the conclusion that there is some deep meaning on our part in trying to prevent their having guns.[47]

There was another aspect of the law on firearms. It was forbidden to remove a gun from the Colony without a licence for removal. In 1876 some Basotho returning from the Eastern Cape to Basutoland had their guns taken away near the border at Herschel. In the ensuing outcry they were fully supported by their magistrates, even Austen. It was wrong, Bell argued, to take away with the left hand what had been granted with the right. The guns were restored, and Chalmers was instructed to issue permits of removal in future.[48]

The Basotho's eagerness to get guns continued to fuel rumours that they were disloyal at heart and were planning to rebel, and in May 1876 Letsie held another *pitso* at Thaba-Bosiu in order to repudiate them. He and his principal men were 'astonished', he told Griffith, 'grieved', and 'pained beyond expression' by these rumours: 'we have not a thought nor a desire of turning away from the government of our glorious Queen'. But at the same time he protested about the seizure of his subjects' guns in terms that were almost a mirror image of Chalmers' representations:

> They are apprehended as if they were enemies and their guns are taken from them by their own Government, and thus they are treated exactly as if they were an enemy's people. This matter has indeed alarmed us and we ask why, if we are really so much trusted as Government men, does this take place? Is it because of our *Sesuto colour*? Why, we believe ourselves to be the servants of the Queen just as much as if we were white .... Our guns will not be fired against the Queen .... [49]

Letsie's declaration of loyalty satisfied the British authorities but did not put an end to the alarms and panics. In June Griffith had to assure the Free State government that the Basotho had no plans to attack the Free State and that there was no truth in reports that two whites had been murdered.[50]

There were other reasons for unease. This was the year in which the prophets flourished, bringing messages from Moshoeshoe that he wanted the Basotho to regain their independence. It was also the year in which Nehemiah Moshoeshoe ran into trouble in the adjoining territory of Griqualand East. The Basotho laid claim to this area on the strength of a cession by the Mpondo chief, Faku, to Moshoeshoe, but this claim had been repudiated by the Cape government. Nehemiah and his people, however, were allowed to live there, alongside the Griqua of Adam Kok and several other chiefdoms. His influence increased as more of his followers joined him, and when Matthew

---

[47] A.23-'77, pp. 5-6, W.B. Chalmers, 'Report on the Trade in Gunpowder and Firearms by the Resident Magistrate, Cradock', 28 December 1875. Chalmers was defending the practice of the local JPs as well as his own.
[48] CA, NA 273, Austen to Griffith, 25 April 1876; LNA, L2/1/1, Bell to Griffith, 21 May 1876; CA, NA 273, Bright, memorandum, 25 May 1876.
[49] CA, NA 273, Letsie to Griffith, 21 May 1876.
[50] LNA, S9/1/3/3, Griffith to F.K. Höhne, 12 June 1876; LNA, S9/1/2/1, Griffith to SNA, 14 June 1876.

Blyth, the Chief Magistrate, attempted to arrest some of his men for refusing to obey a summons, they opened fire and fled into the Drakensberg. Nehemiah, though not present, was arrested by Blyth for inciting his people to rebellion. This created a sensation in Basutoland, and soon there was an alarming but unfounded report that 300 Basotho were marching over the Drakensberg to help him.[51] When Nehemiah was brought to trial he was acquitted, but the Basotho's dislike of Blyth was later to resurface when he was appointed after the Gun War as Governor's Agent.[52]

In the rest of South Africa there were new disturbances and new causes for alarm. Beyond the Vaal Sekhukhune's Pedi were at war with the commandos of the South African Republic. Like the Basotho, they had acquired guns at the Diamond Fields, and for the time being they more than held their own. Theophilus Shepstone believed that the Pedi's defiance had demonstrated a profound change in the relative strength of Africans and whites in southern Africa and placed every white community in peril.[53]

In 1876 there were widespread scares and panics on the Cape's Eastern Frontier. Farmers abandoned their isolated homes, convinced that a hostile African alliance was about to fall on them and their families. When war came, however, in August 1877, it was sparked off by a drinking quarrel between the Gcaleka and the Colony's old allies, the Mfengu. The underlying issue was land, exacerbated, it seems, by severe drought. Others were drawn in, among them the Ngqika of Sarili, and in the early months of 1878 both the Gcaleka and the Ngqika were crushed by a combined force of imperial and colonial troops, fighting alongside Mfengu and Thembu allies.

Griffith had been called on to command the colonial forces, and Bowker had been appointed to take his place, but when Bowker was unable to continue because of ill health Griffith was recalled. During his absence there had been two main developments.

First, the new Governor and High Commissioner at the Cape, Sir Bartle Frere, had sacked the ministry of John Molteno because it had insisted on its own independent command in the war against the Gcaleka and the Ngqika. He appointed Gordon Sprigg as Prime Minister instead, and Sprigg embarked on the more 'vigorous native policy' which will be discussed more fully in Chapter 7 below. As part of this new thinking Sprigg was resolved on removing any serious military threat to the Colony, and in 1878 the Peace Preservation Act gave the Cape executive the power to issue proclamations requiring all persons, in territories to be defined, to hand in their arms, for which compensation would be paid. At first it seemed that this would be merely a permissive measure which the government could apply to areas where disturbances had arisen or were likely to arise, but soon it became clear that Sprigg was resolved on disarming every African under Cape jurisdiction. The Basotho were alarmed by reports of this measure, and Bowker, still in charge, assured Letsie that it would not be applied to them, but only to Africans who had been disloyal.[54] Sprigg, however, without a word of consultation with Bowker, Griffith or anyone else in the country, announced that it was the government's intention that the Act would be extended to Basutoland, and in October 1878 he instructed Griffith to inform the Basotho accordingly.

---

[51] *The Little Light of Basutoland*, December 1876; LNA, S9/1/2/1, Griffith to SNA, 5 December 1876.
[52] For a brief account of this affair, see Burman (1981: 105-6).
[53] Delius (1983: 225).
[54] *Cape Argus*, 24 September 1878, quoting a letter sent to *The Journal* by 'a correspondent in Basutoland'; C.2755, p. 69, 'The Petition of the Basuto Chiefs and People' to Frere, 21 January 1880; C.2821, p. 13, Mabille to Frere, 24 March 1880; C.2964, p. 4, Lerotholi and others to Strahan, 10 January 1881.

Second, a petition had been drawn up by Tsekelo, now dismissed from the police and in disgrace, at the bidding of Letsie and others, setting out a series of grievances against the government. It was said that Rolland, acting as Governor's Agent between Bowker's departure and Griffith's return, had invited the chiefs to express their concerns openly, though Rolland himself denied this; and when the petition gave rise to trouble Letsie disowned it. It seems clear, though, that the whole petition had been read out to and accepted by Letsie, that it had the support of his advisers and leading subordinates as well as that of Masupha, but that Molapo in the north knew nothing about it. Tsekelo performed the useful function for the chiefs of being adviser and secretary on the one hand and scapegoat when things went wrong on the other.

The petition was a long list of complaints of bad treatment and accusations of bad faith, and Griffith was infuriated by its tone and by what he regarded as its lies and misrepresentations. It was alleged that when Moshoeshoe had agreed to a hut tax it was understood that part of it would be paid to him; that he was to provide for the Queen's representatives only a small plot sufficient for a house and garden (and not the large reserves appropriated by the government); and that the government's regulations had been introduced without any proper consultation with the Basotho. It was proposed that laws should be introduced only after proper consultation; that the government should reprove those (such as George, Sofonia and Ntsane) who were pouring scorn on the chieftainship of Moshoeshoe's sons; that any increase in hut tax should be approved by the chiefs; that the chiefs should have the right to put forward proposals on how the territory's revenue should be spent; that payments to headmen for helping to collect the hut tax should be stopped; and that a Council of the Basuto Nation should be established to make proposals and give advice to the government.[55]

Rolland was clearly embarrassed by the petition, since such a document would never have been submitted while Griffith was still in charge. He dismissed it as a hole-in-the-corner affair, aimed at enhancing Letsie's authority and reducing the power and influence of the sub-chiefs and headmen, most of whom were loyal to the government, and of George, Sofonia and Ntsane, who as police officers were strong supporters of the government.[56]

This then was what faced Griffith on his return in September or October 1878 – instructions from Sprigg that he must tell the Basotho that it was government's intention to disarm them, and a petition from Letsie and others setting out their grievances. At the annual *pitso* on 24 October he pitched straight in. He spelt out in vivid terms the punishment that had been inflicted on the Gcaleka and Ngqika for rebelling against the government. All their cattle had been taken, hundreds of them had been killed, including the Gcaleka chief Sandile, and the most senior chief of all, Sarili, was in hiding. They had been living in their country with no interference, but their chiefs had listened to bad advisers and brought themselves and their people to destruction. 'And thus will it ever be with people who rebel against the just and mild rule of the Queen.'

This lesson he applied at once to the Basotho chiefs and their petition. It was 'a disgraceful document, and an insult to the Government. If I had been here when it was brought to the Governor's Agent's Office by Tsekelo, I should have thrown it in his face and turned him out of my office.' He described those who had written it as rebels, and urged those who were loyal not to be dragged into trouble.

---

[55] CA, NA 275, 'Petition of the Chiefs and People of Basutoland ….', enclosed with Letsie and others to Rolland, 3 July 1878.
[56] LNA, S 9/1/2/1, Rolland to SNA, 26 July 1878.

Chapter 5: 'Success' and fear

Most of those at the meeting protested that they knew nothing about the petition, and those who were implicated tried to throw the blame on Tsekelo. Letsie, who was not present, had sent a message to say that there were only one or two things in the petition that he agreed with. The overwhelming response was one of regret and abject apology. Several speakers were alarmed to hear themselves described as rebels – according to the mission newspaper, *Leselinyana*, 'Everyone present was frightened' – and again there were fervent declarations of loyalty to the Queen and satisfaction with her government.[57]

In all this furore Griffith's announcement that the government intended to disarm the Basotho was passed over almost in silence. And before any action could be taken Moorosi, chief of the Baphuthi, rose in rebellion in the south.

---

[57] G.33-'79, pp. 29-37, report on *pitso*, 24 October 1878. See also *Cape Argus*, 16 November 1878 (from an occasional correspondent of *The Journal*), and *Leselinyana*, December 1878.

CHAPTER 6: THE MOOROSI WAR

Moorosi's chiefdom and the Quthing magistracy

In the great sweep of progress under colonial rule one part of the country had been left almost untouched. This was the mountainous and rugged territory of the Baphuthi, the people of Chief Moorosi, south-east of the Orange River. At first it formed part of the Cornet Spruit District, but it was a long way from the magistracy at Mohale's Hoek and it was often cut off when the Orange was running high. In 1877 Griffith decided to bring Moorosi and his people under closer control by making their country the new sub-district of Quthing with its own magistrate. This move set off a chain of events that was to lead to a full-scale rebellion.

Moorosi's subjects numbered about 5,000 and Griffith looked on them as 'about the wildest and most uncivilized' in the country.[1] Most of them were Baphuthi, who were of Nguni, not Basotho, origin, who still spoke Sephuthi as their primary language, but who had lived among the Basotho for so long that there was no great barrier between them. There were also some Thembu and other Nguni groups, and a few surviving San. Moorosi, who was only about 140 centimetres tall,[2] probably had some San ancestry himself. In 1877 he was about 82 years old, but he retained all his old vigour and fighting spirit. He had a reputation for stubbornness, and he was described by his new magistrate, Hamilton Hope, as 'rash and fearless to an extraordinary degree for a native'.[3]

The Baphuthi had come under Moshoeshoe during the *lifaqane*, having been conquered by his brother, Mohale. After several migrations they moved eastwards during the Seqiti War and established themselves on the mountain fortress overlooking the Orange that is still known as Mount Moorosi. When Wodehouse annexed Basutoland in 1868 his first plan was to establish the Orange as the boundary. This would have excluded the Baphuthi, and under pressure from the French missionary at Masitise, Frédéric Ellenberger, Moorosi went to meet the High Commissioner and it was agreed that his territory should form part of Basutoland.[4] He apparently had second thoughts, however, and it was only after a further meeting with Bowker and Austen in 1870, and after 'a very long argument', that he finally declared, 'plainly and formally', 'that he was a subject of the late paramount chief Moshesh, and that he would follow in the footsteps of his master'.[5]

John Austen's headquarters at Mohale's Hoek were far enough away to allow Moorosi the freedom he wanted, and for the first few years of colonial rule relations between the Baphuthi and the administration were fairly harmonious. This relatively quiet period came to an end in 1877, when the new sub-district of Quthing was created and Hamilton Hope, who had been the clerk in the Mafeteng magistracy, was appointed as its first magistrate.

In May that year Griffith and Austen introduced Hope to Moorosi on his mountain. For a whole day the old chief argued against the new arrangement, but in the end he accepted the magistrate and agreed to allow him to choose a site for his magistracy.[6] In return he was granted an allowance of £50 a year, which was intended to bind him in loyalty to the administration. Hope had only 13 African

---

[1] CA, NA 273, Griffith to Brownlee, 9 September 1876.
[2] PEMS (Morija), Ellenberger Papers, Henry Stevens, 'Reminiscences' (1906).
[3] Taylor (1972: 48); A.49-'79, p. 10, Hope to Rolland, 24 November 1877.
[4] Ellenberger, article in *Leselinyana*, February 1902.
[5] BR VI.151, Austen to Griffith, 29 February 1872.
[6] A.17-'79, p. 39, Austen to Griffith, 7 May 1879.

policemen to support him: he would need to act with discretion.

His first, temporary, office was an old store at Alwyn's Kop, near the Tele river, but he then moved to a site at the end of the wagon road, near the present site of the Leloaleng Technical School. It was closer to Moorosi's mountain, but useless for defence, so useless in fact that when the crisis came it was immediately abandoned.

It soon became clear that Hope was an unfortunate choice as magistrate in such a difficult and sensitive situation. Bowker, during the short period he took over from Griffith, quickly concluded that he was 'an irritable and hasty man',[7] and Ellenberger described him as 'an irascible, impatient character greatly feared by the Baphuthi because of his free and lavish use of the sjambok on them'.[8] He was determined to stamp his authority on the district, and Moorosi was equally determined to resist him.

The events that led up to the rebellion have been described perceptively and in great detail by Atmore and Burman, and the account that follows relies heavily on theirs.[9]

The first crisis

There were four crises which led up to war. The first followed immediately on Hope's appointment. He ordered Raisa, an influential headman under Moorosi's son, Lehana (also known as Doda), to appear before his court for destroying a widow's cornfield (when according to custom that cornfield belonged to Raisa as a relative of the dead husband) and then fined him for contempt when he refused to come. On 22 June Moorosi and a large following of armed men converged on the magistracy and demanded a meeting with Hope. They were persuaded to lay aside their arms, but when the meeting was held the conflict that emerged was stark and uncompromising. Moorosi called on his people to say whom they obeyed, himself or Hope, and they called out that they obeyed Moorosi. Hope and his clerk, Maitin, withdrew with their police, Moorosi's followers took up their arms again, a man was shot dead, accidentally it seems, and it was only with great difficulty that Hope was able to restore order. In the discussions that followed Moorosi told Hope that he should follow what he claimed was Austen's practice, and not adjudicate in any case until he, Moorosi, had given his consent. Hope described this as 'preposterous impertinence'.[10]

Almost immediately afterwards Hope piled on the pressure by refusing to accept that Moorosi had the right to fine villages for selling beer without his permission. Moorosi retorted that he would do as he liked and that Hope was destroying his independence. He was the supreme chief in the Quthing District and Hope was merely his subordinate. He had never given his country to the government: 'you may kill me', he said, 'but I will not submit or resign any of my privileges.'[11]

This was an outright challenge to the magistrate's authority, and Moorosi's advisers told Hope privately that they disagreed with the line their chief was taking. It was perhaps because of this that on the following afternoon, 26 June, Moorosi gave what Hope described as 'a most manly and complete apology'.[12] Later, however, he said that he had done so grudgingly, and that Hope had treated him

---

[7] CA, NA 275, Bowker, undated memorandum, quoted in Bradlow (1968: 140).
[8] Ellenberger, '*History ea Basotho*', *Leselinyana*, 25 June 1915. Another missionary described him as '*un mauvais brouillon*', 'a terrible bungler': PEMS Archives, Paris, Germond to Casalis, 28 March 1878.
[9] Atmore (1970) and Burman (1981: 108-31).
[10] A. 49-'79, p, 114, Hope to Griffith, 23 June 1877.
[11] A. 49-'79, p. 115, Hope to Griffith, 25 June 1877.
[12] A.49-'79, p. 116, Hope to Griffith, 26 June 1877.

unjustly in taking away his judicial authority. 'I am no longer anybody in this land', he said.[13]

In Maseru Griffith watched anxiously as Hope waded in, and warned him 'to be most careful and judicious' in carrying out the judgements and orders of his court; he should 'substitute diplomacy and moral persuasion for physical force or high-handed proceedings'; and he could expect no armed support 'if Moorosi were forced into open resistance'.[14] Hope paid no attention to this warning. When Moorosi and his son, Lehana, persuaded Raisa to submit to the authority of the magistrate's court, Hope fined him three sacks of millet, whereupon Moorosi ordered him not to pay and turned to Letsie for advice.

At this point Griffith intervened more actively, sending George and Sofonia Moshoeshoe to warn Letsie of the dire consequences that would follow if Moorosi continued to defy the magistrate, and Letsie sent a messenger with George and Sofonia to instruct Moorosi to give way. Faced by this united front of colonial and Basotho authority, Moorosi backed down and Raisa complied with the magistrate's judgement. The first crisis was over.

The second crisis

The Raisa affair was a victory for Hope. He had insisted on his magisterial authority, he had not been cowed by Moorosi's show of force, he had been supported by Griffith and Letsie, and the danger of rebellion had been averted, at least for the time being.

Then, in August 1877, fighting broke out in the Transkei between the Colony and the Ngqika and the Gcaleka, Griffith was transferred to take command of the colonial forces, Rolland was appointed temporarily to take his place, and the small detachment of white soldiers just over the border at Palmietfontein was withdrawn to take part in the war. Of all the important Basutoland chiefs Moorosi had the closest connections with the Transkei, and it is possible that these developments encouraged him to embark on a new trial of strength. When Hope returned from the annual *pitso* in Maseru he found groups of armed men assembling at various villages and rumours on every side that Moorosi intended to force him either to acknowledge his supremacy or to leave the district. Moorosi told him that he was coming 'on a friendly visit', but insisted that, in accordance with custom, he and his men would be armed. Hope, without reference to Rolland, sent a telegram to the Colony asking for a detachment of troops to be sent to Palmietfontein. But Rolland cancelled the meeting, believing that no good would come of it, and countermanded Hope's request for troops. Again he brought Letsie into play, arranging for him to send a messenger to Moorosi to remind him of his subordinate position. Moorosi was duly reprimanded, and by early December the country was calm again. In the following month Rolland reported that Moorosi's 'conduct and professions' were now 'of the most loyal and satisfactory description'.[15]

The third crisis

This was the end of the second crisis, and again Hope appeared to have come out on top. Perhaps emboldened by this, he continued to wield his magisterial powers to the full. In January 1879 he gave judgement that certain men, including Maikela, a subject of Moorosi's favourite son, Lehana, should pay hut tax for their widowed mothers. Maikela claimed that Austen had exempted widows from paying tax, and Hope gave him two weeks to get written proof of this from Austen. But neither

---

[13] A.49-'79, p. 117, Moorosi's statement, 16 July 1877.
[14] CA, NA 274, Griffith to Hope, 4 July 1877.
[15] A.49-'79, p. 18, Rolland to Brownlee, 25 January 1878.

Maikela nor anyone else went to Mohale's Hoek. Instead Lehana called his men to arms and, when Hope's policemen came to serve a writ on Maikela, Lehana declared that he had nothing to do with *Makhooa* (white men): he knew only Moorosi. Since the policemen were not able to serve the writ, Hope then issued criminal summons against Lehana, Maikela and others and demanded that Moorosi should arrest his son. Moorosi, anxious to avoid a confrontation, twice offered money as if paying a fine. But Hope insisted on the surrender of Lehana, and though Letsie sent Lerotholi to put pressure on Moorosi he could not persuade him to give up his son. Nor could Ellenberger persuade Lehana to give himself up. Hope would never listen to an African's side of the case, Lehana explained: 'When a man answers back the magistrate threatens him. It is better that Hope should kill me rather than I should be whipped like a dog.'[16]

Hope was pushing his authority too far – at least that was the view of William Ayliff, the Secretary for Native Affairs in Gordon Sprigg's new administration[17] – but even so that authority had to be upheld. At a meeting in Morija on 19 March James Bowker, who had taken over from Rolland as Governor's Agent, called on Letsie to organise an armed force to act against Moorosi, and about 700 men were reluctantly assembled.

Within a few days Bowker's force was gathered on the north bank of the Orange – the 700 Basotho, 80 policemen, Bowker and five white officials to command them, and Dr Taylor, the medical officer from Hlotse Heights. An equal number of Baphuthi were drawn up on the opposite bank. Bowker was wary of crossing the river, which the Baphuthi would have seen as an act of war, and he also had to wait several days for a wagon-load of cartridges. The Basotho began to drift away and by the time the cartridges arrived Bowker was in no position to attack Moorosi's mountain, if indeed he ever was.

There followed several days of tense negotiation, with Bowker knowing that he had to avoid a fight and Moorosi being afraid to come in, suspecting the sort of treachery that had trapped Langalibalele. At last, through the efforts of Lerotholi, a *pitso* was arranged at the camp. Unlike Hope, Bowker had no objection to the Baphuthi coming armed, and Moorosi crossed the river with 800 horsemen.

What followed is best described by Dr Taylor. Bowker and his staff took up their positions on a bench placed against the wall of the camp's mess hall. Their police were drawn up in two sections, to the right and to the left, while 'what was left of the Basuto levy stood some distance off in the foreground'. Presently Moorosi emerged from the crowd and seated himself alone on an ammunition box that had been placed for this purpose a few yards in front of the bench,

> an old man with an impassive face and quiet manner, quaintly dressed in an old silk hat, and a cloak. Immediately behind him were ranged a double row of his sons, grandsons and head men, about eighty in number, all having superior rifles. Just behind them congregated the rest of his people, and near Moorosi stood Doda [Lehana], a black-browed, sullen-looking ruffian, with a deep scowl on his face.
>
> Presently Moorosi rose to his feet, and, addressing Colonel Bowker in quiet tones, said: 'By the order of the Government I have brought Doda here; there he is. .... take him!'
>
> But eighty rifles brought to the 'ready' said 'No! Touch him if you dare!' ....

---

[16] Ellenberger, '*History ea Basotho*', *Leselinyana*, 25 June 1915. See also A.49-'79, pp. 20-24, Rolland to SNA, 6 March 1878 and enclosures, and pp. 26-8, Hope to SNA, 14 March 1878.

[17] A49-'79, p. 25, Ayliff to Rolland, 16 March 1878.

As I looked at the gleaming eyes of the eighty, just behind Moorosi, kneeling on one knee, clutching their rifles, holding them ready to put to their shoulders and fire, I felt that the crisis had come and could not last many seconds longer. Colonel Bowker saw it too, and rising from his seat, he spoke as follows:

'Moorosi, I am glad to see that you have listened to the word of the Government, and have brought Doda here today to be judged. I shall not put Doda back in prison, out of consideration for you, his father, but he must be punished for what he has done, so I fine him twenty head of cattle. Now the matter is finished, go home in peace.'

As soon as these words were spoken, the situation was relieved. Loud cries of 'Pula! Pula!' ('Rain! Rain!') broke from the ranks of the Baphuti, rifles were lowered, the ranks broke up into a confused crowd and the affair was over.[18]

In fact Lehana was fined 24 head of cattle, Maikela ten, and the rest between three and five. Bowker's own account was less dramatic: since Moorosi and his sons had advanced in front of the 'human wall' of their own followers not one of them 'could have escaped our bullets' if they had opened fire, and so he did not expect any trouble.[19]

So ended the third crisis. But this time the administration could not claim success. Bowker had not been able to rely on his Basotho levies and had been forced to compromise. The whole conduct and demeanour of the Basotho at this time must have convinced Moorosi that they would not fight against him. The Baphuthi, on the other hand, had been united and defiant, and they no doubt regarded it as a moral victory when Hamilton Hope was removed and replaced by Austen. Bowker believed that Hope had acted 'injudiciously', Rolland that he had been 'uncompromising'.[20] Moorosi complained about the move, perhaps on the ground he had not been consulted. But, according to Rolland, his real ground of objection was that he thought he could 'manage' more easily with Hope. He 'knew Mr. Austen of old, and was afraid of him.'[21] It soon transpired, in fact, that Austen was determined to avenge what he regarded as the 'ignominious compromise' which Bowker had been forced to make with Moorosi and Lehana,[22] and this contributed to the fourth and final crisis.

The fourth crisis

By mid-1878 the war in the Transkei was over, and the defeat of the Ngqika and the Gcaleka must have had a sobering effect on the Baphuthi. It was against this background that Griffith returned to the country and at the *pitso* on 24 October announced that the government would call on the Basotho to give up their arms. In the following month, November 1878, Austen arrested Lehana and some of his men for stock theft. Seven months before they had stolen horses from the Colony. Lehana had not taken part himself, but was apparently an accomplice after the fact, and he was sentenced to four years' imprisonment. Moorosi left the court room 'grumbling and murmuring all sorts of abuse against Mr. Austen'.[23]

The sentence was severe for a man who was merely an accomplice after the fact, and Lehana's position as Moorosi's favourite added to the old man's anger. The Baphuthi were far from united. Lehana had made common cause with his father against Letuka, the senior son and heir, who was

---

[18] Taylor (1972: 52-3).
[19] A.49-'79, pp. 29-31, Bowker to Ayliff, 18 August 1878.
[20] A.6-'79, Report of the Select Committee ..., pp. 50, 74.
[21] A.6-'79, Report of the Select Committee ..., p. 74, Rolland's evidence, 26 August 1879.
[22] Atmore (1970: 21).
[23] Ellenberger, '*History ea Basotho*', *Leselinyana*, 25 June 1915.

much more compliant and conciliatory. Letuka had been out of the country for some while, and when he returned Moorosi refused to give him a placing in the Quthing District for fear that he would co-operate with Austen in enforcing law and order. While Moorosi muttered against Austen's judgement Letuka and most of the old chief's councillors gave it their full support. Letuka clearly stood to benefit if his main rival was locked away in the Cape for four years.[24]

Austen was determined to be firm, but at this stage he fell short of the vigilance needed to carry his policy through. Lehana and his fellow prisoners were kept in a flimsy and insecure lockup at the magistracy until authority could be obtained for them to be transferred to Cape Town. There was a police guard, but at night it did not maintain a watch and retired to sleep in its own quarters. Keeping the prisoners there at all was a risk, and yet they stayed there for the rest of November and the whole of December. On 23 December the required authorisation was received, but still no move was made. Perhaps Austen was waiting for a white police escort from Palmietfontein, but in any event he saw no reason for alarm. In his annual report, written in the last week of December, he assured Griffith that since Lehana's conviction there had been a general feeling of contentment throughout the district and that the chiefs now realised that their power was crumbling away.[25]

No sooner had Austen sent off this bland report than the crisis broke. It was widely believed among the Baphuthi that white police from Palmietfontein would come on 1 January 1879 to escort Lehana and the other prisoners to the Cape. Up to this point Moorosi had kept quiet, perhaps hoping for mitigation of his son's sentence. But he was not prepared to let him be moved to the Cape, and he was under heavy pressure from Lehana's mother, who declared she had not produced sons for the white man and that if Moorosi refused to take action he should exchange his trousers for her skirt.[26]

On New Year's Eve Austen's policemen watched over the prisoners while they had their supper, and then locked them up, as they believed for the night, and retired to their own quarters about 60 metres away. They spent the rest of the evening drinking Cape brandy and enjoying themselves and then 'slept a peaceful sleep'.[27] In the middle of the night a band of armed men released Lehana and five others and they made their getaway on horseback.[28]

Griffith angrily charged Austen with 'great carelessness'[29] and ordered him to gather information and to build up a case against Moorosi. On 22 January 1879, however, the Zulu gained their great victory at Isandhlwana. Throughout Basutoland the whites were thrown into alarm. Those Africans, such as Moorosi, who were bent on resistance were heartened and elated. There was also news of trouble with the Pedi and with the burghers in the Transvaal. One of Austen's men, after visiting Moorosi's mountain on 21 February, reported that the Baphuthi were encouraged by all these reports and were saying that the government was quite powerless.[30] Sprigg and his colleagues determined on a show of military force to overawe Moorosi and, without any reference to Griffith, sent two troops

---

[24] CA, NA 275, Austen to Griffith, 20 November 1878, enclosure in Griffith to Ayliff, 26 December 1878; A.49-'79, p. 34, Austen to Griffith, 12 November 1878.
[25] G.33-'79, pp. 14-16, Austen to Griffith, 30 December 1878.
[26] Statement of Likatana Sesoane to AA, 21 January 1966, quoted in Atmore, p. 23.
[27] Ellenberger, article in *Leselinyana*, 25 June 1915.
[28] For accounts of the escape, see A49-'79, pp. 45-9, 52-3, 61-3, 63-6, 65-6.
[29] LNA, S 9/1/3/3, Griffith to Austen, 5 February 1879. See also A49-'79, pp. 70-71, Griffith to SNA, 26 February 1879.
[30] CA, NA 276, Austen to Griffith, 22 February 1879; Austen to Ayliff, 31 July 1879.

of yeomanry militia from King William's Town to reinforce the one troop of regular Cape Mounted Riflemen who were permanently stationed at Palmietfontein.

Moorosi viewed the sending of white reinforcements to Palmietfontein as a clear indication that his country was about to be invaded. According to Ellenberger, he regarded it as no less than a declaration of war when Austen, discovering that one of the men who had escaped with Lehana, his half-brother 'Ditlame', was hiding in Phahameng, came with his police to arrest him and opened fire on him when he fled: 'You want war', he told Austen, 'and therefore we must fight.'[31]

The outbreak of war

Because the Basotho were so disturbed by the threat of disarmament Moorosi was sure that he would not have to fight alone,[32] and he later told one of the Cape commanders that 'a large number' of Basotho had promised to join him.[33] But Letsie, though unhappy about the way in which Moorosi had been treated, was at the same time exasperated by him. He had already been irritated by Moorosi's refusal to allow him to place some of his sons high up in the Orange valley,[34] and he was angry now that Moorosi was jeopardizing the peace by refusing to hand over Lehana for punishment: 'how is it', he demanded, 'if Moorosi be a servant of Moshesh's, that his sons should be held so much more precious than the sons of Moshesh – for eight of Moshesh's sons have been in prison and yet no man opened the prison for them.'[35]

On 6 and 7 February Griffith had long discussions with Letsie at Morija, warning him that, if white forces had to be used, the Quthing District would have to be confiscated to pay for them. Letsie claimed later that it was this threat alone that induced him to co-operate.[36] It seems more likely that, in spite of the threat of disarmament, Letsie was not going to run all the dangers of rebellion for the sake of the Baphuthi, who were not even Basotho.

Moorosi sent messengers to every part of his country to call his men to arms, and Austen became convinced that they were going to attack the magistracy. He called on the Commanding Officer at Palmietfontein to send up as many troops as he could in order to defend him – a move which Griffith roundly condemned[37] – but on 23 February, before they arrived, he and his clerk Maitin, their policemen and a few traders, abandoned the magistracy and fled over the Tele River.

Austen was widely condemned for his cowardice in abandoning his post, which might have been unjust,[38] but which intensified his sense of being looked down on by his colleagues.[39] Rolland later testified that, if Austen had remained at the magistracy, it would have had a quieting effect and

---

[31] Ellenberger, article in *Leselinyana*, 25 June 1915. See also *Cape Argus*, 29 April 1879, reproducing article from *Northern Post*, 19 April 1879, and 29 May 1879, reproducing letter from Sauer in *Northern Post*.

[32] A.6-'79, Report of the Select Committee ..., p. 90, Rolland's evidence, 27 August 1879; PEMS report, undated, quoted and translated in Germond (1967: 336); G.20-'81, pp. 10-16, Austen's annual report for 1880.

[33] CA, ACC 459, Life of General Sir E.Y. Brabant, p. 73. See also CA, NA 276, Barkly to Griffith, 19 July 1879.

[34] A.49-'79, p. 27, Hope to SNA, 14 March 1878.

[35] CA, NA 276, Letsie to Austen, 9 February 1879, enclosed in Griffith to Ayliff, 19 February 1879; A49-'79, p. 75, Letsie to Griffith, 24 February 1879.

[36] CA, NA 277, Griffith to Ayliff, 12 March 1880, and enclosed letter from Letsie to Griffith.

[37] A.49-'79, pp. 67-9, Griffith to Ayliff, 24 February 1879.

[38] C.2755, p. 84, statement of 'Mofetudi', 'Moorosi's late Official Messenger', 23 February 1880: 'Mofetudi' said that Moorosi had intended to kill Austen. See also A.49-'79, pp. 131-3, Austen to SNA, 8 July 1879, enclosing statements of J.B. Thomas, 4 July 1879, and 'Molutsi', 21 February 1879.

[39] CA, NA 276, Austen to Ayliff, 5 August 1879.

nothing would have happened.[40] As it was, his flight was the signal for a general uprising among the Baphuthi. Two of Moorosi's sons broke into the magistracy and Austen's house and plundered the contents, looted a trader's store and seized a loaded wagon that was being sent by another trader to the Tele. Even the conciliatory Letuka now joined his father.[41] On 27 February Griffith told Letsie that Moorosi 'has thrown off the cloak under which he has been hiding for so long and has openly rebelled against the Government of the Queen'. He called on him to muster his fighting men and to send them to the Orange at once.[42] At the very time, therefore, that the government was proposing to disarm the Basotho it was also asking them to use their arms against the Baphuthi – an argument that the Basotho and their supporters were to use repeatedly in the debates that were to follow.

In spite of all the doubts about his loyalty, Letsie immediately ordered his sons to call out their regiments, and his brothers, Molapo and Masupha, sent contingents under their sons, Jonathan and Lepoqo respectively. But Letsie acted unwillingly, and so did at least two of his sons. Maama's praises described his unease and unhappiness.

> I left my home on horseback,
> I left the Korokoro at a gallop.
> Going to Letsie for my orders.
>
> My father asked me no questions.
> I saw that his eyes were full of tears,
> He told Setha to tell me to pass on.
> I left my home, but it wasn't pleasant.   …
>
> We came to the Orange, we camped a long time.
> At dawn I was given orders about my regiment,   ….
>
> It was then that I felt my body stiffen,
> Then too I felt my hands grow cold:
> I could hardly take my gun.[43]

Lerotholi's praise poet told of his chief's reluctance to enter into the waters of the Orange, which symbolised all the troubles of the war against Moorosi, and concentrated his rage on Letsie's advisers, especially Ntho Mokeke, whom he accused, in effect, of persuading Letsie to sanction their expedition.

> Oh, Mokeke's son's a terrible rogue.
> He spoiled our relations with Maseru,
> He spoiled them and made them disgusting.
> He'd throw the Koena into deep water.
> Lekena drew back ….
>
> Saying 'I'm afraid when Moorosi is fought.
> Beyond the river only paupers should fight,
> Ntho the son of Mokeke and his friends,
> Those who flatter for sugar among the whites!'[44]

---

[40] A.6-'79, Report of the Select Committee …, pp. 77-8, Rolland's evidence, 26 August 1879.
[41] A.49-'79, p. 86, Griffith to Ayliff, received 9 March 1879.
[42] LNA, S9/1/3/3, Griffith to Letsie, 27 February 1879.
[43] Damane and Sanders (1974: 165-6). Translation slightly changed.

At the same time there were others who, whatever they thought about Moorosi, relished the chance of seizing cattle. Both Jonathan and Joel Molapo went into the Maloti and swept off some of the herds that the Baphuthi had sent there.[45] And Letsie's son Bereng was keen to take part in the hope of being placed in Moorosi's land. According to one oral tradition, 'The Basotho didn't like fighting the Baphuthi, except for Bereng.' He was a 'cruel man, very harsh. He wanted to own this land, to drive the Baphuthi from it.'[46]

The Basotho regiments moved south, riding their 'shaggy little horses', not in any order, but in twos and threes, each man armed with a gun and with the ends of his assegais sticking up from a sheath at his back.[47] Griffith left Maseru on 1 March and joined them. He had been appointed Commandant-General of all the Cape Forces, though he had not distinguished himself as a military commander in the war on the eastern frontier and he had not been popular with his men. One of them described him as a police officer of the old school, with ideas and sympathies that belonged to the past, a criticism that was especially damning at a time when the Cape forces were being transformed from a police force to a military organisation.[48] He would be no more successful in the campaign against the Baphuthi. His troops would refer to him as 'an old woman', since he was said to dally so long over every decision,[49] and at the end one of them commented that he had made as great a mess of the Moorosi war as he had of the war against the Gcaleka.[50]

From the beginning he misjudged the magnitude of the task ahead of him. Like many others he was thinking in terms of a short campaign, of a short, sharp blow that would destroy Moorosi's strength.[51] But the forces at his disposal were too weak for this. The Cape's military organisation will be described in Chapter 11 below. Here it is sufficient to note that the only regular soldiers available to Griffith at first were the 100 Cape Mounted Riflemen (CMR) who were based at Palmietfontein. He also had 300 men from the 2nd and 3rd Regiments of the Cape Mounted Yeomanry. But this latter force, the brainchild of Sprigg, had been in existence only a few months, its organisation was not complete, it was well below complement, and it was regarded by the CMR with deep suspicion, bordering at times on contempt. The only artillery at Griffith's disposal was two small seven-pounder guns which did not reach him until 6 April.

His Basotho forces would have been a powerful asset if he had been able to rely on them, but, as he was well aware, Moorosi was in constant communication with their chiefs, trying to persuade them to defect and to join him.[52] In the event they remained loyal, and they plundered stock with some enthusiasm, but at times of crisis they were not prepared to put their lives at serious risk. There were also 100 Mfengu from the Herschel Reserve, but these too were half-hearted and unreliable. To add to Griffith's difficulties the roads between Palmietfontein and Moorosi's mountain were so rough that they had to be repaired before supplies could be sent up with any ease.

---

[44] Damane and Sanders (1974: 153). The Bakoena (Koena) are the clan to which the ruling family belonged.
[45] *Leselinyana*, May 1879; LNA, L2/1/2, Bell to Griffith, 19 August 1879; LNA, S9/1/3/3, Griffith to Bell, 26 August 1879.
[46] Likatana Sesoane of Mokanametso (Villa Maria), interview with AA, 21 January 1966.
[47] Browning (1880: 274-5).
[48] Granville (1881: 154-5)
[49] Witwatersrand University Library, Historical Papers, A 1631, Diary of Arthur Aaron Boss, 7 April 1879.
[50] Granville (1881: 202). See also Lewsen 1982:68; *Cape Argus*, 19 January 1878.
[51] Atmore (1970: 29). See also PEMS Archives, Paris, Dr. Casalis, letter dated 19 March 1879.
[52] Ellenberger, '*History ea Basotho*', *Leselinyana*, 20 August 1915.

On the other side Moorosi had about 1,500 men at his command.[53] Only about 300 of them were on the mountain at any given time, but they were available when needed, and many were ensconced in fortified caves throughout Moorosi's country. Moorosi had been preparing for war for several years. His men were well armed, he had accumulated a huge stock of ammunition, and his fortress, at the junction of the Orange and the Quthing rivers, was strongly and skilfully fortified. His great weakness was his inability to hold onto his herds and flocks. He sent many of them into the Maloti and, apart from those that he kept on his fortress, which were rapidly consumed, he dispersed the rest throughout his country. With his limited forces there was no way of protecting them against the Basotho and the white colonial troops. Even if he held out on his mountain he would be ruined.

Moorosi sent his regiments to stop Griffith's force crossing the Orange and the Tele, and he was hoping at this stage that many of the Basotho would join him. Some of his younger sons, in defiance of his orders, crossed the Tele and tried to round up some colonial cattle. They suffered several losses, the Basotho did not join them, and Moorosi then decided that his men should withdraw to his mountain and to the various fortified caves in his country.[54]

On 16 March Griffith led his Basotho regiments across the Orange and effected a junction with his white troops at Palmietfontein. About 700 men under Lerotholi stayed behind to guard the stock that had been allocated to the force and to harass the Baphuthi on the north bank of the Orange, which Griffith then referred to as Lerotholi's side of the river. The rest of the Basotho were now under the overall command of Letsie's son, Bereng.[55] On the following day, 17 March, Griffith crossed the Tele and began working his way up the Orange valley towards Moorosi's fortress, a journey of about 60 kilometres upriver.

There were two serious encounters on the way. In the first Bereng and his regiments attacked some Baphuthi in the valley of the Sebapala river, in a deep gorge, killing about 30 men and capturing 1,500 head of cattle and several hundred sheep and goats. About five men were killed on the Basotho side, among them 'the brave old chief Lenkoane', as Griffith called him, a junior brother of Moshoeshoe.[56] In the second an attack was made on a fortified cave, led initially by the Yeomanry and some Mfengu, and 43 Baphuthi were killed, including four of Moorosi's sons and two of his grandsons. On the Cape side a white sergeant was killed, and several men were wounded.[57]

The first attack on Mount Moorosi

On 25 March Griffith's force arrived before Moorosi's mountain fortress and pitched the colonial camp at its foot. It rose nearly 130 metres above the waters of the Orange and the Quthing rivers. Three sides were protected by sheer rockfaces. The fourth fell steeply, in part at an angle of about 30°, in a series of nine rocky ledges over a distance of about 700 metres. Each of these ledges was two metres high, and

---

[53] Granville (1881: 206).
[54] *Cape Argus*, 7 April 1879, 'Basutoland. News from Morosi's Country' (from a correspondent of *The Journal*); CA, ACC 459, Life of General Sir E.Y. Brabant, p. 73.
[55] CA, ACC 459, Life of General Sir E.Y. Brabant, p. 82; Damane and Sanders, (1974: 166), Maama's praise poems.
[56] *JME*, 1879, p. 201, Paris, quoting 'one of our missionaries', Morija, 26 March 1879. See also A.17-'79, p.11, C.J. Maitin's Diary of Events, 22 March 1879; Deare (1930: 3 May); PEMS Archives, Morija, Ellenberger Papers, Henry Stevens, 'Reminiscences'.
[57] A.17-'79, p. 11, C.J. Maitin's Diary of Events, 23 March 1879; Witwatersrand University Library, Historical Papers, A 1631, Boss, Diary, 23 March 1979; Browning (1880: 279-88); Deare (1930: 3 May 1930); Ellenberger, '*History ea Basotho*', *Leselinyana*, 27 August 1915.

was surmounted by a wall a further metre high, made of solid earth and faced with stones, and each wall was pierced by a double row of loopholes, one at the base, the other about 60 centimetres up. Flanking walls had been built on either side, so that any attackers would be assailed from three sides at once. The top of the mountain, on which Moorosi had built his village, was about 800 metres by 200 metres. There were several caves on the mountain which were used as granaries, kraals and shelters, and there were several springs of water, though not a plentiful supply. Moorosi's stores of ammunition were kept in a specially constructed magazine on the mountain.[58] At the bottom of the slope there was a rise, which became known as the Saddle, where the Cape forces threw up their own fortifications. Soon there was constant fire from sharpshooters on both sides, the Baphuthi firing from their lowest wall and the Cape forces from the Saddle. They were only 200-300 metres apart.

Griffith disposed his troops on every side of the mountain, but he never had enough to mount an effective siege. The Baphuthi were able to slip through at night almost at will, collecting grain and firewood from their supportive hinterland, and sometimes they were even able to drive up stock.[59] At the beginning the mountain was crowded with stock of every description. Oxen kept up an incessant bellowing day and night. Several goats came down in search of water and were captured.[60]

For the next two weeks, while Griffith waited for his artillery, he and his forces constantly harried the Baphuthi, and large numbers of captured animals were brought in by the Basotho from the mountains.[61] Some Baphuthi, driven from their villages and deprived of their cattle, gave themselves up.[62] Letsie argued that Moorosi had now been punished and urged that the troops should be withdrawn. Griffith brushed him aside: rebellion had to be punished and a rebel like Moorosi was not to be treated with.[63] He was confident that the mountain could be easily taken.

At last, on 6 April, the two seven-pounder guns arrived with about 30 men of the CMR's Artillery Troop. Griffith placed them on the southern side of a rise about 200 metres from the line of the walls, and began at once to prepare his attack. It was to be led by 100 CMR under Captains Grant and Surmon (a brother of the Assistant Commissioner at Mafeteng) and 100 men of the 3rd Regiment of the Cape Mounted Yeomanry under Lieutenant-Colonel Minto. Two troops of the 2nd Yeomanry regiment were held in reserve. The plan was for an assault in three stages. First, on the night of 7 April the attacking force would advance silently up the mountain and take up its positions in a cave about halfway up; second, from 6 to 8 a.m. on the next morning the two seven-pounders would be used to smash holes in the defenders' walls; and third, at 8 a.m. the bugle would sound and the attacking party would rush out and storm the first wall.

All three parts of the plan went disastrously wrong. The attacking party got halfway up the mountain on the night of the 7th, but then the moon rose and the Baphuthi saw them and started to roll down rocks and stones. Some of the attackers made a dash for the cave and waited for the others to join them, but by the time appointed less than half the force was there. On the following morning the so-called bombardment by the two seven-pounders made no impression on the strongly-built

---

[58] For descriptions of the mountain, see A.17-'79, p.12, Maitin's diary, 25 March 1879; Browning (1880: 295); Granville (1881: 208); Deare (1930: 3 May); Featherstone, quoting James Grant (1991: 44).
[59] *Leselinyana*, July 1879.
[60] Browning (1880: 299).
[61] Boss, op. cit., 25 March 1879; articles in *Leselinyana*, June and October 1879; Browning (1880: 299).
[62] A.49-'79, pp. 89-90, Griffith to SNA, 17 April 1879; pp. 91-2, Austen to SNA, 22 April 1879; p. 94, Return drawn up by Austen, 26 April 1879; *Leselinyana*, June 1879.
[63] A.6-79, Report of the Select Committee ..., p. 88, Rolland's evidence, 27 August 1879.

walls. Their deafening roar could be heard for miles around, but, as the troops caustically remarked, they were no better than pea-shooters.[64] At 8 a.m., when the bugle sounded, the depleted attacking party under Grant and Surmon bravely dashed out, and were joined by a small party of the 3rd Yeomanry, but they came under withering fire. Several were killed or wounded at once, Surmon being shot through the lungs and dying later, and the rest, when they reached the wall, found it too high to be scaled and too strong to be pulled down. All they could do was to cower behind rocks or crouch at the foot of the wall and call out for reinforcements. Most of the Yeomanry, however, never came close, and their commander, Minto, was heavily criticised for sheltering all day under a rock, waving his men on but not moving himself. The support force, men of the 2nd CMY under Southey, tried to move up, but they were forced to take cover behind rocks and in caves by the bullets and rocks that rained and ricocheted down from the Baphuthi's defences. An officer who was close to the first wall decided to use some of the shells from the seven-pounders as hand grenades. The first shell that he tossed over the wall did not explode, and the Baphuthi tossed it back again. The second exploded in his hand and shattered it. After that there was nothing to be done but to wait for nightfall, when the troops made the best retreat that they could, suffering more casualties as they ran down the mountain, reaching their camp at 8.30 p.m.

In all, on the Cape side five men were killed and 17 wounded. On the Baphuthi side the losses were negligible. The Basotho's part in this engagement was of no account. They were ordered to cause a diversion by attacking up a gully to the west of the main attack, but they merely fired off their ammunition at long range and withdrew.

In the post-battle analysis much blame was attached to Minto and his men for their 'cowardice' in not joining in the attack. But even if they had been as brave as the men who reached the wall they could never have gone any further. The whole plan was misconceived. The two seven-pounders on which Griffith had placed so much reliance were too light to support a frontal assault and, by attacking only at one point, he had allowed Moorosi to concentrate all his defensive effort there.[65] He had also been totally unprepared for the strength of the Baphuthi's opposition. One of those who took part in the attack confessed afterwards that he and most of his colleagues had been under the impression 'that our day's work would consist of an undisturbed march up to the top of the hill, a general scrimmage for pots, pans, assegais, &c., &c., with perhaps a shot or two at a few of the enemy as they fled down the hill on the other side.'[66] 'I fear this is the first example in our colonial warfare', wrote John Austen, 'in which we have had to encounter such determined opposition and good engineering generalship. We were all, more or less, taken by surprise.'[67]

The second attack

Griffith had to wait for over a month while more troops and heavier artillery were sent up. The two little seven-pounders kept up a desultory shelling and more of the Baphuthi's livestock were captured.

---

[64] Browning (1880: 306).
[65] For this first attack, see A.17-'79, pp. 2-9, Griffith to Colonial Secretary, 24 April 1879, enclosing Grant to Griffith, 11 April 1879 and Return of Casualties, and pp. 13-14, C.J. Maitin, Diary of Events, 8 April 1879; Boss, op. cit., 8 April 1879; *Cape Argus*, 15 and 29 April 1879; Browning (1880: 301-7); Moodie (1888: 302-7); Hook, (1906: 267-8); Deare (1930: 3 May); National Army Museum, Tylden Papers, Box 34056, Notebook IX, p. 66, 'Memories of 50 Years Ago'; Uys (1973: 51-8).
[66] Correspondent of *Northern Post* in *Cape Argus*, 29 April 1879, reprinted in Moodie (188: 302-7).
[67] A.17-'79, p. 40, Austen to Griffith, 7 May 1879. See also *Cape Argus*, 29 April 1879.

But Moorosi's men harassed the troops as well, firing whenever they saw a target and making repeated sorties on the picquets that Griffith had posted round the mountain. In a surprise attack on 6 May they killed one man and wounded four,[68] and in the early hours of 29 May, while it was still dark, they attacked a Yeomanry picket that had neglected to maintain a proper watch and killed eight men and wounded 12, stabbing some of them through the canvas while they were still sleeping in their tents.[69]

By this time the reinforcements had arrived. Colonel Brabant brought with him 140 men of his own Yeomanry regiment and a 12-pounder Armstrong gun which had been borrowed from the Free State, and he was joined by about 300 burghers from various towns in the Colony.[70] There were now 600 white troops in the country, supported by 'native levies' – a large force by colonial standards.

For some days Brabant carried out punitive expeditions up the Orange, dynamiting several fortified caves, destroying grain and capturing stock so that Moorosi and his men on the mountain would have fewer supplies on which to draw.[71] On 30 May he took over the command from Griffith, who was being heavily criticised in the colonial press and by his own troops.[72] But it was doubtful if Brabant could do any better.

The cold weather was now setting in, and Brabant could not afford to delay his assault on the mountain. This time the artillery bombardment was much heavier. Instead of a two-hour shelling by two small seven-pounders, the Armstrong, from 3 June onwards, battered the defences continuously for 48 hours. Several breaches were made in the walls, but then the gun broke down and the defenders had time to repair the damage. Even when the gun was brought into action again the Baphuthi were able to throw up temporary earth works in the breaches.

The attack took place on 5 June, and there were three lines of advance. The main force, consisting of 50 CMR, 75 1st Yeomanry and 25 burghers, was to storm the principal face of the mountain. A feint meanwhile was to be made on the gully to the left of the main attack by the 2nd Yeomanry under Southey and an Mfengu force under Tainton: if the opportunity arose this would be turned into a serious attack. And on the eastern side, to the right of the main attack, a force of 500 Basotho under Davies and a troop of the 1st and 3rd Yeomanry under Minto were detailed to advance.

At 6 a.m. the attacking force took up its positions. In spite of the bombardment Moorosi's men were still at their posts. At 7.30 a.m. the assault party advanced, but, as in the first attack, it came under heavy and accurate fire. Some rushed forward and reached the ledge of rocks below the first wall, and by mid-day about 70 men had gained this position. But the two flanking parties had made no progress at all. According to Brabant, at the first sign of any serious fighting the Basotho fired off a wild volley and bolted down the mountain. It is clear from Davies' account, however, that they were being asked to assail an impregnable position and it would have been suicide for them to advance any further.[73] For the main assault party the situation was hopeless. The order was given for withdrawal,

---

[68] Boss, op. cit., 3 May 1879; Deare (1930: 3 May); Tylden (1950A: 133).
[69] A.17-'79, pp. 15-20, Griffith to Commandant-General, 1 June 1879, with enclosures; Woon (1909: 62-3).
[70] Boss, op. cit., 25 and 27 May 1879; CA, ACC 459, Life of General Sir E.Y. Brabant, p. 82. See also C.6-'79, p. 2, return of troops in the field on 7 July 1879.
[71] A.17-'79, pp. 20-21, Southey to Brabant, 2 June 1879; CA, ACC 459, Life of General Sir E.Y. Brabant, pp. 80-82.
[72] *Cape Argus*, 26 April and 6 May 1879, quoting correspondents of *Burghersdorp Gazette* and *Northern Post*, and 17 May 1879, quoting occasional correspondent of *Grocott's Paper*; PEMS Archives, Paris, Germond, 26 June 1879.
[73] A.17-'79, pp. 21-24, Brabant to A.A. General Colonial Forces, 7 June 1879, and pp. 30-31, Davies to Brabant, 7 June 1879; CA, ACC 459, Life of General Sir E.Y. Brabant, p. 83.

and there were more casualties as the troops dashed down the mountainside for shelter. In all, four whites were killed and 10 wounded. Again many of the attackers had held back, leaving their colleagues in the lurch in a futile attempt to achieve the impossible. The Baphuthi's losses were again insignificant.[74]

Negotiations

The Cape's troops were now thoroughly demoralised. Winter had set in, and the nights were bitterly cold with hard frosts. The camp was plagued by sickness, and horses were dying daily for lack of pasture.[75] Any further attack was unthinkable, and it was decided to invest the mountain and to wait for warmer weather. In the meantime the greater part of the force was disbanded, including most of the Basotho, leaving equal numbers of CMR, yeomanry and burghers, as well as a few African levies, mainly Mfengu.

The Baphuthi were under even greater strain. They had lost nearly all their livestock, and hundreds of them came down from the mountains and surrendered. The fighting men on the mountain still managed to descend at night and to get food, grain and wood, but they were reduced to gnawing the hides of oxen at times.[76]

Throughout the siege Moorosi had tried to open negotiations, sometimes venturing down the mountain with a white flag to the lowest line of defence. Every time he was told that only unconditional surrender would satisfy the Cape, and he preferred, as he said, to die on his mountain.[77] Early in September he tried again with Brabant, and at a meeting halfway up the mountain he said that he and his people would accept a magistrate wherever the government might want to place them. He had 'completely broken' with Letsie, who had promised to come to his assistance if he was attacked and who had betrayed him. 'I acknowledge myself beaten', he said. 'You have taken all my cattle and killed a number of my people. Surely the Government ought to be satisfied.' Brabant was 'a good deal impressed by the old chief', but the Government was not satisfied and the war went on.[78]

The last of Moorosi's exchanges was with Gordon Sprigg towards the end of October. The Cape Prime Minister was coming from Maseru, where he had just told the assembled Basotho that the government wanted them disarmed, as described in Chapter 8 below – a development that must have been reported to Moorosi and which no doubt made him all the more determined to resist. He would not come down to the camp, and so the meeting had to be held on the mountain slope, within a few yards of the Baphuthi's first wall. The old chief was accompanied by 13 councillors and headmen. Sprigg went up with five colleagues, including Brabant of the Cape Mounted Yeomanry and Bayly of the CMR, who was about to take over from Brabant. Moorosi tried to obtain conditions, but Sprigg still insisted on unconditional surrender. Sprigg told Moorosi that he was as good as a dead man. Pointing to the troops below, he said they would take the mountain within a few days and make an

---

[74] For this second attack, see A.17-'79, pp. 21-33, Brabant to A.A. General Colonial Forces, 7 June 1879, and enclosures; Hook (1906: 270-1).

[75] Granville (1881: 213-4); CA, ACC 459, Life of General Sir E.Y. Brabant, p. 90.

[76] *JME* 1879, p. 375, Ellenberger, letter of 31 July 1879; LNA, S9/1/2/1, Barkly to Griffith, 16 August 1879; CA, NA 276, statement of 'Mophuphi Ntlue', 26 August 1879; CA, ACC 459, Life of General Sir E.Y. Brabant, pp. 87-8; Hook (1906: 271); Ellenberger, articles in *Leselinyana*, 27 August and 3 September 1915.

[77] Boss, op. cit., 28 March 1879; *Leselinyana*, August 1879; *JME* 1879, p. 375, Ellenberger, letter of 31 July 1879.

[78] CA, ACC 459, Life of General Sir E.Y. Brabant, p. 91. See also *Cape Argus*, 15 July 1879, 'Basutoland' (from the *Northern Post*).

end of the Baphuthi. Trying to drive a wedge between the chief and his followers, he instructed the interpreter to convey this warning to Moorosi's councillors and headmen and to ask for their response. For a long time they remained silent. At last came a single reply: 'We are Moorosi's people.'[79]

The third attack

For political and financial reasons Sprigg could not tolerate any further delay. The warm weather had returned, the commissariat had improved, and the CMR had been strengthened to 350 men and four guns. It was time to mount the third attack. Sprigg gave Brabant one more chance. He declined. He was, as he admitted, 'fairly played out', suffering from insomnia and plagued by difficulties with the Dutch burghers. 'My troops', he wrote later, were 'too disheartened.'[80]

The new man in charge, Colonel 'Zach' Bayly, was much more decisive. Learning from the failures of Griffith and Brabant, he had devised a new plan of attack. He had sent out reconnoitring parties at night to find a place suitable for an escalade, and they had discovered a large fissure in the perpendicular cliff on the Quthing side of the mountain. Bayly had decided that the Cape's main attack would be concentrated on this point, while a supporting attack would be made on the walls, more as a feint than an all-out offensive. He sent for scaling ladders to Aliwal North, where they had to be specially constructed, and for stronger artillery, a mortar, a 16-pounder, from King William's Town. He decided to rely almost entirely on his own force, the CMR. In a bold move he sent the demoralised Yeomanry away.

When the mortar arrived the artillerymen were dismayed to find that it was inscribed 'George Rex, 1802' and that it needed serious adjustments and improvements before it could be used. And the scaling ladders, each supposed to be 30 feet long, were some of them too short and all of them too weak. They collapsed under the weight of four men, and the only way they could be rendered serviceable was by tying two of them together and strapping them with iron bands.[81] But Bayly determined to press ahead.

For three days – 17, 18 and 19 November – the Cape's three guns and the ancient mortar maintained an incessant bombardment, firing about every ten minutes. For the first time the Baphuthi on the mountain suffered serious casualties. Several small breaches were made in the walls, but the real damage was inflicted by the mortar shells landing on the hillside and rolling down, and then bursting among the men defending the walls. After the battle captured Baphuthi admitted that the mortar and the guns drove them mad: go where they would they could not get out of the way of these bits of iron flying about in every direction.[82] Many Baphuthi had already left the mountain because of starvation

---

[79] Anon. (1896).
[80] CA, ACC 459, Life of General Sir E.Y. Brabant, pp. 91-2.
[81] Granville (1881: 221-2, 226).
[82] Granville (1881: 224-5, 235). Granville, who was in charge of the mortar, may have exaggerated its success. Tylden (1929) says that the shells rolling down behind the walls killed 60-70 men, but does not give his source. According to Woon (1909: 70) the firing did not inflict many casualties, but kept the enemy on the alert and made sleep impossible for many of them. Baphuthi prisoners told Pattison after the battle that 'on account of the bombs dropping about all night they could not sleep', and that on the night of the attack many of the men behind the walls were so tired that they could not keep awake: CA, ACC 88, Pattison Papers, 'The Taking of "Quitini" or Moirosi's Mountain, Basutoland, Nov. 21st 1879'; Kennan, who also took part in the assault, makes no mention of the artillery: Rhodes House Library, Oxford, MSS. Afr. S.969, Letters home from South Africa, 1874-1900, Kennan to his mother, 28 November 1879.

and hardship. More deserted under the ferocious bombardment. According to a Mophuthi prisoner after the battle, there had been 500 men on the mountain a day before the attack, but only 300 men at the time of the attack.[83]

The assault force consisted of 275 CMR, 40 men of the Wodehouse Border Guard who had arrived the day before, 410 'Fingoes and Tambookies' and 50 Basotho. Five parties were formed, two to take the lead in the attack with the ladders and two to follow them up, while a 'native contingent' supported by some CMR was to threaten the walls. Fifty Basotho were to carry the ladders. At around midnight on 19/20 November, after the dipping of the moon, the assailants took up their positions.

When the order for advance was given the troops went forward as silently as they could, most of them wearing dark clothing and 'carrying rifles and bayonets, or carbines, as they preferred'. The Basotho who were to carry the ladders dropped them and left, leaving the troops to do this work themselves. As they made their way in the dark along a steep and winding path they were heard by the Baphuthi, who began to roll down rocks onto them. For several minutes they stayed still and silent, and after a while the rocks ceased. The Baphuthi did not suspect an attack: they thought the noise was made by a picket going to guard some water. The troops went on, and after a further tough climb they reached the fissure, fixed their ladders against it and climbed up to a ledge from which they could see the top of the mountain. They erected their ladders again and began their final and most dangerous ascent, made all the more dangerous because the ladders were so short. Lieutenant Sprenger, specially chosen because of his height, was the first man to reach the top. There was only one sentry there, and he, it seems, had been asleep. Accounts vary. But whether the sentry fired at Sprenger and missed, or flung an assegai which went through his helmet, or was taken by surprise before he could do anything, Sprenger raised his carbine and shot the man, whose body then came toppling over, just missing the ladder and falling a hundred or more feet below. Sprenger then dragged a sergeant up and in the space of a minute about twenty CMR were standing on the edge of the mountain. At the same time the Wodehouse Border Guard and the African levies were attacking the front face of the mountain, where the Baphuthi had concentrated their defences. Moorosi and his men were now caught between two fires. Many of them rushed back from the walls to confront the troops who had mounted the escalade, but the CMR made a bayonet charge and the Baphuthi were overwhelmed. Most of them were killed or met their deaths jumping over the cliffs. Moorosi and five of his sons were killed, including his most senior son, Letuka, who in spite of his disagreements with his father had stayed with him loyally to the end. Lehana (Doda), who had caused so much trouble to Hope and Austen, was able to make his escape.

John Austen counted 38 bodies, among them that of Moorosi, on the fortress on the morning after it was captured, and there must have been many more whose bodies were not found. On the Cape side only two whites had been wounded, while one Mfengu had been killed and another wounded.[84]

---

[83] Granville (1881: 233). The number of men on the mountain is disputed. Deare (1930: 3 May) gives it as 200; 'Nkuetsana', a surrendered rebel, said that there were only 60-70 (CA, NA 276, Nkuetsana's statement, 19 December 1879). For Moorosi's loss of support at the end, see also Barkly (1893: 105).
[84] For accounts of this final assault, see *Cape Argus*, 2 December 1879; Deare (1930: 3 May); Granville (1881: 220-234); Rhodes House Library, Oxford, MSS Afr. S.969, Letters home from South Africa, 1874-1900, Robert Kennan to his mother, 28 November 1879; *Leselinyana*, December 1879; CA, Acc. 88, Pattison Papers, 'The

On the following days the walls were broken down, the magazine destroyed and the gunpowder blown up. When Moorosi's body was brought down to the camp the army doctor had the head removed and sent down to King William's Town on its way to exhibition in a London hospital – until the home government heard in horror what had happened and ordered that it should be returned and given a decent burial. But that was not the only indignity: the troopers got hold of Moorosi's corpse and paraded it round the camp with a spear stuck up the rectum. Then they dismembered it with the help of their African allies (who no doubt used some of the parts for medicine). The Basotho present were told that if they rebelled their chiefs would be treated in the same way.[85]

The Quthing district was now largely depopulated. Herds of cattle had been captured and distributed among the white forces and their African allies. The known leaders of the rebellion, those who were captured, were sentenced to terms of imprisonment. Ordinary men, women and children were sent as labourers to white farms in the Cape. The Baphuthi ceased to exist as a significant chiefdom.

Major Tylden, the military historian, concluded that 'The lesson of the final assault was plain enough; given a commander who understood the use of artillery, no hill fortress could hope to hold out against white troops.' Linking it with the fall of Sekhukhune's stronghold a week later in the Transvaal he declared: 'The day of the Bantu mountain stronghold was over.'[86] The use of artillery had been a powerful factor in the final assault on Moorosi's mountain, but the critical element in the Cape's success had been the surprise attack with the scaling ladders. If the single unfortunate sentry on that side of the mountain had been awake and alert the ladders would have been thrown down and Lieutenant Sprenger would never have got to the summit. Moreover the fall of Sekhukhune's stronghold owed very little to the use of artillery.[87]

But there was another lesson that the Cape should have drawn. As its new Commanding General, Sir Garnet Wolseley, observed, when warning against disarmament, Moorosi, an 'insignificant' chief with 'only a handful of followers', 'from one of those strong mountain positions in which the country abounds', had defied 'all the local military force of the Cape Colony for about six months [in fact eight].' To take on the entire Basuto chiefdom would be beyond the Cape's resources.[88]

About 50 white troops had been killed, or had been mortally wounded or had died of illness, and there had been similar casualties among the 'native allies'.[89] These were heavy losses for a colonial

---

Taking of "Quitini" or Moirosi's Mountain, Basutoland, Nov. 21st 1879'; Hook (1906: 272-4) Tylden (1929); Woon (1909: 69-74).

[85] Smith (1939: 245). For a discussion of this incident, see Atmore (1970: 32).

[86] Tylden (1950A: 136).

[87] Delius (1983: 244).

[88] C.2569, p. 37, Wolseley to Hicks Beach, 10 March 1880.

[89] C.16-79, p. 2, W.M. Cochrane, 'Return ....', 14 July 1879, which gives the figures of 18 whites dead and 46 wounded as on 7 July 1879. According to the Wesleyan missionary, Giddy, writing on 28 June 1879, 23 whites were buried at the foot of the mountain, and 27 native allies (WMS, Queenstown 1877-85, Giddy to General Secretaries of Wesleyan Missionary Society, 28 June 1879). After that there were very few casualties. Some men were buried at Fort Hartley, the base hospital during the war (communication from David Ambrose). The official figures for 'the Colonial Forces' were 28 men killed and 65 wounded: G.5-'83, p. 42, Appendix E to Gordon's 'Report: Colonial Regular Forces', enclosed with Gordon to Colonial Secretary, 6 June 1882. Tylden (December, 1969) identified 36 dead, of whom 32 were whites. These included not only those who were killed, but those who died of wounds and disease. He also wrote (Tylden: 1945) of 84 'attackers' being wounded. I.T. Tavender (1985), relying on a wide range of sources, identified by name 56 dead and 34 wounded.

war. The cost had been £300,000.[90] The Moorosi War had weakened the Basotho's respect for Cape arms.[91] It should have weighed heavily in the Cape's deliberations. Instead Sprigg pressed ahead with disarmament, demanding that the Basotho should give up those very guns which it had called upon them to use against Moorosi. And, contrary to the assurances given to the chiefs, and as if to intensify their fears about losing their territory, it decided to divide up the Quthing district and allocate it to white farmers. To many observers it seemed that the government was hell bent on provoking the Basotho into rebellion.

---

[90] *Cape Argus*, 24 July, 'Cape Parliament, House of Assembly', 23 July.
[91] PEMS Archives, Paris, Germond, letter of 26 June 1879; A.6-'79, Report of the Select Committee ..., p. 79, Rolland's evidence, 26 August 1879.

CHAPTER 7: CONSPIRACY AND CONFEDERATION

An African conspiracy?

The events of the past two years should have persuaded even the most prejudiced observer that the Basotho were not involved in any conspiracy to drive the whites out of South Africa.

Throughout the war with the Gcaleka and the Ngqika they had remained unmoved. They watched carefully and asked for news. But they had no sympathy with the Xhosa in their resistance to the whites, and they saw no reason to jeopardize their own safety for people they regarded as their long-standing enemies.[1] When, at the *pitso* in October 1878, Griffith condemned Letsie's petition and upbraided the Basotho as rebels, one of Letsie's advisers, Ramabilikoe, protested: 'We are not like the Xhosas. Do not put us in the same scale with the Xhosas who are always ready to rebel against the Government.'[2]

They had better relations with the Zulu.[3] Letsie, conscious of their military strength, had continued Moshoeshoe's policy of regularly sending them tribute (*nyehelo*), mainly, it seems, in the form of feathers,[4] but he did nothing to help Cetshwayo when the British army invaded Zululand. The Zulu's astonishing victory at Isandhlwana in January 1879 gave rise to fears among many whites that the long-dreaded African uprising was about to take place, but among the Basotho it caused little excitement.[5] They saw it as merely a temporary success: in the end the British were bound to win.[6] It is possible, as some believed, that Moorosi was encouraged to rebel by the distractions and disasters of the Zulu War, perhaps even by prompting from Zulu messengers.[7] But, apart from the Baphuthi, there were no signs of disaffection, and the Basotho's temper was perhaps best shown by a minor incident in February 1879. Shortly before the war, in October 1878, Major Bell had arrested four Zulu messengers on their way to Letsie, suspecting they were up to no good. When one of them escaped at the end of January 1879 he was recaptured with the help of information from Ramanella who immediately claimed a government reward.[8]

Finally the Basotho's help against their old friend and subordinate, Moorosi, though half-hearted and not very effective, was another proof, if not of their unqualified loyalty, at least of their unwilling-

---

[1] LNA, S9/2/3/1, Davies to Rolland, 1 January 1878; LNA, MF2/1/1, Surmon to Rolland, 7 January 1878; LNA, S9/1/2/1, Rolland to SNA, 28 January 1878; PEMS Archives, Paris, Dr. Casalis to his parents, 4 May 1878; CA, NA 275, Rolland to SNA, 19 July 1878; C.2482, p. 9, Dyke to President of PEMS Conference, 20 February 1879.

[2] *Leselinyana*, December 1878. Lerotholi and Masupha said the same: see official account of the same *pitso*, G.33-'79, pp. 32, 33.

[3] CA, NA 275, Rolland to SNA, 19 July 1878.

[4] A.6-'79, Report of the Select Committee ..., p. 79 evidence of Emile Rolland, 26 August 1879; LNA, L2/1/1, Bell to Griffith, 15 November 1878; Sanders (1975: 141, 282-3).

[5] PRO, CO 51/205, G.33-'79, Griffith to SNA, 29 January 1879, enclosing reports from Major Bell (24 January), Austen (25 January) and Barkly (25 January); LNA, S9/2/3/1, Davies to Griffith, 15 February 1879; LNA, MF2/1/1, Surmon to Griffith, 17 February 1879.

[6] CA, NA 276, Austen to Griffith, 15 February 1879; A.6-'79, Report of the Select Committee ..., pp. xxxiii-xxxiv, Griffith to Ayliff, 17 February 1879.

[7] C.2755, p. 84, statement of 'Mofetudi', Moorosi's 'late Official Messenger', 23 February 1880; A.6-'79, Report of the Select Committee ..., pp. 35 and 47, evidence of Wood and Bright respectively, 23 July 1879; LNA, L2/1/2, Bell to Colonial Secretary, Pietermaritzburg, 30 April 1879.

[8] LNA, L2/1/2, Bell to Griffith, 19 February 1879.

ness to take up arms against the Cape. The Baphuthi chief had expected support from Letsie, but had been left to fight alone.

Confederation, 'vigour' and disarmament

But the Basotho now had cause for anxiety themselves. While there was no African conspiracy against the whites, there was a real possibility of the whites coming together against the blacks. In 1875 Lord Carnarvon, Disraeli's Secretary of State for the Colonies, embarked on the bold enterprise of trying to bring together the disparate and disunited white communities of southern Africa – the Cape Colony, Natal, Griqualand West, the South African Republic and the Orange Free State – in a single confederation. In this way a strong and viable unity would be created which would make every African in the sub-continent understand that resistance and rebellion would be futile. It would also enable Britain to withdraw its regiments, except those that were needed for the defence of imperial interests at Simon's Bay. And in 1878 Sprigg's ministry came to power in the Cape with the promise of a more vigorous native policy. For the Basotho the most worrying manifestation of this policy was the government's determination, through the Peace Preservation Act of 1878, to disarm all the Africans within its jurisdiction, even those, like the Mfengu and the Basotho, who had been conspicuously loyal. At the same time, alarmed by the weaknesses exposed in the war against the Ngcika and the Gcaleka, the new ministry embarked on a series of military reforms designed to strengthen the Cape's forces so that they would not have to rely in future on help from imperial regiments. These linked initiatives – the confederation proposed by the imperial government, and the colonial government's new policy of vigour, incorporating disarmament and backed up by military reform – resulted in a swift and dramatic heightening of tension.

The man Carnarvon appointed to push forward confederation was Sir Bartle Frere. Now over 60, he was old enough to retire, but he was persuaded to take on the post as Governor and High Commissioner at the Cape by the promise and prospect of becoming the first Governor-General of the new South African confederation if he was able to bring it about. His appointment was warmly welcomed in Britain. He had a reputation as a brilliant and energetic administrator and as a humanitarian as well. His previous career had been mainly in India, where he had narrowly missed out on becoming Viceroy, and he had recently induced the Sultan of Zanzibar to sign a treaty prohibiting the slave-trade. He was a fervent Evangelical and a member of the Aborigines Protection Society, the main pressure group in Britain for the defence and promotion of African interests. Throughout South Africa, even in far-off Basutoland, missionaries welcomed his appointment. Mabille was full of hope, having heard, he told Frere, of 'your noble actions in India, at Zanzibar, and elsewhere, of your Christian character, of your love and enthusiasm for missions, for all the outcast, and those that are trampled under foot'.[9] The fact that he was an avowed expansionist and imperialist was a recommendation to the missionaries. They shared his belief that the best future for the African was under European rule, under magistrates rather than chiefs, advancing in civilization and Christianity and engaged in useful work and trade.[10]

Frere arrived at the Cape in April 1877. When Carnarvon resigned as Secretary of State in January 1878 – over a crisis in Europe, not an imperial issue – his successor, Sir Michael Hicks Beach, continued his policy of confederation, but the initiative now rested much more with the Governor

---

[9] C.2821, p. 3, Mabille to Frere, 29 December 1879. See also *The Little Light of Basutholand*, March 1873.
[10] Campbell (1959: 142).

and High Commissioner on the spot. It was Frere who forced on the war with Cetshwayo's powerful Zulu. He saw that it would be impossible to persuade any of the other white communities to link themselves with Natal if this entailed the risk of becoming involved in a Zulu war. He was also convinced that the young men in Cetshwayo's standing army were eager to 'wash their spears', and he was persuaded by Shepstone that the Zulu chief was trying to build up a hostile African combination with the object of expelling the white man from South Africa.[11]

North of the Vaal the South African Republic had to be won over. After its reverses at the hands of Sekhukhune's Pedi the state was bankrupt and discredited. Shepstone had been sent in with a small force, and eight days after Frere's arrival at the Cape he formally annexed the country to the Crown. For years the SAR's farmers had been involved in a border dispute with the Zulu. Shepstone, who had formerly supported the Zulu, now switched sides in an attempt to win over the Boers' support. With the same end in view, winning support for confederation, the war against the Pedi was resumed, and in November 1879 Tsate, Sekhukhune's capital, was taken by a combined force of imperial troops under Sir Garnet Wolseley and a powerful contingent of Swazi. The Pedi, with their Diamond Fields guns, had put up a long and fierce resistance. There was a lesson there for the Cape to learn, but the warning signs were ignored.[12]

The Free State was still smarting, first because of the British annexation of Basutoland, and second because its claims to the Diamond Fields had been rejected. In speeches at the beginning of 1876, in order to win over its support for confederation, Carnarvon's unofficial emissary, James Anthony Froude, had suggested that Basutoland should be handed over to the Free State as compensation for the loss of the Diamond Fields.[13] In a powerful and passionate outburst Griffith demanded to know whether Froude was expressing government policy or merely his personal opinion. If these reports were widely believed, he wrote, the Basotho's confidence in the government would be destroyed. It would be an act of betrayal. Already rumours of confederation had disturbed men such as Nehemiah and Tsekelo. What would be the effect of these new reports? He had poured his 'whole soul' into his work, not just because he had been trusted by government, but also 'for the sake of the people towards whom I have conceived a real attachment. I have ... led them to believe that [the government] would never perpetrate or tolerate any act of injustice to people under its rule'. How could he continue to rule in this way if these reports of Froude's speeches gained credence among the Basotho?

In view of the later policy of disarmament Griffith's final argument takes on a particular poignancy. There had recently been a report that the government intended to disarm the Basotho. 'I was able to allay the fears of Chief Letsie, and the Basutos, by treating the rumour with contempt, and telling them how unlikely and absurd it would be of us, first to grant permits at the Fields, and thus to arm those we intended shortly afterwards to disarm.' He could not dismiss Froude's speeches so easily: it was the government's duty to issue an authoritative repudiation.[14]

The matter was referred back to Carnarvon in London, and in the end Griffith was given authority to issue a denial on his behalf that there was any intention on the government's part to cede Basutoland to the Free State.[15] With the abandonment of the Orange River Sovereignty in 1854 still in Basotho

---

[11] De Kiewiet, (1937: 216, 222); Goodfellow (1966: 159).
[12] Delius (1983: 217-46).
[13] Lewsen (1960: 24), Merriman to J.B. Currey, 25 February 1876.
[14] G.52-'76, pp. 7-9, Griffith to SNA, 21 April 1876.
[15] LNA, S9/1/3/3, Griffith to all Magistrates and Assistant Resident Magistrate, Maseru, 18 July 1876.

minds, however, this episode must have shaken their confidence in the permanence of Cape rule.

In the Colony the ministry of John Molteno had been opposed to Carnarvon's plans, not wanting to expose the Cape, the largest and most prosperous of the white communities, to the obligations and dangers involved in assuming federal commitments to the others. In February 1878 the dispute over the conduct of the war with the Gcaleka and the Ngqika gave Frere the opportunity of dismissing Molteno and replacing him with John Gordon Sprigg, a frontiersman who, though at first opposed to confederation, soon became one of its strongest supporters. When Frere sent for Sprigg to form a ministry he was in laager at his farm on the Kei border defending it with his neighbours against insurgents who had destroyed and plundered many other farms around. Two other Ministers, and most of their local advisers, had 'considerable experience in frontier warfare', and, as Frere noted later, this stiffened their resolve to disarm the Basotho.[16]

Sprigg's new Secretary for Native Affairs was William Ayliff, the son of an Eastern frontier missionary, but Ayliff made very little impact – it was considered a joke that he was associated with a policy of 'vigour' – and it was Sprigg who took the initiative. A short, stocky man, with bushy eyebrows and moustache, he was a combative debater and an effective politician. He had no high view of Africans: to treat a Kafir leniently, he once said, was to throw away your kindness, but 'if you treat him like a dog he is at your feet'.[17] He would certainly be throwing away no kindness on the Basotho. He soon formed a close working relationship with Frere.[18] Like the Governor, he was an expansionist who regarded independent chiefdoms as an anomaly. Following the war with the Gcaleka and Ngqika he wanted to annex and to integrate all the territory between the Cape and Natal, while within the area of the Cape's control he would continue the former policy of undermining the chiefs but with more 'vigour' and determination than before: 'it is our intention', he announced to his constituents in East London, '… not to talk about breaking the powers of the chiefs, but really to break their power … Our intention is to recognize no chief whatsoever within the Colony. …. Our object will therefore be to break up all the tribes; that a tribe shall not live together as a tribe; that certain small locations only shall be established.' There would no longer be large stretches of native territory, 'but you shall have white people intervening.' Private ownership of land would be allowed and encouraged. This destruction of the old order was essential, he believed, if the whites in South Africa were to carry out their civilising mission. So too was disarmament. 'We intend', he declared to his cheering audience, 'to disarm all the natives within the colony.' And he announced the strengthening of the Cape's military capacity that will be described in Chapter 11.[19] In other speeches at this time he went further: children would be compelled not only to be educated, but also to work. This would be good for them and beneficial to the Colony. 'Properly managed these natives ought to be a source of wealth, and not a loss to the country, as was now the case.' What the Cape needed was compliant workers, not hostile warriors. And he protested that he would be taking arms from Africans, not because of the colour of their skin, but because they were not fit to be trusted with them.[20]

---

[16] C.2755, p. 49, Frere to Kimberley, 26 July 1880.
[17] Lewsen (1982: 27-8).
[18] Lewsen (1960: 41).
[19] *Cape Argus*, 14 March 1878. 'The Premier on the Situation'. For Sprigg's policy, see de Kiewiet (1937: 132-3) and Bradlow (1968: 140-1).
[20] *Cape Argus*, 28 March 1878, 'The Premier on the Situation', and 21 May 1878, Sprigg's speech to the

Frere was in complete agreement with him, and may indeed have been the first to suggest the policy of disarmament: 'among the natives of Africa', he wrote, 'a tendency to self-esteem is a common weakness; and, in a vain, uncivilized race, the possession of a gun is apt to encourage the most pernicious amount of self conceit'. It was therefore a duty, indeed a kindness, to disarm them.[21] He also saw disarmament as 'only a branch … of … Union or Confederation; self-defence against African enemies and good government …'[22]

It was in this context that Sprigg and his Attorney-General, Thomas Upington, pushed through the Peace Preservation Act, which gave the government the power to disarm all persons living within a proclaimed area. Although it applied to whites as well as blacks, the Act made provision for trustworthy persons to hold arms under licence and the government made no attempt to disguise the fact that the new measure was aimed at Africans. And although the Act could be applied to any area within the Colony, and although the intention was to 'disarm all the natives within the colony', Sprigg and Upington professed that they were primarily concerned with those areas which were likely to be disturbed and those people who were likely to misuse their guns. They were well aware, they said, of the dangers involved and would proceed with caution. The opposition, agreeing with the principle of disarmament, accepted these assurances and the Act was passed.[23]

The new policy was put into effect, however, in ways that took the opposition by surprise. In the immediate aftermath of the war against the Gcaleka and the Ngqika, without going so far as to apply the Act, Sprigg called on the Thembu and the loyal Mfengu to hand in their arms on an informal and voluntary basis. There was discontent, but no opposition. Then, in October 1878, he gave his instructions to Griffith as he made his way back to resume his post in Basutoland. He told him that disarmament was 'proceeding very successfully' on the Cape's eastern frontier and that he should now

> commence with the Basutos. Assemble the leading men and acquaint them with the native policy of the present Government, which I believe you thoroughly understand to be a Government of a barbarous people in the proper sense of the word – that they are not to be allowed to ruin themselves and everybody else, but that our superior intelligence is to be beneficially exercised on their behalf, that they are to be held in hand and guided and trained with the view of raising them out of barbarism into civilization. That the proof of manhood is not in the possession of a gun but the capacity to observe and maintain order and to assist in advancing the moral and material prosperity of the community. The guns after delivery will be valued and each man will receive compensation, and an assurance that the Government recognises its duty to protect the people from aggression and will perform that duty.

If the people were willing to give up their arms then a day would be appointed for them to hand them over. If not, Griffith was to inform them 'that the Government are resolute on the matter, and are determined to carry it out'.[24]

Griffith decided to inform the Basotho of their impending disarmament at the annual *pitso* on 24 October. As described in Chapter 5, this was dominated by his enraged condemnation of the petition setting out the Basotho's grievances. After that he announced the government's policy on disarma-

---

House of Assembly.
[21] For a more complete statement of Frere's views see p. 100 below. See also Bradlow (1968: 144-5).
[22] Quoted in Schreuder (2009: 71).
[23] For the debates on the Peace Preservation Bill, see *Cape Argus*, 18 and 21 May 1878.
[24] CA, NA 279, Sprigg to Griffith, 5 October 1878.

ment. The Thembu, the Mfengu and 'all the tribes in the Colony and under British rule' would have to disarm. Many had already shown their loyalty by giving up their arms when called upon to do so. He hoped the Basotho would do the same. Compensation would be paid. The government wanted the country to be at peace. The Basotho had no use for guns: if they were allowed to keep them they would only fight with each other.

Because of the furore over the petition few speakers responded to this announcement. Two of the policemen sons of Moshoeshoe, George and Sofonia, said they would be willing to give up their guns, but George, like Ntho, Letsie's chief councillor, reminded Griffith that the Basotho had chosen the Colony and not Natal because they had had heard that in Natal 'the Queen's subjects were disarmed'. The nearest to any expression of dissent came from Ramabilikoe, another of Letsie's councillors: 'With regard to our being disarmed, we do not know what to say, but we cannot be classed with the other tribes who have given up their guns. Perhaps we have been deceived by the Government leading us to believe that it trusts us.'[25]

Because of the wars in Zululand and the Transvaal, and because of the troubles with Moorosi, no further action was taken for the time being, and it was against the background of these disturbances that the Basotho's reaction was framed. The Moorosi War, as well as weakening the prestige of the Cape's forces, gave them another powerful argument against disarmament. How could the Queen order them to give up the very guns which they had used so loyally to support her against the Baphuthi rebels? But the same war hardened Sprigg's resolve to press on. Moorosi, he believed, would never have dared to resist the Cape if his people had not been well armed, nor would they have been able to hold out for so long.

Although the response at the *pitso* had been so muted Griffith's announcement had profoundly disturbed the Basotho, and soon the issue of disarmament was being fiercely debated throughout the country and was the subject of anxious consultations among the chiefs.[26] Davies, the Assistant Magistrate at Maseru, reported that the Basotho were divided into two parties. There was no strong support for disarmament. The Basotho prized their guns too highly for that. But on the one hand there were those who would be prepared to give them up simply because they were loyal to the government, and on the other there were those who protested that they had obtained their guns legally and with the government's full knowledge, that they had not been guilty of any misconduct, and that they should therefore not have to suffer disarmament.[27]

The veteran PEMS missionary, Hamilton Dyke, spelt out this hostile reaction more strongly. Griffith's announcement of impending disarmament had changed the people's demeanour, he wrote. It had engendered a spirit of mistrust. The Basotho were being treated as a conquered tribe, and their neighbours – no doubt the Xhosa chiefdoms – were pointing the finger of scorn and asking what the Basotho had gained by trusting the English – a slower death, perhaps, but a death just as sure as theirs. They had been induced to work on the Diamond Fields by the prospect of being able to get guns. They had worked hard for many months to get them. How could they be asked to give them up?[28]

---

[25] G.33-'79, p. 35 report on *pitso* held on 24 October at Maseru.
[26] CA, NA 276, Bell to Griffith, 24 January 1879.
[27] G.33-'79, p. 20, Davies to Griffith, 11 January 1879.
[28] C.2482, p. 8, Dyke to President of Conference of PEMS, 20 February 1879.

The country was swept by rumours and alarms, some of them put about by chiefs who were already exploiting the issue to whip up hostility against the government. They told their people that, in spite of Griffith's assurances, the government had an ulterior object in view. One of Letsie's sons said 'that after the Basutos were disarmed ... they would be made slaves of and oppressed in every way.'[29] Referring to Moorosi's recalcitrance, the government clerk in Quthing, C.J. Maitin, declared that 'Agitators have used the question of disarmament with great skill, thence the whole evil. Natives are trying to play a deep game with us...' At an entirely different level Tsekelo, it seems, was linking Sprigg's policy of disarmament with Frere's policy of confederation. 'Directly [Sir Bartle Frere] came to Africa', he said later, 'he had wars all over Africa. As Letsie was asking, what fault had the Basutos that they should be disarmed? There was no fault till Sir Bartle Frere was here; he was only sweeping away everything so that there might be confederation afterwards.'[30]

None of the magistrates responded to disarmament with any enthusiasm. All, more or less, recommended caution. Some, notably Griffith himself, had warned as early as 1873 of the dangers of allowing the Basotho to obtain arms so easily, and they all agreed with disarmament in principle. But with South Africa so unsettled the questions of manner and timing became critically important.

Griffith believed that, with the exceptions of Moorosi and Masupha, he might be able to persuade the Basotho chiefs to give up their arms quietly, but he was 'not quite sanguine' that they would. The only way to prevent opposition was 'to show a bold front and to have a sufficient force to put down at once any attempt at resistance'.[31] Austen, at Quthing, advised that a distinction should be made between those who were loyal and those who were not. If a few respectable men in each village could keep their guns on licence, there would be no opposition. Davies, at Maseru, believed that even those who were strongly opposed to disarmament would, if called upon, give up their arms, however aggrieved they might feel. Charles Bell, at Advance Post, in the heart of Masupha's country, warned that the people regarded disarmament as a very serious matter, 'the gun being the most valuable article a Mosotho possesses, and which he considers it his duty to retain at any sacrifice'. If the matter was approached with caution, in the course of time arms would be delivered up without any resistance or trouble, but it would be premature to demand them now. His father, Major Bell at Hlotse Heights, was more forthright. Disarmament would give rise to the greatest dissatisfaction and could not be properly carried out. In the country as a whole there were about 10,000 good firearms purchased at the Diamond Fields and elsewhere at a cost of about £75,000. To deprive the Basotho of their weapons would 'probably alienate them from the rulers whom they have hitherto looked up to with loyalty and respect.' Instead he recommended a licence of 20 or 30 shillings a year, which he thought would be paid without demur.[32]

After the Moorosi rebellion had broken out the Cape's House of Assembly set up a Select Committee to consider and report on the hostilities. Several officials gave evidence, and all who expressed an opinion advised against disarmament at this particular juncture. James Bowker, now free from official responsibilities, said that he was 'dead against disarming friendly tribes'. There was 'a very bitter feeling' in the country about disarmament, and 'if the Peace Preservation Act was put into operation in Basutoland, you would at once have 20,000 men against you.' The Basotho were well

---

[29] LNA, S9/1/2/1, Griffith to SNA, 3 January 1879.
[30] G.26-'82, pp. 48-9, Memorandum of Pitso held at Matsieng, 29 August 1881.
[31] LNA, S9/1/2/2, Griffith to Sprigg, 16 October 1878.
[32] For these reports, see G.33-'79, p. 6 (Major Bell), p. 12 (Charles Bell), p. 15 (Austen), p. 20 (Davies).

armed, and to try to enforce disarmament 'would be insanity, unless you accompany the order with six regiments'. It would unite 'every black face in South Africa against us.' It was no less than 'moral castration'.[33]

Though expressed in less colourful language than Bowker's, the testimony of Emile Rolland was even more important. With his missionary background and his fluent Sesotho he understood much better than most the intensity of feeling in the country. He confirmed that Griffith's announcement of disarmament had 'an unsettling effect' on the Basotho – 'Upon every man, woman and child; the whole country was profoundly moved by it' – and so far from 'wearing off' the feeling had strengthened and he believed it lay at the bottom of Moorosi's rebellion.[34] In response to further questioning he said that the Basotho might accept disarmament if their white neighbours were disarmed as well. 'The Basutos always feel that we may one day abandon them and that then they would be face to face with the Free State, their hereditary enemies.' And it would be 'very unjust' to leave them 'defenceless'.[35]

A month later, according to Frere, Rolland told him that there were 'designing and interested people' who were constantly telling the Basotho that 'we mean to leave them to themselves, to defend their country as best [they] can against the OFS'. This impression had gained a 'great hold on the people' and was the reason for their 'dislike to disarmament'.[36] The 'designing and interested people' to whom Rolland referred appear to have certain Free Staters, who were working to undermine the Basotho's loyalty to the Crown and who may even have hoped to provoke a war in the hope of gaining land.

The PEMS missionaries, like the magistrates, had been worried about the Basotho's easy acquisition of arms, but now that these guns had been acquired they were even more worried about the dangers of trying to disarm them. In an editorial in *Leselinyana* Adolphe Mabille set out the two arguments that were to form the basis of the PEMS position. First, looking to the Cape authorities, he did not understand why the disarmament of loyal subjects was necessary. Second, looking to the Basotho, he strongly advised them, if the government insisted on disarmament, not to rebel and sacrifice their lives for the sake of guns. Even if they drove the whites out of Basutoland today the government would send in powerful armies tomorrow, supported perhaps by volunteers from the Free State. The Basotho would be defeated and dispersed like a flock of pigeons and their country would be occupied by whites. If the government ordered them to give up their guns they must do it. It was the only way to save their country: 'if you refuse disarmament you will be committing national suicide....'[37]

In February 1879 Frere took the unusual step of asking the missionaries for their views on political issues. Hamilton Dyke, in a long paper already referred to, spelt out the Basotho's hostility to disarmament and strongly advised against it,[38] and in April his views were endorsed by his fellow missionaries at their annual conference. If only disarmament were laid aside, they told Frere, Griffith,

---

[33] A.6-'79, Report of the Select Committee, p. 17, evidence of Orpen, 15 July 1879; pp. 51, 56, 61, evidence of Bowker, 7 August 1879.
[34] A.6-'79, Report of the Select Committee, p. 77, evidence of Emile Rolland, 26 August 1879.
[35] A.6-'79, Report of Select Committee ..., p. 93, Rolland's evidence, 27 August 1879.
[36] C. 2482, p. 299, Frere to Hicks Beach, 22 September 1879.
[37] *Leselinyana*, December 1878.
[38] C.2482, pp. 7-10, Dyke to the President of Conference, 20 February 1879. See also CA, Griffith Papers, Dyke to Griffith, 26 April 1879.

'our most able Administrator', 'would have no trouble to maintain tranquillity and loyalty among the Basutos'.[39]

The traders, who were also asked for advice, expressed themselves unanimously against disarmament.[40] One of them, James Morisse, warned that to deprive the Basotho of their guns would 'convert a firm and reliable friend into a dangerous and troublesome enemy'. 'A Basuto', he wrote, 'has an intense affection for his gun, he looks upon it as a mark of manhood....'[41]

In London the Aborigines Protection Society was also beginning to voice some criticism of disarmament, partly on the prompting of Eugène Casalis, the PEMS Director in Paris, but mainly because of what it believed was 'the reckless manner' in which it had been carried out on the Eastern Frontier in that loyal Africans had been disarmed as well as rebels. Drawing on Frere's reports, the Colonial Office put forward the argument that was to become standard in the coming debate: that disarmament was not a punishment, but a necessary step for the security and welfare of all Her Majesty's subjects in the Colony.[42]

The same arguments were reflected in a debate in the Cape Parliament at the end of August and the beginning of September 1879. The opposition protested that, when the Peace Preservation Act had been passed the year before they had been led to believe that it would be applied only to districts that were disturbed and people who were disloyal, and they were opposed to its being extended to Basutoland. The Attorney-General, Thomas Upington, replied that Africans would never be civilized if they retained their guns, but then, in language that would be flung up against the government time and again, cut through all the elaborate justifications and hypocrisy: the safety of the white man made the surrender of guns by Africans imperative because the African was the white man's 'natural enemy'. There were some who thought that the black man could 'rise as high, if not higher, than the white man; but that was a mistake, for in this country the black man would never rise beyond the position of tiller of the soil, and the history of the world showed that it must be so …. The great and all-important question was, could the white population in this country grow up side by side safely with an armed black population? He contended that it was impossible, and therefore it was that the government intended taking the guns from the natives.' Ayliff declared that natives had a 'natural love of warfare', and so it was necessary to take away from them the means of carrying it out. Sprigg was more circumspect, advancing his familiar arguments that the possession of guns incited Africans to war and that it was therefore a real kindness to deprive them of these dangerous weapons which would only lead to their own destruction.[43]

Following this debate government ministers, trusting the magistrates ('on whose ability and discernment the Government places every reliance'), ignoring the missionaries, and discounting the traders ('who have a direct interest in keeping up the trade in firearms'), concluded that 'The weight of

---

[39] C.2482, p. 11, Dieterlen, Secretary PEM, to W. Littleton, 25 April 1879. See also PEMS Archives, Paris, Dr. Casalis to his parents, 5 February 1879; *JME* 1879, pp. 121-2, '*Nos dernières nouvelles du Cap*'.
[40] C.2482, pp. 299-300, Colonial Ministers' Minute, 18 September 1879. See also *Cape Argus*, 30 October 1879, reprinting article from *Cape Mercury*.
[41] C. 2482, p. 1, Morisse to Colonial Office, 7 May 1879.
[42] C.2569, pp. 1-2, APS to Colonial Office, 5 April 1879; p. 2, Colonial Office to APS, 17 April 1879.
[43] Debate reported in full in *Cape Argus*, 28 and 30 August and 2 September 1879. See also C. 2755, pp. 294, 297, 315, 316-7. Sprigg denied that Upington had used the term 'natural enemies', but Upington himself later confessed that while in office he had 'eaten' the phrase and that once out of office he felt free to use it again: *Cape Argus*, 13 April and 2 May 1881.

evidence ... is decidedly in favour of the possibility, with caution and forbearance, of disarmament without open resistance'. For the time being, however, in view of the possible risks involved, they were not taking any action.[44]

Frere too was advising caution. In October 1878 he had suggested that if annual licences were issued, as in England, they should not be denied to responsible Africans. He now repeated this advice. 'In Basutoland', he added, 'there are circumstances not met with elsewhere, which modify the question considerably.'[45]

It was at this point that Sprigg set off for Basutoland. Moorosi was still holding out on his mountain fortress, and Sprigg hoped to induce his surrender. But first, in spite of all the warnings from magistrates, missionaries and traders he was determined to press on with disarmament. The Basotho had to be told that there would be no wavering or retreat. Who better to impress this on them than the Cape Prime Minister himself?

---

[44] C.2482, pp. 299-300, Minute, 18 September 1879.
[45] C.2482, p. 299, Frere to Hicks Beach, 22 September 1879.

CHAPTER 8: DISARMAMENT AND THE CONFISCATION OF QUTHING

Sprigg's mission

> White Man left home and was swearing,
> Thumping and beating his chest;
> One day he took off his hat,
> He stamped all over it with his boots,
> Yes, he trampled it underfoot:
> 'Bring the guns here, you Kaffirs!'[1]

The praises of Maama, Letsie's fiery son, and soon to be one of the most fearless of the *Mabelete*, give a lively and dramatic picture of the Cape Premier, Gordon Sprigg, here referred to contemptuously as *Lekhooa*, 'White Man', presenting his demand for disarmament at the *pitso* at Maseru on 16 October 1879.

Between 6,000 and 10,000 men had turned out to hear what Sprigg had to say. They were nearly all mounted on horseback and dressed in European style, which afforded the missionaries great pride. Many had brought along colourful umbrellas to protect them from the sun. Of the three great chiefs only Letsie and Molapo were there, and Molapo was so unwell that he was unable to speak and others spoke on his behalf. As well as the magistrates and missionaries, several traders were present and some farmers from the Free State.

Sprigg did not impress the Basotho. Henry Taylor, the doctor from Hlotse Heights, described him in terms just as unflattering as Maama's: 'Being of insignificant stature, having a short staccato manner of speech, and dressed in a tweed suit and a straw-hat furnished with a long puggaree, he looked anything but an important and powerful personage, while his general manner was fussy and wanting in dignity....'[2]

His speech, of course, amounted to much more than 'Bring the guns here, you Kaffirs!' Short of admitting that the government was determined to make the Basotho powerless in order to make itself safe, it was a strikingly frank exposure of the arrogant and patronising thinking that lay behind the demand for disarmament, and it caused great offence.[3] Sprigg spelt out three basic arguments. The first was the foundation story of British rule in Basutoland: 'In the day of your calamity, when you appeared to be doomed to destruction as a people, you cried to the Government of the Queen to help you, and that Government listened to your cry ... everything that you ... possess this day, you owe to the Government of Her Majesty the Queen.'

The second was the justification of all colonial rule in Africa, the superiority of the white man:

> like the rest of the natives in South Africa, you possess very much the character of children, and the Government knows that children cannot at all times trust even themselves; that they are led away by excitement, and that when the war fever is abroad in the land, the natives often become infected by it, ... and then they use these guns, which they had no intention of using, for the purpose of fighting against the Government and their fellow-creatures. .... the Government knows better than yourselves what is good for you .... [It] acts as a father does towards his own child .... it is simply for your own interests, advantage, and prosperity, that the Government exists in this country.

---

[1] Damane and Sanders 1974: 160-1. Translation slightly changed.
[2] Taylor (1972: 56).
[3] C.2821, p. 10, Mabille to Frere, 17 February 1880.

The third was the argument of the white Juggernaut. He had been told that the Basotho would fight rather than surrender their guns. He could not believe that they would be so foolish, and he pointed warningly to the dire examples of the Ngqika, the Gcaleka and the Zulu.

All this was contained within the vision of Sprigg's 'vigorous' native policy, both on the narrow issue of guns and on the wider issue of helping the Basotho to advance in 'civilization'. 'The Government wants you to become like the white man, and not to regard it as a proof of manhood that you possess guns. If you go into the larger towns of the Colony, or across the sea to England, you will find that few white men have guns.' Just a few had arms for the defence of the country, and in the same way the government was proposing to establish in Basutoland a small African militia under European officers. The government also wanted to press ahead with more schools, an industrial school, a model farm, new roads and bridges, and an increase in the police force. All this was needed if the Basotho were to make progress. For these reasons there would have to be an increase in the hut tax, from 10s. a year to £1, an increase that was justified because the Basotho were so much wealthier than before.

The Basotho chiefs on the whole accepted the increase in the hut tax, though several of the poorer men said they would be unable to pay. But on the issue of guns every speaker protested, both those who would later be *Mabelete* and those who would later be *Maketetoa*. So far from committing any fault, they argued, they had helped the government against Langalibalele and Moorosi, and Griffith had told them when they turned out against Moorosi it was unlikely that they would be disarmed. It was wrong to treat them like rebels. Taking away their guns would be like tearing their hearts from their bosoms. They would not resist, but they would suffer great pain. They had joined the Cape, and not Natal, because the Cape allowed them to keep their guns (this argument was now in full flow). The government did not trust them because they were black. And Tsekelo, who was abreast of the latest news, flung up the comment of the Attorney-General, Thomas Upington, that blacks were the natural enemies of whites. What kind of language was that?

On the following day there was a meeting with the chiefs in the schoolroom at Maseru. Letsie, though present the previous day, was now said to be unwell, and Molapo was so ill that he had to go back to Leribe. In their absence the lead on the Basotho side was taken by Tsekelo, Sofonia and George. In response to their old, familiar arguments Sprigg told them he had heard nothing to make him change his mind: the Basotho were being disarmed not because they were black but because they were children. They had said they had no cause of grievance, but nor did the Gcaleka, the Ngqika and the Zulu. But once these people had guns they had embarked on war. In reply the Basotho acknowledged the futility of resistance – they were as helpless as a fieldmouse being held up by its tail, George said – but Sofonia pointed out that they still remembered the abandonment of the Orange River Sovereignty in 1854 and they believed the government might abandon them again. How would they hold their own if they did not have guns?

According to the official report Sprigg rounded off the meeting by impressing on the Basotho that the government stood firmly by the policy of disarmament and that when 'the proper time' came the magistrates would be instructed to take their guns. He assured them that the whole government were at one in their desire 'to raise and civilise the native races of South Africa. We think that the European race is endowed by the Almighty with superior intelligence', and this gave them a great responsibility .... we shall use our utmost endeavours to raise you in the scale of civilisation, to make you better men in this world, and to fit you for the higher and better life which is to come'. This, according to the official report, was greeted with 'loud cheering'.[4]

---

[4] C.2482, pp. 488-509, 'Official Report of ... Pitso ... held at Maseru, on ... 16th and 17th October 1879'.

According to the report which appeared in *Leselinyana*, however, Sprigg closed the meeting by saying he would transmit what the Basotho had said to the Cape and to England, and then added: "If you are intelligent you will understand that your duty is to surrender your arms, but the Government cannot take them away from you by force and with bloodshed. They will remain in your hands until you have understood that it is your duty to surrender them." 'When [the Basotho] heard these words, they expressed their gratitude with loud applause.'[5]

In a letter written ten days later Hamilton Dyke gave a similar account. Since Sprigg had been unable to persuade the Basotho willingly to give up their guns, 'the Government would certainly not employ force in disarming them. Thus a great danger has been averted from the land ....'[6] Thomas Irvine, a trader who was present, wrote that the chiefs' faces 'brightened' when Sprigg conceded that nothing would be rushed, but that 'when the Basutos were prepared to give up their guns, Government would receive them.'[7] Major Bell too came away from the meeting with the clear understanding, as he wrote to Griffith, that Sprigg had given an undertaking that 'the arms should not be taken by force' – though these words were omitted from Bell's letter as printed.[8] There were similar reports in the *The Cape Argus* and *The Cape Mercury*.[9] Sprigg protested about both,[10] but it is clear that he regretted his last-minute concession and that the official account was doctored accordingly.

Those Basotho who were present were certainly under the impression that the Cape Premier had promised not to use force.[11] When Letsie later complained to Griffith that Sprigg's assurance had been omitted from the official report the Governor's Agent could not deny that it had been given.[12] In later negotiations Masupha would refer to Sprigg's 'last words' that force would not be used,[13] and at a critical meeting shortly before the outbreak of hostilities he would get his son Lepoqo to read out the account from *Leselinyana* as proof of what he saw as the government's bad faith.[14]

The order to disarm

There was general agreement that the meeting had been a bad reverse for the Cape Premier. He had been hoping to win the Basotho over, but had been taken aback by the intensity of their opposition and in the end had made his much regretted concession. A month later Moorosi's mountain was captured, and a week after that there was news of the final defeat and overthrow of Sekhukhune's Pedi in the Transvaal. Sprigg was relieved and encouraged – 'our troubles are I hope at an end', he wrote[15] –

---

[5] *JME* 1880, pp. 11-18, *Le Pitso ... des Bassoutos, tenue le 16 Octobre,* the account given in *Leselinyana*. See also Sekese's articles in *Leselinyana*, 15 September 1893, 1 February 1905 and 15 September 1907.

[6] PEMS Archives, Paris, Dyke to Casalis, 27 October 1879. See also Mabille's comments in *Leselinyana*, November 1879: he had feared 'a terrible storm', but the meeting had 'passed without touching the Basuto nation'.

[7] Irvine (1881:26).

[8] LNA, L2/1/2, Bell to Griffith, 19 July 1880. For the printed version, see C.2755, p. 115.

[9] *Cape Argus*, 4 November 1879 and 11 December 1879; *Cape Mercury*, 31 October 1879. The *Argus* and the *Mercury* were the only two papers with representatives at the *pitso*: *Cape Argus*, 18 November 1879.

[10] C.2482, p. 370 Frere to Hicks Beach, 28 October 1879; *Cape Argus*, 6 and 18 November 1879.

[11] C.2755, p. 155, interview between Sprigg and Letsie, 26 August 1880.

[12] C.2821, p. 9, Mabille to Frere, 17 February 1880.

[13] C.2755, p. 129, *Cape Argus*, 24 August 1880: account of an interview with Masupha, 6 August 1880; C.2755, p. 142, letter from Makhobalo quoted in communication from Webster's Special Correspondent in Basutoland, 27 August 1880.

[14] C.2755, p. 55, 'Minutes of Meeting' held at Thaba-Bosiu, 3 July 1880. See also C.2755, p. 161, *Cape Times*, 9 September 1880, report of Interview held between Sprigg, Tsekelo, Sofonia and Ntsane, 25 August 1880.

[15] CA, Griffith Papers, Sprigg to Griffith, 8 December 1879.

and as soon as the Baphuthi were defeated he determined to press ahead with disarmament. The Peace Preservation Act had not yet been applied to Basutoland, but on 22 December, acting on Sprigg's instructions, Griffith issued a circular to Letsie and to the chiefs and people of Basutoland calling on every man to give up his gun in return for fair compensation. 'Now is the time to show whether you are truly subjects of the Queen or not....'[16]

Letsie was alarmed and confused. In view of what had been said at the October *pitso* he had believed that Sprigg, having heard the Basotho's case, would make representations on their behalf at the Cape. He had not expected that Griffith would call on the Basotho to give up their arms. He understood well enough, however, that the Basotho were not being coerced at this stage, and, no doubt acting on Mabille's advice, he decided to send petitions to the High Commissioner and to the Queen. In the meantime he instructed his people that they were not to give up their arms. If the Peace Preservation Act was proclaimed he would obey, but not until then.

His petitions, dated 21 January 1880, were drafted for him by Mabille[17] and were signed also by Jonathan and Lepoqo on behalf of their fathers, Molapo and Masupha. As well as the earlier arguments, he protested that if control over the country had been transferred from the High Commissioner to the Cape Parliament, the Basotho had never been told of this, and they still claimed to be 'dependent' on the High Commissioner; that Bowker, during his brief spell as Governor's Agent, had assured them that the Peace Preservation Act would not be applied to Basutoland; and that Sprigg had told them that no force would be used to make them put down their arms. They did not dare to disobey a government order, but it would be a painful duty to give up their arms and they felt 'terrified', 'afraid and anxious', 'disgraced'.[18]

Letsie's policy of refusing to give up his arms while he submitted his petitions was supported by almost the entire people, including, as Arthur Barkly put it, the 'more moderate and intelligent' section.[19] When two of his headmen wanted to hand in their guns he told them that they were not to do so because he was still talking with government. 'If the Government insisted upon his giving up his guns he would do so', but no one was to take action before him.[20]

Masupha was less cautious. When one of his Hlubi headmen, Mpoba, wanted his people to hand in their guns, he was reported to have sent a force of 300 or 400 armed men to summon them to a meeting and to instruct them not to take action. When called to account by his Magistrate he replied that he had merely held a meeting to inform Mpoba of Letsie's wishes, that only 30 armed men had been present, and that it was the Basotho's custom to carry arms to such meetings. Griffith was unconvinced. He warned Letsie that if he heard of any more such cases of intimidation he would ask government 'to send up a body of Troops to ... protect the loyal people',[21] and he punished Masupha by withholding his percentage of the hut tax collection.[22] The ferocity of his response was a portent of things to come. Meanwhile on the Basotho side initiation schools, with their attendant military training, were on the increase.[23]

---

[16] C. 2755, pp. 101-2, Griffith's Notice of 22 December 1879.
[17] PEMS Archives, Morija, Mabille to Hamilton Dyke, n.d. See also Smith (1939: 255).
[18] C.2755, pp. 67-70, 'The Petition of the Basuto Chiefs and People' to Frere, 21 January 1880.
[19] LNA, MF2/1/1, Barkly to Griffith, 8 May 1880.
[20] LNA, S9/1/3/4, Statements of Matsepa and 'Seithleko', 30 January 1880.
[21] LNA, S9/1/3/4, Griffith to Letsie, 13 February 1880.
[22] LNA, S9/1/3/4, Griffith to Charles Bell, 25 February 1880; C.2755, p. 103, Sprigg to Griffith, 28 February 1880.
[23] G.13-'80, p.26, Davis to Griffith, 3 January 1880; C.2821, p. 10, Mabille to Frere, 17 February 1880.

When issuing his circular Griffith had called on the French missionaries to do everything in their power to persuade the Basotho to hand in their guns. In the mission newspaper, *Leselinyana*, Adolphe Mabille referred to the circular as an instruction and urged the Basotho to comply, drawing attention once again to the terrible fate of those who had defied the government – the Ngqika, the Gcaleka, the Zulu, the Pedi and the Baphuthi.[24] Hermann Dieterlen assured his readers that the government had no ulterior motives and was worthy of their trust.[25] At the same time the missionaries regarded disarmament as unjust and unwise, likely at best to alienate the people and at worst to provoke rebellion. Mabille helped to draft and translate Letsie's correspondence and clearly inspired some of his arguments.[26] He also wrote personally to Frere, appealing to the Governor's humanitarian record,[27] and meanwhile, with the support of the mission's headquarters in Paris, the Aborigines Protection Society was mounting a strong campaign in London.

The opposition in the Cape also seized on the issue of disarmament to attack the government, and fiercely critical articles began to appear in the press, particularly the *Cape Argus*, mixed up, inevitably, with the usual rumours and dire predictions.[28]

The confiscation of Quthing

There were many Basotho who feared that disarmament was merely a prelude to some more general attack on their rights and their property, and at the beginning of 1880 these fears seemed to be startlingly confirmed when they learned of the Cape government's decision to punish Moorosi's rebellion by confiscating the district of Quthing, dividing it up into farms and throwing it open for private ownership. Individual Basotho would be free to bid for farms, but most of the land would be taken by whites. A commission for surveying and laying out the farms was established under the chairmanship of none other than the Basotho's old enemy, John Austen.

The Basotho had good reason to believe that this was merely the beginning of the break-up of their country. Sprigg told one of their missionaries, François Coillard, that he regarded Basutoland as now constituted as an anomaly,[29] and he later elaborated on this in a debate in the House of Assembly at a time when Masupha was beginning to give trouble. If, he said, one chief after another went into rebellion their land would be taken

> and Basutoland would disappear as a native territory. Some people might deplore that; but he was one of those who thought it desirable that the Basutos should not exist as a separate nation, while nobody outside was to set foot in Basutoland. He thought it better, in the interests of civilisation, that the black tribes should be segregated [i.e. split up], and not kept together as a tribe. By that means they would advance the interests of the people themselves, and of the Colony.[30]

So the alienation of Quthing from Basutoland, like disarmament, was all part of Sprigg's vigorous native policy of breaking up and civilising the 'black tribes' of southern Africa.

For the Basotho throwing Quthing open for white settlement was a shocking breach of faith, and Letsie and his fellow chiefs poured out their anger in a series of anguished letters and petitions: 'we

---

[24] *Leselinyana*, January 1880.
[25] '*Keletso*' ['Advice'], *Leselinyana*, February 1880.
[26] See fn. 17 above. See also LNA, S9/1/2/1, Griffith to Ayliff, 18 May 1880.
[27] C.2821, pp. 2-3, Mabille to Frere, 29 December 1879.
[28] CA, Griffith Papers, Sprigg to Griffith, 19 January 1880; C.2755, p. 102, Griffith to Sprigg, 28 January 1880.
[29] C.2821, p. 9, Mabille to Frere, 17 February 1880.
[30] C.2755, p. 25, *Cape Argus*, 1 July 1880, proceedings of the House of Assembly, 30 June 1880.

have no words at our command', Letsie told Griffith, 'whereby to express our deep grief and astonishment'. When Wodehouse had taken over Basutoland it was on the clear understanding that it would be kept as a whole for the Basotho alone. Moorosi had been Moshoeshoe's subordinate, his land had formed part of Moshoeshoe's land, and it had all been included within the boundaries of Basutoland as annexed by Wodehouse and governed by the Cape. In taking it away the government was therefore punishing the Basotho, not just the Baphuthi, and this was all the more unjust because the Basotho had helped in the military operations against the Baphuthi. It was also alleged that Griffith had promised the Basotho that if they helped to fight Moorosi Quthing would remain part of their country.[31]

Griffith denied making any such promise, though he admitted warning the Basotho that if they did not help the colonial troops he feared that the district of Quthing would be confiscated to pay for the expenses of suppressing Moorosi.[32] But apart from this he supported the Basotho's case and shared their sense of outrage. To deprive them of Quthing, he wrote, 'would ... be acting most unjustly to the Basutos, and would entirely shake their confidence in the British Government'.[33] It would be subversive of the moral authority he had taken so much care to build up: 'they will naturally conclude that this is only the thin end of the wedge, and that, upon one pretence or another, they will eventually be deprived of all their country'.[34]

The French missionaries, like Griffith, shared the Basotho's shock, particularly Ellenberger, who was to be allowed to maintain his mission station at Masitise but would now find himself surrounded by a sea of white farms. If they were strong in their protest against disarmament they were even stronger in their protest against the confiscation of Quthing, which they regarded as the naked exercise of might over right.[35] The case was taken up in similar terms by the opposition in the Cape and the Aborigines Protection Society in London.

Griffith was now deeply concerned by the excessive strain that was being placed on the Basotho's loyalty, not just by disarmament and the confiscation of Quthing, but by the doubling of the hut tax and the appropriation of £12,500 from the surplus revenues of the country in order to meet, in small part at least, the costs of the Moorosi rebellion. He did not want to lose the 'unsullied reputation' which he had built up over 32 years of service, and he felt bound to raise a 'warning note'. Had these measures been introduced at different times, and at sufficient intervals, the strain would not have been so great. As it was, they would now 'create a wide gap in that good feeling which has hitherto existed between the whole nation and myself as their "Father"'.[36]

The Peace Preservation Act
Letsie had pinned his hopes of avoiding disarmament on his two petitions. He still believed that Frere and the Queen were the great centres of authority, but he was soon put firmly in his constitutional

---

[31] CA, NA 277, Letsie to Griffith, 6 February and 9 March 1880.
[32] CA, NA 277, Griffith to Letsie, 12 March 1880. See also LNA, S9/1/2/1, Griffith to Ayliff, 12 March 1880.
[33] C.2569, p. 34, Griffith to Ayliff, 27 November 1879.
[34] LNA, S9/1/2/1, Griffith to Ayliff, 6 January 1880. See also LNA, S9/1/2/1, Griffith to Ayliff, 31 January 1880 and 12 March 1880.
[35] CA, Griffith Papers, Mabille to Griffith, 3 February 1880; C.2821, p. 9, Mabille to Frere, 17 February 1880; PEMS Archives, Morija, Dyke to Irvine, n.d.; PEMS Archives, Paris, '*Divers* 1880', Dyke to Orpen, 27 April 1880; Rhodes House Library, Oxford, Anti-Slavery Papers, MSS.Brit.Emp. S.18, C 128/190, Coillard to Chesson, 15 May 1880.
[36] C.2755, pp. 73-4, Griffith to Ayliff, 26 January 1880.

place. It was not Frere who replied, nor the Queen, but Bright, the Under Secretary for Native Affairs, in a letter to Griffith. The Governor's Agent was to tell Letsie that his petition to the Queen had been forwarded to her by the Governor, who had been unable to support it, and that his petition to the Governor had been submitted to his Ministers, who had directed that it should be rejected. Letsie had misunderstood Basutoland's constitutional standing: the Governor could not act alone in the affairs of the country, and all his executive acts were performed upon the advice of his Ministers in the Cape.[37]

At the same time, before any reply from the Queen had been received, Sprigg informed Griffith that a proclamation would now be issued applying the Peace Preservation Act to Basutoland. A copy of the Proclamation was sent up, reaching Griffith on 18 March, and he straightaway sent it to Mabille at Morija asking him to translate and print it. He would allow one month for the arms to be handed in, but at this stage did not name a date because he did not know how long Mabille would need to carry out the work.[38]

Sprigg now bombarded Griffith with instructions to press ahead as quickly as possible.[39] It was six months since the *pitso* in October 1879, and he felt he had been strung along by the Basotho. On 31 March Griffith wrote to Mabille with the missing dates: the proclamation was to come into effect on 6 April, and it would be unlawful to possess a gun after 7 May.[40]

Mabille refused to print the proclamation. He had been under the impression that it would not come into force until the Queen had responded to the Basotho's petition. He was aware too that Letsie was intending to send a delegation to the Cape Parliament. To print the proclamation would be to collude with the government in depriving the Basotho of these possibilities of constitutional redress, and he was not prepared to put either himself or the mission in this position.[41] When Griffith protested, Mabille's fellow missionaries fully backed him up.[42] Griffith then rushed to have the proclamation printed in Bloemfontein, but because of the delay the period for surrendering weapons was extended to 21 May.

Formally the Peace Preservation Act extended not only to 'guns and pistols', and to all 'gunpowder or other material capable of being used in the explosion of guns and pistols', but to 'swords, bayonets, daggers, pikes, spears, assegais'. The whole focus of the government's policy and action, however, was on guns, and so was the Basotho's protest against it. It was of no great concern to the government that very few assegais were surrendered, and for the Basotho the ensuing war was known as the *Ntoa ea Lithunya*, the War of the Guns.[43]

In one respect, acting in part on Frere's advice, the government was exercising caution. Sprigg fully expected that 'a large number' of guns would be handed in by 21 May, but after that, although the possession of arms would be unlawful and no compensation would be paid for any arms surrendered, no force would be used in order to seize them. Carrying arms in public would be stopped, but that was all. Over time the arms that were concealed at home would rust away and

---

[37] C.2755, pp. 70-3, Bright to Griffith, 26 February 1880.
[38] C.2755, p. 104, Griffith to Sprigg, 19 March 1880.
[39] C.2755, p. 104, Sprigg to Griffith, 17, 20 and 30 March 1880.
[40] C.2755, p. 87, Griffith to Mabille, 31 March 1880.
[41] C.2755, pp. 87-8, Mabille to Griffith, 2 April 1880.
[42] C.2755, pp. 90-91, Duvoisin and Dieterlen to Griffith, 10 April 1880.
[43] C.2569, pp. 43-5, 'Proclamation ...', 6 April 1880.

become worthless. In this way disarmament would be effected gradually and peacefully.[44] Sprigg also agreed that the £12,500 taken from the Basutoland Treasury would be restored, though this was no generous concession since the sum would be paid out of the funds received from the sale of farms in Quthing.[45] And on the great issue of Quthing itself the government was immovable. The district had been 'forfeited by rebellion'.[46]

Letsie was distressed and appalled. By rushing through the proclamation the government was making his position impossible. The Peace Preservation Act was being applied to Basutoland before his petition to the Queen had been answered, and he also wanted to send a deputation to the Cape Parliament because he believed that his petition had not been properly understood.[47] He was advised through Griffith that there was no point in doing so, since Parliament had entrusted the government with these affairs, and, when he insisted on going ahead, he was warned that, although he could not be stopped, he must not expect anything from the deputation and he must obey the law in the meantime.[48] There was, however, one concession. To avoid giving the impression that Parliament's response to the deputation was merely a matter of form the time limit for the surrender of arms was extended from 21 May to 21 June.[49]

It is a striking indication of the trust that Letsie still placed in Griffith that he asked him for his advice on the composition of the deputation,[50] and the six men who were sent were clearly chosen to make the best possible impression – Ntho and Ramabilikoe, two of Letsie's chief councillors, both highly respected by Griffith; Nathanael Makotoko and Abel Matete, two of Molapo's chief councillors, both staunch members of the church; and Letsie's son, Mojela, and Jacob Moletsane, the son of the aged Bataung chief Moletsane.[51] They were to be accompanied by the young French missionary, Irénée Cochet, whom Frere later described as 'very enthusiastic' but politically ignorant and naive,[52] and they took with them two petitions to the House of Assembly, one on disarmament and one on Quthing.[53]

Their arrival in Cape Town coincided with a major debate in the House of Assembly on what was formally a constitutional issue, an opposition motion that the government should be censured for applying the Peace Preservation Act to Basutoland without Parliamentary authority, but what was in fact a substantive issue, the application of the Act itself and the government's native policy in general. The debate was spread over eight days, from 22 May to 1 June, with the Basotho deputation in daily attendance. Again the arguments against disarmament were repeated and elaborated, and again the official justifications were spelt out. In an earlier debate the Attorney-General, Thomas Upington, had notoriously referred to Africans as 'natural enemies'. Now he declared his belief that 'the entire native

---

[44] CA, NA 279, Sprigg to Griffith, 26 February 1880; C.2569, p. 7, Frere to Hicks Beach, 2 March 1880; C.2755, p. 4, Frere to Ministers, 6 March 1880.
[45] CA, NA 279, Sprigg to Griffith, 26 February 1880.
[46] C.2755, p. 104, Sprigg to Griffith, 17 March 1880.
[47] C.2755, p. 81, Letsie to Griffith, 16 March 1880.
[48] LNA, S9/1/3/4, Griffith to Letsie, 3 April 1880; CA, NA 279, Sprigg to Griffith, 6 April 1880.
[49] CA, NA 279, Sprigg to Griffith, 14 May 1880.
[50] C.2755, p. 89, Letsie to Griffith, 11 April 1880.
[51] C.2755, p. 9, Frere to Kimberley, 8 June 1880.
[52] C.2755, p. 9, Frere to Kimberley, 8 June 1880.
[53] C.2755, pp. 10-11, two petitions to the House of Assembly dated 22 April 1880.

population should be disarmed'.⁵⁴ William Ayliff, the Secretary for Native Affairs, advised that, although they had been told of Basotho's 'loyalty and progress', 'savage nations' must always be looked upon with 'distrust and suspicion'. The impulse in them to take human life was so strong that arms had to be taken out of their hands.⁵⁵

Sprigg himself gave vivid expression to these fears when he responded to the debate in a long and impassioned address. Two experiences in Basutoland had made a powerful impression on him. The first was standing on Moorosi's mountain, and seeing 'men armed to the teeth with weapons purchased in this Colony and other parts of South Africa, the guns bristling tier above tier, not 30 yards distant'. The other was facing the Basotho at the *pitso* in October 1879, where he saw

> a large body of cavalry almost as numerous as that which enabled Marlborough to win his great victory of Blenheim. The force amounted to something like 7,000 or 8,000 men. I thought what a terrible thing it would be for this country if such a body of men, disciplined and trained to the use of their horses, and, to a certain extent, to the use of their arms, were to break out into open rebellion.

Confronted by such a threat he would have been failing his country if he had hesitated a moment longer than necessary before putting the Peace Preservation Act into force.⁵⁶ After this *tour de force* the government carried the day by 38 votes to 29.

Shortly afterwards Frere, with Sprigg and Ayliff present, met the Basotho deputation and conveyed to them the Queen's answer to their petition. Over the previous months the Aborigines Protection Society, with advice and support from the Paris Mission, had been mounting a powerful campaign against disarmament, and, partly to answer Letsie's petition, and partly to answer the APS, Frere had sent a series of long and brilliantly argued despatches, replete with historical comparisons drawn from the Scottish Highlands, Ireland and India, America and Australia and Albania and Montenegro. He insisted that disarmament was not a punishment, but merely a precautionary measure, necessary among civilized as well as barbarous peoples. He repeated what Sprigg had said at the *pitso*, that the Basotho were like children, and just as a wise parent took a knife from a child who might otherwise destroy himself or his friends, so the government must take their guns from the Basotho. He fully supported his government's policy, although he recognised it was fraught with danger. 'It must not be forgotten', he thundered, 'that this question of disarmament is one of the most important branches of the great contest between barbarism and civilization in South Africa.' It was necessary not only for the safety of the Cape Colony, but for 'the practical civilization of all native races'. The APS, instead of attacking the government, should give it every support.⁵⁷

As early as February 1880 Hicks Beach, Disraeli's Colonial Secretary, had indicated that, since these matters were the Colony's responsibility, he was not prepared to intervene, but that extreme caution should be exercised. If the Colony provoked a rebellion, it must deal with it on its own. No imperial troops would be supplied.⁵⁸ With an impending general election, however, the APS had hopes that if the Liberals won Frere might be recalled and the policy of disarmament might be

---

⁵⁴ C.2755, p. 297.
⁵⁵ C.2755, pp. 311 and 316.
⁵⁶ C.2755, pp. 344, 350, 351.
⁵⁷ C.2569, pp. 6-9, Frere to Hicks Beach, 2 March 1880; pp. 17-22, Frere to Hicks Beach, 15 March 1880; pp. 38-41, Frere to Hicks Beach, 17 March 1880; C.2676, pp. 42-4, Frere to Kimberley, 6 May 1880.
⁵⁸ C 2569, p. 6, Hicks Beach to Frere, 20 February 1880.

reversed. The Liberals did win, but they kept Frere in office, at least for the time being, and Kimberley, Gladstone's Colonial Secretary, took much the same line as Hicks Beach. In his formal reply to the petition he merely indicated that the Queen, while appreciating the Basotho's expressions of loyalty, wanted them to understand that disarmament should not be regarded as degrading them, but as a necessary step in their progress towards civilization. The Basotho were being asked to do no more than the Queen's subjects in other parts of her dominions.[59] In an accompanying letter, however, he acidly remarked that, since the Peace Preservation Act had been applied to Basutoland, and since the Cape government was responsible and thought this necessary, there was nothing more that he could say to any advantage. He repeated that, in the event of trouble, the Cape could expect no help from imperial troops. It would be 'much to be lamented' if the Basotho, who had been so distinguished for their loyalty, were treated with any want of consideration. While stopping short of outright criticism, he could hardly have made his dislike of the policy any plainer.[60]

The Basotho's representations about the confiscation of Quthing were no more successful. In the Cape Joseph Orpen, who consistently championed their interests, introduced a motion in the House of Assembly on 30 June against the alienation of any part of Basutoland without the prior consent of the Crown and an Act of Parliament, but he was persuaded to withdraw it on receiving an assurance that Sprigg would make a thorough inquiry into the matter.[61] And in London Kimberley responded that the confiscation of Quthing, like disarmament, was now a matter for the Cape government. At the same time, however, he made it clear that he agreed with Griffith that it was both unjust and a flagrant breach of faith.[62] It was in vain for Frere to claim that, although Moshoeshoe had asked for Basutoland to be kept as a native reserve, Wodehouse had never promised this.[63] Those who were present at the time remembered Wodehouse's undertaking that Basutoland would be kept for ever for Moshoeshoe and his people and their children's children, and Wodehouse himself assured Kimberley that 'Basutoland for the Basutos' was 'the very thing to the attainment of which all my efforts were directed'.[64]

Frere and Sprigg had been able to hold their position, but it had been badly undermined. They believed that after the disturbances of the past few years disarmament would lead to long-term peace, and that it was in the interests not just of the colonists, who would enjoy stronger security and control, but of the Basotho themselves, who without guns would be spared the temptation of a futile uprising against a force incomparably more powerful than their own. In this wise, noble and yet dangerous endeavour, they declared, they were entitled to the support of all men of goodwill, but instead they had to face a concerted campaign of opposition from missionaries and politicians alike. Their adversaries, by expressing their disagreement, were in effect inciting the Basotho to disobedience and rebellion. If war broke out it would be their responsibility.

The PEMS missionaries protested that they had always insisted on obedience to the law, and they were in fact horrified by the prospect of rebellion. They were convinced it would destroy the Basotho

---

[59] C.2569, p. 46, Kimberley to Frere, 13 May 1980.
[60] C.2569, pp. 46-7, Kimberley to Frere, 13 May 1880.
[61] C.2755, pp. 17-26, *Cape Argus*, 1 July 1880, account of proceedings in the House of Assembly, 30 June 1880. According to Merriman and Fuller, Orpen made the mistake of relying on legalities instead of the moral issue: *Cape Argus*, 17 June 1880.
[62] C.2569, pp. 49-51, Kimberley to Frere, 20 May 1880.
[63] C.2569, pp. 32-3, Frere to Ministers, 3 January 1880.
[64] PRO, CO 48/494, memorandum by Wodehouse, c. 15 March 1880. See also Smith (1939: 201).

chiefdom and therefore their own achievements over the past fifty years. But their opposition to disarmament was well known and must surely have confirmed the Basotho in thinking of themselves as victims of injustice. Mabille's refusal to publish the disarmament proclamation was merely the most dramatic expression of this opposition. Shortly afterwards, much to Letsie's distress, Mabille was recalled to Europe for an enforced rest for almost two years. But by this time, his critics argued, the damage had been done.

The opposition in the Cape came under attack in much the same way as the PEMS missionaries, with the added charge that they were endangering the peace by exploiting the crisis for party political ends. As John Merriman protested in the debate on disarmament, 'You cannot take up the cause of any oppressed nationalities, or of any race that is being, as you think, unjustly treated, without it being said that you are inciting those people to rebellion.'[65] Again, however, as with the missionaries, their attacks on government policy must have confirmed the Basotho in their belief in the justice of their cause. Several of the chiefs, Masupha for one,[66] took colonial newspapers and kept themselves informed of colonial politics, and the deputation which sat through the long Parliamentary debate on disarmament must have come back with a lively appreciation of the strength of the opposition.

Even Griffith and his magistrates were giving cause for concern. They had no great enthusiasm for disarmament. In their official reports the predominant view was that, if care was exercised and due concessions made, it could be successfully carried through, but since then Griffith's 'note of warning' had been published in a Cape Parliamentary Blue Book, and in the missionaries' correspondence and elsewhere it was frequently asserted that neither he nor his magistrates were in favour of disarmament.[67] A new note crept in to Sprigg's communications. Griffith had been asking for leave, which Sprigg felt unable to grant at this time. 'I hope you feel strong enough to carry this business through', he wrote. 'If you are in doubt I will sanction your application for leave and appoint someone to act for you, but I should much prefer your remaining at your post just now if you feel equal to it'.[68] In the following month he told Griffith that the matter was now in his hands. 'You have always impressed upon the Basutos the majesty of law and the necessity of implicit obedience. The results of your teaching are now to be tested. *I rely very greatly* upon your *influence* with the people and the *great respect* they entertain for you.'[69] The Governor's Agent had to be kept up to the mark.

The home government's support was lukewarm and distant. The old confidence in Frere had gone. His appointment had been generally welcomed. His dismissal was now generally demanded. He had been appointed to push through confederation. Instead he had presided over a series of costly wars and confederation was further away than ever. The disaster at Isandhlwana had been a hammerblow to his reputation, and Shepstone's annexation of the Transvaal had spectacularly backfired, stirring up demands for the restoration of independence and giving rise to a growth in political

---

[65] C.2755, p. 301, Merriman's speech on 21 May 1880.
[66] C.3708, p. 47, report of meeting at Maseru, 19 March 1883. PEMS Archives, Paris, Dieterlen to Lautré, 29 November 1880. During the war the missionaries at Morija were without newspapers, and Masupha sent them his: '*les marena rebelles [rebel chiefs] sont toujours au courant et communiquent à M. Jousse les derniers journaux, "Empire" et autres dont ils semblent abondannement pourvus.*'
[67] See, e.g, C.2821, p. 7, Coillard to Frere, 12 January 1880; C.2755, pp. 306-7, Sauer's speech in House of Assembly, 24 and 25 June 1880, and p. 343, Sprigg's speech, 1 June 1880; *Cape Argus*, 20 April 1881, 'Colonial Parliament. Notes in the Gallery'.
[68] CA, NA 279 (also Griffith Papers), Sprigg to Griffith, 12 March 1880.
[69] CA, NA 279 (also Griffith Papers), Sprigg to Griffith, 6 April 1880.

consciousness among the Afrikaners that embraced those in the Cape no less than those beyond the Orange and the Vaal.[70] Frere had a close and harmonious relationship with Sprigg, who, in response to the attacks of the APS, described him as 'the most high-minded Governor who ever set foot in South Africa'.[71] But he was now loathed by the humanitarians, all the more so because of their initial high expectations of him. 'What misery, what ruin he has caused to the natives', wrote Hamilton Dyke. 'Truly we may class him as the greatest enemy of the *freedom* of the Native that ever put his foot on Africa'.[72] His 'smooth tongue', his 'fine phrases' and his 'unctuous' manner made him all the more dangerous.[73] When, in June, Sprigg failed to carry a vote on confederation in the Cape House of Assembly Frere's doom was finally sealed. Three months later he was recalled.

This then was the context in which Letsie's deputation made its long way back from the Cape to Basutoland to report the failure of its mission.

---

[70] See, e.g., Schreuder (1969:27 and 1980:86-7) and Lewsen (1982:83).
[71] C.2755, p. 350, Sprigg's speech in House of Assembly, 1 June 1880. See also *Cape Argus*, 2 March 1882: in a speech at Grahamstown Sprigg described Frere as 'the most noble and high-minded Governor the Colony had ever had'.
[72] PEMS Archives, Paris, Dyke to Casalis, 14 April 1880.
[73] *Ibid*. See also Lewsen (1960: 43 and 1982:83); PEMS Archives, Paris, Chesson to Casalis, 13 March 1880.

CHAPTER 9: THE DESCENT TO WAR

Divisions among the Basotho and the intimidation of the loyalists

Not all of the Basotho's deputation made its way back immediately. Three of them, headed by Ramabilikoe Matete, left on 15 June. The others, headed by Ntho, stayed behind in order to strengthen their representations about the loss of Quthing.

On 11 June, four days before Ramabilikoe and his two colleagues set off from Cape Town, Griffith conveyed to Letsie the rejection of his petition by both the Queen and the Cape Parliament, and reminded him that all guns had to be handed in by 21 June, a period that was extended to 12 July to allow time for Ramabilikoe and his two colleagues to return and to make their report.[1]

Letsie had already made it known that if the petitions failed he would hand in his guns, and even before Ramabilikoe and his two colleagues had arrived he sent out a circular explaining the Queen's decision in the terms in which it had been explained to himself – that the Basotho were not being degraded, but were being treated in the same way as the rest of the Queen's subjects – announcing that he was handing in his arms, and calling on his people to do the same.[2] He ran into a storm of criticism for issuing instructions before the deputation had reported back, and for sending out a circular instead of calling a *pitso*,[3] but the real ground of objection was the order to surrender guns itself. Letsie's brother Molapo, in spite of all their old rivalries, had given him every support on disarmament, but at this critical juncture Molapo was on his deathbed. His sons were sharply divided between Jonathan, who had been appointed to act as Molapo's successor because his older brother, Josefa, was mad, and Joel, another older brother but from a less senior house. No one knew which way they would go.[4]

It was Masupha who took the lead for the opposition. At a *pitso* at his village on 21 June he and others denounced Letsie for 'betraying the tribe' and made it clear that they would not give up their guns.[5] In the south Arthur Barkly at Mafeteng already had his suspicions about Lerotholi's intentions, and he was soon to withdraw his tax gratuity on the ground that he was 'seditiously and rebelliously inclined',[6] while the missionary at Siloe, François Maeder, was despairing of the aged Moletsane, the chief of the Bataung, who had said at one time that he would follow Letsie, but now forbade his people to surrender any arms and was clearly in league with Masupha and Lerotholi: 'The Bataung say that the English will take their children and their cattle.'[7]

At the same time many of those who wanted to obey the government were being threatened with all sorts of pains and penalties. And there were now the first real signs of panic among the white population. Nerves were beginning to fray. The traders, who had already given up their arms, were

---

[1] LNA, S9/1/3/4, Griffith to Letsie, 11 June (2 letters) and 19 June 1880.
[2] A.22-'81, p. 3. Griffith to Sprigg, 16 June 1880.
[3] CA, Griffith Papers, Surmon to Griffith, 25 June 1880; C.2755, p. 129, *Cape Argus*, 24 August 1880.
[4] C.2755, pp. 12-3, Griffith to Sprigg, 23 June 1880.
[5] C.2755, pp. 28-9, Charles Bell to Griffith, 25 June 1880, enclosing statement of 'Lefuyane', 25 June 1880. For the criticisms of Letsie, see C. 2755, pp. 12-3, Griffith to Sprigg, 23 June 1880; C.2755, pp. 36-7, statement of Zakaria 'Mokhithlanyane', 29 June 1880; C.2755, p.54, 'Minutes of Meeting' held at Thaba-Bosiu on 3 July 1880, Ramatseatsana's speech.
[6] LNA, MF2/1/1, Barkly to Griffith, 12 July 1880.
[7] Ellenberger Papers, Maeder to Ellenberger, 30 June 1880.

now at the mercy of their Basotho neighbours and the rumours had already begun of impending attacks on their stations.[8]

On 23 June, two days after the *pitso* at Masupha's, Griffith sent a telegram to Sprigg reporting these developments: affairs had 'very much changed' and were now 'in a very critical state'. Letsie's sons, he said, had 'thrown him over' and joined Masupha, who had now come out into the open as the leader of 'the anti-Government or rebellious party'.[9] On the night of 28/29 June Molapo died.

In the face of all this pressure Letsie had summoned a *pitso* to be held on 3 July at Thaba-Bosiu, the day after Molapo's funeral there, to hear the report of his deputation to the Cape Parliament. Its spokesman, Ramabilikoe, gave a full account of its activities in Cape Town and of the debate in the House of Assembly. He also announced what he had not known before, but what he heard in the debate, that Griffith had 'interceded' for the Basotho and that Major Bell had told the government that he disapproved of disarmament. But his final message was blunt and uncompromising: the petitions had been refused. 'We say, let us give up all hope and do our duty .... Surrender your guns ....'

The debate that followed was fierce and impassioned, the argument swaying back and forth. The pain and the anger leap out from the printed record. Two issues were now inextricably intertwined – disarmament and Letsie's paramountcy.

Jonathan, Molapo's son, who had just been placed as his father's acting successor, supported both disarmament and Letsie's authority, and several others did the same, notably Sofonia, Tsekelo and Ntsane. Jonathan invoked the blessings of peace and prosperity: 'there can be only one Bull', he told Letsie, 'and you are that Bull.' But when Tsekelo called on the Basotho to give up their guns only a few voices responded.

It was Masupha who led the counter-charge, and who defied Letsie, not in his own name, but in that of the people. 'It is the custom to follow the Chief, but ... if the chief does wrong he must not be followed; the voice which must be listened to is the voice of the people'. And he reminded the meeting of Sprigg's words at the October *pitso*, that the government would not disarm the Basotho by force. Lerotholi spoke with characteristic bluntness: 'we cannot part with [our guns]'. Speaker after speaker said the same. 'Men without arms are not men', said one. Another pointed to the confiscation of Quthing: 'Morosi's country is taken from you, and Austen is cutting it up into farms to be sold. If our guns are taken from us we will be killed.'

The normal procedure at the end of a *pitso* was for the chief, having heard his followers' views, to announce his decision, and for that decision to be the final word. But Letsie's position was so weak that he was unable to bind his followers in this way. 'I cannot speak, my heart is full of grief. ... Are we disputing for the chieftainship? .... even my own son (Lerothodi) has turned against me. ... If the people were still *mine* I would say that all the guns will be surrendered. ... O, my people, my gun is going to the Government. All those who like me will follow my example. If a house is divided that house will not stand.' But Letsie knew only too well that the Basotho's house was badly divided.[10]

Letsie had declared that his guns were going to the government. Five days later, on 8 July 1880, the cart carrying them from his village to Maseru was cut off by some of his junior sons, mere boys he

---

[8] C.2755, pp. 12-3, Griffith to Sprigg, 23 June 1880, pp. 15-16, Griffith to Ayliff, 23 June 1880, and p. 16, Davies to Griffith, 21 June 1880. See also C.2755, p. 37, statement of Zakaria 'Mokhithlanyane', 29 June 1880.
[9] C.2755, pp. 12-3, Griffith to Sprigg, 23 June 1880.
[10] C.2755, pp. 51-7, 'Minutes of Meeting' held at Thaba-Bosiu on 3 July 1880. See also C. 2755, p. 30, Griffith to Sprigg, 7 July 1880.

called them, who were clearly acting with the approval of their more senior brothers and no doubt on their authority as well. Lerotholi and Bereng were both strongly implicated. It was an act of defiance against both their father and the government.[11]

Eleven days after that, on 19 July, Masupha ate up his Hlubi subordinate, Tokonya, for surrendering his guns on his own initiative. In this way he was asserting his right as a chief to exercise authority over people whom he regarded as his own subjects, and not as subjects of the Crown.[12] It implied a rejection of both the Cape and Letsie. Masupha was virtually declaring independence. About the same time his neighbour and nephew, Leshoboro Majara, ate up at least one of his own subordinate headmen, 'the first man ... to obey the orders of the Government and surrender his guns'.[13]

Throughout the period for giving up guns Masupha and Lerotholi sent messages throughout the country urging defiance, and by 12 July, the date set down in the Proclamation, very few arms had been handed in. At Maseru in the Thaba-Bosiu District Davies reported that 23 guns, 9 revolvers and 1 sword had been surrendered by 20 whites, and 28 guns, 1 sword, 2 assegais and 1 battle-axe by 27 'natives'.[14] At Mohale's Hoek Surmon reported that only 82 persons – 9 whites and 73 'natives' – had handed in their guns, fewer than one in 30 of those who had guns.[15] The only exception was the Leribe District, where Major Bell had over 600 guns in his court room at Hlotse Heights, most of them handed in by Jonathan Molapo and his followers, and some by Selebalo Moshoeshoe, but he frankly confessed that he was embarrassed to have them, since Masupha and others were now threatening Jonathan and Selebalo, and by 20 July he had handed them all back.[16]

Throughout the country men who wanted to hand in their guns were being threatened and intimidated, and several of those who ignored these threats suffered the same fate as Tokonya and were eaten up. In the north, when Jonathan and Selebalo ordered their men to hand in their guns, many of them defected and went over to Masupha.[17] George Moshoeshoe fled with 1,000 head of cattle into the Free State, and when President Brand protested Griffith begged that they should be allowed to stay since he could afford no protection until such time as troops arrived.[18] 'The loyal people are cowed', he told Sprigg, '...because they see we have no means at hand of protecting them.'[19] The only force in the country was that of the chiefs.

Among the Basotho rumours flourished that they were being disarmed so that their children could be taken as soldiers, so that their cattle could be seized, so that every kind of injustice could be imposed on them.[20] Among the whites there were scares of impending attacks on the magistracies and trading stations. In the Berea District, according to local reports, Masupha was telling his people to keep their horses in good condition for an attack on Charles Bell and his policemen at Advance

---

[11] Introduction, pp. 1-2 above.
[12] *JME* 1880, p. 373, Duvoisin to Casalis, 31 July 1880.
[13] LNA, S9/1/2/2, Griffith to Ayliff, 19 July 1880; C.2755, p. 116, Griffith to Ayliff, 27 July 1880, enclosing statement of Moleko, 22 July 1880; C.2755, pp. 134-5, statement of Mokhitle, 27 July 1880; C.2755, p. 135, statement of 'Thomas Ditshaba', 28 July 1880; G.20-'81, pp. 8-10, Charles Bell to Griffith, 24 December 1880.
[14] C.2755, p. 120, Davies to Griffith, 13 July 1880.
[15] C.2755, p. 125, Surmon to Griffith, 17 July 1880.
[16] CA, Griffith Papers, Bell to Griffith, 16 and 20 July 1880; C.2755, p. 115, Bell to Griffith, 19 July 1880.
[17] CA, Griffith Papers, Bell to Griffith, 16 July 1880; C.3112, p. 113, Bell to Griffith, 10 January 1881.
[18] C.2755, pp. 60-1, Brand to Frere, telegram received 7 July 1880.
[19] C.2755, p. 13, Griffith to Sprigg, 23 June 1880.
[20] PEMS Archives, Paris, Committee Members to Directors, 28 July 1880.

Post.[21] At Mohale's Hoek William Surmon reported that some of the local traders were 'very much scared, and it is all I can do to keep them from clearing out helter-skelter'.[22] At Korokoro, at the end of June, the local chief, Koali Makhobalo, advised the trader, Samuel Brummage, to send his family away at once and himself to leave in a week's time.[23]

The 'eating-up' of the loyals had transformed the position. The French missionaries were in despair over what they saw as the chiefs' stupidity. If they had wanted to hold on to their guns all they had to do was to sit quiet and follow a policy of passive resistance. There was no need to embark on a course of rebellious criminality that no self-respecting government would be able to overlook.[24] And on the government side, while Sprigg had acknowledged the possibility that many guns would not be handed in, he had believed he could deal with this by not forcing the issue – by not going out to seize arms through house-to-house searches, for example, but by forbidding any public display of arms, so that eventually they would fall into disuse and rust away. He had said that he would not use force, albeit in a concession which he had regretted and disowned, but he could not sit by and watch loyal subjects being ruthlessly attacked and plundered merely for obeying the government's orders. He was not yet ready, however, to bring his troops into action, and he still had hopes of a peaceful settlement.

Colonial delays

For the present the authorities in Basutoland were powerless. Apart from the police, who were not even 100 strong, they had no forces available to them in the country. It would take some time before troops could be mobilised and in the meantime the loyal Basotho were being intimidated and plundered and the magistrates and traders were vulnerable to attack. The magistrates began to fortify their headquarters and to call for more arms and ammunition, and several of them begged for reinforcements. Only Surmon dissented, afraid that the sudden appearance of troops would be the signal for a general uprising.[25]

The strain was beginning to tell even on the normally imperturbable Griffith. On 28 June he telegraphed for authority to recruit a force of 200 Europeans, men, as he explained later, who could be 'dribbled' into the magistracies one by one (to avoid the danger feared by Surmon),[26] and when this was refused he felt humiliated and betrayed. 'If matters come to the worst', he wired Sprigg, 'what protection are you going to give us? Are we quietly to wait and have our throats cut?'[27] He threatened to leave the country if the government failed to give him the means of protecting those men who were loyal: 'I will not remain here to be subjected to such indignity and injustice ....'[28] 'You don't seem to grasp the position up here .... Our position is becoming a laughing-stock to the whole country.'[29]

Sprigg's response merely added to Griffith's despair and exasperation. The rest of Letsie's deputation would soon be back in Basutoland. Sprigg placed an absurd faith in the impressive Ntho, in

---

[21] C.2755, p. 29, statements of 'Lefuyane', 25 June 1880, and 'Umahashe', 26 June 1880.
[22] CA, Griffith Papers, Surmon to Griffith, 11 July 1880.
[23] C.2755, pp. 27-8, affidavit of Samuel Brummage, 28 June 1880.
[24] PEMS Archives, Paris, Committee members to Directors, 28 July 1880.
[25] CA, Griffith Papers, Surmon to Griffith, 4 and 19 July and 7 August 1880; C.2755, p. 125, Surmon to Griffith, 17 July 1880, and p. 66, Surmon to Sprigg, 8 August 1880.
[26] A.22-'81, p. 5, Griffith to Sprigg, 28 June 1880; CA, NA 279 and Griffith Papers, Griffith to Sprigg, 14 July 1880.
[27] A.22-'81, p. 5, Griffith to Sprigg, 30 June 1880.
[28] A.22-'81, p. 11, Griffith to Sprigg, 28 July 1880.
[29] A.22-'81, p. 14, Griffith to Sprigg, 2 August 1880.

Frere's view 'the most experienced, trusted, and well affected' of Letsie's councillors,[30] who had assured him that if the Basotho were dealt with patiently there would be no rebellion, and he naively believed that the arrival of Ntho and his colleagues would 'produce a beneficial effect'. So while he was discussing contingency plans with the Commandant-General he had no plans to send up troops straightaway. 'You know that you have all the sympathy of Government with you at this very anxious time....'[31]

Griffith's response was explosive:

My dear Mr. Sprigg,

You who are comfortably settled at Cape Town *out of all danger* no doubt take a very calm view of the situation up here, but we who have our families here with us and so many people looking to us for advice and protection cannot take the same view as you do and I cannot help feeling that we are being cruelly treated by you. My request for arms and ammunition etc. was pooh, poohed, in the coolest manner as if I was the most ordinary of alarmists whereas the history of my thirty-two years service will prove to the contrary.

Before this policy of disarmt. was forced upon the Basutos the Government ought to have taken the precaution of supporting the officers who were to carry it out instead of leaving everything to chance. Warnings have not been wanting from all the officials in this Territory.

The very worst feelings of the Basutos have now been roused and the state of the Country cannot be better described than as an armed truce. How you can support us now it is impossible to tell. For if you move troops up it will be the signal for a general rising and massacre of all the whites and loyal people.

You say the Govt. sympathize with me, but that is poor consolation at a time when you are just waiting to see a mine spring at your feet. Sympathy won't assist you to protect the lives and property of people around you.[32]

Over the next two months Griffith and his colleagues had to stand by, impotent and humiliated, as the country lurched towards war. Masupha and Leshoboro Majara had already eaten up subordinate headmen who had handed in their guns. Over the next two months others did the same, among them Letsie's three sons, Lerotholi, Bereng and Nkuebe, and his cousin Ramanella.[33] Hundreds of loyal Basotho fled or were driven from their villages and sought refuge at the magistracies or in the Free State.[34] Many more would have fled, but could not get away with their families and their stock because they were watched continuously by hostile neighbours.[35]

---

[30] C.2755, p. 30, Frere to Ministers, 11 July 1880.

[31] CA, NA 279 (also Griffith Papers), Sprigg to Griffith, 10 July 1880.

[32] CA, NA 279 (also Griffith Papers), Griffith to Sprigg, 14 July 1880. See also *Cape Argus*, 27 July 1880, quoting Griffith: 'You have persevered in your ill-considered policy, all my remonstrances to the contrary notwithstanding. Moral force I now longer consequently have. With physical force you must furnish me, if I am to maintain my authority.'

[33] There are many references to these punishments in the reports of the magistrates in the LNA files and in C.2755. Griffith listed the main offenders as Masupha, Lerotholi, Leshoboro, Lesaoana [Ramanella], Lepoqo Masupha, Mapeshoane, Bereng Letsie, Nkuebe Letsie, Alexander (Maama) Letsie, Peete Lesaoana, Smith Posholi and Jeremiah Jobo: C.2821, p. 19, Griffith to Ayliff, 18 August 1880.

[34] LNA, S9/2/3/1, Davies to Griffith, 17 July 1880; *JME* 1880, p. 362, Dieterlen, letter of 23 July 1880; *Mission Field*, 1880, p. 401, letter from Stenson, 9 September 1880.

[35] E.g. LNA, MF2/1/1, Barkly to Resident Magistrate, Mount Frere, 30 July 1880; C.2755, p. 142, Koali

The potential rebels pressed on with their preparations for war. Masupha was fortifying Thaba-Bosiu, 'night and day' according to one report.[36] Lerotholi and Bereng were fortifying Kolo and Masite and calling on their followers to send in stocks of grain to these strongholds.[37] Guns were being cleaned,[38] and a brisk trade in arms, powder and ammunition sprang up with Free Staters who, although the trade was unlawful, were happy to make a quick and handsome profit out of it and in some cases actively incited rebellion, assuring the Basotho that the Cape was militarily powerless and that the imperial forces had suffered such heavy losses at Isandhlwana that they would not be able to offer any help.[39] The manufacture of assegais was stepped up, and Lerotholi and no doubt others distributed assegai heads to their followers.[40] Armed patrols rode along the borders and manned the drifts, making it difficult for the magistrates to import the arms and ammunition they needed.[41] Even before the winter ended there were reports of cattle being sent into the Maloti.[42] Perhaps most significant of all, there was an exodus of 4,000 Basotho from the Diamond Fields, no doubt at the chiefs' instigation,[43] while in the Free State it was impossible to get Basotho labour.[44]

In July several traders fled the country, pursued by Griffith's angry order to return and acquit themselves like Englishmen and his threat to confiscate their property if they did not.[45] Within a day or two, however, of Masupha's attack on Tokonya, Griffith was ordering Charles Bell and his police to abandon the magistracy at Advance Post, advising the French missionaries, Duvoisin and Jousse, to leave their stations at Berea and Thaba-Bosiu respectively, and sending his own family into the Free State. At the same time Major Bell at Hlotse Heights sent his family to Ficksburg and Arthur Barkly at Mafeteng sent his wife to join their children who were already at Wepener. In the event no attacks on whites took place, though the store abandoned by Samuel Brummage at Korokoro was plundered in spite of Maama's undertaking to protect it.[46]

Makhobalo to Sprigg (?), undated, towards end of August 1880.

[36] C.2755, p. 142, Koali Makhobalo to Sprigg(?), undated, towards end of August 1880.

[37] G.96-'83, Commission on Basutoland Losses, p.46, evidence of Mr. Donald Fraser, 8 August 1880; C.2755, p.159, Interview between Sprigg and George Moshoeshoe, 30 August 1880; C.2755, p. 162, *Cape Times*, 9 September 1880, Interview between Sprigg and Tsekelo, Sofonia and Ntsane, 25 August 1880, statement of Tsekelo.

[38] C.2755, p. 127, Surmon to Griffith, 26 July 1880.

[39] E.g. C.2755, p. 109, Frere to Brand, 10 August 1880; C.2821, p. 27, Tsekelo to Griffith, 14 August 1880; CA, Griffith Papers, Bell to Griffith, 16 August 1880; C.2755, p. 130, *Cape Argus*, 24 August 1880; C.2755, p. 65, Griffith to Sprigg, 7 August 1880; C.2755, p. 158, Interview between Sprigg and George Moshoeshoe, 30 August 1880.

[40] CA, Griffith Papers, Barkly to Griffith, 18th [July 1880]; C.2755, p. 127, Surmon to Griffith, 26 July 1880.

[41] CA Griffith Papers, Barkly to Griffith, 2 August 1880; C.2755, pp. 139-40, Austen to Ayliff, 5 August 1880 and enclosures.

[42] C.2755, p. 43, Barkly to Sprigg, 24 July 1880.

[43] *Cape Argus*, 25 August 1880, 'Our Basuto Mistake. How it affects the Diamond Fields', quoting *Diamond Fields Advertiser*: 'In fourteen days, almost four thousand British Basutos deserted from their employers on the Fields; this took place about a month ago ....' Worger (1987: 100) describes a more gradual process: 'Accounting for one-third of the mine workers in 1877, their [the Basotho's] numbers dropped as war threatened; by the time hostilities erupted in 1880-81 they formed only one-tenth of the work force.'

[44] *Cape Argus*, 24 July 1880.

[45] LNA, S9/2/3/1, Davies to Griffith, 14 and 17 July 1880; LNA, S9/1/3/4, Griffith to Messrs. Windell, Breen(?) and Humphries, n.d..

[46] C.2755, pp. 125-7, Griffith to Ayliff, 26 July 1880, and enclosures; C.2755, p. 136, Griffith to Ayliff, 4 August

The magistrates were now doing everything they could to convert their headquarters into fortified camps and to build up such forces as they could muster for their defence. As well as their small bands of police, they enlisted some of the loyal Africans who had fled to the magistracies and several white volunteers. For the most part their men were still poorly equipped, and at the end of July and the beginning of September several wagon-loads of rifles and ammunition were brought in to Maseru and the other magistracies. Even so the most they could hope for was to defend themselves for a few weeks until such time as colonial troops arrived.

The two magistracies that were in the greatest immediate danger were Mohale's Hoek and Mafeteng in the south. At Mohale's Hoek by the middle of August Surmon had only 94 men under his command, 14 white volunteers and about 80 Africans, but they had only enough ammunition to resist the first onslaught and if they were cut off their provisions would last only a month. Most of the chiefs in the area were disaffected and every day Surmon was in fear of an attack. He was determined to hang on. 'Nothing short of a direct order or the most dire necessity will cause me to leave my Post and abandon the loyals that have rallied round me ....'[47]

At Mafeteng Barkly had little more than 100 men at his disposal – 20 Basotho police, 76 Africans and 9 whites – and there were constant alarms and panics as Lerotholi threatened to 'trample him underfoot'.[48] Over the court house Barkly defiantly ran up the Union Jack, the flag that had 'braved a thousand years': it made, he said, 'a fine effect'.[49] Across the border at Wepener Fanny Barkly was terrified by rumours that Lerotholi had offered £100 for her husband's head, and was told by the Civil Commissioner of Aliwal North that it was terrible to think of the way he had been left to the mercy of savages.[50]

Major Bell had no greater force at his command at Hlotse Heights, and did not even have enough men to mount a proper guard at night.[51] At this stage, however, he was not under the same serious threat of attack. Nor was Austen at Quthing, who had about 200 men at his disposal.[52]

At Maseru there was a stronger force – 'thirty whites and a lot of loyal natives', according to one report[53] – and after the initial scare following Masupha's attack on Tokonya there were no immediate crises and Griffith was apparently confident that if attacked he could hold his own, at least in the short run.

As the government delayed, the magistrates' demand for troops became increasingly insistent and exasperated. It was widely believed that, if the government had sent in troops at an earlier stage, the chiefs would not have dared to attack the loyalists and the magistrates' authority would have been maintained. 'I cannot comprehend the action of Govt.', wrote Arthur Barkly at Mafeteng: 'It seems

---

1880, enclosing letter from 'a missionary' to Mr. Trower, 27 July 1880; C.2821. pp. 23-4, Griffith to Letsie, 5 August 1880.

[47] CA, Griffith Papers, Surmon to Griffith, 7 and 15 August 1880; LNA, S9/1/1/2, Griffith to Sprigg, 25 August 1880. (The quotation is from the letter of 15 August.)

[48] LNA, MF2/1/1, Barkly to Griffith, 8 August 1880, and CA, Griffith Papers, Barkly to Griffith, 8 and 15 August 1880.

[49] CA, Griffith Papers, Barkly to Griffith, 1 August 1880.

[50] Barkly (1893: 155-6).

[51] CA, Griffith Papers, Bell to Griffith, 16 August 1880.

[52] *Mission Field*, 1880, p. 401, letter from Stenson, 9 September 1880.

[53] Barkly (1893: 175). See also *Mission Field*, 1880, p. 401, letter from Stenson, 9 September 1880, referring to 'a good force' at Maseru.

simply fatuous to wait till the country is up instead of promptly suppressing the whole affair.'[54] Without any government force in evidence, the chiefs were able to reassert their old authority and the waverers had little choice but to obey their orders.

It was only at the end of July that the government despatched two columns of the Cape Mounted Riflemen from King William's Town and Kokstad. They were fewer than 500 strong (Griffith commented that he would have preferred 3,000),[55] their progress was slow, and even at this stage they were under strict orders not to enter Basutoland since Sprigg believed, with good reason, that this would provoke immediate hostilities.

The Cape Premier and his Ministers, and the Governor too, still hoped that law and order could be restored without any military intervention, and that the mere proximity of the troops, the mere threat of their arrival, would help to cow the rebels. In retrospect their reports seem absurdly optimistic – prospects brighter, the situation improving, the rebels losing strength. Even the flight of loyal Basotho was presented as their gathering around the magistracies in order to defend themselves in case of attack.[56] They were trying to rebut the criticisms of the opposition, but there were also genuine grounds for hope. It still seemed madness for the Basotho to pit themselves against the government. And while Griffith and his magistrates might have lost control, old Letsie now bestirred himself to reimpose his authority.

Letsie's initiative

Letsie was alarmed that the rebels were leading the country to disaster, but they were also defying his paramountcy, weak as that paramountcy might be. He told Griffith not to send in troops. Like Sprigg, he knew that this would lead to war. Let him, Letsie, make one final effort to bring his people to their senses.[57] Within his personal ward he made Lerotholi and Bereng hand back the cattle they had seized from those loyal to the government and prevented further attacks. He sent round messengers to order his subordinates not to block the roads or to close the drifts, and in spite of their doubts about his sincerity both Barkly at Mafeteng and Surmon at Mohale's Hoek acknowledged the effect of these efforts.[58] In the north he was even able to make Ramanella hand back the cattle he had captured.

Above all, he called up his forces and marched north and, on 10 August, occupied Thaba-Bosiu. Griffith had been urging him to take this step, since he was afraid that if, in the event of war, Masupha occupied the mountain he would be even more difficult to dislodge than Moorosi.[59] But for Letsie his ascent of the mountain was essentially an assertion of his authority over the Basotho chiefdom as a whole. Moshoeshoe's old stronghold, with the ruins of his village and the graveyard of the chiefs, was the symbolic centre of the Basotho chiefdom. Letsie was angry that Masupha had 'usurped' it.[60]

---

[54] CA Griffith Papers, Barkly to Griffith, 9 August 1880.
[55] C.2755, p. 65, Griffith to Sprigg, 7 August 1880.
[56] C.2755, pp. 58-9, *Cape Argus*, 29 July 1880, and p. 60, *Cape Argus*, 30 July 1880; C.2695, item 40, Frere to Kimberley, 3 August 1880.
[57] C.2755, pp. 137-8, Letsie to Griffith, 30 July 1880.
[58] E.g., A.22-'81, p. 13, Griffith to Sprigg, 1 August 1880; CA, Griffith Papers, Surmon to Griffith, 7-9 August 1880; C.2755, p. 66, Surmon to Sprigg, 8 August 1880; C.2755, pp. 110-1 and 111-12, Barkly to Sprigg, 11 and 12 August 1880.
[59] C.2755, p. 138, Griffith to Letsie, 31 July 1880; C.2755, p. 62, Griffith to Sprigg, 1 August 1880.
[60] LNA, MF 2/1/1, Barkly to Sprigg, 2 August 1880.

Masupha, who had gathered his forces on the flat summit of the mountain, made no resistance as Letsie and his regiments made their way up through the fortifications of the Khubelu Pass. He had drawn up his men, about 800 in all, in a horse-shoe formation, and Letsie drew up about 1000 men in a similar formation opposite. The ends of the two horseshoes were about 50 metres apart. On Letsie's side were several of his sons, including Lerotholi, and some of the loyal chiefs, such as Nehemiah, Sofonia and, after some delay, Jonathan Molapo. Masupha was supported by his own sons, and by Leshoboro Majara and Mapeshoane Posholi.

After long discussions between Letsie and his subordinates Jonathan was sent to try to persuade Masupha to come to terms, probably because as Masupha's son-in-law – his senior wife was Masupha's daughter – it was thought he had the best chance of winning him over. Masupha, however, was immovable, and on 13 August, three days after he had ascended the mountain, Letsie received a message from Griffith that he was required by the government to arrest his brother and to destroy his fortifications.[61] About two days later he was further informed that the government wanted all arms surrendered and that if this was done willingly it would deal leniently with 'those who have been led astray by mischievous and designing men'. If however Masupha did not surrender Letsie was to keep possession of the mountain until the CMR arrived to support him. Lerotholi could be dealt with by a fine.[62]

The government, unable to enforce obedience itself, was turning to Letsie to do the job for it and in doing so to risk a major civil war in which he might well be defeated. Having done nothing over the past decade to strengthen his authority over his powerful subordinates, now, in its hour of need, it expected him to exercise that authority on an issue, disarmament, that was deeply unpopular throughout the country. Its demands were unrealistic, as Griffith himself well knew. 'As to Letsie apprehending Masupha and Lerothodi', he wrote, 'you might as well ask him to fly.'[63] There were too many cross-cutting loyalties and rivalries. Letsie's sons were worried that Masupha was trying to throw off his allegiance to the house of Letsie, but on the issue of disarmament they were more in sympathy with him than with their father. Jonathan Molapo supported Letsie on disarmament, but was reluctant to move against Masupha – as he said later, to take the shield out of his wife's house against her father.[64] Both Masupha and Lerotholi distrusted the government, and were afraid that if they submitted they would be sent to Robben Island, like Langalibalele. Even a paramount younger, more energetic and more determined than Letsie would have found it impossible to do what Griffith had asked him. 'I understand what you say in your letter', Letsie wrote, 'but all the people have become wild [no doubt his original Sesotho was *mabelete*], and I do not see anyone to carry out the orders I have received.'

While assuring Griffith that he still belonged to the Queen and that he would do everything he could to 'prevent the peace ... being destroyed',[65] Letsie knew he was not strong enough to make Masupha come to terms, and on 14 August he told Griffith that Lerotholi had now left the mountain and that he himself wanted to leave in order to get a stronger force together. Griffith urged him to stay where he was until the CMR arrived, but it was hopeless. Letsie's men were cold and hungry, and with the first rains many of them were slipping away in order to start ploughing their lands.[66] On 16

---

[61] C.2821, p. 24, Griffith to Letsie, 11 August 1880.
[62] C.2755, p. 113, Ayliff to Griffith, 13 August 1880, and Griffith to Ayliff, 15 August 1880.
[63] C.2755, p. 65, Griffith to Sprigg, 7 August.
[64] C.3717, p. 155, Orpen to Sauer, 12 January 1883.
[65] C.2821, p. 24, Letsie to Griffith, 13 August 1880.
[66] C.2821, p. 27, Tsekelo to Griffith, 14 August 1880.

or 17 August he sent Griffith a pathetic message begging for permission to return to his village. The government must believe in his sincerity, he said, but he was 'old without legs, without arms and without an eye'. He was 'alone on the mountain, because those he had called to help them went away one after the other to their own homes'.[67] A few days later, in spite of all Griffith's remonstrances, he left, bereft of support and afraid, or so he said, that Masupha would kill him or take him prisoner.[68]

There were many who suspected that Letsie was merely playing for time while the Basotho fortified their mountains,[69] and these suspicions were intensified by the claims of many disaffected Basotho to be acting on Letsie's authority. He had every reason, however, to try to assert his paramountcy and to avoid a war which he believed would be disastrous, and men such as Tsekelo and George Moshoeshoe assured the authorities that he was acting honestly and sincerely.[70] And there were many who ascribed his retreat from Thaba-Bosiu, not to duplicity, but to personal defects – in Frere's words, to 'the fatal weakness and indolence for which he has always been noted'.[71] The truth was more simple: he was not strong enough to do more.

Sprigg's final mission

Sprigg now played his final card in his efforts to achieve a peaceful settlement. Towards the end of August he set off once again for Basutoland, this time accompanied on the one side by Joseph Orpen, Moshoeshoe's old friend and a great champion of Basotho interests, who he hoped would be able to use his influence to persuade the chiefs to come to terms, and on the other by Commandant Schermbrucker, a veteran of the Crimean War who had served with Griffith in the war against the Ngqika and the Gcaleka, and who, in the event of war with the Basotho, would be placed in charge of the Basutoland Police.[72]

In one respect Sprigg's position was stronger, for the CMR were now poised to enter Basutoland. Their commander, Colonel Mansfield Clarke, the Commandant-General of Colonial Forces, was Sprigg's travelling companion as he made his way to Basutoland. But in another respect he was much weaker. With an adverse vote in the Cape House of Assembly the policy of confederation, with which he and Frere had been so closely identified, had finally collapsed. Frere had been recalled and was on the point of leaving, and with his withdrawal Sprigg was losing a powerful ally. The new Governor and High Commissioner, Sir Hercules Robinson, would not arrive until early in 1881, and in the meantime imperial responsibilities were exercised by an Administrator, General Clifford and then Sir George Strahan, both of whom were critical of Sprigg. Meanwhile, in the United Kingdom, in spite of Gladstone's earlier statements in support of disarmament, the government was now openly hostile. In a debate in the House of Commons in July Joseph Chamberlain, as President of the Board of Trade, declared that 'No more imprudent thing at a more imprudent time could have been suggested than the

---

[67] C.2821, p. 26, message of Letsie as stated by Ntho, 16 or 17 August 1880.

[68] C.2755, p. 128, Griffith to Ayliff, 21 August 1880.

[69] E.g. CA, Griffith Papers, Barkly to Griffith, 8 August 1880, quoting 'Labane'; C.2755, p. 66, Barkly to Griffith, 8 August 1880.

[70] C.2821, p. 27, Tsekelo to Griffith, 14 August 1880; C.2755, p. 160, interview between Sprigg and George Moshoeshoe, 30 August 1880. Griffith too was convinced of Letsie's sincerity: A.22-81, p. 20, Griffith to Sprigg, 17 August 1880; LNA, S9/1/1/2, Griffith to Sprigg, 5 September 1880.

[71] C.2755, p. 114, Frere to Kimberley, 24 August 1880.

[72] *Cape Argus*, 24 August and 1 and 20 September 1880. LNA, S9/1/1/2, Griffith to Sprigg, 6 September 1880.

disarmament of the loyal Basutos .... the Government disagreed with the policy he [Frere] had pursued on the grounds alike of expediency and justice ....' The House greeted these statements with cheers.[73] A few months later, in a confidential minute, Kimberley commented: 'The Cape Government seems to me to have committed every possible error in dealing with this Basuto question ... It is inconceivable to me that a governor of Sir B. Frere's undoubted abilities could have lent his support to such blundering ....'[74]

Before leaving the Cape, Frere had urged Sprigg's ministry to exercise clemency in the terms offered to the rebel leaders,[75] but in Basutoland Griffith, tired of being defied and humiliated, argued that the time had come for vigorous measures. The rebel chiefs should be made to submit to the law, and large forces should be assembled at Maseru, Advance Post, Mafeteng and Mohale's Hoek in order to enforce the government's demands.[76]

Sprigg seems to have come with a more open mind – 'Cannot form a decided opinion yet', he told Frere[77] – and while he sent Orpen to see Lerotholi he embarked on a series of discussions with the Basotho chiefs and their advisers. Griffith was ill and unable to take part.

On 26 August the Cape Premier met Letsie at the French mission station of Morija. He asked him for his advice, but Letsie, after his humiliation at Thaba-Bosiu, could only confess his helplessness: 'I do not know what to say .... I am like a blind man and require to be led. ... If I were still a chief I could speak for others, but as I am not I cannot do so.' Lerotholi had become mad with drink, and Masupha was wild. There was nothing more he could do with them.[78]

Sprigg then went on to Maseru, where he met the loyal sons of Moshoeshoe, Tsekelo, Ntsane, Sofonia and George. They were pleased that the CMR were at last on the border, and insisted that the government should now take firm action. Anything less would be seen as a victory for the rebels. They also confirmed Sprigg's suspicion that the rebel chiefs were exploiting the issue of disarmament in order to throw off all government authority. Some rebels, perhaps, wanted to remain under British protection, but they wanted the magistrates to be removed completely.[79]

Orpen meanwhile, with the help of his brother-in-law, Emile Rolland, was trying to win over Lerotholi. Their talks were friendly, he reported to Sprigg, but Lerotholi was in a turmoil and could not be relied upon.[80] He was at one with Masupha on the issue of disarmament, but he resented his uncle's pretensions to independence and still more any pretensions that he might have to the paramountcy. He was also grimly aware that rebellion might lead to the destruction of his chiefdom. He was drinking heavily at this time. At one point he was reported to have come back drunk from his father's village and to have flung his gun on the ground, telling his people that it was Letsie's body and that he, Lerotholi, was the new chief of Basutoland.[81] His magistrate, Arthur Barkly, described him at this time as 'a very bad subject, violent, treacherous and I believe slightly insane – very

---

[73] C.2821, pp. 90-1, Report of Proceedings in House of Commons, Thursday, 22 July 1880, published in *The Times* of 23 July.
[74] PRO, CO 48/495, minute, 4 October 1880.
[75] C.2755, p. 41, Frere to Kimberley, 13 August 1880.
[76] C.2821, pp. 92-3, Griffith to Ayliff, 18 August 1880.
[77] C.2755, p. 141, Sprigg to Frere, 24 August 1880.
[78] C.2755, pp. 154-8, interview between Sprigg and Letsie, 26 August 1880.
[79] C.2755, pp. 158-161, Interview between Sprigg and George Moshoeshoe, 30 August 1880; C.2755, pp. 161-3, *Cape Times*, 9 September 1880, interview between Sprigg and Tsekelo, Sofonia and Ntsane, 25 August 1880.
[80] C.2755, p. 141, Sprigg to Frere, 24 August 1880.
[81] CA, Griffith Papers, Barkly to Griffith, 18 (July?) 1880.

intemperate also'.[82] There could be no hope of peace in his district as long as this 'firebrand' was there.[83]

Orpen and Rolland also went to see Masupha, but he refused to meet them. For the sake of form he professed to be ill, but in fact he was now completely intransigent, and his resistance was being strengthened by prophetesses who told him that the Queen had very few soldiers and that the Basotho would eat them up.[84] He also refused to attend when Letsie summoned him to a meeting, this time saying that he was afraid of being arrested. According to a missionary source at this time he was determined to undermine Moshoeshoe's elaborate arrangements for the succession to Letsie (which united the houses of Letsie and Molapo and cut out his own house completely), and was using disarmament as a way of drawing support away from Letsie to himself.[85]

The meeting which Letsie had summoned was designed to unite his principal chiefs and headmen in a final attempt to avoid hostilities. But Masupha was not the only absentee. No one of any significance came from outside Letsie's ward – not the sons of Molapo, not Leshoboro Majara, not Ramanella – and in the end, on 3 September, tired of waiting for them, Letsie, his advisers and subordinates, including Lerotholi, submitted a plea for mercy to Sprigg, humbling themselves, condemning themselves, casting themselves at his feet, promising to submit to punishment for destroying the property of those loyal to the government, interceding on behalf of Masupha, but begging for the law on disarmament to 'sleep' while Letsie continued to persuade the people.[86]

Two days later Griffith spelt out Sprigg's reply. The offending chiefs were to appear in court and to submit to the sentences imposed, which would be fines (so there would be no transportations to Robben Island). All goods and stock seized from whites or Africans were to be restored. If Masupha made due submission the government would entertain his supplication. Detachments of troops would be placed at Maseru and Mafeteng to preserve order and to give confidence to the well disposed. As for the law on disarmament, that was already in force, but for the time being the government would be content if 'some guns' were given up by Lerotholi and those chiefs who had been 'actually in arms against law and order'. As for the rest of the guns, the government would wait until the country was at peace.[87]

Orpen took this reply to the chiefs, and three days of tense negotiations followed. When Orpen was asked what was meant by 'some guns' he agreed that ten would be enough. Lerotholi was receptive, saying he was ready to give up ten guns and to pay a fine, though he was afraid of appearing in court and of the CMR being placed so close to him. He did not want to act without Masupha, and it was agreed that he would go to Thaba-Bosiu with several loyally disposed chiefs and councillors and try to get Masupha to join him in accepting the terms offered. As he and his companions were riding off, however, he met some men who had been sent by Letsie to sort out some difficulties at Mafeteng, an action which for some reason he regarded as being directed against himself, and he galloped back to his home at Likhoele.

---

[82] LNA, MF2/1/1, Barkly to Sprigg, c.25 July 1880.
[83] C.2755, pp. 110-1, 111-2, Barkly to Sprigg, 11 and 12 August 1880.
[84] C.2755, p. 158, interview between Sprigg and George Moshoeshoe, 30 August 1880.
[85] PEMS Archives, Morija, Dyke to Sprigg, 27 August 1880.
[86] C.2755, pp. 163-4, Letsie to Griffith, 3 September 1880.
[87] C.2755, pp. 164-5, Griffith to Letsie, 5 September 1880; CA, ACC 302, press cutting, n.d., 'Political Reminiscences of Hon. Joseph Orpen, ex-M.L.A.'

That evening Orpen heard that Letsie had sent out instructions that no chiefs should obey Lerotholi's orders as he had gone mad. Ntho, Letsie's chief councillor, warned him, however, that disarmament was so unpopular that Letsie had little support, and Josiah, one of Letsie's sons, added that the feeling about disarmament was so strong that it had almost 'paralysed' Letsie's power.[88]

In the meantime Sprigg had ordered the CMR to cross the Caledon 'to give confidence to the loyal people'.[89] Colonel Bayly with 300 men was to cross the Caledon at Jackman's Drift and establish himself at Maseru. Colonel Carrington with 200 men was to take up his position at Mafeteng.

Carrington and his men crossed into Basutoland shortly after 6 a.m. on Monday, 13 September. Lerotholi at once appeared in force with about 700 men, supported by 400-500 of Moletsane's Bataung. Arthur Barkly rode out from Mafeteng with 20 men, 16 Basotho policemen and four whites, to reconnoitre. Lerotholi sent a message that he wanted to see him, and Barkly rode forward with his chief constable of police, Lichaba, and a white volunteer. 'As I came up', he wrote, 'I saw a queer spectacle. Lerotholi dismounted was engaged in a violent struggle with two of his men, who were forcibly holding him back'. Lichaba told Barkly they were afraid of his revolver, and so he put it aside and rode in among them unarmed. Lerotholi then threw off his followers and rode forward to greet him. They shook hands. Barkly advised Lerotholi to surrender himself for trial, which he agreed to do if Barkly would stop 'the policies', which of course he had no power to do. The two men then shook hands again and parted. Barkly rode down to join Carrington, and as the CMR advanced a gunshot rang out. Was it a Mosotho opening fire, or, as some believed, a loaded rifle going off by accident? Lerotholi, it was said, had given no orders for an attack. Whatever the cause, the tension had broken and after one or two volleys the CMR charged. The Gun War had begun.[90]

---

[88] Cory Library, Grahamstown, MS 10,060, Orpen to Sprigg, Morija, 9 September 1880. See also PEMS Archives, Paris, Dr. Casalis to Maeder, 8 September 1880.
[89] C.2755, p. 149, Sprigg to Ayliff, 5 September 1880.
[90] Barkly (1893: 181-6). See also C.2755, pp. 191-3, Barkly to Griffith, 13 September 1880; C.2755, pp. 170-1, Sprigg to Ayliff, 15 September 1880; C.2755, p. 166, Carrington to Ayliff, n.d.; C.2755, pp. 200-1, Carrington to Assistant Adjutant General, Colonial Forces, 16 September 1880. For the opening gunshot, see *JME* 1880, p. 406, Dieterlen, 15 September 1880; Woon (1909: 113).

CHAPTER 10: GUNS, CHIEFTAINSHIP, LAND AND DROUGHT

When the loyal sons of Moshoeshoe, George, Sofonia, Tsekelo and Ntsane, urged Sprigg to take action, they also confirmed his suspicion that the rebel chiefs were exploiting the issue of disarmament in order to throw off all government authority.[1] This was the message which he was hearing from all sides – from other well-disposed Basotho, such as Nehemiah and Koali Makhobalo, from Griffith, and from Orpen[2] – and he was easily persuaded, if indeed he needed any persuasion. 'The outbreak ... has nothing to do with disarmament,' he wrote a few weeks later, after the war had started, 'though it shows the imperative need of it; but is a struggle for independence.'[3] And in a speech a month later he assured his audience that 'So long as chieftainship is endured, we shall have wars with the natives.'[4] This was the defence in which he now entrenched himself and his government. His opponents berated him for provoking hostilities by enforcing disarmament, but if the real cause of the war was the chiefs' determination to throw off the government, and if they were merely using disarmament to whip up support, this criticism lost much of its force. Similarly he would be at pains to protest that the Cape had not gone to war in order to enforce disarmament, but because it could not stand by and watch its loyal subjects 'eaten up'.[5] When he was accused of rushing into war he pointed out that at first he had sent in only a few troops, being advised by many who knew the country well that this would be enough to bring the Basotho back into obedience.[6]

For the big chiefs Sprigg's argument had some force. They did want to recover their powers and they did use disarmament to turn the people against the government. But disarmament was not a mere pretext. It was a terrible threat. Not only had the gun become the symbol of manhood. For all the Basotho, chiefs as well as commoners, there was still the danger that the Cape, having stripped them of their arms, might one day abandon them, and they would then be defenceless against the Free State. There was also the threat from the Cape itself. It was already planning to take Quthing and to dismember the rest of the country. All this the Basotho dreaded as the resumption of the seemingly inexorable process whereby the whites had already swallowed up the greater part of their country.

To this extent de Kiewiet was plainly right when he argued, in his influential study of *The Imperial Factor in South Africa*, that competition for land was the underlying cause of tension and conflict in Basutoland as well as in the rest of South Africa. 'It was the want of land', he wrote, that the Basotho found 'most oppressive.' Deprived of the Conquered Territory, they were pressed up hard together and there was no longer sufficient pasture for their cattle. In order to obtain the goods they needed and to pay their taxes and fines they had to export their labour, and 'perhaps from no other territory

---

[1] C.2755, pp. 158-161, Interview between Sprigg and George Moshoeshoe, 30 August 1880; C.2755, pp. 161-3, *Cape Times*, 9 September 1880, interview between Sprigg and Tsekelo, Sofonia and Ntsane, 25 August 1880.
[2] C.2755, p. 142, Makhobalo to Webster's Correspondent, n.d.; C.2821, p. 92, Griffith to Ayliff, 18 August 1880; LNA, S9/1/1/2, Griffith to Sprigg, 25 August 1880; C.2755, p. 176, Sprigg to Ayliff, 14 September 1880; CA, ACC 302, press cutting, n.d. 'Political Reminiscences of Hon. Joseph Orpen, ex-M.L.A.'
[3] C.2755, p. 183, Sprigg to Administrator, 20 September 1880. See also C.2755, p.176, Sprigg to Ayliff, 14 September 1880, and *Cape Argus*, 13 November 1880, 'The War. Its Cause'.
[4] *Cape Argus*, 11 October 1880.
[5] See, e.g. *The Journal*, 25 February 1882, 'Mr. Sprigg at Peddie'.
[6] See, e.g. *The Journal*, 25 February 1882, 'Mr. Sprigg at Peddie'.

did the labourers go forth in greater numbers. ..... Disarmament was a provocation, but the causes of war were deeper.'[7]

Although de Kiewiet's core argument was valid, he overstated his case by painting too gloomy a picture of Basutoland's economy. More and more pastureland was ploughed up, but this was partly in response to the high price which the Basotho could command for their grain in the Diamond Fields and elsewhere. They produced much more than they needed for themselves, and their income from their agricultural exports was far in excess of their income from labouring and transport-riding, five times as much according to Rolland in 1879.[8] For the most part the men who went to the Diamond Fields and elsewhere were not driven by necessity, but attracted by a widening field of opportunity, above all, though de Kiewiet fails to mention this, by the prospect of purchasing guns. Similarly the Basotho's desire for more land arose, not just from economic need, but from political ambition. As well as individuals who suffered poverty and hardship, there were chiefs who complained that their wards were not big enough for men of their dignity and standing, especially chiefs who had been compelled to withdraw from the Conquered Territory and who had been resettled among resentful neighbours, and especially too those sons of chiefs for whom it became increasingly difficult to find free and unoccupied territory when the time came for them to be 'placed' in villages of their own. As a refinement of his general thesis de Kiewiet asserted that the 'loyalists' in the coming war were 'those with most land' – the implication being that they had less reason to rebel.[9] In fact the opposite was the case. Jonathan Molapo was the only important chief to throw in his lot with the government, and other leading *Maketetoa*, such as George, Sofonia, Nehemiah, Tsekelo and Ntsane, were junior sons of Moshoeshoe whose landholdings were small.

Even though there is abundant evidence that the Basotho enjoyed a great increase in their standard of living under Cape rule, it is clear that at the same time they felt increasingly constricted and confined, and that they were all the more determined to resist disarmament because they were determined to defend their territory. It is also clear, though de Kiewiet makes no reference to it in this context, that the colonists were keen to grab more land. Hence the proposed expropriation of Quthing.

But was de Kiewiet also right when he went on to argue that the timing of the Gun War, as of the other wars in this period, was in part determined by 'the scourge of drought, that laid the land in dust, and the plague of cattle disease that decimated the herds'? 'The decision of the Cape Government to disarm the Basuto', he declared, 'affected a people shaken by an economic revolution and whipped by intemperate seasons.' And so 'the hard times that helped to provoke or exasperate conflict on the Eastern Frontier, in Zululand and the Eastern Transvaal, played their part in Basutoland as well.'[10]

To de Kiewiet it was of profound significance that the series of wars at the end of the 1870s coincided with one of the worst droughts that the region had experienced.

> The real seriousness of the economic condition of the natives was not immediately evident. Their level of subsistence was naturally low [and] against serious adversity the weak structure of native economic life could not prevail. And it came about that in 1877 a great area which included much of the Transvaal, Zululand, Natal and the entire area down to the Cape border was afflicted by a

---

[7] C.W. de Kiewiet (1937: 265).
[8] A.6-'79, p. 83, Rolland's evidence, 27 August 1879.
[9] De Kiewiet (1937: 264).
[10] De Kiewiet (1937: 263-5). See also Eldredge (1993: 80).

cruel and ruinous drought. South Africa was used to droughts …. [b]ut such a drought as oppressed natives and Europeans in month after month of unbroken tyranny was beyond the experience of all. …. the drought started in Fingoland, Emigrant Tambookieland, Herschel and parts of Basutoland in 1875 …….

In South African farming communities, whether they be white or black, a protracted and depressing drought has ever been a frequent cause of political unrest and sometimes of violence. The normal irritations of life during busy and profitable seasons become galling; petty discontents swell until they become unendurable grievances. And under the tyrannous sun men on both sides of the frontier looked upon their neighbours with hard eyes, reading peril in one another's discontent. Cattle and sheep died by the thousand; stock thefts reached a height unprecedented in frontier annals.[11]

It is apparent, even from these brief passages, that de Kiewiet extrapolated too much from the Eastern Frontier to Basutoland. The Basotho's economy did not collapse under the impact of drought. No 'plague of cattle disease … decimated the herds'. There was no increase in stock theft. And in fact Basutoland, though suffering badly, was less affected by drought than the surrounding areas.

De Kiewiet claimed that at the time when disarmament was applied to the Basotho they had suffered 'intemperate seasons', and that the crucial harvest of 1879/80 was a failure. To support this he quoted Henry Davies' annual report from Maseru at the end of 1879, during the growing season for that harvest: 'The chief characteristic of the year 1879 is the protracted and severe drought which has prevailed throughout the land, the effects of which are only too plainly visible in the parched up country and withering crops ….'[12]

The impact of drought, however, was very uneven. The Basotho grew three main crops – millet ('Kafir corn'), which was their 'staple diet',[13] maize, and winter wheat, the main export crop, which had a shorter growing season, being harvested in December and January rather than May. Because of the variability of the rainfall it sometimes happened that one crop failed while others did comparatively well, and that some parts of the country flourished while others were stricken. And because of the inequalities of distribution some families had ample supplies while others went hungry.

In 1876/77, a year of severe drought in much of South Africa, Griffith reported that in Basutoland the millet had 'failed to a considerable extent' and the maize crop had been 'poor'. The people would still have enough food to eat, but more than usual would have to go as migrant labourers to the public works in the Cape 'to earn what they require.'[14] A few months later Surmon, writing from the south of the country, reported that, although the harvest had been small, the Basotho were still selling large quantities of grain because of the failure of crops elsewhere.[15]

In 1877/78 there was again a 'very severe and protracted' drought, but following rains in January it was expected that the crops would be 'fairly up to the average'.[16] Looking back in May 1878, the French

---

[11] De Kiewiet (1937: 161, 164).
[12] De Kiewiet (1937: 265).
[13] LNA, S9/1/2/1, Griffith to SNA, 3 July 1877.
[14] *Ibid.*
[15] LNA, MF2/1/1, Surmon to Governor's Agent, 7 January 1878.
[16] G.17-'78, p. 4, Rolland to SNA, 28 January 1878.

missionaries expressed their relief that the threat of famine had been averted,[17] but even so there was distress in the south of the country. According to Stenson, the Anglican missionary at Mohale's Hoek, 1878, after three successive years of drought, was a season of unusual scarcity and want.[18]

In 1878/79 there was again a drought during the early months of the growing season, but the rains began on Christmas Day and, though the wheat crop was poor, there was an excellent harvest of millet and maize in most parts of the country.[19] One visitor, looking at the crops in January, commented that they were 'far the best' she had seen in South Africa.[20] Even in the far south of the country, in the Quthing district, Austen reported that the 1879 harvest was 'exceptionally good'.[21] This was the harvest which preceded the Moorosi War, and so even although the previous three harvests had been 'very light', and the people had had 'very hard times', it seems unlikely that Moorosi had been 'impoverished by drought', as de Kiewiet argued, with the implication that this was one of the reasons for his rebellion.[22]

In 1879/80, as de Kiewiet noted, Davies at Maseru reported a long and severe drought, and so too did other magistrates. But these reports dated from the end of 1879. A month or so later there were 'splendid rains' and the crops made at least some recovery.[23]

It is not easy to judge the effect of all this. The south of the country, it seems, suffered more than the north. In July 1879 Paul Germond reported that this was the third year in which the people at the Thabana-Morena mission station were suffering a scarcity of food;[24] in September 1880 Dr Casalis at Morija reported that people were beginning to go hungry in several districts;[25] and in December 1880 he reported famine 'in certain districts. I am beset by natives who need kaffir corn and it is difficult to keep on refusing.'[26] Yet at Hlotse Heights in the north an Anglican visitor, Canon Crisp, noted in July 1880 that 'During the last few years a sufficient rainfall has given them [the Basotho] good harvests, while in the Free State the crops have been destroyed by drought. They have thus had a ready market for their corn, and they have grown rich in oxen.' He was careful to add, however, that 'In the southern part, near Mohali's Hoek, the harvest has failed, and great scarcity threatened.'[27] In the documents on the opening months of the Gun War there are many references to the Basotho's stores of grain, some of which they moved up into the Maloti.[28]

---

[17] *JME* 1878, p. 282, Report of Missionary Conference, 21 May 1878; pp. 185-6, R. Henry Dyke, letter of 24 February 1878; and p. 180, Maeder to Directors, 26 February 1878.

[18] Rhodes House Library, Oxford, USPG Archives, Missionaries' Reports, E 33A, Stenson to Bullock, 30 June 1878, and report for quarter ending 31 December 1878.

[19] G.33-'79, p.19, Surmon to Governor's Agent, 2 January 1879, and p.20, Davies to Governor's Agent, 11 January 1879; G.13-'80, p. 20, Charles Bell to Griffith, 19 January 1879.

[20] *Quarterly Paper of the Bloemfontein Mission,* No. 44, April 1879, pp.27-8, letter from Mrs. McKenzie, 12 January 1879.

[21] G.13-'80, p. 37, Austen to Governor's Agent, 24 December 1879.

[22] De Kiewiet (1937: 238).

[23] *Cape Argus*, 16 March 1880, 'Basutoland. A Stranger and Pilgrim in the Land'.

[24] PEMS Archives, Paris, Germond to Directors, 20 July 1879.

[25] PEMS Archives, Paris, Casalis to '*parents et amis bien chers*', 14 September 1880. See also Casalis's letter of 2 December 1880.

[26] *JME* 1881, p. 59, as translated by Germond (1967:367).

[27] *Quarterly Paper of the Orange Free State Mission*, no. 49, July 1880, p. 10, account by Canon W. Crisp of 'The Bishop's Visit to Basutoland'.

[28] E.g. *JME* 1880, p. 458, Dieterlen, letter of 19 September 1880.

At times there was widespread hardship during these years, mainly, it seems, in the south of the country. But in 1880, although the drought was severe in some areas, none of the magistrates, and none of the missionaries, suggested that anything exceptional was happening. There was hunger, but nothing like famine. In the events leading up to the Gun War drought was perhaps an aggravating factor, but not enough to have made the difference between peace and war. The political imperatives were so powerful that even if the harvest had been abundant the Basotho would have rebelled.

De Kiewiet, trapped by his Eastern Frontier analogies, concentrated too much on the Basotho and their economy, and perhaps we should be looking at their white neighbours instead. Among them the drought was much more severe, and it is possible, as Eldredge has suggested,[29] that this sharpened their appetite for the Basotho's better watered land and was a factor in the proposed confiscation of Quthing, which so shook and disturbed the Basotho. It is also possible that, rather than looking at these simple lines of cause and effect, we should see drought as part of a wide concatenation of interlocking events. It might well, for example, have exacerbated the unrest on the Eastern Frontier, and the war there was certainly a major factor in the determination of the Sprigg Ministry to enforce disarmament. De Kiewiet overstated his case, but there is still a case to be made.

.

---

[29] Eldredge (1993: 80).

PART II

THE GUN WAR

> The chief who goes back when men are dying,
> Bullets splitting men's heads,
> Swords striking men's necks,
> Grenades bursting and fires blazing,
> Blazing, and showing their darting flames,
> And many are saying: 'It's the last day!'[1]

---

[1] Damane and Sanders (1974: 159), Maama's praise poems.

CHAPTER 11: PREDICTIONS AND PROPHECIES

Fears and expectations

As they entered on the Gun War the Cape's politicians, officials and soldiers were confident of victory. The Basotho would be unable to hold their own in the open field, they would be driven back to their mountain strongholds, and their capitulation would be merely a matter of time.

Griffith had urged the chiefs to come to their senses and not to bring defeat and ruin on their country. 'The Government of the Queen is strong', he told Letsie, 'and could easily, as you are aware, bring up a large force to destroy the Basuto people ....'[1] Barkly believed that once the troops had arrived 'there ought to be no difficulty at all. What fools the people are to pursue a struggle which the most ignorant men among them must know can only have one ending.'[2] Sprigg was convinced that with an adequate force the Basotho rebellion could be 'squashed' within three months,[3] and the soldiers on the spot had no doubts about their superiority. When the CMR arrived at Wepener they were reported to be 'in capital spirits, and delighted at the idea of "tackling the Basutos"'.[4]

The missionaries feared the worst for the Basotho. Hamilton Dyke wrung his hands as he saw 'deluded men' such as Masupha throwing over their allegiance to the government and bringing 'misery and destruction on the land'. 'In the long run', wrote Hermann Dieterlen, 'there can be but one outcome to the struggle: defeat and the nation's ruin.' 'Poor Lerotholi', wrote Paul Germond, 'to be killed in combat or imprisoned for life, that is what awaits him.'[5]

These fears were shared by many Basotho, and not just by those who were loyal to the government. They too believed that the war would resolve itself into a struggle around their mountain strongholds. In the south Letsie's sons were fortifying Kolo and Masite, and at Thaba-Bosiu Masupha, following Moorosi's example, was building two double stone walls packed with earth to resist the onslaught of the Cape's artillery.[6] But they had no great confidence in their ability to hold out. George Moshoeshoe's words have already been quoted, that the Basotho 'had always looked upon the British Government as invincible and as far superior in strength to all the native races of South African combined'.[7] Letsie believed that it would be madness to take up arms against the Cape,[8] and according to George even Masupha's followers knew that the government would be too strong for them.[9] In the south old Moletsane, chief of the Bataung, refused to submit to the 'outrage' of disarmament and threw in his lot with the rebels, but without any hope of success. 'I know we are heading for our ruin', he said.[10]

---

[1] C.2755, pp. 164-5, Griffith to Letsie, 5 September 1880.
[2] CA, Griffith Papers, Barkly to Griffith, 1 July 1880.
[3] C.2755, p. 173, Sprigg to Ayliff, 20 September 1880.
[4] Barkly (1893: 180).
[5] PEMS Archives, Morija, Dyke to Sprigg, 27 August 1880; PEMS Archives, Paris, Dieterlen, letter dated 24 September 1880, and Germond, November 1880. See also PEMS Archives, Paris, Dr. Casalis to parents, brothers and sisters, 22 September 1880; *JME* 1880, p. 463, Dieterlen, 24 September 1880; PEMS Archives, Paris, Jousse to Casalis, 16 September 1880.
[6] C.2755, p. 65, Griffith to Sprigg, 7 August 1880. See also Tylden (1950C: 22).
[7] Tylden (1950A: 176-7).
[8] C.2755, p. 56, Letsie's speech at the *pitso* on 3 July 1880.
[9] C.2755, p. 159, interview between Sprigg and George Moshoeshoe, 30 August 1880.
[10] Maeder, 1880, quoted in Germond (1967: 364).

In the event none of these expectations was realised. The Basotho were never confined to their mountain fortresses, and they never came close to defeat. Why then was the Cape government so confident?

First, it looked to the Seqiti War of 1865-8, when Moshoeshoe's Basotho had been humbled by the Orange Free State, which was smaller and less powerful than the Cape. At no time in the war did the Free State have more than 2,500 men under arms, and at the end it was deploying just two commandos each numbering over 500.[11] The wealthier and more populous Cape would be able to mobilise a much larger force.

Second, they were swept along by the seemingly irresistible advance of white power throughout the whole of southern Africa, especially in the last few years. At the *pitso* in July 1880 Griffith had pointed warningly to the fate of the Baphuthi, the Gcaleka and the Ngqika, the Zulu and the Pedi. The Basotho, if they rebelled, would meet a similar fate.

Third, there was a widespread assumption that, unlike the Zulu, the Basotho were not a warlike people. According to one authority at the time, they had 'no martial instincts.'[12] The Cape politician John Merriman had described them as 'a very cowardly people ... certainly the most cowardly race I have ever seen',[13] and after the very first engagement in the Gun War Sprigg was writing them off as 'utterly destitute of pluck'.[14]

On all three grounds the Cape's confidence was misplaced.

First, the situation had changed dramatically between 1865 and 1880. In the Seqiti War, because of the restrictions on the trade in arms and ammunition, most of the Basotho were still equipped with old and often defective muskets and they were short of powder and lead, whereas the Free State commandos were armed with modern rifles and were well supplied with ammunition. The Free State also had heavy artillery in the form of new Whitworths and Armstrongs, though this was not used to the best effect. The Basotho heavily outnumbered their opponents, but, as the sympathetic Joseph Orpen noted, 'an infinite superiority in weapons and ammunition is what makes the Boers victorious'.[15] By 1880 the Basotho were much better equipped because of their acquisition of firearms from the Diamond Fields and elsewhere. Many were still armed with old-fashioned muskets, but a considerable proportion now had breech-loading rifles, mainly Sniders, Enfields and Whitworths, but also some Martini-Henrys (the favoured weapon of the imperial army) and the sporting Westley-Richards.[16] By

---

[11] Fraser (1922: 417); Sanders (1975: 299). At the beginning of the war, in 1865, President Brand had mobilised 1,600 men, and at the beginning of 1866 he had sent in four commandos, each 400 to 600 men strong. See Tylden (1950A: 93), and Sanders (1975: 293).

[12] Kilpin (1912: 243).

[13] BR VI.66: Committee on Basutoland Annexation Bill, Minutes of Evidence, Merriman's evidence, 20 July 1871.

[14] C.2755, p. 173, Sprigg to Ayliff, 20 September 1880. See also *Cape Argus*, 3 September, quoting the Rouxville correspondent of *The Friend*: 'Basutos are not the stuff to cut warriors from. They are ... enormous brags; but they are also rank cowards' Look at what happened in the last war with the Free State: 'the Basutos have not the courage to face the white man ....' 'They skedaddled like springboks.' In the same way Shepstone had dismissed the Pedi as 'a Makatee or Basuto tribe, unwarlike, and of no account in Zulu estimation'. Later he admitted he had underestimated them: subduing Sekhukhune was 'a more difficult task' than subduing Cetshwayo: Delius (1883: 227, 240).

[15] CA, G.H. 10/7, Orpen to Wodehouse, 6 November 1865. See Sanders (1975: 284) and Thompson (1975: 279).

[16] There was possibly a tendency for the Cape's military commanders to exaggerate the excellence of the

contrast the CMR had Snider carbines, which had a much shorter range than the Martini-Henrys and Westley-Richards.

Second, none of the recent wars offered a close parallel with the forthcoming struggle with the Basotho, and some of them, so far from inspiring confidence, should have made the Cape more cautious.

The war against Moorosi's Baphuthi has already been described, and the views of Sir Garnet Wolseley have already been quoted. The Cape forces had taken eight months to defeat Moorosi, an 'insignificant' chief with 'only a handful of followers'. How could they defeat the entire Basotho nation?[17]

The war against the Ngqika and the Gcaleka was fought by a combination of colonial and imperial troops, whereas in the Gun War the Cape would have to fight on its own. And although the Ngqika and the Gcaleka had acquired firearms, they were not as well equipped as the Basotho.[18] Yet this war cost the lives of 60 whites and £1,750,000.[19]

The war against Cetshwayo's Zulu offered even fewer parallels. It was fought overwhelmingly by imperial troops, and the immense effort involved could never have been matched by the Cape. By the end of the war about 5,000 troops were in the field. Seventy-six officers and 1007 men were killed in action, and about a thousand African auxiliaries from Natal. The extra cost incurred amounted to over five million pounds.

The Zulu were about twice as numerous as the Basotho, and their regiments numbered about 40,000 men. They did not have cavalry, but they had acquired guns – not from the Diamond Fields, but from the trade through Delagoa Bay – and at Isandhlwana they added to their stock by capturing about a thousand Martini-Henrys and 500,000 rounds of ammunition. At times they made good use of these,[20] but for the most part they adhered to the strategy and tactics laid down in the time of Shaka, attacking the enemy as a massed, highly disciplined infantry armed with shields and broad stabbing spears. They achieved their great victory at Isandhlwana by breaking through and getting to grips with the enemy at close quarters. Yet even there they suffered terrible losses, and in other encounters their attacks were kept at bay by the rifle fire from the troops' Martini-Henrys.[21] The Basotho's methods of fighting would be very different.

With a population between 70,000 and 100,000, Sekhukhune's Sesotho-speaking Pedi were much more like the Basotho. They had acquired firearms at the Diamond Fields, where their workers far outnumbered those of any other African chiefdom. They did not make extensive use of horses, but when pressed fell back on mountain fortresses. In their first war against the South African Republic, in 1876, they successfully fought off a force of 2,000 burghers, supported by 2,400 Swazi and 600

Basotho's arms in order to emphasise the difficulties which they faced. In the fighting between the former rebel Joel and the former loyalist Jonathan after the Gun War it was noted that Joel's men were mainly armed with 'muzzle-loaders of a very inferior type', whereas Jonathan's had been given breech-loaders, mainly Sniders and Martini-Henrys, on the orders of the Cape government. See Chapter 19, p. 241 below.

[17] P. 80 above. Sir George Colley, Wolseley's successor, held similar views: de Kiewiet (1937: 262).

[18] *Cape Argus*, 28 March 1878, quoting *Kaffrarian Watchman*: the troops owed their safety to the superiority of their weapons; Deare (1930: 10 May).

[19] Walker (1963: 371).

[20] C.2569, p. 18, Frere to Hicks Beach, 15 March 1880.

[21] Guy (1971) and Morris (1966).

Africans from the Transvaal. The Republic, then financially ruined, was annexed by the Crown, and in 1879 the struggle against the Pedi was taken up by Sir Garnet Wolseley. In November that year he attacked with 3,500 imperial troops and volunteers and 3,500 African auxiliaries from the Transvaal, assisted by 8,000 Swazi. Even then the troops' frontal attack on Tsate, the Pedi capital, was halted by the Pedi's intense fire from their rocky defences, and it was only when the Swazi climbed the heights and suddenly appeared behind them that the Pedi were broken and finally defeated.[22]

In all these conflicts, therefore, except the war against Moorosi, imperial troops had played a decisive role, and both the Cape government and the Basotho chiefs were well aware that in the Gun War no imperial help would be provided.[23] Sprigg, however, welcomed the opportunity of showing what the Cape forces could do on their own, especially against the Basotho, whose alleged lack of 'martial instincts' provided the Cape with its third ground of confidence.

But here again was a misconception. According to one officer in the CMR, the Basotho turned out to be 'a well-armed and mounted race of men, far superior in every way as fighting men and as natives to any tribe in South Africa – Zulus not excepted'.[24] He might have been exaggerating in order to lessen the disgrace of the CMR's lack of success, but the effectiveness of the Basotho as a fighting force came as an unpleasant surprise for the Cape. After only a few months of fighting the *Cape Argus* was acknowledging that the Basotho had 'displayed qualities of pluck and resolution for which neither friend nor foe had given them credit.'[25]

Organisation, resources, strategy and leadership: the Basotho

Moshoeshoe had made no attempt to imitate the Zulu's military system, with its powerful standing army and its centrally controlled regiments. There was no standing force among the Basotho. At times of war each subordinate chief was called upon to raise his own regiment, and the core of each regiment was the chief's *lithaka*, his comrades in the initiation school, or if, like Maama and Nehemiah, he had not been initiated, simply the men of his own age. The names of these regiments are still well remembered – Maama's Vultures, for example, and Jonathan Molapo's Buffaloes.

Nor did Moshoeshoe adopt the Zulu's tactics of fighting in close, disciplined formations, or the large oval shield that was suitable for such tactics. The Basotho's small shields were designed to deflect missiles, not to be strong defences in the cut and thrust of hand-to-hand fighting. Shaka had insisted that, instead of carrying a bunch of spears which he could throw from a distance, each man should be armed with a single short-handled, broad-bladed stabbing spear which he would hold on to and wield at close quarters. The Basotho's spears, which they carried in a quiver on their back, could be used for throwing as well as stabbing,[26] and in fighting at close quarters they relied on the

---

[22] Delius (1983: 181-216 and 239-50).
[23] Barkly (1893: 22); C.2755, p. 196, Clarke to Treasurer General, Cape Town, 1 October 1880. The missionaries had been told as early as March 1880 that no imperial regiments would be made available: Rhodes House Library, Oxford, Anti-Slavery Papers, MSS Brit. Emp. S.18, C 128/189, Coillard to Chesson, 6 March 1880.
[24] Woon (1909: 118).
[25] *Cape Argus*, 3 December 1880, Editorial.
[26] Kimble (1978: 38), without citing any authority, says that the Basotho adopted the Zulu's 'short stabbing spear, lerumo'. Atmore and Sanders (1971: 535), citing an article by Sekese, *Leselinyana*, 6 July 1917, say that the short stabbing spear was not adopted. Thompson (1975: 62-3) says the same. The spear illustrated in Casalis (1861: 132) is not broad-bladed, nor is the spear carried by the foot soldier in illustration no. 53. No doubt some men used a broad-bladed spear, but by the time of the Gun War the usual practice was to carry three or six spears in a quiver which could be thrown from the saddle or used for stabbing: Browning (1880: 277); Army Museum,

knobkerrie and the battle-axe as well.

During the *lifaqane* Moshoeshoe and his followers had retired to the mountain fortress of Thaba-Bosiu, where they erected fortifications and defied their enemies by hurling down spears and rolling down rocks. Towards the end of the *lifaqane* they began to acquire horses and guns from the Kora, and over time they became highly skilled cavalrymen and the famous Basotho pony was developed. According to a CMR officer in the Gun War,

> The Basuto pony is without exception the best of its kind in Africa. Standing anything from twelve to fourteen hands in height, they are very strongly built, with short, thick legs, broad quarters, and strong shoulders. They will carry a Basuto all day, up and down mountains, as surefooted as a goat; they will scramble over rocks and down the sides of mountains where a man would hesitate to walk. A Basuto never dismounts ....[27]

'You can hardly imagine the pace these Basutos can go on their ponies', wrote another officer, 'up and down hill, over rocks, at a breakneck pace; our horses are not in it with them.'[28]

Not every man had his own horse. Of a fighting force of 25-30,000 men about half were mounted, and in the reports on the Gun War there are many references to large bodies of men on foot.[29] But over a short period the Basotho army changed from a lightly-armed infantry to a mixture of infantry and highly mobile musket and rifle firing cavalry. Their regiments fought more like Boer commandos than like the Zulu army. At long range they were able, with their modern rifles, to outrange the Cape forces and, in the words of one volunteer officer, 'to make things very lively' for them. And when the cavalry charged it was the spear and the battle-axe that did the most damage:

> they used to come tearing down, holding rifle and reins in their left hand, a sheaf of assegais slung at their back, and this terrible axe in their right. Others used to sling their rifles over their back, and have an assegai in their right hand.[30]

The Basotho's military strategy reflected their political and military organisation. Each important subordinate chief controlled his own followers in his own area, and the degree to which he subscribed to central control was determined by his assessment of his own interests and of the duties he owed to his paramount. In the first war with the Free State, in 1858, known to the Basotho as *Ntoa ea Senekane*,

---

Tylden Papers, Box 34057, Notebook III, p. 84, information from 'Every, ex C.M.R.'. See also illustration no. 54. For a discussion of the use of stabbing spears see Norman Etherington (2001: 104-5).

[27] Woon (1909: 136-7).

[28] Shervinton (1899: 65).

[29] In 1875 Rolland estimated that there were 25,000 able-bodied men: G.16-'76, p. 8, Rolland to Griffith, 31 December 1875. Deare (1930: 10 May) estimated that the Basotho could 'place certainly over 23,000 mounted men in the field'. Shervinton (1899:66) estimated that the fighting force numbered 40,000 men, of whom half were mounted. In the space of a few months François Maeder gave estimates of 20,000, 25,000 and 30,000 armed men: PEMS Archives, Paris, Maeder to President and Directors, 28 August 1880 and 23 November 1880, and *JME* 1881, p. 99, Maeder to Committee members, 21 December 1880. See also, e.g. C.2755, p. 174, enclosure with Clifford to Kimberley, 21 September 1880; C.2755, p. 271, Schermbrucker to Bayly, 11 October 1880. There was a tendency on the part of the Cape's military commanders to exaggerate the number of their enemies in the field: a 'skirmish' became 'a pitched battle': *Cape Argus*, 10 August 1881, 'The Basuto War'.

[30] Deare (1930: 10 May). See also Browning (1880: 277); Woon (1909: 133). When the Basotho charged in the battle of 'Tantje's Berg' they had guns over their shoulders and assegais and battle-axes in their hands: *The Journal*, 8 March 1881, 'Battle of Tantje's Berg'.

Senekal's War, Moshoeshoe was still at the height of his powers, but even then he was unable to enforce total compliance with his orders. His strategy was simple: the Basotho were to offer no serious resistance to the invading commandos but were to fall back on Thaba-Bosiu and wait for them there. Many of his subordinates were unwilling to abandon their villages and crops and tried to resist the commandos, but in the absence of any unity or combination among them, and in the absence of any support from the centre, their resistance was easily overcome. As the commandos advanced on Thaba-Bosiu, however, Basotho regiments swept round behind them and raided deep into the Free State. Moshoeshoe claimed that he had not authorised these raids, and this might well have been true, because he was now making his preparations for the decisive confrontation at Thaba-Bosiu. In the event the Basotho were hardly put to the test. The Free Staters, confronted by the formidable defences of Thaba-Bosiu, from which the bullets were coming down 'like hail', and disturbed by news of the raids behind them, made no attempt to storm the mountain, but broke up their laager and went home.[31]

By the time the Seqiti War broke out in 1865 Moshoeshoe was almost 80 years old, and his overall control was even weaker than it had been in Senekal's War. Ideally, he would have re-enacted his earlier strategy and withdrawn all his forces to the Basotho heartlands. His subordinates, however, wanted to resist the Free Staters on the outskirts of the country and to raid their exposed farms as soon as possible. Moshoeshoe apparently sanctioned both parts of this plan, even if he did not approve of them. This time the Basotho's raids were unsuccessful, all local resistance was overcome, and soon Moshoeshoe's main strength was concentrated on Thaba-Bosiu. Among members of his own family Letsie was the only man of consequence to have deserted him, and even he, though wandering fearfully through the Maloti, had sent in his sons with Lerotholi at their head. The Free Staters' attacks on the mountain were repelled, but this time, instead of breaking up and going home, they continued hostilities, laying siege for some months to the mountain and then, in January 1866, mounting a new invasion, capturing livestock and laying waste crops and villages. Moshoeshoe had enough men on the mountain to defend him, but otherwise resistance to the commandos seems to have been organised locally by the subordinates most immediately threatened. Molapo concluded a separate peace, and in April Moshoeshoe made peace himself, but only to give his people breathing-space in which to harvest their crops.

When war broke out again it resumed the pattern of the earlier fighting. Several subordinates, including Letsie and Moshoeshoe's brother Mopeli, entered, or tried to enter, into separate agreements with the Free State. Others tried to maintain their local positions, but with little success. At Thaba-Bosiu Moshoeshoe felt deserted. Of his senior sons only Masupha was still with him, and that was probably because his own area was so close to Thaba-Bosiu. Yet the Basotho refused to abandon their land, and in the end it was only Wodehouse's intervention that brought the fighting to an end.[32]

Whereas in the two wars against the Free State Moshoeshoe had been at the heart of the Basotho's resistance, in the Gun War Letsie did not want to fight and so the question of his imposing an overall strategy did not arise. Even before the CMR had crossed the border he was asking Griffith for protection if hostilities broke out.[33] The conduct of the war was therefore in the hands of those

---

[31] Sanders (1975: 228-32); Thompson (1975: 239-42).
[32] Sanders (1975: 284-301); Thompson (1975: 278-302).
[33] Cory Library, Grahamstown, MS 10,060, Orpen to Sprigg, 9 September 1880. According to Eldredge there

who were nominally his subordinates. They consulted among themselves and sometimes mounted combined operations, but there was no one in overall command.

Masupha might perhaps have assumed this role if the Basotho had been driven back on Thaba-Bosiu. As it was he was unable to control even his near neighbour and cousin, Ramanella. When by way of preparing for war he told Ramanella that he must come to Thaba-Bosiu and bring his grain, Ramanella retorted that he was not Masupha's servant, and that if war came it would find him at his own place and not at Thaba-Bosiu.[34] In the event Masupha worked closely with Ramanella and with Joel Molapo in the north, and with Leshoboro Majara and Letsie's sons Maama and Theko in the centre, and at times of crisis he sent help to Lerotholi in the south. He had the support of his many sons, and he seems to have dominated Leshoboro, the head of the house of Moshoeshoe's fourth son, Majara, whose village was close to Maseru.

Lerotholi, as the most senior of Letsie's sons, was able to exercise some control over his junior brothers, and he worked very closely with Moletsane's Bataung. But he had little or no influence over Masupha, who saw him as a threat to his own pretensions to independence.[35] Unlike many of his brothers, he was uneducated and illiterate, and he was also a heavy drinker, but he had great force of character and was popular with his followers. He was more direct and forthright than his father, but more open to negotiation and compromise than Masupha. Based at Likhoele, only a few kilometres east of Mafeteng, he was well placed to lead the resistance in the south. Many stories were told about his dash and gallantry in the Seqiti War, and his reputation for bravery would be enhanced in the Gun War. About this time a white visitor described him as

> a man of about 5 ft. 7, and of compact build. .... His eyes are prominent and slightly bloodshot but generally have a pleasing expression of easy good nature. When I took a sketch of him, Lerothodi sent for his red braided smoking cap, putting aside his Basuto straw hat ... he was constantly receiving messengers and transacting business .... The principal of his councillors and others sat round him on the hillside and hardly took their eyes off his face for a moment ....

He was a splendid rider, it was said, and kept beautiful horses.[36]

Another white observer described him at this time as stout and 'well-grown', about five feet ten, shrewd, with a certain natural dignity, and 'taciturn to a degree', rarely opening his mouth 'except to give the briefest of brief instructions to his attendants'.[37]

Lerotholi had two full brothers, Bereng and Theko. Bereng's village was at Masite, close to the Morija mission station, Theko's just south of the Phuthiatsana, in the foothills east of Thaba-Bosiu.

---

was a 'preconceived plan agreed upon by the BaSotho as a whole'. Letsie would continue to profess loyalty, but would pretend to be too weak to impose his will on his followers, and the *Mateketoa*, notably Jonathan Molapo in the north, would throw in their lot with the colonial troops. So the Basotho's strategy was 'to take both sides' and Letsie 'designated' some of his followers as *Mateketoa* and others as *Mabelete*. (Eldredge 2007: 82-9) But the evidence is clear: Letsie was genuinely opposed to the war, since he was afraid that the Basotho would be defeated, but he lacked the power to enforce his will. The *Mateketoa*'s support for the colonial government was not part of some hidden conspiracy, but the obvious outcome of where they saw their own advantage. The post-war bitterness against them was so fierce that many had to leave the country.

34 C.2755, p. 162, *Cape Times*, 9 September 1880.
35 Tylden (1950A: 147).
36 CA, ACC 88, Papers of Arthur J.T. Pattison.
37 *The Journal*, 27 October 1880, 'Rebel Leaders. I. LEROTHODI'.

Both were fully committed to the rebellion. Bereng, who had had commanded the Basotho's forces against Moorosi, is remembered as an aggressive man, difficult to control, much in the tradition of Posholi and Ramanella.[38] Theko was to play a major part, not just in helping his brothers in the south, but in supporting Masupha in his operations around Maseru.[39]

Letsie's third house was in disgrace, and after Lerotholi the most prominent of his sons was Maama, the eldest son in his fourth house. He was Letsie's favourite, and his father would have wanted him, rather than Lerotholi, to be his successor. He had been converted by the French missionaries and baptized as Alexander, but he gradually moved away from the church and was later to become close to the Roman Catholics. After the Seqiti War he had been sent to the Cape to be educated at Zonnebloem, where he learned to speak English fluently, and on his return he was placed in the north of his father's ward, in the area still known as Maama's. His senior wife was a daughter of Masupha. At the time of the Moorosi War he was described as 'most courteous' by one English officer, welcoming every opportunity to speak English, and being fond of long words and polite exchanges.[40] He was later described as 'a winning lad, of good appearance, bold, educated and ambitious.'[41] He was outraged by disarmament, unable at times to contain his 'repugnance and bitterness' when the issue was discussed.[42] Since his village was in the north of his father's ward it was natural that, like his brother Theko, he should operate closely with Masupha as well as with Lerotholi. His Gun War praises, which he composed himself, are among the finest and most dramatic in all Sesotho poetry. After the war his hostility to Lerotholi was a constant factor in the Basotho's internal politics.

Among other sons of Letsie who played a prominent part in the war were Seeiso, Maama's full brother, still in his early twenties, who was to win renown in the battle of Qalabane and was greatly admired by at least some of his white opponents, and the mild-mannered but resolute Nkuebe, who became the senior son in the fifth house when his brother Mpiti was killed in the war.[43]

Other chiefs who were heavily involved in the south were those of the Bamohale and Baposholi (the followers of Moshoeshoe's brothers, Mohale and Posholi), and those of the Bataung, now Moletsane's sons, since Moletsane himself was over 90 years old.

In the north the Gun War became also a civil war in the house of Molapo between Jonathan, who had been named by Molapo and confirmed by Letsie as his father's successor, and who was the only important chief to support the government, and Joel, an older brother but from a junior house, who disputed Jonathan's succession and was an out-and-out rebel.[44] Because of the enmity between the two Molapo had placed them as far apart as he could, Jonathan in the south-west at Fobane and Joel in the north-east, beyond the Caledon, at Futhane. After the Seqiti War all Joel's land north of the Caledon was taken over by the Free State as part of the Conquered Territory, and he had to be pulled

---

[38] Bereng and Lehloenya (1991: 73).
[39] Mangoaela (1957: 241).
[40] Browning (1880: 292-3). See also CA, Acc. 459, Brabant's autobiography, p. 115.
[41] Lagden (1901: 584-5). See also Kilpin (1912: 244-5).
[42] C.2755, p. 129, *Cape Argus*, 24 August 1880.
[43] *Cape Argus*, 9 July 1881, 'Occasional Notes', and 28 March 1882, Sauer's speech in the House of Assembly, 27 March; Bereng and Lehloenya (1991: 88, 90).
[44] Jonathan was the second son in Molapo's senior house. Since his elder brother, Josefa, was insane, he was named by his father as his successor, acting as regent for Josefa. This was disputed by Joel, the eldest son in Molapo's second house, who was about two years older than Jonathan. After Jonathan's death the chieftainship reverted to Josefa's line.

back to Qalo, where his limited holding was always a brake on his ambitions.⁴⁵ Henry Taylor, the doctor at Hlotse Heights, knew the two brothers well.

> Jonathan when a boy had been at school in Cape Town [at Zonnebloem] for a time; he could read and write and spoke a little English, although he always preferred to converse in Sesuto. Joel was uneducated and illiterate, but a man of considerable force of character – not so smooth in his manners as Jonathan, but perhaps none the worse for that.⁴⁶

Austen, writing in 1880, also compared the two to Joel's advantage. Jonathan, he wrote, was 'always well disposed, but is a weak-minded young man, while Joel is quite the opposite.'⁴⁷ Within a few years, however, Jonathan, no doubt toughened by adversity, emerged as one of the most powerful and formidable chiefs in the country.

When fighting broke out Joel had the support of most of Molapo's sons, Hlasoa and Khethisa being the most important, and he also received help from Ramanella and, to some extent, Masupha, whose commitment might have been tempered because Jonathan was married to his senior daughter.⁴⁸ Because of their respective roles Joel was almost demonized in white sources while Jonathan was held up as a faithful ally – 'a noble specimen of the Mosuto', wrote one visitor, '... with an intelligent and frank expression of countenance'.⁴⁹

In the event the Basotho's lack of overall direction did them no harm. There was local co-operation between the chiefs, and the initial strategy that had failed in the Seqiti War – of resisting the enemy at once, of fighting on several fronts and not falling back – this time proved to be highly successful. In the words of Lerotholi's praises,

> The war is fought on the outskirts, Mokoena,
> It's fought at Likhoele, there's fighting at Leribe.⁵⁰

Because they were fighting close to their homes the Basotho regiments, unlike the Zulu regiments of Cetshwayo, had no serious commissariat problems. Their food on campaign was *lipabi,* ground roasted maize or millet, and when necessary they could either slip back home for more or women and boys from their villages could bring them more in the field. In the same way they could replenish their stocks of ammunition and gunpowder.

Unlike the Cape regiments, they were familiar with every configuration of their country – its valleys and its rivers and its rock-strewn hills, its plateaux ringed by steep cliffs, and the mountainous hinterland of the Maloti where they could send their stock for safety. And they were helped by one great stroke of good luck. The summer of 1880/81 was the wettest for many years, with heavy rains setting in early. The troops' movements were often barred by swollen rivers and bogged down by heavy roads, and for long periods it was impossible to move the artillery. Whereas the Cape camps

---

⁴⁵ C.3112, p. 110, Bell to Orpen, 30 September 1881; G.8-'84, p. 44, 'Continuation of pitso', 23 May 1883, statement of Letsie (where Botani must be an error for Futhane); Lelosa, interview with AA at Qalo, 21 May 1966.
⁴⁶ Taylor (1972: 46). For Jonathan's education at Zonnebloem, see LNA, S9/1/2/2, Orpen to Sauer, 11 March 1882. For a crude and unflattering description of Joel and his rough ways, see Fenton (1905: 333-340).
⁴⁷ G.20-'81, p. 15, Austen to Griffith, 31 December 1880.
⁴⁸ Widdicombe (1895: 237-8).
⁴⁹ Matthews (1976: 376).
⁵⁰ Damane and Sanders (1974: 147). *Liqola* (translated as 'outskirts') are the holes made at the edge of a skin when it is pegged to the ground for tanning. For Mokoena, the singular of Bakoena, see page 72, fn. 44 above.

became waterlogged and unhealthy, the Basotho could find shelter in their villages throughout the country. And during the winter, as in every winter, the frosts and the lack of rain turned the country to an arid, pastureless brown, rendering any prolonged mounted operations impossible.

Two years before the war began Rolland had declared, with inadvertent foresight, that the jealousies among the chiefs made 'any combination of the whole tribe in the highest degree improbable', and that 'No such combination could be formed or carried out except through gross mismanagement on our part'.[51] He also predicted that in any confrontation between the chiefs and the government the Christians would support the government 'to a man'.[52] Now gross mismanagement had united the chiefs against the government, with the sole major exception of Jonathan Molapo, and had even driven most of the Christians into rebellion.[53] Though opposed to disarmament, men such as George and Sofonia Moshoeshoe remained loyal to the Cape because their only hope of realising their ambitions was through government favour, and they also believed that the Cape would win.

Dr. Casalis, reporting back to Paris that most of the people at the mission stations had taken up arms, explained that war fever had now taken possession of '*tous les esprits*', women as much as men.[54] They were fighting for their homeland and they were convinced of the righteousness of their cause. For the Cape soldiers, as will be seen, the war was at best an adventure and at worst an imposition. For the Basotho it was a struggle for national survival.

Organisation, resources, strategy and leadership: the Cape

One of the main objects of the policy of confederation and the development of a strong, united South Africa was to relieve the imperial government of the burden of defence. And it was part of Sprigg's policy of 'vigour' to build up the colonial forces so that they could deal with the Cape's African subjects and neighbours without any need for imperial help. Within the past few years the imperial garrison had been sharply reduced, while the Cape forces, following their poor showing in the war against the Ngqika and the Gcaleka, were being reorganised and strengthened.[55] On the eve of the Gun War Sprigg and his Ministers assured Frere that they had no doubts about the ability of these forces to cope with the Basotho.[56]

The Cape's Commandant-General, Charles Mansfield Clarke, had formerly been an officer in the imperial army. He had served in the Zulu War and was an efficient commander of regular troops, but the men now under his command found him unsympathetic and 'conventional to a degree', keeping even his immediate staff at arm's length.[57] One of his officers described him as 'one of the best organisers in the British army' and 'a man of the greatest personal courage', but he was 'totally deficient in the qualities which make a successful leader of troops in the field'. He 'looked down on and did not trust Colonial officers and Colonial troops', though with rare exceptions the forces under

---

[51] CA, NA 275, Rolland to SNA, 19 July 1878.
[52] CA, NA 174, Rolland to SNA, 28 December 1877, quoted in Burman (1976A: 73).
[53] See, e.g., PEMS Archives, Paris, Dr Casalis to parents, brothers and sisters, 22 September 1880; Dieterlen to Lautré, 29 November 1880; Jousse to Casalis, 16 September 1880; and Maeder to President and Directors, 21 December 1880. But the people at Berea fled from the station fearing an attack from Masupha, the people at Masitise took no part in the fighting, and the congregations at Thabana-Morena, Thaba-Bosiu and Leribe were badly divided: see *JME* 1882, pp. 299-309, Report of Missionary Conference, 4 May 1882.
[54] PEMS Archives, Paris, Dr. Casalis to parents, brothers and sisters, 22 September 1880.
[55] De Kiewiet (1937: 174).
[56] C.2755, p. 49, Frere to Kimberley, 26 July 1880.
[57] Scully (1913: 124).

him were entirely composed of colonials. He stuck to the rule book, neglected opportunities, and gradually seemed to lose confidence in himself.[58]

The five branches available to Clarke were the Cape Mounted Riflemen (CMR), the newly created Cape Mounted Yeomanry, the burghers, the volunteer corps, and 'native' levies. The single regiment of the CMR was the Colony's only standing army. This force, which had its origins in 1852, had been reformed three years later as the Frontier Armed and Mounted Police (FAMP). In its early years the FAMP had consisted mainly of young colonials, sons of farmers and others, who knew the country well and could ride and shoot and generally look after themselves. In the 1870s, however, with the development of the Diamond Fields and the Cape's economy generally, there was more lucrative employment to be found elsewhere, and it became necessary to mount a vigorous recruitment campaign in England. Hundreds of young men responded, few with any experience of the horse or the gun, and many straight out of their public schools, 'young sparks', as one Cape newspaper described them, eager for excitement and adventure.[59] When they arrived they found that their terms and conditions were much less favourable than they had been led to expect, and, in the words of General Sir Arthur Cunynghame, 'A general discontent therefore pervaded the force'. When he inspected it in 1874 he found it, 'as a rule, miserably mounted, very indifferently clothed, wretchedly armed and equipped, and wanting in all the accessories necessary for taking the field.'[60]

As commander of the imperial forces Cunynghame had no direct control over colonial troops and the reforms he was able to push through were limited. At the beginning of the 1877-78 campaign against the Ngqika and the Gcaleka the FAMP were still 'badly equipped for the field, and their system was so incomplete, and their arrangements so faulty, that it was difficult, nay impossible, to discover the whereabouts of a large portion of them.'[61] They performed indifferently in the campaign, and when the fighting was over it was decided that they should be should be converted into a military force. By an Act of 1878 the FAMP became the CMR, they were placed under military command, and their Inspectors and Sub-Inspectors became Captains and Lieutenants. These changes, and the imposition of tough military discipline, were resented and even resisted by many in the FAMP, particularly the older men, who had enlisted as policemen and not as soldiers. One troop went on strike, and 250 out of 600 men were made prisoner.[62] When the Gun War broke out the CMR was still in the process of transition, with its new military officers trying to knock both the old policemen and their new recruits into shape. Drunkenness was rife and discipline was still a serious problem. Morale had been lifted, however, by the capture of Moorosi's mountain, which was almost exclusively a CMR exploit.

At the beginning of the Gun War the overall complement of the CMR was about 1,000 men, divided between its depot, an artillery troop, and nine troops, each troop being about 100 men strong and under the command of a captain. For the purposes of its operations in Basutoland it was organised into two wings, each wing consisting of five troops.

The left wing was commanded by Colonel Z.S. (Zach) Bayly, formerly an imperial officer, 'a man of about forty years of age, medium height, with fair hair and moustache, rather inclined to stoutness;

---

[58] CA, Acc. 459, Brabant's autobiography, p. 117. See also Deare's comments in National Army Muscum, Tylden Papers, Box 34057, Notebook V, p. 95, and Grant's comments in Box 34057, Notebook VII, p. 123.
[59] *Cape Argus*, 9 July 1881, 'Occasional Notes'.
[60] Cunynghame (1879: 50, 51).
[61] Cunynghame (1879: 306).
[62] Granville (1881: 156-7); Woon (1909: 68-9).

but a thorough-looking soldier all through'.[63] He was popular with his men, especially after his triumph at Moorosi's mountain, but he soon fell out with Clarke and their mutual hostility became well known among the troops. He had formerly been the sole commanding officer of the CMR, and was furious when his command was divided and the right wing was placed under Colonel Frederick Carrington, or 'Fighting Fred' as he was known, and when Carrington was given equal rank with himself; and he was even more furious later when Clarke had to leave Basutoland for several months and Carrington was given overall command.

Carrington, like Bayly, had formerly served in the imperial army, and with his dash and bravado, his hot temper and unconventional tactics, was reckoned by some to be 'an ideal leader' of men such as those who made up the CMR.[64] But he was not clear thinking or well organised. According to one volunteer officer

> He used to get very tight & next morning would say he would go & have a scrap, but with no fixed idea in his head of what to do or how to do it. He used to say quite openly they thought nothing of him unless he could show a big butcher's bill. ... He was plucky enough personally, but it was like hunting with him, a case of "gone away", devil may care, with no idea of anything.[65]

The officers under Bayly and Carrington were most of them well thought of. They were all 'gentlemen', according to one newspaper report: several had served in the imperial forces, one had the V.C., another the Iron Cross, another was 'the *beau ideal* of the British soldier'.[66] These men imposed a fierce discipline and training on their troops, many of whom were dismissed for drunkenness and insubordination. When the CMR was summoned to Basutoland Carrington left 100 recruits behind for further training because he did not yet regard them as fit to take the field. Others were left in reserve, and in the event Bayly took up about 300 men and Carrington about 200.

While the Basotho's miscellany of arms included a significant number of Martini-Henrys and Westley-Richards, which had a range of over 1,000 metres, the CMR were armed with Snider carbines, many of which had been discarded by the imperial troops when they had been equipped with the superior Martini-Henrys.[67] The Snider was a short, breech-loading rifle suitable for use on horseback, but with a range, at best, of about 600 metres, and at worst of about 100.[68] Their only other weapon was a Colt revolver. They did not even have swords or lances for clashes at close quarters.[69] Towards the end of 1879 one new recruit found himself issued with 'a very ancient Snider carbine with a barrel like a gas-pipe, which had evidently seen a lot of service', and 'a revolver, an old-fashioned article which threatened more damage to the man behind it than any one in front'. The whole regiment, he wrote, was 'very badly armed'.[70] On the other hand, the CMR, as regular soldiers,

---

[63] Woon (1909: 13). A good account of Bayly is given in the *Cape Argus*, 4 November 1881. He favoured those who were good at 'manly sports' and was 'quite incapable of official drudgery'.
[64] CA, Griffith Papers, Barkly to Griffith, 20 September 1880; Scully (1913: 124). For Carrington generally, see Gon (1984).
[65] National Army Museum, Tylden Papers, Box 34057, Notebook IV, p. 14: comments by Major Deare.
[66] Quoted in Shervinton (1899: 75-6).
[67] Cunynghame (1879: 309).
[68] Woon (1909: 118, 130); Deare (1930: 10 May).
[69] C.2755, p. 174, undated enclosure with Clifford to Kimberley, 21 September 1880; Shervinton (1899: 65); Deare (1930: 10 May).
[70] Woon (1909: 21, 23).

were well trained as marksmen whereas the Basotho were generally wild and inaccurate.[71]

Another source of discontent was that the CMR, though professional soldiers, had to provide their own horses and provisions: this was to cause trouble when the fighting began, leading to many desertions.[72] The commissariat was badly organised and there were constant shortages of fuel.

The Yeomanry, the second main branch of the colonial forces, had been established following the 1877-8 campaign with three regiments with a complement of 1,000 men each. They were not a standing army, but had committed themselves to serve and could be called out for a fixed period as and when required. They were to a great extent Sprigg's own creation, and he looked on them, as he said, with 'a kindly feeling', like a father looking on his son.[73]. Their poor performance in the Moorosi War had reflected badly on him,[74] but at the outbreak of the Gun War he was so confident of success that he thought it would be enough to call out 700 men for a period of three months. Clarke wanted to call out only such numbers as he could keep permanently in the field, which he estimated at 600 rather than 700, and in the end it was decided that these 600 should be required to serve for up to six months.[75]

It was already becoming evident, however, that many of the Yeomen, in spite of their initial enthusiasm, were unwilling to leave their farms and businesses for any length of time, and some paid substitutes to serve in their stead.[76] The gaudiness of their uniforms – blue tunics with white, red or yellow fronts according to which regiment they belonged to – only showed up the deficiencies of their drill and discipline, and like the CMR they were armed only with the short-range Snider carbines.[77]

The third branch consisted, potentially, of the burghers, a reserve which in times of trouble could be compelled to come forward under the old Burgher Law. Clarke, however, wanted nothing to do with them. 'The burgher force, as at present constituted', he wrote, 'is of little or no use as a military force; its members ... possess no military training, leave their homes unwillingly, and hamper rather than assist the commander of any force in the field.' Unless training was given 'the force is valueless ....'[78] He would later describe them as 'shy of control, and officered for the most part by men having no experience of the work they are called upon to perform'.[79] At first Clarke's wishes were respected, but the crisis quickly became so severe that the burghers had to be called up, with results that were as disastrous as Clarke had predicted.

Clarke thought more highly of the fourth branch of the Cape's forces, the volunteer corps: 'these men have some knowledge of the use of arms', he wrote, 'and possess a certain amount, however limited it may be, of military training'.[80] They had performed more creditably in the Moorosi War

---

[71] National Army Museum, Tylden Papers, Box 34057, Notebook V, p. 3, evidence of W. Richards.
[72] Shervinton (1899: 77).
[73] *Cape Argus*, 18 November 1879, 'Mr. Sprigg at Aliwal'.
[74] Browning (1880: 303-4); Granville (1881: 118).
[75] C.2755, pp. 182-3, H.H. Clifford to Ministers, 18 September 1880; Pearson, Minute, 17 September 1880; Clarke to Treasurer-General, Cape Town, 17 September 1880.
[76] A.23-'80, Report of the Select Committee appointed to consider and report on the Cape Yeomanry; Browning (1880: 316); Woon (1909: 147-8).
[77] Woon (1909: 147-8); Laurence (1881: 74).
[78] C.2755, p. 197, Clarke to Strahan, 17 September 1880. See also Hofmeyr (1913: 182), quoted in Smith (1939: 273).
[79] *Cape Argus*, 31 March 1881, 'The Colonial Force. Report of the Commandant-General', 24 January 1881
[80] C.2755, p. 197, Clarke to Strahan, 17 September 1880. Cunynghame (1879: 52, 112, 308, 368) also had a high opinion of them.

than the Yeomanry[81] but, like the burghers, they tended to look to captured livestock for their reward, they were not as disciplined as regular troops, and drunkenness among them was to become notorious.

There were several volunteer corps, ready to serve when called upon under the Volunteer Act. Initially it was decided to call out contingents from the Duke of Edinburgh's Own Volunteer Rifles, based in Cape Town; the Prince Alfred's Guard, Port Elizabeth; the 1st City Volunteers, Graham's Town; and the Stockenstrom Rifle Volunteers – a total of 25 officers and 620 men.[82] These numbers were well below the full strength of the corps involved, and in Cape Town ballots for those to serve were held before an apathetic and unenthusiastic crowd. Sprigg was beginning to sound a note of anxiety: 'We are suddenly in the presence of a great difficulty, and if the Colonists have any patriotism they should answer the call with alacrity. ... I wish I could be in Cape Town to-night to meet the volunteers; I would stir them up to a sense of duty.'[83]

Other bands of volunteers, such as the Kimberley Horse and Stanton's Light Horse, were formed in response to the crisis. The lead was usually taken by some public-spirited individual, but for the most part the men were inspired by mercenary considerations rather than patriotism. At the outset of the war these volunteer corps were still in the process of formation, but in the later stages they were to play an important role in the north, in the defence of Hlotse Heights.

Some corps were more disciplined and better armed than others, and there was the usual mixture of men, from high-minded and adventure-seeking public schoolboys to what one old officer described as the rakings of hell.[84] Drunkenness again was a serious problem, and on their way to Basutoland several bands were involved in rioting and disorder. In one notorious incident the town of Aliwal North was looted and several men were killed.[85]

The fifth main branch of the Cape's forces was made up by African levies. At the outset of the war Sprigg was thinking of raising a force of 2,000 Zulu, and Griffith suggested 'four or five thousand Natal Zulus' – 'they would be delighted to come and loot the Basuto cattle' – but nothing came of these ideas.[86] Major Hook, the Magistrate at Herschel, raised an armed force of Mfengu, but Sprigg had no great confidence either in them or in the 'Hottentots' of the Kat River Settlement. He wanted white troops: 'do not depend upon the Fingoes and Hottentots', he wrote. 'We want men who will charge the rebels and disperse them.'[87] Later in the war, however, the number of men in the African levies was to match that of those in the white forces involved.

There were also the members of the Basutoland Police, armed with Sniders and now placed under the control of white officers and strengthened in numbers to well over 100,[88] and the forces of

---

[81] Woon (1909: 118).
[82] C.2755, p. 178, Pearson, Treasurer-General, Minute, 21 September 1880. In the event men from five volunteer corps went in with Clarke: see p. 153 below.
[83] C.2755, p. 173, Sprigg to Ayliff, 20 September 1880.
[84] Scully (1913: 113).
[85] CA, ACC 102, Wavell to his wife, 6 April 1881; Scully (1913: 130-2). For similar, though less serious, disturbances involving volunteers passing through the Free State, see C.2821, p. 65, Brand to Strahan, 12 November 1880, and Strahan to Brand, 12 November 1880; Laurence (1882: ix).
[86] A.22-'81, p. 9, Griffith to Sprigg, 26 July 1880; C.2755, p. 159, Interview between Sprigg and George Moshoeshoe, 30 August 1880.
[87] C.2755, p. 173, Sprigg to Ayliff, 20 September 1880.
[88] Tylden (1944B).

the loyalist chiefs, notably those of Jonathan Molapo in the north. These men were particularly useful in the defence of the magistracies.

In the opening phase of the war, while Clarke sent in the 500 CMR under Bayly and Carrington, he himself remained in King William's Town until he was able to move up with reinforcements. A month later he entered Basutoland with about 2,000 men, sufficient, he thought, for the task ahead.[89] But as the fighting dragged on more and more men were called upon, until in December Sprigg claimed that a force of nearly 18,000 men was being placed in the field, one half of them whites.[90] These plans were never realised, however. There was no great enthusiasm for the war:[91] volunteers came forward slowly and reluctantly and as the struggle dragged on from month to month desertions became endemic. Throughout the early months of 1881 Clarke was repeatedly calling out for reinforcements.[92]

At first Clarke had intended to concentrate his forces at Maseru, but he was persuaded by Griffith and Barkly to divide them between Maseru and Mafeteng, and later to send volunteer corps to Hlotse Heights. This division of the Cape's main forces between Mafeteng, Maseru and Hlotse Heights matched the Basotho's divisions between the houses of Letsie, Masupha and Molapo respectively, and since, except at Mafeteng, the Cape's forces were not able to break out of their camps they remained separated throughout the war. Although they had an overall commander, first Clarke and later Carrington, the jealousies and rivalries between their officers further bedevilled their operations.

There were other causes of division and demoralisation. The policy of disarming the Basotho was already an issue in party politics. The opposition blamed the government for, as they saw it, driving the Basotho into rebellion, and the government accused them of inciting the Basotho to resist. And there were growing tensions between the British and the Cape Dutch. Shepstone's annexation and administration of the South African Republic had gone badly wrong, and in December the Boers rose in rebellion. The sympathies of the colonial forces were divided, with the Cape Dutch among them supporting their kinsmen beyond the Vaal and the British supporting the imperial forces.

On the Basutoland borders the Orange Free State was ambivalent. Although it was officially neutral, and although President Brand allowed a free passage to those of the Cape's troops who had to pass through its territory, there were strong anti-British feelings in the towns and on the farms, especially after the outbreak of rebellion in the Transvaal, and there were many who sold guns and ammunition to the Basotho. One of the Lerotholi's praise poets likened Brand (the Free Staters) to Peete, Moshoeshoe's grandfather, one of the ancestors watching solicitously over the Basotho:

> To us too the Boers will give help:
> This Brand is now Peete
> For he forges weapons to give us.[93]

---

[89] C.2755, p. 167, Clarke to Acting Under-Colonial Secretary, 15 September 1880.
[90] C.2821, p. 91, Sprigg, minute to the Administrator, 8 December 1880.
[91] The *Cape Argus* (7 September 1880, Editorial) described it as the most unpopular war ever waged in South Africa.
[92] For Clarke's repeated requests, see *Cape Argus*, 6 April 1882, 'Parliament. House of Assembly', 5 April 1882, Sauer's speech.
[93] Damane and Sanders (1974: 146). See also PEMS Archives, Paris, Maeder to President and Directors, 28 August 1880, and Dieterlen to Lautré, 29 November 1880; C.3112, p. 93, Orpen to Sauer, 19 November

To add to the Cape's difficulties the rebellion was immediately taken up by the Basotho in East Griqualand, below the Drakensberg, and by their old enemies there, the Batlokoa of Lelingoana and the Griqua of Adam Kok. The Thembu and the Mpondomise on the Cape's eastern frontier joined in, and the colonial forces, already pressed to the limit, were even further extended. For much of the Gun War Clarke had to leave the operations in Basutoland in Carrington's hands while he stamped out the resistance below the Drakensberg.

For all these reasons the war did not take its expected course. The Cape forces did not sweep all before them. The Basotho were not driven back onto their mountain strongholds. Instead there were three main theatres of war – the south, where Lerotholi and his brothers faced Fighting Fred Carrington; the centre, where Masupha and his sons faced the disillusioned and disgruntled Bayly; and the north, where Joel Molapo confronted Major Bell, who had no CMR or Yeomanry to support him, but only volunteers, his police and Jonathan Molapo's loyal Basotho.

1881; Barkly (1893: 232).

Map 2: The Gun War in the South

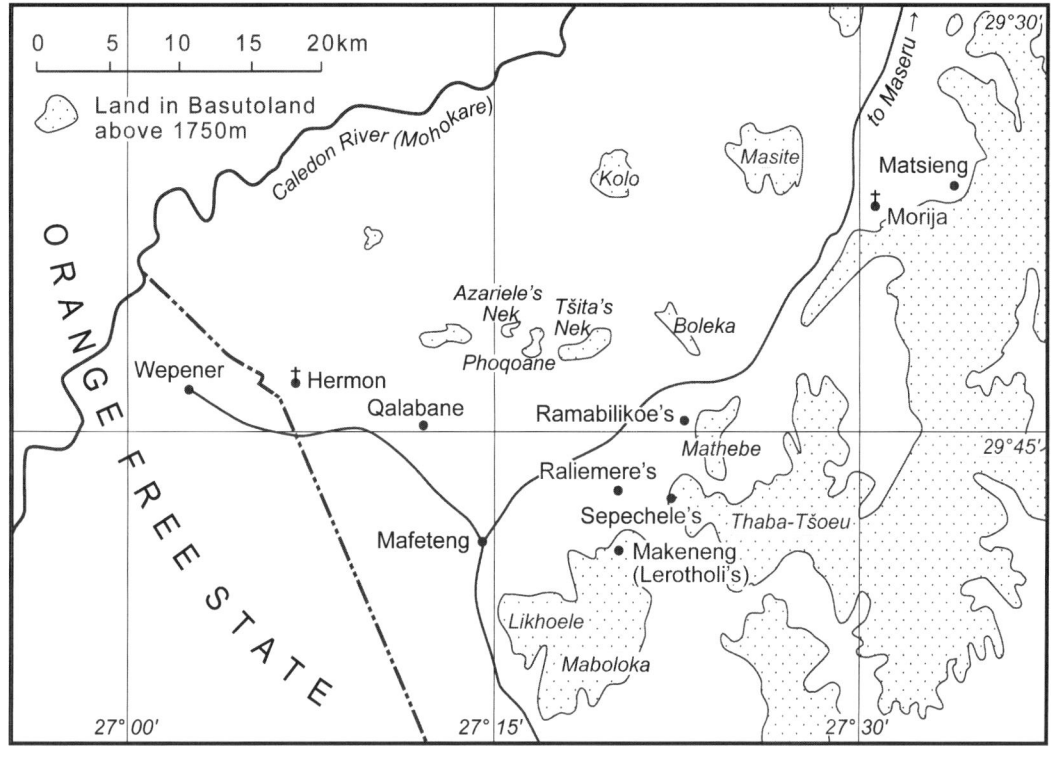

CHAPTER 12: THE FIRST PHASE OF THE WAR

Introduction

The first phase in the war lasted just over a month – from 13 September, when the CMR entered Basutoland and the first shots were fired, until 19 October, when Clarke arrived with reinforcements. Sprigg might have hoped that as soon as the troops appeared the rebels would back down, but they did not. The *Mabelete* did not come to their senses. Instead they launched all-out attacks on four of the five magistracies which were still occupied by the government – Maseru, Mafeteng, Mohale's Hoek and Quthing – and in the absence of any protection many Basotho who had looked to the government now joined the rebels' ranks.

The Cape was shaken by the strength of the Basotho's resistance, but the limited number of troops initially sent up, about 500 men in all, ruled out any serious offensive operations. The most that Carrington and Bayly could do was to defend the magistracies (or the camps, as they came to be known), to try to keep lines of communication and supply open, and to inflict as much local damage as they could until Clarke's reinforcements arrived.

The war in the south

Carrington and his 200 men, with their 23 wagons, rode into Mafeteng at 11 a.m. on Monday, 13 September. The first sight of the little village was 'decidedly pleasing' – 'a cluster of green trees and clean, whitewashed houses' set out along a street about 200 metres long. At one end of the street was Barkly's residence, 'a brick, iron-roofed house, with a long, thatched mud building, generally used for bedrooms and offices', but soon to be turned into a hospital for the sick and wounded. Next to this was a cattle kraal, on the other side of which Carrington established and entrenched his camp. At the other end of the street was Aschmann's store, also a stone building with kraals. Between them the street was lined with stone houses occupied by the loyal Basotho and their families, and in the centre was the court house, which had been sandbagged and loopholed so as to form a fort. The small hill above the court house had been heavily fortified with 'three large schanzes or defences', which were occupied by Barkly's police, now to be reinforced by some of the CMR.[1] About four kilometres to the north was Liphiring, a large trading store, which the Fraser brothers, 'rich gentlemen traders',[2] had fortified in expectation of a war. About nine kilometres to the east was Lerotholi's village of Likhoele on the slopes of the flat-topped mountain of that name.

Carrington had every reason to be pleased with his progress. As he had approached Mafeteng Lerotholi had positioned hundreds of men on a ridge overlooking the road. They fled when charged by the CMR, tried to rally at each rocky place they came to, but were driven off until they were completely routed. After the CMR had laagered their wagons in Mafeteng they heard reports that the rebels were attacking some loyalists nearby. Carrington sent 70 men who put the rebels to flight and pursued them for 21 kilometres. About 10 Basotho were believed to be killed, among them one of Letsie's junior sons. Lerotholi's horse was injured under him.[3] Sprigg was exultant: the CMR, with

---

[1] Shervinton (1899: 62); Woon (1909: 116-7). The quotations, except the last, are from Shervinton. See also C.2755, p. 201, Carrington to Assistant Adjutant General, Colonial Forces, 16 September 1880.

[2] Barkly (1893: 120).

[3] C.2755, pp. 191-3, Barkly to Griffith, 13 September 1880, and pp. 200-1, Carrington to Assistant Adjutant General, Colonial Forces, 16 September 1880; CA, Griffith Papers, Barkly to Griffith, 20 September 1880; Barkly (1893: 181-9).

Barkly's native police, 'drove the rebels before them like sheep'.⁴ Barkly was contemptuous: '[The rebels] showed no courage whatever'. In the countryside around it was widely reported that Lerotholi had suffered a severe defeat.⁵

Over the next few days the CMR set about destroying the rebel villages around Mafeteng, setting fire to the houses and seizing whatever grain had been left. At first they encountered little opposition, but all round the camp large bands of Basotho could be seen riding in to Likhoele, and in the initial skirmishes the troops noted apprehensively that some of the Basotho's rifles had a much longer range than their own.⁶ Gradually Lerotholi stifled their initiative, pouring in mounted men whenever they showed themselves outside the camp, and Carrington quickly came to realise that an attack on Likhoele would be beyond the strength of his present force. The most he could do at this stage was to hold Mafeteng and to keep the road to Wepener open. 'It soon became evident', wrote one of his officers, 'that we were not in for a picnic ....' When, on the 16th, Gordon Sprigg was brought in to camp by a mounted and armed escort the troops hoped that he would be attacked *en route* to give him a lesson.⁷

A day after Sprigg's arrival 27 men under Captain Shervinton set out to seize some grain and to clear the Basotho from hills near the trading station of Liphiring. They expected 'a stiff fight', but, as one of their number noted later, it was an act of madness to send out such a small force so far from the camp. About five kilometres from Mafeteng the troops were cut off by 800 Basotho under Lerotholi and one of their videttes was killed, the first white casualty of the war. They made a stand on some rising ground and reinforcements were rushed out, but they were short of ammunition, and when they made a frantic dash for Liphiring two men, a lieutenant and a private, were stabbed to death. Towards evening the whole party made its way back to camp. They had been lucky to escape with their lives. 'I never expected to get out with a single man', wrote Shervinton, and he himself had a lucky escape when his field-glasses were shot out of his hands. As they approached Mafeteng they saw a cart and four, with an armed escort, starting out for the Free State border. Gordon Sprigg was making his escape. He got out, as he admitted later, 'by the skin of his teeth'.⁸ On the same day Sir Bartle Frere left Cape Town for England.

Carrington claimed that 50 Basotho had lost their lives, which might have been true, though it was difficult to judge because the Basotho immediately removed the bodies of their dead,⁹ and it was later freely admitted that the numbers of enemy killed were sometimes grossly exaggerated.¹⁰ It was Lerotholi, however, rather than Carrington who took heart from the battle. While Carrington gave up all offensive operations for the present, because 'the instant a party moves out the rebels turn up in

---

⁴ C.2755, p. 170, Sprigg to Ayliff, 15 September 1880.
⁵ CA, Griffith Papers, Barkly to Griffith, n.d. (in fact 14 September 1880), and Surmon to Griffith, 13/15 September 1880.
⁶ Barkly (1893: 188); Woon (1909: 118-9, 123).
⁷ Woon (1909: 119, 121).
⁸ Woon (1909: 121-8). See also CA, Griffith Papers, Barkly to Griffith, 20 September 1880; C.2755, p. 174, enclosure with Clifford to Kimberley, 21 September 1880; Barkly (1893: 196-7); Shervinton (1899: 63-6).
⁹ Barkly (1893: 205); Woon (1909: 136).
¹⁰ Scully (1913: 123). In this instance Barkly (CA, Griffith Papers, Barkly to Griffith, 20 September 1880) gave the number as 30 killed and wounded. See also *Cape Argus*, 25 September 1880, 'The Basuto War. Conflicting Reports of Casualties', and 7 October 1880, Editorial; PEMS Archives, Paris, Dr. Casalis to beloved parents and friends, 1 November 1880; *JME* 1881, p. 28, Ellenberger to '*ses amis de la Maison des Missions*', 11 November 1880.

swarms on all sides',[11] Lerotholi pressed ahead with his arrangements for an all-out attack on the camp.

It came on Tuesday, 21 September, at 10.45 a.m., and it was a much bigger operation than any that Lerotholi had so far mounted. At least 7,000 mounted men were involved – his own regiments, together with those of his brothers and Moletsane's Bataung. The defending force consisted of 171 CMR, 120 Basotho policemen and a few volunteers, and there were a further 25 CMR and 25 volunteers at Frasers' store at Liphiring.[12]

The attack took the defenders by surprise. Some were sitting round the mess fire at breakfast when they saw 'an unending stream of horsemen coming round the side of the mountain' below Likhoele.[13] Although the trumpets immediately sounded the alarm all the garrison's cattle were swept off, and half of the horses of the Basutoland Police. As soon as the cattle had been driven to the rear the Basotho charged repeatedly, waving their guns and their battle-axes. One charge was led by a chief – the colonial sources do not give his name – right down the main street of Mafeteng, but it was repelled after he and several others had been killed.[14] Lerotholi himself was in the thick of the fighting, advancing with 300 of his men, having his horse shot under him, and gaining the protection of a rocky ledge and a wall near Aschmann's store. He and his men were repeatedly reinforced, in spite of heavy fire, and were sheltering, it was thought, with the intention of rushing the defences at dark. In the late afternoon a charge of 25 CMR under Shervinton, supported by heavy fire from the schanzen, dislodged them and forced them to retire. The Basotho remained in the ruined villages around Mafeteng, firing randomly into the camp, but they mounted no further attack. The fighting had lasted from 11 a.m. until darkness fell around 7 p.m. The camp's defences had been well prepared. The Basotho had suffered heavy losses. Barkly reckoned that nearly a hundred had been killed or wounded, and they had to leave a hundred dead and wounded horses. Among the CMR only five men had been slightly wounded, and among the Basotho police just two men killed.[15]

The garrison remained under arms all night, but the Basotho did not renew the attack. The CMR's fire from prepared positions had been deadly, and to strengthen their defences still further they levelled every wall and enclosure around to deny the Basotho any cover nearby. It was the last time that Lerotholi was to attempt an outright assault of this kind, and it was rumoured that when he made his report to Letsie he was blamed for attacking so strong a place and losing so many men.[16] He now settled down to invest the camp. The garrison had lost all their cattle and were reduced to slaughtering some of the CMR's horses. There were four wagon loads of supplies on the Free State border, only eleven kilometres away, but it was too dangerous to attempt to bring them in. The defenders made light of their privations, livening up their horse-meat with curry powder and rice, and trying out dried horse-dung when their tobacco ran out.[17] The *Mabelete* mocked them:

---

[11] CA, Griffith Papers, Barkly to Griffith, 20 September 1880.

[12] C.2755, p. 214, Carrington to A.A. General, King William's Town, 22 September 1880.

[13] Woon (1909: 132-3).

[14] Sprigg says that one of Letsie's sons was killed in the attack: C.2755, p. 186, Sprigg to Treasurer-General, 27 September 1880.

[15] C.2755, pp. 214-5, Carrington to A.A. General, King William's Town, 22 September 1880; Barkly (1893: 190-6 and 203-6); Shervinton (1899: 66-9); Woon (1909: 132-7).

[16] C.2755, p. 232, Clarke to Sprigg, 21 October 1880.

[17] Woon (1909: 138); Rhodes House Library, Oxford, MSS Afr. S.696, Kennan Papers, notes compiled by Miles Kennan based on the letters of his father, Thomas Kennan, who was one of the CMR under siege. See also *Cape Argus*, 1 November 1880, 'Mafeteng and its Investment'.

The Whites were besieged in the Mafeteng Office,
They had to live on horse gravy,
They even finished up their donkeys' ears![18]

On the 23rd, two days after the battle, the post cart from Wepener was seized. All communication with Maseru was lost. On 4 October Frasers' store at Liphiring was looted and burnt. Ammunition was running low.[19]

The only course now open to Carrington was to wait for Clarke's reinforcements, but every day the Basotho rode out *en masse* from Lerotholi's village towards the Free State border. As one CMR officer observed, 'it looked as if our relief column would have their work cut out to get to us'.[20]

Meanwhile, at Mohale's Hoek, William Surmon was in an even more perilous position. No CMR had been sent to protect him, and the only forces at his disposal were 14 white volunteers and about 80 Africans. His supplies of ammunition were 'scanty'.[21] By the 19th he was desperate.

> It is really shameful the way Govnt. is treating me by leaving me to face such a fearful danger almost single handed .... Austen was blamed for leaving his Post but how the devil can the Government expect their servants to remain, in the face of such great danger, when they are so slow in sending them any assistance at all?[22]

On 20 September, a day before the attack on Mafeteng, 1,200 *Mabelete* poured down on Mohale's Hoek, all local regiments under their chiefs and with the sons of Posholi prominent among them. They were beaten off, but one of the Basotho defenders was killed, another was wounded, and nearly all the horses and cattle were seized. The magistracy was then besieged, and on the night of the 25th another attack was made in which several houses, including Surmon's, were burnt. A relieving column was rushed up under the command of Colonel Southey, and the siege was raised on 4 October. The Basotho, it was reported, fought well, and, since some of them were armed with 'superior' weapons, it was only by charging that the troops could get near them.[23]

The troops were needed at Mafeteng, and Mohale's Hoek had to be abandoned. Surmon and his men were ordered to leave, and the whole force, encumbered with numerous refugees, made their way into the Free State, where they waited to join the main relieving column that was just then setting out from King William's Town under Clarke's command.

---

[18] Mangoaela (1957: 191), the praises of Moiloa, one of Lerotholi's men. Translated from Sesotho.
[19] C. 2755, pp. 226-7, Carrington to A.A. General, 5 October 1880; LNA, MF2/1/2, Barkly to Griffith, 27 September 1880; Barkly (1893: 208); Woon (1909: 134, 138-40); Walton (1958A: 23-4).
[20] Woon (1909: 141).
[21] See p.110 above. See also C. 2755, p. 188, memorandum of 29 September 1880 attached to Minute by H.W. Pearson, 29 September 1880, where the number of volunteers is given as 12.
[22] Griffith Papers, Surmon to Griffith, 19 September 1880.
[23] *Quarterly Paper of the Bloemfontein Mission*, January 1881, No. 51, pp. 15-18, Stenson, 'The destruction of Mohale's Hoek'; National Army Museum, Tylden Papers, Box 34057, Notebook VII, p. 21, newspaper cutting, Southey to A.A. General, Colonial Forces, 8 October 1880; C.2755, pp. 275-6, Clarke to Sprigg, 16 October 1880, and Surmon to Clarke, 16 October 1880; G.20-'81, p. 8, Surmon to Griffith, 30 December 1880; Rhodes House Library, MSS Afr. s.969, Kennan Papers, 'Siege of Mohale's Hoek - September/October 1880', notes made by Myles Kennan, based on letters home from his uncle, Robert Kennan; National Army Museum, Tylden Papers, Box 34057, Notebook V, p. 146, statement of Samuel Lefoka, 12 July 1938; National Army Museum, Tylden Papers, Box 34057, Notebook VII, p. 21, information supplied by R.C. Grant.

Further south, at Quthing, John Austen was in no serious danger. As well as a few white volunteers, he had 100 special police and a considerable following of loyal Africans in camp. It was not a powerful force, but after the Moorosi War the district was half deserted, and the main opposition seems to have been led by Tyali, an elderly Thembu chief who lived on the other side of the Orange. At dawn on 21 September, the same day as Lerotholi's attack on Mafeteng, a combined force of Basotho and Thembu attacked the camp, but were driven off without any great difficulty. Austen had a point to prove: he was still smarting under the accusations of cowardice for abandoning his post at the outbreak of the Moorosi War. 'You will doubtless be pleased to hear that I am still here', he wrote to Griffith after the battle; and, having given a breathless account of the fighting, he assured him that he was well able to hold his own.[24]

The war in the centre

The Maseru front was Masupha's responsibility. In the south Lerotholi had confronted the troops as soon as they crossed the border. In the centre Masupha allowed Bayly and 278 CMR to cross the Caledon with their two guns, a twelve-pounder and a nine-pounder,[25] and to make their way to Maseru unopposed.

Griffith's headquarters were described as a 'prettily situated village'.[26] On either side of the main road were government offices, traders' stores, houses, a hospital and a school, all set amidst trees and gardens, while the police camp and gaol were on a little eminence to the south which became known during the war as Koali's Kopje. Further to the south, beyond the kopje, was the larger hill of Qoaling; to the south-east were the three hills which the troops called the World, the Flesh and the Devil, and to the north was the rise where Bayly established his camp, Fort Gordon, named after Gordon Sprigg. This was described a few months later as having 'a strong sod wall with a good trench round it in the shape of a parallelogram' with 'two bastions for cannon' at diagonal corners, but since it was some distance from the main body of the village 'whoever selected the site for the camp could not really have hit upon a spot where the camp could have been of less use ....'[27] The traders, who had been waiting impatiently for the CMR to come and protect them, were angry and disappointed: 'in the event of an attack', wrote one of them, 'they would be of little use except for their own protection'.[28] During the previous few months, however, all the main buildings in the village had been fortified, the walls being loopholed and bastions of mealie-bags piled up.

It was not until Sunday, 10 October, that Masupha launched his attack. He might well have delayed because he wanted to muster as many forces as possible and needed the help of Letsie's sons, who had previously been fighting around Mafeteng. It seems that the *Mabelete* chiefs had learnt from Lerotholi's experience at Mafeteng that in an attack on fortified positions cavalry had no advantage over infantry. On the contrary, at Mafeteng they had sometimes been encumbered by their horses and about 100 animals had been killed or injured. The attack on Maseru was conducted mainly on foot.

---

[24] CA, Griffith Papers, Austen to Griffith, 23 September 1880. See also C.2755, pp. 178-9, Austen to Ayliff, 21 September 1880, and G.20-'81, pp. 11-12, Austen to Griffith, 31 December 1880.
[25] *Cape Argus*, 3 September 1880, 'Orange Free State', citing *The Friend of the Free State*.
[26] Matthews (1887: 374).
[27] 'Rienzi', *The Friend*, 24 March 1881, quoted in David Ambrose (1993: 75-76) See also photographs in Ambrose (1993: 56, 57), and map on p. 147. 'Rienzi' says that the fort was named after Gordon Sprigg, but according to James Walton (1958B: 3) it was named after the subaltern responsible for the work
[28] Walton, quoting George Hobson (1958B: 3).

Chapter 12: The first phase of the war

Map 3: The Gun War in Maseru

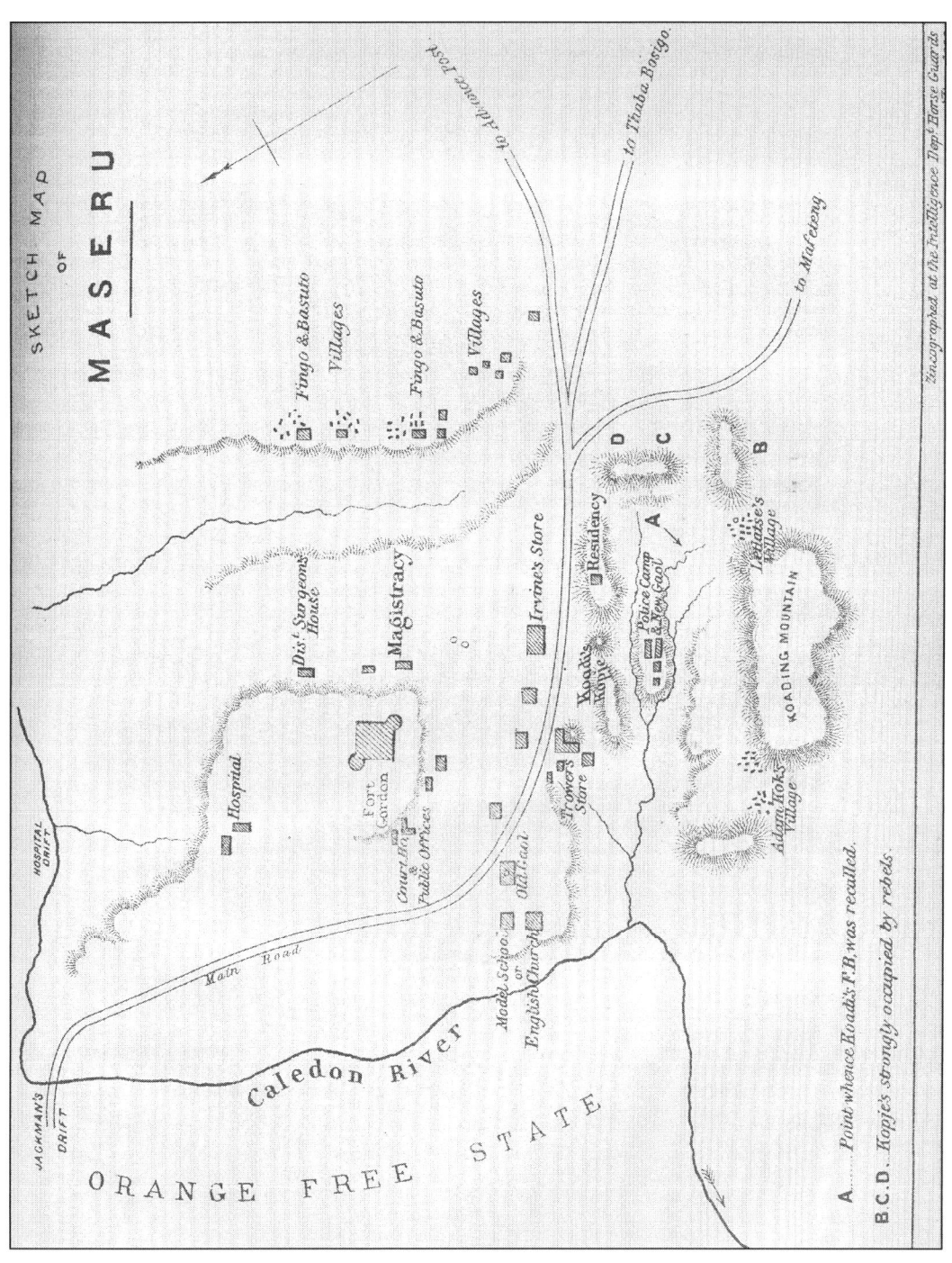

The attacking regiments were in two main divisions. The first, from the south, of about 3,000 men, was commanded by Letsie's son, Bereng, supported by his brothers, Maama and Theko. The second, from the east, of about 2,000 men, was under the command of Lepoqo Masupha, with the support of his brother, Martins, and of Leshoboro Majara and Peete Lesaoana (Ramanella's son). All of Bereng's forces, and most of Lepoqo's, were on foot. Masupha was said to be in overall command and watched the battle from one of the hilltops nearby, but the two divisions were kept separate.[29]

As well as his own CMR, Bayly had 33 white volunteers and 261 Africans – 30 Basutoland Police under George Moshoeshoe and 231 Basotho in 'levies' under various *Mateketoa* chiefs such as Sofonia Moshoeshoe (supported by his brothers Tsekelo and Nehemiah) and Koali Makhobalo. All these men had been placed under the command of Commandant Schermbrucker, the military adviser who had served under Griffith against the Ngqika and Gcaleka and who had come up with Sprigg in his last mission before the war.[30] Griffith himself was away in the south at this time.

On 9 October, the day before the attack, Schermbrucker, in accordance with Bayly's instructions, had distributed his men among five defensive positions – Griffith's Residency, Koali's Kopje, 'the English Church-ground' (an area that had been designated for the building of a church), Trower's Store, and Irvine's Store. The CMR were to remain in Fort Gordon, where Bayly himself was in command.

During the night of the 9th and the 10th Letsie's sons occupied the World, the Flesh and the Devil, and as the mist cleared at 6 a.m. some of their men could be seen building stone walls while others were advancing through the pass between the Devil and Qoaling. At the same time Lepoqo Masupha's force advanced on the village from the east, from the direction of the Berea plateau.

Lepoqo's regiments concentrated on Fort Gordon, where they had to confront not just the rifles of Bayly's CMR but the two guns as well, the twelve-pounder and the nine-pounder. They advanced to within 70 metres of the camp and tried to gain the protection of the hospital nearby, but the CMR thwarted this move by setting fire to the building and shelling Lepoqo's men when they tried to put out the flames. Bayly ordered a lull in the firing, which lured the Basotho out into the open, and then drove them to take cover by a volley of rifle fire and a shell from the bastion. After that the Basotho kept up a continuous but ineffective fire, while the CMR in the fort responded only when the Basotho exposed themselves. Around 1 p.m. the main body of Lepoqo's men retired.[31]

Meanwhile the Basotho's other division, under Bereng Letsie, occupied various heights around the village and opened fire, advancing gradually from one position to another. Around 4 p.m. about 500 of them launched a direct attack on the men under Sofonia Moshoeshoe at the English Church-ground. Sofonia, with the help of Tsekelo and Nehemiah, 'held out to the last cartridge', but at 5.30 p.m., with his ammunition spent, he had to withdraw to the Court House.

By this time the Basotho were attacking all the Cape's positions – Koali's Kopje, the Residency, and Trower's and Irvine's stores. Around 6.45 p.m. Koali's men also ran out of ammunition and had to retreat to the Residency, but within the hour the Kopje was recaptured in a counter-attack. At Trower's store there was hand-to-hand fighting over the wall, the *Mabelete* set fire to one of the store-rooms and Trower was severely wounded in the neck. At the Residency they came to within 20

---

[29] C.2755, p. 271, Schermbrucker to Bayly, 11 October 1880.
[30] LNA, S9/1/1/2, Griffith to Sprigg, 6 September 1880.
[31] C.2755, pp. 269-70, Bayly to Assistant Adjutant-General, 13 October 1880. For Schermbrucker, see National Army Museum, Tylden Papers, Box 34-057, Notebook VII, p. 71.

metres of the ramparts. Many cattle and horses were seized, and it was about 11 p.m. before the attacks were beaten off and past midnight before the firing finally subsided.

Although the *Mabelete*'s fire was variously described as 'galling', 'heavy and continuous', 'intense' and 'determined', the casualties on the Cape side were negligible. Two Africans were killed, one Mosotho and one Mfengu. One African and one white, Richard Trower, were seriously wounded. The CMR suffered no casualties at all, and merely reported five wounded horses. Fort Gordon had never been in serious danger. As Schermbrucker pointedly reported, 'Unlike any of the other engagements fought in Basutoland since the outbreak of the rebellion, the fight at Maseru was sustained chiefly by European civilians and Basotho refugees, not belonging to any of the regularly organized corps of the colonial forces ....'[32]

The *Mabelete*'s losses are not known, but one of the white volunteers reckoned that between 40 and 60 men were killed.[33] Schermbrucker calculated that their losses must have been severe: 'blood spoors, pieces of human skull and human brain were scattered in several places, and the traces of bodies having been dragged along the ground were found frequently; three dead bodies of rebels were left on the field ....'[34] It was reported that among those killed were two of Masupha's sons.[35] The defenders had been fighting from well-prepared positions. The attackers had been much more exposed.[36]

The engagement was hailed as a victory for the Cape, but the fighting had been brought right into the heart of its administrative headquarters. The court room had been sacked and several important buildings destroyed – the police barracks and stables, the school and some houses, while the hospital had been burnt by the defenders themselves. For the *Mabelete* the blazing fires of Maseru became a symbol of their own destructive power. Maama, one of the attacking chiefs, likened himself to a bolt of lightning:

The black lightning bird from the house of Seeiso
Burned Maseru as the sun was going down.
So Trower left, out he was thrown
In mid-afternoon.[37]

The attack also had the effect of pinning down Bayly's troops in Maseru. Shortly before he had had twice been ordered to move to the relief of Mafeteng with 250 men and one gun, leaving 50 men and the other gun for the protection of Maseru. With Griffith's support he had refused, arguing that the risk to Maseru would be too great. The order was countermanded and the attack proved him

---

[32] Walton (1958B: 4).

[33] C.2755, p. 273, Hobson to Major Bailie, 11 October 1880. Newspaper reports gave the number killed as about 50: Ambrose (1993: 61).

[34] C.2755, p. 272, Schermbrucker to Bayly, 11 October 1880.

[35] *Quarterly Paper of the Bloemfontein Mission*, January 1881, no. 51, pp. 11-15, Douglas, 'The attack on Maseru'. Douglas was wrong, however, in reporting that Lepoqo Masupha was killed. Sekese (*Leselinyana*, 15 February 1905) says that Mosiuoa Masupha was killed at Maseru, but does not identify the particular battle.

[36] C.2755, pp. 269-275: Bayly to Assistant Adjutant-General, 13 October 1880; Schermbrucker to Bayly, 11 October 1880; Hobson to Major Bailie, 11 October 1880; Sidwell to Bayly, 11 October 1880; *Cape Argus*, 14 October 1880, 'Basutoland. Desperate Attack on Maseru'; Walton (1953B: 4-6). See also *Quarterly Paper of the Bloemfontein Mission*, January 1881, No. 51, pp. 11-15, Douglas, 'The attack on Maseru'.

[37] Damane and Sanders (1974: 155). The translation has been slightly altered. Seeiso was Maama's brother. See also Damane and Sanders (1974: 149), the praises of Lerotholi.

right.[38]

It had been hoped that the CMR would be able to rally the *Maketetoa* in the country as a whole, but it now transpired that Bayly could barely defend them in Maseru itself. Immediately after the battle the loyalist chiefs there, George, Sofonia, Ntsane, Nehemiah, Tsekelo, Koali Makhobalo and others, declared that their present position was untenable and that in the event of another attack they would be forced to seek shelter in the Free State. Bayly ordered the Diamond Fields Native Contingent, which had arrived on the border the previous day, to come through the Caledon and reinforce them.[39]

The war in the north

Throughout this time there was no fighting in the north. Jonathan Molapo was still loyal to the government, but his great rival, his brother Joel, was more inclined to join the *Mabelete*, and so were their junior brothers, Khethisa, Hlasoa and Seetsa. In the west Ramanella was firmly in the rebel camp. A month before the war began Major Bell at Hlotse Heights acknowledged that 'the greater part' of his district was in sympathy with Masupha.[40] As well as the issue of disarmament, Joel still disputed the succession with Jonathan and there were unresolved conflicts about Molapo's property. In these early weeks of the war he pretended that his argument was not with his 'father', Major Bell, but only with Jonathan.[41]

Jonathan's village of Fobane, on the western border of the Molapo ward, was dangerously close to Masupha and Ramanella. Griffith proposed to send Charlie Bell with 50 whites and a detachment of Basutoland Police to support him, but Jonathan, 'timid' and 'in a great fright' according to Major Bell,[42] thought it better to move closer to the centre of his ward, to the flat-topped mountain fortress of Tsikoane, about five kilometres south-west of the magistracy at Hlotse Heights. Charlie Bell and his men, together with Tokonya's Hlubi, then joined his father, Major Bell, at Hlotse. Masupha, who still claimed the Mfengu as his subjects, constantly sent Bell messages to enquire after the welfare of his 'scabby goats' and to assure him that one day he would be sending to fetch them.[43] Before the war many of Jonathan's followers had deserted him when he had handed in his guns. In the continuing absence of any strong government force others were now slipping away.

Major Bell had chosen Hlotse Heights for his magistracy because of its defensibility. It was not a mountain fortress surrounded by cliffs, but on every side it was flanked by steep slopes and on the north and the west it was skirted by the Caledon and Hlotse rivers. Bell had already built what the local doctor, Henry Taylor, described as 'an oblong enclosure, some fifty yards by thirty, surrounded by a rough stone wall', with a round stone tower at one corner that had been a storeroom and was now to serve as a look-out. This enclosure contained the prisons for men and women, but by a convenient coincidence these now escaped and the whole area was turned into a fort.[44] The sod walls around the police barracks were also loopholed, and the church was put into a state of defence. With the scanty forces available to him Bell decided that these were only positions he was able to hold.

---

[38] *Cape Argus*, 4 October 1880, and *The Journal*, 4 October 1880.
[39] LNA, S9/1/3/4, Davies to Bayly, 13 October 1880; LNA, S9/1/2/2, Davies to Ayliff, 13 October 1880.
[40] CA, Griffith Papers, Bell to Griffith, 16 August 1880.
[41] CA, Griffith Papers, Bell to Griffith, 22 and 26 September 1880; LNA, L2/1/2, Bell to Joel, 24 September 1880.
[42] CA, Griffith Papers, Bell to Griffith, 19 and 22 September 1880.
[43] CA, Griffith Papers, Bell to Griffith, 9 October 1880; Widdicombe (1895: 169).
[44] Taylor (1972: 60-1).

Chapter 12: The first phase of the war

Map 4: The Gun War in the North

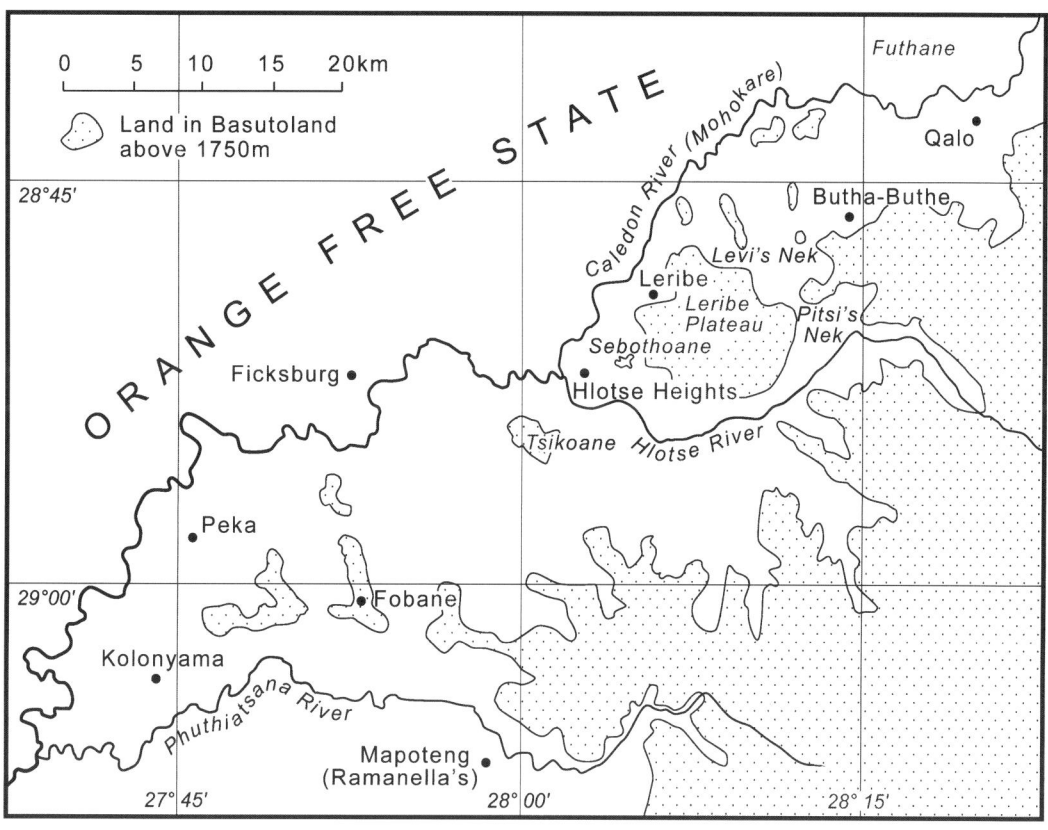

With only 56 African police Bell desperately needed more men. He constantly asked for forces from Natal, but there were bureaucratic delays – the request had to be channelled through the Governor at the Cape – and there was no response beyond assurances of help and expressions of sympathy. Just across the Free State border, however, even before the fighting began, a farmer, John Stanton, volunteered to raise a group of men – the first man, Griffith wrote later, to come to the government's defence.[45] Taylor described him as 'a rather remarkable man. Though very poorly educated he was a born leader of men, and had had great experience in former native wars ....' At first

> he raised about thirty rapscallions, tramps, and such like, a most disreputable lot ... though there were a few decent fellows among them. The Government supplied them each with a horse, saddle and bridle, and a Snider carbine, and gave them 5s a day pay, with rations for themselves and their horses. .... No quarters or tents being available, they slept on the ground. Commandant Stanton himself had a native hut for his quarters, which he used as dining-room, bedroom, and orderly room combined.[46]

Taylor referred to them as 'the noble thirty', but their official title was Stanton's Light Horse.

At about the same time Tokonya and his Hlubi also came into the camp, and by the end of the month Bell's force amounted in all to about 110 Africans and 47 whites.[47] Stanton was trying to recruit more, but by 31 October he had added only 30 to his number.[48] Hlotse Heights was in a fairly good state of defence, but the position was becoming daily more perilous.

Bell complained repeatedly about the government's failure to send him more men and its demoralising effect upon the loyalist Basotho in his district. He had been promised 200 men, but on 10 October he was told that these were being sent to Kokstad instead to deal with the Basotho and others who had risen in rebellion below the Drakensberg.[49]

All hopes were pinned on General Clarke and his reinforcements, which were now on the point of crossing the border and relieving the siege at Mafeteng. But Clarke could no longer devote all his forces to Basutoland alone. The war below the Drakensberg would be a costly distraction.

---

[45] LNA, S9/1/1/2, Griffith to Sprigg, 26 October 1880.
[46] Taylor (1972: 59-60).
[47] Widdicombe (1895: 166).
[48] LNA, L2/1/2, Bell to Sprigg, 22 October 1880; CA, Griffith Papers, Bell to Griffith, 31 October 1880.
[49] CA, Griffith Papers, Bell to Griffith, 11 October 1880.

CHAPTER 13: THE SECOND PHASE OF THE WAR

The war in the south

In spite of the sobering events of the previous month Clarke was confident of rapid success. With Carrington's agreement he had held up his advance from Wepener until every section of his new force was present. He thought it advisable, he explained, 'to enter Basutoland with a large force, in order to strike a decisive blow at the outset'.[1]

At 4.45 a.m. on 19 October Clarke's troops set off from Massyn's Farm on the Free State border, the same starting point as Carrington's a month before. His force was about eight times larger, consisting of 101 officers, 1,495 white troops and 75 Africans. As well as contingents from the three Yeomanry regiments, there were reinforcements for the CMR, five volunteer corps – the Diamond Fields Horse, Captain Hunt's Volunteers, the (Graham's Town) 1st City Rifles, Prince Alfred's Guard and the Duke of Edinburgh's Own Volunteer Rifles – and the contingent of Basotho from Mohale's Hoek under the command of William Surmon. About 1000 of these men were mounted – the CMR, the Yeomanry and the Diamond Fields Horse – and the rest were on foot. Clarke had five guns, more than 40 wagons, and several spans of slaughter oxen.

The column moved off with its wagons in the centre, flanked by the infantry, and with the mounted men outside them. Groups of Basotho opened fire, but the troops advanced without serious opposition as far as Qalabane, a small height on the left of the road. The CMR took possession of this so that the column could move through safely without being fired on from above. Behind Qalabane was a ridge, and behind this, out of sight, was a mounted force of Basotho under Letsie's sons, Bereng, Maama, Seeiso, Nkuebe and Mojela. Since there was no sign of the Basotho Clarke despatched about 120 men of the 1st Yeomanry under Captain Dalgety to the left of Qalabane 'to feel for the enemy in an easterly direction'. Without sending out scouts, Dalgety's men dismounted and made their way up the ridge in loose formation. This was the Basotho's opportunity. A mass of horsemen suddenly appeared over the ridge, rode down at full speed and cut right through the Yeomanry, who had no time to rally. In the hand to hand fighting that followed 31 Yeomen were hacked or stabbed to death and 11 were wounded, one of whom died within the day. Reinforcements were rushed out from the column and the Basotho were driven off.[2]

Having gathered up its dead and wounded, the column made its way to the camp at Mafeteng, where the besieged men were eagerly waiting for the luxuries of fresh meat, tea, coffee and tobacco. As they went towards the wagons they came across what one of them described as 'a ghastly sight'.

> Two wagons, which had contained fresh meat for us, were piled up with dead bodies of men .... They were lying in all positions, just as they had been hurriedly picked up and thrown on the first wagon which came along and which happened to contain the meat intended for us. It was a

---

[1] C.2755, p. 229, 'Summary of News for Week ending October 19, 1880', Colonial Secretary's Office, Cape Town. Sprigg too was confident of a rapid victory: *Cape Argus*, 27 September 1880.

[2] C.2755, pp. 230-2, Clarke to Sprigg, 19 October 1880; *The Journal*, 25 October, Supplement 29 October, and 3 November 1880; CA, Acc. 459, Brabant's Autobiography, pp. 97-100; Barkly (1893: 234-6, 242-4); Shervinton (1899: 70-1); Woon (1909: 143-50); Deare (1930: 10 May); National Army Museum, Tylden Papers, Box 34057, Notebook IV, p. 77, letter from G.H. Bruce, 1930, and Notebook VII, p. 22, information from R.C. Grant; Tylden (1950A: 154-6); Bereng and Lehloenya (1991: 88, 90).

gruesome sight to look at. They had all been either battleaxed or assegaied, and were covered with gashes or stabs – in some cases half their heads were nearly cut off – and the jostling of the wagons caused these half-severed heads to open and shut as they moved along, and made most of us half-starved creatures very sick.[3]

The victory at Qalabane boosted the Basotho's confidence after the failures of their attacks on Mafeteng and Maseru. On the Cape side Clarke was no longer talking of inflicting a swift and decisive blow. Within 24 hours of crossing the border he had been brought to understand that his present force was 'not adequate for the work that evidently will be necessary'. In spite of his poor opinion of the burghers he called for 1000 of them to be sent up at once and estimated that a further 1000 would probably be required. He also decided, like the CMR officers at Mafeteng, that his men needed swords for fighting at close quarters.[4]

While maintaining the garrison at Mafeteng Clarke established his main camp just outside the magistracy, on the high ground between Mafeteng and Liphiring. It was important for him to seize the initiative, and he decided that the best way to do this was to launch an attack on Lerotholi's village at Likhoele. He wasted no time. While it was still dark on the morning of 22 October, three days after his arrival, he set out with about 1000 men, mounted and on foot, together with a seven-pounder gun and two five and a half inch mortars. He put Carrington in charge of the attack, while he himself followed behind as an onlooker with Arthur Barkly. The force consisted of CMR, volunteers, and the Basotho contingents from Mafeteng and Mohale's Hoek. The three Yeomanry regiments were left to protect the magistracy and the camp.

Lerotholi's village was built on a ridge and had not been heavily fortified. As daylight broke a troop of the CMR, together with the contingents from Mafeteng and Mohale's Hoek, seized a height, variously described as a kopje or a plateau, about 800 metres from the village, where they dragged up the gun and mortars by hand. They began to advance on the village, but had to retire when they were suddenly confronted by a large force of Basotho. They kept them at a distance with the artillery, but could not dislodge them. Then a large force of Moletsane's Bataung swept in and occupied a rocky gorge, in this way cutting the troops off from Mafeteng. The CMR, backed up by infantry volunteers, charged and dislodged them with carbines and revolvers. The way was then clear for a direct attack on the village, and by 1.30 p.m. it was in the Cape's possession. Clarke himself followed up the attack, clambering up the steep ridge, unable to speak because he was out of breath, laughing and waving the men forward with his sword. The village was burnt, and by four in the afternoon the troops were back in camp.

According to one account about 6-8,000 Basotho had been engaged. They had kept up a heavy fire, but they were poor shots. Barkly reported that, although 'a large percentage of them' had 'excellent rifles', they used smooth bores 'a good deal' and many of their bullets were spent before reaching their target. On the Cape side only 11 men were wounded, one of whom died later from his wounds. On the Basotho side the losses are not known, but 31 bodies were found in the rocky gorge and 200 rifles and many horses were captured.[5]

Clarke was pleased with his troops' performance, and the seizure and burning of Lerotholi's 'capital' made good reading in the colonial press. The Basotho, it was said, were now badly demoral-

---

[3] Woon (1909: 145).
[4] C.2755, pp. 230-2, Clarke to Sprigg, 19 October 1880.
[5] C.2755, pp. 233-4, Clarke's 'official' report, 22 October 1880; Barkly (1893: 239-42); Shervinton (1899: 71-3); Woon (1909: 150-6); Deare (1930: 17 May).

ised, and Clark was confident that with the reinforcements he had asked for he could 'end the war quickly'.[6] Tactically, however, he had achieved very little. The Basotho remained in control of the country around Mafeteng, and during the day the hills around Likhoele 'were constantly occupied by large numbers of the enemy'.[7]

On 31 October, nine days after the attack on Likhoele, having brought in further supplies, Clarke mounted another attack. This time his main target was Moletsane's stronghold of Maboloka (often referred to as Makoaisberg), about ten kilometres beyond Likhoele, and Clarke himself was in command. He took 1,450 men – 700 under Carrington in advance, mainly CMR and volunteers; 500, mainly Yeomanry, under Brabant in reserve; and a separate force of 250 CMR and volunteers under Major Grant who were ordered to turn aside and to seize Likhoele again. Carrington took two seven-pounder guns and one five and a half inch mortar. Brabant took a seven-pounder gun.

Because of the distance to be covered the troops left at 1 a.m., under cover of darkness. Their progress was slow. They got stuck in rivers, their wagons were upset, they lost their way, and they made so much noise that the Basotho must have been aware of their movements. To their surprise, however, they were not attacked, and by daybreak Carrington's advance column was drawn up on a plateau opposite Maboloka. To some of the old hands 'the quietness seemed ominous'. A few Basotho appeared and fired some shots, but rode off as soon as the artillery was brought into action, and a few more rode round the side of the mountain and opened fire. It seemed as if they were deliberately luring the troops on. The mountain was heavily fortified, but when Carrington's men attacked there was no serious resistance. A few shots were fired, some rocks came bouncing down, and two men were wounded (one of them died later). When they finally reached the summit all they could see was a few Basotho disappearing down the other side of the deserted plateau. Clarke came up and admired the view, while the troops sat down on the rocks and ate their breakfast and enjoyed a smoke. They were uneasy. They felt they had 'been done by the wily natives, and wondered what mischief they were up to, and where'.

They did not wonder long. As Clarke surveyed the scene heavy firing was heard from the direction of Likhoele, and he could see Grant's men confronting a large Basotho force on the plain to the north. It was now apparent what the Basotho had been up to: their resistance was centred on the burnt-out ruins of Likhoele, where they were hoping to move in and destroy Grant's force. Clarke gave orders that the reserve force should move back as quickly as it could to relieve Grant and his men.

Grant had occupied the village soon after dawn without having to fire a shot and he had posted groups of his men on the surrounding heights. At first few Basotho were to be seen, but by 8 a.m. about 2,000-3,000 men had gathered in the open country to the north. All the sons of Letsie were said to be there. Grant, having signalled for help to the main column and to Mafeteng, began to concentrate his men on one of the heights close to the village. In the confusion his orders were not passed on to a group of 25 men from the 1st City Volunteers, and they started to pull back only when they saw the others retreating. It was too late. The Basotho closed in, and in hand-to-hand fighting like that at Qalabane they killed six men and wounded their commander. The survivors struggled through to join their comrades, but Grant and his troops were now completely cut off. Their position was critical, and according to Clarke the relief force, the 2nd Yeomanry, arrived not a minute too soon. There was then more fighting as the entire column made its weary and painful way back to

---

[6] C.2755, p. 234, Clarke's 'official' report, 22 October 1880, and p. 260, summary of events, 27 October 1880.
[7] Woon (1909: 158).

Mafeteng. It reached camp at half past six, having been under arms for over 18 hours.[8]

This time there was no euphoria. One CMR officer commented:

> It now became manifest that it was useless for a column to attempt any further operations in the direction of the last two engagements, the country being so mountainous and treacherous that an invading force could not do more than burn a few kraals or drive the enemy out of their positions, without achieving permanent results. The Basutos let themselves be driven out of their positions, but only to take up others in the vicinity, and on our retiring to our base of operations they invariably followed us up, re-occupying the positions and generally harassing us pretty severely the whole return journey. The last engagement clearly showed the risk incurred by an isolated force left at any one position, of being surrounded and suffering heavy losses.[9]

Lerotholi rebuilt and reoccupied his village at Likhoele, and he and his followers were now 'stronger than ever'.[10]

By this time the Cape was embroiled in serious fighting not just in Basutoland, but below the Drakensberg as well. Even before Clarke had set out from King William's Town the Basotho in Griqualand East had risen. They had reasons of their own for rebellion, since they too feared disarmament, but according to Charles Brownlee, the Chief Magistrate of East Griqualand, they had been encouraged to take up arms by messages from Letsie, warning them that their turn would come next. Lerotholi had attacked the troops against his orders, he said, but he must now be supported.[11] These Basotho were joined by the Batlokoa of Lelingoana and some of the Griqua, and the Thembu on the Cape border also rebelled. Hamilton Hope, the man who had so provoked and exasperated Moorosi, and who was now the magistrate with the Mpondomise, decided to enlist their help against the rebels but was murdered by one of their chiefs, Mhlonhlo, when he met him to hand over arms and ammunition. The Mpondomise then invested Maclear and Tsolo, while the Thembu invested Umtata in the Transkei. The crisis was so serious that on 7 November Clarke had to leave Basutoland and to organise the forces below the Drakensberg, and many of the men who might have been sent to Basutoland were detained on the Cape's eastern frontier. Clarke was confident that he would have 'no great difficulty' in stamping out the rebellion, and that he would then be able to send a large force into Basutoland,[12] but in the event he did not return until 27 February the next year.

Although Bayly with the CMR at Maseru and Brabant with the Yeomanry at Mafeteng were the officers with the highest seniority in the country, Clarke appointed Carrington to take charge while he was away and gave him 'the hitherto unknown rank of Colonel-Commandant'.[13] Both Bayly and Brabant were offended and resentful. Bayly refused to accept orders from Carrington, and Clarke was

---

[8] C.2755, p. 263, Clarke's official report, 31 October 1880; C.2821, pp. 28-30, Clarke to Sprigg, 1 November 1880; C.2821, pp. 30-2, Grant to Assistant Adjutant-General, Colonial Forces, 1 November 1880; CA, Acc. 459, Brabant's Autobiography, pp. 101-2; Barkly (1893: 254-6); Woon (1909: 157-66); Deare (1930: 17 May); Rhodes House Library, Oxford, MSS Afr. S.969, Kennan Papers, notes compiled by Myles Kennan from the letters of his father, Thomas Kennan, pp. 7-8; National Army Museum, Tylden Papers, Box 34057, Notebook III, p. 39, evidence of A.F. Ward. The quotations are from Woon.
[9] Woon (1909: 166).
[10] *The Journal*, 1 December 1880, 'With the First Yeomanry', 11 November 1880. See also PEMS Archives, Paris, Dieterlen to Lautré, 29 November 1880.
[11] Brownlee (1916: 194).
[12] CA, Griffith Papers, Clarke to Griffith, King William's Town, 26 November 1880.
[13] Gon (1984: 43-4).

Chapter 13: The second phase of the war

unable to make him obey. Brabant decided, as he wrote later, to place his country's interests above his 'personal dignity', but although he remained on good personal terms with Carrington the decision confirmed him in his view that Clarke had no confidence in colonial officers or soldiers.[14]

Carrington was left with a force at Mafeteng of almost 2,000 men. In a jocular letter to a friend he commented that his new command was 'no sinecure' as he did not have a tenth of the number of men he needed, and that he had cut off his beard for fear a Mosotho would get hold of it in close fighting.[15] He expected reinforcements in due course, as well as more heavy artillery, Martini-Henry rifles to replace the obsolete Sniders, and swords for fighting at close quarters. But in the meantime he could not afford to be inactive. The Yeomen and the volunteers had enlisted for only six months, and according to Brabant it was impossible to keep them 'living in fixed camps without fighting'. They had left their usual occupations at great loss to themselves, and they objected to what they regarded as 'useless procrastination'.[16] Carrington also had to keep his political masters and the colonial press satisfied: as he cynically observed, he had to show some sort of butcher's bill, otherwise it would be thought that he was doing nothing.[17]

Carrington shifted his line of attack to the more open country to the north of Mafeteng, and on 10 November he set out with 1,400 men, leaving Brabant and 450 men to defend Mafeteng. Instead of marching through the night, making a lightning attack at dawn and returning the same day, he planned to be away for seven days and to set up camp each night. Elaborate precautions were taken against any risk of being rushed by the Basotho. The expedition was like a moving square, with the wagons massed in the centre, the infantry on all four sides of them, the guns at the corners, the CMR forming the advance and rear guards and the Yeomanry on both flanks.

As the Cape forces made their way north-eastwards, roughly parallel with the Free State border, they were closely watched by the Basotho. On the first night they camped near the French mission station of Hermon, and on the following day, 11 November, they moved on to Tsakholo. They spent the next day destroying the local villages, and on 13 November set off at 4 a.m. towards the mountain of Kolo. The small plateau at the summit of the mountain was edged with cliffs, but Kolo's main strength was its steep rock-strewn slopes extending on every side down into the valley. As well as the local population, many Basotho whose villages had been destroyed were now living there. A missionary who visited the mountain a few weeks later described its appearance as 'extraordinary', with 'improvised villages everywhere'. It was a 'natural fortress', he wrote, a 'chaos of terraces and boulders'.[18] Even with their heavy artillery, it was too dangerous for the Cape troops to attack the mountain. Carrington's tactics were to lure the Basotho into the open and into the range of his men's carbines. The Basotho's tactics were to attack and cut off any forces that broke away from the main column, but they were also prepared to storm the Cape

---

[14] A.6-'81; CA, Acc. 459, Brabant's Autobiography, pp. 103-4. See also CA, DD 1/275, Carrington's War Diary, transcripts of relevant correspondence; *Cape Argus*, 30 November 1880, 'Opinions at Mafeteng', quoting correspondent of *Cape Mercury*. For the dispute between Clarke and Bayly see Tylden Papers, Box 34057, Notebook VII, p. 129.

[15] CA, Acc. 232, Carrington to Mrs. Kingsley, 18 November 1880.

[16] CA, Acc. 459, Brabant's Autobiography, p. 103.

[17] Army Museum, Tylden Papers, Box 34057, Notebook IV, p. 14, information from G.R. Deare; Tylden, (1950A: 159).

[18] *JME* 1881, P. 111, Hermann Dieterlen to his family, 28 December 1880.

lines. In the last resort they could fall back on the mountain and the surrounding heights and harass the troops with their rifle fire.

Carrington sent out the 2nd and 3rd Yeomanry with supporting forces, the 2nd Yeomanry to seize a village about 1,000 metres to his right, and the 3rd Yeomanry to occupy a hill on the left. As the Yeomen moved forward the Basotho, about 3,000 men in all, 'dashed out from their concealment and charged furiously', according to Carrington's official report – 'in a splendid manner', he wrote to a friend, 'as if they were riding for the Derby'.[19] The Yeomanry fell back on their supporting forces, but too late for some, who were cut off and killed. In spite of heavy fire from the artillery the Basotho tried to press home their charges, being stopped at one point 'almost at the muzzles' of the guns. They then retired out of sight, taking cover behind some rocky ledges and keeping up 'an almost harmless long range fire'. The serious fighting was now over. Six of the Yeomanry had been killed. On the Basotho side 20 bodies were left on the field, and more must have been carried away. The Cape forces remained for several hours, trying in vain to draw out the Basotho, but at 1.30 p.m. they began to retire and reached the site of their previous night's camp at 4.30 p.m. Carrington believed they might have stormed the positions in front of them, but only with heavy losses.[20] As for Kolo, as one of his officers observed, it would have been 'sheer madness' to attack it.[21]

At the end of November Carrington decided to establish his camp at a site near the Boleka ridge. Again leaving a strong garrison at Mafeteng, he took with him three seven-pounder guns and just over 1,300 troops – about 250 CMR, 360 Yeomanry, 690 volunteers (from the Kimberley Horse, Prince Alfred's Guard and the Duke of Edinburgh's Own Volunteer Rifles), and 120 Basotho policemen and loyalists. Although Boleka formed part of a line of ridges and mountains barring the way north-eastwards, and although it overlooked the road that led to Letsie's village of Matsieng, and ultimately Bayly's camp at Maseru, Carrington seems to have had no intention of trying to break through. His aim was merely to keep the troops actively employed and to maintain at least some pressure on the Basotho until reinforcements arrived.

Within a few days the Cape forces were being confronted by about 8,000 Basotho, no doubt under the overall command of Lerotholi. All the sons of Letsie were there, as well as the Bamohale, the Baposholi and the Bataung. Masupha had sent help under the command of his son Senekane.[22] As soon as Carrington struck camp the Basotho took up strong positions all round and subjected his men to constant harassment. On 28 November his cattle and horses stampeded out of the camp in a heavy hailstorm and were recovered only with luck and difficulty, and that evening the Basotho crept close to the camp and for at least an hour poured in heavy volleys of rifle fire without, though, inflicting much damage. During a lull in the firing the troops' morale was lifted when the band of the Prince Alfred's Guard suddenly struck up with 'St Patrick's day in the morning', 'Rule Britannia' and 'The Campbells are coming', to be greeted with a burst of cheering. According to one of the Guard's officers 'the effect was electrical' and not another shot was fired that night. The story was no doubt

---

[19] CA, Acc. 232, Carrington to Mrs Kingsley, 18 November 1880.
[20] C.2821, pp. 74-5, Carrington to A.A.G. Colonial Forces, 16 November 1880; CA, Acc. 232, Carrington to Mrs Kingsley, 18 November 1880; C.2821, pp. 36-7, 'Summary of Events reported from Basutoland since the 10th November'; Woon (1909: 171-5); Deare (1930: 17 May). At first Carrington estimated that 5,000 Basotho had been engaged and that their losses were well over 100. Later (C.2821, p. 68, 'Summary of Events reported since the 16th November') these figures rose to 10,000 and 600.
[21] Woon (1909: 173).
[22] C.2821, p. 87, 'Summary of Events reported since the 30th November, Basutoland'.

often repeated, complete with the detail of the drummer who begged to be moved to a more sheltered spot in case his drums should be damaged by bullets. (Another story was that the Basotho, being loyal subjects, stopped firing when the band struck up 'God Save the Queen'.) [23]

Over the next few days Carrington and his men set out on a series of probing expeditions. In the west they destroyed villages at Azariele's Nek and at Tšita's Nek, but when they tried to move south-eastwards towards Thaba-Tšoeu thousands of Basotho immediately appeared, occupied the heights around them, and constantly threatened to charge and to cut off any parties that might become detached from the main force. They inflicted few casualties, and they avoided any engagement in the open field, but they kept the troops under constant pressure. 'We could do nothing but hold our ground', one of Carrington's officers reported.[24] Shortly afterwards Carrington moved camp to a better position at Tšita's Nek.

The Basotho's confidence was growing every day. They had been warned of the folly of resistance, but it was now almost three months since the colonial troops had entered the country and they were still confined to Maseru, Hlotse Heights and the environs of Mafeteng. According to the Paris missionaries, the English now admitted that they were

> faced with a resistance which they had not expected. ... the rebels are fighting with the courage born of desperation, more than ever convinced that their national existence is at stake. That is the reason why the losses which they sustain do not discourage them; this also explains why one by one those who had hitherto been most in favour of peace are going over to join their ranks.[25]

On 2 December Dr. Casalis provided a vivid picture of what could be seen from the summit of Morija mountain, only a few kilometres behind the Basotho's lines. The camp, then at Boleka, was clearly visible and the missionaries could

> follow the various evolutions of the two armies. For days they have been firing at each other from a distance. The Basuto are entrenched behind the hills and rocks which the Whites dare not storm, for fear of the assegais. More often than not, their shells fall beyond the retreats of the natives and their bullets merely strike the rocks behind which they shelter. Much noise and smoke, but relatively speaking, little damage done. The Cape papers no doubt say that the Basuto are dying by the hundred, perhaps even in their thousands. They delude themselves.

In some districts, because of the recent drought, people were suffering from famine, but this year, because of the rain,

> the standing crops are magnificent .... Hitherto Morija has been very quiet; except for the almost

---

[23] Deare (1930: 17 May); Woon (1909: 184); Rhodes House Library, Oxford, MSS Afr. S.969, Kennan Papers, notes compiled by Myles Kennan from the letters of his father, Thomas Kennan, p. 8. See also *Cape Argus*, 3 December 1880, Editorial, 6 December 1880, 'The Native War', and 21 December 1880, 'The Basuto War. With Carrington on Patrol'. For the official report, see C.2821, p. 86, 'Summary of Events reported since the 30th November, Basutoland'.

[24] C.2821, pp. 87-8, Tennant to Sprigg, 1 December 1880. See also C.2821, pp. 86-7, 'Summary of Events reported since the 30th November, Basutoland'; National Army Museum, Tylden Papers, Box 34057, Notebook VII, p. 38, newspaper cutting, Carrington to A.A.G. Colonial Forces, 10 December 1880; Rhodes House Library, Oxford, MSS Afr. s.969, Kennan papers, Letters Home from South Africa, 1874-1900, No. 60, Thomas Kennan to his parents, December 1880; Deare (1930: 17 May).

[25] *JME* 1880, pp. 446-7, Paris, November 1880, as translated by Germond (1967: 365-6).

total absence of the men of the station and the constant passage of warriors armed to the teeth, one would not suspect that a stubborn conflict is waging twenty odd kilometres from here.[26]

The Basotho's mounting confidence was mirrored by the Cape's increasing frustration and concern. On every side the cry went up for more troops. 'The present state of affairs ... is very critical', wrote one of the CMR. 'The natives are every day gaining in strength and confidence and if the Government do not at once send up strong reinforcements this war may last for the next twelve months or more.'[27] According to Arthur Barkly, now acting as Clarke's Staff Officer, the Cape forces could barely hold their own. 'In a month or two's time it will be necessary to destroy the crops, ... which would require a very large force, and if we fail in doing it ... we are in for two years of it.'[28] It was 'no use going on without more men to hold the ground', Carrington reported. As well as his own attacking force he needed another 1,700 men – '700 men to keep communication open with Mafeteng, 600 to bring in supplies from Wepener, and 400 to garrison Mafeteng'.[29]

On 4 December 830 burghers rode in, and on 10 December 36 more – about half of Carrington's requirements. Although they were good shots and were well armed and mounted, they added, as Clarke had predicted, very little to the Cape's fighting effectiveness. They were conscripted men, most of them 'Dutchmen', with no interest in the war and no enthusiasm for fighting in it, and when the Transvaal broke out in rebellion two weeks later their sympathies were with Kruger and the rebels.[30] One of the CMR officers described them as 'tall bearded men' in 'smasher hats' and 'cord coats', most of them following the Dopper fashion of wearing one spur upside down. 'They were all well armed with the best rifles of that day – chiefly Westley-Richards and Winchester repeaters – and their bodies were hung about with crossed bandoliers or leather breastplates, with cartridges sticking out of leather holders.'[31] On their very first night in camp near Mafeteng, although there was no cause for alarm, they were seized by a panic and began firing off their rifles, causing their horses and cattle to stampede out of the laager in all directions. Most of the animals were recovered, but it was not the kind of start to inspire Carrington with confidence in his new men.[32]

A week after their arrival Carrington enlisted 500 of them in their first serious military operations. The Basotho, mainly, it seems, Bereng's and Maama's regiments, were occupying the heights opposite him during the day and retiring to nearby villages at night. If Carrington was to make any progress towards Matsieng and Maseru he would have to take command of these heights, and as a first step he decided to destroy the villages. He divided his attacking force into two columns. The first, under Brabant, was 645 men strong, with almost half, 300, made up by the burghers. The second, under himself, was 485 men strong, of whom 200 were burghers. Each column was supported by a seven-pounder gun. Brabant's column was to break through Azariele's

---

[26] *JME* 1881, p. 59, Dr. Casalis to his family, 2 December 1880, as translated by Germond (1967: 367).
[27] Rhodes House Library, Oxford, MSS Afr. s.969, Kennan Papers, Letters home from South Africa, 1874-1900, No. 60, Thomas Kennan to his parents, December 1880.
[28] Barkly (1893: 257).
[29] C.2821, p. 86, 'Summary of Events reported since the 30th November, Basutoland'.
[30] CA, Acc. 459, Brabant's Autobiography, pp. 104, 117; Germond (1967: 371), *The Times*, 19 January 1881, referred to by the Paris Mission; Woon (1909: 207-8).
[31] Woon (1909: 188); *Cape Argus*, 11 December 1880, 'The Native War'; Deare (1930: 24 May).
[32] C.2821, pp. 100-1, Greer, 'Summary of Events ....', 14 December 1880, *Cape Argus*, 9 December 1880.

Nek and to destroy the villages beyond. Carrington's column was to create a diversion by moving off to the right, towards Phoqoane.

As soon as Carrington moved out a large Basotho force appeared from the south and threatened to seize a hill on his right. Carrington sent off the CMR to forestall them, and the burghers, acting without orders, dashed off after them, leaving Carrington with just 200 men in a dangerously exposed position. As the Basotho closed in on him he formed a square, and as they charged he slowly moved to higher ground. In a letter to a lady friend he described the battle as 'rare pretty'. He had 'got surrounded', he wrote, 'by some 4000 to 5000 and only had 200 men, but real good ones, and it was all the more exciting because the enemy thought they had got us and could eat us up at their pleasure. I felt in all my glory and would not have missed it for £1000 paid down. I really felt as safe as in London and so it was as long as the men stood steady.'[33] In the meantime the CMR and the burghers had taken only part of the hill, and were now given orders to retire to the square.

While this was going on Brabant's column, confronted by about 1,000 Basotho, had been brought to a halt, and Carrington, hearing of this, ordered it to fall back, and by 11 a.m. the entire force was back in camp. Only two men had been killed, but there were several casualties, mainly men struck by spent bullets and ricochets, including Carrington himself, who was wounded slightly on the knee. On the Basotho side the casualties were much higher, but once again the Cape had achieved very little.[34]

In his official report Carrington wrote that the burghers had 'behaved well', even though they had dashed off without orders and had been 'rather wild in retiring from the hill'.[35] His men were less diplomatic. According to one officer they quickly fell behind in the attack on the hill, 'lying behind stones in a helpless manner'. The CMR went on, calling out to the burghers to follow them, but although they made some advance they 'would not come up to the firing line', pretending not to understand their orders. Only one man came and stood with the CMR, and he was an Englishmen who begged them not to mix him up 'with this – set of curs'. They did, however, understand the order to retreat, and rushed down so quickly that they put the CMR in danger.[36]

In spite of Carrington's official report word got round the camp that 'the Dutchmen' were responsible for the day's failure, and Carrington's command was now plagued, especially after the outbreak of the Transvaal rebellion, by having volunteers and conscripts living in separate camps, divided by language and even by loyalty. On 18 December about 70 more burghers arrived from Hope Town, but he was still far short of the reinforcements he needed. The war below the Drakensberg was going well and soon more troops could be expected from there, but at the same time the war in Basutoland was coming under increasing criticism in the Cape because it was diverting resources away from the Transvaal. Carrington was also still waiting for the swords and the Martini-Henry rifles he so badly needed. For the time being, therefore, he brought all the troops back to the camp at Mafeteng for a Christmas party and a week of sport and races.[37]

---

[33] CA, Acc. 232, Carrington to Mrs Kingsley, 31 December 1880.
[34] C.2821, pp. 112-3, Tennant to Sprigg, 13 December 1880; C.2821, pp. 119-21, Carrington to Assistant Adjutant-General, 17 December 1880; C.2821, p. 112, Greer, 'Summary of Events which have been reported since the 14th December', 21 December 1880; Woon (1909: 188-93); Deare (1930: 24 May); Gon (1984: 45-6), relying in part on the *Graaff-Reinet Herald*, 1 January 1881.
[35] C.2821, p. 121, Carrington to Assistant Adjutant-General, 17 December 1880.
[36] Woon (1909: 188-93).
[37] Gon (1984: 47) based on the *Graaff-Reinet Herald*, 2 February 1881.

On their side the Basotho now realised that the war was going to be won or lost in the south. According to a Mosotho prisoner, the sons of Letsie held all the heights barring the road to Morija and Matsieng, Masupha had already sent help under the command of his son Senekane, and his eldest son Lepoqo was coming up with more men. The Basotho's force was not less than 8,000. 'They were so confident that they were grazing cattle only a few miles behind their lines, and only those cattle which were normally sent to the cattle posts had in fact been sent to the Maloti.[38] Dr. Casalis, at Morija, confirmed this report. The women, he wrote, were 'busy weeding the lands' while the cattle were 'fattening themselves in the fine pastures of the Lerato valley. .... each battle inspires the Basuto with renewed courage'.[39] Hermann Dieterlen, the missionary at Hermon, close to the Mafeteng/Wepener road, set out shortly before Christmas to visit his colleagues at Morija. After leaving the war zone, he wrote,

> the aspect of the country alters. There are women reaping fields of native corn and a few herds of cattle in the pastures which, thanks to the recent rains, are now green, and flocks of white sheep with a six-months' fleece on their back.[40]

Maeder, the missionary at Siloe in the south, reported that all the local Bataung men had gone north to the fighting zone. The Basotho, he wrote, were 'strong and well armed. They have no difficulty in procuring the rifles and ammunition which they need.' The tribe was 'exasperated and determined to die for its arms'.[41]

Shortly before Christmas the long-awaited Martini-Henry rifles and swords arrived, and also more artillery – four 75-pounder howitzers as well as some seven-pounder guns – under the newly formed Cape Field Artillery which had replaced the CMR Artillery Troop. Although Carrington was still not up to the strength he wanted, and although heavy rains had now set in, he had to resume the initiative. He moved his forward camp to Phoqoane, and early in the New Year he began sending out his patrols again. At first he enjoyed some minor success. In an engagement on 10 January it was claimed that about 60 Basotho were killed, and Shervinton, now back in the fray after being wounded, believed that the Basotho had 'found out the difference of the Martini already'.[42]

Then, on Friday 14 January, in one of the most significant engagements in the war, Carrington sent out a large force under Brabant's command in the direction of Thaba Tšoeu, about 16 kilometres east of Mafeteng. It was almost a thousand strong – 180 infantry and 750 mounted men, including about 400 burghers, while men from the Native Contingent (made up of police and *Maketetoa*) acted as scouts. They set off at dawn in a damp mist, and after several kilometres they came to two villages, Raliemere's in the open country and Sepechele's on the higher ground towards Thaba-Tšoeu. Brabant ordered the burghers to attack and destroy Raliemere's. They raced off, seized the undefended village and put it to the torch. Excited by this easy victory, and acting without orders, they then galloped off towards Sepechele's to do the same again. Before they could reach the village Maama and his regiment suddenly rode out of the mist. The burghers turned and fled back

---

[38] C.2821, p. 112, Greer, 'Summary of Events which have been reported since the 14th December', 21 December 1880. See also *Cape Argus*, 8 December 1880, 'The Native War'.
[39] *JME* 1881, p. 104, Dr. Casalis to his family, Christmas 1880, as translated by Germond (1967: 368).
[40] *JME* 1881, p. 107, Dieterlen to his family, 28 December 1880, as translated by Germond (1967: 369).
[41] *JME* 1881, pp. 99-100, Maeder to Committee members, 21 December 1880, as translated by Germond (1967: 367-8).
[42] Shervinton (1899: 78-80). See also *Cape Argus*, 13 January 1881, 'The Fight in Basutoland (Official)'.

towards the main column, but the Basotho, on their tough little ponies, caught them up and swung out with their battle-axes and assegais. Ten burghers, including their Commandant, Erasmus, were killed before the rest reached the safety of the square. The Basotho's attack on the square was beaten off, and in the pouring rain the two forces then fired blindly at each other for some time. At first Brabant's men had the advantage because of their heavy artillery, but then the gun carriages collapsed and they were put out of action. At this point the 2nd Yeomanry were ordered to charge with their new swords, but this proved a fiasco: without proper training they effected very little, and finally it was the fixed bayonets of the infantry that drove the Basotho from the field.

As Brabant himself acknowledged, it was an 'empty victory', and one of the Cape newspapers frankly described the engagement as 'disastrous'.[43] In all the Cape forces lost 16 killed and 21 wounded, but it was not so much their casualties that disheartened them. The Yeoman had failed to make good use of their new swords, and when charged by Maama's men the burghers had failed to make a stand. The burghers had already been threatening to return home, only falling into line after Carrington had 'blown them up'.[44] Now they were so angered by Carrington's official report, damning them for turning around and taking flight instead of dismounting and holding their ground, and by his assistant staff-officer's telegraphic report, in which one of the headings was 'Burghers bolted', that within a few weeks most of their force slipped out of the country and only 300 remained.[45] 'If this is what we may expect from this branch of the service', wrote one disillusioned observer, 'the sooner a less rotten reed is provided for the Colony ... the better'.[46]

By contrast, the Basotho had shown great courage and resolve. According to Shervinton, whose horse was shot under him, 'The fighting lasted from 5.30 to 9.30, and was the hottest I have been in, either in Zululand or elsewhere'.[47] 'The rebels never fought with such desperation', one newspaper correspondent reported. 'They coolly received our charges, and fired at ten paces, and to the final moment showed no more sign of broken power and waning pluck than on the first day at Qualabane.'[48] For Maama the battle was a personal triumph. He claimed to have killed Erasmus, the Boer commander, himself,[49] and his praises were like a great shout of victory:

> I struck White Man, I threw him down:
> He fell before the face of my horse,

---

[43] Army Museum, Tylden Papers, Box 34057, Notebook V, p. 63, letter from Port Elizabeth paper, undated, quoted in Tylden (1950A: 163).

[44] CA, Acc. 459, Brabant's Autobiography, pp. 108-9. National Army Museum, Tylden Papers, Box 34057, Note-book IV, p. 15, Deare's evidence.

[45] *Cape Argus*, 17 January 1881, 'The Native War', Tennant to Colonial Secretary, 14 January 1881; *Cape Argus*, 5 February 1881, 'The Battle of Tweefontein', Carrington to Assistant Adjutant-General Colonial Forces, 16 January 1881, reprinted from Government Gazette, 4 February 1881; *The Journal*, 24 January 1881. 'The War in Basutoland'; Shervinton (1899: 82); Deare (1930: 24 May); Gon (1984: 49) quoting *Graaff-Reinet Herald*, 13 March 1881. For departures (because of the expiry of the three month period of service) and desertions (because of the 'bolting' accusation and the war in the Transvaal), see also *Cape Argus*, 3 February 1881, 'The Native War'; 4 February 1881, 'The Native War. The Mutiny of the Burghers'; and 5 February 1881, 'The Native War'; *The Journal*, 9 and 25 February 1881.

[46] *The Journal*, 9 February 1881, quoting a letter from *The Friend*, 22 January.

[47] Shervinton (1899: 81).

[48] Gon (1984: 49), quoting *Graaff-Reinet Herald*, 2 February 1881.

[49] Mangoaela (1957: 241).

> He fell before the face of my horse, Koloboi;
> His friends gathered up a nonentity,
> They took up a corpse, the spirit was gone,
> They collected it up, they dumped it on a wagon,
> They acted as if he would wake!
> ....
> The owner of the grey horse was sleeping.
> Why are you sleeping, White Man's child,
> While the steady rains are falling?[50]

Lerotholi's praise poet gloated that the Cape commanders should now look for their men on the ground:

> You can choose them from the corpses, they're dead![51]

In the Cape papers the battle was referred to as Tweefontein, a name that is not known locally. Among the Basotho it was called *Ntoa ea Lisabole*, the Battle of the Swords.[52]

About a fortnight later, on 28 January, the Cape forces suffered another serious reverse. In the war below the Drakensberg the Basotho and their allies had been defeated and driven into the Maloti – a great success for the colonial troops there. But then John Austen, the old magistrate of the Quthing District, pursued the fugitives up the Orange and in an ill-judged attack he and eight of his men were killed. Austen's body was badly mutilated, and his head (no doubt to be used for medicine) was sent by the Batlokoa chief Lelingoana to Letsie as a gesture of goodwill.[53] According to one official, 'The melancholy fate of Mr. Austen ... seemed for the time to have spread a gloom and panic through the whole of the District ....'[54]

There was further fighting on the Mafeteng front in February, but again Carrington and his men could make no significant advance. The Basotho's resistance was as determined as ever, and in one engagement, near the village of Ramabilikoe's, about three hundred men charged right on to the bayonets of the waiting infantry, and two of them, whose names were long remembered with honour, Setaka Ranthako and Lefu Ramarothole, broke through and were killed inside the line. 'It was the most desperate charge I have seen yet ...' Shervinton wrote.[55]

Carrington had intended to move back towards Mafeteng, but the rains were now so torrential that he had to remain where he was. The enforced immobility further lowered morale. The rain-soaked roads became impassable for the seven-pounder guns, which could no longer be taken out on offensive operations and could only be used for defence. The camps became sodden and water-logged. The tents were inadequate. For weeks on end neither officers nor men had anything dry to wear. They had to throw away meat for want of fuel to cook it. Fever and dysentery were becoming

---

[50] Damane and Sanders (1974: 155, 156). Translation slightly changed.
[51] Damane and Sanders (1974: 145). Translation slightly changed.
[52] Damane and Sanders (1974: 155).
[53] Mangoaela (1957: 80), translated from the Sesotho; National Army Museum, Tylden Papers, Box 34057, Notebook V, pp. 144-5, statement of Ramuso Makhoana, 10 July 1938; Tylden (1950A: 164).
[54] A.25-'81, p. 2, E. Ayliff, Acting RM Quthing, to Griffith, 8 March 1881.
[55] Shervinton (1899: 83-4); CA, Accessions 459, Brabant's Autobiography, pp. 111-2; Deare (1930: 24 May); Tylden (1950A: 165).

widespread.[56] There were desertions even among the men of the CMR, the cream of Carrington's force, their old grievances about their terms and conditions resurfacing in the disappointments of the war.[57] To add to the Cape's troubles there was bad news from the Transvaal, where the Boers had defeated the imperial forces at Laing's Nek and were soon to inflict the humiliation of Majuba. There were fears in London that the Dutch-speaking colonists and Free Staters would join the rebels beyond the Vaal in a hostile and united Afrikaner front, fears which were soon to induce the Gladstone government to make what many regarded as an ignominious peace with Kruger and his colleagues.[58]

On the other two fronts, Maseru in the centre and Leribe in the north, there was even less reason to believe that the war could be drawn to a quick conclusion.

The war in the centre

In the opening stages of the war it had seemed that the Maseru front would be more important than the Mafeteng. The greater part of the CMR's forces was posted there – 300 men as against 200 in Mafeteng, and with artillery support as well – and Lerotholi's attack on Mafeteng on 21 September was fully matched by Masupha's attack on Maseru on 10 October.

There was a further attack on 28 October. At ten in the morning, according to Bayly's report, 'the rebel cavalry' came charging in from the south and south-west and captured some horses and oxen. A mass of infantry followed, about 500 men taking up their positions in the rocks and dongas around the town and in the ruins of the school that had been destroyed in the first attack. They could not be dislodged by rifle fire, but were eventually driven out by 'a most gallant charge' by the African forces, including the loyal Basotho contingent, reinforced by a few white volunteers and 20 CMR. Three men were killed on the Cape side, while the rebels left 21 dead on the field. An attack on Fort Gordon was easily beaten off.[59]

This, however, was the last serious fighting on the Maseru front. Clarke, instead of marching into Maseru, had been diverted to Mafeteng and made his headquarters there, and after that Maseru was merely a side-show. In the initial attack on the village Masupha had been helped by some of the sons of Letsie: in the later stages of the Mafeteng fighting the sons of Letsie were helped by Masupha. Some reinforcements were sent to Bayly at Maseru, but most of the new men were allocated to Carrington. The way to Ladybrand was kept open, and heliograph communication through the Free State with Mafeteng was established, but otherwise the Cape's forces were completely hemmed in. The *Mabelete* occupied the hills around Maseru, firing into the village at will, and it was not considered safe 'to go beyond the end of the garden of the Residency.'[60] At the beginning of the year Bayly's

---

[56] CA, ACC. 232, Carrington to Mrs Kingsley, 31 December 1880; Rhodes House Library, Oxford, MSS Afr. S.969, Kennan Papers, undated letter (No. 61) from Thomas Kennan; Deare (1930: 31 May).

[57] G.5-'83, pp. 61-2, Gordon, 'Report on the Colonial Regular Forces', 5 October 1882; Gon (1984: 49). According to Gordon men recruited in England were more likely to desert than men recruited in the Colony, since there were 'no near deterrent social ties against deserting'. See also *Cape Argus*, 13 December 1880, 'Capture of Deserters'.

[58] Schreuder (1969: 3-4).

[59] C.2821, pp. 32-3, Bayly to Assistant Adjutant-General, 30 October 1880; Walton (1958B: 6), quoting George Hobson; Ambrose (1993: 73), quoting *The Friend*, 4 November 1880; *The Journal*, 10 November 1880, 'At The Front'.

[60] Laurence (1881: 97). See also *The Journal*, 7 January 1881, 'Maseru', and A.25-'81, p. 3, Davies to Griffith, 21

forces drove the rebels off the two nearest hills, the World and the Flesh, but they were not strong enough to capture and hold the third, the Devil.[61] And at the beginning of February, when they were ordered to create a diversion to relieve the pressure on the Mafeteng front, they sent out a patrol which burnt a few villages, drove off Lepoqo Masupha when he attacked, killing about a dozen of his men, but again had to retreat to the camp because they lacked the strength to hold on to their position.[62]

According to Davies, the local magistrate, there was only sufficient force to garrison Maseru, and this might well have been the case.[63] There were about 1,000 Basotho women and children who had taken refuge at the camp and who had to be protected.[64] Even so it seems surprising that Bayly did not take more initiative, and that, while Carrington was engaged in such heavy fighting in the south, he was allowed to keep 300 of the CMR, the pick of the Cape's fighting men, relatively inactive in Fort Gordon. In February 1881, as a result of his refusal to obey Carrington's orders, he was recalled to Cape Town 'to show reason why he should not be dismissed',[65] but there was no change in strategy after he had gone.

As the troops looked out towards the Berea plateau, they could see

> the smoke rising daily from the Berea villages, the cattle and horses grazing along the grassy slopes, and the nightly watch fires upon prominent peaks and ridges', all proclaiming 'the presence of the enemy in sufficient force to prevent any forward movement by the meagre garrison at Maseru. Contemptuously enough do they ride to and fro, till their lands, and pursue their ordinary avocations and pleasures, conscious that no aggressive movements of ours can take place without timely notice being given of them.

And all the time the garrison was kept on the alert by rumours of an impending third attack.[66]

The war in the north

In the first stage of the war there had been no fighting on the Leribe front. The loyalist Jonathan Molapo had withdrawn from Fobane to the mountain fortress of Tsikoane, while Major Bell, with the help of his police, Stanton's Light Horse and Basotho *Mateketoa*, had put Hlotse Heights into a state of defence. Joel Molapo and Ramanella might have held back because they were waiting on the outcome of the first battles around Mafeteng and Maseru, and several of the chiefs around them still felt constrained by loyalty to Jonathan.[67] But there were repeated messages from Masupha and

---

March 1881.

[61] *The Journal*, 7 January 1881, 'Maseru'.

[62] *Cape Argus*, 10 February 1881, 'The Native Wars. A Patrol from Maseru', and *The Journal*, 10 February 1881, 'The Fight at Maseru', both quoting Bayly's official telegram, 6 February 1881; *The Journal*, 17 February 1881, 'The Battle of Mejametalane'; PEMS Archives, Paris, Jousse to Casalis, 10 February 1881; National Army Museum, Tylden Papers, Box 34057, Notebook V, p. 36.

[63] G.25-'81, p. 3, Davies to Griffith, 21 March 1881. For the same judgement see also *The Journal*, 31 December 1880, 'Maseru'.

[64] LNA, S9/1/2/2, Griffith to Ayliff, 30 November 1880.

[65] *Cape Argus*, 21 February 1881, 'The Native War. Colonel Bayly's Case'; Ambrose (1993: 76-7), quoting article by 'Rienzi' in *The Friend*, 17 March 1881. See also Rhodes House Library, Oxford, MSS Afr. S.969, Kennan Papers, Letter no. 61, Thomas Kennan to his parents, undated.

[66] *The Journal*, 7 January 1881, 'Maseru'.

[67] CA, Griffith Papers, Bell to Griffith, 31 October 1880.

Lerotholi urging them to take action, and they must have been encouraged to respond when they heard that the Cape forces were being held in check.

The attack when it came was not on the scale of the attacks on Mafeteng and Maseru, but because of recent heavy rains it took the defenders by surprise. Shortly before six on the morning of 8 November 600 of Joel's horsemen raced in. As the defenders rushed to their positions Joel's men split into two detachments. The first managed to get into the police barracks, but after several hours' fighting was driven off. The second was eventually repelled by the men in the church under Jervis, Major Bell's clerk, but not before some of the attackers had thrust their rifles through the loopholes in the walls. Jonathan and some of his men rode in from Tsikoane, but too late to play any significant part. On the Cape side three men were severely wounded, several buildings were burnt and some stock was captured.[68]

The rebels left 17 bodies on the field and must have lost more, but for Joel, as for the chiefs at Maseru, it was symbolic that he had been able to wreak destruction right in the heart of the enemy's stronghold. His praise poet told how he had fought against 'strange, foreign regiments', against Griffith and Barkly, and 'against Major Bell, the mighty champion from the Cape.' Even the doctors with their protective medicine horns had been powerless against him:

> He's just gone into the Magistrate's,
> There was a blaze, the doctors' houses were burnt,
> Burnt was the house of Potse the Letebele,
> Where the medicine horns were kept in the pass.[69]

After the battle Joel withdrew to the heights of Sebothoane, only about two kilometres away, and other rebel forces began to appear, the regiments of Ramanella and of Khethisa and some of the other sons of Molapo, about 2,000 men in all. A further attack on the camp was feared, but instead, on Thursday, 11 November, the rebels turned their forces against Jonathan's mountain fortress of Tsikoane. In the camp it was confidently expected that Jonathan, though weakened by desertions, would have no difficulty in keeping them at bay. Instead, he was betrayed by one of his leading councillors, many more of his followers turned against him, and Tsikoane was quickly taken. Jonathan's village was burnt to the ground, most of his cattle and horses were taken, and he himself fled to the camp, where eventually he was joined by about 260 men.[70]

Joel's praise poet mocked their headlong flight to the camp, where the head policeman, Jan Mokhahlane, could only provide them with a skinny, unsalted beast for their food:

---

[68] LNA, L2/1/2, Bell to Griffith, 9 November 1880; C.2821, p. 36, 'Summary of Events reported from Basutoland since the 10th November'; *Quarterly Paper of the Bloemfontein Mission*, January 1881, No. 51, pp. 19-21, Champernowne, 12 November 1880, 'The Attack on Thlotse'; Laurence (1881: 136-8), quoting *The Friend*, 25 November 1880. Widdicombe (1895: 172-5) and Taylor (1972: 62-4) increase the number of attackers and say Ramanella's forces would have joined them if they had been able to cross the Caledon. It is clear from the account in *The Friend* that these extra forces began to appear only after the engagement was over.

[69] Damane and Sanders (1974: 189). Translation slightly altered.

[70] CA, Griffith Papers, Bell to Griffith, 11 November 1880; LNA, L2/1/2, Bell to Ayliff, 19 November 1880; *Quarterly Paper of the Bloemfontein Mission*, Jan. 1881, No. 51, pp. 19-21, Champernowne, 12 November 1880, 'The Attack on Thlotse', and pp. 21-23, Widdicombe, 4 December 1880, 'Siege of Thlotse'; Widdicombe (1895: 178-9); Taylor (1972: 68-9); Mangoaela (1957: 146), the praises of Seshophe Ramanella.

> The poor men have run a long way,
> Perhaps they'll cough and be ill,
> Perhaps they'll have a pain in the chest!⁷¹

'I remember so well the scene', wrote Canon Widdicombe later.

> The men cowed, beaten, and demoralized, ... coming in by twos and threes, ... all of them hungry and exhausted, and most of them stark naked, having thrown off their blankets when the hand-to-hand struggle began. By the time they all reached us it was quite dark, and Mr. Charles Bell [Major Bell's son] and I went out with lanterns and distributed among them several bales of coloured blankets, which had fortunately been left at a local trader's ... They were, of course, utterly destitute, ... and until they could build for themselves they had to huddle together for several weeks outside the fort, sleeping in rows round its walls.⁷²

Afterwards they were formed into a 'Native Contingent', together with Tokonya's Hlubi and others, under the command of Charlie Bell.

Most of Jonathan's men had now gone over to Joel. At Leribe, about ten kilometres to the north, some of his father's old followers, under Nathanael Makotoko, still remained loyal, but Joel soon 'ate them up' and they too had to take refuge at the camp.⁷³ In Maseru and Mafeteng it was still being argued that many of the common people would have sided with the government but for their fear of the chiefs. The events in the north suggested otherwise. Here was a strong chief who stood by the government, but his people deserted him. Jonathan's power was broken, and it would be several years before he recovered it.

The situation at Hlotse Heights was now desperate. The rebel forces around the Camp numbered between 3,000 and 4,000, with Joel and his brothers to the east and Ramanella and his sons to the west. Canon Widdicombe described how they

> formed a cordon which surrounded us on all sides .... They poisoned the water in one of our springs, and cut off our supply from another .... From daylight to dark they kept up a desultory, dropping fire upon us, which was exceedingly irritating, though it did but little real harm. They burnt all the outlying huts ... There were now over seven hundred half-starved natives to be fed daily, besides fifty Europeans .... food was rapidly failing, and there was no means of getting a fresh supply.⁷⁴

Ammunition was also running low, and it was unsafe for the stock to go out to graze.

Immediately after the attack on the camp Major Bell had sent a message to Maseru calling for ammunition and reinforcements.⁷⁵ On 11 November, the very day on which it was thrust into Griffith's hands, 200 men of the Diamond Fields Horse (otherwise known as the Kimberley Horse) reached Jackman's Drift on the Caledon, the crossing point for Maseru, and without a moment's delay Griffith despatched them to Hlotse Heights. Four days later, on the morning of 15 November, after a difficult journey through the rough terrain of the Free State, they fought their way across the Caledon and up to the summit of the camp. They then regrouped, and with the help of the rest of the garrison drove the rebels from their positions around the camp,

---

⁷¹ Damane and Sanders (1974: 200). Translation slightly changed.
⁷² Widdicombe (1895: 180).
⁷³ CA, Griffith Papers, Bell to Griffith, 11 and 18 November 1880; Widdicombe (1895: 180-2).
⁷⁴ Widdicombe (1895: 182). See also Taylor (1972: 67-8).
⁷⁵ CA, Griffith Papers, Bell to Griffith, n.d. (received 11 November 1880).

destroyed their fortifications, and set fire to several of the nearby villages. According to Bell they were only just in time.[76]

The Diamond Fields Horse were a powerful addition to Bell's garrison. They were drawn from several different nationalities and many of them, like the men of Stanton's Light Horse, were rough, hard-drinking adventurers out for excitement and loot, and their 'irregularities' as they passed through the Free State had already given rise to official complaint from President Brand.[77] But they wore proper uniforms and had good horses, and they were the first men on the colonial side to be armed with the new Martini-Henrys, which they had used to good effect in their attack on the rebels. They were also ably led by Captain William Moorsom Laurence, the son of an Anglican clergyman, who prided himself on his descent from Admiral Sir Robert Moorsom, the commander of "The Revenge" at Trafalgar. Laurence had taken part in the Zulu War and had been editing the *Diamond News* at Kimberley. Though only 24 when he was appointed to the command, he quickly imposed a strong discipline on his troops. The contrast between Laurence and Stanton was striking – Laurence, who had won prizes for Latin verse at his public school, Haileybury, and the uneducated Stanton, whose battle-cry as he killed each rebel was 'There go *your* brains into your hat!'[78]

After this initial engagement Laurence was full of confidence. The slopes of Hlotse Heights were free from the enemy and the road to the drift across the Caledon was open. The Basotho had at last encountered troops who were better armed than themselves, and he fancied they would now give no trouble for some time.[79]

Two weeks later, on 25 November, another volunteer corps fought its way into Hlotse Heights, about 200 men of the Transvaal Horse under Captain Ferreira, with two heavy guns, one six-pounder and one three-pounder.[80] Ferreira's men, like those of the Diamond Fields Horse, belonged to many different nationalities, and according to Dr Taylor were made up of 'thieves, ruffians, deserters from the Army, and bad lots generally'. His two guns, however, were 'very well served by some deserters from the Royal Artillery'. As for Ferreira himself, he was

> an illiterate Dutchman, and a good type of the medieval mercenary commander, who sold the services of himself and his men to the highest bidder. ... [He] was not a bad fellow on the whole, an adventurer who had some genius for commanding men, and who by rough and ready means kept a certain amount of discipline among his wild followers.[81]

'A certain amount of discipline', perhaps, but not very much. In order to boost his income Ferreira opened a canteen in his camp, which made him more inclined to overlook his men's drunkenness and even to encourage it.[82]

With the arrival of the two corps of volunteers Bell now had about 500 white troops as well as

---

[76] CA, Griffith Papers, Bell to Griffith, 18 November 1880; LNA, L2/1/2, Bell to Ayliff, 19 November 1880; Laurence (1881: 76-80, 139-40) quoting Laurence's account and article in *The Friend*, 25 November 1880; Widdicombe (1895: 183).

[77] C.2821, p. 61, Strahan to Kimberley, 23 November 1880; C.2821, p. 63, President Brand to Strahan, 9 November 1880; Laurence (1882: ix); Taylor (1972: 72).

[78] Taylor (1972: 64). See also Laurence (1882: 1-5); Taylor (1972: 81-2).

[79] Laurence (1882: 80).

[80] LNA, L2/1/2, Bell to Carrington, 3 December 1880.

[81] Taylor (1972: 74-5).

[82] Taylor (1972: 79).

about 700 in the Native Contingent made up of his police, Tokonya's Hlubi and the *Mateketoa* of Jonathan and some other chiefs. Like Maseru, Hlotse Heights was no longer in serious danger and its supply route was secure, but, again like Maseru, its garrison was too weak to mount any significant offensive. The new Martini-Henrys were not as effective as they should have been because of a shortage of ammunition.[83]

Meanwhile, in spite of Laurence's confidence, the rebels maintained their positions on the hills and in the villages around Hlotse Heights. They were so well supplied with ammunition from the Free State that at times it seemed that they were firing it off merely to demonstrate how well provided they were.[84] They knew that they could not mount an attack on the main fortifications at the camp, but they could threaten the more exposed and outlying positions, they could plunder stock, and above all by their constant presence they could prevent any serious outbreak by the colonial forces. Beyond two or three kilometres around Hlotse Heights the country was entirely under rebel control.[85] Like the Basotho at Mafeteng and Maseru, Joel and his comrades in arms were showing a courage and determination that their enemies had never expected. 'They are brave', wrote Amos Dormoy, the PEMS missionary at Leribe, 'in the manner of men who have been deprived of everything and who therefore have nothing to lose. They are brave because they fight like desperate men and prefer death to servitude.'[86] Faced with this resistance, the most that the garrison could do was to provoke and harass the rebels until, as they hoped, reinforcements arrived. The result was a series of inconclusive engagements and skirmishes which left the two sides in much the same positions as before.

For a few weeks after the arrival of Ferreira and his men there was a lull in the fighting, and there were those who believed that the rebels were 'cowed' as they saw the camp's fortifications being strengthened and well guarded convoys to the Free State established.[87] But it was not long before fighting began again. The camp was suffering from a lack of firewood, and on the morning of 2 December Bell sent out Ferreira with 300 men and six wagons in the direction of Tsikoane. At the same time Jonathan, 'most imprudently' and without orders according to Bell, went off with two wagons to the Khomokhoana river in order to get grain from a nearby village. Joel and Khethisa, seeing this, sent in their regiments. Jonathan's wagons were seized, 15 of his men were killed, and he himself barely escaped with his life to the Free State before making his humiliated way back to the camp.[88]

Soon after dawn on 14 December there was another engagement when the rebels began attacking one of the camp's pickets, which was manned by the Transvaal Horse. Ferreira sent out reinforcements, the Diamond Fields Horse were drawn in, and by 11 a.m. the fighting was general. Most of the Basotho were driven off, but some were trapped among some rocks near the camp, and when the fire became too hot for them they had to dash back over 200 yards of exposed country to the hills behind. After the battle twenty bodies were found among the rocks, and at least as many must have been killed in the open. On the Cape side several men were wounded, and one of the Diamond Fields officers was killed.[89]

A month later, on 6 January 1881, the rebels attacked in force. Just before sunset, according to

---

[83] LNA, L2/1/2, Bell to Colonial Secretary, 28 November 1881; Laurence (1882: 95).
[84] Laurence (1882: 95). See also Widdicombe (1895: 188).
[85] *JME* 1881, pp. 178-9, Dormoy to Director, 28 January 1881.
[86] *JME* 1881, p. 179, Dormoy to Director, 28 January 1881, as translated by Germond (1967: 372).
[87] Widdicombe (1895: 184).
[88] LNA, L2/1/2, Bell to Carrington, 3 December 1880; Widdicombe (1895: 193-4).
[89] LNA, L2/1/2, Bell to Sprigg, 19 December 1880; Laurence (1882: 90-2).

Widdicombe,

> large commandos were seen advancing ... from all quarters .... and soon there poured forth, stream upon stream, the whole rebel host. Down they rushed from the slopes and gorges of Sebotoane, and over the "neck" from Khethisa's; upwards they clambered from Ramanella's and Tlasua's .... In twenty minutes we were completely surrounded, and for six hours – from sunset until one in the morning when the moon went down – an incessant fusilade was kept up; but as our men were all well under cover only very few of them were hit.[90]

'It was a desperate fight', wrote Dr Taylor. 'The constant volleys were deafening ... The air seemed alive with bullets .... In the darkness one hardly knew what was happening ....'[91]

The attackers' object was to seize the camp's stock, which was kraaled close to the huts of Jonathan and his men on the side of the camp overlooking the Hlotse River. Although outnumbered the *Mateketoa*, led by Molapo's old adviser, Nathanael Makotoko – 'a brave Christian chief', as Bell described him – had the advantage of a rocky height from which they were able to hold off their assailants, and about midnight, when their ammunition was exhausted, the *Mabelete* finally withdrew. Two of Jonathan's men had been killed and four wounded. The rebels' losses were known only to themselves.[92]

On 29 January there was another engagement, which in Laurence's view was 'likely to redound very little to our credit with the enemy, or to our military reputation'.[93] It began, however, with a bold sortie by the Hlubi chief, Tokonya, the man who had been ousted by Masupha before the fighting began. Throughout the war Tokonya and his men had been posted at Hlotse Heights, and had won the admiration of everyone in the camp – 'the bravest lot of men I ever met with', wrote Taylor, 'always in the very front of the fight'.[94] About 50 of them set out from the camp before sunrise, rode six or seven kilometres to the south, fired into the village of one of the leading rebels, Khethisa, and then retreated. They were pursued by Khethisa's men, who were soon joined by Joel's. Ferreira's Transvaal Horse turned out in support, but according to Laurence 'in a state of utter disorder'. As Joel's men poured down from Leribe mountain, threatening Ferreira's flank, the Diamond Fields Horse rode out from the camp and provided cover as the Transvaal Horse retreated. After a while the enemy retired, not, as Laurence admitted, because they had been defeated, but 'because they wanted their breakfast'. By 11 a.m. the fight was over. There were hardly any casualties on either side.[95]

The next significant engagement was on 11 February. Three kilometres south of the camp was a low flat-topped hill overlooking the Hlotse River. Joel's men had established their position close by, and many of them used to go down every morning to gather mealies in the surrounding fields. Bell sent out a mixed force of 500 men under Ferreira to occupy the hill and to gather some mealies themselves. Setting off at 3.30 a.m., Ferreira sent forward 100 men of the Diamond Fields Horse with

---

[90] Widdicombe (1895: 189-90).
[91] Taylor (1972: 80).
[92] LNA, L2/1/2, Bell to Staff Officer, OC Basutoland, Mafeteng, 7 January 1881; Laurence (1882: 93-5); Widdicombe (1895: 189-90); Taylor (1972: 80).
[93] Laurence (1882: 101).
[94] Taylor (1972: 87-8).
[95] Laurence (1882: 101-4).

60 of the Native Contingent to achieve these objectives, while the rest of the force under his own command occupied another height halfway between the hill and the camp. Khethisa's village was about four kilometres further south. While it was still dark 500-1000 of his men rode out and then, leaving their horses behind, crept up to within 200 metres of the hill and, according to Laurence, 'opened up a hot fire upon our men, who were fortunately well covered by the rocks surrounding the kopje which they held'.

Observing all this, about 1000 of Joel's men set out to attack the camp, thinking it was now defenceless, but were checked first by 'two tremendous volleys' from the Transvaal Horse and then, when they went round to the other side of the camp, by Stanton and 50 of his Light Horse.

In the meantime the Diamond Fields Horse were so outnumbered and hard pressed that Ferreira gave the order to retire.

On the Cape side several men were wounded and one officer killed. The rebels were rumoured to have lost up to 200 men, but Laurence's own estimate was that 70 were killed outright and about 140 wounded. According to Laurence, 'Never during the present war has a fight been maintained as this was for five hours (from 5 a.m. to 10 a.m.) against such tremendous odds'. But after gathering what Bell described as 'a quantity of maize' the colonial troops had been forced to make a hazardous retreat and the two sides were left in much the same position as before.[96]

The real significance of the encounter, however, lay in what happened outside the field of battle. Part of the large force of conscripted burghers that had arrived at Mafeteng at the beginning of January consisted of 200 men from Colesberg, who had been ordered to ride northwards to Hlotse Heights. They had taken their time, and it was 27 January before they reached Ficksburg in the Orange Free State, about 20 kilometres from Hlotse Heights. Over the next week or so they advanced a further eight kilometres, and when Bell went over and expostulated with Theunissen, their Commandant – 'an excellent specimen', wrote Laurence, 'of an ancient "dopper"' – he was told that it was 'impossible for him to march when it rained, or when it appeared likely to rain'. And when Bell suggested he should move on that day 'the Commandant held up his hands in pious horror at the idea of marching on a Sunday'.[97]

By 11 February, the day of the battle, the burghers had at last reached the banks of the Caledon opposite Hlotse Heights, where they could safely lie on the grass, smoke their pipes, and watch the engagement between Stanton's Light Horse and Joel's regiments. With the exception of the few Englishmen among them and 'about a dozen Dutchmen of a different stamp to the others', and in spite of Stanton's 'riding within earshot of them and obliging them with a string of epithets in their native language', they made no attempt to cross the river and help.[98]

According to Taylor, however, Theunissen at least made a show of ordering his men to cross the river, and a few days later came to the camp

> and entreated Colonel Bell to go over and see if he could do anything with the men, in the way of persuading them to do their duty. Colonel Bell rode over to their camp, and I accompanied him. When we got there, we found they had struck camp and disappeared bodily, men, horses, tents and wagons. Hearing they had gone to Ficksburg, we rode thither, and came upon them just outside the village, where they had off-saddled. Colonel Bell got them together and addressed

---

[96] LNA, L2/1/2, Bell to SO to OC Mafeteng, 17 February 1881; Laurence (1882: 106-11); Taylor (1972: 80-81).
[97] Laurence (1882: 105).
[98] Laurence (1882: 107).

them, telling them it was a most disgraceful and cowardly action to refuse to serve their country in its need, and asking them to reconsider their action and return to duty. When he had finished speaking, there was a dead silence in the ranks for a few moments, then a voice called out, '*Huis toe!*' ('Home!'), and without another word they rapidly saddled their horses and rode away in a cloud of dust. That was the last we ever saw of them.[99]

The desertion of the Colesberg burghers was the northern counterpart of the desertion of the main part of the burgher force in the south after they had 'bolted' at the battle of Sepechele's. As Taylor observed, they had little interest in the war, 'and resented being compelled to leave their farms and occupations, their wives and families, and proceed to an unknown and savage country, with the off-chance of being killed or badly wounded.'[100] Their departure was all the more serious because, as Bell reported at the beginning of January, his force was gradually decreasing from 'discharge, death and desertion'.[101] By the middle of January, according to Laurence, the Diamond Fields Horse had lost 10 men by desertions, Stanton's Light Horse about 20 and the Transvaal Horse nearly 30.[102]

'Desertions', wrote Taylor, 'were frequent …. They generally took place about dusk; a man would be seen leaving the lines and stealing down towards the river, the cry 'Deserter!' would be raised in camp, and out we would sally with our revolvers to pot at the deserter, who had to run the gauntlet of a hot fire or surrender, but he generally took his chance and made for the river.'[103]

The loyalty of the volunteers was placed under greater strain when the government fell into arrears with their pay. Mutiny and disbandment were threatened, and it needed all of Bell's persuasion and authority to make them stay.[104]

Throughout the campaign drunkenness was rife. Ferreira's canteen was only one among several, and the men could also get drunk in Ficksburg. Taylor, no doubt making the best of a good story, related how some of the men would 'enter Ficksburg quite sober, go straight to the magistrate's office, and place £2 on his table, stating that they intended to get drunk, and wished to pay the fine beforehand ….'[105] More seriously, Ficksburg, being neutral ground, was frequented by the rebels as well. 'Our men', wrote Taylor, 'used to take over rifles, revolvers, and ammunition and sell them to the enemy, the very men with whom perhaps they had been fighting the day before, and then spend the proceeds in a drunken orgy.'[106] In January, after serious disturbances, the Free State town was placed out of bounds.[107]

---

[99] Taylor (1972: 86-7). In fact 37 of the burghers, mainly Englishmen, stayed, but it seems that some if not all of these soon left as well: L2/1/2, Bell to CO Mafeteng, 17, 19 and 21 February 1880, and Bell to Sprigg, 20 February 1881.
[100] Taylor (1972: 86).
[101] LNA, L2/1/2, Bell to Staff Officer, O.C. Basutoland, 7 January 1881.
[102] Laurence (1882: 96).
[103] Taylor (1972: 79).
[104] LNA, L2/1/2, Bell to Staff Officer to CO Mafeteng, 5 and 24 February 1881, and Bell to Clarke, 24 February 1881.
[105] Taylor (1972: 79).
[106] Taylor (1972: 78).
[107] LNA, L2/1/2, Bell to Brand, 21 and 30 January 1881; Bell to Ferreira, 21 February 1881; Bell to Staff Officer to OC Mafeteng, 24 February 1881. According to Griffith about 1600 guns went missing during the war, believed to have been sold and fallen into rebel hands: A.24-'83, p. 84, Orpen to Sauer, 10 January 1882. One former NCO in the CMR set up as the garrison butcher in Maseru: 'He abstracted any rifle he saw lying

At times the camp's security was more directly threatened: 'the very sentinels', wrote Widdicombe, 'were often unfit for duty'.[108] In March one of the stores was closed by Bell 'because of drunkenness which seriously endangers the Garrison'.[109] Fights broke out between men from different corps, and the camp was plagued by thefts.[110]

The camp was relatively free of disease, though it suffered for a time from the effects of a spring that had been poisoned by the enemy and from 'a curious malady', as Taylor described it, which came to be known as 'fly sickness', since it seemed to be brought on by the swarms of flies that were infesting the camp.[111] A much greater hardship was the rain, which had been heavy since the outset of the war but which became an almost constant downpour from February onwards. As well as the obvious discomforts for men living under canvas, it made the task of keeping the camp supplied even more demanding and onerous. Taylor spelt out what was involved. The Caledon river became

> impassable for wagons, while the drifts down which the wagons had to come were a mass of sticky, slippery mud. When the wagons reached the edge of the water, they had to be unloaded into a small boat, which brought across their loads, then the oxen were taken out and made to swim the swollen river; next the wagon itself had to be floated across, then loaded up again with the goods brought over in the boat, and it had finally to make its way up a dreadfully steep road towards the camp.
>
> All the time this was going on we were subject to constant attacks by the enemy, and a large force had daily to be detailed to hold the road at all odds, and protect the workers in the river. The strain on the men's energies and our resources was immense. Men, stripped to their shirts, were up to their shoulders in the water, working to get oxen, wagons and goods over, while others struggled through the mud of the drifts, carrying the heavy cases uphill to the bank, and slipping back at every step .... This work had to be carried on all day and every day, and at night the men returned to camp worn out and drenched. ....
>
> Under these conditions there was small opportunity for us to make any important military moves, as all our time and strength were occupied in getting in supplies of food and ammunition to keep the camp going.[112]

Widdicombe depicted the hardships of the sentries at night, standing hour after hour in the driving, pitiless rain, and returning to their quarters in the morning sodden and exhausted.[113]

Heavily outnumbered by the rebels, the garrison often fought with outstanding bravery. But, as Laurence admitted in January, 'we hold just as much ground as we can cover with the fire of our rifles, and no more.' '... no sane man', he wrote, 'imagines that the slightest impression has been made upon the resistance of the Basutos.'[114]

Overtures for peace

Only a few days before, however, on 10 January 1881, Lerotholi and Joel had added their marks to a

---

about' and sold it to the rebel Basotho for the oxen which he slaughtered: Army Museum, Tylden Papers, Box 34057, Notebook II, p. 74.
[108] Widdicombe (1895: 86).
[109] LNA, L2/1/2, notice by Bell, 7 March 1881.
[110] Taylor (1972: 75-6, 78, 79).
[111] Taylor (1972: 76-7).
[112] Taylor (1972: 85-6).
[113] Widdicombe (1895: 195).
[114] Laurence (1882: 97).

petition to Sir George Strahan, the Imperial Administrator at Cape Town, assuring him of their loyalty to the Queen, complaining about their treatment at the hands of the Cape government, and begging him to intercede for them and to lay their case before the Queen – 'to beseech Her Majesty to allow us to retain our arms and our country'. In a characteristically Basotho display of *boikokobetso*, which may be roughly translated as 'self-abasement', a quality which Moshoeshoe had famously exercised to make it possible for others, supposedly grander than himself, to climb down without loss of face, they concluded:

> We pray you also to beseech Her Majesty to cause war and bloodshed to be stopped in our country. Our fields are being devastated, our homes destroyed, our wives and children have to flee to the mountains for shelter, where many perish of hunger and disease. ... We know we are unable to fight the white man. We do not want war. We want peace. Give us peace! We have always been told that Her Majesty is powerful, but just also. Therefore we believe she will hear this our prayer.[115]

---

[115] C.2964, pp. 3-5, Lerotholi and Joel to Sir George Strahan, 10 January 1881.

CHAPTER 14: THE THIRD PHASE OF THE WAR

Negotiations for peace

In the Seqiti War with the Free State the Basotho had begged for the High Commissioner's intervention because they were on the brink of defeat. In the Gun War they had more than held their own, and they were in a stronger position than when hostilities began. They had suffered hardships and heavy losses. According to prisoners captured by the Cape 'the people were war-weary and only continued the struggle because they were compelled by the chiefs. .... they spoke of Lerotholi's tyranny, and said that he "ate up" those of his men who wished to surrender; and killed the cowards or took away their horses lest they should gallop away from the battle fields.'[1] The PEMS missionary Hamilton Dyke reported that many Basotho were under arms 'by coercion'.[2] And according to C.J. Maitin many years later, Lerotholi told him that if the Cape had not stopped fighting 'he must have given in as his Basuto had no fight left in them'.[3] They were short of food, and would remain so until the harvest, and Lerotholi had to take the unpopular measure of commandeering cattle to feed the regiments.[4] But the military reports were unanimous that the Basotho were fighting with great courage and commitment,[5] and whereas at the end of the Seqiti War their country was being devastated by the Free State commandos, in the Gun War, except around Mafeteng, their fields and homes were almost untouched. The statement in the petition that 'Our fields are being devastated, our homes destroyed', was an exaggeration, meaningful for Lerotholi and some of his brothers, but not for the rest of the Basotho, and should be regarded as a flourish of *boikokobetso*. Around Mohale's Hoek, for example, it was reported that they were 'hoeing their crops as calmly as if there was no such thing as war in their land.'[6] And a few years later Letsie's sons would tell Masupha that they had borne the brunt of the fighting, and that he did not know what it meant.[7] But war with white men was full of danger, and the Basotho were receiving disturbing reports from below the Drakensberg that the rebellion there was being crushed. Their kinsmen and allies in the Matatiele District had been driven into the Maloti, the Thembu's siege of Umtata had been lifted, Mhlonhlo's Mpondomise had suffered a decisive defeat and Mhlonhlo himself had taken refuge in Basutoland. At the end of 1880 the Cape had 17,000 men in the field – 7,000 whites and 10,000 Africans – and more than half of these were

---

[1] Mohapeloa (1971: 64). There were similar reports from other prisoners (*Cape Argus*, 21 December 1880, 'The Basuto War', and 22 December 1880, 'The Basuto War'; CA DD 1/175, Carrington's War Diary, statement of prisoner taken on January 14 1881); from a loyal headman (*Cape Argus*, 6 January 1881, 'The Native War'); and from a rebel who gave himself up (*Cape Argus*, 24 January 1881). See also *The Journal*, 14 February 1881, 'Peace Prospects', reporting that the Basotho seemed demoralised and that Lerotholi shot men if they wavered in a fight.
[2] PEMS Archives, Morija, Dyke to Sauer, 14 January 1881.
[3] National Army Museum, Tylden Papers, Box 34057, Notebook IV, p. 2.
[4] CA, DD 1275, Carrington's War Diary, statement of Petrus Rakhomo of the Mafeteng Contingent, 16 January 1881; *Cape Argus*, 24 January 1881, 'The Native War'. For the shortage of food, see also *The Journal*, 9 February, quoting a letter from *The Friend*.
[5] As well as sources already quoted, see *Cape Argus*, 8 January 1881, 'Occasional Notes', and 8 February 1881, 'Occasional Notes'.
[6] *The Journal*, 9 February 1881, quoting letter from *The Friend*, 22 January 1881.
[7] *Cape Argus*, 13 December 1883, 'Telegrams. Masupha Holds a Pitso'.

deployed below the Drakensberg.[8] When the rebellion there was finally put down many of these troops could be redeployed in Basutoland.[9] Sprigg and his supporters were confident that the Basotho's defeat was only a matter of time.[10]

But the arguments for seeking peace would not have prevailed if the Basotho had not been receiving intimations that if they approached the High Commissioner they would be offered generous terms. This message was conveyed to them by the Catholic missionary, François Lebihan, and, according to Laydevant, Lebihan's biographer, it originated from 'a Colonial politician'.

Lebihan was based at the central mission station of Roma, and he had taken the bold step of acting as chaplain to Maama's men, sharing their hardships in the field and living, like them, off *lipabi* (roasted maize). In late December 1880 or early January 1881 he was passing through the Free State town of Ladybrand where 'a Colonial politician begged him to use his influence to persuade the Basotho chiefs to ask for peace, assuring him that ... they would obtain good terms.' Lebihan enlisted Maama's support, and together they went to see Letsie and persuaded him to draw up a petition for peace.[11]

The 'Colonial politician' who had approached Lebihan was J.W. Sauer, one of the members of the House of Assembly for Aliwal North, a leading member of the opposition, and destined later to become Secretary for Native Affairs. Sauer took a close interest in Basotho affairs, and he was acting on his own initiative and without government authority. On 10 January Letsie wrote a covering letter to Sauer, asking him to send the petition to the Governor, and at the same time he wrote to the Governor himself, begging him to bring the war to an end.[12] The PEMS missionaries, though uncertain of the origins of the petition, added their signatures as witnesses and gave it every support.

There was some delay in sending the petition. Masupha had refused to add his name, and there was much argument about who should sign as the 'principals in the war'. Eventually it was agreed that Joel Molapo could sign as well as Lerotholi, but not any lesser chiefs and headmen. Letsie was anxious that no further time should be lost 'now he has thus far succeeded in gaining over his sons to desire peace'.[13]

The old Paramount Chief was now coming back into the action. Before the war, although he detested disarmament, he had wanted to obey the government, but once the fighting had started, unlike the *Maketekoa* chiefs, who fought on the government's side, he adopted a largely passive role. When Anthony Atmore conducted his research in 1965-6 he found a strong tradition that while professing obedience Letsie was secretly encouraging resistance. In the words of Chief Leshoboro Majara, 'During the Gun War Letsie was playing dumb ... During the night he secretly told Lerotholi

---

[8] Smith (1939: 274). The *Cape Argus* (18 December 1880, Editorial) gives the figure of 18,000 men, 4,000 in Basutoland and 14,000 in Griqualand East and the Transkeian Territories.

[9] CA, NA 279, Statement of Sergeant Chert, Basutoland Police Force, 9 February 1881; Smith (1939: 283, 286).

[10] See, e.g., *The Journal*, 24 December 1880, Editorial; 9 February 1881, quoting a letter from *The Friend*; and 14 February 1881, Editorial.

[11] Laydevant (1935 and 1943): see Tylden (1950A:168) and National Army Museum, Tylden Papers, Box.34056, Notebook VI, p. 76. Smith (1939: 286) ascribed the initiative to the PEMS missionaries, but in a letter to Orpen Dyke said that he did not know who had drawn up the petition and praised the Catholic missionaries for 'advising the leaders of the revolt to make those overtures': CA, Acc.302, Dyke to Orpen, 23 March 1881; Maama's role is confirmed in LNA, S9/1/2/2, Orpen to Sauer, 16 January 1882.

[12] C.2964, pp. 2 and 5, Letsie to Sir George Strahan, 10 January 1881, and Letsie to Sauer, 10 January 1881.

[13] PEMS Archives, Morija, Dyke to Sauer, 14 January 1881.

and others that they mustn't hand over their guns. During the day-time he said the opposite.'[14] Mosebi Damane spelt out the logic of this position:

> Supposing Letsie was to come out openly as Masupha did, then it meant that the head of the state was rebelling against the Government. ... if Government succeeded in quelling the rebellion, Letsie could say, this was caused by people who have no authority in the country, not by the head of the state; if [the] rebels succeeded, he would still retain their confidence. The Basutos had nothing against Letsie's attitude in this matter – they thought it was perfectly correct.[15]

To some extent this is borne out by the praise poems. Nowhere is Letsie referred to as a *Leteketoa*. Every mention of him is respectful. He is fully represented in the associative praise-names of his kinsmen,[16] he is depicted, like the ancestors, as bringing good fortune, he is said to have given a pistol to Maama, and in the most striking reference of all he is called on by Maama and his warriors to reward them for their exploits:

Letsie, give us cattle, we're yours,
We're your dogs, your bulldogs,
You'll strike with us at the nations![17]

But it was natural for chiefs to exaggerate the support of their senior kinsmen and so to give their actions more authority. No doubt Letsie took pride in the unexpected success of the Basotho's resistance, and, once the rebels had embarked on hostilities, he might have offered them some encouragement. But he had never wanted war.[18] He still believed that if the Basotho were to survive they would have to make peace, and his greatest fear was that the Cape forces would advance on Matsieng and that he himself would become embroiled: '... the war is drawing nearer and nearer to me', he noted nervously in his petition to the Governor.[19] To avoid this he wanted the government to draw a circle around his village and to declare it a war-free zone – a proposition which Sprigg rejected.[20] Now at last, however, Letsie had the backing of two of his most influential sons, Lerotholi and Maama, and Joel Molapo too was supportive. The war party, headed by Masupha, was still strong, but Hamilton Dyke believed that 'the good order party was gaining the ascendancy' and that if there was a favourable reply to the petition the nation would rally behind Letsie and his sons.[21]

Although the petition was addressed to Sir George Strahan, the Basotho chiefs would have known, since they were acting with missionary advice, that it would be dealt with by the new High

---

[14] Interview with AA, 18 November 1965.
[15] Mosebi Damane, interview with AA, 17 November 1965. Stephen Pinda said much the same: interview with AA, 7 October 1965.
[16] Associative praise-names (or eulogues) link the person being praised with his relatives, his friends and the places of his home: Damane and Sanders (1974: 42-3).
[17] Damane and Sanders (1974: 161). Translation slightly altered.
[18] See, e.g., *Cape Argus*, 8 June 1881, 'The Basuto Question': according to Jonathan Molapo Letsie 'all along had wished for peace but had really no authority'; and *Cape Argus*, 8 August 1881, 'The Basuto War': Lerotholi said 'Any blame for being led into hostilities he took to himself, as his father Letsea had told him that "no good could come of it".'.
[19] C.2964, p. 2, Letsie to Strahan, 10 January 1881.
[20] PEMS Archives, Morija, Ayliff to Griffith, 30 December 1880; LNA, S9/1/3/4, Griffith to Letsie, 22 January 1881; CA, NA 279, Letsie to Griffith, 6 February 1881.
[21] PEMS Archives, Morija, Dyke to Daumas, 25 January 1881.

1. Matsieng, Letsie's village

2. Morija, the headquarters of the Paris Evangelical Mission

3. Thaba-Bosiu, Moshoeshoe's stronghold

4. Moshoeshoe

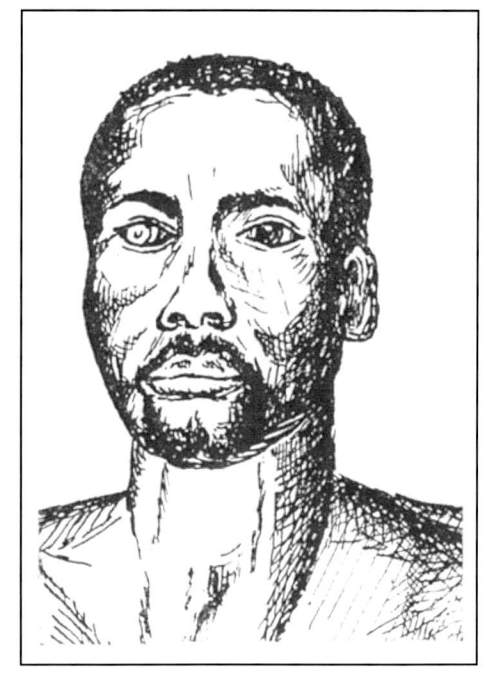
5. Letsie

6. Molapo

7. Masupha

8. Lerotholi

9. Maama

10. Seeiso

11. Bereng

12. Mojela, who lost his right hand in 1898 in the war against Masupha

13. Nkuebe

14. Theko

15. Jonathan Molapo in old age

16. Joel Molapo

17. Moletsane, Chief of the Bataung

18. Moorosi, Chief of the Baphuthi

19. Nehemiah (Sekhonyana)

20. Sofonia (Pii)

21. George (Tlali)

22. Tsekelo

23. Molomo Mohale

24. The delegation to Cape Town, 1880: In the back row: Ntho, Mojela Letsie, Abel Matete. Seated in centre: Irénée Cochet. Seated at the front: Nathanael Makotoko, Ramabilikoe Matete, Jakobo Moletsane.

25. Philip Wodehouse

26. Henry Barkly

27. Bartle Frere

28. Hercules Robinson

29. James Bowker

30. Charles Duncan Griffith

31. Matthew Blyth

32. Joseph Millerd Orpen

33. J.S. Moffat

34. Major Charles Harland Bell

35. Charles G.H. Bell (son of Major Bell)

36. Arthur Barkly

37. Emile Rolland

38. Fanny Barkly

39. J. Gordon Sprigg

40. General Charles Gordon

41. The Scanlen Cabinet, 1884: John Merriman, Jacobus Sauer, James Leonard, Cecil Rhodes, Thomas Scanlen

Illustrations

42. Adolphe Mabille

43. Dr. Eugène Casalis

44. Hamilton Moore Dyke

45. D.F. Ellenberger

46. John Widdicombe

47. Dr. Henry Taylor

48. Charles Mansfield Clarke

49. E.Y. Brabant

50. 'Zach' Bayly

51. 'Fighting Fred' Carrington

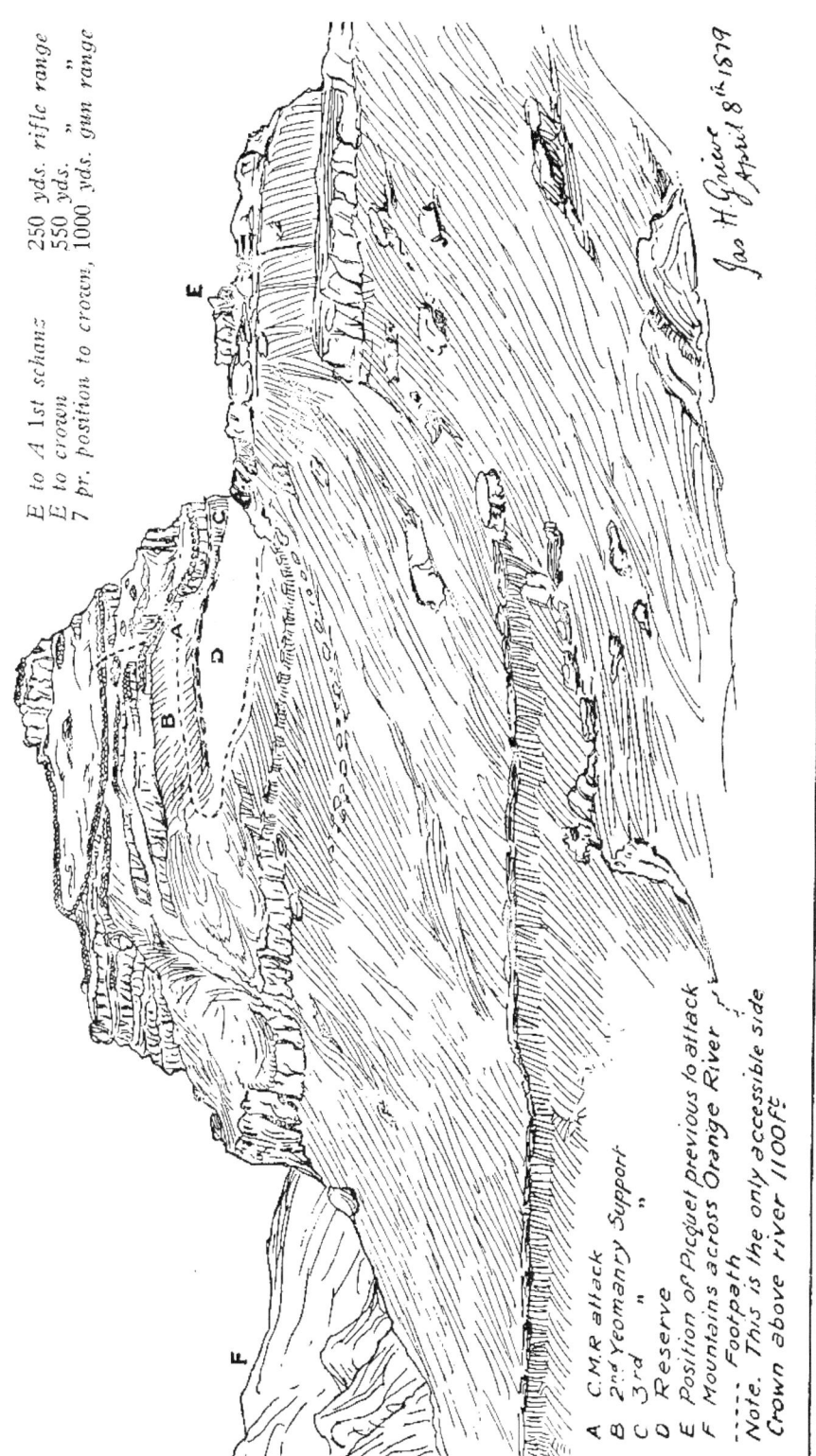

52. Moorosi's Mountain: A sketch made on 8 April 1879 after the first attack

'Throwing Down White Man'

53. Mosotho foot-soldier. Contemporary illustration.

54. Mosotho cavalryman. Later reconstruction.

55. 'Colonial Volunteers Reconnoitring – Return of the Scout'

Illustrations

56. Maseru: the view looking southeastwards across Maseru, December 1880, with the World, the Flesh and the Devil in the background

57. Fort Bell at Hlotse Heights, 1881

58. The burning of the Model School at Maseru, 10 October 1880

'Throwing Down White Man'

59. Commandant Schermbrucker and Basotho police during Gun War

60. Marshal Clarke

61. Godfrey Lagden

Commissioner, Sir Hercules Robinson, who assumed office at the Cape on 22 January. In England sympathies lay strongly with the Basotho.[22] The Aborigines Protection Society and the PEMS had been campaigning vigorously, and Gladstone's Secretary of State for the Colonies, Lord Kimberley, had instructed Robinson to respond to any Basotho request for peace and to use his influence on the side of leniency and moderation.[23] When Robinson told Kimberley that he had received the petition, the Secretary of State wired back at once: 'Overture from Basutos important. Press earnestly upon your Ministers to enable you to take advantage of it to arrange terms by which war may be brought to close.'[24]

There were strong reasons for Sprigg and his colleagues to bring the war to a close – the casualties, the troops' hardships in the field, and the heavy strain on their limited financial resources.[25] They could hardly afford to go on. But lenient terms would discredit them in the Cape and undermine their authority in Basutoland, and with the prospect of reinforcements from below the Drakensberg they still believed that they would prevail. Sprigg himself was absurdly optimistic. When a relief detachment of the First City Rifles told him that they did not want to serve for more than three months, he cheerfully replied 'It's all right, my lads, we shall not want you for half that time.'[26] He also doubted the petitioners' sincerity. Robinson therefore told Griffith to inform Lerotholi and Joel that they should lay down their arms, and that then, if they placed themselves 'unreservedly' in his hands, they could rely upon him to exert his influence 'to obtain for them not only just but generous terms'.[27]

During the hostilities Griffith had been left very much to one side, not even being consulted or informed when his staff had been given military commands. Like Letsie, however, he was now back centre stage. Before the war, although he had not wanted disarmament, he had insisted on a hard negotiating line in the belief that any concessions would weaken the Colony's standing and the Basotho would become ungovernable. He adopted the same argument now. The rebels did not yet feel beaten and would never give up their arms, but on the contrary felt elated, saying that it was the government that was asking for peace.

> 'I do hope and pray', he wrote prophetically, 'that no patched-up peace will be made with the rebels, for, if they are not thoroughly humbled and brought to terms, they will be so overbearing that neither the loyal Basutos nor the magistrates will be able to live in the country.'[28]

The chiefs had asked for an armistice to enable them to consider the Governor's reply, and Robinson granted them a week, from 18 to 24 February. The leading *Mabelete*, except Masupha and Ramanella, met in the area of Morija and Matsieng and were attended by at least four of the PEMS missionaries. Their reply, like their petition, was in the names of Lerotholi and Joel, and it was witnessed by, among others, three of Letsie's sons, Maama, Theko and Seeiso. As always, the chiefs professed their

---

[22] John Benyon (1980: 186-7), referring to letters by Barkly and Wodehouse in *The Times*, 24 and 27 December 1880. See also *JME* 1881, p. 52, 'Les Délégués du Comité des Missions à Londres'; Smith (1939: 282).
[23] C.2754, pp. 3-7, Kimberley to Robinson, 30 December 1880.
[24] C.2964, p. 1, Kimberley to Robinson, 31 January 1881.
[25] Smith (1939: 284). See also Benyon (1980: 187).
[26] *Cape Argus*, 3 February 1881, Editorial.
[27] C.2964, p. 7, Robinson to Griffith, 4 February 1881.
[28] A.44-'81, p. 8, Griffith to Robinson, 11 February 1881.

loyalty to the Queen, but the main burden of their reply was that before laying down their arms they wanted to know the terms which Robinson would grant. They did not distrust Robinson's intentions, but they could not forget what they had heard of 'the taking of our country and arms, and of some of the Chiefs being doomed men ....'[29] Masupha and Ramanella wrote separately to say that they had not signed because of a misunderstanding but fully supported the contents of the reply.[30]

It was clear, and it soon became even clearer, that there were three issues on which the rebel leaders were not prepared to compromise. They were determined to retain their arms, they were determined to keep Quthing as part of their country, and they would not submit to any punishment for themselves except perhaps a fine.

It was during this armistice that Brabant rode out from the headquarters camp and had an interview with Lerotholi. 'At that time', he wrote later, 'he had been drinking heavily and was in an excessively nervous state. He was, however, very civil and very frank.' He showed a wound he had received earlier in the war, and when Brabant remonstrated with him on the Basotho's practice of not taking prisoners, and of killing wounded men who fell into their hands, 'He admitted this, but said he could not restrain his people when excited by fighting'. The two men parted 'very good friends'.[31] Another portrait of the chief at this time was given by the missionary, Hermann Dieterlen. He described him arriving at Morija by cart, 'in great pain from an old inflammation of the bladder which had been greatly aggravated by the fatigues of war and the long hours spent on horseback every day. The poor man is indeed very ill ....'[32]

Robinson interpreted the rebel leaders' response as a rejection of his offer of arbitration, since they had refused to lay down their arms and to place themselves unreservedly in his hands. At the same time he was receiving reports, not just from Griffith, 'that the Basutos did not really mean to desist from armed rebellion unless they were permitted to retain their arms', and that they would 'only use the suspension of hostilities to reap their crops and strengthen their positions'. In these circumstances he felt bound to withdraw his offer of arbitration, to revert to his constitutional position as Governor and to act on his Ministers' advice. And his Ministers proposed that the Basotho should surrender their arms immediately; that an amnesty should be granted to all the rebels except Masupha, Lerotholi and Joel, who would have to stand trial, but whose lives would be spared; that the Basotho should pay a fine to be determined by Parliament; and that Quthing would be dealt with as Parliament should decide. The rebel leaders were to be given 24 hours in which to respond, failing which hostilities would recommence.[33]

These terms were despatched to Lerotholi on the morning of 24 February, and to give the chiefs time to consider them the armistice was extended to 26 February. No answer was received in the time allowed, and the armistice came to an end. The terms offered were completely unacceptable to the rebel leaders. In a letter to Griffith dated 26 February, the last day of the armistice, Lerotholi said they were 'deeply grieved' by the Governor's reply.[34] Later, in a letter to a Free State official, he was more frank. The Basotho had asked for arbitration, he wrote, but

---

[29] C.2964, pp. 8-9, Lerotholi and Joel to Robinson, 19 February 1881.
[30] C.2964, p. 9, Masupha and 'Ramenella', n.d.
[31] CA, Accessions 459, Brabant's Autobiography, p. 115.
[32] *JME* 1881, p. 172, '*Un peu de relâche parmi nos missionnaires pendant l'armistice*', quoting letter from Dieterlen, undated, as translated in Germond (1967: 376).
[33] C.2964, pp. 12-3, Robinson to Kimberley, 5 March 1881, and p. 160, Sprigg to Griffith, 22 February 1881.
[34] C.2964, p. 19, Lerotholi to Griffith, 26 February 1881.

instead of having a reply from the Governor we got it from the old Sprigg, and he (Sprigg) spoke the old thing which caused this unjust war of disarmament, and our answer was that of old, that is, we will not submit to his terms, because we are not yet defeated by them ....[35]

Together with Letsie, Masupha and others, he later told Griffith that Sprigg's reply 'put us into despair. We saw that we must only prepare for death ....'[36]

The PEMS missionaries were incensed. After all their efforts to gain peace, wrote Hamilton Dyke, Robinson's reply

was as oil to the flames. The rage of despair succeeded to the calm we had tried to bring about. It is now considered as a struggle for life and for honour, as the giving up of leaders would have been the lowest depth of dishonour to the nation ....[37]

In the House of Commons the home government expressed its regret at the 'severity' of the terms that had been offered, and this was splashed all over the colonial press and confirmed the Basotho in their determination to hold out.[38]

Sprigg had never expected that the rebel leaders would accept his terms. He had merely put them forward to avoid any criticism that he had failed to respond to their initiative. He had learnt nothing from the previous five months' campaigning. He was confident that, with the war below the Drakensberg now coming to an end, and with extra troops available, Clarke would be able to bring the Basotho to heel.

The resumption of fighting

Clarke returned to Basutoland to resume his command on 27 February, the day after the armistice came to an end. He could hardly have been encouraged by what he found. In the north, at Hlotse Heights, Major Bell was warning that the whole garrison was in danger of breaking up: the periods of service for the Kimberley Horse and the Transvaal Horse would expire at the end of April, the troops were threatening to defect because they had not been paid, and Ferreira was declaring that there was no point in going on unless 500 extra men were made available.[39] In Maseru there were only sufficient men to defend the town, and for the most part they kept themselves fit by playing football and hockey. Their popular commander, Colonel Bayly, was soon to return vindicated and unpunished after refusing to obey orders, but still no serious offensive was taken.[40] In the south, apart from the garrison at Mafeteng, the main striking force at the Boleka ridge consisted of only 1,500 men. Many of the burghers had proved unwilling to fight, and those who had stayed were on the point of completing their terms of service and leaving.[41] Because of the unpopularity of the war men were increasingly

---

[35] FS, GS 1173, Lerotholi and others to 'Diedericki' [Diederichs?], 28 February 1881.
[36] A.44-'81, p. 24, Lerotholi, Letsie, Masupha and others to Griffith, 8 April 1881.
[37] CA, Accessions 302, Dyke to Orpen, 23 March 1881.
[38] C.2964, p. 13, Robinson to Kimberley, 5 March 1881; p. 6, Robinson to Kimberley, 28 February 1881; pp. 11-12, Reuter's Telegram of 25 February 1881. See also C. 2964, p. 6, Kimberley to Robinson, 25 February 1881, and p. 11, Sprigg, minute, 1 March 1881, and Martineau (1895: II: 385).
[39] LNA, L2/1/2, Bell to Staff Officer to Officer Commanding, Mafeteng, 24 February and 5 March 1881.
[40] Woon (1909: 225). There was a skirmish in mid-March, which resulted in several Basotho being killed and on the Cape side a white sergeant and an African trooper: *Cape Argus*, 24 March 1881, 'The Native War. A Skirmish at Maseru'.
[41] C.2964, p. 16, B. St. John, Summary of events reported since the 1st March 1881.

reluctant to volunteer, and some of those who had already volunteered for the war below the Drakensberg refused to be transferred to Basutoland. Two hundred men of the Western Levies and the Cape Town Rangers, for example, refused to go, and the officer who had to preside over their trial for disobeying orders found them in a state of 'flagrant mutiny'.[42] In the following month 100 burghers were called out from the Tarka division: only 50 put in an appearance, most of them substitutes, and nearly 20 of these had deserted by the time they reached Aliwal North.[43] The reinforcements on which Sprigg had placed such excessive hopes fell far short of expectations, barely making up for departures and desertions. Clarke later likened his force to a stage army, constantly disappearing and reappearing, except that it never reappeared.[44] He needed 10,000 men, but he could not reckon for a month on holding 2,000 together.[45] Meanwhile, in the far south, the death of Austen was still unavenged.[46]

By contrast, the defeat of the rebels below the Drakensberg had the effect of adding to the Basotho's strength in the form of the fugitives under Makoae and the Batlokoa chief Lelingoana. Both chiefs were called upon to give help to Lerotholi, and the praise poems of Lelingoana make it clear that he identified fully with the Basotho cause and responded enthusiastically.[47] And in February and March the Basotho's morale and fighting capacity were strengthened by the ripening of a prodigious harvest, which brought their food shortage swiftly to an end. 'The food supply in the country is simply enormous', wrote one newspaper correspondent in March. Even in the fields on the Boleka front there was 'an abundance' of green mealies, marrows and pumpkins.[48]

After the armistice came to an end there was what the French missionaries called a 'divine truce': the rains were so constant and heavy that the colonial forces were completely immobilised. About 580mm. fell in twelve days. 'Every ditch has become a roaring torrent, every road a bog ....'[49] In their waterlogged camps, under their leaking tents, having to forage miles for a scrap of fuel, the troops suffered increasing discomfort and illness. By contrast, as the French missionaries pointed out, the Basotho had 'no lack of shelters in the thousands of uninvaded villages and the caves and grottos of every dimension which abound in their country'. Far from being discouraged, the chiefs were now raising a public subscription of cattle and food, a *sethabathaba*, 'to enable them [the combatants] to remain in their camps and thus avoid the necessity of dispersing after every battle to provide for their sustenance'. 'Numerous cattle', it was reported, 'were promptly subscribed.'[50]

---

[42] Scully (193: 117-9). See also *Cape Argus*, 22 February 1881, 'Refractory Western Levies. A Trial at Clarksburg' (where 'Culley' is presumably Scully).

[43] *Cape Argus*, 21 March 1881, 'Native War Items'.

[44] *Cape Argus*, 6 April 1882, 'Parliament. House of Assembly', Sauer's speech on 5 April.

[45] *Cape Argus*, 7 April 1881, 'The War in Basutoland', quoting *The Friend*'s correspondent.

[46] Rhodes House Library, Oxford, MSS Afr. S.969, Letter no. 63, Robert Kennan to his mother, 17 February 1881.

[47] CA, NA 279, Setha Matete to Griffith, 6 March 1881; Mangoaela (1957: 78-90). See also PEMS Archives, Paris, Maeder to Casalis, 16 March 1881.

[48] *Cape Argus*, 21 March 1881, 'Native War Items', quoting a correspondent of *The Friend*. See also PEMS Archives, Paris, Germond to Casalis, 17 February 1881: '*Le blé a été recolté, la famine a disparu et les champs ont magnifique apparence.*'

[49] *JME* 1881, p. 133, '*Nouvelles de la Guerre*', Paris, 21 March 1881, as translated by Germond (1967: 375). See also *Cape Argus*, 21 March 1881, 'The Native War', 'Native War Items', and 30 April 1881, 'Occasional Notes'.

[50] *JME* 1881, p. 133, '*Nouvelles de la Guerre*', Paris, 21 March 1881, as translated by Germond (1967: 375). See also FS, GS 1174, Orpen to Brand, 16 September 1881.

Chapter 14: The third phase of the war

By the middle of March, in spite of the rain, Clarke decided to mount another offensive. He had received some volunteer reinforcements, but even so the fighting column at his disposal amounted to only 1,800 men.[51] Nor was morale very high. According to the Wesleyan chaplain, Henry Cotton, everyone wished that 'this wretched war' was over: it could so easily have been avoided.[52]

From the camp Clarke could see the Basotho position stretching from Mathebe on his right to Boleka on his left, with the road running northwards to Morija between them. Further up the road was the fortified mountain of Masite, where Lerotholi had been accumulating supplies for some time.[53] On 22 March Clarke despatched 1,000 troops, mostly on foot, to advance up this road. On the Basotho side Lerotholi kept his men hidden behind their fortifications, but as the column neared the saddle between the two mountains they opened up such an intense fire that Clarke at once gave the order to retreat. The Basotho continued firing on the departing troops and four men fell, one of them Carrington, who was seriously wounded in the chest.[54]

Two days later, on 24 March, the Basotho made a surprise raid and swept off the whole of the CMR's horses, killing three men as they did so,[55] and it was mainly because of this that the next colonial expedition was made with infantry and guns. After a few rounds, however, the guns began to sink in the rain-sodden ground, the Basotho charged, and it was only with the greatest difficulty that the infantry were able to form a square and hold them at bay before retreating to the camp.[56]

There were further advances, followed by further retreats, with the Basotho, as Brabant described them, falling on the troops like a swarm of hornets.[57] One newly arrived volunteer described the stalemate as 'chronic'. 'Something like general demoralization reigned. Wholesale desertions depleted the ranks of the Cape Mounted Riflemen.'[58] Burghers whose time was up refused to wait until replacements arrived. The wounded Carrington had to give up his command to Shervinton and Grant. From the Transvaal there was news of the British defeat at Majuba.

The reinforcements who did appear were too few to tip the scales. At the beginning of April, for example, Colonel Wavell (later General Wavell) arrived with 241 men of all ranks (several weeks after they had been expected, and only after they had run riot and looted Aliwal North on their way). He immediately recognised the hopelessness of the situation. 'The more I see of [my new command] the less I like it', he wrote to his wife. 'I have not enough men to do anything of any use.' He likened Clarke to 'the King of France marching up a hill to march down again. ... If he does not attack tomorrow or the next day, and carry the Boleka Ridge, I shall be puzzled to know what he does mean to do'.[59] But the Boleka ridge was too strongly held for the cautious Clarke to think of attacking it. The Basotho, according to one report, had put their largest force in the field, with Lerotholi and his

---

[51] SOAS, MMS/South Africa/Correspondence/Queenstown/FBN21, Cotton to Kilner, Headquarters Column, Basutoland, 24 March 1881.
[52] SOAS, MMS/South Africa/Correspondence/Queenstown/FBN21, Cotton to Lamplough, Ramabilikoe Camp, 9 March 1881.
[53] Tylden (1950A: 166).
[54] CA, Accessions 459, Brabant's Autobiography, p. 112; Gon (1984: 50); Tylden, (1950A: 167).
[55] Scully (1913: 124-5); Woon (1909: 208-9); Tylden (1950A: 167).
[56] Woon (1909: 209-10).
[57] CA, Accessions 459, Brabant's Autobiography, p. 114.
[58] Scully (1913: 132). See also *Cape Argus*, 1 March 1881, '"They all Want to Go"'.
[59] CA, Accessions 102, Colonel G.A.G. Wavell to his wife, 11 April 1881.

brothers, determined to prevent any breakthrough to Matsieng and Maseru, being strengthened by Masupha, Ramanella and Joel. Clarke believed they had 16,000 men in the field.[60]

Clarke sank more and more into despair: 'it is a farce', he wrote on 30 March, 'to think of carrying on operations with a small force, which continually decreases, against a nation of natives well armed, and occupying strong positions in a difficult country. I might, of course, run my head against the Boleka position, but I am not going to incur the risk of needless loss of life without a definite object, for even supposing we could take the ridge, we could not advance a yard beyond it with our present force ….' On 5 April he described the war as 'a waste of both money and time'.[61] He did not want to be responsible for another Isandhlwana.

Meanwhile, in the north, the rebels maintained their grip on Hlotse Heights, and by the beginning of March the camp had been beleaguered for four months. On 9 March Joel and his rebel brothers, supported by Ramanella, tried to sweep off the camp's stock. They were driven off, but only after an engagement which lasted four to five hours. They were reported to have suffered heavy losses, but the garrison too suffered a grievous loss through the death of Major Laurence, the commander of the Diamond Fields Horse, who had exposed himself 'too freely' in directing a counter-attack.[62] A few days later Jonathan Molapo joined Bell in begging for reinforcements. If Ferreira left with the Transvaal Horse, he wrote, 'we shall be like a man with one arm'. If only 800-1,000 men had been sent earlier the war in the Leribe District would have been finished long ago. As it was, 'Every day the enemy are laughing and mocking us ....'[63]

By the beginning of April Bell's position was becoming desperate. A volunteer corps, Landry's Horse, was on its way to help him, but in the meantime, he reported, he was 'hanging on' with only 150 troops.[64] On 10 April a cattle-raid on the camp was beaten off,[65] and a week later, on the morning of 17 April, the rebels suddenly 'poured down ... from all quarters'. From nine till twelve 'the firing was almost continuous', but by half-past twelve the rebels had retired to the heights of Sebothoane.

This, however, as Widdicombe observed, was the last fighting day of the Gun War. In the afternoon a flag of truce came in 'with the information that Lerothodi had sued for peace'.[66]

Sir Hercules Robinson's award

The collapse of the initial peace negotiations had seemed final, but as Robinson found his feet in the Cape he determined to take up the initiative again. He was under pressure from the home government to bring the war to an end. He could see that there was no realistic prospect of an early victory. His task was to enable the Cape to back out of the war with as little loss of face as possible. In

---

[60] *The Journal*, 'Basutoland', 1 April 1881; *Cape Argus*, 6 April 1882, 'Parliament. House of Assembly. 5 April 1882, Sauer's speech.

[61] *Cape Argus, op.cit.* At the beginning of April his white troops numbered 1286 infantry and 3893 cavalry, and he had 'Hottentot' and 'native' support as well, but these numbers included not just men in the country but those *en route* and being raised: *The Journal*, 29 April 1881, 'Our Diary', quoting the Gazette of 22 April. He also had 14 guns, 6 mortars and 3 howitzers.

[62] LNA, L2/1/2, Bell to Staff Officer to OC, Mafeteng, 12 March 1881; Laurence (1882: 141-6, 146-9); Taylor (1972: 81-2).

[63] LNA, L2/1/2, Jonathan to Robinson, undated, enclosed with Bell to Griffith, 8 March 1881.

[64] LNA, L2/1/2, Bell to officer commanding Landrey's Horse, *en route* to Hlotse Heights, 8 April 1881. For Landry's Horse, see Taylor (1972: 82-3).

[65] LNA, L2/1/2, Bell to A.A.G. Mafeteng, 13 April 1881.

[66] Widdicombe (1895: 204).

spite of all their huffing and puffing, Sprigg's Ministry could hope for nothing better.

Soon after the conclusion of the earlier armistice Robinson had received a letter from Lerotholi asking the Governor to explain what was wanted of him and begging him not to cast the Basotho off.[67] This gave him the opening he needed: on 20 March he sent a telegram to Griffith that his offer of arbitration was still open, but only, as before, if the rebels laid down their arms and placed themselves unreservedly in his hands.[68] This came as a surprise to the PEMS missionaries,[69] and no doubt to the rebel leaders as well. Lerotholi was eager to exploit the opportunity, but at the same time he did not want to find himself confronted by the same terms as those put forward by Sprigg. On 29 March, writing from the mountain fortress of Masite, he responded positively, begging for a cessation of hostilities, but in terms so vague that Robinson was at a loss to know exactly what he meant.[70] 'Does he merely want to know what my arbitration would be before he submits', he wrote, 'or is he willing to accept absolutely my arbitration; and, if so, is he ready to prove the sincerity of his determination to abide by my decision by laying down his arms beforehand and submitting to the law?'[71]

Letsie summoned the rebel chiefs to a meeting – Lerotholi was still so ill that he had to be fetched by cart – and in their reply, framed with the help of missionary advice, they assured the Governor that they were ready to accept his arbitration and to lay down their arms. What had 'frightened' them before was Sprigg's reply. As Dyke explained in a letter to Griffith, the chiefs were reassured by the idea of Robinson's acting as an umpire, and they believed he would visit Basutoland and hear what they had to say.[72]

Robinson's emphatic condition – that the Basotho should lay down their arms before he would arbitrate – was his first attempt to dig in his heels on behalf of the Cape government as he began to slide down the slope of humiliation. And it was the first position that he had to abandon. Griffith was confused. What exactly was meant by 'laying down of arms', he asked: did it mean surrendering them? Robinson replied that he would be prepared to arbitrate 'if the people in armed opposition disperse to their homes'.[73]

He then began consulting Griffith about the terms which he was proposing to put forward. These were:

1. that the Basotho should accept the policy of disarmament, with or without such modifications as special permits to be arranged by Griffith and his magistrates;
2. that the Basotho should pay a moderate fine;
3. that there should be a complete amnesty;
4. that no part of the country [i.e. Quthing] should be confiscated.[74]

---

[67] C.2964, p. 19, Lerotholi to Griffith, 26 February 1881.
[68] C.2964, p. 19, Robinson to Griffith, 20 March 1881.
[69] *JME* 1881, p. 260, Dr. Casalis, 20 April 1881.
[70] A.44-'81, p. 19, Griffith to Robinson, 30 March 1881 (in which Lerotholi's letter, received the previous evening, is quoted).
[71] A.44-'81, pp. 19-20, Robinson to Griffith, 3 April 1881.
[72] A.44-'81, p. 24, Lerotholi, Letsie, Masupha, 'Mokhale' (for Moletsane) and 'Ramahopu' (for Joel Molapo) to Griffith, 8 April 1881. For the background to this letter, see Hamilton Dyke's letters to Griffith, 6-8 April 1881 (PEMS Archives, Morija).
[73] A.44-'81, pp. 22, 23, Griffith to Robinson, 5 April, 1881, Robinson to Griffith, 8 April 1881.
[74] A.44-'81, p. 23, Robinson to Griffith, 8 April 1881.

Griffith believed these terms were too generous. Before any leniency could be shown, he argued, the Basotho had to be '*punished first*'. They had to be made to give up their arms.[75] Being 'in a barbarous heathen state', the rebels 'cannot appreciate or understand the motives which move a civilized Government to offer them just and generous terms. From their standpoint they put it down to weakness ....'[76] He still clung to the hope of a military victory. The common people, he believed, were tired of the war but they were too much controlled by their chiefs to show it. If the colonial forces could strike a decisive blow, such as taking Boleka and advancing on Morija, the people would press the chiefs to accept terms.[77] A few days later the *Mateketoa*'s leaders wrote in the same vein. A *Mabelete* victory would be disastrous for them. Contrary to all appearances, they argued, the rebel chiefs were still perverse and obstinate, and more rigorous steps should be taken to put them down.[78]

Robinson argued that his terms were not too generous, but he had to be more generous than Sprigg, since otherwise he could be accused of 'entrapping them [the Basotho] into submission by raising false expectations'. He was still insisting that he would not arbitrate until the rebel regiments had dispersed, and colonial troops would then occupy the positions which they had abandoned. In view of Griffith's reservations, however, he asked him to summon the rebel chiefs to Maseru and to ask them frankly if they were ready to surrender their arms to the Governor. If they were, they could trust to him for the rest. If not, it would be better if they did not accept him as an arbiter.[79]

Griffith invited Lerotholi to meet him at Letlatsa's village, near Maseru, on Good Friday, 15 April, and suggested that some of the missionaries should be there too in order to give him confidence. There was some delay, since Lerotholi still had to travel by cart because of his illness, and the meeting took place on Easter Sunday, 17 April. There were many among Lerotholi's followers who believed that it was all a trap and that their chief would be captured and killed. Lerotholi insisted on going, but, as Dyke observed, 'Thousands and thousands of people were round about us watching every movement'.[80] To allay any suspicion Griffith rode out with just five unarmed followers.

In response to Griffith's questions Lerotholi assured him that he wanted peace, but on the central issue he would make no promise. Griffith's record of the meeting is plain and direct:

> Griffith. – I want to be straightforward with you. What answer am I to give the Governor about the guns? Will you surrender them or not?
>
> Lerothodi. – I cannot bind myself by saying that the Basutos will surrender their guns .... I put our case in your hands, and beg of you to intercede for us, in order that we may be allowed to retain our guns.

Griffith urged him to show his sincerity by instructing his people to disperse to their homes, and Lerotholi agreed to give orders to this effect.[81] Griffith then instructed Clarke and the other military commanders to suspend hostilities if the Basotho dispersed.[82]

---

[75] A.44-'81, pp. 22-3, 24-5, Griffith to Robinson, 10 and 5 April 1881 respectively.
[76] LNA, S9/1/1/3, Griffith to Robinson, 15 April 1881.
[77] A.44-'81, pp. 23-4, Griffith to Robinson, 9 April 1881.
[78] LNA, S9/1/1/2, Griffith to Robinson, 15 April 1881, enclosing letter of 13 April.
[79] A.44-'81, pp. 25-6, Robinson to Griffith, telegram and letter, 12 April 1881.
[80] PEMS Archives, Morija, Dyke to Orpen, 18 April 1881.
[81] A.44-'81, pp. 28-9, Griffith to Robinson, 18 April 1881. See also A.44-'81, p. 27, Griffith to Robinson, 17 April 1881; PEMS Archives, Morija, Dyke to Orpen, 18 April 1881.
[82] LNA, S9/1/3/4, Griffith to Clarke and others, 17 April 1881; A.44-'81, p. 27, Griffith to Robinson, 18 April 1881.

Although Lerotholi had begged Griffith to intercede for them, and although Griffith assured Dr Casalis that the Governor's award would be most generous, behind the scenes he was doing everything that he could to make the terms as strong as possible. Lerotholi's response had confirmed him in his belief that the Basotho would never willingly give up their arms, and he was against any concessions in the way of licences or any other modifications:

> 'if the unconditional surrender of arms is not now enforced', he wrote, 'it would be better to withdraw from the country and let the Basutos manage their own affairs: if they are allowed to keep their arms, now, after all that has been gone through, the magistrates, and the loyal people who have stuck to them, will return humiliated to their respective stations, without "prestige," and without power to do any good, and the Government of the country will be virtually back again in the hands of the chiefs, as it was before they became British subjects.'[83]

In response Robinson put several plain questions to Griffith.

> If I were to announce as my award the unconditional surrender of arms, do you believe the chiefs and people would comply with such a decision? If not, how would you enforce compliance? Have you estimated the force it would require, the time it would occupy, and the cost?[84]

Griffith replied that the chiefs and people would not comply, that he would enforce compliance by 'vigorous military operations', and that General Clarke would be better able to answer the questions about the force required, the time and the cost.[85] Two days later Clarke told Robinson that the continuance of the war would involve 'the moving of the existing force into winter quarters, the resumption of hostilities in the spring with 10,000 men, and the expenditure of several additional millions'.[86]. He must have known that this would be impossible. And the reference to moving into winter quarters was significant. The frosts had started and soon there would be no pasture for the horses. Even in the Seqiti War the Free State had abandoned operations in the winter. Confirmed by these gloomy assessments, Robinson knew he had to bring the war to an end.

Before he could announce his award, however, there was still an awkward presentational hurdle to be overcome. He had declared that he would not act as an arbitrator unless and until the rebel forces were dispersed. Although there had been some movement, the Basotho regiments were still maintaining their positions. Clarke reported, however, that they were 'perfectly quiet',[87] and this gave Robinson his opening for backing down, for slipping further down the slope. Dispersal, he now declared, was a 'side issue', a 'minor point'. He acknowledged that the Basotho might not have fully complied with the order to return to their homes, but, rather than insisting on the 'strict letter of the condition as to dispersion' he would prefer to 'accept the present submissive attitude of the people' and go ahead with his arbitration.[88]

---

[83] A.44-'81, pp. 29-30, Griffith to Robinson, 20 April 1881.
[84] A.44-'81, p. 30, Robinson to Griffith, 20 April 1881.
[85] A.44-'81, pp. 30-1, Griffith to Robinson, 20 April 1881.
[86] C.2964, p. 24, Robinson to Ministers, 27 April 1881. The words quoted are Robinson's. More precisely, Clarke had stipulated 8,000 men, 'exclusive of the garrisons': A.44-'81, p. 33, Clarke to Colonial Secretary, Cape Town, 22 April 1881.
[87] A.44-'81, p. 33, Clarke to Colonial Secretary, 22 April 1881.
[88] C.2964, p. 24, Robinson to Ministers, 27 April 1881.

Sprigg and his Ministers reluctantly agreed, and Robinson announced his award. It fell under three heads. Under the first, 'Disarmament', the law remained in force, and all guns had to be surrendered, but any person who wanted to keep his gun could, with the approval of a magistrate, have it registered and returned to him on the payment of a licence fee of £1, to be payable annually. (In a letter to London Robinson euphemistically described this as 'disarmament, tempered by a system of registration'.)[89] Under the second, 'Compensation', all the losses of the loyalists, traders and government should be restored or made good. Under the third, 'Fine', the Basotho should pay 5,000 head of cattle. If these conditions were met there would be a complete amnesty and no confiscation of territory.

The award was conveyed immediately to Lerotholi, and a meeting was summoned at Letsie's village. Lerotholi was in favour of acceptance, but there was strong opposition from Masupha and other chiefs who, unlike Lerotholi and his brothers, had not suffered in the war, and who distrusted the colonial government and wanted to hold out.[90] The provisions relating to disarmament were generally accepted, being regarded simply as a 'tax' on rifles, but it was the provisions under the second heading, about compensation to the *Mateketoa*, that gave rise to the greatest difficulty. These men had taken up arms against the rebels and what they had lost they had lost through war. In the end, on 12 May, Letsie, Lerotholi, Joel Molapo and ten other chiefs wrote to accept the award, in spite, as they said, of the compensation required. 'We shall endeavour to act as we are ordered,' they wrote, 'but we may be overcome by the weight of some of the conditions in Clause 2.' As in all the negotiations so far, Masupha did not sign.[91]

The Sprigg Ministry's formal acceptance of the award was almost its last act. The final negotiations had taken place against a background of a no confidence debate in the House of Assembly dominated by opposition attacks on the government's policy of disarmament and its conduct of the war. Sprigg, now a sick man, looking 'pale and feeble', 'not at all robust', desperately defended his record and the government survived, but only by 37 votes to 34, and a few days later Sprigg handed in his resignation.[92]

---

[89] C.2964, p. 20, Robinson to Kimberley, 29 April 1881.
[90] PEMS Archives, Morija, Lerotholi to Griffith, 4 May 1881, and Dyke to J.J. Irvine, 9 May 1881.
[91] C.2964, p. 21, Robinson to Kimberley, 16 May 1881; *JME* 1881, p. 296, Dieterlen to Mabille, 31 May 1881.
[92] For a detailed record of the debate see *Cape Argus*, 12 April 1881 and following. The vote was taken on 27 April and Sprigg resigned on 6 May. For Sprigg's health, see *The Journal*, 2 May 1881, 'Gossip from the House'.

PART III

THE COLLAPSE OF CAPE RULE

Now those who began the war have drawn in their claws:
You provoke it, and then you run away![1]

---

[1] Damane and Sanders (1974: 147), Lerotholi's praise poems.

CHAPTER 15: THE MISSION OF J.W. SAUER

J.W. Sauer
The new Cape government assumed office on 9 May 1881, just three days before Letsie, Lerotholi and Joel wrote to accept Robinson's award. The new Premier, Thomas Scanlen, was a country lawyer, quiet, dependable and hard-working, and, unlike Sprigg, not the sort of man to arouse great passions either for or against himself. He was supported by most of the 'big guns' of the House such as Molteno, Merriman and Hofmeyr.[1] But for the Basotho the most important appointment was that of J.W. Sauer as Secretary for Native Affairs. Sauer, now 31, had been brought up at Aliwal North, not far from the Basutoland border. He was beginning to build up a reputation as a champion of African interests and the Cape liberal tradition, and the PEMS missionaries had been impressed by his 'sympathy for the natives'.[2] It was Sauer who, back in January, had initiated the peace process, and he had consistently opposed Sprigg's policy of disarmament. With his debating skills and his 'calm, self-possessed manner' he had already made his mark in the House of Assembly.[3]

In the previous administration Sprigg had taken charge of 'native policy' almost to the exclusion of William Ayliff, his Secretary for Native Affairs. In the new government Scanlen gave the lead and was reassuringly supportive, but it was Sauer who was invariably at the forefront of the action. Overruling the objections of Merriman and Hofmeyr, who did not believe that the award would be carried out by the Basotho or could be enforced by the Cape, but with full support from Sauer, Scanlen announced to a cheering house, 'in tones of peculiar emphasis' it was said, that his ministry accepted the award and would ensure, if necessary by military action, that the Basotho complied with it.[4] It was Sauer's responsibility to get this decision carried out.

He had been given a poisoned chalice. The award was based on the fiction that the Basotho had been defeated and that the mildness of its terms was due to Robinson's generosity, whereas in fact it was the Cape that had been forced to back down, and the terms were mild because anything more severe, like Sprigg's earlier terms, would have been rejected by the chiefs out of hand. And if the Basotho failed to comply even with the watered-down provisions of the award the demoralisation and paralysis of the last few months of the war had shown, contrary to Scanlen's assurance, that it could never be enforced by Cape troops alone. Sprigg and his colleagues were still smarting under the humiliation of failure, which they blamed on their opponents' treachery. They were determined to exact their revenge, to undermine Scanlen's government just as they themselves claimed to have been undermined. For the time being they lay in wait, licking their wounds, but when they saw their chance they would come out fighting.

---

[1] Lewsen (1982:90).
[2] Smith (1939: 292); Lewsen (1960: 93); Rhodes House Library, Oxford, Anti-Slavery Papers, MSS. Brit. Emp. S.18, C140/242, Mabille to Chesson, 7 April 1881; PEMS Archives, Paris, Maeder to President and Directors, 7 July 1881.
[3] *Cape Argus*, 14 May 1880, 'Notes in Parliament'.
[4] Lewsen (1982: 96).

The talks at Morija

Towards the end of June Sauer set out for Basutoland. In his determination to effect a lasting settlement he stayed for almost three months, with just a break of ten days in July when he went back to Aliwal North. He arrived at the headquarters camp near the Boleka ridge on 19 June. It was mid-winter, cold 'almost beyond endurance'.[5] He had ridden in with Clarke and Griffith, and two days later they set out for Morija. At Boleka Nek they were met by 400 armed and mounted Basotho, who cheered and fired salutes, and as they approached the mission station Lerotholi and Joel joined them with another 400 armed horsemen. According to Sauer,

> The chiefs and people were most respectful in their demeanour and civil in their language …. Though apparently in no way boastful, it was evident that the Basutos had pretty accurately guaged [sic] the results of the campaign …. They saw that Mohali's Hoek had been abandoned; no advance made from Maseru, or Thlotse Heights; and that our forces had only proceeded some nine miles beyond Mafeteng and seemed paralysed before the Boleka Nek.[6]

On the following day a meeting was held in the school-room at Morija. Seventy chiefs and councillors were there and a thousand more Basotho waited outside. Sauer set the scene. In a code that was easily deciphered he characterised Sprigg's Ministry and Scanlen's. There were people in the Colony, he said, who thought that there was 'only one way of dealing with native tribes', and that was 'under threat of compulsion by force of arms'. There were others who thought that the Basotho could be 'treated as a reasonable people'. The Basotho must not throw away their sympathy. They must prove their loyalty by complying with the award.

The discussion that followed went on for three days. There were complaints about the heaviness of the £1 licence fee for guns. Sauer responded sympathetically: if the Basotho conducted themselves well this burden might be made lighter for them. This possible concession was welcomed, and Masupha declared that if it was only a question of the fine and the registration of guns, matters would be much simplified. But the real difficulty, he said, was the compensation to be paid to the traders and the *Mateketoa*. These men had taken up arms against them. The traders' stores had been turned into forts, and the *Mateketoa* had handed in their guns before they had any authority to do so. When a dog bit its master it must be given a beating.

On the final day there were no formal speeches, but 'a desultory conversation', mainly about the clause on compensation.

> The chiefs stated that though they were willing to comply with it, the bulk of the property taken had been distributed among the people, who regarded it as portion of the spoils of war; that it would be difficult to enforce restitution in many cases; that much of the property had been parted with, and that some of it had not fallen into their hands, but was lost, stolen, or destroyed. They stated further that the claims of the loyal people were exaggerated.[7]

Sauer said that the government would not change the clause on compensation, but it would be willing to appoint a commission to enquire into the loyalists' losses. 'This was agreed to by all present but Masupha, who evaded the question.' But Lerotholi was clearly agitated: he had

---

[5] *Cape Argus*, 'Basutoland', 24 June 1881.
[6] G.26-'82, pp. 6-7.
[7] G.26-'82, p. 29.
[7] G.26-'82, p. 28.

promised his people that what they had taken in war would be theirs, and now he was being made a liar.

Several speakers raised another important theme that had nothing to do with the award: they did not want the Cape administration to revert to magisterial rule. The Basotho wanted their chiefs to judge their cases, and only if a chief was unable to deal with a case should it be referred to 'the ruler … sent by the Queen'.[8] Two Bataung speakers made a revealing comparison between Cape rule and Moshoeshoe's rule. In the words of Popolosi Mopheti,

> In Moshesh's time we were Moshesh's, but Moletsani's children were his children, and his people were his people, although Moletsani was the subject of Moshesh. That is why Letsie should be under the Queen and Letsie's subjects his own subjects, and why only matters that Letsie cannot arrange should by his reference be placed before you.[9]

But it was Masupha who spoke most strongly. There had been too many magistrates before the war.

> We wish that our chief Letsie may continue to be our chief and govern us, and that the magistrate may govern the chief …. The magistrates have taken all power away from the chiefs …. And they tell us that when we have once given ourselves to the Queen's Government we have nothing whatever to say. Consequently before the gun question arose the affairs of the Basutos were in troubled waters as it were on account of this.[10]

If Sauer made any response to these protests they were not recorded. His first priority was to deal with the enforcement of the award.

Another interesting feature of the discussions was the Basotho's determination to protect Letsie against any charge of disloyalty and to reinstate him in the government's good books. Letsie himself defended his record at great length. He had wanted to obey the government but Lerotholi had been 'headstrong'. He had been left unsupported. His people had 'killed' him.[11] Matela, the chief of the Makhoakhoa, urged that no blame should be attached to Letsie, who had wanted to keep the peace but had been overcome by his people.[12] Masupha declared that Letsie had 'always been loyal to the Government'.[13]

The fine, 'disarmament' and compensation

Sauer had insisted that the only way for the Basotho to prove their loyalty was to comply with the award, and on the issue of the fine of 5,000 head of cattle he had a quick response. The chiefs had ordered a *sethabathaba*, a public subscription, and although there were some who had 'murmured' about paying, Letsie, Lerotholi and Joel were all firm that the payment had to be made.[14] Shortly after the meeting Lerotholi delivered up about 1,000 head of cattle, and on the day after the meeting Letsie and Joel each handed over a further 1,000 head. Masupha was less forthcoming. At first he asked why the Basotho should give cattle to people they had beaten, but in the end he

---

[8] G.26-'82, p. 20.
[9] G.26-'82, p. 28.
[10] G.26-'82, pp. 21-2.
[11] G.26-'82, pp. 24-7.
[12] G.26-'82, p. 14.
[13] G.26-'82, p. 21.
[14] *JME* 1881, p. 296, Dieterlen to Mabille, 31 May 1881.

relented and paid about 400 head – a relatively meagre contribution, especially as he had suffered so little in the war. Although the fine now disappeared from the government's list of concerns, it was never paid in full, and there were some who alleged that the cattle handed over were wretchedly inferior – 'ancient, scraggy animals in the shape of oxen', said one.[15] Sauer, however, was willing to be satisfied.

On the issue of guns the Basotho were less compliant. Although the relevant article in the Robinson Award had been set out under the heading of disarmament, it would have been more accurate, and more honest, to have used the term registration. Not a single Mosotho would be disarmed. As Orpen, the next Governor's Agent, freely confessed later, 'Everyone in Basutoland knows that the first article of the award did not lay down disarmament, but a liberal construction with regard to licences …. And all know that disarmament is impracticable ….'[16] On the very issue that had given rise to the war, on the very issue that given the war its name, the Basotho had prevailed. Even registration was only partial. On the day following the meeting Letsie, Lerotholi, Joel and several other chiefs and councillors set an example by handing over their licence fees, and over the next few months between 4,000 and 5,000 guns are known to have been registered.[17] They represented only a fraction of the Basotho's guns, and at first no guns at all were brought in by Masupha. Sauer turned a blind eye to this, except that he demanded at least some compliance from Masupha in what became the much more important context of demanding compensation for the *Mateketoa*.

It was already clear that compensation was the issue on which Robinson's settlement was likely to founder. In the initial discussions at Morija Sauer had suggested a commission of enquiry to assess the *Mateketoa*'s losses. This proposal was not pursued, and in the weeks following the Morija discussions the magistrates were busy collecting information about the losses sustained by the *Mateketoa* and the white traders, officials and missionaries. The amounts claimed were huge. In the Leribe District the *Mateketoa* claimed 15,000 cattle, 1,650 horses, 15,000 sheep and goats, 200 pigs, 150 ploughs, 3000 muids of grain, and miscellaneous property to the value of £5,000 – and these figures did not include the cattle and other property belonging to the estate of Molapo which Joel and his brothers had seized and which were claimed by Jonathan as Molapo's heir and successor.[18] In the same district the local whites submitted claims to the value of almost £23,000, while those in the Mafeteng District claimed over £19,000 (which Surmon, the local magistrate, regarded as excessive) and those in the Thaba-Bosiu and Berea Districts between £8,000 and £9,000 each.[19]

---

[15] Woon (1909: 234). See also *The Friend*, 28 July 1881 (quoted in Mohapeloa 1971: 68).

[16] G.89-'82, p. 34, Orpen, 'Remarks on the Clauses of the petition', 8 November 1881.

[17] C.2964, p. 29, Robinson to Kimberley, 13 July 1881 (600 registered by 13 July); G.26-'82, pp. 34-5, Charles Bell to Orpen, 30 September 1881 (1,400 guns registered by Joel Molapo's people, but at 5s. a gun); G.26-'82, p. 35 (2,000 registered at Morija by 19 August); LNA, MF2/1/2, Surmon to Orpen, 3 October 1881 (360 registered at Siloe).

[18] LNA, L2/1/2, Davies to Griffith, 26 July 1881.

[19] LNA, S9/1/2/2, Griffith to Orpen, 22 August 1881; MF2/1/2, Surmon to Griffith, 7 September 1881. These figures varied over time: in February 1882 the claims submitted by the *Mateketoa* were valued in all at £153,326 10s, the bulk being made up of 27,326 cattle valued at £4 each, while the claims of the officials, missionaries and traders amounted to £81,158 14s. 6d.: see G.89-'82, pp. 14-16, Orpen to Sauer, 15 February 1882. Lerotholi had protested at Morija that he had promised his people that they could keep all the cattle which they had captured in war. Sauer and Robinson accepted that the only stock to be restored were those taken before the war began. In

There was little prospect of these claims being met in full or even in large measure. The popular rage against the *Mateketoa* was too strong,[20] especially against George Moshoeshoe, who was believed to have killed one of Masupha's sons.[21] Letsie and Lerotholi promised to do what they could, and early in August Joel handed over 'some 2,400 head of cattle, 1,400 sheep and goats, and 500 horses, the property of, and compensation to, loyal Basutos'.[22] But Masupha was still refusing to budge. On 7 August Sauer met him at the mission station at Thaba-Bosiu and castigated him for being the only principal chief who refused to accept the award. If he went on in this way he might well find himself on Robben Island. Masupha politely thanked him for the interview and said he would think over what Sauer had said.[23]

The *Mateketoa* were in despair. They had lost everything in the war. They and their families had been driven from their homes and had taken refuge at Mafeteng, Maseru and Hlotse Heights. By the end of the war there were several thousand refugees in and around each of these magistracies. So long as the fighting men received their pay they could afford to support their families, but the 'native contingents' would soon be disbanded and they would all become dependent on government rations. As well as compensation for their losses there was the even more important issue of whether or not they would be allowed to return to their homes. They were nervous about going back and living among hostile neighbours, and in most cases their lands had been allocated to others.[24] Sauer was already proposing that some of them should be moved to the Quthing District, Moorosi's old home.[25] During the war they had basked in government approval, fighting alongside the white troops and being praised for their loyalty and bravery. Now they saw the *Mabelete* restored to favour and courted by a government anxious to secure compliance with the award. Sauer spent three days talking with Joel, they complained, and only an hour with the loyal Jonathan.[26] After all their sacrifices and sufferings, after cutting themselves off from the main body of the people, they felt cruelly neglected, shoved to one side. When they complained to Letsie he merely replied that it was a *tsietsi*, a trouble, like war.[27]

There was peace, said the Basotho, but it was not a white peace.[28]

Among the missions in Basutoland there were mixed reactions. The PEMS missionaries, especially Adolphe Mabille, had vigorously campaigned against disarmament, and while they had advocated obedience to the law, and while many in their congregations had handed in their guns, in the course of the war itself their sympathies for the most part had rested with the *Mabelete*. In spite of their own dire predictions they were relieved that the Basotho had escaped defeat and dispersal, and they took

---

practice, however, this concession was ignored. See C.2964, p. 29, Robinson to Kimberley, 13 July 1881; LNA, S9/1/2/2, Orpen to Sauer, 30 September 1881.

[20] *JME* 1881, p. 296, Dieterlen to Mabille, 31 May 1881.

[21] In his praise poems he was described as *khomo ea se itja mohlana*, a cow which eats its own rump: Bereng and Lehloenya (1991: 45). See also the praise poems of Lerotholi, Damane and Sanders (1974: 145): 'We commoners and chiefs are distressed,/Whom shall we see and call our friend?/Our uncles behave like Matebele'. (Translation slightly changed.)

[22] G.26-'82, p. 34.

[23] G.26-'82, p. 34.

[24] G.89-'82, p. 8. George Moshesh to Sauer, 18 August 1881.

[25] G.26-'82, p. 35, account of a meeting held at Maseru on 24 July 1881 between Sauer and 'the loyal chiefs and some of the principal headmen'.

[26] *The Journal*, 8 September 1881, quoting a correspondent of *The Friend*.

[27] PEMS Archives, Paris, Maeder to President and Directors, 3 September 1881.

[28] *JME* 1881, p. 430, Germond to Committee, 25 August 1881.

pride in their bravery and in their victories in the field. Now they urged the Basotho to comply with the award and gave Sauer all the help they could.

The Catholics, having initiated the moves towards peace, no doubt shared the French Protestants' relief that the war was over and that the Basotho were still in possession of their country. But the Anglicans, who had been so closely identified with the government, and who had suffered so much at the hands of the rebels, deplored what they regarded as the headlong rush to peace at any price. Canon Widdicombe at Hlotse Heights, who had been appointed chaplain to the forces there, believed that until the rebels were 'really humbled' there would be 'no real peace or safety in the country'.[29] Instead, 'in their desire to bring the war to an end, the Cape Ministers were ready to go any lengths in the direction of concession or accommodation'.[30]

The main reason why the new government made so many concessions was that it had no viable alternative. There had been proposals in the Cape House of Assembly that Basutoland should be handed back to the imperial government, but the imperial government would have none of this:[31] after its recent defeat in the war in the Transvaal it was all the more determined not to get embroiled in the affairs of the interior. And it was impossible to maintain a strong force in the country. Sprigg later criticised the government for disbanding its troops before the terms of the award were carried out.[32] But the Colony was already £3m. in debt, and even if the money had been available it was impossible to keep irregulars in the field when there was no fighting to be done. Men whose terms of service came to an end insisted on going home, others deserted, and those who remained were demoralised and often drunk. The torrential rains of the summer had now been succeeded by the biting cold of the highveld winter. Oxen and horses suffered from lack of pasture. By the beginning of September all the irregulars had been disbanded. The only white troops in the country were the Cape Field Artillery and the CMR, one wing of which was about to leave, and the only black troops were the now militarised Basutoland Police and the 'native contingents', shortly to be disbanded, at Maseru and Hlotse Heights.[33]

At the same time the payment of (most of) the fine and the registration of at least a few thousand guns were encouraging signs that the Robinson Award would be complied with. Just as Sprigg had been too optimistic about the prospects of disarmament, so Sauer was too optimistic about the prospects of compliance with the award.[34]

Sauer was also having to look for a new Governor's Agent. Griffith was sure that, since they had not been defeated, the Basotho would be ungovernable, and in June he told Sauer that he wanted to get out. The Basotho would no longer look upon him 'with the same unbounded confidence as they did before'. His usefulness had been 'greatly impaired'.[35] It was not easy to find a replacement. The difficulties that Griffith had highlighted would not be removed by his departure. Bowker, who had twice been Governor's Agent before, turned down the job, and so did Chalmers, the Civil Commissioner at King William's Town.[36] Eventually the man appointed was Joseph Orpen. In the

---

[29] *Quarterly Paper of the Bloemfontein Mission*, No. 53, July 1881, p. 155, Widdicombe to Webb, 10 May 1881.
[30] Widdicombe (1895: 207-8).
[31] C.2964, pp. 172-3, 176-8.
[32] *The Journal*, 25 February 1882, 'Mr Sprigg at Peddie'; *Cape Argus*, 2 March 1882, Editorial.
[33] C.3112, p. 65, Sauer to , 5 September 1881.
[34] C.2964, p. 29, Robinson to Kimberley, 13 July 1881.
[35] LNA, S9/1/2/2, Griffith to Sauer, 17 June 1881.
[36] Bradlow (1968: 176), referring to *Cape Argus*, 6 August 1881 (for Bowker) and 23 May 1882 (for Chalmers).

negotiations immediately before the war Sprigg had tried, without success, to use Orpen's influence with the Basotho to head off the coming rebellion. Scanlen and Sauer now decided that their best hope of re-establishing law and order was to make use of his influence again. On 25 August Griffith went on a year's leave prior to retirement. On the same day, at a meeting in Maseru, Sauer introduced Orpen to the Basotho *Mateketoa* as the new Governor's Agent.

It was not an auspicious welcome. Griffith had already uttered his grim warnings. Now, in a powerful and eloquent speech, George Moshoeshoe spoke bitterly and bluntly. He had no time, he said, for flattering words. 'Not one single item of the Governor's award had yet been accepted and fulfilled by the rebels.' Before the war the loyal chiefs had been wealthy and respected. But then,

> At the call of the Queen they had given up their guns, had left all their property behind, and had come to Maseru, where they were promised the protection of government …. But when they arrived at Maseru … they were told that, instead of being able to protect them, the Government expected to be protected by them, and they had to fight for their lives and for the protection of the lives of the white men against their own brothers and against men of their own race and tribe. And now what could they think of a peace by which the rebels obtained all they chose to ask for, whereas the loyals lost everything they were possessed of?

They had killed many of their own people, including one of Masupha's sons. Did Sauer and Orpen really imagine that the rebel chiefs would ever forgive them? George was astonished that, although the whites had suffered grievously in the war, they had submitted to a humiliating award and 'did not even wink at the non-fulfilment of that award'. How could the loyalists now live among the rebels? The very lands which George had ploughed last year had been disposed of by the rebel chiefs to other men. Would the Queen help him to get them back again?

> They had a cry in Basutoland that once upon a time a lion died and then the carcase all rotted away except the lion's skin, and all the people, not knowing the lion was dead, were very much frightened and would not go near the place, so that the hare had a good and quiet time of it under cover of the lion's skin; but one day a little boy came and threw a stone at the lion and then the skin gave a hollow sound and the hare jumped out and ran away. So the people all laughed heartily at the dead lion's skin and were no longer frightened.

Before the war the Basotho

> had always looked upon the British Government as invincible … but now all that had been changed. Pride had now taken possession of the Basuto; they considered their chiefs now superior to the Queen's Government ….

> One example was sufficient to show what the Basuto really did think in their hearts, and this was the new song which they had adopted and was now sung wildly at their dances … 'We refused to give up our guns, and we have them still, and we will not give them up.'[37]

Sauer did not record this speech in his official account. He simply wrote that some spoke

---

[37] Tylden (1950A: 173-8), quoting article from the *Eastern Star*, n.d. The speech was also reported at length in *The Journal*, 9 September 1881, 'The Pitso of the Sons and Grandsons of Moshesh', which took it from *The [Kaffrarian] Watchman*.

strongly against the prospects of continued peace, others strongly in favour.[38] He was determined to bring about a lasting basis for peace before he left the country, and George's pessimism was not what he wanted to hear.

Masupha's 'submission'

Four days later, at a *pitso* at Matsieng, Sauer and Orpen succeeded in bringing the *Mabelete* and the *Mateketoa* together, though at first there was no sign of the recalcitrant Masupha. They urged the two sides to become reconciled and to live in harmony together, and on both sides the chiefs professed their attachment to peace. But while these encouraging speeches were being made Masupha and 20 armed followers burst in on the meeting. They had come across a wagon of brandy on the way and Masupha was 'under the influence of drink'. Letsie and several others left the *pitso* in disgust, and although it was resumed it was quickly brought to a close.[39]

The real business took place after the *pitso*. For Sauer there was one overwhelming priority: Masupha had to be brought to heel. He still had not accepted the Robinson Award, and Sauer now turned to Letsie and Lerotholi to compel him by force of arms, 'failing which', he said vaguely and unconvincingly, 'the Government would take the necessary measures to enforce submission.'[40] Letsie (after much pressure) and Lerotholi were prepared to take action, if only to remove a threat to their own position, and within a day or two 600 armed men were collected at Matsieng, ready to advance on Thaba-Bosiu, to repossess the loyalists' captured cattle and to 'eat Masupha up'.[41]

Masupha, now very respectful in his manner, brought in 140 head of cattle, which Sauer contemptuously rejected; and when, on 3 September, he sent word that he was prepared to carry out the conditions of the award, Sauer demanded that he should come himself or hand over his son Lepoqo as a hostage. Masupha sent in Lepoqo two days later.

In Sauer's view matters had come to a crisis. Masupha, he believed, could see that he was isolated. He did not expect him to resist. But if he did Letsie would eat him up and remove him from Thaba-Bosiu and Masupha, the arch-rebel, would be politically dead. He would release Lepoqo only if Masupha handed over no fewer than 6000 head of cattle and registered at least 100 guns.[42]

On 9 September Masupha rode in with 20 followers, begged for forgiveness, and delivered up 706 head of cattle. It was also reported that his people had registered 303 guns. His two allies, Ramanella and Leshoboro, handed over 170 and 200 cattle respectively.[43] On 10 September Masupha handed in a letter expressing his contrition and formally assuring Sauer of his humble submission to the Governor's award.[44]

Although the cattle handed over fell far short of the 6,000 he had demanded, Sauer accepted this letter at its face value and released Lepoqo. Had he pressed on and demanded the full amount, while Masupha still felt under serious threat, he might possibly have been able to enforce the award. But privately – and inconsistently with his public declarations – he told Orpen that he

---

[38] G.26-'82, p. 35.

[39] G.26-'82, pp. 41-50, 'Memorandum of the Pitso held at Matseing [sic], Letsie's residence, August 29th, 1881'.

[40] G.26-'82, p. 50.

[41] C.3112, pp. 60-2, Sauer to Scanlen, 29, 30, and 31 August and 2 September, 1881.

[42] C.3112, pp. 61-2, 65, Sauer to Scanlen, 31 August, 2 and 5 September 1881.

[43] G.26-'82, p. 51.

[44] G.26-'82, p. 51. Masupha to Sauer, 10 September 1881.

did not think that Letsie's sons would really have coerced Masupha: 'we are very lucky in his giving in.'[45] Moreover, although there was no record of this in his reports at the time, he apparently indicated that for the present he was prepared to accept 3,000 cattle as an 'earnest' of the payment of the award in full, a statement that was misrepresented by Masupha and others as indicating that no further payment was required.[46]

Sauer now believed that he had accomplished his mission and set out for the Colony: 'we have rounded the corner', he wrote to Scanlen, 'and it is now merely a matter of detail and perseverance. I have no doubt that law and order will soon be completely re-established, and that there is little or no danger of an attempt to resist our authority ….'[47] On the way he held meetings at Mafeteng, Mohale's Hoek and the mission station of Masitise. Everything went as well as he could have wished. 'I only hope', he said at Masitise, 'that very soon matters will in these parts be as if no war had existed, and that you will be contented and prosperous under the rule of the Government.' 'The meeting concluded amidst hearty cheers and waving of hats.'[48]

The final enforcement of the award now rested in the hands of the new Governor's Agent.

---

[45] Cory Library, MS 1248, Orpen, 'Major General Charles Gordon's visit to Basutoland in 1882 and my administration of the government of that territory from August 1881 to March 1883', p. 12.
[46] LNA. S9/1/2/2, Orpen to Sauer, 16 (in fact 17) January 1882, report on *pitso* held on 16 (in fact 17) January 1882, speeches of Orpen and Lerotholi.
[47] C.3112, p. 66, Sauer to Scanlen, 9 September 1881.
[48] G.26-'82, pp. 59-60, 'Memorandum of proceedings at a meeting held at Masitisi on September 14, 1881'.

CHAPTER 16: JOSEPH MILLERD ORPEN

Orpen and his magistrates

Joseph Millerd Orpen is one of the most controversial and intriguing characters in the Basotho's history. He was born in 1828, the fourth of seven sons of a Dublin physician, and came to South Africa in 1846. He worked as a surveyor in the Orange River Sovereignty, took part in the fighting against the Basotho at that time, and after the Sovereignty was abandoned became a member of the Volksraad of the newly established Free State. President Hoffman sent him on a special mission to establish friendly relations with Moshoeshoe. The young Irishman was quickly convinced that the Basotho had been wrongly deprived of much of their land, and from that time on he became a passionate and committed supporter of Moshoeshoe and his people. His *History of the Basutus of South Africa*, published in 1857, was an uncompromising statement of their case. His connection with the country was strengthened in 1859 by his marriage to Elise, the daughter of the missionary, Samuel Rolland, and the sister of Emile Rolland. He continued to work closely with Moshoeshoe, visiting him frequently and constantly advising him to seek British intervention in his disputes with his powerful neighbours, and when Moshoeshoe made his famous declaration that what he wanted was that the Queen should send a man to live with him, the man that he had in mind was Orpen.[1] Such an appointment, however, would have been unacceptable to the Free State.

In 1872, after the Seqiti War, Orpen was elected from Queenstown to the Cape Parliament, and from 1873 to 1875 he was the British Resident in Griqualand East. In 1877 he supported Nehemiah Moshoeshoe when he was accused of fomenting rebellion in that territory,[2] a bold stand that won him gratitude and admiration throughout Basutoland. In 1879 he was re-elected to the Cape Parliament, this time as one of the members for Aliwal North, and he often spoke up in the Basotho's interests. While arguing that, 'from an abstract point of view, disarmament was no doubt an excellent thing', he disagreed profoundly with the timing and the manner of its application.[3] Many found it strange that he should have accompanied Sprigg on his final mission to Basutoland before the outbreak of war, but he pointed out, to good effect, that Sprigg had said that he would not use force in order to bring about disarmament, and that he felt himself under a moral obligation to do what he could to try to secure peace.[4]

He was not always the most effective of advocates, and the very qualities that made him acceptable to the Basotho attracted criticism in the Colony. The *Cape Times* described his appointment as 'a gross and a lamentable mistake'. Personally he was 'a very estimable gentleman', 'very well meaning' and 'possessed of personal courage'. But he was 'vague in his ideas' and 'decidedly prosy in his speeches', and his only qualification for the post was 'the fact that he is well-known to the Basutos as ... one who has – judiciously or injudiciously – never failed to take their part'.[5] The *Cape Argus*, which was generally sympathetic and supportive, found him 'terribly in earnest' but 'terribly tedious', 'one of the greatest bores in the House of Assembly'. He was 'not the happiest of orators': his speeches were too long and

---

[1] Sanders (1975: 256).
[2] Chapter 5, pp. 60-1 above.
[3] *Cape Argus*, 28 August 1879, 'House of Assembly', 25 August.
[4] *Cape Argus*, 10 November 1880, Editorial, and 18 November 1880, 'Mr. Orpen and the Basutos'.
[5] *Cape Times*, 9 August 1881.

his manner was 'halting'.[6] Later one critic in the House of Assembly described him as 'conscientiously mad on native affairs'.[7]

He was a man of great energy, and his 'vigorous frame' enabled him to put up with considerable discomfort and hardship.[8] In 1873 the Basotho had given him the name of Ramaloti when, at the time of the Langalibalele affair, he had gone with a small body of men into the mountains, and as the Governor's Agent he moved around extensively, spending at first almost as much time at Morija and Matsieng, working with Letsie and Lerotholi, as at his desk in Maseru. But he was not as clear-thinking or as well-organised as Griffith, and he lacked Griffith's presence and authority.

He badly needed the support of a strong and loyal team of magistrates. Three of Griffith's stalwarts were no longer there. John Austen was dead. At the end of May Arthur Barkly resigned, his health shattered by the hardships of campaigning. A month later Major Bell, worn out by the strains and privations of the war, died of double pneumonia at Hlotse Heights. And those who remained, instead of supporting Orpen, were out of sympathy with what he was trying to do. Like Griffith, they believed that the rebels should have been humbled and they were opposed to what they regarded as a scamped and patched-up peace. As Henry Davies in Maseru frankly acknowledged, they were 'partial to the loyals, who have fought side by side with us & risked their lives to save ours'.[9] They had no faith in the goodwill of Letsie, Lerotholi and Joel, and Orpen's efforts to win the co-operation of the *Mabelete* were perceived and portrayed as betrayals of the *Mateketoa*.

Except for Surmon they declared themselves 'incapacitated through late events' and were anxious to leave. Davies, however, stayed on until the end of the year. Of all the old magistrates he was the most embittered and outspoken.[10] His communications to Orpen became increasingly disrespectful and hostile, to the point where he had to be censured and working relations between them broke down. In the south a new man, Colonel Marshal Clarke, was appointed to take Austen's place at Quthing; Surmon was restored to his post at Mohale's Hoek; and another new man, Alexander Bailie, was posted to Mafeteng. In the north Charlie Bell took over from his late father as Magistrate of the Leribe District, but he was in such profound disagreement with the new policies that in December he was transferred at his own request to the Transkei. His place was then taken by Bailie on transfer from Mafeteng, and a new magistrate, Nettelton, was appointed in Mafeteng. Meanwhile, because of Masupha's resistance, it was impossible to re-establish a magistrate at Advance Post.

As well as Davies, Surmon and Bell, several of the clerks remained in post, at least until the following year, and for the most part they too were out of sympathy with the new administration. The opposition to Orpen was particularly strong at Hlotse Heights, where, as well as Henry Jervis the clerk, Dr Taylor and Canon Widdicombe were heavily involved. Nor did it help Orpen that the magistracies were crowded with *Mateketoa* refugees, whose sufferings and complaints formed the immediate backdrop against which most of these men carried out their duties. As Rolland commented on Surmon later, he lived among loyals, he had little or no communication with the former rebels, and his opinions

---

[6] *Cape Argus*, 3 July 1879, 'Notes in Parliament'; 5 July 1879, Editorial; and 12 August 1880, 'Notes in Parliament'.
[7] *Cape Argus*, 14 April 1882, 'Parliament. House of Assembly', 13 April 1882.
[8] *The Journal*, 1 February 1881, 'Basutoland'.
[9] CA, N.A. 280, Davies to Orpen, 17 November 1881.
[10] *The Journal*, 28 December 1881, 'Basutoland': 'He has always borne the character of a frank, outspoken man as well as a clever and able magistrate.'

were affected accordingly.[11]

Those who believed that the *Maketetoa* were being betrayed found a ready outlet for their disgust in the opposition press. The supporters of the previous administration blamed their political opponents and the PEMS missionaries for the failure of disarmament. Now they could take their revenge.

After the withdrawal of most of the Cape forces, and with barely enough CMR to garrison the magistracies, Orpen had to rely almost entirely on 'moral force'. But that 'moral force' was now spent and there was no other kind of force in reserve. Unlike Griffith, he could not browbeat or threaten any chiefs who defied him – except perhaps with abandonment, which was precisely what some of them wanted and which would only have encouraged them in their resistance. He was therefore completely dependent on the co-operation of the principal chiefs, the very men who had recently been in rebellion against the government.

Trying to get justice for the *Maketetoa*

One issue now dominated all others – the treatment of the *Maketetoa*, and in particular their rights to compensation and to return to their villages. Later it would be recognised that the whole attempt to recover the *Maketetoa*'s stock from the *Mabelete* was misconceived and impracticable. Instead of pretending that it had won the war, the government itself should have paid the compensation, or, if it had to insist that the Basotho should pay, it should have imposed a fine or raised a general tax. As it was, the methods that Orpen adopted were quickly bogged down in muddle and mutual recrimination. He did not call upon the *Mabelete* chiefs to pay specified numbers of animals, but instead instructed them, in general terms, to recover and to return all the *Maketetoa*'s stock. At the same time he called on the *Maketetoa* to go among their former enemies in order to find and identify their animals and to reassert their claims to their former villages and land. He became personally immersed and embroiled in many individual cases, sometimes to the detriment of his dignity and authority.

To add to the confusion the *Maketetoa* and their white sympathisers exaggerated their plight and the difficulties they faced, while Orpen talked up the prospects of success and painted too rosy a picture. The gulf between Orpen's reports and those of the magistrates, particularly Davies, Bell and Surmon, was often so wide that it must have been impossible for their political masters to know what was going on.

Because of the methods that Orpen adopted the *Maketetoa* were often exposed to unpleasantness and danger, particularly in those areas where Masupha was in control or influential. In September several chiefs and headmen tried to recover their property and reclaim their land in the Berea District and in the Maseru division of the Thaba-Bosiu District. In every case they met with evasion or downright refusal, and in some cases abuse and threats to their lives.[12] At a *pitso* with the *Maketetoa* in the same month, according to a hostile newspaper report, Orpen told them to go about the country 'as if nothing had happened', to go home and plough their lands. When one of them, Moleko, said they had no ploughs or oxen, Orpen told him to borrow or to hire them. When Moleko said they no longer had any friends or money, Orpen told him to use 'a Kafir hoe'. Moleko was outraged: he used to have six to seven spans of oxen, he protested, but when war broke out he had to flee and leave them behind. If he went to look for them he would be killed, and now, 'because of my faithful

---

[11] LNA, S9/1/2/2, Rolland to Sauer, 6 April 1882.
[12] G.89-'82, pp. 38-43, Davies to Orpen, 20 September 1881, with enclosures.

adherence to the Government, I am told go and till the ground with a Kafir hoe!'[13]

For Orpen the central question was whether or not the principal chiefs would be able and willing to overcome this opposition. Masupha of course had no intention of complying with the Robinson Award. In discussions with his followers he misrepresented Sauer's acceptance of an 'earnest' of cattle as an acceptance of a settlement in full, and at a meeting with Orpen he told him that he was Orpen's 'very great friend' but he would not return a single head of cattle to the *Mateketoa*. In a later meeting he was even more forthright, brandishing a stick and saying that this was what would happen to any *Mateketoa* who tried to go back to their villages.[14] He now had what he had always wanted – his independence, free from magisterial control, and indeed from any control by Letsie. He punished those chiefs who had offended him before the war, instructed his people not to return the *Mateketoa*'s cattle, and told them that 'no loyals would be allowed to return'.[15] He was also placing his sons in new villages without any reference to Letsie or the government.[16] By fomenting unrest and instability he could maintain his freedom of action. He knew only too well that if the country was brought to order his branch of the family would be overshadowed by Letsie's, especially when Lerotholi succeeded his father.[17]

In the north, however, in the Leribe District, Joel was anxious to win back the government's approval. His magistrate, Charles Bell, reported that, because of his defiance in the war, he was now 'the paramount Chief in the district'. 'Being an intelligent, cautious, and ambitious man, he has succeeded in gaining sufficient influence over the people to enable him to rule them without the slightest opposition. …. All matters are referred to him, and no one dares to act contrary to his decision.'[18] But in the long term his position was insecure. His brother Jonathan had been recognised as Molapo's rightful successor, albeit in an acting capacity for his deranged brother Josefa. And although Joel enjoyed the support of several of his other brothers, notably Khethisa and Hlasoa, he considered he deserved more from the *Mabelete* in the rest of the country. In his praise poems he described himself as

> The young warrior who's rejected by his kinsmen,
> Today the Bakoena have deserted him,
> Masupha and Lerotholi.[19]

And again:

> Last year, in the Gun War,
> They said: 'Hey, Mokoena!
> Blood-child of Molapo, Fierce-Visaged!'
> The war ended, they said 'You're a Letebele!'
> If only I'd known I'd have left the fight![20]

---

[13] *The Journal*, 11 October 1881, 'A Pitso with the Loyals in Basutoland', from a correspondent of *The Watchman*, Maseru, 24 September.
[14] *The Journal*, 2 November 1881, 'Basutoland'; G.33-'82, p. 229, *pitso* held 16 January 1882.
[15] C.3112, p. 112, Charles Bell to Orpen, 4 October 1881. See also LNA, S9/2/3/1, Davies to Orpen, 27 September 1881.
[16] LNA, S9/1/2/2, Orpen to Sauer, 30 September 1881.
[17] PEMS Archives, Morija, Dyke, 11 November 1881.
[18] C.3112, p. 110, Bell to Orpen, 30 September 1881.
[19] Damane and Sanders (1974: 192). For Bakoena, see page 72, fn. 44 above.

Furthermore, his territorial base was weak, since he had lost most of his territory during the last war with the Free State and his much-diminished ward, now based at Qalo, was 'hardly large enough for himself and his people'.[21] Jonathan, at least nominally, had a much more extensive territory, and after all his sufferings in the war demanded total and unequivocal government support. Joel, he reckoned, was merely his subordinate.[22] Bell was completely on Jonathan's side. 'The object of the Government, it is to be presumed,' he wrote, 'is to break Joel's power and to reduce him to his former status in the district.'[23]

This then was the context in which Joel had to operate. He needed to soften the Cape's hostility, but if he restored all Jonathan's stock and allowed him to reoccupy all his former land he would be preparing the ground for his own defeat. Orpen later declared that Joel did more than any other chief to comply with the award.[24] His contribution to the fine, 1,220 head of cattle, was larger absolutely, and much larger relatively, than the contribution of any other chief, and when Letsie and Lerotholi were threatening to attack Masupha he had 600-1000 men ready on the border to help them.[25] Early in August, as noted already, he had handed over to Sauer some 2,400 head of cattle, 1,400 sheep and goats and 500 horses as compensation for the *Mateketoa*.[26] In September Orpen reported that he had 'generally satisfactory accounts from Leribe', where 'more than half' of the *Mateketoa* were 'already reinstated', and in October that they had all returned to their homes and that the district was quiet.[27]

In making these statements Orpen was partly reflecting the views of Charles Bell, who declared on 30 September that the *Mateketoa* were 'returning to their villages in numbers, few remaining in camp', and on 24 November that matters were 'very quiet, not a rumour stirring. Letsie's sons are getting the cattle in gradually ..., small lots come in every day. All loyals are hard at work ploughing in every direction'.[28] But Bell's communications did not all point the same way. On 18 September he reported that Joel was 'obstructing Jonathan in his plans for arranging and settling his people in their former villages .... [He] openly states that he has captured the District by force of arms and intends to retain it'.[29] And the compensation which Sauer had taken delivery of with such evident satisfaction in August Bell dismissed as of little worth – 'old cows and calves', only a small proportion of the *Mateketoa*'s losses, and Joel was refusing to give up the rest.[30] In all this, according to Bell, Joel was supported by his brothers, Khethisa and Hlasoa, and by his old ally in arms, Ramanella.[31]

At the end of November, only six days after informing Orpen that his District was 'very quiet', Bell suddenly sounded a note of alarm. The government was contemplating action against Masupha, and Bell had probably been unsettled by the rumours to which this gave rise. The former rebels, he

---

[20] Damane and Sanders (1974: 202). The translation has been changed.
[21] C.3112, p. 110, Bell to Orpen, 30 September 1881.
[22] G.47-'82, p. 186, Bailie to Orpen, 31 March 1882. See also G.47-'82, p. 193, Orpen's Report, March 1882.
[23] C.3112, p. 110, Bell to Orpen, 30 September 1881.
[24] LNA, S9/1/2/2, Orpen's draft annual report for 1881, 25 February 1882.
[25] C.3112, pp. 65-6, Sauer to Scanlen, 9 September 1881.
[26] Chapter 15, p. 195 above.
[27] LNA, S9/1/2/2, Orpen to Sauer, 23 and 26 September 1881; C.3112, p. 86, Orpen to Sauer, 14 October 1881.
[28] C.3112, p. 111, Bell to Orpen, 30 September 1881; p. 94, Orpen to Under SNA, 29 November 1881, quoting Bell to Orpen, 24 November 1881.
[29] LNA, L2/1/2, Bell to Orpen, 18 September 1881.
[30] C.3112, pp. 110-1, Bell to Orpen, 30 September 1881.
[31] LNA, L2/1/2, Bell to Orpen, 18 November 1881; C.3112, p. 114, Bell to Orpen, 30 November 1881.

wrote, were becoming increasingly independent and defiant. There were rumours of their combining with Masupha in the event of any action against him, and he called for troops to defend Hlotse Heights.[32] On 14 December he announced that 'the Joel faction' were refusing to make any concessions to the loyals on the ground that they were no longer entitled to call themselves Basotho.[33] Orpen asked him to account for this about-turn in his reports, but by this time he had handed over his responsibilities to Bailie and had left on extended leave.

In the south Letsie and Lerotholi made strenuous efforts to recover the *Mateketoa*'s property and were constantly encouraging them to return to their villages.[34] They were supported by at least two other sons of Letsie, Seeiso and Mojela, but not by Bereng, and it was unfortunate for Orpen that Bereng's home was close to the old village of George Moshoeshoe, the most articulate of the *Mateketoa* chiefs. The constant wrangles about George's return to his area are described later in this chapter.

In the Mafeteng division of the Thaba-Bosiu District Orpen's sanguine reports were supported by Bailie who, as a new magistrate, was unencumbered by the past and who had full and active co-operation from Lerotholi. On 14 October Orpen reported that most of the *Mateketoa* in the Mafeteng district had gone home and none were prevented. About a third of their stated losses had been restored and a large part of the rest had been struck off, being found to be in the care of relatives.[35] On 25 November Bailie told Sauer that the situation in his district was 'most satisfactory', and his main complaint was against the *Mateketoa*, who 'spread all sorts of rumours'.[36] A few days later he told Orpen that there was 'a more settled feeling' among the loyals and the rebels, and all traces of the late rebellion were being 'toned down'.[37]

In the Cornet Spruit District, however, where Orpen claimed on 14 October that all the *Mateketoa* had gone home,[38] Surmon's report two weeks later was in flat contradiction. Some *Mateketoa*, he wrote, had returned to their homes on the government reserve, but 'None of those who had their homes off the Reserve are now living at them ....' Two had returned but were so disturbed by 'the bearing of the people towards them' that they had left. There had been little move towards reconciliation. On the contrary, feelings were still running high, 'especially on the part of the late rebels, who are said to taunt and jeer at the loyals whenever they meet'. He confirmed Orpen's report that the *Mateketoa* had received about a third of the cattle taken from them, but said that because of threats from the *Mabelete* they were now afraid to go looking for any more.[39]

---

[32] G.89-82, pp. 43-4 (and C.3112, p. 114), Bell to Orpen, 30 November 1881.

[33] G.89-'82, pp. 173-4, Bell to Orpen, 14 December 1881. For a similar report see *The Journal*, 21 November 1881, 'Basutoland'.

[34] For Letsie's efforts, see, e.g., LNA, S9/1/2/2, Orpen to Sauer, 21, 23, 26 and 30 September 1881; S9/1/3/5, Orpen to J.E. Surmon, 4 October 1881; MF2/1/2, Surmon to Orpen, 6 October 1881; C.3112, pp. 86-7, Sauer to Scanlen, 17 October 1881. For Lerotholi's efforts, see, e.g., G.89-'82, p. 38, Surmon to Orpen, 19 September 1881; postcript dated 20 September 1881; LNA, MF2/1/2, Bailie (at Mafeteng) to Orpen, 12 October 1881. For Seeiso and Mojela, see G.26-'82, pp. 62-3, 'Memorandum of a Meeting held at Mohali's Hoek, on 12th September 1881', and pp. 57-8, 'Memorandum of Proceedings at a Meeting held at Masitisi on September 14, 1881'; LNA, S9/1/2/2, Orpen to Sauer, 29 September 1881.

[35] C.3112, Orpen to Sauer, 14 October 1881.

[36] C.3112, p. 97, Sauer to Scanlen, 4 December 1881, quoting Bailie to Sauer, 25 November 1881.

[37] LNA, MF2/1/2, Bailie to Orpen, 29 November 1881.

[38] C.3112, p. 86, Orpen to Sauer, 14 October 1881.

[39] C.3112, pp. 115-6, Surmon to Orpen, 30 November 1881.

In the Maseru division of the Thaba-Bosiu District the contradiction was even sharper. Orpen reported that the *Mateketoa* were returning to their homes, though some were fearful or reluctant,[40] while Davies, drawing his information exclusively from the *Mateketoa*, piled up one strongly worded account after another of *Mabelete* intransigence and downright hostility. Under Masupha's influence the *Mabelete* chiefs in his district would not allow any *Mateketoa* to return to their villages. And if the *Mateketoa* did go back, unless they continued to receive rations from the government, 'they would in a very short time be reduced to simple starvation, for they would not receive any assistance from the rebels, who hate them most thoroughly and would glory in their distress and persecute them for their loyalty to us'.[41] The *Mateketoa*'s stock had been returned only in individual cases where Letsie or Orpen himself had intervened. 'In all other cases the rebels flatly refuse to restore it.'[42]

There was the further complication that several of the *Mateketoa* chiefs, especially George Moshoeshoe, did not want to go back to their villages. This was partly because they did not want to live among hostile neighbours, but they were also keen to get out from under the authority of their more senior relatives and to find a new home in the Quthing District, which was still largely vacant after the defeat of Moorosi, or in the Matatiele District below the Drakensberg, where there was land vacated by rebels such as Makoae and Lelingoana.[43] In these places they would at last fulfil their old ambitions and become great chiefs in their own right.

Towards the end of his mission in Basutoland Sauer had offered George and a few other *Mateketoa* chiefs the prospect of land in Quthing, and when they had accepted he had told them that, although the time was not yet right, 'liberal provision' would be made for them when all the arrangements were settled.[44] The matter was left in Orpen's hands, and Orpen was more ambiguous. He was concerned that giving up the land to the *Mabelete* would in effect be rewarding them for their rebellion, and it would encourage them to resist the return of the *Mateketoa* throughout the country.[45] He did not explicitly renege on Sauer's offer, but told George that he would 'best please the Government' and serve his own interests if he co-operated with Lerotholi and Letsie in trying to get restitution of his villages and fields within Basutoland. 'This will not prevent any subsequent arrangements for your being placed anywhere else if Government so decides, but will rather facilitate it.'[46] But George was determined not to return to his old home, where he would be dominated by Letsie's son, Bereng.

Over the next few months there was a protracted tussle, with Orpen putting pressure on George to return to his village (to the extent of going there himself to witness what was happening and making George a gift of £5, with £5 more to come), Letsie giving him every encouragement and support (to the extent of arranging for George's lands to be ploughed by a *letsema*, a work party), Bereng playing a double game (telling George he could return but at the same time ordering his

---

[40] C.3112, p. 86, Sauer to Scanlen, 17 October 1881, quoting Orpen to Sauer, 14 October 1881.
[41] LNA, S9/2/3/1, Davies to Orpen, 1 November 1881.
[42] C.3112, p. 115, Davies to Orpen, 26 November 1881.
[43] LNA, S9/1/3//5, Orpen to George Moshoeshoe and six others, 5 October 1881. It was at this time that the Batlokoa of Lelingoana were given land in the Maloti, in what became the Mokhotlong District.
[44] G.26-'82, p. 35; C. 3112, pp. 95-6, Sauer to Scanlen, 2 December 1881; G.89-'82, pp. 161-2, 'Koadi M. Moshesh on behalf of Tsitsa and Rampa' to Orpen, 31 December 1881.
[45] G.89-82, pp. 34-5, Orpen, 'Remarks on the Clauses of the Petition', 8 November 1881, and p. 11, Orpen to George Moshoeshoe, 9 December 1881. Sauer agreed with Orpen: C.3112, pp. 94-6, Sauer to Scanlen, 2 December 1881.
[46] LNA, S9/1/3/5, Orpen to George Moshesh and six others, 5 October 1881.

subordinates to make him unwelcome), Davies making no secret of his view that it was dangerous and irresponsible to ask George to go back, and George himself determined not to move but to hold out for his promised land in Quthing. While Orpen exaggerated the ease of the move, George exaggerated its difficulties. But for the prospect of land in Quthing he might have tried to go back, but whether he would have been allowed to settle down is doubtful.[47]

George's refusal to return to his village was part of the much wider opposition to the new administration that was developing among the *Mateketoa* and that was most powerfully expressed in a petition to the High Commissioner from the leading *Mateketoa* in the Maseru and Leribe Districts, Jonathan Molapo, George, Sofonia and Ntsane Moshoeshoe, Piet Mokolokolo and 36 others. The account that they gave was one of unrelieved bleakness and despair. Robinson's award was just, they wrote, but it had not been complied with. Only the fine had been paid. Disarmament was a dead letter, and only a small part of their property had been restored. The rebels were ploughing their lands and living in their villages, and when Orpen sent them to claim their stock they were fobbed off to Letsie, who did nothing. 'As for peace, there is no such thing.' They bemoaned the loss of Griffith, 'a man in whom we had great confidence'. What they wanted, they said, was their rights and justice.[48]

The *Mateketoa* at Mafeteng drew up a similar petition to Gordon Sprigg, despairing, as they said, of any approach to Sauer, who when in Basutoland had spent all his time listening to the *Mabelete*. Their grievances were in stark opposition to the bland reports being submitted by Bailie. They had lost all their property, and all they had received by way of compensation were some 'poor miserable old bulls and cows that have been divided amongst us in twos and threes'. They had identified and claimed some of their plundered stock, but in no case had they been able to recover them, and when they had gone back to their villages they had been 'told by the rebels that we have no right to come back again, that they have beaten the white man, and that we had better return and live under the care of the white man, for that some harm would befal [sic] us if we came back ....' What they wanted was an area of land around the government reserve where they could live under government protection.[49] Some of the *Mateketoa* tried to provoke action against the *Mabelete* by spreading rumours – for example that Masupha was preparing to attack Maseru, that Joel was acting in concert with him, and even that Letsie and Lerotholi would support him.[50]

The *Mateketoa*'s opposition to Orpen was encouraged and supported by many whites, some of whom felt deeply ashamed that the *Mateketoa* should suffer so much for their loyalty, while others

---

[47] G.89-'82, p. 33, Orpen's 'Remarks on the Clauses of the Petition', 8 November 1881; G.89-'82, pp. 1-2, Orpen to George Moshoeshoe, 1 December 1881; pp. 2-3, George Moshoeshoe to Orpen, 1 December 1881; p. 3, F.E.C. Bell to George, 1 December 1881; and p. 3, George to F.E.C. Bell, 1 December 1881; C.3112, p. 105, Orpen to Colonial Secretary, 6 December 1881; and p. 122, Davies to Orpen, 6 December 1881; G.89-82, pp. 7-8, George Moshoeshoe to Orpen, 6 December 1881; pp. 9-11, Orpen to George Moshoeshoe, 9 December 1881; and p. 12, George Moshoeshoe to Orpen, 27 December 1881; *Cape Argus*, 20 December 1881, 'The Basuto Loyals. A Ploughing Bee'.

[48] G.89-'82, pp. 28-31, George Moshesh to Orpen, 23 October 1881, enclosing petition to Robinson, 20 October 1881.

[49] G.47-'82, pp. 107-8, petition from 'the loyal Basutos, Mafeteng', to Sprigg, 31 October 1881.

[50] E.g., LNA, S9/2/3/1, Davies, 'Official diary of reports made in connection with the carrying out of the Governor's Award, and Affairs in General', entries under 14 and 23 November and 9 December 1881; C.3112, p. 97, Bailie to Sauer, 25 November 1881, quoted in Sauer to Scanlen, 4 December 1881.

exploited their plight in order to embarrass the new government. In the colonial press Orpen was under constant and virulent attack as the great enemy of the *Mateketoa*.[51]

The only logical outcome of this opposition was the renewal of war. Sauer suspected that this was what some of the *Mateketoa* wanted, since in no other way would they be able to recover their position in the country,[52] and among the officials who had served under Griffith it was commonly held that it was only through force that the government could regain control. According to Orpen, Davies had 'from the first ... consistently held the view that restoration of peace but by armed force was impossible, and the return of the loyals unadvisable and dangerous till the rebellious feeling was stamped out by a Colonial army'.[53] Bell too believed that 'coercion' would be needed to restore the government's authority.[54] There were others who wanted war for less respectable reasons. With a scarcely veiled allusion to the parliamentary opposition Sauer referred to 'the "string the nigger up" party', while Orpen believed that they were inciting hatred in order to 'show that there is nothing for it but a war of confiscation and extermination'.[55] After the expense and humiliation of the Gun War, however, the colonial government was in no position to take up arms again.

For their part Sauer and Orpen believed that the Robinson Award offered the best hope for a lasting settlement. They knew they had to be patient and to make concessions, but they had, as they thought, two grounds for optimism. First, they believed that the hostility between the *Mabelete* and the *Mateketoa* was much exaggerated and that a reconciliation could be brought about.[56] Second, they had faith in the goodwill of Letsie, Lerotholi and others.

In his response to the *Mateketoa*'s petitions Orpen accused them of sweeping misrepresentations. He acknowledged that there were difficulties, especially in Masupha's area, but claimed that the *Mateketoa* had recovered 'a considerable number' of their stock, that many of them had been reinstated in their villages, and that others, like George, were refusing to go because they wanted to become independent chiefs in Quthing. 'There is nothing which hinders more the establishment of peace than the reiterated bitter cry that there is no peace.' As for the implication of prejudice against the *Mateketoa*, 'The loyal Basutos have indeed the first claim upon Government. My whole time is devoted to carrying out the fulfilment of this claim'.[57] Sauer's response was much the same. He spelt out every step he had taken to help the *Mateketoa*, and Orpen, he declared, was 'at this very moment ... straining every nerve to obtain satisfaction' for them.[58]

---

[51] G.89-'82, p. 35, Orpen, 'Remarks on the Clauses of the Petition', 8 November 1881; C.3112, p. 94, Orpen to Under SNA, 29 November 1881, and p. 107, Orpen to Colonial Secretary, 13 December 1881.
[52] C.3112, p. 95, Sauer to Scanlen, 2 December 1881, and p. 97, Sauer to Scanlen, 4 December 1881.
[53] C.3112, p. 118, Orpen to Sauer, 4 December 1881.
[54] C.3112, p. 114, Bell to Orpen, 30 November 1881.
[55] C.3112, p. 95, Sauer to Scanlen, 2 December 1881, and p. 94, Orpen to Under SNA, 29 November 1881. In February 1880 in a speech to his constituents in East London, Sprigg said that Masupha was trying to intimidate his people into not giving up their arms to the government. Schermbrucker (later to be put in charge of the Basutoland police in the Gun War) called out 'String him up!', and there was then a 'chorus', 'String him up, string him up!': *The Journal*, 'The Premier at East London', 13 February 1880.
[56] C.3112, p. 87, Orpen to Sauer, 14 October 1881; p. 94, Orpen to Under SNA, 19 November 1881; p. 96, Sauer to Scanlen, 2 December 1881.
[57] G.89-'82, pp. 33-5, Orpen, 'Remarks on the Clauses of the Petition', 8 November 1881. For Mokolokolo, see also LNA, S9/1/2/2, Orpen to Sauer, 23 September 1881, and MF2/1/2, J.E. Surmon to Orpen, 30 September and 6 October 1881.
[58] C.3112, pp. 94-6, Sauer to Scanlen, 2 December 1881.

At the same time, however, Sauer pressed Orpen for hard factual information about the *Mateketoa*'s losses and the numbers who had returned to their homes. Orpen had to admit that he could not immediately provide it, and the returns that he later obtained from his magistrates could not have reassured the government. The claims submitted by the *Mateketoa* were valued in all at £153,326 10s., the bulk being made up of 27,326 cattle valued at £4 each; the balance still owing to them was valued at £130,659 10s., 85% of the total claimed. The *Mateketoa* exaggerated their losses, but they had powerful reasons for complaint. Meanwhile not a penny had been paid of the claims submitted by the officials, missionaries and traders, which amounted to £81,158 14s. 6d. – a grievance which bound them in sympathy and interest even more closely to the *Mateketoa*.[59]

On the numbers of *Mateketoa* who had returned to their lands it was even more difficult to provide information since, as Orpen pointed out, the position was constantly changing.[60] There is clear evidence, however, about the numbers of people who were still receiving government rations at the camps. Towards the end of November 1881 910 persons, including 273 children under 10, were receiving rations at Mafeteng; in January 1882 1,690, including 768 children, at Maseru (a number which had not 'perceptibly altered' over the past 18 months); and in the same month 3,652 people, including 992 children, at Hlotse Heights.[61] There were some *Mateketoa*, such as George Moshoeshoe, who were reluctant to return to their homes because they wanted more extensive holdings elsewhere, and, as Bailie pointed out at Hlotse Heights, the payment of government rations was an inducement in itself for some to remain in the camps.[62] Jonathan Molapo, however, had every interest in getting his people back on the land and, though many did in fact return and large areas were brought under cultivation, the fact that at Hlotse Heights there were still 3,652 receiving rations is a powerful indication that many were still afraid to move.

The attempt to coerce Masupha

On one issue, however, there was no disagreement between Orpen, his magistrates and the *Mateketoa*, and that was Masupha's intransigence and the need to subdue him. His influence extended far beyond his own ward. He was the head of all resistance to the government. Cut off that head, it was argued, and the resistance would collapse.[63]

On 7 November Sauer instructed Orpen to call on Letsie and Lerotholi to compel Masupha to submit, but before resorting to force he should use every precaution to secure success, as failure would be calamitous.[64] At first Orpen was uncharacteristically apprehensive. He had no doubt about the sincerity of Letsie and Lerotholi in their hostility to Masupha, but 'all authority for good is weak, and there are evil influences at work ....' He doubted if Letsie would take action unless he could be

---

[59] G.89-'82, pp. 14-16, Orpen to Sauer, 15 February 1882. The amounts claimed by the *Mateketoa* varied considerably, and there was great confusion in working out how much they had received. In a speech to the House of Assembly on 27 March 1882 Sauer gave detailed figures showing that 7,071 head of cattle 518 horses and 1,492 sheep and goats had been restored to the *Mateketoa*. *Cape Argus*, 28 March 1882.
[60] C.3112, p. 105, Orpen to Colonial Secretary, 7 December 1881.
[61] LNA, MF2/1/2, Bailie to Orpen, 23 November 1881; LNA, S9/2/3/1, Hatchard to Orpen, 9 January 1882. LNA, L2/1/2, Bailie to Orpen, 7 January 1882. For the numbers in February 1882, see G.47-'82, pp. 1-72.
[62] G.33-'82, p. 211, Bailie to Orpen, 7 January 1882.
[63] G.89-'82, p. 45, Davies to Orpen, 26 November 1881; C.3112, pp. 118, 119, Orpen to Sauer, 4 and 23 December 1881; LNA, S9/1/2/2, Orpen to Sauer, 29 September 1881.
[64] A.24-'83, pp. 4-5, Sauer to Orpen, 7 November 1881; C.3112, p. 93, Orpen to Sauer, 19 November 1881.

assured of military support, if needed, from the colonial and imperial governments.[65] Sauer was unable to give him that assurance, but instead asked him to warn Letsie that if Masupha did not submit 'Basutoland may be abandoned' and the government would hold on to Quthing.[66]

Having expressed his reservations, however, Orpen then threw all his energies into building up the coalition against Masupha, and by the beginning of December he was brimming over with his usual confidence and optimism. Letsie, he reported, had consulted his sons and had agreed to punish his brother. Lerotholi in particular was resolute and determined. In the south Orpen went personally to Mohale's Hoek and won over the support of Molomo Mohale, who had at first held aloof because of some disagreement with Letsie. In the north Joel pledged his support, no doubt because he wanted the administration's goodwill in his dispute with Jonathan. Jonathan, however, refused to take part unless he was given the security of white troops alongside him. He was afraid, he said, of an attack from his former enemies, he did not trust Letsie and Lerotholi to go through with their projected action, and he was also bound, though he did not say so, by his strong family ties and affections to Masupha.[67] In the meantime Masupha was gathering his men at Thaba-Bosiu and had sent many of his cattle into the mountains. As in the crisis before the war, he had called on Ramanella to join him, but only a few men had been sent. Orpen was sure that in the country as a whole opinion was moving firmly against Masupha.[68] 'The game is in our hands', he assured Sauer, 'and is only a matter of time.'[69]

As always, the old magistrates did not share Orpen's optimism, and viewed the proposed expedition against Masupha with a mixture of incredulity and alarm. While Orpen claimed to have won over Molomo Mohale, Surmon warned him that the chiefs in his part of the country sympathised with Masupha and would rise in the event of failure.[70] And while Orpen declared that Joel had committed himself to support Letsie and Lerotholi, Bell reported the strong belief among the *Mateketoa* that Joel was in league with Masupha. 'One false step on the part of Letsie', he warned, 'would set the whole district in a blaze, the feeling of the people being that Masupha is upholding a cause in which they are all more or less implicated.'[71] Of all the magistrates Davies was the most contemptuous and dismissive. There was no chance, he wrote, of Letsie or Lerotholi making any aggressive movement against Masupha, 'for the sympathies of the majority of the Chiefs and people are with Masupha, so that even if Letsie and Lerothodi were inclined to take action ... which I am of opinion is not the case, they could not do more than make a mere demonstration.'[72] Orpen had to act almost completely on his own. Apart from Bailie, his only strong supporter in the administration was his brother-in-law, Emile Rolland.

On one issue the magistrates were plainly right: there was no strong shift of feeling against Masupha. In the opinion of Hermann Dieterlen, the PEMS missionary at Hermon in the south,

---

[65] C.3112, p. 93, Orpen to Sauer, 19 November 1881.

[66] A.24-'83, p. 5, Sauer to Orpen, 24 November 1881, and p. 6, de Smidt to Orpen, 8 January 1882.

[67] G.89-'82, p. 138, Jonathan to Orpen, 8 December 1881; G. 89-'82, p. 180, 'Minutes of a meeting held privately at the office of the Resident Magistrate, Leribe District, on the 30th December 1881 ....'

[68] C.3112, pp. 105-8, Orpen to Colonial Secretary, 6, 7, 8, 10, 11 and 13 December 1881. See also p. 118, Orpen to Colonial Secretary, 20 December 1881.

[69] A.24-'83, p. 50, Orpen to Sauer, 25 November 1881.

[70] G.89-'82, p. 52, Surmon to Orpen, 7 December 1881; C.3112, p. 107, Orpen to Colonial Secretary, 13 December 1881.

[71] G.89-'82, p. 173, Bell to Orpen, 14 December 1881.

[72] C. 3112, p. 122, Davies to Orpen, 6 December 1881.

Masupha was 'the most popular chief' in the country and most of the Basotho sympathised with him. Letsie and his sons (though not all of them, it transpired) were sincere in wanting to punish him. Mojela Letsie confided to Dieterlen 'that Masopha intended to usurp Letsie's right to the chieftainship and that the sons of Letsie would die rather than consent to this'. The coming confrontation was therefore driven, not just by the government's resolve to punish Masupha, but by the determination of Letsie and his sons to thwart Masupha's ambitions. In view of Masupha's popularity, however, Dieterlen doubted if they would be able to succeed.[73]

By mid-December Letsie's forces were ready to move into action. There was a delay because Lerotholi was laid low by an attack of dysentery and Orpen judged that he could not go ahead without him. By the first weeks of January, though still in pain, Lerotholi had sufficiently recovered to take the field, and a force consisting of several thousand horsemen advanced towards Thaba-Bosiu. Meanwhile in the north the regiments of Joel Molapo and several of his brothers moved towards the Phuthiatsana river, the boundary between the Leribe and Berea Districts, where they were to wait for further orders. The plan was that when they crossed the Phuthiatsana their places would be taken by Jonathan and his men, who would then keep Ramanella in check.

The reports from Masupha's country were encouraging: he was anxious to avoid a struggle and many of his people wanted to break away from him.[74] Orpen was now confident that there would be no bloodshed, only 'peaceable coercion'.[75] He was worried, however, that Letsie insisted on keeping overall command, when he himself wanted Lerotholi to take charge, since in spite of his illness he was much more active and decisive.[76] And with Rolland's help he had to work hard to overcome what he described as 'a good deal of adverse feeling and unwillingness among the people'.[77]

By 14 January 1882 the main body of Letsie's army was established just five kilometres south of Thaba-Bosiu. The bulk was provided by Letsie, his sons and their immediate subordinates, and they were supported among others by Leshoboro (the son of Moshoeshoe's fourth son, Majara, a timid man who was usually under Masupha's domination but had committed himself nervously to Letsie's side), by Molomo Mohale (who had come from the south, but whose loyalty Surmon had doubted), and also by Moiketsi Moletsane of the Bataung. While there they were joined by some deserters from Masupha. The men were in cheerful spirits, Orpen reported. He was merely waiting for Joel and others to join him before authorising the final advance.[78]

Masupha's strategy was clear. As with Sauer a few months earlier, he was hoping to make a show of submission with a few trivial concessions, in this way to induce his enemies to disperse, and then to go on his independent way as before. As he well knew, there were many on the other side who were anxious to avoid fighting. Molomo Mohale went on his own authority to sound him out and brought back the message that Masupha 'submits, and throws himself entirely on our mercy'. This time, however, Orpen and Letsie were determined to take possession of Thaba-Bosiu.[79]

---

[73] *JME* 1882, p. 58, Dieterlen, '*La situation politique au Lessouto*', undated, as translated by Germond (1967: 391).
[74] G.89-'82, pp. 182-3, Orpen to Bailie, 8 January 1882; C.3112, p. 127, Orpen to Sauer, 10 and 12 January 1882.
[75] C.3112, p. 127, Orpen to Sauer, 10 January 1882. See also G.89-'82, pp. 180 and 182-3, Orpen to Bailie, 5 and 8 January 1882.
[76] C.3112, pp. 127 and 131, Orpen to Sauer, 11 and 18 January 1882.
[77] C.3112, p. 127, Orpen to Sauer, 11 January 1882.
[78] C.3112, p. 128, Orpen to Sauer, 12 and 14 January 1882.
[79] C.3112, p. 128, Orpen to Sauer, 14 January 1882.

Joel and his brothers crossed the Phuthiatsana and joined Letsie on the evening of Saturday, 14 January, and on the Monday morning the whole force was ready to advance. Just as it was about to start, however, there were objections from what Orpen described as 'a deputation of men of considerable influence'. No names are given, but it is clear from what followed that Maama took the lead, with support from his brothers Bereng and Nkuebe, and perhaps Seeiso as well. They proposed that the chiefs alone should visit Masupha and enter into discussions with him. Lerotholi angrily dared anyone to leave, declared that if necessary he would do the work alone, and set off in a wagon at the head of his men. Letsie, with encouragement from Orpen and others, 'made a passionate appeal' which apparently brought his reluctant sons into line, at least for the time being. The old chief was then helped into his cart, and the entire force, now 10,000 cavalry strong, swept on. Thaba-Bosiu, not being defended, was 'swarmed over'. Masupha, soon to be reinforced by Ramanella, was occupying the passes of the mountain opposite.[80]

But already the divisions among the sons of Letsie were having a baneful effect. Two of Leshoboro's brothers deserted him and went back to Masupha, and Leshoboro himself was afraid that 'living so mixed up with Masupha's people, he should be exposed to revenge when Letsie returned home'. There were also complaints about Jonathan. Only 30 of his men had moved up to the Phuthiatsana, so leaving Ramanella free to send reinforcements to Masupha, and he was reported to have sent a message to Masupha telling him that he had no quarrel with him, but only with Joel.[81] That evening Letsie sent for Masupha. He refused to come, but said he repented like the prodigal son, adding that he had nothing left to restore and that the people should pay a fine for him.[82]

On the morning of Tuesday, 17 January, Letsie held a *pitso* on the summit of the mountain. By this time the whole army was buzzing with talk about the conflict between Letsie and Lerotholi on the one hand and Maama, Bereng and Nkuebe on the other. Orpen began by spelling out the provisions of the Robinson Award, and he warned that the districts of Matatiele and Quthing were being 'held in pawn' pending the fulfilment of the award, like an ox being held as a receipt for a debt. It was now nine months since the award had been made. Only Masupha was refusing to honour it. Letsie must stand up and do his duty.

It was Maama who spoke first in opposition. When Lerotholi and others had come to his village looking for the *Mateketoa*'s stock, he had co-operated and given up what was required. In just the same way the *Mateketoa* should be allowed to look for their stock in Masupha's ward. He was willing to obey Letsie's orders, but, he said, 'do not let us sacrifice lives'. Another speaker, a junior son of Moshoeshoe, suggested that the whole nation should pay a fine on Masupha's behalf, just as Masupha himself had proposed.

Lerotholi responded with what Orpen described as 'a powerful, loyal and determined speech, declaring his affection for Masupha but exposing his breaches of faith. He then rounded on his brothers, Bereng, Maama and Nkuebe: 'You have bound yourselves to this peace and you must fulfil it. .... I will not hide it. I say it to you. We are dissatisfied with you. .... If you are afraid then I say, stand aside and let the Government punish Masupha.'

---

[80] C.3112, pp. 130-1, 132, Orpen to Sauer, 16 and 18 January 1882.
[81] LNA, S9/1/2/2, Orpen to Sauer, 16 [in fact 17] January 1882; Annual Blue Book 1882, G.47-'82, p. 194, Orpen's Report, March 1882. (In his letter of 18 January Orpen refers to the *pitso* being held 'yesterday morning'.)
[82] C.3112, p. 131, Orpen to Sauer, 18 January 1882.

Letsie described himself as 'a deserted old ruin'. His authority had been defied by Masupha. He was not being harsh. He did not want to kill Masupha. His only object in coming to Thaba-Bosiu was 'to get cattle to wipe out the fault of the rebellion'. He was astonished to find that the 'loyal' Jonathan was hindering rather than helping him. 'Now I sit down', he concluded, 'and entreat you to fulfil the Award.'[83]

After the *pitso* Orpen directed Letsie to order Masupha to bring up his cattle. If Masupha refused, force would have to be used. He then went down the mountain and pitched his tent at its foot. On the following morning, 18 January, he waited impatiently for developments, but there was no movement. When he went up the mountain he found Letsie in great anxiety. Maama and Bereng, who were encamped to the south, had not come when called and had pleaded sickness, and he believed that they were in secret and separate communication with Masupha. He was unwilling to give instructions until he could be sure that his orders would be obeyed. The next morning, when everyone was there, and when Orpen told Letsie to give the order to attack, Maama suggested instead that all the leading chiefs should go to Masupha and remonstrate with him for the last time. Only if he refused again should they attack. Lerotholi, for the sake of unity, reluctantly agreed.

The chiefs went off, while Orpen once again waited on developments. When they returned, they reported that Lerotholi, supported by Joel, had 'put the case thoroughly and strongly' before Masupha; that he had remained 'obdurate'; that Maama and Seeiso had held themselves aloof, but afterwards had stayed behind with Masupha; that Bereng had suddenly gone home, pleading illness, leaving his men under Maama's command; and that three or four other chiefs were suspected of acting with Maama or to be hesitating. Letsie, 'timid and suspicious', now begged to be allowed to go home. Lerotholi wanted to go ahead, and his brothers Theko, Mojela and Tšepinare were prepared to back him up, together with Joel and Moiketsi Moletsane. They had to admit, however, when pressed by Orpen, that 'there was a great risk of failure through the disorganization which had taken place, and the impossibility of having confidence in the commanders, or in the obedience of the people, a considerable number of whom had already surreptitiously gone home.' Sauer had impressed on Orpen that he should go ahead only if he was sure of success. Lerotholi was now advising him to retire, and in these circumstances he abandoned the action.[84]

The withdrawal of Letsie's army was a body blow from which Orpen's reputation and authority never recovered. Why had he failed? For the opposition press the answer was simple. Letsie and Lerotholi had never been sincere in their promises to attack Masupha, and Orpen had been 'hoodwinked' and 'humbugged' by them.[85] But this crude analysis was inspired mainly by animosity to the government, especially to Sauer and Orpen, and the reasons for the failure were less obvious and more complex.

There were close ties of kinship and friendship between Letsie's followers and Masupha's, and for many in Letsie's forces it would have been hard to fight one of their national heroes to recover the cattle of the despised *Mateketoa*, all the more so as the leading *Leteketoa*, Jonathan Molapo, was refusing to give them any help. Lerotholi asked if, in the event of failure, colonial forces would be

---

[83] C. 3717, pp. 16-21, 'report of a Pitso held on Thaba Bosigo on the 16th January 1882 ....'; LNA, S9/1/2/2, Orpen to Sauer, 16 [in fact 17] January 1882; C.3112, pp. 131-2, Orpen to Sauer, 18 January 1881.

[84] C.3112, pp. 132-3, Orpen to Sauer, 19 January 1882.

[85] See, e.g., the reports and editorials in *The Journal* at this time.

used, and Orpen, to his embarrassment, could give him no assurance.[86] Orpen also emphasised the uncertainties caused by divisions in the Colony. At this very time there was a bill before the House of Assembly calling for the abandonment of Basutoland. In Orpen's words, it was like flag being hauled down in token of surrender.[87] Yet Letsie, and even more Lerotholi, sincerely wanted to put down Masupha, and the expedition might well have been carried through successfully but for the divisions among Letsie's sons.[88] Maama, Bereng, Seeiso and Nkuebe were reluctant to attack their old comrade-in-arms, but they were also motivated by their rivalry with Lerotholi. Maama in particular felt over-shadowed by his elder brother. In his Gun War praises he reminded his listeners how Lerotholi had found the fighting too much for him and had called on Maama to come to his aid:

> You're always saying the Makena are brave,
> You forget they've just called on the Vultures, the Young
> Vultures of Lineo's father[89] –

and in later years the two chiefs were in continual conflict with each other. It was helpful for both Maama and others to use Masupha as a counterweight to Lerotholi. The expedition was in part a potential civil war between the house of Letsie and the house of Masupha, but there was also a potential civil war within the house of Letsie, and it was this factor that Orpen had not sufficiently appreciated. As he admitted at the time, 'the harm done by the malcontents among some of Letsie's sons and headmen had been more than I understood at first'.[90] The fierce jealousies between the chiefs had given Orpen his chance to mount a campaign against Masupha. They also brought about the failure of that campaign.

In this way the first policy initiative of the Scanlen government collapsed. It was now time for a reappraisal.

---

[86] C.3112, p. 133, Orpen to Sauer, 19 January 1882; C.3717, p. 14, Orpen to Sauer, 30 January 1882.
[87] C.3112, p. 127, Orpen to Sauer, 6 January 1882.
[88] C.3717, p. 2, Orpen to Sauer, 22 January 1882: among the Basotho Maama was blamed for the failure of the expedition.
[89] Damane and Sanders (1974: 162-3). The translation has been slightly changed. The Makena, those who enter the thick of the battle, were Lerotholi's regiment, the Vultures were Maama's regiment, and Lineo was one of Maama's daughters.
[90] C.3112, p. 131, Orpen to Sauer, 18 January 1882.

CHAPTER 17: FROM 'ULTIMATUM' TO 'EXPECTATION'

'Ultimatum'

The one man who emerged triumphant from this confrontation was Masupha. While professing respect for Letsie, he had defied and frustrated him. He had demonstrated the depth of his popular support and exploited the divisions among Letsie's sons. The break-up of Letsie's conglomeration of regiments left him with his independence confirmed.

Letsie had been correspondingly weakened and humiliated. His own sons had conspired against him. He explained his failure by the Basotho's lack of organisation and his people's refusal to obey him. He added, perhaps under Orpen's influence, that there was no government force to help him, 'whilst Masupha found support amongst the people, and was strengthened by the report of the probable abandonment of Basutoland'. He would try to get the people to respect government authority, and it might be that Masupha would fall into line. But he could punish Masupha only if the government helped him: 'the Government must not lay a burden upon me that is beyond my strength'.[1]

The Cape's attempt, however, to coerce Masupha through Letsie had been its last bold initiative to regain control. It had been unable to enforce compliance with the Robinson Award. It now had to reappraise its policy. Even before Letsie had retreated from Thaba-Bosiu Ministers were considering their options.[2] They identified three possible courses of action – withdrawal, the re-establishment of colonial authority through the use of colonial force, and the use of imperial troops.

Most whites in the Colony would have favoured withdrawal.[3] They were tired of the trouble and expense involved in ruling the ungrateful Basotho, and Upington, Sprigg's old Attorney-General, now leading the opposition while Sprigg was in England, had a bill before Parliament proposing the dis-annexation of Basutoland from the Cape. But Ministers believed that withdrawal would lead to an all-out war between the Basotho and the Free State, a 'lamentable contingency' which they had a duty to prevent, and they knew it would not be countenanced by the home government. They also knew that the home government would not agree to the use of imperial troops, and if they were in any doubt about this Kimberley spelt it out yet again.[4]

That left them with their second course of action, the re-establishment of colonial authority through the use of colonial force. They were proposing to recommend this to Parliament when it reconvened in March 1882, but before doing so they wanted an assurance from the home government that, if they went to war, they could impose whatever settlement they wanted, since without this Parliament would never sanction hostilities. Kimberley gave them this assurance, since, as he explained, by failing to comply with the award the Basotho had forfeited the home government's sympathy. This opened the way, if the Cape so decided, to the confiscation of the Quthing District, and the prospect of cheap farms might make a war more popular and encourage recruitment.[5]

---

[1] C.3717, pp. 43-4, Letsie to Orpen, 10 March 1882.
[2] C.3112, p. 102, Robinson to Kimberley, 29 December 1881.
[3] C.3493, p. 31, Scanlen to Gordon, 7 August 1882.
[4] C.3112, p. 129, Robinson to Kimberley, 6 February 1882; C.3112, p. 125, Kimberley to Robinson, 2 February 1882.
[5] C.3717, pp. 1-2, Scanlen, Minute, 24 January 1882; pp. 15-6, Scanlen, Minute, 6 February 1882; *Cape Argus*, 16 March 1882, Editorial, and 28 March 1882, 'Parliament. House of Assembly'.

On 13 February Sauer sent Orpen what came to be seen as an ultimatum to the Basotho. They were to comply with the Robinson Award by 15 March, two days before Parliament was due to reconvene, failing which the award would be cancelled. The Cape government could then dispose of the Quthing District as it wished. In the rest of Basutoland the government would undertake the enforcement of law and order, and if any chief resisted it would be free to confiscate his property and land. The government now called on Letsie, Lerotholi and Joel to make 'a supreme effort' to secure the advantages of the award. This policy, Sauer was at pains to emphasise, had the full backing of the imperial government.[6]

This apparently fearsome ultimatum, however, rested on the premise that the mobilisation of the Cape's troops was still a viable option. Although Sauer, it seems, still adhered to this, Scanlen recognised that, even with the bait of land in Quthing, the resumption of hostilities was not a realistic possibility. Instead he favoured a policy of 'expectation': of gradually trying to impose law and order, reducing the hut tax and gun licence to ten shillings each, establishing a Council of Chiefs to help in the administration of the country, and in this way isolating Masupha.[7] The ultimatum, if read carefully, papered over this disagreement. It did not say that if the Basotho failed to comply with the award the confiscation of Quthing and the use of force would inevitably follow, merely that these courses of action would then be open for the Cape.

In Basutoland the ultimatum caused consternation. The *Mateketoa*, of course, were surprised and delighted. Those at Hlotse Heights listened to the ultimatum 'in breathless silence and astonishment', and then gave three hearty cheers for the government.[8] But when Letsie 'received the ultimatum he wept bitterly, and seemed in blank despair.'[9] It was impossible, he declared, to comply with the award in the time set down. The Basotho were neither united nor obedient. But what really alarmed him was the threat to take Quthing and the country of any chiefs who resisted the settlement. 'These words ... are death to us and make the hearts of the people desperate. Therefore I humbly entreat that this terrible word of taking away Basuto country may be removed.....'[10] Orpen said the same. It was unrealistic to expect the Basotho to comply with the award in a month. He recommended that, instead of calling on the *Mabelete* to restore what they had taken, a general tax should be levied. The threats of confiscating land, he warned, might drive the Basotho to rebellion. They would believe that they were being 'entrapped in order to seize their country'.[11] The entire nation would unite to fight for Quthing: 'I do not believe a man will remain loyal at heart'.[12] Rumours of war swept the country, and, having checked on his defence capabilities, Orpen warned that in the event of hostilities Mohale's Hoek would have to be abandoned, and probably Mafeteng and Hlotse Heights as well.[13]

About this time, on 10 March, Adolphe Mabille arrived back at Morija after a two-year fur-

---

[6] C.3717, pp. 27-8. Sauer to Orpen, 13 February 1882.
[7] Smith (1939: 300), quoting Mabille to Dr E. Casalis, 7 February 1882.
[8] *Cape Argus*, 1 March 1882, 'The Basuto Ultimatum'.
[9] A.24A-'83, p. 6, Orpen to Sauer, 17 February 1882.
[10] C.3717, p. 41, Letsie to Orpen, 6 March 1882.
[11] C.3717, pp. 28-9, Orpen to Sauer, 15 February 1882.
[12] C.3717, p. 33, Orpen to Sauer, 23 February 1882. For a similar view see *Cape Argus*, 15 March 1882, 'Public Opinion. The Basuto Ultimatum', quoting the *Natal Mercury*.
[13] C.3717, pp. 30-1, 33-4, 42, 43, Orpen to Sauer, two letters of 18 February, 24 February, 5 March, 9 March 1882; LNA, S9/2/3/1, Hatchard to Orpen, 22 February 1882. See also C.3717, p. 37, Surmon to Orpen, 31 January 1882.

lough in France. He was dismayed by what he found. Military success against white opponents had strengthened the Basotho's confidence in the validity of their own beliefs and customs, and many were turning their backs on Christianity and school education. A new spirit of 'arrogance' was abroad. Boer traders were bringing in brandy by the wagonload. Mrs. Mabille found Letsie drinking heavily; he was aged, she wrote, and pitifully emaciated. The church was torn between *Mabelete* and *Mateketoa*.[14] While on furlough in Europe Mabille had been heavily involved in lobbying the home government, and on his way back he had long discussions with Scanlen and Sauer. He supported Scanlen in his policy of expectation, and on 12 March, two days after his arrival, he wrote to Sauer that this policy would succeed, but only if the Basotho were not hurried and 'threats of confiscation' were left out.[15]

In the face of all these warnings and representations the government backed down. Scanlen claimed that the situation had improved, but even his supporters openly acknowledged that the government had issued an ultimatum which it did not have the ability to enforce, and the policy which the Premier spelt out in Parliament on 27 March was a further retreat from the pretensions of power.[16] The Robinson Award had already been cancelled, but Basutoland would not be abandoned; there would be no renewal of war and no territorial confiscations, except as a last resource; the disarmament proclamation would be repealed; and a commission would be appointed to evaluate and pay for the losses of the traders and the loyal Basotho. With these concessions it was hoped to overcome the Basotho's dis-affection and to restore law and order. The opposition moved a vote of no confidence, arguing that the government's authority had broken down and criticising it for sending away nearly all the troops instead of keeping them in the country in order to enforce obedience. Scanlen and Sauer argued that the situation was not as dire as the opposition pretended and that a lot of the trouble was due to the agitation of 'white agents' encouraging the *Mateketoa* not to return to their homes but to hold out for better terms; and by quoting Clarke at length Sauer was able to demonstrate that military action had been out of the question. The vote of no confidence failed, and on 12 April Upington's bill proposing the repeal of the Annexation Act was defeated by 34 votes to 23. The government's policy was approved.[17]

At the same time the Legislative Council, the Upper House, appointed a Select Committee to enquire into the affairs of Basutoland, and Orpen was summoned to Cape Town to appear before it. In the event the Committee was unable to complete its work,[18] but, for reasons to be considered below, Orpen, who had left Basutoland on 25 March, did not return until 19 June, and in the meantime Emile Rolland acted in his stead.

---

[14] Smith (1939: 304-5).
[15] C.3717, p. 45, Mabille to Sauer, 12 March 1882. See also *JME* 1882, pp. 186-7, Mabille to PEMS Committee, 15 March 1882.
[16] *Cape Argus*, 18 March 1882, Editorial; 28 March 1882, 'Parliament. House of Assembly', 27 March; 4 April 1882, Editorial; 16 May 1882, Editorial. Burman (1981: 160), relying on Benyon's thesis, 'Basutoland and the High Commission', pp. 509-13, says that the ultimatum drew a storm of criticism from humanitarians in England, colonial press, and members of the Cape Parliament and therefore had to be withdrawn.
[17] C.3717, p. 34, Robinson to Kimberley, 28 March 1882; accounts of House of Assembly debates in *Cape Argus*, 28 March, 4, 6 and 13 April 1882. Originally it was intended that the commission investigating claims for compensation would also consider the question of possible self-government by the Basotho, but this fell away.
[18] C.5-'82, Report of Select Committee … on Basutoland Affairs.

The campaign against Orpen

Although Scanlen and Sauer had been able to push through their new policies, the debate in the Assembly was notable for the virulence of the opposition's attacks on both the government generally and Orpen personally. Sprigg sneered at Orpen as a '*wonderful administrative genius*', and declared that he was bringing '*shame and everlasting infamy on the British name in Basutoland*'. The government had 'shown every black man in South Africa that loyalty does not pay'. Masupha's rebellion should have been suppressed. Instead the government 'go to Lerothodi, red-handed rebel as he is, and almost on bended knees they implore him to do that duty which they have not courage to do themselves ....'[19] Upington denounced Orpen as 'a weak and hopeless administrator' who had been 'continually hoodwinked and outwitted by the Basutos', and quoted some doggerel verse from a frontier newspaper:

> Rolland, we dare not sneeze
> In Masupha's land, says Orpen. [20]

One of the main weapons in the opposition's attacks was a petition drawn up by Jonathan Molapo and 898 others:

> from the first day when Mr. J.M. Orpen took over the government of Basutoland, your petitioners are grieved to say their rights and interests as her Majesty's loyal and obedient subjects were ignored, they themselves were treated in every respect as if they had committed a crime by remaining loyal, whereas the rebels were encouraged in every way ....

They had been forcibly expelled from their lands when they tried to reoccupy them, their cattle had not been restored, and yet Orpen had persisted in assuring the government that matters were satisfactory and that 'things were quieting down'. As a result the petitioners were kept in the greatest misery, dependent upon government rations, cooped up around the fortified camps of the magistracies. They were 'exposed daily to insults and injuries' not just from the rebels but from Orpen as well, and they begged the House of Assembly to inquire into their cause and to give them relief.[21] Orpen gave a detailed rebuttal of these charges,[22] but they were merely part of a powerful and concerted campaign against him conducted mainly through the pages of the colonial press and centred on the treatment of Jonathan.

The new magistrate in the Leribe District, Alexander Bailie, who was one of Orpen's few white supporters in the country, found Joel much easier to deal with than Jonathan. He believed that he had fully complied with the award, and in the final confrontation with Masupha he and his men, unlike Jonathan, had been ready and willing to fight alongside the sons of Letsie. When the collection of hut tax was renewed Joel and his *Mabelete* brothers, again unlike Jonathan, gave Bailie every satisfaction.[23] In the context of another dispute, in which the *Mateketoa* at Hlotse Heights refused to obey his orders, Bailie told them 'they were loyals only in name, and that the late rebels were showing a very good example and one which they as loyals should be ashamed not to follow'.[24] 'Joel is a good man,' he told Hlasoa Molapo, 'he has fulfilled the Governor's Award and Govern-

---

[19] Quotations from *Cape Mercury* and *Cape Argus* in G.47-'82, p. 171.
[20] *Cape Argus*, 13 April 1882, 'Parliament. House of Assembly', 12 April 1882.
[21] A.2-'82, 'Petition of Jonathan Molapo and other Basuto Chiefs', 14 March 1882.
[22] G.47-'82, pp. 168-78, Orpen to Sauer, 20 March 1882, and enclosures.
[23] LNA L2/1/2, Bailie to Jonathan, 29 March 1882.
[24] G.47-'82, p. 82, Bailie to Orpen, 27 February 1882.

ment has great confidence in him. No trouble can come to this district while you follow Joel with your whole heart.'[25]

He sometimes wrote to Jonathan as 'My Friend', but his usual form of address to Joel was 'My good friend'.[26] When Joel complained about certain actions of Jonathan Bailie wrote to reassure him: 'You need not be afraid that Jonathan and his friends can injure you. We ... must not let the idle gossip of wanderers bother us. .... I have told the Government that you and I can keep all quiet in our district.'[27]

The reference to 'our district' would have been anathema to Jonathan. He had innumerable complaints against Joel and the other *Mabelete* chiefs, but his main grievance, as he freely declared, 'was about his chieftainship'.[28] What irked him most was the recognition accorded to Joel, as when Orpen called on him to help against Masupha. This, wrote Orpen, was 'gall and wormwood to Jonathan',[29] and it was gall and wormwood to his white supporters as well. In his reminiscences Henry Taylor, the doctor at Hlotse Heights, set out their views in simple and emotive terms:

> New officials were appointed, with instructions to favour the rebel party as much as possible, and to do all in their power to crush and oppress Jonathan and his few followers ....
>
> This infamous policy was much resented by all the old officials .... A cabal was formed in official circles, and while ostensibly obeying orders, they secretly did all they could to counterbalance them by aiding and sympathising with Jonathan, and by keeping the opposition Press in the Colony fully informed of what was going on in Basutoland.[30]

Prominent in this 'cabal' was Henry Jervis, the clerk at Hlotse Heights, who, as 'a very brave young fellow of 22', had distinguished himself in the Gun War[31] and who repeatedly spoke up for Jonathan and the *Mateketoa*. In March 1882 he was transferred to Maseru, and in May he was suspended from duty on the suspicion of leaking documents to opponents of the administration. It was impossible to prove anything against him, and in July he was transferred at his own request to Thembuland.[32]

One of the men to whom Jervis was suspected of passing documents was Colonel Schermbrucker, who had been the officer in charge of the Basutoland police at Maseru during the Gun War and who was now the leading spirit among the men whom the government condemned as white agitators and agents. Before the war, when Sprigg told a meeting of his constituents in East London that Masupha was stopping men handing in their guns, he had attracted much notoriety by shouting out 'String the nigger up!' – words which were now flung up against him by the government and which he said he regretted.[33] He was a member of the Legislative Council, and in that position was

---

[25] LNA, L2/1/2, Bailie to Hlasoa, 11 March 1882.
[26] E.g., LNA, L2/1/2, Bailie to Jonathan, 29 March 1882, Bailie to Joel, 15 March 1882.
[27] G.47-'82, p. 146, Bailie to Joel, 7 March 1882.
[28] G.47-'82, p. 186, Bailie to Orpen, 31 March 1882. As Molapo's successor, acting on behalf of Josefa, Jonathan claimed the right to administer Molapo's inheritance, and this too was disputed by Joel: C.3-'83, p. 2, Jonathan to 'Governor's Agent, Leribe District', 29 December 1882.
[29] G.47-'82, p. 193, Orpen's Report, March 1882.
[30] Taylor (1972: 93). See also Widdicombe (1895: 232-3).
[31] Taylor (1972: 62).
[32] LNA, files S9/1/3/5 and S9/2/3/1; A.24-'83, p. 100, Rolland to Sauer, 3 May 1882. See also Taylor (1972: 93).
[33] For Schermbrucker, see, e.g., *Cape Argus*, 20 December 1881, Editorial; 26 and 29 April, 'Parliament.

well placed to launch his attacks. He advised Jonathan that Orpen and Bailie had no legal right to call on him to help in the war against Masupha, advice which Jonathan was happy to receive,[34] and shortly before Parliament was recalled in March he and a Member of the House of Assembly, Dr. J.W. Matthews, visited Basutoland to hold meetings with the *Maketetoa* at Maseru and Leribe and to see the position for themselves.[35] The upshot was the petition already referred to, signed by Jonathan Molapo and 898 others, which Matthews presented to the House of Assembly on 21 March to support the opposition's attack on the government.

In spite of Orpen's exertions in trying to recover the *Maketetoa*'s stock, and in spite of his attempted coercion of Masupha, it was now the received wisdom among the *Maketetoa* that he was hostile to them and that the new magistrates had been chosen 'because they hated the loyals'.[36] He was even described as a rebel himself. 'We always call you a Rebel', one Mafeteng loyalist told him, '*because you are living amongst the Rebels at Morija*, giving them all your time, and do not come to see us Loyals ....'[37]

Under the government's new policy, however, with the appointment of a commission to assess and to pay for the *Maketetoa*'s losses, and with authorisation being given for their moves to Quthing or elsewhere, there was at last a real possibility of some justice for them. Towards the end of 1882 George Moshoeshoe and others left Basutoland and settled in the Matatiele area, in the country which George named The Queen's Mercy. Others, among them Nehemiah, moved to the Quthing District. But the most prominent *Leteketoa* of all, Jonathan Molapo, resolutely held on in the Leribe District.

The policy of expectation

The new policy was immediately put into effect. On 29 March Sauer sent a telegram to Rolland: 'The effect of the cancellation of the Award is that no more gun tax nor restoration of cattle belonging to loyals nor compensation to traders and others will be demanded or payable ....'[38] Throughout the first months of Orpen's administration he had been at full stretch trying to recover the *Maketetoa*'s stock, and his failure had been a cause of constant wrangling and hostility. From now on the *Maketetoa* would look to the new commission, not to Orpen, to make good their losses, and the pressure on the administration would be eased.

On 6 April the Peace Preservation Proclamation was revoked – a revocation that finally declared to the world that the rebellious Basotho had won the day – and shortly afterwards the *Maketetoa* were informed that the government had now decided, if that was what they wanted, to locate them in 'Quthing, Matatiele or Emigrant Tembuland'.[39] Many of them, in fact, elected to

---

Legislative Council'. See also p. 208, fn. 55 above.

[34] E.g., LNA, S9/1/2/2, Orpen to Sauer, 6 March 1882; G.47-'82, pp. 139-40, Orpen to Sauer, 11 March 1882, and Jonathan to Orpen, 13 February 1882.

[35] Matthews (1976: 373-90).

[36] G.47-'82, pp. 160-1, 186, Bailie to Orpen, 14 and 31 March 1882.

[37] G.47-'82, p. 176, 'Solomon "Matsepi" (or properly termed "Leballo"), a Loyal, living at Mafeteng', statement of 9 March 1882.

[38] A.24-'83, p. 17, SNA to Rolland, 29 March 1882.

[39] G.74-'82, pp. 2-11, Rolland to Sauer, 5 April 1882, forwarding Hatchard to Rolland, 4 April 1882, with 'Minutes of a Meeting held at Maseru on the 3rd day of April, 1882, ... to give the loyal Basutos notice of the intentions of the Government'. See also LNA, S9/2/3/1, Hatchard to Rolland, 21 April 1882;

stay,⁴⁰ and there were long delays before others were authorised to go, but many set off over the next few months.⁴¹

The settlement of Quthing was one of the few occasions of conflict between Letsie and Orpen. Letsie wanted to place his son Nkuebe in the area, but Orpen refused. Quthing had been promised to the *Mateketoa*, and they had no wish to be placed under a rebel chief – the very plight from which they wanted to escape by moving.⁴²

After the panic induced by Sauer's ultimatum Letsie welcomed the new policy with 'joy and gratitude',⁴³ and at Korokoro Maama and other chiefs were 'overjoyed at the course taken by Government, and promised to give it all the support in their power.'⁴⁴ Mabille wrote to Sauer congratulating him on the vote setting aside the Peace Preservation Proclamation: 'The difference in the minds of the people from the time I arrived here on the 10th of March to this day is very marked …. I have much hope for the future.'⁴⁵ The Paris mission was now solidly behind the government. Eugène Casalis, the Mission's Director in Paris, declared that the Basotho were bound to welcome the new dispensation because it met their grievances so fully. 'Consequently, we may straightway give free rein to our gratitude to God for this deliverance….'⁴⁶

The aim of the new policy was to re-establish the government's authority, and central to this was the collection of the hut tax, which now replaced compensating the *Mateketoa* as the touchstone of the Basotho's loyalty.⁴⁷ Letsie and his sons and Joel Molapo were all willing to co-operate (though Bereng and Maama were initially reluctant),⁴⁸ and many of the people were prepared to follow their lead. At a national *pitso* on 12 April Letsie was 'repeatedly cheered when urging on people to pay tax and return to order'. After the *pitso* Lerotholi and others went to Maseru to convey their thanks and renew their allegiance.⁴⁹

There was one principal chief, however, who did not attend the *pitso*. Masupha, as so often, refused to fall into line. He objected, he said, to 'the imperative language' that Letsie had used in summoning him to the *pitso*, telling him that he must come and take orders.⁵⁰ He held out, it was reported, against the disapproval of his followers,⁵¹ and he also held out against a powerful deputation that was

---

⁴⁰ LNA, MF2/1/2, Nettelton to Sauer, 6 July 1882; Nettelton to Orpen, 26 July 1882.

⁴¹ LNA, MF2/1/2, Nettelton to Resident Magistrate, Quthing, 28 August 1882; LNA, S9/1/3/6, Orpen to Resident Magistrate, Quthing, 27 August 1882; PEMS Archives, Morija, Ellenberger Papers, Ellenberger to Orpen, 23 September 1882.

⁴² LNA, S9/1/2/2, Orpen to Sauer, 13 September 1882; C.3717, p. 87, Orpen to Sauer, 31 August 1772; G.54-'83, p. 58, Letsie's speech at meeting with Scanlen and Sauer on 26 March 1883. Bereng wanted to go to Quthing, but Letsie refused because he was so assertive and confrontational: A.24-'83, p. 61, Orpen to Sauer, 1 September 1882, and Bereng and Lehloenya (1991: 73).

⁴³ C.3717, p. 54, Rolland to Sauer, 31 March 1882.

⁴⁴ *Cape Argus*, 6 April 1882, 'Parliament. House of Assembly', 5 April.

⁴⁵ C.3717, p. 58, Mabille to Sauer, 9 April 1882.

⁴⁶ Germond (1967: 398), extracts from the minutes of the General Assembly of the PEMS, 27 April 1882.

⁴⁷ PEMS Archives, Paris, copy of Circular No. 14 of 1882, 31 March 1882, Orpen to Surmon, enclosed with Maeder to Boegner, 7 August 1882; *The Journal*, 11 April 1882, 'Basutoland'.

⁴⁸ LNA, MF2/1/2, Nettelton to Sauer, n.d. (but either 13 or 14 April 1882).

⁴⁹ C.3717, p. 59, Rolland to Sauer, 13 April 1882. See also Smith (1939: 303).

⁵⁰ C.3717, p. 60, Nettelton to Sauer, 14 April 1882. See also C.3717, pp. 59-60, Rolland to Sauer, n.d., received 17 April 1882.

⁵¹ LNA, MF2/1/2, Nettelton to Sauer, n.d. (but either 13 or 14 April 1882)

sent by Letsie following the *pitso* consisting of all his important sons, two sons of Molapo, and the French missionaries Mabille and Jousse. He accepted the Queen's peace, he said, but he refused to pay tax. Lerotholi and the other chiefs solemnly renounced him. 'They all seem to think that Masupha is not sane', Rolland reported. 'He is much altered and would not look anyone in the face.'[52] Yet Rolland believed that Masupha might still give way. Letsie's sons were 'extremely angry' with him. They had 'refused to shake hands or return his greeting when they left him', but they were confident they would be able to overcome his resistance, without necessitating warlike interference by Government'.[53]

For a while Rolland's hopes seemed be well founded. Masupha had been trying to relieve the pressure on his ward and to extend his influence by placing his sons beyond his own borders. Letsie's sons forced them to retire.[54] Payments of hut tax came in steadily, especially in the north, where Joel and his followers were the most forthcoming, and in Letsie's district of Mafeteng, where in a single week more than £400 was brought in.[55] But then the payments fell sharply away, and by the end of the 15-month period ending on 30 September 1882 only £6,405 out of £30,000 had been handed in.[56] Masupha not only stopped his own followers paying, but influenced others not to pay, even as far south as Mohale's Hoek.[57] According to Orpen, however, the main disincentive was the build-up of rumours that the Cape was planning either to remove its magistrates and to grant the Basotho self-government, or else to abandon the country entirely.[58] For why should an ordinary man, not well-off, make the sacrifice of £1 when the government demanding it was likely to be withdrawn? And why should the chiefs risk unpopularity by insisting that their followers should pay?

On 1 April the Legislative Council, the Cape's Upper House, contrary to the vote in the House of Assembly, had adopted a resolution that, in view of the humiliating and unsatisfactory situation in Basutoland, the Annexation Act should be repealed. This was rejected by the home government, and it is not clear if it had any effect in Basutoland. But the colonial newspapers were soon carrying further unsettling reports that emanated, not from the opposition in the Cape Parliament, but from the activities of the newly appointed Commandant-General of the Colonial Forces, Charles George Gordon, already famous as Chinese Gordon for his victories in the Far East, and later to become even more famous as the dying hero of Khartoum.[59]

How Gordon came to be involved in Basutoland's affairs was beset with the muddle and confusion that were to characterise all his proceedings there.

---

[52] C.3717, p. 61, Rolland to Sauer, 19 April 1882.

[53] C.3717, pp. 61-2, Rolland to Sauer, 19 April 1882.

[54] C.3717, p. 81, Orpen to Sauer, 2 July 1882; p. 152, Orpen, 12 January 1883, Annual Report for 1882; G.8-'83, p. 288, Orpen to Sauer, 22 July 1882; *JME* 1882, p. 362, Mabille, letter of 26 July 1882; *The Journal*, 27 July 1882, 'Basutoland'; *Cape Argus*, 1 August 1882.

[55] C.3717, p. 60, Nettelton to Sauer, 14 April 1882; p. 62, Rolland to Sauer, 28 April 1882; *Leselinyana*, July 1882.

[56] LNA, no reference noted, 'Revenue collected 1 July 1881 to 30 September 1882'. According to *Leselinyana*, July 1882, about £6,000 out of £30,000 was collected. According to Orpen about £7,000 was collected between 1 April and 30 September 1882: LNA, S9/1/2/2, Orpen to Sauer, 24 October 1882.

[57] A.24-'83, p. 8, Surmon to Orpen, 12 July 1882; *Leselinyana*, August 1882.

[58] LNA, S9/1/2/2, Orpen to Sauer, 13 September 1882; C.3717, p. 152, Orpen to Sauer, 12 January 1883, Annual Report for 1882. Rolland, however, reported that part of the reason for the falling away of payments was 'the action of Mama, Bereng, and others, who insist on people paying through them, and then embezzle a part of the money ....': C.3717, p. 71, Rolland to Sauer, 29 May 1882.

[59] C.3717, p. 79, Orpen to Sauer, 20 June 1882; p. 87, Orpen to Sauer, 31 August 1882.

CHAPTER 18: GENERAL GORDON

Gordon's appointment

As early as 1880 Hicks Beach, Disraeli's Secretary of State for the Colonies, had suggested to Frere that Gordon should be offered the post of Commandant-General, but Gordon had turned this down on the ground, or so he claimed later, that the Basotho were not being fairly treated.[1] Then in April 1881 Gordon himself, serving in Mauritius, had offered his services to the Sprigg Ministry 'to assist in terminating war and administering Basutoland'.[2] Sprigg did not reply – his Ministry was about to collapse and the war was almost over – but Gordon's letter was found on file by the incoming Ministry, and on 3 March 1882, prompted by John Merriman and with clearance from the home government, Scanlen telegraphed asking him if he would renew the offer which he had made to the previous ministry: 'Position of matters in Basutoland grave, and of utmost importance that Colony secure services of some one of proved ability, firmness, and energy'.[3] This cable took almost a month to reach Gordon, but within two days of receiving it he set off for the Cape where he arrived on 3 May.

In turning to Gordon the Cape was drawn by his military reputation, based mainly on his suppression of the Taiping rebellion in China. When Scanlen asked him to come to South Africa Sauer had just issued his ultimatum and war seemed a serious possibility. It was even more drawn, however, by his reputation in the 'management of native peoples'. Though publicly supportive, some Ministers, especially Merriman, had serious doubts about Orpen. He had been appointed because of his supposed influence over the Basotho, and he had worked well with Letsie, Lerotholi and Joel, but he had made no impression on Masupha and he had antagonised the *Maketetoa*. They were not yet ready to dismiss him, but they were casting around for a new saviour. Gordon seemed the ideal man.

From the beginning there was a lack of clarity about Gordon's role. The post to which he was appointed was that of Commandant-General, but the purpose for which he was appointed was to sort out Basutoland. How he was to do this was not clear, since there was no plan for him to resume hostilities as Commandant-General (with the Government's new policy the danger of war had receded) and for whatever reason (either the post was not offered to him or it was offered and he refused) he was not going to replace Orpen as Governor's Agent.[4] The Cape politicians were putting their faith in the extraordinary 'mesmeric' power that Gordon was reputed to exercise over 'native

---

[1] C.3493, p.70, 'Report of Proceedings of Meeting in Schoolroom at the Morija Mission Station, on the 16th September, 1882'; Bradlow (1970: 225-6).
[2] Gordon (1886: 180).
[3] C.3493, p. 7, Scanlen to Gordon, 3 March 1883.
[4] According to Gordon (Boulger (1896: 2.84), Robinson, Scanlen and Merriman wanted him to replace Orpen, but Gordon himself 'deprecated any such change'. According to H.W. Gordon (1886: 182) Robinson and Merriman wanted Gordon to take charge of Basutoland, but were reluctant to remove Orpen, and so Gordon finally accepted the military post. According to Merriman (*Cape Times*, 26 November 1896), Gordon was offered an appointment as Governor's Agent but rejected it on finding that Orpen was in post. According to Orpen, Gordon told him soon after his arrival that he had been offered the post of Commandant-General, but he had suggested to Robinson that he wanted to go to Basutoland as Orpen's private secretary, which Orpen thought was inappropriate (Cory Library, MS 1248, p. 22). Again according to Orpen (Cory Library, MS 1248, p.23) Scanlen told him that the only post offered to Gordon was that of Commandant-General (Cory Library, MS 1248, pp. 16-7). In fact the post of Commandant-General was open while that of Governor's Agent was not. Initially Gordon turned it down (Gordon Correspondence: 1905:5) and it was only on 18 May that he was formally appointed.

peoples'. They had not thought through how this power was to be harnessed, or how it fitted in with their policy of expectation, of slowly building up the authority of the administration and so gradually isolating Masupha. The most that could be suggested was that, in the midst of his duties as Commandant-General, he should visit Basutoland, see the situation for himself and give the Colony the benefit of his advice.

Gordon was not the man for gradualism. He believed that he was an instrument of the Divine Will and that he took his orders from God. With his simple, direct and unaffected manner, coupled with his sense of divine purpose, he won the admiration and even adulation of many of those he met. At the same time he was commonly regarded as eccentric, especially in matters of religion.[5] He was convinced that in a previous incarnation he had been a Roman centurion at the crucifixion of Christ, and that in his present incarnation he had discovered the Garden of Eden in the Seychelles and identified the forbidden fruit. He was headstrong and impulsive, quick to change his mind about both policies and people. As Gladstone was to find out two years later, when Gordon was sent to report on the Sudan, he was an impossible man to control. When he thought it right he had no hesitation in ignoring or stretching his instructions. He freely admitted as much himself: 'I cannot help it', he said once, 'I know if I was chief I would never employ *myself*, for I am incorrigible.'[6]

He admired the Cape government: it was 'very well inclined towards the natives ... and very considerate', he wrote to a friend in England: 'I hope by God's active aid to ... heal their stripes.' He yearned to do good to the Basotho as well, the 'poor Black sheep of this fold'. He had no thought of personal glory, he said, but would want to 'hand over the command of the Colonial Forces to the Captain of the Hosts of the Lord'.[7]

Gordon's policy
He began gathering as much information about the country as he could. One of the first men to call on him was Orpen, who had been summoned to Cape Town to appear before the Select Committee which had been set up to enquire into the affairs of Basutoland but which was discharged on the day that Gordon arrived. Orpen supplied him with a mass of documents, and the two men met frequently and talked at great length. Orpen, by his own account, was 'charmed' by Gordon. 'The more I saw,' he wrote, 'the more I liked him. I thought him very eccentric but transparent, honest, kind and loveable'.[8] Gordon described Orpen as 'a just, kind gentleman'.[9]

The two men travelled up-country together as Gordon made his way to his military headquarters at King William's Town and Orpen returned to Basutoland. On the way Gordon drew up a memorandum on 'The Basuto Question' in which he advocated that bygones should be bygones, that a national *pitso* should be called to discuss the best means of securing the settlement of the country, and that the Loyals should 'at once be paid off' with a sum of £30,000.[10] It was surprising, as he acknowledged himself, that he should be offering this advice before he had even set foot in Basutoland. There were other disturbing signs. So far he had got on well with Orpen, but on reaching King William's Town he read a letter from Schermbrucker in a newspaper and on the strength of this

---

[5] Cory Library, Orpen, MS 1248, p. 22.
[6] Lewsen (1982: 102).
[7] Rhodes House Library, Oxford, Mss.Afr.S.16, Waller Papers, Vol. II, f. 207, Gordon to Waller, 13 May 1882.
[8] Cory Library, MS 1248, Orpen, 'Major General Charles George Gordon's Visit ...', pp. 21, 27.
[9] C.3493, p. 8, Gordon to Robinson, 26 May 1882.
[10] C.3493, pp. 8-9, Gordon, 'The Basuto Question'. See also Cory Library, MS 1248, p. 33.

told Orpen that his policy was 'all wrong'.[11] There were also reports in the press that he was planning to go with a small force to capture Masupha – reports which he later denied but which were to lead to serious embarrassment for him in Basutoland.[12]

At this time, without informing Orpen, he wrote confidentially to Masupha's missionary, Théophile Jousse, setting out his proposals, asking for his advice, and begging him to assure Masupha – no doubt to counter the newspaper reports – that he would be coming to Basutoland as a friend of the Basotho and was 'desirous to conciliate them'. In particular he wanted to meet Masupha, suggesting that this should be a 'private visit'.[13]

Orpen left King William's Town on 1 June with the understanding that Gordon would shortly be coming up to Basutoland to stay with him. After he had left, and again without consulting him, Gordon wrote to Scanlen proposing to remove all troops from Basutoland. There were still 310 Cape Mounted Riflemen in the country. They were expensive to maintain, their morale had been undermined by inactivity, and in Gordon's view they served no useful purpose. A reply was sent from Scanlen's office to say that the troops should be retained for the present until a new police force was organised, but in the meantime, according to Orpen, Gordon gave it out through the CMR officers in Basutoland that their removal was imminent.[14]

Over the next two months Gordon busied himself mainly on military matters, but he was also consulting widely on Basutoland affairs. The man who had the greatest influence on him was Mansfield Clarke, his predecessor as Commandant-General, who told him that Orpen's view was 'too rose-coloured', and who recommended a new system of government with as little interference as possible in the internal affairs of the Basotho.[15] When Gordon came to make his own recommendations he followed these suggestions very closely. He proposed the appointment of a Resident and two Sub-residents; 'the government of the Basutos in all internal affairs' to 'remain under the jurisdiction of the Chiefs'; the establishment of a Supreme Council consisting of the leading Chiefs and the Resident; a hut tax of 10s. a year which would be used to pay for the Resident and the Sub-residents, the balance to be spent on education, roads etc.; the payment to the chiefs of 10% of the hut tax they collected; arrangements for the prevention of stock theft; and communications with the Free State to be conducted through the Resident. He suggested that Griffith should be appointed as the Resident, and he believed that Letsie and Masupha could be induced to propose a settlement along these lines.[16]

In brief, if Gordon's proposals were accepted the system of magisterial rule would be abandoned and the Basotho would have complete self-government, with the Colony remaining responsible for defence and external affairs. Merriman and Scanlen pointed out to him that until the next session of

---

[11] Cory Library, MS 1248, p. 33.
[12] *Cape Argus*, 31 May 1882, 'Parliament. House of Assembly', 30 May; Cory Library, MS 1248, pp. 28-31.
[13] C.3493, pp. 22-3, Keck to Gordon, 20 June 1882. Gordon claimed that Orpen knew that he had written to Jousse: C.3493, p. 21, Gordon to Colonial Secretary, 19 July 1882. Orpen, it seems, knew about it only through press reports (G.8-'83, pp. 294-7, Orpen to Sauer, 13 September 1882; Cory Library, MS 1248, pp. 35-6). Gordon told Scanlen that he wanted to go, 'as it were, privately', to Basutoland 'and see Masupha and other chiefs and hear what they had to say'.
[14] C.3493, pp. 10-11, Gordon to Colonial Secretary, 1 June 1882; p. 12, Acting Under Colonial Secretary, Hampden Willis, to Gordon, 21 June 1882; Cory Library, MS 1248, pp. 36-7.
[15] Gordon Correspondence (1905: 5), Gordon to Scanlen, 2 June 1882.
[16] C. 3493, pp. 20-22, Gordon to Colonial Secretary, 19 July 1882.

Parliament the government was committed to try to bring about the restoration of law and order through the gradual re-establishment of magisterial rule, and that it could consider alternatives only if this failed. Scanlen emphasised the need for patience: the Colony would not sanction more vigorous moves.[17]

Gordon's proposals, therefore, were in direct conflict with government policy, and whereas the government was seeking to isolate Masupha Gordon had been in contact with him through his missionary and was keen to meet him personally. He had also taken a strong dislike to Orpen. According to Merriman he was '*terribly down*' on him because he had 'found him straying from the strict paths of veracity'. Merriman gave no details, but later Gordon accused Orpen of misleading him by telling him that Masupha had only ten followers – which, as Orpen pointed out, was so far from the truth that he could not conceivably have said such a thing – and that Masupha had little or no support among the rest of the Basotho – which he doubtless said, since that was his belief.[18] It was on the basis of this information that Gordon had spoken about capturing Masupha, and since this had got him into such trouble he might well have turned against Orpen for this reason. There was no place for Orpen in Gordon's proposed settlement, and his hostility to Orpen soon became common knowledge. So too did his proposals to remove magisterial control and to establish Basutoland as a Protectorate or a Suzerainty.

Gordon goes to Basutoland.

Although Gordon was pursuing his own agenda Merriman was still one of his greatest admirers. 'He is a queer fellow', he wrote, 'but I like him as much as ever I did .... the man makes a great impression on me ....' Like Gordon, he had no confidence in Orpen, who in his judgement was not strong enough to carry the government's plans into action.[19] He dreaded having to go back to Parliament with nothing to show but Orpen's memoranda.[20] Something more decisive had to be done.

Merriman therefore pressed strongly for Gordon, acting as a private individual, to join Sauer in a visit to Basutoland. At the beginning of September, after Scanlen had given his consent, Sauer and Gordon travelled up together. They were accompanied by Arthur Garcia, who was acting as Gordon's secretary, and by W.G. Bellairs, Sauer's secretary, and at some point they were joined by Captain David Hook and Captain Nettelton. Gordon was still determined to visit Masupha, since that, he believed, would lead to the solution of 'the Basuto question', while Sauer had not the slightest confidence in Gordon's ability to win over Masupha and generally regarded him as 'erratic and peculiar'.[21]

On 14 September they were greeted by Orpen as they entered Basutoland, and they spent that night at Mafeteng. On the following day they went on to Morija, escorted by thousands of Basotho horsemen. Sauer and Orpen went to lodge with Hamilton Dyke, while Gordon spent the night at Adolphe Mabille's.

Orpen was vehemently opposed to any meeting between Gordon and Masupha. It ran counter to everything that he was trying to do. In a long letter which he handed to Sauer at the border he argued

---

[17] Lewsen (1960: 108-9, 110); Gordon Correspondence (1905: 15), Scanlen to Gordon, 14 August 1882.
[18] Lewsen (1960: 110), Merriman to Scanlen, 30 July 1882; C.3493, p. 78, 'Meeting. - General Gordon with Masupha at Thaba Bosigo', 26 September 1882.
[19] Lewsen (1960: 109-11), Merriman to Scanlen, 30 July 1882.
[20] Lewsen (1960: 112), Merriman to Sauer, 30 July 1882.
[21] C.3493, p. 84, Sauer to Scanlen, 16 October 1882, and Garcia to Scanlen, 18 October 1882; pp. 85-6, Hook's memorandum of 16 October 1882; p. 86, Bellairs' memorandum, 19 October 1882. The quotation is from Hook.

that Masupha was now the only serious obstacle to the realisation of the Government's policy, and that ranged against him were 'the mass of the people', who were 'disgusted and alarmed' by his 'violence, drunkenness and depravity', and all the best sons of Letsie, with Lerotholi pre-eminent among them. Letsie himself was hopelessly weak, but he had sounded out Masupha's subordinate chiefs and subjects and found them 'generally willing and desirous for the restoration of order and payment of Hut Tax'. Acting with Letsie's authority, Lerotholi was now preparing to 'proceed with force' to carry this out. Orpen claimed later that what was intended was not a 'sudden assault with all its dangers', but 'simply a renewal of what Letsie some time before had been carrying out – placing a force in Masupha's neighbourhood and collecting hut tax, protecting those who paid, and restoring authority.'[22]

For the success of this initiative it was essential 'that the policy of the Government should be clear and stable'. Instead there had been constant reports, many of them connected with Gordon's name, that Basutoland would be made a Protectorate, 'leaving the management of affairs in the hands of the Chiefs', and that failing this the country would be abandoned. These reports had spread 'like wild fire' among the Basotho, and Masupha had bluntly told Letsie that there was no point in carrying out Orpen's instructions since the government was about to abandon the country. The only way to undo this harm was to return to the proper channels of communication – not to have any dealings with Masupha, but to declare that the government would be firm and consistent in carrying through its policy and in this way bring Masupha's resistance to an end.[23]

In the meantime Mabille was impressing on Gordon that what Orpen was doing 'was the only right and judicious thing and that Masupha was absolutely incorrigible and must gradually be sup[p]ressed'.[24] It is possible that this accounted for Gordon's unexpected intervention at the meeting that took place the next day in the schoolroom at Morija.

The official side was led by Sauer, with Gordon, Orpen and several others in attendance, the Basotho side by Letsie, supported mainly by his sons and councillors. No chiefs from the Leribe District were there. Nor was Masupha. Sauer harangued the Basotho for not having complied with Robinson's award and criticised Letsie for not enforcing obedience. But he stated categorically that the government would not abandon Basutoland. He had spelt out what the government required in his telegram in March – that hut tax should be paid, that the magistrates should be obeyed and supported, and that there should be peace and order throughout the country. As far as he could see, little had been done.

Then Gordon rose to his feet. The Colony would not give Basutoland up, he said: 'the Basutos are the only really good tribe, the only tribe who have shown that they really wish to get on and progress'. But Letsie was old and could not enforce obedience. 'Why should not Letsie let Lerothodi act for him, who is young and strong and brave?' He had 'some sort of feeling for Masupha', but if he continued to defy Letsie he 'must be suppressed'. 'I must tell Lerothodi that his chance of being paramount chief is not worth one shilling unless Masupha's power is put down ....'

But the real business took place at an interview between Sauer and the chiefs immediately after the meeting. Orpen was not present, nor it seems was Gordon. The chiefs had been stung by Sauer's rebukes and Gordon's warnings, and wanted to show that they were determined to act. Letsie asked for the government's permission to compel Masupha to submit. He believed he was now strong

---

[22] Cory Library, MS 1248, p. 53. See also LNA, S9/1/2/2, Orpen to Sauer, 24 October 1882.
[23] G.8-'83, pp. 294-7, Orpen to Sauer, 13 September 1882.
[24] Cory Library, MS 1248, p. 52.

enough to carry this through, but he needed first to ascertain the feeling of the people throughout the country and to collect an armed force. Sauer agreed to this course of action, and Letsie said he would be in a position to give more definite information by Monday, 25 September.[25]

The officials decided that, while they were waiting, they should take advantage of the delay to visit Hlotse Heights. Letsie asked Sauer and Orpen to reinforce his call on Jonathan and Joel to come in force against Masupha, and Sauer promised he would.[26]

On 19 September, after spending the night at Maseru, Sauer and Orpen set off early in order to reach Hlotse Heights that evening, while Gordon branched off to the Anglican mission at Modderpoort in the Free State, where he put down his views in a document which he entitled 'The Basuto Embroglio'. At the meeting in Morija he had urged Letsie and Lerotholi to suppress Masupha. Now he urged the opposite. An attack on Masupha was unlikely to succeed, and if it failed the magistracies would probably be attacked and the Colony would be drawn into a war for which it was not prepared. He recommended that Letsie should not be pressed into action; that Orpen should be replaced as Governor's Agent; that there should be as few magistrates as possible; that the loyalists should be quickly paid off; that the troops should be removed and the police force built up; and every effort should be made to isolate Masupha and support Lerotholi, 'but this in a gradual manner'. 'With respect to Mr. Orpen, I believe him to be quite sincere, and that he has done his best, but that best has failed, and I think that, considering that he has lost the confidence of both the Basutos and Colony, it would be better for his sake and Colony that he should resign.'[27]

The next day he went on and joined Sauer and Orpen at Hlotse Heights. By this time the commission which had been appointed to enquire into the *Mateketoa*'s losses was gathering information at Hlotse Heights. It consisted of Charles Griffith as chairman and Cecil Rhodes and two others as members, and they too became peripheral players in Gordon's drama.

As soon as he arrived Gordon was drawn into the maelstrom of Jonathan's dispute with Joel. Dr. Taylor's account is revealingly frank:

> Some of us went to Jonathan and told him the truth, that Sauer was a member of the Ministry that had basely abandoned him and that he had come up to Thlotsi with the intention of ... encouraging the rebel party to destroy him; but that General Gordon was a just and upright man who would do all he could for him. Sauer was received in the camp in stony silence, but, when the General arrived a few days afterwards [in fact a day later], Jonathan rode out to meet him with some 500 men on horseback, and brought him into Thlotsi amid clamorous shouts of welcome.[28]

Orpen, though writing from a different perspective, confirms Taylor's account:

> Before we reached Leribe, the white opposition there ... prepared a big native demonstration by Jonathan and his men, to ignore Mr Sauer and myself and worship the supposed rising sun, General Gordon, who was expected to revolutionise everything.[29]

---

[25] C.3493, pp. 69-71, 'Report of Proceedings of Meeting in Schoolroom at the Morija Mission Station', 16 September 1882, and pp. 71-2, Sauer to Letsie, 18 September 1882.
[26] Cory Library, MS 1248, p. 56.
[27] C.3493, pp. 74-5, Gordon, 'The Basuto Embroglio', 19 September 1882.
[28] Taylor (1972: 93-4).
[29] Cory Library, MS 1248, pp. 60-1.

Rhodes warned Gordon that he should not allow himself to be used in this way, but should make it clear that he was subordinate to Sauer.[30] Up to a point Gordon followed that advice. When a petition setting out the *Maseketoa*'s grievances was presented to him he handed it over unopened to Sauer, and when he met Jonathan he told him that although he felt deeply for him he was unable to help him. All that he could do was to give him advice – that he should never desert the Queen of England and that he should rule his people justly. In this way he would recover his rightful position.[31] At the same time he made it clear that his sympathies lay entirely with the opposition. According to Widdicombe, he was in profound disagreement with the Government's plans.

> He trusted neither the measures nor the men. Rightly or wrongly, he had come to regard them as crooked. "I feel," he said, ... "as if I should go up yonder," pointing to where the chief officials were, "and explode."[32]

And he told Griffith that the turning point had been reached and that the present system was 'doomed'.[33]

At some stage, perhaps even as Gordon was threatening to 'explode', Sauer, Orpen and Bailie were holding a private meeting with Joel and other *Mabelete* chiefs. Letsie had asked Sauer and Orpen to back up his instructions to Joel and Jonathan to join him against Masupha. According to Orpen, Sauer spoke only to Joel, telling him to act as Letsie had directed.

> Joel asked quietly: "I wish to know where I come in". Mr Sauer answered with the greatest deliberation that when Masupha was coerced he would give Joel the very ground we were standing on, where Jonathan was living, and up to the river Khomokuana. .... Joel said "All right".

On leaving this meeting, however, Sauer was waylaid by Nathanael Makotoko, Molapo's old councillor, who extracted an undertaking that he would return in a fortnight's time to settle the disputes between Jonathan and Joel.[34] So while Sauer was promising Joel that he would have Jonathan's land if he helped Letsie to humble Masupha, he was also assuring Jonathan that he would come in two weeks' time to settle their dispute. As Orpen remarked, if Gordon had known what Sauer was saying to Joel he would have had good reason to 'explode'.

Gordon meanwhile was applying relentless pressure on Sauer to allow him to visit Masupha. According to Bellairs, he exhibited more than his usual impatience at Hlotse Heights – 'Why are we sticking here? What good can we do here?' – and 'it was his ever constant and growing desire to visit Masupha, and that, if possible, alone'.[35] Orpen advised strongly against allowing him to go, pointing out that it would run contrary to the arrangements with Letsie. 'Besides that, Gordon is quite uncontrollable; he will say exactly what comes uppermost at the time and not what you may wish him to say to Masupha. He seems quite mad sometimes.' Sauer replied:

---

[30] Cory Library, MS 1248, pp. 60-1; Rotberg (1988: 143-4).
[31] Widdicombe (1895: 225-6). See also C.3-'83, pp. 3-4 and 4-6, Jonathan to Gordon, 18 September 1882, and Jonathan and others to Gordon, 18 September 1882; C. 3717, p. 154, Orpen to Sauer, 12 January 1883, Annual Report for 1882.
[32] Widdicombe (1895: 223).
[33] CA, Griffith Papers, Gordon to Griffith, 22 September 1882.
[34] Cory Library, MS 1248, pp. 61-3. See also C.3717, p. 154, Orpen to Sauer, 12 January 1883, Annual Report for 1882.
[35] C.3493, Bellairs, Memorandum, 19 October 1882.

I can not say I think him very wise, but you see he has a very great name, and if he should succeed with Masupha, we should have the credit and advantage, and if he failed people would say that if Gordon could not succeed, then nobody could.

The corollary of this was that if Sauer did not let Gordon visit Masupha, and if Masupha continued along his defiant path, Sauer would be blamed for missing a heavensent opportunity to bring Basutoland's troubles to a close.

Sauer still had not made up his mind by the time the party left Hlotse Heights. Orpen was then sent on to Morija, where Letsie was gathering his forces, while Sauer and Gordon returned to Maseru. It was there, on the evening of Sunday, 24 September, that Sauer finally agreed to allow Gordon to go.

Gordon claimed later that he had visited Masupha only because Sauer had asked him to go. His own secretary, Arthur Garcia, however, testified later that Gordon was anxious to see Masupha because 'he believed that such an interview would give a solution to the Basuto question', and that Sauer was uneasy about it because the General 'seemed so easily to alter his mind' and he did not share the General's optimism.[36] Hook declared that he never saw any sign that Sauer wanted Gordon to go, but on the contrary thought the General 'rather eccentric or peculiar' and had no confidence in him for 'native work'. On the other hand Gordon 'seemed most anxious to go to Masupha and talked of it often, and said he would go and live with him and seemed quite pleased the morning he started'.[37] Bellairs, Sauer's secretary, testified that the General was 'in high glee' at dinner on the night of the 24th, and that after breakfast the next morning he told Sauer 'It will all be settled in a fortnight', to which Sauer replied, non-committally, 'I hope so'. Later that afternoon Sauer told Bellairs that he knew Masupha well: 'the General would not be able to do anything with him; Masupha would meet him, would be very polite and civil, but would laugh at him in his sleeve.'[38]

Sauer was worried that Gordon would act contrary to government policy, and when giving his permission for the General to go he made him write down exactly what it was that he had been authorised to do – to visit Masupha 'in a completely private capacity'; to hear what he had to say about accepting a magistrate and paying hut tax; to impress on him that abandonment was impossible; and then to hear what Masupha wanted so that Sauer could consider whether his wishes were acceptable to government.[39] Sauer also told Garcia how uneasy he was, and Garcia said the General was 'a strange old fellow' but he would keep him to what was required.[40]

Gordon, as he frankly admitted later, had no intention of abiding by these instructions. Formally he was under Sauer's direction and control, but as Chinese Gordon, the great imperial hero, he far outweighed the young and inexperienced colonial politician. To his own perception, he was being guided by the Divine Will to bring peace and stability to the poor black sheep of Basutoland. The present policies were 'doomed', Orpen and his magistrates were not up to the job, and the only hope was to turn to himself. He was even trying out the idea that he should work as a magistrate with Masupha for two years (though not, of course, under Orpen).[41] He protested that he wanted no glory

---

[36] C.3493, pp. 84-5, Garcia to Scanlen, 18 October 1882.
[37] C.3493, pp. 85-6, D. Hook, Memorandum, 16 October 1882.
[38] C.3493, p. 86, Bellairs, Memorandum, 19 October 1882.
[39] C.3493, p. 72, Gordon to Sauer, 24 September 1882.
[40] C.3493, p. 84, Sauer to Scanlen, 16 October 1882.
[41] Hook (1906: 303). See also C. 3493, p. 88, Gordon to Scanlen, 8 October 1882.

for himself, but only for God, but he was clearly excited by the opportunity to exert his 'mesmeric' influence over Masupha and so to add to the lustre of his own name.

Masupha had his own agenda. He had defied both Letsie and the administration. Lerotholi and others had renounced him, and the administration had tried to isolate him. And then, in June, he had received the confidential message from Gordon, telling him that he wanted to conciliate the Basotho and that he wanted a private meeting with Masupha. To which Masupha had responded that he would welcome such a meeting, but because of the rumours about Gordon's intentions to capture him he should come only with a private secretary and two servants.[42] As in all dealings with powerful whites, he would have to tread carefully, but there would seem to be a chance here to use Gordon to his own advantage.[43]

Gordon, accompanied by Garcia and Nettelton, arrived at the mission station of Thaba-Bosiu at 11 a.m. on Monday, 25 September. At 1 p.m. they were joined by two of Masupha's sons, Thebe and Senekane. Masupha had sent them with two questions. First, why, after writing that he wanted to meet Masupha, had the General gone first to Maseru and Hlotse Heights? Gordon's reply was recklessly indiscreet: Sauer had wanted to visit these places, and Gordon had gone with him because he was afraid to leave Sauer in the hands of Orpen, whose views he did not share. Second, what was the purpose of his visit? In reply Gordon wrote a letter to Masupha which went far beyond what he had agreed with Sauer. The Basotho were a fine people: he would not fight them in 1880 and he would not fight them now. He wanted to see Masupha because he had heard that he was a warrior who spoke his mind. Masupha should tell him what he wanted and he would then tell this to Sauer. The government would never abandon Basutoland, since that would lead to war with the Free State and the Basotho would be driven over the Drakensberg. So it was only right that they should pay hut tax for the expenses of their own protection. But if, as the government insisted, Masupha was to have a magistrate, he could ask for a magistrate whom he wanted, and this magistrate should consult with him on all large matters and treat him with all proper respect as a great chief, and he and the magistrate should agree on how to spend 'the hut-tax money of your country'. Letsie was Paramount Chief of Basutoland, 'but I would not set him or Lerothodi against you'.[44]

Having received this letter Masupha sent a message that he wanted to consult his people and would let Gordon know that evening if he would be able to meet him. Garcia in the meantime sent a copy of the letter to Sauer and told him of developments.

Meanwhile Orpen was at Morija giving support to Letsie and Lerotholi as they mustered their forces against Masupha. Thousands of men had gathered together and there were severe commissariat problems. Action had to be taken quickly. When Orpen had last spoken with Sauer no decision had been reached on Gordon's visit to Thaba-Bosiu. Now he was told that Gordon was going there with the intention of staying three or four days. He was shocked, and at once wrote to Sauer to warn him of the possible consequences. If Gordon stayed and Lerotholi advanced, he could well be detained by Masupha or even murdered. If he stayed and the advance was delayed, that would be fatal, because the force could not long be kept in the field. Nothing that Masupha might tell Gordon could possibly justify postponement because, as Sauer knew from his own experience, his

---

[42] C.3493, p. 23, Keck to Gordon, 20 June 1882.
[43] C.3717, p. 153, Orpen to Sauer, 12 January 1883, Annual Report for 1882.
[44] C.3493, pp. 76-7, Gordon to Masupha, 25 September 1882.

promises could not be relied upon. The only possible course of action was for Sauer to order Gordon to return to Maseru at once.[45]

Letsie too was profoundly disturbed to hear that Gordon was going to see Masupha, and on Sauer's instructions Orpen sought desperately to reassure him that Gordon was merely trying to extinguish the rumours linked with his name. But the tales of divisions among the whites were unsettling. Letsie was about to embark on a hazardous undertaking, his men were ready to advance, and he wanted to make absolutely sure that what he was doing would receive government support.[46] Sauer, who had now come to Morija, not only gave this assurance: he told Letsie that he fully expected him to carry out what he had undertaken, 'and that without delay'.[47]

Having been persuaded by Gordon to let him go to Thaba-Bosiu, Sauer was now persuaded by Orpen to recall him. On the morning of the 26th, before receiving Garcia's report, he sent off an urgent message to Gordon to tell him that Lerotholi's force was ready to advance. Masupha would try to drag out the negotiations in the hope that this force would disperse in the meantime: 'already the men are complaining of hunger'. 'I must therefore ask you not to stay longer than tomorrow morning at Thaba Bosigo.'[48]

Then Sauer received Garcia's note and the copy of Gordon's letter to Masupha. He was 'angry' and 'astonished',[49] and he at once dashed off another note to Garcia:

> I see the General says he does not agree with the policy of Mr. Orpen. This may or may not be, but the present Government is responsible for the policy pursued by Mr. Orpen .... I am not prepared to say that the Government will go as far as the General indicates in his letter to Masupha, ...

Sauer then repeated Orpen's argument: even if Masupha agreed to pay hut tax there was no guarantee that he would do so. 'Don't let Masupha prolong negotiations and so destroy the chance of getting Letsie to act.'[50]

On the morning of the same day, the 26th, before receiving Sauer's letters, Gordon heard from Masupha that he was prepared to see him, and he and his party went to the chief's village. About 200 of Masupha's people were present. Gordon, it seems, spoke in pidgin English – that was the way his words were recorded. He repeated what he had said in his letter, and advised Masupha to see Sauer, not Orpen. 'Mr. Sauer big man of Colony, and Masupha big man here.' Masupha should say 'give me good magistrate', and Masupha should then pay for this magistrate and also for police on the frontier. 'Then Mr Sauer would say, all right, good friends.' The magistrate would advise, but Masupha would govern his people. 'Masupha first, and Magistrate, adviser.' He then turned to religion. 'I believe God made you Christians in your heart. You are sheep of Jesus .... I cannot make Masupha and his people do what I want, so I leave it to Jesus, who works everything.' Finally he dealt with the rumours that he had been intending to capture Masupha:

> I came from the Cape. .... I heard Mr. Orpen said Masupha had ten men with him, and all Basutos not like Masupha. This is two-tongue business; and then I would say to Masupha, come to

---

[45] LNA, S9/1/2/2, Orpen to Sauer, 25 September 1882.
[46] C.3493, p. 73, Tsekelo to Sauer, 25 September 1882; LNA, S9/1/2/2, Orpen to Sauer, 25 September 1882.
[47] C.3493, p. 73, Sauer to Letsie, 26 September 1882.
[48] G.6-'83, pp. 7-8, Sauer to Gordon, 26 September 1882.
[49] C.3493, pp. 85-6, memorandum by Hook, 16 October 1882, and memorandum by Bellairs, 19 October 1882.
[50] C.3493, p. 79, Sauer to Garcia, 26 September 1882.

Maseru with your ten men, and I should take Masupha. But when I heard that most Basutos' hearts were with Masupha, I said it was a lie.

He urged Masupha to think over what he had said and to give his answer to Sauer. 'If you jump over precipice, I cannot help it.'

Masupha's responses gave nothing away: 'I am still waiting for other councillors and people, and scarcely can answer you now. ... I am very glad to see you with your present purpose. ... I can hardly ask any question, because I must think over matters. ... That is all right. May God give us rain, and a peaceful and rightful settlement. ... You put these matters in my ears and I will give them due consideration.'[51]

The position at the close of the meeting was that Masupha was planning to consult his people and then tell Gordon whether or not he would see Sauer. In the meantime Gordon would wait for Masupha's answer at the mission station.

In the afternoon Garcia received Sauer's letters telling Gordon not to stay beyond the morning of the next day, 27 September. Gordon's immediate reaction was that he would leave for Maseru at once, but then he decided to stay until the next morning in the hope of receiving a reply from Masupha. He was sure, however, that Lerotholi's advance would cause Masupha to reject the terms he had proposed.[52]

At the same time Gordon informed Masupha that he had received instructions from Sauer to return to Maseru the next day, and that if Masupha had anything to say to him he should send it before 9 a.m. the next morning. Over the next hours, right up to midnight, messages went to and fro between Masupha's village and the mission station, and all the while rumours were swirling around that Lerotholi and his force would be attacking Masupha at daybreak. Masupha asked why Sauer was instructing the General to withdraw. Gordon told Masupha to ask Sauer. Masupha said he was astonished by Lerotholi's action; he had determined to agree to Gordon's proposals. Gordon told him he had nothing to do with Lerotholi and referred him again to Sauer. On the following morning, at 9 a.m., the General left Thaba-Bosiu.[53] There was no sign of Lerotholi. Contrary to all the rumours, he and his force had only moved about 20 kilometres from Morija.

Before leaving Thaba-Bosiu Gordon sent a letter to Sauer saying it was an error that he had ever come to Basutoland, and enclosing the telegram to Scanlen which he was about to send:

> As I am in completely false position up here and can do more harm than good, I am leaving for Colony, whence I propose coming to Cape Town, when I trust Government will accept my resignation.[54]

Gordon's departure

Sauer and Orpen were expecting Gordon at Maseru, but instead he went direct to Morija, and from there he returned to the Colony without seeing them. While at Morija he had passed several groups of Lerotholi's men and, according to Orpen, 'harangued and abused them', no doubt to their astonishment, 'for being there assembled in arms against their kinsman Masupha!'[55]

---

[51] C.3493, pp. 77-9, 'Meeting. - General Gordon with Masupha at Thaba Bosigo', 26 September 1882.
[52] C.3493, pp. 79-80, Garcia to Sauer, 26 September 1882.
[53] C.3493, p. 80, Garcia to Sauer, 27 September 1882.
[54] C.3493, pp. 80-1, Gordon to Sauer, 27 September 1882, enclosing telegram to Under Colonial Secretary, Cape Town, and Merriman, Graham's Town.
[55] Cory Library, MS 1248, p. 78. See also Mackintosh (1907: 307): according to Christina Coillard, he met 'some native police' and 'shook his fist in their faces'.

Gordon did not in fact resign immediately. He had previously undertaken to remain in post until Parliament met again, but he told Scanlen he had overlooked this, 'being put out', when offering his resignation from Thaba-Bosiu.[56] Scanlen responded icily that he had no wish to keep Gordon to his undertaking:

> After the intimation that you would not fight the Basutos, and considering the tenor of your communications to Masupha, I regret to record my conviction that your continuance in the position you occupy would not be conducive to the public interests.[57]

Lerotholi's action, as Gordon had predicted, came to nothing. On 26 September, while Gordon and Masupha were holding their meeting, he set out with a large force from Morija, but he only got as far as Mofoka's Nek when he was held up by heavy rain. He himself was willing to go on, but his brothers Bereng, Maama and Nkuebe were refusing to march against Masupha if the intention was to do anything but talk. He had sent messages to Joel asking for help, but because of the delay Joel's men went home, and in the end Lerotholi's own force broke up and left him powerless.[58] Orpen blamed the failure on the rains and the flooded rivers, and on the demoralisation arising from the confusion and conflict between Sauer and Gordon.[59] Letsie's explanation was closer to the truth: although he had explained that he was not embarking on war, but was only insisting that Masupha's people should pay tax, the Basotho said that they did not wish 'to handle Masupha's blood'.[60]

Though Gordon himself was no longer in the country his initiative had not yet run its full course. Shortly before leaving he had advised Sauer to go to see Masupha 'who I believe would come to terms if Orpen is kept out of it'.[61] Just as Orpen claimed that, but for Gordon's visit to Thaba-Bosiu, Lerotholi would have brought Masupha to heel, so Gordon argued that, but for Lerotholi's action, Masupha would have come to some agreement. Sauer sent Hook to sound out Masupha, and at the end of what Hook described as 'a pleasant meeting' the old chief responded, with no great enthusiasm, that he would be glad to see Sauer if he came 'and if he does not it will be all the same. .... Please convey my compliments to him.'[62] On 18 October Sauer came to Thaba-Bosiu. As Gordon advised, he did not take Orpen. He spelt out the settlement that was on offer – the payment of taxes, the establishment of magistracies, but the chiefs to be recognised as chiefs and treated accordingly. According to the official record Masupha praised Sauer as 'the Peace Bringer', but nothing could have been plainer than his final words: 'we are subjects of the Queen, but we wish to be ruled in the same way as in the time of Moshesh. I and my people do not want a magistrate, also we do not want to pay taxes.'[63] According to another account of the meeting, 'Mr. Sauer's manner and tone' was 'nearly that

---

[56] C.3493, Gordon to Under Colonial Secretary, 3 October 1882.
[57] C.3493, p. 82, Scanlen to Gordon, 5 October 1882.
[58] *Cape Argus*, 2 October 1882, 'Who'll Bell the Cat? Maama Holds Aloof'; 5 October 1882, 'News from Basutoland'; 16 October 1882, 'Letsie and Masupha. Friendly but Useless'. See also *The Journal*, 30 September 1882, 'Basutoland Affairs', 7 October 1882, 'Lerothodi's Forces Dispersing', 16 October 1882, 'Affairs in Basutoland', and 23 October 1882, 'Basutoland'.
[59] Cory Library, MS 1248, pp. 80-1.
[60] G.6-'83, pp. 27-8, Letsie to Sauer, 17 October 1882.
[61] C.3493, p. 81, Gordon to Sauer, 29 September 1882.
[62] C.3493, pp. 90-2, 'Note of Semi-private Interview between the Chief Masupha and Captain Hook....', 12 October 1882.
[63] C.3493, pp. 93-5, 'Report of Proceedings of Meeting at Thaba Bosigo, on the 18th October 1882'.

of a suppliant' while Masupha, though very polite, was most sarcastic.[64]

In communications with his fellow Basotho Masupha was even more outspoken. His son Thebe told a messenger from George Moshoeshoe:

> I shall tell you the plain truth: We are all agreed with what Masupha says .... We fear to agree to a Magistrate coming, because if they come again, they will try their old dodges .... If Lerothodi comes and attempts to make Masupha's people pay hut-tax, ... there will be a fight. .... There will never be peace between us and the English, who want to crush us down by equalizing the common people with the chiefs. These are Masupha's words, and we all agree with them.[65]

Gordon's visit to Thaba-Bosiu, his readiness to negotiate directly with Masupha and his recognition of him as the 'big man' of Basutoland – a course which was then followed by Sauer in his official capacity as a government minister – coupled with yet another failure on the part of Letsie and Lerotholi, left Masupha in a stronger position than ever before, while Letsie's impotence had been exposed yet again. 'From that day to this', he told Sauer, 'I have been continuously seized with *shame and dejection*'. The visit of General Gordon, 'far from producing the smallest good ... has only come to greatly increase perversity on the part of Masupha and others.'[66]

Gordon had hammered away at Ministers that Orpen had to be removed, and he went on hammering away after leaving Basutoland. And it was not just Orpen who had to go, but his 'wretched ner-do-well [*sic*] Magistrates', these 'men of doubtful reputation', these 'broken down creatures' – Rolland, Bailie and Nettelton (though not Surmon).[67]

Merriman confessed later that it had been 'possibly a blunder' for which he was 'chiefly to blame' to involve Gordon in the affairs of Basutoland, a man who was a 'brilliant genius' but 'full of impulses often noble but often singularly bewildering'.[68] More specifically, it was a blunder on Merriman's part to encourage Gordon to go to Basutoland when he knew that he disagreed so profoundly with government policy and disapproved so strongly of the Governor's Agent. And it was a blunder on Sauer's part to agree to this proposal, and then to allow Gordon to visit Masupha at the very time when Letsie and Lerotholi were trying to take action against him. The notion that a man of Gordon's reputation, holding the post of Commandant-General of the Colonial Forces, could be regarded as no more than a private individual was absurdly unrealistic.

The making of a myth

At the time Gordon shifted between justifying himself – that he had only gone to Basutoland 'at the earnest request of Government' and against his own 'repeated protestations'[69] – and confessing

---

[64] *Cape Argus*, 23 October 1882, 'Mr. Sauer at Thaba Bosigo'. See also *The Journal*, 31 October 1882, 'Basutoland', and A.7-'83, p. 17, translation of leading article in the *Zuid-Afrikaan*, 24 October 1882.
[65] A.24B-'83, pp. 25-6, statement of Tsinyane, 2 October 1882.
[66] G.6-'83, p. 28, Letsie to Sauer, 17 October 1882. See also *Cape Argus*, 16 October 1882, 'Letsie and Masupha'.
[67] CA, Acc. 611, Southey Papers, Vol. 66, Gordon to Southey, 16 October 1882. For a gentler judgement see *Cape Argus*, 24 October 1882, 'General Gordon in Basutoland'. Orpen was 'sincere' but 'mistaken'. If he were wiser he would resign. 'He cannot hope to do any good even were his policy best, considering the dead-set that his political and personal enemies make upon him. I have told him so.'
[68] Lewsen (1960: 117), Merriman to Editor of *Cape Times*, 24 November 1896.
[69] C.3493, p. 83, Gordon to Scanlen, 11 October 1882; pp. 83-4, Gordon to Scanlen, 11 October 1882; pp. 86-8, Gordon to Scanlen, 8 October 1882.

frankly, as in his letter to Scanlen as he left Cape Town:

> I did not even attempt to follow the wishes of the Government, [n]or did I in the least weigh my words with a view to suit the Government. I acted entirely upon my own responsibility, and was and am perfectly convinced that what I said was and is the best thing that could be done ....[70]

Gordon's biographers and apologists, relying not just on the contemporary documents but on later statements by the General, shaped and built up these events into a myth of near martyrdom that took on even greater force after the tragic events at Khartoum – a myth of crooked, mean-spirited Cape politicians who were determined to rid themselves of a fine Christian man who was telling them too many uncomfortable truths, and who therefore persuaded him, much against his wishes, to go alone and unarmed to negotiate with Masupha, promising at the same time not to send in Lerotholi's force, but then, even as he was in discussions with the chief, ordering Lerotholi to advance, and so leaving him with no honourable alternative but to withdraw and to resign. But for the shining sincerity of the man, but for his 'power of inspiring savages with confidence in his complete uprightness',[71] Masupha would have had him put to death. Sauer was guilty of 'an act of treachery that has never been surpassed'.[72]

This myth was fully subscribed to by Gordon's admirers at Hlotse Heights. Widdicombe and Taylor had fallen completely under his spell. Widdicombe spent 'four of the most delightful hours' of his life discussing mission work, theology and the Bible with him, prayed with him in the House of God, and came to revere him almost as a saint. There were many tales about Gordon's 'madness' – about his weeping over 'those dear black lambs of the Saviour' as he addressed the Sunday School at Morija, of his being found in the veld, kneeling in prayer and with his arms outstretched, of his yearning to spend his last years in a monastery on Mount Carmel where he could instruct some Syrian boys of the lower classes – but for Widdicombe such stories were merely confirmations of Gordon's goodness and his greatness.[73] Taylor was ill with ophthalmia at the time and was confined to a dark room, but Gordon used to come down and sit on his bed 'and while away a weary hour with his pleasant chat'. The young doctor was so affected by his 'extraordinary hypnotic power' that, in his own words, 'if he had said to me, 'Leave all and come with me', I should have done so without the slightest hesitation'.[74]

Jonathan Molapo, too, was grateful for Gordon's sympathy and advice – it was a long time, he said, since he had heard such words from a government officer – and Widdicombe was convinced that it had a profound influence on him and played a great part in turning around his fortunes.[75] This

---

[70] C.3493, p. 88, Gordon to Scanlen, 16 October. See also *Cape Argus*, 28 October 1882, 'Saturday Sallies'. Before going to Thaba-Bosiu Gordon said that the Ministry had made a big mistake in approaching him: it had bought 'a pig in a poke'. His companion said 'And a very big pig too'. 'Yes, and a very obstinate pig', said Gordon.

[71] Hake (1884: 396).

[72] Boulger (1896: II.82-3). See also Hake (1884) 394-6; Butler (1891: 183); Boulger (1896: II.82-5).

[73] Widdicombe (1895: 220-31). For the story of Gordon at Morija see Cory Library, MS 1248, pp. 57-8; Smith (1939: 310).

[74] Taylor (1972: 95). For another adulatory account of Gordon's doings, which must have been based largely on Widdicombe and Taylor, see Christina Coillard's letter to her sister, 8 May 1881, quoted in C.W. Mackintosh (1907: 306-7).

[75] Widdicombe (1895: 224-5, 232, 233).

seems unlikely – there were many other good reasons for Jonathan's recovery – but it added to the myth of Gordon's prophetic wisdom and insight.

Sauer failed to return to Leribe to settle Jonathan's differences with Joel, and in November full scale hostilities broke out. The government had already been badly shaken by developments in Basutoland and was already thinking about a change of policy. The outbreak of an extensive civil war, which it was unable to damp down or extinguish, and which led to complications with the Free State as refugees fled over the Caledon, gave an added urgency to its deliberations. The pressure for abandonment was building up, but one last policy remained to be tried – the withdrawal of magisterial control and the grant of internal self-government. It was of course the policy that Gordon had been pressing the government to adopt.

CHAPTER 19: RETREAT AND DESPAIR

Picking up the threads

Gordon's intervention had cut right across the government's policy of isolating Masupha, weakening his power and bringing him under control. Six months had been lost. Orpen now wanted to pick up the threads and to resume where he had been forced to leave off. What was needed, he argued, was patience and perseverance. The government must gradually build up its authority through the collection of hut tax and the re-establishment of magisterial control. It must resist the pressure of those who argued that the situation was too humiliating to be endured and that 'something must be done'.[1]

In the face of so many setbacks and disappointments, in the teeth of so many calls for his removal, Orpen's buoyancy and resilience were remarkable. He was genuinely encouraged by every sign of goodwill and support. He still believed that the bulk of popular opinion was behind him and that he could achieve the government's goals by working through his trusted allies, above all the energetic and determined Lerotholi.

Most whites in the country were convinced that he was wrong. Among them was the new magistrate in Maseru, John Smith Moffat, son of the famous missionary, Robert Moffat of Kuruman, and brother-in-law of David Livingstone. Moffat, who had taken up his appointment in May 1882, wrote that in the view of the most experienced men in the country there were only two alternatives for the government – 'either to reconquer the Basutos, which the Colony is not prepared to do ... or that we relinquish the pretence of governing the country'. Instead the government was 'trying a middle course' and was not being honest with the public. He despised Orpen's 'policy of sham' and after falling out with him on various issues expressed the view that 'sooner or later he will break down with all his shams on top of him'.[2]

In his efforts to collect the hut tax Orpen achieved some limited success. In the three years before the war, when the annual tax had been 10s per hut, payments had averaged about £15,000 a year. Sprigg doubled the tax to £1 a hut, but in 1881, during the war and its immediate aftermath, only £463 was paid. From 1 January 1882 to the end of February 1883, a period of 14 months under Orpen's stewardship, payments amounted to about £9,000.[3] This was not a bad achievement in the circumstances. No tax was paid in the Berea District, and the *Maketetoa* were not paying until they received their compensation.[4] Many people were still recovering from their losses in the war, there was stagnation in trade and in mining enterprise, the harvest of 1882 had been ruined by drought, and there had been the disruption of Gordon's intervention. In the context of a policy of patience and perseverance, an overall payment of £9,000 laid the ground for some hope in the future. The practice of paying the chiefs 10% of what they collected had fallen into abeyance: its revival could be expected

---

[1] LNA, S9/1/2/2, Orpen to Sauer, 24 October 1882; *Cape Argus*, 30 October 1882: the 'occasional correspondent' who wrote the article on 'Basutoland Affairs' was probably Orpen himself.

[2] Moffat (1969: 195, 197, 198).

[3] C.3708, p. 75, report on meeting at Morija, 26 March 1883. In October 1882 the figure of £8,000 was given: *Cape Argus*, 30 October 1882, 'Basutoland Affairs'. For finances generally, see C.3708, pp. 12-3, statements of revenue and expenditure enclosed with L. Smyth to Earl of Derby, 5 May 1883.

[4] *Cape Argus*, 30 October 1882, 'Basutoland Affairs'; C.3708, pp. 53 and 87, reports on meetings at Morija, 19 and 26 March 1883 respectively.

to lead to better results. More recently the rains had been good and in 1883 a good harvest was expected.

Hardly any progress was made in reimposing magisterial rule. There were reports of the chiefs oppressing their people and preventing cases being taken to the magistrates.[5] At Maseru Moffat declared that it was impossible to enforce the law beyond the boundaries of the camp. Maama was particularly resistant, receiving CMR deserters at his village and refusing to give them up on the ground that desertion was not a crime in 'his' country.[6]

Even Letsie defied the administration where his vital interests were involved. The *Maketetoa* were gradually making their way back to their own villages or to the districts of Quthing (within Basutoland) and Matatiele (below the Drakensberg). No unauthorised settlement was allowed in Quthing, but in December Letsie's son Nkuebe arrived at the camp declaring that he had been sent by Orpen and Letsie as district chief.[7] The *Maketetoa* were immediately up in arms. Orpen said that Nkuebe was to act merely 'in a police capacity', helping the magistrate in much the same way as Mohapi, another son of Letsie, had been helping the magistrate at Mohale's Hoek.[8] The *Maketetoa* protested to the Cape Parliament, but to no effect. The government was powerless. Nkuebe rapidly came to assume the position of district chief, which was exactly the position that Letsie had wanted for him.

In the unsettled and agitated state of the country there were constant rumours of impending hostilities, and in December the *Maketetoa* at Maseru sent out pickets because they were afraid of an attack by Masupha.[9] It was only in the north, however, that fighting broke out, and that did not arise from any resistance to the government but from the struggle for power between Jonathan and Joel.

Civil war in the house of Molapo: Jonathan and Joel (1)

The first serious engagement took place on 30 November. An old headmen, Qacha, was looking after certain cattle which belonged to Jonathan's mother, 'Mamosa, and so formed part of the Molapo estate. 'Mamosa and Jonathan sent for these cattle because they were making arrangements for the payment of *bohali*, marriage-cattle, for Moliboea, one of Molapo's junior sons. Joel protested that Jonathan had no right to start disposing of Molapo's estate, and he and his brothers called their men to arms. Bailie intervened and persuaded them to return home, but it seems that one of the brothers, Khethisa, did in fact recover some of the cattle. Jonathan then called up his forces and determined to assert his claims. Joel, who had already sent most of his forces home, went to intercept Jonathan, at the same time sending a peremptory message to Bailie telling him not to interfere. At this stage Joel had no more than 1,000 men while Jonathan had about 700. Jonathan ascended the Leribe plateau and prepared to confront his brother. On both sides, it was said, there was a reluctance to fight, and a

---

[5] Smith (1939:309), quoting letter, not dated, by Adolphe Mabille.
[6] G.8-'83, pp. 257-9, Moffat to Orpen, 26 December 1882; LNA, S9/2/3/1, Moffat to Officer Commanding CMR, 29 November 1882.
[7] A.24B-'83, p. 27, S. Barrett to Orpen, 9 December 1882; LNA, S9/1/2/2, Orpen to Sauer, 18 and 25 December 1882.
[8] LNA, S9/1/3/6, Orpen to Barrett, 23 December 1882. Later Orpen claimed that it was Sauer who, in his absence and against his advice, had made an agreement with Letsie that Nkuebe should be stationed in Quthing: Cory Library, No. 1248, pp. 82-4. Orpen had certainly advised against Nkuebe's being placed in Quthing: C. 3717, p. 87, Orpen to Sauer, 31 August 1882.
[9] A.24B-'83, pp. 28-9, Masupha to Moffat, received 11 December 1882, and Moffat to Masupha, 11 December 1882.

meeting was arranged to settle the dispute. Joel went forward to parley, but Jonathan's men, either on his orders or, as he claimed, because they were out of control, opened fire and attacked. According to a report that reached Letsie at Matsieng, Jonathan treacherously attacked Joel as he was riding away. Whatever the truth of this, Joel's men scattered without much of a fight, and the battle became known as *Ntoa ea Lepatla-patla*, the Battle of Helter-skelter Flight. At least nine of Joel's men were killed there and then, and they suffered further losses as they were driven back to their homes. All Joel's villages were burnt, including his own village at Qalo, and many of his people fled across the Caledon into the Free State.[10]

Widdicombe later described this battle as the turning point in Jonathan's fortunes: more and more of his old adversaries were coming across and joining him. This was partly because Letsie had acknowledged him as the leading chief in the district,[11] but there was another development which was passed over in silence in official sources but which is strongly emphasised in Basotho tradition. As already described, Moshoeshoe, in an effort to hold his chiefdom together after his death, had decreed that Letsie's eldest daughter, Senate, should be accounted a man, that Molapo's senior son, Josefa, should be accounted her wife, that their offspring, Motšoene, should be accounted the child of Letsie's senior wife, 'Masenate, and that Motšoene should therefore succeed to the paramountcy when Letsie died. This arrangement had never been widely accepted, but after Moshoeshoe's death the young Motšoene was brought up under Letsie at Matsieng. At the same time, since Motšoene's father, Josefa, was Molapo's senior son, in due course Motšoene could expect to succeed to Molapo's ward. Jonathan was merely acting as ward chief because Josefa was mad. Motšoene still held land in the Leribe District, not far from Joel's village at Qalo, and Joel had taken advantage of the confusion of the Gun War to seize control of this land. Because he was getting the worst of it against Joel, Jonathan went to Matsieng and persuaded Motšoene to return with him to the north, warning him that his father's followers and property were being taken over by Joel. In this way he attracted Motšoene's following to himself, as well as all those who were disposed to support the lawful chief, and this was a considerable addition to his strength. When exactly he did this is not clear, but Motšoene had certainly come to the north by the time fighting broke out.[12]

It appears, however, that as well as this increase in his fighting strength Jonathan was also better armed than Joel. When Griffith was at Hlotse Heights chairing the commission of enquiry into the payment of compensation, he made an impassioned plea to Sauer, as a matter of honour, to supply

---

[10] A.24B-'83, pp. 19-24, Bailie to Orpen, 1 December 1882 and enclosures; C.3717, pp. 94-5, Brand to Robinson, telegram received 2 December 1882, and p. 95, Brand to Robinson, 4 December 1882; C.3717, p. 98, Orpen to Sauer, 3 December 1882; Germond (1967: 399), Coillard, letter of 11 December 1882; C.3717, pp. 100-2, Robinson to Kimberley, 12 December 1882, with enclosures; C.3-'83, pp. 2-3, Jonathan to Orpen, 29 December 1882; G.9-'83, Annual Report for 1882 of the Resident Magistrate of Leribe, and Proceedings of the Trial of Chiefs Jonathan and Joel Molapo; C.3717, pp. 156-7, Orpen to Sauer, 12 January 1883; A.7-'83, pp. 24-5, Makotoko's statement, 9 December 1882; *Leselinyana*, 1 January 1883, Samson Nasone, 'Tsa Lesotho'. According to Widdicombe (1895: 235-6), hostilities were provoked by the *Mabelete*'s 'continued ill treatment of those of Jonathan's people who had gone out ... to plough and sow their fields.' This was no doubt an underlying factor, but not the immediate cause.

[11] Widdicombe (1895: 233).

[12] C.3717, p. 103, Orpen to Sauer, 10 December 1882; Widdicombe (1895: 240); LNA, S3/5/3/8, Letsie to Resident Commissioner, 28 May 1889; LNA, S3/5/12/4, Joel's statement of 1 March 1913; interviews by AA with Motsarapane J. Molapo (Leribe), May 1966, Lelosa (Qalo), 21 May 1966, and Goliathe Malebanye, 4 June 1966.

Jonathan with arms so that he could defend himself and so by degrees regain his position as 'the head chief of this District'. The Loyals, he claimed, were '*unarmed and without ammunition*'.[13] This advice seems to have been followed. Neither Orpen nor Bailie was directly involved, though they soon became aware that some change had taken place.[14] When Bailie attempted to prevent hostilities he noted that 'Jonathan's men were better armed than Joel's, nearly all being armed with breech-loaders, principally Sniders and Martini-Henri [*sic*], while Joel's men with few exceptions were armed with muzzle-loaders of a very inferior type'. And Orpen noted that many of Jonathan's breech-loaders were government property.[15] Sauer claimed that these guns had been given to Jonathan during the rebellion, and that he had merely allowed him to retain them.[16] Whatever the truth of this, Jonathan's breech-loaders gave rise to exaggerated reports, which according to Orpen were widely believed, that 'in revenge for Joel's rebellion' the government had put up Jonathan 'to massacre Joel's faction' and had given him a wagon-load of guns and ammunition to do so.[17] There was even a rumour that the CMR had fought alongside Jonathan with blackened faces.[18]

Although Jonathan had won a striking victory, he knew he was likely to face reprisals. While begging Masupha and Ramanella not to intervene, he called on Letsie to try to settle the dispute. Letsie, working closely with Orpen, prevailed on both sides to lay down their arms, and Orpen then made arrangements to hear the case himself with Lerotholi and other chiefs in support.[19]

Even while proceedings were pending, however, Hlasoa Molapo, with a motley of allies – one of Masupha's sons, Seshope Lesaoana, some of Maama's and Bereng's followers, Jobo, Moshoeshoe's brother, and even some of the sons of Posholi from the south – attacked Jonathan's villages in the west, destroying Kolonyama, Peka and Fobane, killing about 12 of Jonathan's followers, seizing cattle, and driving his people into the Free State. In all about half of Jonathan's villages were burnt to the ground.[20]

Both Joel and Jonathan had suffered great losses, Jonathan now even more than Joel, and both were ready to come to terms. Lerotholi came up with 250 men to help Orpen to restore law and order, and then sat with Orpen to hear the case. A large, excited crowd gathered outside the court room, and Orpen, anxious to get things over, fined Jonathan 15 head of cattle for starting the fight and Joel 10 head of cattle for leaving his village with an armed force. A month later, in January 1883, with the help of Letsie's sons, he laid down a boundary which satisfied Joel but not Jonathan, though

[13] LNA, S9/1/2/2, Griffith to Sauer, 20 October 1882.
[14] LNA, S9/1/3/6, Orpen to Bailie, 30 November 1882.
[15] A.24B-'83, p. 19, Bailie to Orpen, 1 December 1882. See also C.3717, p. 98, Orpen to Sauer, 3 December 1882: See also *Cape Argus*, 31 May 1883. Masupha complained that the *Mateketoa* had received ammunition from Bailie, who denied it.
[16] A.24-'83, p. 24, Sauer to Orpen, 6 December 1882.
[17] C.3717, p.102, Orpen to Sauer, 10 December 1882. See also LNA, S9/1/3/6, Orpen to Bailie, 4 December 1882.
[18] C.3717, p. 104, Orpen to Sauer, 14 December 1882.
[19] LNA, S9/1/3/6, Orpen to Bailie, 5 December 1882; C.3717, pp. 100-03, Orpen to Sauer, 7 and 10 December 1882, Bailie to Sauer, 8 December 1882.
[20] A.24B-'83, pp. 29-30, Jonathan's statement before Orpen, 15 December 1882; *JME* 1883, pp. 114-5, Duvoisin, n.d.; C.3717, pp. 103-5, Orpen to Sauer, 13, 18 and 20 December 1882, Rolland to Sauer, 19 December 1882; Samsone Nasone, 'Tsa Lesotho', *Leselinyana*, 1 January 1883; C.3717, p. 157, Orpen to Sauer, 12 January 1883, Annual Report for 1882.

it is not clear if Jonathan objected to this particular boundary or to having any boundary at all, since he claimed to be chief of the whole of the Leribe District. Orpen now declared that peace had been restored, and throughout the country it was reported that Jonathan and Joel had been reconciled.[21]

The fighting among the sons of Molapo was bad enough in itself, but as a consequence thousands of Basotho, Jonathan's followers as well as Joel's, had fled to the Free State. President Brand remonstrated with the High Commissioner that this was a breach of the undertakings given at the time of the Aliwal North Convention, under which the home government had guaranteed to safeguard the borders. There could be no assurance that it would not happen again.

A further retreat

Because of the fighting between Jonathan and Joel the session of the Cape Parliament that was due to begin in March 1883 was brought forward to January. Ministers had lost patience. As Merriman had feared, Orpen's optimistic reports were all that they had to show. Throughout the country, especially among the Dutch farmers, there was a strong movement in favour of abandonment that found expression in fifty petitions to Parliament.[22]

Ministers were not prepared to go as far as that, but decided instead on a radical new policy that was almost exactly the same as that put forward by General Gordon. On 19 January Robinson addressed the Parliament: ' ... my ministers ... have arrived at the conclusion that the best interests of the Colony will be served by withdrawing from the management and responsibility of their [the Basutos'] internal affairs, whilst retaining that control over their external relations which is necessary to the maintenance of order on the Free State border'.[23] To use the Irish analogy, the Basotho were to be granted Home Rule. In the debate that followed there were many who pressed the case for abandonment, but in the end, on 4 February, 34 members voted for the new policy and 27 against.

The proposed withdrawal of magisterial rule, the latest retreat in a long series of retreats, was contrary to all Cape precedent and principle, and the government used this change of direction as the occasion for changing the Governor's Agent. In conveying this decision to Orpen Sauer stressed that no blame attached to him in any way. On the contrary, he had been doing his best to carry out the policies laid down by the government, and Ministers were conscious of his 'devotion, energy and single-mindedness' in carrying out his 'grave and onerous duties'. But circumstances made it 'imperative' that he should be replaced.[24] In truth there had been so much criticism of Orpen, most recently in the Parliamentary debate, that it was impossible for the government to retain him in office. Very few members of the House, it was said, had any confidence in his judgement. The opposition denounced his administration as a failure: it was 'a discredit to the country, and degraded the Queen's government in the eyes of every native in the land.' Perhaps the kindest stricture was that he was 'a good sort of man, but fanatical, and led away by his hopes, and incapable of managing men.'[25]

The man who replaced him, Captain Matthew Blyth, Chief Magistrate of the Transkei, was very different from Orpen. He was widely acknowledged as 'an experienced and able official', but he was

---

[21] C.3717, pp. 104-5, Orpen to Sauer, 18 and 21 December 1882; Samsone Nasone, '*Tsa Lesotho*', *Leselinyana*, February 1883; C.3717, p. 157, Orpen to Sauer, 12 January 1883, annual report for 1882;

[22] Bradlow (1970: 191).

[23] C. 3717, p. 107, Robinson's speech to Parliament, 19 January 1883.

[24] A 24-'83, p. 10, Sauer to Orpen, 9 February 1883.

[25] *Cape Argus*, 4 April 1882, 'Parliament. House of Assembly', reporting a no confidence debate a few weeks later. The quotations are from the speech of John Laing.

also, 'to say the least', as the *Cape Argus* noted, 'firm in his government of natives', and his appointment was 'more popular on the European than on the native side'.[26] After the long campaign of vituperation against Orpen the government was anxious that its new appointment should win the confidence of the country, and in this at least it was successful. The opposition press, led by *The Kaffrarian Watchman*, combined its welcome of Blyth's arrival on the scene with another kick at the departing Orpen:

> We colonists may congratulate ourselves upon having a gentleman at the head of Basutoland affairs whose name is a sufficient guarantee that his administration will be honest and above-board, and a blow will at last be struck at the whispering, lying, and dodging policy, which has been so prevalent for many months.[27]

Blyth himself soon made his opinion known that for the past two years the administration of the country had been 'one lie',[28] and publicly criticised Orpen's lack of financial control and the disorganisation of his office – 'books, papers, telegrams, all muddled together without order or regularity'.[29]

In March 1883 Scanlen and Sauer came up to introduce Blyth to the Basotho and, before putting their new policy into effect, to ascertain their views. They ran into a storm of anger from Letsie and the *Mabelete* chiefs, not just about Orpen's dismissal but also about Blyth's appointment. Their first meeting, at Morija on 16 March, with Letsie and his sons and councillors, was almost entirely taken up with these grievances. The Basotho complained that they had not been consulted. They got on well with Orpen, and they wanted to know why he had been removed. When Scanlen and Sauer replied that this was a matter for the government and was not open for discussion several chiefs left the room in disgust.[30]

The Basotho had particular reason to object to Blyth, since to them he was notorious as the man who, in Griqualand East in 1876, had arrested and imprisoned Nehemiah Moshoeshoe on a charge of fomenting rebellion. Nehemiah had been championed by Orpen, and several chiefs had attended the trial at King William's Town in which he had been acquitted.[31] Blyth, it was reported, had 'a very wrathful and hard-hearted way'.[32] Letsie was also offended when, because of a misunderstanding, Blyth went direct to Maseru instead of going with Scanlen and Sauer to greet him at Morija, but in the end he resigned himself to the inevitable. He had been given two wives he had not liked by Moshoeshoe, he said, but he had come to like them. Perhaps it would be the same with Blyth. His son Seeiso said that the Basotho would accept Blyth, not because of himself, but because they had confidence in the men who had appointed him.[33]

---

[26] *Cape Argus*, 19 February 1883, Editorial.
[27] Quoted in *Cape Argus*, 12 March 1883.
[28] *Cape Argus*, 12 July 1883, 'Parliament. House of Assembly'.
[29] *The Journal*, 27 October 1883, 'Basutoland'.
[30] C.3708, pp. 43-5, report of meeting at Morija, 16 March 1883. See also A.24-'83, pp. 69-70, Letsie to Sauer, 26 February 1883; C.3708, pp. 69-72, report of meeting at Maseru, 21 March 1883; p. 101, report of meeting at Morija, 27 March 1883. See also *Leselinyana*, March 1883.
[31] See Chapter 5, pp. 60-1 above; C.3708, pp. 69 and 74, report of meeting at Morija, 21 March 1883; p. 76, report of meeting at Morija, 26 March 1883; pp. 92-3, report of meeting at Morija, 27 March 1883.
[32] C.3708, p. 92, report of meeting at Morija, 27 March 1883, speech by 'Malipani'. One of Blyth's admirers described him as having 'a good heart and a most awful temper': Streatfeild (1911: 235).
[33] C.3708, pp. 68-9, 70, report of meeting at Maseru, 21 March 1883; pp. 76-7, report of meeting at Morija, 26

Scanlen and Sauer then held a series of meetings to find out what the Basotho really wanted – with Letsie and his councillors at Morija; with the *Mateketoa* chiefs at Maseru; with Letsie's messengers at Maseru; and with Letsie and his subordinates at Morija. The detailed records of these discussions give the clearest evidence of what the Basotho thought about Cape rule before the war and what they wanted now.

Scanlen asked three questions. First, did the Basotho want to be under the Queen at all, or did they want their independence? Second, if they wanted to be under the Queen, did they want imperial or colonial rule? Third, what kind of rule did they want?

The reply to the first question was an almost unqualified yes, though it was acknowledged that both Masupha and Ramanella wanted independence. According to Nehemiah, Letsie's sons, Maama and Bereng, were also in favour of independence, and in view of what happened later he might well have been right.[34] For the rest there was a clear recognition that abandonment would lead to war with the Free State and, in Letsie's firm belief, to 'the destruction of the Basuto people'.[35] The *Mateketoa* chiefs stressed that the common people were terrified of abandonment because it would leave them defenceless against the oppression of chiefs. 'They are afraid of being eaten up', said Nehemiah, 'and that if the Government were to abandon the country each chief would be his own law to himself.'[36]

On the second question, Sofonia asserted that most of the common people did not know the difference between imperial and colonial rule,[37] but at the final meeting, after an 'animated' exchange, Letsie and his immediate subordinates replied that ideally what they wanted was imperial rule, failing that colonial rule, and in no circumstances abandonment.[38]

The responses to the third question, about the type of rule the Basotho wanted, revealed a distinction, not always sharp, between those who favoured magisterial rule and those who favoured rule by the chiefs – or, in Sofonia's formulation, between those who loved the government and those who merely wanted the flag. For the most part, according to Sofonia, it was the common people who loved the government. Their reasons for disliking chiefly rule were the same as their reasons for rejecting independence: 'they see the Government protects them. If the Basotho were left to manage their own affairs the chiefs would be like jackals among a flock of sheep'.[39]

The *Mateketoa* acknowledged that there were some chiefs who loved the government: as well as Jonathan and themselves, they named Lerotholi, Mojela, Leluma Posholi, Molomo Mohale and Joel.[40] But most of the chiefs, and certainly most of the big chiefs, were opposed to magisterial rule and wanted only protection under a British Resident. 'A man like Letsie', Sofonia said, '... would be quite

---

March 1883; pp. 99-100, report of meeting at Morija, 27 March 1883; *Cape Argus*, 31 March 1883, 'Ministers in Basutoland'.

[34] C.3708, pp. 45-6, report of meeting at Maseru, 19 March 1883.

[35] C.3708, p. 121, report of meeting at Hlotse Heights, 2 April 1883.

[36] C.3708, p. 46, report of meeting at Maseru, 19 March 1883. In the same report, covering 19 as well as 20 March, see also pp. 54, 63, 65, 66 and 68, evidence of Tlalinyane, 'Lefiyani', son of 'Nico' [i.e. Neko], Nkau, Tšita [Mofoka] and Tlaele respectively.

[37] C.3708, p. 52, report of meeting at Maseru, 19 March 1883.

[38] C.3708, p. 82, report of meeting at Morija, 26 March 1883.

[39] C.3708, pp. 50-52, report of meeting at Maseru, 19 March 1883, evidence of Sofonia. For similar evidence by Nehemiah, see p. 48.

[40] C.3708, pp. 46-7, report of meeting at Maseru, 19-20 March 1883, evidence of Nehemiah; p. 50, evidence of Sofonia. See also p. 66, evidence of Tšita Mofoka.

satisfied so long as the Resident is here to protect him from the Free State, and leave him to govern the people, because he would be able to do as he pleased.'[41] Even the *Mateketoa*, in their capacity as chiefs, had grievances about the Cape's rule before the war, and Letsie and the *Mabelete* chiefs poured out a long catalogue of complaints about land allocation, the administration of justice, the lack of consultation and the interference with Sesotho custom.[42]

In the light of all these discussions Scanlen drew up his draft regulations, which he sent to Letsie on 31 March. Cases in which whites were involved, and cases of murder or culpable homicide, were to be reserved for the Governor's Agent and his officers. All other cases would be heard by the chiefs, though there would be a right of appeal (presumably to the Governor's Agent and his officers, though this was not explicitly stated). Otherwise the Paramount Chief and his subordinates would be responsible for 'the arrangement of the internal affairs of Basutoland'. The laws would continue to be made by the Governor, but there would a Council of Advice, consisting of chiefs and headmen, which would meet at least once a year to discuss public business and to suggest any changes in the law that it wanted. Hut tax would continue to be paid to defray the expenses of government.[43]

Sauer described this as the most liberal and generous constitution ever offered to a native tribe in South Africa, and Scanlen tried to impress on Letsie the enormous importance of the Basotho's response: their future welfare depended on it.[44] If the Cape was to go on governing the country the regulations would have to be accepted by all the Basotho, not just some of them.[45] And that meant winning over Masupha.

It was arranged that a national *pitso* should be held to consider the draft regulations in about three weeks' time, and at this point Scanlen left the country, shortly followed by Sauer. On 9 April Blyth, accompanied by Surmon, Moffat and the PEMS missionary, Daniel Keck, undertook the thankless task of trying to sell the proposed arrangements to Masupha at Thaba-Bosiu. They found him 'half-drunk' and 'insolent', with about 150 followers 'who acted in much the same way'. After Blyth had explained the regulations Masupha 'said he did not want the Government in the country, but to go back to the days before Moshesh handed the country to the Government. This he emphatically repeated ....'[46] In other discussions at this time Masupha likened the Basotho to a well-trained team of oxen which had been pulling contentedly under the English yoke, but the owner had then treated them harshly. Now the owner wanted them to come back under the yoke and to work in the same way as before, but how could they?[47]

What was meant to be the all-important, decisive *pitso* was held at Piet Mokolokolo's village on 24 April. Alfred Boegner, the new Director of the PEMS Mission who was then visiting the country, described the scene – a great gathering under a grey sky set in a frame of mountains, horses grazing around, the ground strewn with red saddles, the crowd talking, shouting, laughing.

---

[41] C.3708, p. 50, report of meeting at Maseru, 19 March 1883.
[42] C.3708, pp. 77-9.
[43] C.3708, pp. 122-4, report of meeting at Hlotse Heights, 2 April 1883.
[44] C.3708, p. 122, report of meeting at Hlotse Heights, 2 April 1883; LNA, S9/2/2/3, Scanlen to Letsie, 31 March 1883.
[45] C. 3708, pp. 103-4, report of meeting at Morija, 27 March 1883.
[46] LNA, S9/1/2/3, Blyth to Sauer, 11 April 1883.
[47] C.3493, p. 91, interview between Masupha and Captain Hook, 12 October 1883.

They are awaiting Masupha. Horsemen by the score continue to arrive – but Masupha comes not. The Pitso begins without him. The men arrange themselves in a huge hollow square, those in front sitting on the ground, those behind standing. The chiefs and missionaries take their places within the square: Letsie, Captain Blyth and the six magistrates seat themselves there apart. The Captain has a soldierly bearing and inspires confidence. Mabille opens with a prayer. Then Letsie rises. "*Lumelang!* Hail!" he cries, and the thousands of voices respond with a long-drawn-out "*Eh!*".

Blyth presented himself as a man of plain speaking who was going to sweep away the confusions and obfuscations of his predecessor. Everything that had happened over the past two years he damned as 'lies, one thing said one day, another the next, consequently all got wrong'. He stood there as the government's representative and he demanded a plain answer: 'do you or do you not accept the regulations proposed by Government?' At one point the officials withdrew to give the Basotho the opportunity to discuss the matter among themselves, and Mabille seized the opportunity to implore them to give a clear and decisive reply. If they could not accept these proposals then sooner or later the country would be abandoned. And once the British had gone the Boers would come.

> They will say: 'Mojela, clear out! Lerothodi, clear out! Letsie, clear out! All this land is ours.' .... One man troubles you – Masupha. ... He kills us all by his selfishness. ... And ... when some day you are scattered abroad or serving the Boers in the land that was yours, ... – then your children will say, and you will say to yourself: 'A curse upon Masupha! It is he who brought us to destruction'. To-day it is not too late. Reflect – act – be men!

Letsie, Lerotholi, Jonathan and others all declared, with varying degrees of firmness and clarity, that they were prepared to accept the regulations, but Masupha and Ramanella were not there and Blyth was not prepared to compromise: 'Why go on hoping and hoping against hope and nothing but a lie?'[48]

The meeting ended, the horsemen rode off. On the following morning Blyth met the chiefs again: he wanted to give them every opportunity to achieve some kind of unanimity. But there was still no indication from Masupha that he was prepared to accept the regulations, and now Letsie turned to shuffling and evasion. Blyth became increasingly exasperated: 'do you, or do you not accept the regulations?' Lerotholi pressed his father to accept, and so did Letsie's adviser, Setha Matete. When the people around 'acclaimed' what Setha said, Letsie at last gave his assent: 'I say to you, Maama and others as Moshesh gave us over to the Queen I have accepted these laws with my whole heart.'[49]

Why was Letsie so hesitant? The *Mateketoa* chiefs provided the answer. He wanted to be under the government, but, being an old man, was increasingly dominated by his sons, Bereng and Maama, who sided with Masupha and Ramanella.[50] Blyth agreed: 'the arrogance and general bearing of these two chieflets', he reported, 'bode but little good to the general peace of this country.'[51]

---

[48] Boegner's account, originally given in French in *JME* 1883, pp. 250-7, is translated and quoted in Smith (1939: 315-6). For the official account, see G.8-'84 (Appendix), pp. 14-17.
[49] G.8-'84 (Appendix), pp. 17-21, report of meeting held on 25 April 1883.
[50] C.3708, pp. 46, 50, report of meeting at Maseru, 19 March 1883, evidence of Nehemiah and Sofonia respectively; C.3708, p. 127, report of meeting at Hlotse Heights, 2 April 1883, evidence of Abel.
[51] G.8-'84 (Appendix), p. 13, Blyth to Sauer, 27 April 1883.

Even before the *pitso* Blyth was sure that Masupha was 'at the head of a large body of the Basutos who desire to get rid of the government and to be left to themselves', and he was already advising Ministers to face up to the facts, with the clear implication that they should now abandon the country.[52] The decision not to use force was so much a settled part of government policy that Blyth now dispensed with the services of the remaining CMR and even cut back the police force – steps which he wrongly believed would help to win the Basotho's confidence.[53] He also disclaimed any intention of setting one part of the nation against another in order to bring Masupha to heel: 'God forbid that I should do this', he said.[54]

Civil war in the house of Molapo: Jonathan and Joel (2)

In the discussions with the *Mateketoa* chiefs Nehemiah had told Scanlen and Sauer that, 'as regards Joel and those who sided with him during the rebellion, ... they show themselves now to be more for the Government than any other people in any part of Basutoland.'[55] Yet a few days before the *pitso* Joel was telling the missionary Coillard that he wanted the government to leave,[56] and a few days after the *pitso* he and his allies were involved in the heaviest and bloodiest fighting with Jonathan that had taken place since the war. His confidence in the government had been shaken by its alleged loan or gift of guns to Jonathan, and perhaps the reports of possible abandonment made him believe that there was nothing further to be gained from courting government approval.

The immediate causes of the outbreak are not clear, and in the inquiry that followed Letsie confessed that he was unable to find out who was in the wrong. It was harvest time, and there was a dispute over the millet in certain fields. There was also a dispute over some cattle.[57] But whatever it was that gave rise to the fighting, at the end of April and the beginning of May Joel and his allies began advancing on Jonathan's forces at Hlotse Heights, burning Jonathan's villages on their way.[58]

Canon Widdicombe, watching from the Camp, and passionately committed to Jonathan's cause, gave a vivid description of what he saw. On the morning of 3 May the regiments of Khethisa, Hlasoa and Ramanella came into view from the east and took up their positions on some rising ground above the Hlotse river. The forces of Lepoqo Masupha were reported to be massed behind Tsikoane mountain to the south. In the north Jonathan had posted Motšoene with 300 men at the Leribe pass to hold up Joel's advance, and there was as yet no sign of Joel's regiments.

Jonathan and his men, 1,700 strong, rode out, crossed the Hlotse river and, after a desultory exchange of fire, charged right in among the forces of Khethisa, Hlasoa and Ramanella. For about ten minutes there was a fierce struggle at close quarters, but then the *Mabelete* broke rank and fled. 'The Mabelete ran for dear life', wrote Widdicombe. 'But the Matikete pursued them everywhere, cutting down every straggler ... setting fire to village after village.'

Jonathan's pursuit had left the camp unprotected, but Lepoqo Masupha and his men made no

---

[52] LNA, S9/1/2/3, Blyth to Sauer, 11 April 1883.
[53] LNA, S9/1/2/3, Blyth to Sauer, 7 April 1883; C.3708, p. 73, report of meeting at Maseru, 21 March 1883; C.3708, p. 115, report of meeting at Hlotse Heights, 2 April 1883.
[54] G.8-'84 (Appendix), p. 18, report of meeting at Piet Makolokolo's [Mokolokolo's] village, 25 April 1883. See also LNA, S9/1/2/3, Blyth to Sauer, 7 April 1883.
[55] C.3708, pp. 55-6, report of meeting at Maseru on 20 March 1883.
[56] LNA, S9/1/2/3, Blyth to Sauer, 18 April 1883.
[57] G.8-'84 (Appendix), pp. 40-9, reports on meetings held on 22, 23, 24 and 26 May, 1883.
[58] LNA, S9/1/3/6, Blyth to Letsie, 1 May 1883; Favre (1931:347-8, quoting Coillard's letter of 8 May 1883).

attempt to attack it. Nor did they give any help to their allies. Instead they returned to their homes, laying waste the whole country along their line of march, burning villages, trampling down the crops, and seizing whatever grain they could find. At no risk or cost to themselves they had once more weakened Jonathan and ensured that Masupha would be free from any pressure on his eastern boundary.

Meanwhile in the north Joel's regiments had forced their way through the Leribe pass and by noon they were advancing on Hlotse Heights. The camp was defenceless as they approached. But then Tokonya, the Hlubi chief, rode out with 30 men and began taking potshots at the *Mabelete*. To Widdicombe it seemed an act of madness to challenge such a multitude, but then he saw Joel's men wheel round and quietly retire towards Sebothoane. 'It seemed a dream, an optical illusion, an impossibility, but it was a simple, downright fact. They had actually abandoned the prey when it was absolutely within their grasp. It was inexplicable but it was true.'

But the camp was not in such peril as Widdicombe described. It would have been foolish for Joel to attack it, just as it would have been foolish for Lepoqo Masupha to attack it. This was not the Gun War between the *Mabelete* and the Cape, but a civil war between the sons of Molapo. Joel's 'prey' was not the white community in the Camp, but Jonathan and his regiments. He would probably have attacked the camp if Jonathan had still been there, but if he had attacked it in Jonathan's absence he would have antagonised the Cape administration irrevocably.

It was now one o'clock. Three hours later Jonathan and his men returned 'exulting in their victory'. Having rested their horses they rode out, just as the sun was setting, and launched their attack on Joel's regiments on Sebothoane. In the gathering darkness Widdicombe watched, and then listened, from Hlotse Heights, and as he heard the firing becoming more and more distant he knew that the *Mabelete* had been driven away. Jonathan and his men gave chase through the night, returning only in the small hours of the morning.[59]

Widdicombe gives the impression that the *Mabelete* were utterly routed, but early on the following day, 4 May, Joel and his men continued their work of destroying Jonathan's villages in the east. Many women and children had taken refuge at the French mission station at Leribe. Coillard (who had now returned to the station) begged Joel to spare them, but he was implacable.[60] Several women were stripped of their clothes and took flight over the Caledon into the Free State. Among them was Letsie's daughter, Senate. Several old men were killed. A young boy was castrated and put to death.[61] Two days later Molapo's European-style house at Leribe was burnt – an act which was said to have been widely condemned as an insult to Molapo's ancestral spirit.[62]

Jonathan and his regiments, according to Widdicombe, 'celebrated their double victory by such a war-dance as I have never witnessed either before or since, making the air resound for miles with their repeated shouts of joy'.[63] About 50 men were said to have been killed, most of them on the side

---

[59] Widdicombe (1895: 238-55). See also G.8-'84 (Appendix), pp. 38-9, Blyth to Sauer, 30 May 1883; Taylor (1972: 98-103).
[60] Favre (1931: 348-9).
[61] LNA, S9/1/2/3, Blyth to Sauer, 28 May 1883; *Quarterly Paper of the Bloemfontein Mission* No. 61, July 1883, pp. 154-5, Widdicombe to Webb, 18 May 1883; Rhodes House Library, Oxford, USPG Archives, E 38B, Widdicombe to Tucker for quarter ending 31 May 1883.
[62] Widdicombe (1895: 245); Favre (1931: 349-50), quoting Coillard's letter of 8 May; Mackintosh (1907: 309). Widdicombe places the burning of Molapo's house before the confrontation at Hlotse Heights. It is clear from Coillard's letter of 8 May that it took place on Sunday, 6 May.
[63] (1895: 254).

of the *Mabelete*. But all Jonathan's country had been devastated, many of his people had taken refuge in the Free State, and when Coillard begged him not to take vengeance he confessed that he was too weak to take any action but would do so as soon as he was strong enough.[64]

With the exception of Bailie, the whites fell back into Gun War mode. Jonathan was again the sturdy loyalist whose bravery had saved Hlotse Heights. Joel was again the bloodthirsty rebel. Even before conducting an enquiry Blyth declared that Jonathan was completely blameless, and he found it 'humiliating' and 'shameful in the extreme' to see this loyal man surrounded and oppressed by 'a horde of rebels determined on his destruction, not one of whom has ever obeyed a lawful command of the Government'. He was convinced that Masupha lay behind it all, and that his aim was to instal Ramanella as his puppet chief of Leribe with Joel as his leading subordinate.[65]

Blyth went up as soon as he could to conduct enquiries. Letsie, after some characteristic hesitation, also went up, and in due course almost every important chief was there – Letsie, Lerotholi, Masupha, Jonathan, Joel and many others – with thousands of men in attendance. A crowded *pitso* was held near the Hlotse River on 22-23 May, and a further *pitso* at Tsikoane on 26 May. There was so much tension and excitement that it seemed that at any moment fighting would break out. Masupha and Ramanella were criticised on all sides for interfering in the Molapo family's quarrel. They in turn criticised the government for making guns available to Jonathan. Letsie, pulled this way and that, was in a turmoil of indecision. He loved Jonathan, who had given up his guns at the time of the Gun War, and he loved Joel, who had paid his hut tax after the war. How could he condemn either of them? But the people insisted that he make a decision – you are the *senohe,* they called out, the diviner or prophet who can tell the truth – whereupon he 'walked away about one hundred yards, weeping and sobbing like a man in hopeless despair'. He came back, asked the same question, was given the same answer and again walked away and wept. He came back again and asked Blyth to judge, but Blyth insisted that he should make the decision himself. He then confirmed Jonathan as the head chief of the Leribe District, saying he should go back to his old village at Fobane, declared that whoever broke the peace in future 'would be set upon and eaten up by the whole tribe', and announced that boundaries would be arranged between the different chiefs so as to prevent further disputes.[66]

Among Letsie's sons there was a clear divide between Lerotholi, who supported Jonathan, and his rivals, Maama and Bereng, who supported Masupha and to a lesser extent Joel. Letsie had given judgement in favour of Jonathan, and Blyth commended him for the care he had taken. But he had also directed him to arrest and try the *Mabelete* who were alleged to have killed the young boy and the old men at Leribe (he also believed some women had been killed), since that was 'not fighting, but murder'. Letsie had been evasive, and in his final judgement had ignored this demand, but it was an issue that would not be forgotten.[67] And in spite of Letsie's judgement Jonathan felt unable to return to Fobane, since it was so far from the protection of the camp and so close to Masupha's land.[68]

---

[64] Favre (1931: 350).

[65] LNA, S9/1/2/3, Blyth to Sauer, 13 and 15 May 1883. See also C.3708, p. 24, Blyth to Sauer, 11 May 1883, and G.8-'84 (Appendix), pp. 38-9, Blyth to Sauer, 30 May 1883.

[66] G.8-'84 (Appendix), pp. 48-9, minutes of a meeting held on 26 May 1883, and pp. 38-9, Blyth to Sauer, 30 May 1883; A.24-'83, p. 78, Blyth to Sauer, 27 May 1883; *Cape Argus*, 31 May 1883, 'Telegrams', and 11 June 1883, 'Letsie at Thlotsi Heights'.

[67] G.8-'84 (Appendix), p. 48, minutes of a meeting held on 24 May 1883.

[68] *Cape Argus*, 19 June 1883, 'Jonathan Molapo's position'.

Preparing for the last retreat

Blyth had already reported to Sauer that Masupha and Ramanella had refused to accept the new regulations for governing the country, and that it was only after many evasions that Letsie had finally agreed to accept them. There was already good reason for the Cape to try to offload its responsibility for the country onto the imperial government. The outbreak of fighting in Leribe added a new urgency.

On 30 April, even as the *Mabelete* were preparing to attack Jonathan Molapo, the Cape had prepared for its final retreat. In a despairing minute to the High Commissioner Scanlen spelt out the failure of all the Cape's efforts to control the Basotho, the impossibility of its continued rule in the country, and the appalling consequences that were likely to follow abandonment. Before taking any step, however, the government was sending John Merriman by the next steamer to England in order to consult with Her Majesty's Government.[69] The message was now clear. The Cape wanted the imperial government to resume responsibility for Basutoland. Failing that it would abandon the Basotho to their fate.

---

[69] C.3708, pp. 1-3, Scanlen's minute, 30 April 1883.

CHAPTER 20: THE FINAL RETREAT

Merriman's mission to London

Up to this point the Basotho's destiny had been fought out, and argued out, within Basutoland itself and in the Cape. In the next few months it would be decided in England, in the imperial offices and corridors of power. In the end it would be Gladstone, the Prime Minister himself, who would set the Basotho on the course they were to follow over the next century.

Merriman arrived in London in the latter half of May 1883. He had two objects – to raise a loan to tide the Cape over its economic difficulties, and to persuade the Earl of Derby, Gladstone's Colonial Secretary, that the home government should resume control of Basutoland. He was not hopeful: the odds, he believed, were heavily stacked against him.[1] Derby, he had been told, did not even admit the possibility of Basutoland becoming a Crown Colony,[2] and Gladstone too was unsympathetic.[3]

He was however supported by unremitting humanitarian pressure, inspired by the Paris mission and the Aborigines Protection Society, and by strong political pressure from the Cape. Robinson, the High Commissioner, was on leave in England at the time, and played a vital role in shifting Colonial Office opinion.

On 29 May Merriman submitted his case. The Cape could no longer control Basutoland, and the only course open to it was the repeal of the Annexation Act, which would need the Queen's consent. He urged the home government to take up the responsibility which the Cape was anxious to lay down. For this there were two compelling reasons. First, the home government was bound by the Convention of Aliwal North to maintain law and order along Basutoland's borders. Second, if the Basotho were abandoned they would not only be torn apart by civil war, they would also provoke the Free State to hostilities which would end in 'a savage war of extermination', a war of the races, with disastrous consequences for South Africa as a whole. At the same time he suggested that the home government should take over 'Fingoland, Tembuland, East Griqualand, and St John's'.[4]

Even before Merriman wrote this memorandum, however, the Cabinet had decided, with great reluctance, to take back Basutoland, but subject to stringent conditions.[5] In replying to Merriman Derby repudiated any treaty obligations, arguing that insofar as they existed they had been assumed by the Cape Government. He also repudiated any obligations to the Basotho, who had taken up arms against the Crown. But the government was willing to contemplate taking on Basutoland on a temporary basis if the Basotho demonstrated that they wanted to remain under the Crown and that they would pay taxes and obey the law; if the Cape paid customs duties arising out of Basutoland's trade and any further sum that might be needed for the police and administration; and if the Free State would provide a frontier force to help to keep peace on the border.[6] He refused to take on any other territories.

---

[1] Lewsen (1960: 131), Merriman to his mother, 14 June 1883.
[2] Lewsen (1960: 121-2), Capt. D. Mills to Merriman, 5 April 1883; Benyon (1980: 188).
[3] Gladstone Papers, Add. MSS 44141, f. 73; Derby to Gladstone, 24 April 1883; Note by Gladstone, 25 April 1883: quoted in Benyon (1980: 188).
[4] C.3708, pp. 14-19, 'Memorandum on the present situation of affairs in Basutoland', 29 May 1883.
[5] Vincent (2004: 547).
[6] C.3708, pp. 19-21, 'Draft of a Despatch' proposed to be sent by Derby to the Officer Administering the Government, June 1883.

Derby was persuaded, mainly by Robinson, to drop his demand for administrative expenses, and, rather than insisting on a Free State border force, he was content merely to look to the Free State to prevent incursions into its territory. On 14 June he sent a formal Despatch to Cape Town conveying the government's decision. It admitted no obligations, but in recognition of the 'strenuous efforts' and the 'heavy expenditure' which the Cape had made it was 'willing to test, provisionally, and for a time, the sincerity of the assurance that the Basutos desire to come under the Crown'.[7]

The issue was still far from settled. In the Cape House of Assembly there were many, led by Hofmeyr and his Afrikander party, who were strongly opposed to any imperial intervention, and others, led by Upington, who objected to the financial provisions.[8] In July the Basutoland Disannexation Bill was carried in the Cape House of Assembly, but only by 36 votes to 28. It was also passed by the Legislative Council. Then, before it was given Crown consent, the Basotho had to demonstrate, as the home government had insisted, that they were indeed willing to come under the direct rule of the High Commissioner, and for this purpose a national *pitso* was to be called.

Marking time in Basutoland

In these circumstances Blyth gave up any serious attempt to introduce the new self-rule regulations. His policy now amounted to no more than reducing expenditure, avoiding giving any cause of offence and irritation, and trying to achieve 'some measure of right and justice' by working through Letsie.[9] Blyth's reliance on the Paramount, 'weak, old and double dealing' Letsie as he called him,[10] led to continual frustration and acrimony. Even in his own ward Letsie was not fully in control, nor did he always do what Blyth would have wanted. Bereng – 'always ... a bad and headstrong man'[11] – was the main source of unrest. He exacted tolls from whites crossing the Caledon, refused to hand over criminals or stolen stock, and for a time gave protection to Mhlonhlo, the Mpondomise chief who had killed Hamilton Hope. There were also disturbances in Maama's ward in which a man was killed. Maama drove off more than a thousand head of cattle but was never called to account.[12] Even Lerotholi took up arms against a neighbouring chief without any reference to Letsie or Blyth.[13] In Quthing, Nkuebe, for all the reputed mildness of his rule, was steadily imposing his authority on the whole district, contrary to Blyth's instructions and much to the alarm of the local *Mateketoa*.[14]

Masupha of course conducted himself with complete independence. He dealt with cases of murder himself, refused to give back the cattle which his people had seized from Jonathan in the recent disturbances, and was dismissive when Letsie tried to frighten him with a message that Merri-

---

[7] C.3708, pp. 37-40.
[8] Hofmeyr's motion that the issue should be referred to the constituencies was defeated 42-21. Upington's motion, for abandonment pure and simple, was defeated 37-27. For accounts of the debates, see contemporary issues of the *Cape Argus*, 10 July 1883 and following.
[9] G.3-'84, p. 81, Blyth's report for 1883, 12 January 1884.
[10] G.3-'84, p. 84, Blyth's report for 1883, 12 January 1884.
[11] LNA, S9/1/2/3, Blyth to Sauer, 26 August 1883. See also LNA, MF2/1/2, Nettelton to Blyth, 29 August 1881.
[12] LNA, S9/1/3/6, Blyth to Letsie, 1 May 1883 and 31 May 1883; G.8-'83 (Appendix), p. 135, Blyth to Letsie, 27 June 1883.
[13] LNA, S9/1/2/3, Blyth to Sauer, 17, 23 and 24 November 1883; LNA, MF2/1/2, Nettelton to Blyth, 20 November 1883, and S9/1/3/6, Blyth to Nettelton, 24 November 1883.
[14] LNA, S9/1/3/6, Blyth to Letsie, 22 June, 2 and 27 August, 7 and 18 September 1883; LNA, S9/1/2/3, Blyth to Sauer, 15 and 18 August 1883; *Leselinyana*, October 1883.

man would be coming back from England with imperial troops: 'Let it be so they do come, let them.' The only solution, he declared, was a return to the days of Moshoeshoe: 'we Basutos are goats, white people are cattle. Goats and cattle cannot be put into the same kraal. Cattle have long horns. They will destroy the goats.'[15]

In the north the conflict between Jonathan and Joel was always threatening to erupt into armed confrontation. Jonathan was gaining in strength, but his following was still smaller than the combined followings of his enemies.[16] Several thousands of his people were concentrated at the magistracy, and after the destruction of their crops in the recent fighting many were suffering from hunger.[17] Blyth was wholly on Jonathan's side, but there was nothing he could do. He was especially disgusted that Letsie refused to punish those followers of Joel who had allegedly murdered the old men and the young boy in the last bout of fighting.[18] The old alliances continued to operate, Joel being supported by his brothers, especially Khethisa and Hlasoa, and by Masupha, Ramanella, Bereng and Maama, and Jonathan being supported by Lerotholi, Theko and Mojela. There were fears at times that the Molapo quarrels would embroil the whole country in civil war.

Blyth was in despair. The Basotho were ungovernable, and the government's position was shameful and humiliating. Matters would never come right 'without a force, and the teaching the Basutos so much want, that the European is superior to them in every way including fighting'.[19] But he knew that no force would be sent.

His denunciations of Letsie became more and more strident. The greatest difficulty in enforcing law and order, he reported, was Letsie's 'unreliable and deceitful character'. 'I have done all in my power to induce Letsea to listen to reason, and govern his people on some principles of justice and right, but it is no use. Such principles have no place in his heart ....'[20] He had been appointed to carry out a fresh policy, but as soon as it became known that the Cape was going to leave the country the Basotho looked on him as a mere stopgap, 'without power and authority'. 'I have had to deal with a Paramount Chief who is *a wily, astute and deceitful savage*, who has not supported me in the least, and no one feels more than I do how little I have been able to do.'[21] Just as in the Gun War there were those who believed that Letsie was secretly encouraging the *Mabelete*, so Blyth was now convinced that Letsie, no less than Masupha, wanted complete independence. He was going about it 'in a different way',[22] and he was 'too deep' to declare himself openly, but in spite of all his protestations of loyalty there was 'a complete understanding' between him and Masupha. 'From my little experience', Blyth concluded bitterly, 'I do not think that at any time except when the Boers were thrashing them, that there was any real loyalty to the government. It was a very thin veneer like much of their boasted civilization. ... a vast

---

[15] G.8-'83 (Appendix), pp. 130-4, Blyth to SNA, 22 June and 1 July 1883; Letsie to Blyth, 27 June 1883; statement of 'Lithlomo', Letsie's messenger to Masupha, 27 June 1883. Both quotations are from Lithlomo's statement (p. 134).
[16] LNA, no reference noted, Bailie, Return, 29 December 1883.
[17] LNA, S9/1/2/3, Blyth to Sauer, 23 November 1883; L2/1/4, Bailie to Blyth, 4 December 1883.
[18] S9/1/2/3, Blyth to Sauer, 28 May 1883; G.8-'83 (Appendix), p. 133, Letsie to Blyth, 27 June 1883, pp. 134-5, statement of 'Lithlomo', 27 June 1883, and p. 131, Blyth to Sauer, 1 July 1883.
[19] G.8-'83 (Appendix), p. 133, Blyth to Sauer, 1 July 1883.
[20] G.8-'83 (Appendix), pp. 142-3, Blyth to Sauer, 15 July 1883.
[21] LNA, S9/1/3/6, Blyth to Sauer, 20 October 1883.
[22] G.8-'83 (Appendix), pp. 142-3, Blyth to Sauer, 15 July 1883.

amount of money and earnest good will has been thrown away upon an ungrateful people.'[23]

Letsie certainly wanted to rule his people with as little government interference as possible, but, as he protested time and time again, he recognised that without government protection the Basotho would be torn apart by civil war and would eventually get caught up in hostilities with the Free State. He admitted that he was failing to carry out Blyth's instructions, but his authority was undermined by his sons and brothers. He could not sleep from anxiety, he told Blyth, and at one stage he even spoke of resigning his position.[24] Most of the chiefs under him, especially Lerotholi, were also anxious not to be thrown on their own resources. As for the common people, as even Blyth acknowledged, they were tired of the chiefs' oppressions and wanted government control, though at present they were afraid to express their views 'as they see no visible power able to protect them'.[25]

The Basotho are called upon to decide

This was the background against which the historic *pitso* was held near Piet Mokolokolo's village on 29 November. Two days beforehand Blyth sent on to Letsie a message from the Earl of Derby. The home government was willing to consider taking over the Basotho again, but before making a decision it wanted to put the following questions to the Basotho chiefs and people:

> Do you desire to remain British subjects under the direct Government of the Queen, and if so, do you undertake to be obedient to the laws and orders of Her Majesty's High Commissioner ... and to pay a hut tax of ten shillings [i.e. a reduction from £1] ...? If you say 'Yes', the Government ask further, 'Are you united?' The Queen does not want unwilling subjects. Her Majesty's Government cannot take over a divided people.[26]

About 3,000 Basotho attended the *pitso*. Blyth was supported by several of his staff, and several missionaries and traders were present. On the Basotho side it quickly became clear that Masupha had not come, and had merely sent two of his junior sons who had been instructed to report back to him, that Joel and Ramanella were not there, and that Jonathan had stayed away for fear of being attacked. So hardly any Basotho were present from the whole of the northern part of the country.

Blyth then put the Queen's questions to the meeting and the home government's message was read out. He again presented himself as the plain man who insisted on getting things clear and who would stand no nonsense. There were two roads, he said. One was the road to peace, the road on which their father Moshoeshoe had put them. The other was the road which led to 'war, ruin, and destruction as a tribe'. Which road would they choose?

Letsie, unusually, spoke first, and he spoke at great length and with great passion. He was determined to seize the initiative and to give a strong lead. The argument which made the greatest impression – it 'brought down' the assembled multitude, according to one observer – was that it was Moshoeshoe who had sought out the British, not the British who had sought out Moshoeshoe, and that he, Letsie, would never forsake the government his father had chosen. 'I am for the Queen's Government. What

---

[23] LNA, S9/1/3/4, Blyth to Sauer, 15 September 1883.
[24] LNA, S9/1/3/6, Blyth to Letsie, 22 October 1883. See also G.8-'83 (Appendix), pp. 133-4, Letsie to Blyth, 27 June 1883, and p. 143, Letsie to Blyth, 13 July 1883.
[25] LNA, S9/1/2/3, Blyth to Sauer, 20 October 1883. See also *The Journal*, 6 August 1883, 'Basutoland', and 11 August 1883, 'Basutoland'.
[26] C.3855, p. 43, Derby to Officer Administering the Government of the Cape of Good Hope, telegraphic, 24 November 1883.

do you say?' 'There were loud cries which shook the air, "So are we, Chief! Mother, do not leave your children to be killed!"' Lerotholi, Theko, Maama, Seeiso and others then spoke in support of Letsie, and they all added their names to a document accepting the Queen's proposals. There was not a single dissentient voice.[27]

But the home government had insisted that the Basotho should be united in their acceptance of the Queen's proposals: it could not take over 'a divided people'. Soon after the *pitso* Joel, Khethisa, Hlasoa and Ramanella sent word that they followed Letsie, but Masupha remained defiant. On 5 December he held a *pitso* at his own village at which he declared 'that he did not desire the rule of the Imperial Government, or any other, but his complete independence, and to be left alone', and that he was 'prepared to fight if the Government came to him'.[28]

Letsie was desperate and begged the Queen not to abandon him even although Masupha refused to follow him. 'Abandonment means our complete destruction. We do not want our independence. Listen, Queen, to my earnest prayer ....'[29]

The final decision
The drama then moved back to London. According to Robinson, who was still in England, it was 'touch-and-go' right up to the last moment.[30] Derby was inclined 'to throw in the sponge',[31] but there was a solid body of Liberal supporters who would never allow the Basotho to be abandoned to the mercies of the Free State, and the Conservatives too were in favour of taking over.[32] Just as in 1868, it was the man on the spot, the High Commissioner, who was the most insistent that the country should be taken over. In meeting after meeting Robinson pounded away, with support from his deputy, Leicester-Smyth, in Cape Town, who pointed out that the Basotho who wanted imperial rule numbered over 100,000, compared with only 20,000 who followed Masupha.[33] At their final meeting on 13 December Robinson was able to win Derby over. Derby's recommendation was sent to Gladstone, who was then at Hawarden, and within a matter of hours Gladstone confirmed that the Basotho were to come under the direct rule of the High Commissioner.[34]

The parallels with 1868 were striking. Throughout the negotiations Ministers and officials alike

---

[27] C.3855, pp. 50-54, Blyth to Administrator and High Commissioner, 1 December 1883 (from which the quotation from Blyth is taken); report in *The Friend*, 6 December 1883, reprinted in Burman (1976A: 116-9) (from which the quotation from Letsie is taken); *Leselinyana*, December 1883. See also C.3855, p. 45, Officer administering the government of the Cape of Good Hope to Derby, received 2 December 1883.

[28] C.3855, p. 47, Officer administering the government of the Cape of Good Hope to Derby, received 12 December 1883, quoting Blyth's telegram of 9 December; *Cape Argus*, 13 December 1883, 'Masupha Holds a Pitso'.

[29] C.3855, p. 45, Officer administering the Government of the Cape of Good Hope to Derby, 3 December 1883.

[30] Benyon (1980: 190), quoting South African Public Library, Cape Town, Merriman Papers, No. 1 of 1884, Robinson to Merriman, 3 January 1884.

[31] Benyon (1980: 191), quoting South African Public Library, Cape Town, Merriman Papers, No. 266 of 1883, Robinson to Merriman, 13 December 1883. See also Vincent (2004: 612).

[32] Benyon (1980: 191), citing South African Public Library, Cape Town, Merriman Papers, No. 232 of 1883, Scanlen to Merriman, 15 November 1883.

[33] C.3855, p. 47, Leicester-Smyth to Derby, received 12 December 1883.

[34] PRO, CO 48/507, Gladstone to Derby, 14 December 1883. See also Benyon (1980: 191), Vincent (2004: 613), and British Library, Gladstone Papers, Add. MSS 44142, ff. 21-2, Derby to Gladstone 13 December 1883, enclosing Minute by Gladstone, approving.

had laid great stress on the Queen's personal role and the wonderful magnanimity of her government. Blyth told the Basotho at the final *pitso* that

> the Queen, in her greatness and goodness, has, at the last moment, had pity upon you misguided people, not because she is afraid of you, but because she is good and loves Christianity .... Remember this, Her Majesty's Government come with no cringing to you .... They come to you in their greatness and goodness of heart.[35]

The humanitarian influence on Gladstone's government was strong. There was a widespread belief that the Basotho had been badly treated and that after years of devoted loyalty they had been rashly goaded into resistance by Frere and Sprigg.[36] This concern, however, was part of the government's broader concern to establish stability in the interior. As Merriman had spelt out so cogently, if the Basotho were abandoned they would be torn apart by civil war and conflict with the Free State would be inevitable. Volunteers would pour in from the Cape and Natal, eager to strengthen the Free State commandos and to grab some share of the spoils, and Basotho refugees would flood down into the Transkei. The Cape's trade with the interior would be badly disrupted, just as it had been disrupted in the Seqiti War of 1865-8. Power politics too were a factor. Again as Merriman had argued, if the home government failed to intervene in Basutoland it would in effect be giving up its claim to paramountcy in South Africa.[37] The northern Cape was in turmoil because of repeated conflicts between the local African chiefdoms and the Boers, and, as in Basutoland, there was powerful humanitarian pressure for the home government to intervene and take control. If the government failed to intervene in Basutoland, especially after the defeats at Laings Nek and Majuba, it would be sending out a clear signal that the Dutch republics and freebooters could do as they liked. It is significant that its resumption of control in Basutoland was followed within the year by the establishment of the Bechuanaland Protectorate.

At the same time the home government's decision to take over Basutoland could be regarded as yet another retreat in the face of Basotho intransigence. Derby had declared that the Queen would not take over a divided people, and yet that was precisely what the government was doing. Just as Masupha had been undaunted by the threat of war, so now he was undaunted by the threat of abandonment.

In 1868 the Basotho had been on the brink of national disintegration, and Wodehouse's message that the Queen would take them over had been greeted with wild acclaim. In 1884 there was no knife against the Basotho's throat, though the long-term threat might have been just as dangerous, and their response was more measured.

> 'I verily believe', wrote Letsie, 'that, had we remained under the direct Government of England the last war, and all the evils that have risen from it, would never have taken place. It is with our whole heart that we put our trust in the Queen's Government .... We have confidence that, being once more under the shelter which our father Moshesh had obtained for us, we shall have peace, prosperity and sleep.'

But at the same time he begged the Queen to bear in mind that the disturbances were not at an end. Masupha had not changed his mind.[38]

---

[35] C.3855, p. 51, report on *pitso* held on 29 November 1883, sent by Blyth to Administrator and High Commissioner, 1 December 1883. See also C.3855, p. 48, Derby to Leicester-Smyth, 17 December 1883.
[36] Schreuder (2009: 105-6).
[37] C.3708, p. 17, Merriman's 'Memorandum' enclosed with Merriman to Derby, 29 May 1883.
[38] C.4263, pp. 8-9, Letsie to Blyth, 9 January 1883. See also *JME* 1884, p. 97, Mabille to Casalis, 29 December

The end of colonial rule

Marshal Clarke, who had served for a year after the Gun War as the Assistant Magistrate in Quthing, was chosen as the new Resident Commissioner, but he could not take up his office until March. The final two months of colonial rule merely prolonged the government's shame and embarrassment. The ordinary people looked forward to imperial rule since they hoped for some protection against the chiefs, but in the meantime the chiefs did very much as they wanted.[39] When his orders were ignored or flouted Blyth's only sanction was the threat of the Queen's disapproval. His only consolation was that the whole sorry business would soon come to an end.

Two other factors added to the depression. The crops were being ruined by drought, and many areas were infected with smallpox from the Diamond Fields, so that all public meetings had to be forbidden.

Throughout the country there were conflicts and disturbances, but the worst trouble, as so often of late, was in the Leribe District, where Motšoene (the son of Josefa and Senate, the putative paramount chief after Letsie) was now insisting on his territorial rights. Letsie, with Blyth's approval, had told Jonathan to reinstate him in his old village near Butha-Buthe, which Joel had taken over during the Gun War. When Joel tried to prevent this Jonathan took action against him, and when Joel and his allies attacked Jonathan at the camp Jonathan drove them off. The *Mabelete* suffered heavy losses, but in the meantime the whole of Jonathan's country towards Masupha, between his village of Tsikoane and the Phuthiatsana river, was deserted.[40]

Relations between Blyth and Letsie continued to be strained. In spite of the strong lead given by Letsie at the *pitso*, Blyth still entertained serious doubts about his loyalty, though he was baffled by the old chief's apparent sincerity. '*Letsie is so astute and clever*', he wrote, 'that at times one feels quite ashamed of suspecting him of any duplicity'. His final view was that while Letsie himself might be loyal, he was allowing and perhaps encouraging Masupha to defy the government 'as a sort of advance guard' to see how far it would allow him to go.[41] He accused Letsie of treating him with disrespect, while Letsie complained that Blyth, unlike Griffith and Orpen, never did what he wanted.[42]

Blyth could hardly wait to get out. He wrote bitterly to Sauer that he and his fellow officers had been placed in a 'painful and false position' in which they had been given 'but little sympathy or consideration'.[43] To Letsie he wrote wearily that he had done his duty; he had given his advice; he hoped for peace; he could do no more.[44]

1883: when Letsie was told of the Government's decision he said 'Now we shall be able to sleep.'

[39] G.3-'84, p. 86, Surmon to Acting Governor's Agent, 31 December 1883; and p. 91, Nettelton to Acting Governor's Agent, 4 January 1884.

[40] LNA, L2/1/4, Bailie to Blyth, 13, 15 (*bis*), 16, 18, 19 and 20 March 1884; LNA, S9/1/3/7, Blyth to Bailie 15, 16 and 17 March 1884; LNA, S8/2/2/1, Clarke to Jonathan, 25 March 1884; *Leselinyana*, April 1884; *Quarterly Paper of the Bloemfontein Mission*, July 1884, No. 65, pp. 125-6, Widdicombe to Archdeacon, 22 March 1884; *The Journal*, 31 March 1884, 'The Late Fighting in Basutoland'. See also *The Journal*, 10 September 1883, 'Basutoland', and 16 October 1883, 'Basutoland'; Widdicombe (1895: 261-2); and Taylor (1972: 109).

[41] C.4263, p. 13, Blyth to Administrator and High Commissioner, 19 January 1884.

[42] LNA, S9/1/3/7, Blyth to Letsie, 19 February 1884.

[43] LNA, S9/1/2/3, Blyth to Sauer, 16 February 1884.

[44] LNA, S9/1/3/7, Blyth to Letsie, 4 (also C.4263, p. 21) and 19 February, 12 March 1884.

CHAPTER 21: IMPERIAL RULE AND THE TRIUMPH OF THE CHIEFS

More of the same

On 17 March 1884, in a torrential thunderstorm, Colonel Marshal Clarke, the new Resident Commissioner, crossed the Caledon and entered Basutoland. Born in Ireland in 1841, he had served in India, where he had lost an arm in a struggle with a tiger, and he had then seen service in Natal, where he had taken part in the campaign against Langalibalele, and in the Transvaal, as Shepstone's ADC, where he had fought in the wars against the Pedi and the South African Republic. After a spell as a magistrate in Quthing in 1881-2 he took command of the Cape Police, was then transferred to the Egyptian Gendarmerie, and from there was appointed as Resident Commissioner to Basutoland. The French missionaries knew and admired him from his days in Quthing. He was calm and unhurried, 'the very man we want', wrote Mabille.[1]

He brought with him Godfrey Lagden, the eleventh child of a Dorset clergyman, who was to succeed him as Acting Resident Commissioner in 1893, when he was posted to Zululand, and as full Resident Commissioner in 1898, when he retired. Lagden later wrote a two volume history of the Basotho that was to hold the field for almost fifty years and was a powerful vindication of imperial rule.[2]

Clarke had wanted to mark the transfer of power from colonial to imperial rule by some suitable ceremony, but the home government had advised against this on the ground of expense. Instead he and Lagden came in, as Lagden wrote later, 'unobtrusively', with no glittering uniforms, but like 'two farmers returning to our homestead'.[3] They were met by Lerotholi and some hundreds of Basotho on horseback, who escorted them to Morija. On the following day they rode on to Maseru where Clarke formally took over from Blyth. At a *pitso* to mark the occasion Letsie and his sons gave the new Resident Commissioner an enthusiastic welcome and Blyth a tactfully courteous farewell. Masupha and Ramanella were not there. Nor were Jonathan and Joel Molapo, who were confronting each other in the north.[4]

Clarke's instructions were simple. On no account was expenditure to exceed revenue, which at first would consist mainly of the annual payment of £20,000 by the Cape Colony in lieu of customs duties. For the present it would not be possible to attempt more than the protection of life and property and the maintenance of order on the frontier. The Basotho were to be encouraged, and assisted, to establish a system of internal self-government sufficient 'to suppress crime and settle inter-tribal disputes'. As for education, public works, hospitals and other 'questions of more advanced administration', these had to stand over until the revenue allowed them to be undertaken.[5] In the meantime it had to be understood that imperial rule was no more than an experiment, a temporary and provisional arrangement. If it did not work out, if the Basotho made trouble, the government would withdraw.

---

[1] Smith (1939: 320). See also PEMS Archives, Paris, Mabille to Boegner, 22 March 1884; *Livre d'Or* (1912: 375); V. Ellenberger (1938: 226-7). For an Anglican view, equally favourable, see Widdicombe (1895: 260-1).
[2] Lagden (1909). For Clarke and Lagden in general, see Cassidy (1967-8).
[3] C.4263, pp. 17-18, Clarke to Robinson, 27 February 1884, and Derby to Robinson, 22 March 1884; Lagden (1909: II.565-6); Cassidy (1967-8: 158), citing Notes on Basutoland, written by Lagden for Lady Milner.
[4] C.4263, pp. 55-7, 'Minutes of Pitso held in front of the Residency, Maseru, Basutoland, on Wednesday the 19th of March 1884'; *JME* 1884, pp. 218-22, '*Le Pitso du 17 Mars 1884. Récit tiré du journal des Bassoutos, "le I ésélinyand"*.'
[5] C.3855, pp. 58-9, Colonial Office to Clarke, 25 January 1884.

The internal administration of the country was left largely with the chiefs. This was partly a matter of necessity: the chiefs were in control and the government could not seize that control without spending money and resources. It was also a matter of choice: Clarke believed that the Basotho were the best judges in their own affairs, that the chiefs were their natural representatives, and that the government should therefore make use of the chiefs and gain their trust and confidence. In particular he believed in building up the paramountcy: as he later wrote to Letsie, 'It is ... my desire and object to support your lawful authority in every way in my power'.[6] Under new regulations drawn up by Robinson, the Resident Commissioner and his magistrates could try cases of every kind, but in practice, while they retained the power to try all cases of murder and all cases in which whites were involved, they made the chiefs responsible in the first instance for administering the 'native laws' of the country. There was a right of appeal ultimately to the Resident Commissioner, but the aim was to make use of the chiefs' courts, not to break them down.[7] Because of the smallpox epidemic and the unsettled state of the country, it was two years before these regulations were presented formally to the Basotho, and they then met with general acceptance.[8]

As a mark of this change of policy the imperial officials in the districts were now called Assistant Commissioners, not Resident Magistrates. There were only four of them, supported by a police force of 130 men under about 20 officers. For the most part police work was carried out by the chiefs, and Lagden noted with approval that the police were employed mainly as messengers.[9]

Like Orpen and Blyth, Clarke had no military force to back him up and had to rely on 'moral force' alone. Lagden characterised Robinson's instructions as 'Do the best you can with your materials; I will encourage you and not interfere; but don't look to me for money or troops; I can give you neither.'[10] The situation was daunting, and during his first 18 months in office, in spite of all the praise that was heaped on him later, Clarke was no more successful than his colonial predecessors.

The chiefs were determined that they should not lose the advantages they had gained during the Gun War. Having recovered their powers they used them to the full, and in many cases abused them as well.[11] They were oppressive to their followers and, as Clarke admitted, there was nothing that the government could do.[12] The people did not appeal to the Assistant Commissioners for fear of being deprived of their cattle: 'the poor miserable people', wrote one observer, 'have to groan under the yoke of their Chiefs without the least hope of redress'.[13] As in the last years of Cape rule, there were also constant outbreaks of disorder as the disputes between chiefs were exacerbated by the increasing pressure on land.

---

[6] PRO, CO 417/34, Clarke to Letsie, 28 October 1887, enclosed with Leicester-Smyth to Knutsford, 21 November 1889.
[7] For the Regulations, see C.4263, pp. 75-80, 'Proclamation by His Excellency ... Sir Hercules George Robert Robinson', 29 May 1884; for the rules for the guidance of Native Chiefs, see C.4263, p. 81, Clarke to Robinson, 12 June 1884, and enclosure.
[8] C.4838, pp. 11-14, 'Notes of a National Pitso', 11 March 1886; p. 45, Letsie to Clarke, 26 March 1886.
[9] Lagden (1909: II. 629).
[10] Lagden (1909: II.564).
[11] Germond (1967: 405), Duvoisin, letter from Berea, 1885.
[12] C.4644, p. 24, Clarke's report, 6 July 1885.
[13] C.4644, p. 18, presumably a missionary, quoted in Chesson to Stanley, 21 August 1885.

In July 1884 Thomas Kennan, one of Clarke's new officials, expressed the widespread exasperation:

> The present policy of the Imperial Government in South Africa is the most misjudged the World has ever seen. .... Colonel Clarke is sent out here to bring the Basuto into subjection without the assistance of any force and with only a limited supply of money. Can anything be more absurd? [14]

Fourteen months later Canon Widdicombe at Hlotse Heights was equally pessimistic. Twenty men had been killed in a clash between Masupha and Ramanella.

> Col. Clarke has done his best to restore peace and order ... But as the Resident Commissioner has no force worthy of the name at his back ... the government is powerless to make their authority felt .... It is indeed sad to think that the great and powerful British Government should permit these scenes of bloodshed to continue unchecked year after year in a country supposed to be ruled in the name of the Queen ....[15]

The PEMS missionaries were also apprehensive. Jacottet complained that the British seemed incapable of being decisive, while Duvoisin was afraid that Clarke was being strung along by the Basotho, a repetition of the comedy that had been played a hundred times before with the Cape administration.[16]

Many of the chiefs, and many of their followers, had become addicted to Cape brandy, or 'Cape fire' as it was commonly known – not just Masupha and Ramanella, but Letsie and his sons Lerotholi, Bereng, Theko, Maama, Seeiso, Mojela and Tšepinare.[17] In July 1885 Surmon, at Mafeteng, referred to the 'inordinate use of brandy now going on in almost every village'. 'Most of the principal Chiefs', he wrote, 'are drunk nearly every day, and totally unfit to attend to the affairs of the tribe.'[18] 'One great difficulty', wrote Clarke, 'is that, since the rebellion, the majority of the Chiefs have become habitual drunkards.' Illegal canteens were set up in many villages, and the Free State authorities made no effort to prevent supplies crossing the border.[19] At the same time President Brand was loudly complaining about the violations of the border as hundreds of Basotho fled from the internal fighting and took refuge with their stock on Free State farms – though, as before, many farmers were keen to encourage this because they charged the Basotho for pasturage.

On 6 July 1885 Clarke gloomily reported that, while to a large extent he had preserved the security of the border and maintained the peace, he was 'unable to ensure the administration of justice with any degree of certainty'. It was time, he submitted, to 'define a limit to the experimental Government, and decide as to the future'.[20] A few weeks later he urged again that the 'present experimental stage of administration' should be brought to a close.[21]

Robinson was already pressing for an end to the uncertainty. In January he had written to

---

[14] Rhodes House Library, Oxford, MSS. Afr. s.969, Kennan Papers, Thomas Kennan to his father, 18 September 1884.
[15] Rhodes House Library, Oxford, USPG Archives, D 73, Widdicombe to SPG, 16 November 1885.
[16] PEMS Archives, Paris, Jacottet to *'cher monsieur'*, 14 October 1885, Duvoisin to *'cher monsieur'*, 31 March 1886.
[17] C.4644, p. 18, Chesson to Stanley, 21 August 1885.
[18] C.4644, p. 28, Surmon's report for the year ended 30th June 1885, 6 July 1885.
[19] C.4644, p. 25, Clarke's report, 6 July 1885.
[20] C 4644, p. 25, Clarke's report, 6 July 1885. See also p. 21, Clarke to Robinson, 21 July 1885.
[21] C.4644, p. 21, Clarke to Robinson, 21 July 1885.

London, applauding the efforts of Clarke and his officers, but drawing attention to the undignified position in which they were placed. Masupha and his adherents were disputing the Resident Commissioner's authority. It was difficult to know what to do.

> The successful resistance which the Basutos opposed to the Colonial Government has completely spoiled them. They have become arrogant, and Colonel Clarke is engaged in an unpromising attempt to govern them by moral force after physical force has failed. On the whole, I am disposed to think that the best course would be for Her Majesty's Government to determine at once, before matters become worse, whether ... Basutoland shall be abandoned, or the contumacious minority coerced.[22]

The home government did not even trouble itself to reply. Clarke and his officers had to soldier on.

This early period of the imperial administration is sometimes portrayed as merely a prelude to the great triumphs that were to come, a prelude in which Clarke waited wisely and patiently for the Basotho to be won over. Writing about thirty years later Édouard Jacottet likened him to Fabius Cunctator, the Roman general who had defeated Hannibal by playing a waiting game.[23] His gloomy reports of July 1885 were dismissed as 'momentary pessimism'.[24]

That was not how it seemed at the time. By July 1885 Clarke had been in office for 14 months, almost as long as Orpen and longer than Blyth. He had good reason for despair. His patience was a factor of powerlessness, not policy. But he had one great advantage that his predecessors had lacked. Basutoland had been removed from the arena of Cape politics and was of negligible political interest in the United Kingdom. It was no longer a burning issue that could bring down governments. The recalcitrance of Masupha and others no longer caused a political crisis. 'Reports of local commotion', wrote Lagden, 'did not attain so much publicity as formerly for the reason that Basutoland affairs were no longer a party question at the Cape.'[25]

Orpen had struggled to impose order through the chiefs, and he had constantly begged for patience, for calm, for an end to all the talk of withdrawal so that he could get on with the job. But the Colony had suffered a humiliating defeat at the hands of the rebels and its government was being treated with contempt. It was an intolerable position, especially for men who took pride in their supposed superiority over the black man. Orpen and his political masters were held up to ridicule and scorn in the colonial press. In the face of opposition attacks the colonial government could not afford to be patient. Just as Sprigg's government had been brought down largely because of its failure in Basutoland, so too was Scanlen's, which was defeated and resigned in May 1884. The imperial government, unlike the colonial government, could afford to take its time.

Another development which helped the new administration was Jonathan Molapo's recovery in the north. It had been a matter of burning shame to the Cape government that Jonathan and his men, who had fought shoulder to shoulder with them in the Gun War, and who had suffered so many losses, should be harassed and tormented by Joel and his allies. The imperial government had not been closely allied with Jonathan and was able to take a more detached view, especially as Jonathan was now recovering his power and was as much sinning as sinned against.[26]

---

[22] C.4589, pp. 13-14, Robinson to Derby, 21 January 1885.
[23] *Livre d'Or* (1912: 375).
[24] Smith (1939: 325).
[25] Lagden (1909: II.570-1).
[26] LNA, S8/2/2/1, Clarke to Jonathan, 25 March 1885.

At the time of Clarke's arrival there had just been a particularly fierce outbreak of fighting between the two sides, and one of his first acts was to call on Letsie to bring them to order. Jonathan already had much more land than Joel. Lerotholi, representing his father, laid down a new boundary which gave him even more at Joel's expense. In a crucial move Khethisa, who had previously supported Joel, went over to Jonathan, while Hlasoa, under instructions from Letsie and Lerotholi, had to leave the land given to him by his father and move across the new border to join Joel. After this the balance of power rested with Jonathan, whose fighting men, together with those of Khethisa, outnumbered Joel's by about two to one, and he was able to leave Hlotse Heights and to reoccupy his old village at Tsikoane.[27]

The submission of Masupha

In July 1885, the month when Clarke was writing in such despair, Masupha had sent him a message begging to be pardoned for his 'long obstinacy' and asking to 'be looked upon with the same eye' as the rest of the Basotho nation. 'I … see that I am being deprived of my rights', he said, 'and all because I am called a rebel, and that I have nowhere to take my case to.'[28] According to his missionary, Louis Duvoisin, he felt 'acutely conscious of his present position in the tribe, a position which has become too isolated'.[29]

In September Masupha clashed with Ramanella, whose son Peete had been allowed to settle on Masupha's land and now tried to shake off Masupha's authority. About 50 men were killed. Both sides appealed to the government for arbitration, and Clarke, with Letsie, conducted an enquiry, fined both sides for breaking the peace, and allowed Peete to stay where he was but only on condition that he should remain subject to Masupha. According to Lagden,

> that quarrel had unforeseen, yet important results. …. A just and impartial decision accepted by both gave the impression that there was now in the country a Court of Final Appeal which had no soldiers behind it but, what was stronger, the force of public opinion.
>
> The growth of that public opinion was not lost upon Masupha. Finding himself more and more isolated and out of touch with the tribe, perhaps also because his pride rebelled against non-recognition by Government, he approached the Resident Commissioner in February 1886 with the request for a Magistrate to be placed in his district to whom he promised respectful obedience. ….[30]

At the beginning of March 1886 Lagden was sent to establish a new government station at Teya-teyaneng. From the start Masupha gave him every assistance, and insisted on his followers doing the same.[31]

---

[27] C.4644, pp. 37, 40, Wolfe, Annual Report, 2 July 1885, and Appendix; LNA, S7/3/1, 'Tlasoa' to Clarke, 26 June 1884; C.4907, p. 27, Wolfe's Annual Report, 1 July 1886. As early as September 1884 Kennan reported that Jonathan's forces could match Joel's: Rhodes House Library, Oxford, MSS. Afr. S.969, Kennan Papers, Kennan to his father, 18 September 1884. Kennan also reported that 'Lots of filibusters' had joined Jonathan.

[28] C.4644, p. 18, 'TRANSLATION of a verbal message from the Chief Masupha to the Resident Commissioner, delivered by messenger on 9th July at Maseru'.

[29] *JME* 1884, p. 411, Duvoisin, 9 September 1884, as translated by Germond (1967: 403).

[30] Lagden (1909: II.574-5). See also C.4907, pp. 16-17, Clarke's Report, 23 July 1886.

[31] C.4907, p. 20, Lagden to Clarke, 1 July 1886.

This was the great breakthrough for which Clarke had been working, and for which Orpen had worked so hard before. Why had the old chief swung round so completely?

Masupha's increasing isolation from the rest of the Basotho and his lack of recognition from the government – the factors stressed by Lagden and Duvoisin, and indeed by Masupha himself – were no doubt the determining considerations. When Clarke had first arrived Letsie warned him against taking action against Masupha, since 'the disaffected were in the majority, and ... a half-hearted support only could be expected from the remainder of the people'.[32] There had clearly been a shift in public opinion. The chiefs were no doubt coming to realise that the government was not the great threat which they had feared. They criticised the right of appeal from their courts, but when they came to discuss the regulations in March 1886 they accepted them with hardly a murmur of complaint.[33] They saw that in all their territorial disputes Clarke worked through Letsie and Lerotholi, and in Quthing he won Letsie's approval (and the disapproval of the *Mateketoa* chiefs) by recognising Nkuebe as the district chief.[34]

Another important factor was Jonathan's triumph in the north. Even before his final victory over Joel Jonathan was gaining the upper hand, and, with the resources of his extensive landholding, he soon emerged as the most powerful subordinate in the country. He owed a lot to Lerotholi's support, but, in the tradition of his father, Molapo, he resisted any attempt by the house of Letsie to interfere in the affairs of his ward. On this issue he and Masupha were united. The main threat to Masupha's rights and privileges was no longer the government, but the paramountcy. In asking to be treated like the rest of the Basotho Masupha had reasoned that he would 'then be able to enter into the same court with Letsea'.[35]

In this way Masupha's reconciliation with the government was linked with the subsequent realignment of alliances among the chiefs. In the final confrontations between Jonathan and Joel Masupha, it seems, took no part. Instead, according to Widdicombe, 'Confidential messages passed and repassed between him and Jonathan .... Jonathan paid a friendly visit ... soon afterwards, and was received very graciously, and in a few days the feud of years was forgotten!'[36]

The Basotho as a whole had further reason to appreciate the value of imperial protection when, in July 1884, President Brand incorporated the territory of Thaba Nchu into the Orange Free State. This land, surrounded entirely by the Free State and situated about halfway between Basutoland and Bloemfontein, had been occupied in 1833 by the Barolong of Chief Moroka with Moshoeshoe's permission and was still claimed by the Basotho. After Moroka's death in 1880 there was civil strife between his sons, Samuel Lehulere and Tšepinare, which culminated in July 1884 when Samuel attacked and killed Tšepinare. This gave Brand the occasion for intervention. Though the Barolong were allowed to remain where they were, over time much of their land was parcelled out to white farmers. Another small step had been taken in the inexorable march of white encroachment. In Basutoland the French mission paper *Leselinyana* spelt out the lesson: do not cause trouble with the

---

[32] C.4644, p. 24, Clarke's report, 6 July 1885.
[33] C.4907, p. 17, Clarke's report, 23 July 1886.
[34] C.4263, pp. 105-6, Clarke, 'Memorandum on Affairs in Quithing District', 17 September 1884.
[35] C.4644, p. 18, 'TRANSLATION of a verbal message from the Chief Masupha to the Resident Commissioner, delivered by messenger on 9th July at Maseru'.
[36] Widdicombe (1895: 277). Widdicombe was probably going too far when he ascribed Masupha's request for a magistrate to Jonathan's new ascendancy.

whites. They can be resisted for a while but they will always spread by one means or another. The only way of salvation is to make friends with them. Only Lesotho has the benefit of imperial protection. So pay your tax and make progress, since otherwise you will perish.[37]

The annexation of Thaba Nchu gave rise to a rumour that the Basotho were about to invade the Free State. President Brand called out his commandos, and disbanded them only when Clarke assured him that the rumour was groundless.[38] There were other causes of annoyance between the Free State and the Basotho, irritants that in the past, in the time of Basotho independence, would have given rise to tension and perhaps even to war. Now they were handled by Clarke and were quietly resolved or laid aside.[39]

The consolidation of imperial rule and the paramountcy

In December 1885 Robinson reported a big improvement in the situation. Masupha had made his submission, and so there was no longer any reason to abandon the territory or to embark on military coercion. He and Clarke now called for a definite statement of the government's intentions, since if the Basotho saw that British rule was permanent they were more likely to give it their support. In the following month they returned to the charge, and in February Lord Granville, the new Colonial Secretary, coolly replied that he did not understand that anything had occurred to give ground for the supposition that there was any intention of terminating the present control of Basutoland, and so he had no objection to Robinson's making it known, if he thought it necessary, that the government contemplated no change in its relations with the Basotho.[40]

After this the administration continued on the course which Lagden later described as the 'drift from masterly inactivity to active guidance and control'.[41] The collection of hut tax, at 10s per hut, rose from £4,600 in 1884 to £19,000 in 1892.[42] The brandy canteens were suppressed. Firm measures were taken, in spite of Letsie's protests, to put an end to the practice of 'eating up'.[43] But the usual chieftainship disputes persisted. Joel could never reconcile himself to Jonathan's supremacy, and the unbalanced Motšoene also turned against Jonathan and was a constant source of trouble.[44] Masupha was at loggerheads with his former allies, Ramanella and the sons of Majara. Above all there were two major confrontations that were powerfully reminiscent of the troubles during the period of Cape rule after the Gun War. The first was the continuing conflict between Lerotholi and his brother Maama, the second that between Lerotholi and Masupha.

Lerotholi became Paramount Chief when Letsie died in 1891, but his authority was repeatedly challenged by some of his younger brothers, especially Maama, Letsie's favourite. Maama laid claim to some land, people and cattle at Korokoro which had always been held as belonging to the Paramount, and when Lerotholi claimed them back Maama defied him. Lerotholi was supported by his sons and

---

[37] *Leselinyana*, October 1884.
[38] PRO, CO 417/1, Robinson to Derby, 13 August 1884; Lagden (1909: II. 569).
[39] E.g., C.4907, pp. 5-6, Brand to Acting High Commissioner, 17 May 1886; Lagden (1909: II. 567-8).
[40] C.4644, pp. 82-4, Robinson to Stanley, 30 December 1885; C.4838, p. 1, Robinson to Stanley, 27 January 1886, pp. 1-3, Clarke to Robinson, 13 January 1886, p. 3, Granville to Robinson, 25 February 1886.
[41] Cassidy (1967-8: 175), citing Rhodes House Library, Oxford, Lagden Papers, Lagden to Clarke, 11 February 1894.
[42] Lagden (1909: II.580).
[43] Cassidy (1967-8: 165, 168).
[44] E.g., C.4644, pp. 37-8, George Wolfe, Annual Report, 2 July 1885; C.5238, p. 5, Clarke, Annual Report, 16 July 1887.

by his younger brothers in his own house, Bereng and Theko. But several junior brothers in other houses supported Maama, and so did Masupha. The house of Molapo remained neutral. In 1893 the government decided the case in favour of Lerotholi, but Maama tried to undermine the judgement and defied Lerotholi's authority to the extent of killing one of his messengers. When he then refused to obey Lerotholi's summons to court, Lagden, Clarke's successor as Resident Commissioner, gave the Paramount leave to attack. Just as fighting was about to break out Maama surrendered himself for trial and a major civil war was averted.[45]

Then, in 1897, after repeated confrontations with Lerotholi, Masupha committed his final act of defiance against the government, and this time fighting did break out. One of Masupha's sons, Moiketsi, raided the Free State with an armed band in search of a woman who had run away from her husband. He was intercepted and arrested by the Free State authorities who tried and sentenced him to be whipped, but before the sentence could be carried out he escaped and fled to Basutoland. The Free State applied for extradition, which was refused, but Lagden demanded that Moiketsi should be handed over to him for trial. Masupha refused to give him up, and Lagden called on Lerotholi to effect the arrest.

The situation was very similar to that faced by Orpen when he had been confronted by Masupha's defiance in January 1882. Once again, rather than sending in its own troops, the government was calling on the Paramount Chief to compel Masupha to obey its orders. But this time there were two big differences. First, Lerotholi was much more resolute than Letsie. Second, Orpen, when asked if the Cape would back up the Paramount with armed force, had to confess that it would not. Now Sir Alfred Milner, the High Commissioner, told Lagden that if Lerotholi failed to hand over Moiketsi 'we must assert our authority with British troops or clear out bag and baggage; we cannot tarry and see our rule dishonoured'. Informed of this, Lerotholi pressed on. On 12 January 1898 Masupha was decisively beaten and five days later Moiketsi was handed over. Over 20,000 men had been engaged in the fighting: 31 were killed on Lerotholi's side, 24 on Masupha's.[46] Masupha was fined and deprived of his district chieftainship.

There were further parallels with 1882. In both confrontations Jonathan Molapo took no part. In 1882 he had failed to bring any effective support to Lerotholi. In 1898 he came with 1,000 men to help Masupha, but then turned around and went home. And just as Maama had undermined Letsie's resolve in 1882, so now he refused to give any help to Lerotholi and was punished for disobedience.[47] In 1882 the divisions between the chiefs proved more important than the authority of the Paramount Chief and the government. In 1898 it was Lerotholi and Lagden who came out on top.

A year later Masupha died, and for the first time Lerotholi enjoyed undisputed supremacy.

---

[45] Lagden (1909: II.584-90).

[46] Lagden (1909: II.594-7). Milner's words are Lagden's paraphrase. For the original correspondence see PRO, CO 417/248.

[47] Basutoland: Annual Report for 1897-8, p. 30.

CHAPTER 22: CONCLUSION

Masupha's defeat largely completed the resolution of the conflicts that had bedevilled Cape rule.

Disarmament had long since ceased to be an issue. The Basotho's guns, which had loomed so large in the fearful imaginings of Frere and Sprigg, were sometimes brandished and fired in chieftainship disputes, and were brought out for display at *pitso*s, but were otherwise tucked quietly away with their spears and battle-axes behind the rafters of their huts. They gave their owners a sense of manly pride, and no doubt an underlying sense of security in case the British ever withdrew and the Free State had to be confronted again. Perhaps too the mere awareness of their presence placed a certain constraint on the imperial administration. In 1908, as South Africa moved towards unification and the question of incorporating Basutoland was being considered, the Basotho's opposition had to be taken a little more seriously because of their guns. 'Basutoland is a very prickly hedgehog', wrote one nervous official. 'The Basutos are already asking questions, they are warlike and armed.' There were many in the Cape who would not want to 'risk repeating the mistakes of ... a quarter of a century ago'.[1]

If the imperial government had reverted to the Cape's policy of disempowering the chiefs there would no doubt have been resistance, the question of coercion would have arisen again, and the Basotho's guns would have been an important factor in the equation. But the imperial government did not want to disempower the chiefs. It depended on them to carry out the day-to-day business of government, it prided itself on its good relations with them, and its policy came to be seen as part of the wider imperial practice of indirect rule (though, as several critics pointed out, it was closer to *laissez-faire*). When Sir Henry Loch, the High Commissioner, visited Basutoland in 1890 Clarke made a special point of inviting the Basotho to come armed to the welcoming *pitso* as a mark of his confidence in them.[2] It was as if he were showing off to the Cape that the imperial government had won the Basotho's trust and had nothing to fear. After Lerotholi had crushed Masupha there was no serious challenge to British rule until the upsurge of African nationalism in the 1950s.[3]

The great underlying issue, the question of magisterial or chiefly rule, had largely been settled in favour of the chiefs. For the most part the administration of the country was left in their hands, and their courts continued to be the main centres of public life. They could not act with total independence and impunity, as Masupha found to his cost in 1898. But the imperial dispensation gave them considerable power and responsibility and on the whole was much to their liking. The general impression of later observers was that the Basotho governed themselves. They enjoyed protection with only the lightest of controls.[4]

Within the chieftainship it was the paramountcy above all that emerged with its position strengthened and confirmed. Under the Cape Letsie had been Paramount Chief in little more than name. With the full backing of Milner and Lagden Lerotholi had now asserted his authority. Masupha's obduracy had been broken. So had Maama's. The great subordinate chiefs still enjoyed a large measure of self-

---

[1] PRO, CO 417/455, minute by Just, 24 June 1908.
[2] C.5897, p. 3, Loch to Knutsford, 8 May 1890.
[3] The last government to be seriously worried about guns was the independent government of Lesotho in 1970. Muskets and rifles were collected throughout the country and thrown into a dam near Maseru - only to be pulled out again when it was realised that many of them were precious antiques.
[4] Murray and Sanders (2005), Chapter 1.

rule in their own wards, just as they had in Moshoeshoe's time, and Jonathan Molapo still hankered after independence, but they had to respect the Paramount's overall supremacy. Letsie II, who succeeded Lerotholi in 1905, was weak and ineffective, but his brother Griffith, who succeeded him in 1913 and ruled until 1939, was very much in command.

The assertion of Lerotholi's authority was also the assertion of imperial authority. The success of Clarke and Lagden's policy depended on the degree to which the Paramount Chief was able and willing to follow their guidance and carry out their instructions. The same had been true of Cape rule after the Gun War. Relying on the weak and vacillating Letsie, Orpen had been humiliated by Masupha's defiance. Relying on the more determined and energetic Lerotholi, Lagden had overcome it.

The people who lost out were the commoners, who had little to protect them against chiefly oppression and abuse. The French missionary, Louis Duvoisin, writing about the chiefs in 1885, was scathing:

> In the intoxication of their triumph and of their reconquered authority – I speak of the majority – they have hastened to abuse it and have succeeded in disgusting the bulk of their subjects who, in their heart of hearts, will never cease to regret the old regime.[5]

A year later Clarke frankly reported that in some cases the chiefs were 'arbitrary and cruel' and the government was too weak to act effectively against them.[6] Over time, as the imperial authorities became stronger and the country became more settled, the worst excesses were checked, but right up to the reforms of the 1930s and 1940s there were many complaints about the injustices of the chiefs' courts and the petty tyrannies of their rule.

There were many in the Cape, and later in South Africa, who came to regret the Cape's decision to withdraw. They were critical of the imperial policy of relying on the chiefs, which ran counter to their own policy of magisterial control, and they were critical of the failure to develop the country more actively. In 1909 John Merriman, as Cape Prime Minister, condemned imperial rule for 'erecting a system of government through the chiefs, instead of breaking down and minimising their power'.[7] And in 1924 Edgar Brookes, in his influential *History of Native Policy in South Africa*, while recognising that the imperial government had 'preserved order perfectly among the Basuto', commented that it had 'done little directly to civilise' them and that the chiefs' courts were 'to-day a crying grievance'.[8] By the 1920s there were many in imperial circles too who believed that more should have been done to reform the chieftainship and to develop the country. And there were critics among the Basotho as well, particularly among the educated élite, the *bahlalefi*, who in 1907 formed the Basutoland Progressive Association (a name which distinguished them from the unprogressive chiefs).

In the early years, however, the overwhelming consensus was that imperial rule was an astonishing success, all the more so because of the contrast with the miseries and humiliations of the last years of Cape rule. In 1889, when Sir Hercules Robinson was on the point of leaving South Africa, the condition of Basutoland was one aspect of his record which gave him particular pride and

---

[5] *JME* 1886, p. 477, Duvoisin, '*Quelques-uns des principaux obstacles aux progrès de l'Évangile chez les Bassoutos. IX. Décadence de l'État politique et social*', as translated by Germond (1967: 405).

[6] C.4907, p. 18, Clarke's report, 23 July 1886.

[7] Quoted in Machobane (1990: 122).

[8] Brookes (1927: 106). See PRO, CO 417/683, letters by 'Mosotho' and Simon Phamotse in *The Friend*, 2 and 16 December 1921 respectively, enclosed with Resident Commissioner to High Commissioner, 24 December 1921.

satisfaction.⁹ And in 1896 an official in the Colonial Office exulted: 'I do not think that even in the British Empire there is a parallel to the Gov't of Basutoland where we have established perfect order and won the complete confidence of the natives at a cost borne almost entirely by themselves.'¹⁰

Even allowing for the temptations and exaggerations of self-congratulation, there seems little doubt that most Basotho were content under imperial rule. They complained about some of their chiefs, but at the same time they had a profound reverence for the institution of chieftainship, and their criticisms were not directed at the imperial government. Under imperial protection there was no longer any danger of renewed war with the Free State. The Basotho were again safe in the cave that Moshoeshoe had provided for them. No more of their land was taken away. No white settlement was allowed. They could follow their own customs. There was a return to prosperity too, at least in the short term. Although there was increasing pressure and overcrowding on the land, exports exceeded imports well into the 1920s, and the opportunities for migrant labour increased dramatically after the opening of the world's richest gold mines on the Rand. Basotho labour was much in demand, and the country's economy benefited from the wealth it brought back.¹¹

Why then did the imperial government succeed where the Cape had failed? Everyone paid tribute to the character and ability of Marshal Clarke. 'No finer selection [as Resident Commissioner] could have been made', wrote Lagden,¹² a view which was shared by Robinson in South Africa and by successive Secretaries of State in London.¹³ Lagden too was well regarded. But similar eulogies had been heaped on Griffith and his magistrates in the period of Cape rule. There was more to success than the individuals involved, and Lagden himself was keen to stress the differences between colonial and imperial policy. He was damning about the Basotho's treatment under the Cape:

> Transferred to the Cape without fair consultation, over-administered by zealous magistrates armed with rigorous laws unsuited then to a quasi-independent people, disarmed by Proclamation, warred against but undefeated, threatened, abandoned and condemned, it is not surprising that they became in turns dejected, arrogant and suspicious.¹⁴

Before 1884, he wrote, 'they were either at war or struggling intermittently against laws and procedures not in keeping with their feelings and aspirations'. The colonial government might have been sincere in its efforts to stimulate improvement, but 'it failed to appreciate the sentiment of the people and, striving to accomplish a good end by repressive measures, not only miscarried but bequeathed a legacy of racial prejudice'.¹⁵

By contrast Clarke's delegation of powers to the chiefs 'appealed to them warmly. It took them apparently into partnership, gave them an intelligent interest in their own affairs – gave them to feel in

---

⁹ Lagden (1909: II.580).
¹⁰ PRO, CO 417/186, minute by Meade, undated, on Lord Rosmead (formerly Sir Hercules Robinson) to Chamberlain, 30 October 1896.
¹¹ For the full impact of migrant labour in the long term, see Murray (1981).
¹² Lagden (1909: II. 559).
¹³ C.4838, p. 1, Robinson to Stanley, 27 January 1886, and C.4907, p. 16, Robinson to Granville, 10 August 1886. For Secretaries of State, see, e.g., Lord Knutsford in 1890, quoted in Lagden (1909: II. 581). See also PRO, CO 417/11, R. Herbert, minute, 2 September 1886.
¹⁴ Lagden (1909: II. 560-1).
¹⁵ Lagden (1909: II. 626).

fact the pride of independence and the similitude of home rule.'[16] 'The system under the Cape Government of pressing minor cases into court and interfering with the allocation of land was abandoned. The Chiefs were given duties, were subsidized and held up to public respect. .... That was a system they liked.'[17]

Over the years these arguments were repeatedly taken up by imperial officials. According to the brief historical resumé which appeared in the Basutoland Government's annual reports from 1946 onwards, 'The people never took kindly to Cape Colonial rule', and after the failed attempt at disarmament the country was handed over to the Imperial Government.[18] In 1960 this account was elaborated:

> The Cape government attempted a policy of direct rule: due to the weakness of the administration this was not a success, and it aroused the hostility of the Chiefs, who saw in it an attempt to usurp their power. The climax of this policy came in 1880, when an attempt was made to disarm the Basuto....[19]

These arguments assumed a particular significance in the debate about incorporation. It was because of their experiences under Cape rule that the chiefs dreaded transfer to the Union of South Africa, and also because of the way in which they saw their fellow-Africans being treated in the Union. Like Moshoeshoe before them, they understood that the imperial government was less likely than the Cape to covet their land. When the new High Commissioner, Sir Henry Loch, visited the country in 1890 Letsie and his councillors begged him for a written promise

> that this country ... will remain in the caretaking of Government (Imperial Government) for ever .... Although we may not touch on the matter of the gun war, which pained this nation in many ways, although this is so, we do not fail to hear from passers-by that this country of ours is wished for by those who are not of our colour; we are in particular afraid if we should again be put under the herding of the Colony; for from what we see those of our colour who are living in the Colony are unable to live comfortably.[20]

In 1909, when the threat of transfer was very real, the chiefs petitioned the King not to hand them over to South Africa. As Lagden wrote, 'their experience of twenty-four years under direct rule by the Imperial Government...left them contented and in a marked degree prosperous; under the colonial Government it had not been so.'[21] This opposition to transfer became all the more determined as South Africa's 'native policy' became more illiberal.

Many of the chiefs had of course been unhappy under Cape rule, even before the Gun War, but the arguments put forward by Lagden and, later, the Basutoland government overlook one major factor – that by 1880 magisterial control had won a surprising degree of acceptance, especially among the ordinary people. Up to that time Cape rule was a success, and a success that was all the more

---

[16] Lagden (1909: II. 565).
[17] Lagden (1909: II. 629).
[18] *Basutoland: Annual Report 1946*, p. 59.
[19] *Basutoland: Annual Report 1960*, p. 117. See also FCO, S262, Baring to Gordon-Walker, 28 November 1950: 'an outstanding feature of the native policy pursued during the last century in the Cape Colony was the deliberate destruction of the powers of the chiefs. This the Basuto have noted, and this they resisted at the time of the Gun War.'
[20] C.5897, p. 5, Letsie to Loch, 25 April 1890.
[21] Lagden (1909: II. 620).

remarkable because of its boldness. And insofar as these arguments portray disarmament as the natural consequence of magisterial control, or the 'climax' or crowning folly of that policy, they are plainly wrong. It was not the logic of magisterial control that required disarmament, but the logic of a 'vigorous' native policy, linked with the imperial policy of confederation – a logic that gave rise to conflicts throughout the region at that time, above all the wars with the Zulu and the Pedi. It was not the imposition of magisterial control that provoked the Basotho to resistance, but the attempt to disarm them. And it was the failure of that attempt that discredited Cape rule. After the Gun War the Colony had neither the will nor the resources to enforce magisterial control again.

Disarmament was a colossal blunder, inspired by mistrust and fear. Before 1880 there was no real danger of the Basotho's turning their arms against the colonial government. Contrary to the narrative told by Frere and Sprigg, and even by Griffith, they were not like children who would be carried away by the excitement of owning guns into defying their wise and benevolent rulers. The only time they turned their guns against the administration was when the Cape tried to take those guns away, and the only legislation that led to war was the so-called Peace Preservation Act.

The Gun War, then, was one of the great turning points in the Basotho's history. Before 1880 they were set on a course of magisterial control under Cape rule. Their successful resistance made magisterial control impossible, and after the war Masupha's continued resistance made Cape rule impossible. After 1884 they were set on a new course, that of chiefly control under imperial rule.

The bitterness between the *Mateketoa* and the *Mabelete* gradually fell away as a serious factor in the Basotho's political life, and today the Gun War is a matter of national pride. Together with the protracted struggles against the Free State, it is remembered and experienced as part of a glorious record of brave resistance to the threat of white encroachment and dominance. Alone of the African polities at the time, the Basotho emerged from the crises of the late 1870s and early 1880s with their position strengthened. The Zulu, the Pedi and the Xhosa had all gone down to defeat. The Basotho had not faced imperial troops, but they had shown that, given firearms and ammunition, they could more than hold their own against the much vaunted whites of the Cape. Maama's killing of Willem Erasmus at Sepechele's symbolised the defeat of the white community. The Basotho had thrown down White Man.

The Basotho were always conscious of the presence of the *balimo*, their ancestors, who were thought to care deeply about their welfare, and throughout the struggles of the Gun War they believed that the *balimo* were at their side encouraging and supporting them. They were the spiritual arm, the spiritual army, of the Basotho people. In the praises of Lerotholi, the 'Deliverer', they not only urged him to resist the invader and to prevent the scattering of the Basotho nation, they took part in the fighting themselves:

> In this war the spirits have fought:
> Those of our father's house are fighting, and those of our mother's house.
> Ramakha and his men commend the struggle,
> Saying 'Seize your chance to act thus, Deliverer!'
> The guardians of the old and of the lame give praise,
> Saying 'Seize your chance to act thus, Deliverer,
> That our old men die at home,
> That they die at home and we bury them ourselves.'[22]

---

[22] Damane and Sanders (1974: 145-6). Ramakha is Setenane, Moshoeshoe's cousin.

Maama also acknowledged how much he had been helped by his ancestors, among whom he numbered his father Letsie:

> Good fortune has come from the ancestors,
> It's come from Peete and Mokhachane,
> It's come from Letsie and Moshoeshoe.[23]

At the beginning of the Gun War Lerotholi's praise poet, quoted at the opening of this book, anxiously depicted Letsie's son refusing to allow the guns to go to the Cape and so incurring huge debts that would ultimately have to be paid by his ancestors. These debts were the wrath and hostility of the supposedly invincible whites. But through their efforts and sacrifices in the Gun War the Basotho, with the help of their ancestors, had warded off their white enemies and so paid off their debts. They would not be dispersed. They would keep their land. Their old men could die at home.

---

[23] Damane and Sanders, (1974: 159).

SOURCES

A   OFFICIAL MANUSCRIPT SOURCES

I   Unpublished

a   National Archives, Kew, London (formerly Public Record Office)

CO 48/440-510. Cape of Good Hope, Original Correspondence from Cape Town to London: Despatches and enclosures (including Offices and Individuals), 1868-1884.

CO 49/60-61. Cape of Good Hope, Entry Books of Correspondence from London to Cape Town, 1866-1872.

CO 51/152-245. Cape of Good Hope, Executive Council and Legislative Council, Assembly, 1866-84.

CO 417/1-248. High Commission for South Africa, Original Correspondence, 1884-1898.

CO 879/16-17. Colonial Office: Confidential Print, including African Nos. 200 (South African Arms Question) and 225 (Correspondence respecting the Affairs of Basutoland).

b   Cape Archives, Cape Town

i.   Native Affairs Department Papers.

N.A. 1-10: Letters from Chief Magistrate, Transkei (1878-81).

N.A. 272-84: Letters from Governor's Agent, Basutoland (1873-84).

N.A. 840-1: Letter Books (1873-6).

N.A. 932: Letters despatched (1879-80).

N.A. 1050: Circulars, Native Affairs Department.

ii.   Government House Papers.

G.H. 10/7: Letters Received, Private and Semi-Official (1863-9).

G.H. 14/7: Letters from Native Chiefs and British Officials in Basutoland (1864-83).

iii.   Prime Minister's Office Papers.

P.M. 259: Prime Minister's correspondence, minutes, memoranda, etc. (1875-81).

iv.   Colonial Office Papers.

C.O. 5488: Basutoland Letter Book (1872-78).

C.O. 5489: Index.

c   Lesotho National Archives, Maseru

i.   Governor's Agent to High Commissioner and Colonial Secretary. S9/1/1/1 - S9/1/1/2 (1871-81).

ii.   Governor's Agent to Secretary for Native Affairs. S9/1/2/1 – S9/1/2/3 (1873-84).

iii.   Governor's Agent: miscellaneous correspondence despatched. S9/1/3/1 - S9/1/3/7 (1871-84).

iv.   Chief Magistrate and Resident Magistrates to Colonial Secretary. S9/2/1/1 – S9/2/1/2 (1872-4).

v.   Chief Magistrate to Magistrates. S9/2/2/1 and S9/2/2/3 (1872-4 and 1876-84).

vi.   Resident Magistrate, Maseru (out). S9/2/3/1 (1876-83).

vii.   Miscellaneous. S7/7/1 (1883-4).

viii.   Pitso Book. S11/1 (1875-6).

Sources

c   Lesotho National Archives, Maseru (cont.)

ix.   Leribe: Letters despatched. L2/1/1 - L2/1/4 (1872-84).

x.   Mafeteng: Letters despatched. MF2/1/1 – MF2/1/2 (1872-84).

xi.   References to the Leribe District in the period of imperial rule: S3/5 series, S7/3/1 and S8/2/2/1.

II   Published

a   British

C.459. *Correspondence re Cape of Good Hope* (GB: Parliamentary Papers, 1871 [C.459]XLVII)

C.732. *Correspondence re Cape of Good Hope*. (GB: Parliamentary Papers, 1873 [C.732]XLIX)

C.1025. *Papers relating to the Late Kafir outbreak in Natal* (GB: Parliamentary Papers, 1874 [C.1025]XLV).

C.1141. *Langalibalele and the Amahlubi tribe; being remarks upon the official record of the trials of the chief, his sons and Induna, and other members of the Amahlubi tribe, by the Bishop of Natal* (GB: Parliamentary Papers, 1875 [C.1141]LIII).

C.1748. *Correspondence respecting the war between the Transvaal Republic and neighbouring native tribes ....* [GB: Parliamentary Papers, 1877 [C.1748]LX).

C.1776. *Further correspondence respecting the war between the Transvaal Republic and neighbouring native tribes ...* (GB: Parliamentary Papers, 1877[C.1776]LX).

C.1961. *Further correspondence respecting the affairs of South Africa (In continuation of [C.1883] of 1877)* (GB: Parliamentary Papers, 1878[C.1961]LV).

C.2000. *Correspondence re South Africa* (GB: Parliamentary Papers, 1878[C.2000]LV).

C.2144. *Correspondence re South Africa* (GB: Parliamentary Papers, 1878[C.2144]LVI)

C.2252, C.2260, C.2318. *Correspondence re South Africa* (GB: Parliamentary Papers, 1878-9 [C.2252, C.2260, C.2318]LIII)

C.2374 *Correspondence re South Africa.* (GB: Parliamentary Papers, 1878-9 [C.2374,)LIV)

C.2454. *Further correspondence respecting the affairs of South Africa. (In continuation of [C.2374] of July 1879)* (GB: Parliamentary Papers, 1878-79[C.2454]LIV).

C.2482. *Further correspondence respecting the affairs of South Africa. (In continuation of [C.2454] of August 1879)* (GB: Parliamentary Papers, 1880[C.2482]L).

C.2505. *Further correspondence respecting the affairs of South Africa. (In continuation of [C.2482] of February 1880)* (GB: Parliamentary Papers, 1880[C.2505]L).

C.2569. *Correspondence respecting the affairs of Basutoland* (GB: Parliamentary Papers, 1880[C.2569]LI).

C.2655. *Further correspondence respecting the affairs of South Africa (In continuation of [C.2586] of June 1880* (GB: Parliamentary Papers, 1880[C.2655]LI).

C.2676. *Further correspondence respecting the affairs of South Africa. (In continuation of [C.2655] of August 1880* (GB: Parliamentary Papers, 1880[C.2676]LI).

C.2695. *Further correspondence respecting the affairs of South Africa. (In continuation of [C.2676] of August 1880* (GB: Parliamentary Papers, 1880[C.2695]LI).

HL 14. *Return to an address of the House of Lords, dated 7 January 1881, for copy of memorial addressed to Her Majesty's Ministers by the committee of the Paris Evangelical Alliance ....* (GB: Parliamentary Papers, 1881(HL14) XII). [8 pp.]

C.2740. *Further correspondence respecting the affairs of South Africa. (In continuation of [C.2695] of September 1880* (GB: Parliamentary Papers, 1881[C.2740]LCVI).

C.2754. *Copy of a despatch from the Right Hon. the Earl of Kimberley, containing the instructions addressed to Governor Sir H. Robinson* .... (GB: Parliamentary Papers, 1881|C.2754|LXVI).

C.2755. *Correspondence respecting the affairs of Basutoland. (In continuation of [C.2569], May 1880)* (GB: Parliamentary Papers, 1881|C.2755|LXVI).

C.2821. *Correspondence respecting the affairs of Basutoland. (In continuation of [C.2755], January 1881)* (GB: Parliamentary Papers, 1881|C.2821|LXVI).

C.2964. *Correspondence respecting the affairs of Basutoland. (In continuation of [C.2821], January 1881* (GB: Parliamentary Papers, 1881|C.2964|LXVII).

C.3112. *Correspondence respecting affairs of Basutoland and the territories to the eastward of the Cape Colony* ...._(In continuation of [C.2964] July 1881* (GB: Parliamentary Papers, 1881|C.3112|XLVII).

C.3113. *Further correspondence respecting the affairs of South Africa. (In continuation of [C.2961] of July 1881* (GB: Parliamentary Papers, 1882|C.3113|XLVII).

C.3175. *Extract from telegram from Sir Hercules Robinson ... dated December 30th, 1881, respecting the position of affairs in Basutoland* (GB: Parliamentary Papers, 1882|C.3175|XLVII).

C.3493. *Correspondence between the Government of the Colony and Commandant-General of Colonial Forces on the subject of the position of affairs in Basutoland* .... (GB: Parliamentary Papers, 1883|C.3493|XLVIII).

C.3708. *Correspondence respecting the affairs of Basutoland and the proposals of the Cape Government with respect to its future administration* (GB: Parliamentary Papers, 1883|C.3708|XLVIII).

C.3717. *Further correspondence respecting the Cape Colony and adjacent territories (In continuation of [C.3113] of February 1882 and [C.3112] of March 1882)* (GB: Parliamentary Papers, 1883|C.3717|XLIX).

C.3855. *Further correspondence respecting the Cape Colony and adjacent territories. (In continuation of [C.3708] and [C.3717], July 1883)* (GB: Parliamentary Papers, 1884|C.3855|LVI).

C.4263. *Further correspondence respecting the Cape Colony and adjacent territories (In continuation of [C.3855] February 1884)* (GB: Parliamentary Papers, 1884|C.4263|LVI).

C.4589. *Correspondence re Cape and Adjacent Territories.* (GB: Parliamentary Papers, 1884–5 [C.4589]LVI).

C.4644. *Further correspondence respecting the Cape Colony and adjacent territories (In continuation of [C.4589] August 1885)* (GB: Parliamentary Papers, 1886, [C.4644]XLVIII).

C.4907. *Further Correspondence respecting the Affairs of Basutoland (In continuation of [C.4838] June 1886).* (GB: Parliamentary Papers, 1886 [C.4907]XLVIII)

Hansard's Parliamentary Debates 3rd series.

Basutoland: High Commissioners' Proclamations and Notices to June 30th 1901, Cape Town: Argus, n.d.

South Africa. Military Report on Basutoland. Vol. I. *General.* (General Staff, 1910).

War Office, Intelligence Branch, *Precis of Information concerning South Africa ... and Basutoland* (1877, 1880 and 1880 revised in 1898).

Basutoland. Colonial Annual Reports.

b   Cape

Votes and Proceedings of the House of Assembly 1872-1884.
Votes and Proceedings of the Legislative Council 1872-1884.
Government Gazette (1871-84)
A.18-'72. *Report of the Select Committee on the Basuto Regulations.*
G.6-'72. *Petition from the Basuto people praying for representation in Parliament* (Cape of Good Hope Government, Cape Town, 1872).
A.12-'73. *Report of the Select Committee on Native Affairs.*

Sources

A.23-'73. *Report of Governor's Agent on working of Basuto regulations.*

G.27-'73. *Report of the Governor's Agent, Basutoland* (Cape of Good Hope Government, Cape Town, 1873). *Report of the Special Commission on the Laws and Customs of the Basuto* (1873).

G.27-'74. *Blue book on native affairs, 1874* (Cape of Good Hope Government, Cape Town, 1874).

C.17-'75. *Census Returns for Basutoland (population).*

G.18-'75. *Census Returns for Basutoland (stock).*

G.21-'75. *Blue book on native affairs, 1875* (Cape of Good Hope Government, Cape Town, 1875).

G.33-'75. *Statement of Revenue and Expenditure in Basutoland during 1874.*

G.46-'75. *Correspondence relating to the rebel chief Langalibalele.*

A.19-'76. *Petition of the missionaries of the Paris Evangelical Missionary Society in Basutoland, printed by order of the House of Assembly, June 1876* (Cape of Good Hope Government, Cape Town, 1876).

G.16-'76. *Blue book for native affairs for 1876* (Cape of Good Hope Government, Cape Town, 1876).

G.37-'76. *Report of a Commission on the Affairs of Griqualand East.*

G.42-'76. *Results of a census …. March, 1875* (Cape of Good Hope Government, Cape Town, 1876).

G.52-'76. *Appendix to the Blue-book on Native Affairs* (G.52-'76).

A.7-'77. *Petition of the chiefs and people of the Basuto tribe* (Cape of Good Hope Government, Cape Town, 1877).

A.9-'77. *Papers re Nehemiah Moshesh.*

G.1-'77. *Report and Proceedings of the Colonial Defence commission.*

G.12-'77. *Blue book on native affairs, 1877* (Cape of Good Hope Government, Cape Town, 1878).

A.12-'78. *Petition of the Chiefs of the People of Basutoland* (Cape of Good Hope Government, Cape Town, 1878).

G.17-'78. *Blue book on native affairs, 1878* (Cape of Good Hope Government, Cape Town, 1878).

A.1-'79. *Speech of His Excellency the Governor at the opening of the 6th Parliament* (Cape of Good Hope Government, Cape Town, 1879).

A.6-'79. *Report of the Select Committee on Hostilities in Basutoland.*

A.17-'79. *Correspondence and papers (in part) respecting the rebellion in British Basutoland* (Cape of Good Hope Government, Cape Town, 1879).

A.27-'79. *Total Amount brought to Charge on War Account in consequence of the Disturbances on the Northern Border and the Morosi Campaign.*

A.49-'79. *Copies of correspondence, telegrams and etc. in re. Morosi's Rebellion, Basutoland* (A.49-'79) (Cape of Good Hope Government, Cape Town, 1879).

A.50-'79. *Further Papers respecting the Rebellion in British Basutoland.* (Cape of Good Hope Government, Cape Town, 1879).

C.16-'79. *Papers respecting the Rebellion in Basutoland* (Cape of Good Hope Government, 1879).

G.33, 33A and 43-'79. *Blue Book on Native Affairs and Appendix.*

G.55-'79. *Report on the Cape Mounted Riflemen under Command of Colonel Z. Bayly* (Cape of Good Hope Government, 1879).

Official report of proceedings at the Pitso or annual gathering of the Basutos and other native tribes residing in British Basutoland (Cape of Good Hope Government, Cape Town, 1879).

Speech delivered by the Colonial Secretary, the Hon. J. Gordon Sprigg on 1st and 2nd June 1880 on the disarmament of the Basutos and the native policy of the Government (Cape of Good Hope Government, Cape Town, 1880).

A.1-'80. *Speech of His Excellency the Governor after opening the 2nd Session of the 6th Parliament* (Cape of Good Hope Government, Cape Town, 1880).

A.10-'80. *Petition of Letsie and other chiefs of Basutoland* (Cape of Good Hope Government, Cape Town, 1880).

A.11-'80. *Petition of Letsie, Paramount Chief, together with other chiefs and headmen of Basutoland* (Cape of Good Hope Government, Cape Town, 1880).

A.12-'80. *Copies of all correspondence between Col. Griffith and Chief Letsie and the Rev. Mabille and between the Government and Col. Griffith and all other persons on the subject of the disarmament of the Basuto* (Cape of Good Hope Government, Cape Town, 1880).

A.31-'80. *Proclamations and Laws for Native Territories annexed to the Colony of the Cape of Good Hope* (Cape of Good Hope Government, Cape Town, 1880)

A.38-'80. *On Disposal of Lands in Quthing*.

A.52-'80. *Return relative to Despatches, with letters, from Mr. Griffith and other Documents.*

A.67-'80. *Despatch from His Excellency the Governor to the Secretary of State, alluded to by Mr. Grant-Duff in the House of Commons.*

G.13-'80. *Blue book on native affairs for the year 1880* (Cape of Good Hope Government, Cape Town, 1880).

A.6-'81. *Correspondence on Command of Troops.*

A.7-'81. *Correspondence on Bright and Rose Innes.*

A.22-'81. *Telegraphic correspondence between the Colonial Secretary and Colonel C.D. Griffith, C.M.G., Governor's Agent, Basutoland* (Cape of Good Hope Government, Cape Town).

A.24-'81. *Correspondence with reference to the Basutos and their Relations with Government* (Cape of Good Hope Government, Cape Town, 1881).

A.25-'81. *Reports from Chief Magistrates and Resident Commissioners, in Basutoland, Transkei etc.: supplementary to the reports printed in Parliamentary blue book on native affairs no. G.20-'81* (Cape of Good Hope Government, Cape Town, 1881).

A.29-'81. *Correspondence and telegrams between the Government and Col. Griffith relating to the question of the disarmament of the Basutos* (Cape of Good Hope Government, Cape Town, 1881).

A.34-'81. *Correspondence between the Government and the several Civil Commissioners, Commanding Officers of Yeomanry, and Volunteer Corps, relative to the appointment of, Substitutes in the Yeomanry and the Volunteer Force especially regarding the appointment of a Substitute in place of Captain Thornton.*

A.44-'81. *Minutes, telegrams and other correspondence with reference to Basuto negotiations for peace from 27 January to 29 April 1881* (Cape of Good Hope Government, Cape Town, 1881).

A.64-'81. *Petition of Residents of City of Cape Town.*

A 69-'81. *A Despatch from His Excellency Sir Henry Barkly to the Lieutenant-Governor of Griqualand West, forwarding a Remonstrance from the Colonial Government against the indiscriminate Sale of Arms to Natives, especially Basutos, at Kimberley, together with the answer to the same.*

A.77-'81. *Petition of Burghers of the Districts of Colesberg and Philip's Town.*

A.81-'81. *Petition of J.A. van Zyl and others, Committee of S.A. Bond.*

G.20-'81. *Blue-book for Native Affairs, 1881* (Cape of Good Hope Government, Cape Town, 1881).

G.38-'81. *Native Laws Commission Report.*

A.1-'82. *Speech of His Excellency the Governor at the opening of the 4th session of the 6th Parliament* (Cape of Good Hope Government, Cape Town, 1882).

A.2-'82. *Petition from Jonathan Molapo and other Basuto Chiefs* (Cape of Good Hope Government, Cape Town).

A.8-'82. *Telegrams of 5, 9 and 11 September from the Hon. the Secretary for Native Affairs to Hon. the Premier having reference to the Basuto Chief Masupa's acceptance of the award made by His Excellency the Governor* (Cape of Good Hope Government, Cape Town, 1882).

Sources

A.19-'82. *Minutes of His Excellency the Governor, enclosing a Despatch, dated 23rd March, 1882, from His Honour the President of the O.F.S., stating the gratification of the Volksraad on hearing that no measure aiming at the abandonment of Basutoland would be proposed by Ministers* (Cape of Good Hope Government, Cape Town, 1882).

A.30-'82. *Return in compliance with a resolution of the Honourable the House of Assembly, adopted on the 12th May 1881* (Cape of Good Hope Government, Cape Town, 1881).

C.5-'82. *Report of the Select Committee appointed by the Legislative Council to consider and report on Basutoland Affairs* (Cape Town, 1882)

G.12-'82. *Correspondence between the Right Honourable the Secretary of State for the Colonies, His Excellency the Governor and Ministers, relative to Basutoland affairs from December 1881 to February 1882* (Cape of Good Hope Government, Cape Town, 1882).

G.26-'82. *Report of the Honourable the Secretary for Native Affairs, on his visit to Basutoland in June 1881* (Cape of Good Hope Government, Cape Town, 1882).

G.33-'82. *Blue book of native affairs, 1882.* Vol.1, pt.1 (Cape of Good Hope Government, Cape Town, 1882).

G.46-'82. *War Expenditure Commissioners report* (Cape of Good Hope Government, Cape Town, 1881).

G.47-'82. *Blue book of native affairs, 1882, compiled in compliance with a resolution of the Hon. the House of Assembly, dated 10th June 1878 and presented to both Houses of Parliament by command of His Excellency the Governor, 1882.* Vol.1, pt.2 (Cape of Good Hope Government, Cape Town, 1882).

G.74-'82. *Report of a Pitso held at Maseru, Basutoland with the loyal Basutos, by the Acting Magistrate Mr. A.G. Hatchard, on the 3rd April, 1882, together with other correspondence relating to affairs in Basutoland* (Cape of Good Hope Government, Cape Town, 1882).

G.75-'82. *Commission on the distribution of prize money: report* (Cape of Good Hope Government, Cape Town, 1882).

G.89-'82. *Return in compliance with a resolution of the Honourable the House of Assembly adopted 23rd March 1882 being reports and correspondence called for by Dr. Matthews, M.L.A. having reference to the state of affairs in Basutoland* (Cape of Good Hope Government, Cape Town, 1882).

A.1-'83. *Petition of Jonathan Molappo* (Cape of Good Hope Government, Cape Town, 1883).

A.3-'83. *Return in part as follows: for the production of all minutes of Minutes addressed to His Excellency the Governor, upon the subject of Basutoland and colonial native affairs generally since last session of Parliament and for the production of copies of all correspondence between the Government and its officials regarding Basutoland since last session of Parliament* (Cape of Good Hope Government, Cape Town, 1883).

A.7-'83. *Copies of all correspondence which have passed since last session of Parliament between His Excellency the Governor and Her Majesty's Imperial Government, relative to Basutoland and to native affairs of the Colony generally* (Cape of Good Hope Government, Cape Town, 1883).

A.24-'83. *Correspondence between present Ministers and officials, chiefs or others in Basutoland and reports of conferences between Ministers and chiefs and people in Basutoland* (Cape of Good Hope Government, Cape Town, 1883).

A.24A-'83. *Further correspondence relating to affairs in Basutoland* (Cape of Good Hope Government, Cape Town, 1883).

A.24B-'83. *Further correspondence relating to affairs in Basutoland: being continuation of correspondence between present Ministers and officials, chiefs, or others in Basutoland, and reports of conferences between Ministers and chiefs and people in Basutoland, laid on table on 3rd July, 1883* (Cape of Good Hope Government, Cape Town, 1883).

A.26-'83. *War claims: general summary* (Cape of Good Hope Government, Cape Town, 1883).

A.27-'83. *Despatches dated 1st and 5th May from the Officer administering the Colony, with a Memorandum addressed to the Right Honourable the Secretary of State for the Colonies by the Honourable J.X. Merriman, and the Earl of Derby's Reply thereto, dated 14th June, on the subject of the future government of Basutoland* (Cape of Good Hope Government, Cape Town, 1883).

A.29-'83. *Correspondence between His Excellency the Officer administering the Government and His Honour the President of the Orange Free State, with reference to the affairs of Basutoland* (Cape of Good Hope Government, Cape Town, 1883).

A.31-'83. *Petition of Jonathan Molapo, Chief of the Leribe District, Basutoland* (Cape of Good Hope Government, Cape Town, 1883).

A.34-'83. *Minute by His Excellency the Officer administering the Government, covering a despatch from His Honour the President of the Orange Free State, transmitting a resolution of the Volksraad approving His Honour's course of action with reference to Basutoland affairs* (Cape of Good Hope Government, Cape Town, 1883).

A.36-'83. *Communications on the subject of Basutoland between the Right Hon. the Secretary of State for the Colonies and the Hon. J.X. Merriman* (Cape of Good Hope Government, Cape Town, 1883).

A.40-'83. *Further papers relating to affairs in Basutoland. Letter from His Honour the President of the Orange Free State* (Cape of Good Hope Government, Cape Town, 1883).

C.3-'83. *Correspondence between Jonathan Molapo and other Chiefs of the Leribe District with [sic] Major-General Gordon; and other Correspondence on the part of the loyal Basutos. With a Return of the cost of Parliamentary Commissions; and of the advance of Lerothodi's army* (Cape of Good Hope Government, Cape Town, 1883)

G.4-'83. *Report and Proceedings, with Appendices, of the Government Commission on Native Laws and Customs* (Cape Town, Richards and Sons, 1883).

G.5-'83. *Correspondence between the Government and the Commandant-General of Colonial Forces (Major-General Gordon, C.B., R.E.) on the subject of the position of affairs in Basutoland and other Native Territories and the reorganisation of the Colonial Forces* (Cape of Good Hope Government, Cape Town, 1883).

G.6-'83. *Minutes of meetings and correspondence on affairs in Basutoland by the Hon'ble Secretary for Native Affairs* (Cape of Good Hope Government, Cape Town, 1883).

G.8-'83. *Blue-book on Native Affairs, 1883* (Cape of Good Hope Government, Cape Town, 1883).

G.8-'83 (Appendix). *Blue-book on Native Affairs, 1883* (Cape Town, 1883)

G.9-'83. *Basutoland: annual report for 1882 of the Resident Magistrate of Leribe and proceedings of the trials of Chiefs Jonathan and Joel Molapo and annual report for 1882 of the Acting Governor's Agent for Basutoland* (Cape of Good Hope Government, Cape Town, 1883).

G.10-'83. *Basutoland: telegrams from Acting Governor's Agent and other officials on progress of events in Basutoland between 17 and 24 January 1883* (Cape of Good Hope Government, Cape Town, 1883).

G.54-'83. *Official report of interviews between Premier and Secretary of State for Native Affairs and certain Basuto chiefs, councillors and headmen, 16 March to 27 April 1883* (Cape of Good Hope Government, Cape Town, 1883).

G.96-'83. *Report and Proceedings of the Government Commission on Basutoland losses* (Cape of Good Hope Government, Cape Town, 1883).

G.106-'83. *Minutes and correspondence relating to claim of Joseph Amos for theft of cattle in Orange Free State, traced to Basutoland* (Cape of Good Hope Government, Cape Town, 1883).

G.109-'83. *Report re Threatened combination in Extra-Colonial Territories* (Cape of Good Hope Government, Cape Town, 1883)

G.3-'84. *Blue book of native affairs* (Cape of Good Hope Government, Cape Town, 1884).

C.3-'85. *Basutoland report of the Resident Commissioner.*

Cape of Good Hope Government Gazette, 1872-1884.

There are also Blue Books for each year on estimates, revenue and expenditure: except for G.33-'75 these have not been listed.

B UNOFFICIAL MANUSCRIPT SOURCES

a Cape Archives
Brabant Collection. Acc. 459.
Carrington's War Diary, 1881. DD 1/275.
Garcia Papers. Acc. 250.
Gordon Papers. Acc. 6.
Griffith Papers. Acc. 1554.
Kingsley collection. Acc. 232.
Orpen Papers. Acc. 302.
Pattison Papers. Acc. 88.
Southey Papers. Acc. 611.
Wavell, Major General A.G. Papers, 1881. Acc. 102.

b Cory Library, Rhodes University, Grahamstown.
MS 1248, 'Major General Charles George Gordon's Visit to Basutoland in 1882 and my administration of the government of that territory from August 1881 to March 1883 by Joseph Millerd Orpen ...'

c Grant Papers
Grant, Lieutenant-Colonel J.M., Manuscript Diary on operations against Langalibalele. Consulted by Tylden when in possession of his son, Brigadier-General R.C. Grant (Tylden 1950A: 242).

d Institute of Southern African Studies, National University of Lesotho: Documentation Centre
A 176, Information by Chief Matlere Lerotholi in two interviews with Rivers Thompson and E.M. Sehalahala in 1966. Includes information on Gun War. [Matlere Lerotholi] [S.l] [s.n.] [1966].

e Jagger Library, University of Cape Town
W.E. Stanford Papers.

f Maitin Papers
Maitin's Journal. Formerly in possession of Chief Leshoboro Majara. Notes on the journal are in the Tylden Papers. See under National Army Museum, London, below.

g National Army Museum, London
Tylden Papers, Boxes 34012/3, 34056, 34057.
These include notes on interviews with Basotho and white informants whom Tylden consulted when writing *The Rise of the Basuto*, and also on material which Tylden consulted for that book.

h Paris Evangelical Mission Archives, Paris
Correspondence from missionaries in Lesotho. See also under School of Oriental and African Studies, London, below.

i   Paris Evangelical Mission Archives, Morija

These archives contain many files of loosely classified missionary correspondence, and also the Ellenberger Papers.

j   Rhodes House Library, Oxford

British and Foreign Anti-Slavery and Aborigines Protection Society. MSS Br. Emp. s.18. Letters received.
United Society for the Propagation of the Gospel (USPG) Archives. D 44A-86, Letters received, 1876-1888; E 32b-40, Missionaries' reports, 1876-1885.
Hall Papers. MSS. Afr. s.54.
Kennan Papers. MSS. Afr. 5969.
Lagden Papers, MSS. Afr. S. 142-214.
J. C. Molteno Papers. MSS. Afr. s.23.
C. J. Rhodes Papers. MSS. Afr. t.5: Misc.
H. Waller Papers. MS. Afr. S.16 - vol. 2: correspondence with General Gordon.

k   School of Oriental and African Studies, London

Microfiche Boxes FBN 5-9, containing copies of PEMS Mission Archives, Paris, incoming letters, 1867-1898.
Methodist Missionary Society Archives. South Africa/Correspondence/Queenstown/FBN 21, 1880-81: letters of Henry Cotton.

l   South African Public Library, Cape Town

J. X. Merriman Papers.

m   Witwatersrand University Library

Historical Papers, A 1631. Diary of Arthur Aaron Boss.

C   NEWSPAPERS AND PERIODICALS

In Basutoland the monthly mission newspaper, *Leselinyana la Lesotho*, was published at Morija throughout this period, except during the Gun War. A shorter and very different English newspaper, *The Little Light of Basutoland*, was published by the mission from 1872 to 1877.

Throughout southern Africa, but especially in the Cape and the Orange Free State, there were many newspapers which carried original articles on Basutoland, especially during the war. I have concentrated on the *Cape Argus*, published in Cape Town, and the *Graham's Town Journal*, published in Graham's Town. The former was broadly hostile to the Sprigg Ministry, the latter supportive. The *Argus* reported Parliamentary debates in great detail. Both reprinted a wide range of articles from other South African papers. About forty such papers were used in this way, and for the purposes of this book the most important were the *Friend of the Free State* (Bloemfontein), the *Northern Post* (Aliwal North), the *Kaffrarian Watchman* (King William's Town), the *Cape Times* and the *Cape Mercury*. During the Gun War many papers relied on articles submitted by members of the armed forces who came from their areas. W.M. Laurence, for example, who commanded the Diamond Fields Horse at Hlotse Heights, was the correspondent of the *Diamond News*.

In Britain *The Times* was the best source, but a few articles on Basutoland also appeared in periodicals, e.g. *The Nineteenth Century* and the *Gentleman's Magazine*, and illustrations in such publications as the *Graphic* and the *Illustrated London News*.

Sources

The Paris Evangelical Mission Society's *Journal des Missions Évangéliques* (Paris) published many articles on Basutoland. The United Society for the Propagation of the Gospel published the *Mission Field*, and there is also the *Quarterly Paper of the Orange Free State Mission*, which became the *Quarterly Paper of the Bloemfontein Mission* in October 1875.

Subsequent issues of *Leselinyana* carried historical articles relating to the period of Cape rule.

D PRINTED BOOKS, ARTICLES, ETC.

Agar-Hamilton, J.A.I. (1929), 'The South African Protectorates', *African Affairs* (UK), no.113, vol.29 (October 1929), 12-26.

Ambrose, David (1972), 'Masupha's village', *Lesotho: Basutoland Notes & Records*, 9, 1970-71, 20-4.

Ambrose, David (1993), *Maseru. An Illustrated History*, Morija, Lesotho: Morija Museum and Archives.

Anon. (1873), 'La mission française du Lessouto', *Journal des Missions Évangéliques*, 13, 286-7.

Anon. (1880), 'Le désarmement des Bassoutos', *Journal des Missions Évangéliques*, 20, 350-1.

Anon. (1896), *Ons Land*, 29 September 1896.

Atmore, Anthony (1969), 'The Passing of Sotho Independence', in L.M. Thompson (ed.), *African Societies in southern Africa*, London: Heinemann, 282-301.

Atmore, Anthony (1970), 'The Moorosi Rebellion: Lesotho, 1879', in Robert I. Rotberg and Ali A. Mazrui, *Protest and power in Black Africa*, New York: Oxford University Press, 3-35.

Atmore, Anthony, and Sanders, Peter (1971), 'Sotho arms and ammunition in the nineteenth century', *Journal of African History* (UK), 12, 4, 535-44.

Atmore, Anthony, and Marks, Shula (1974), 'The Imperial Factor in South Africa in the Nineteenth Century: Towards a Reassessment', *Journal of Imperial and Commonwealth History*, iii, I, 105-39.

Attwell, J.E.M. Thursby (n.d.), *The fighting police of South Africa*, Durban: privately printed.

Barkly, Fanny (1893), *Among Boers and Basutos and with Barkly's Horse: the story of our life on the frontier*, London: Remington.

Basutoland Records (BR.): see under Theal.

Benyon, John (1980), *Proconsul and Paramountcy in South Africa: The High Commission, British Supremacy and the Sub-Continent 1806-1910*, Pietermaritzburg: University of Natal,

Bereng, Patrick Mohlalefi, and Lehloenya, Patrick Lehloenya (1991), *Haboo*, Roma: National University of Lesotho.

Bereng, Patrick Mohlalefi, and Lehloenya, Patrick Lehloenya (2006), *Haboo*, Maseru: Lilala Publications.

Berthoud, P. (1900), *Lettres missionnaires de M. & Mme. Paul Berthoud, de la Mission romande,1873-1879*, Lausanne, Switzerland: Bridel.

Boulger, Demetrius C. (1896), *Life of Gordon*, London: Fisher Unwin.

Bradlow, Edna (1968), 'The Cape Government's rule of Basutoland 1871-1883', *Archives Year Book for South African History*, 1968, II.

Bradlow, Edna (1970), 'General Gordon in Basutoland', *Historia* (SA), 15, 223-42.

Brookes, Edgar [1924] (1927), *The History of Native Policy in South Africa from 1830 to the Present Day*, 2nd revised edn, Pretoria: J.L. van Schaik.

Brown, William Eric (1960), *The Catholic Church in South Africa from its origins to the present day*, London: Burns & Oates.

Browning, F. (1880), *Fighting and Farming in South Africa*, London: Remington.

Brownlee, Charles (1889), *A chapter on the Basuto War*, Lovedale: Lovedale Mission Press.

Brownlee, Charles (1896), *Reminiscences of Kaffir Life and History*, Lovedale: Lovedale Mission Press. [2nd ed. Lovedale, n.d.; Killie Campbell Africana Library Reprint Series, Pietermaritzburg, 1977].

Bryce, James [1893] (1900), *Impressions of South Africa*, London: Macmillan.

Burman, Sandra B. (1976A), *The justice of the Queen's Government: the Cape's administration of Basutoland 1871-1884*, Leiden: Afrika-Studiecentrum and Cambridge: African Studies Centre.

Burman, Sandra B. (1976B), 'Symbolic Dimensions of the Enforcement of Law', *British Journal of Law and Society*, iii, 2.

Burman, Sandra B. (1979), 'Masopha', in C.C. Saunders (ed.), *African Leaders in Southern African History*, London: Heinemann.

Burman, Sandra (1981), *Chiefdom Politics and Alien Law: Basutoland under Cape Rule 1871-1884*, London: Macmillan.

Butler, Colonel Sir William F. (1891), *Charles George Gordon*, London: Macmillan.

Campbell, W.B. (1959), 'The South African Frontier 1865-1885: A Study in Expansion', *Archives Year Book for South African History*, 1959, I.

Casalis, Eugène (1861), *The Basutos*, London: James Nisbet.

Chalmers, J. (1878), *The Native Question*, Grahamstown.

Chesson, F.W. (1881), *The Basuto War: a brief reply to Sir Bartle Frere's article in Nineteenth Century*, London: Aborigines' Protection Society.

Coleman, Francis L. (1988), *The Kaffrarian Rifles 1876-1986*, East London: Kaffrarian Rifles Association, East London.

'Colonial Officer'. See under Woon.

Couzens, T. (2003), *Murder at Morija*, Johannesburg: Random House.

Cripps, G. St.V. (1882), 'A Page in Colonial History', *Cape Quarterly Review*, 1, 1, 684-8.

Crisp, W. (1895), *Some Account of the Diocese of Bloemfontein in the Province of South Africa from 1863-1894*, Oxford: Parker.

Cunynghame, Arthur T. (1879), *My Command in South Africa, 1874-1878*, London: Macmillan.

Damane, Mosebi (1960), *Moorosi, Morena oa Baphuthi*, Morija: Sesuto Book Depot.

Damane, Mosebi (1969), 'The role played by the Paramount Chieftainship in the struggle for freedom in Lesotho', *Fossil: Journal of the U.B.L.S. History Society* (L), 1, 2, September, 26-37.

Damane, Mosebi, and Sanders, Peter (eds.) (1974), *Lithoko: Sotho Praise-Poems*, Oxford: Clarendon Press.

Darwin, Leonard (1886), *A Short history of Basutoland chiefly compiled from Blue Books*, London: War Office, Intelligence Branch.

Davenport, T.R.H. (1966), *The Afrikaner Bond. The History of a South African Political Party, 1880-1911*, Cape Town: Oxford University Press.

Davenport, T.R.H. [1977] (1978), *South Africa: A Modern History*, Toronto and Buffalo: University of Toronto Press.

De Kiewiet, C.W. (1937), *The imperial factor in South Africa: a study in politics and economics*, Cambridge, England: Cambridge University Press.

De Kiewiet, C.W. (1941), *A history of South Africa: social and economic*, London: Oxford University Press.

De Kock, W. (1948), 'Ekstra Territoriale Vraagstukke van die Kaapse Regering 1872-85', *Archives Year Book for South African History*, I.

De Kock, W., Kruger, D.W., and Beyers, C.J. (eds.) (1968-77), *Dictionary of South African Biography*, i-iii, Cape Town: Tafelberg-Uitgevers Ltd..

De Kok, K.J. (1904), *Empires of the Veld*, Durban: J.C. Juta.

Sources

Deare, Major George (1930), articles in *Natal Week End Advertiser*, 3, 10, 17, 24 and 31 May 1930.

Delius, Peter (1983), *The Land Belongs to Us. The Pedi Polity, the Boers and the British in Nineteenth-Century Transvaal*, Johannesburg: Ravan Press.

Dieterlen, H. (1930), *Eugène Casalis (1812-1891)*, Paris: Société des Missions Évangéliques.

Dieterlen, H. (1933), *Adolphe Mabille (1836-1894)*, Paris: Société des Missions Évangéliques.

Dove, Reginald (1975), *Anglican pioneers in Lesotho: some account of the Diocese of Lesotho, 1876-1930*, Mazenod, Lesotho: Mazenod Institute.

Dove, Reginald, 'The history of Basutoland camps: I Leribe (Hlotse)', *Lesotho: Basutoland Notes and Records* vol.1 (1959), pp.22-37.

Duggan-Cronin, A.M. (1933), *The Bantu Tribes of South Africa. Reproductions of Photographic Studies ... The Southern Basotho*, Cambridge: Deighton, Bell & Co. and Kimberley, Alexander McGregor Memorial Museum.

Duncan, Patrick (1960), *Sotho laws and customs*, Cape Town: Oxford University Press.

Duvoisin, Louis (1880), 'Lessouto', *Mission Vaudoise* (SZ), no.39, vol.3, Dec., 225-7.

Eldredge, Elizabeth A. (1993), *A South African kingdom. The pursuit of security in nineteenth-century Lesotho*, Cambridge: Cambridge University Press.

Eldredge, Elizabeth A. (2007), *Power in Colonial Africa. Conflict and Discourse in Lesotho, 1870-1960*, Madison: University of Wisconsin Press.

Ellenberger, Victor (1932), *Un Siècle de mission au Lessouto, 1833-1933*, Paris: Société des Missions Évangéliques.

Ellenberger, Victor, translated by Edmond M. Ellenberger (1938), *A century of mission work in Basutoland (1833-1933)*, Morija, Lesotho: Sesuto Book Depot.

Eloff, C.C. (1984), *Oranje-Vrystaat en Basoetoland, 1884-1902, 'n Verhoudingstudie*, Pretoria.

Etherington, Norman (1978), *Preachers, Peasants and Politics in Southeast Africa, 1835-1880. African Christian Communities in Natal, Pondoland and Zululand*, London: Royal Historical Society.

Etherington, Norman (2001), *The Great Treks. The Transformation of Southern Africa, 1815-1854)*, Harlow, England: Longman.

Fairclough, T. Lindsay. (1905), 'Notes on the Basuto, their history, country, etc.', *Journal of the Africa Society*, 4, 4, 194-205.

Favre, E. (1931), *Les vingt-cinq ans de Coillard au Lessouto*, Paris: Société des Missions Évangéliques.

Favre, E. (1946), *La vie d'un Missionnaire français. François Coillard*, Paris; Société des Missions Évangéliques.

Featherstone, Donald (1992), *Victorian Colonial Warfare: from the Campaigns against the Kaffirs to the South African War*, London: Cassell.

Fenton, Reginald (1905), *Peculiar People in a Pleasant Land*, Girard, Kansas, USA: Pretoria Publishing Company.

Fowler, William (1881), 'The Basutos and Sir Bartle Frere', *Nineteenth Century* (UK), 49, March, 547-57.

Fraser, Sir J.G. (1922), *Episodes in My Life*, Cape Town: Juta.

Frere, Sir Henry Bartle (1880), *Correspondence relating to the recall of the Right Honourable Sir Bartle Frere*, London: John Murray.

Frere, Sir Henry Bartle (1881), 'The Basutos and the constitution of the Cape of Good Hope', *Nineteenth Century* (UK), 9, 47, 177-200.

Frere, Sir Henry Bartle (1882), *On the Laws affecting the Relations between Civilized and Savage Life*, London: Harrison and Sons.

Gérard, Joseph (1969), *Le Père Gérard nous parle ...*, vol.2: *Son Premier Séjour a Roma 1862-1875*, Roma, Lesotho: The Social Centre.

Gérard, Joseph (1970), *Le Père Gérard nous parle ...*, vol. 3, *Son Séjour a Ste-Monique 1876-1897*, Roma, Lesotho: The Social Centre.

Germond, Robert C. (1967), *Chronicles of Basutoland: a running commentary on the events of the years 1830-1902 by the French Protestant missionaries in Southern Africa*, Morija: Sesuto Book Depot.

Glanville, T.B. (1876), 'A "Pitso"', *Gentleman's Magazine* (UK), 17, 9, Sept., 428-46.

Goiran, H. (1931), *Une action créatrice de la mission protestante française au sud de l'Afrique*, Paris: Editions "Je Sers" Paris.

Gon, Philip (1984), *Send Carrington! The story of an imperial frontiersman*, Craighall, South Africa: Ad. Donker.

Goodfellow, C. (1966), *Great Britain and South African Confederation (1870-1881)*, Cape Town: Oxford University Press.

Gordon, H. W. (1886), *Events in the Life of Charles George Gordon*. London: Kegan Paul.

Gordon Correspondence (1905), 'Correspondence between Major-General Gordon C.B. and Mr. Scanlen, Prime Minister of the Colony of the Cape of Good Hope ...', Cape Town: privately printed.

Grant, Lieutenant-Colonel J.M. (1893), *Historical Record of the Cape Mounted Riflemen*, Cape Town.

Granville, A.K. (Ex C.M.R.) (1881), *With the Cape Mounted Rifles: four years service in South Africa*, London: Richard Bentley & Son.

Griffith, Charles D. (1878), 'Some Observations on Witchcraft in Basutoland', *The Transactions of the South African Philosophical Society*, 1, 2, 87-92.

Guest, W.R. (1976), *Langalibalele: The Crisis in Natal 1873-1875*, Durban: University of Natal.

Guy, Jeff (1971), 'A note on Firearms in the Zulu Kingdom with special reference to the Anglo-Zulu War, 1879', *Journal of African History*, 12, 4, 557-70.

Guy, Jeff [1979] (1982), *The destruction of the Zulu Kingdom*, Johannesburg: Ravan Press.

Hailey, William Malcolm (1953), *Native administration in the British African territories. Pt.5 the High Commission Territories: Basutoland, the Bechuanaland Protectorate and Swaziland*, London: HMSO.

Hake, A.E. (1884), *The Story of Chinese Gordon*, London: Remington.

Haliburton, Gordon (1977), *Historical Dictionary of Lesotho*, Metuchen, New Jersey: Scarecrow Press.

Hance, Gertrude R. (1916), *The Zulu yesterday and to-day: twenty-nine years in South Africa*, New York: Fleming H. Revell.

Hicks Beach, V. (1932), *Life of Sir Michael Hicks Beach*, i, London: Macmillan and Co.

Hirschmann, D. 'The battle of Thlotsi Heights' (1973), *New Nation* (UK), 6, 10, 15-17.

Hofmeyr, J.J. (1913), *The Life of Jan Hendrik Hofmeyr*, Cape Town: Van de Sandt de Villiers.

Hook, David Blair (1906), *With sword and statute on the Cape of Good Hope frontier, republished with additions and further photographs*, London: Greaves, Pass and Co.

Hulme, J.J. (1972), 'Moorosi's War, 1879', *Paratus* (SA), 24, 9, Sept., 58-9.

Irvine, T.W. (1881), *British Basutoland and the Basutos*, London: H.J. Infield.

Jacottet, Edouard (1912), 'Histoire de la mission du Lessouto' in *Livre d'or de la mission du Lessouto*, Paris: Maison des Missions Évangéliques, 156-440.

Jousse, Théophile (1889), *La mission française évangélique au sud de l'Afrique, son origine et son développement jusqu'à nos jours*, Paris: Librairie Fischbacher.

Kikebusch, Pastor (1881), 'Die Basoetokrieg', *Allgemeine Missions-Zeitschrift* (GE), 8, 508.

Kilpin, Sir Ernest (1912), 'The Basutos in 1883', *The State* (South Africa), 8, 243-6.

Kimble, Judith M. (1982), 'Labour migration in Basutoland c.1870-1885', in Marks and Rathbone, *Industrialisation and Social Change in South Africa*, London: Longman.

Kimble, Judith M. (1999), *Migrant Labour and Colonial Rule in Basutoland, 1890-1930*, Grahamstown: Institute of Social and Economic Research, Rhodes University.

Lagden, Sir Godfrey (1901), *The Basutos: the mountaineers and their country; being a narrative of events relating to the tribe from its formation early in the nineteenth century to the present day*, London: Hutchinson.

Laurence, P. (1930), *The Life of John Xavier Merriman*, London: Constable & Co.

Laurence, William Moorsom (1882), *Selected writings of the late William Moorsom Laurence*, Grahamstown: Richards, Slater.

Laydevant, F., and Tjokosela, J.F.I. (1965), *Histori ea Lesotho*, Mazenod, Lesotho: The Catholic Centre.

Laydevant, F. (1935), 'R.P. François Le Bihan, 1833-1916', *Missions O.M.I.* vol. 59, pp. 329-50.

Laydevant, F. (1943) '*Roles des Pères Gérard et Lebihan, Sequiti et Fusils*'. See Tylden (1950A), p. 168.

Lelimo, Martin Moloantoa (1998), *The Question of Lesotho's Conquered Territory: It's Time for an Answer*, Morija, Lesotho: Morija Museum and Archives.

Lewis, Cecil, and Edwards, G.E. (1934), *Historical records of the Church of the Province of South Africa with an introductory letter from the Archbishop of Cape Town*, London: S.P.C.K.

Lewsen, P. (1942), 'The First Crisis in Responsible Government in the Cape Colony', *Archives Year Book for South African History*, I, Cape Town: Cape Times Ltd.

Lewsen, P. (ed.) (1960) *Selections from the Correspondence of J.X. Merriman 1870-1890*, vol. i, Cape Town: van Riebeeck Society.

Lewsen, P. (1982), *John X. Merriman. Paradoxical South African Statesman*, New Haven and London: Yale University Press.

Livre d'Or de la Mission du Lessuoto, soixante-quinze ans de l'histoire d'un tribu Sud-Africain, 1833-1908 (1912), Paris: Maison des Missions Évangéliques.

Macgregor, J.C. (1910), 'Some Notes on the Basuto Tribal System, Political and Social', *The South African Journal of Science*, v. 7, 276-81.

Machobane, L.B.B.J. (1990), *Government and Change in Lesotho, 1800-1966*, Basingstoke and London: Macmillan.

Machobane, L.B.B.J. (2000), 'Gender, Succession and Dynastic Politics: The Saga of Senate and her son Motšoene Molapo Moshoeshoe, 1858-1930', *Review of Southern African Studies*, iv, 1, 19-41.

McCracken, J.L. (1967), *The Cape Parliament 1854-1910*, Oxford: Clarendon Press.

Mackenzie, John (1888), 'Austral Africa: extension of British influence in trans-colonial territories', *Journal of the Manchester Geographical Society* (UK), 4, 201-31.

Mackintosh, C.W. (1907), *Coillard of the Zambesi*, London: Unwin.

Macmillan, M. (1970), *Sir Henry Barkly: Mediator and Moderator*, Cape Town: A.A. Balkema.

Macquarrie, J.W. (ed.) (1958), *The Reminscences of Sir Walter Stanford*, Cape Town: van Riebeeck Society.

Mairot, François (1962), *Suivez le guide s'il vous plait!*, Mazenod: Catholic Centre.

Makoro, J.C.K. (c.1958), *Histori ea Batlokoa*, Mazenod, Lesotho: Catholic Centre.

Malan, C.H. (1878), *La Mission Française du Sud de l'Afrique* (translated from English by Mme G. Mallet), Paris: Bonhoure.

Malan, C.H. (1876), *South African Missions*, London: Nisbet.

Malherbe, V.C. (1972), *Eminent Victorians in Africa*, Cape Town: Juta.

Mangoaela, Z.K. (ed.) [1921] (1957), *Lithoko tsa Marena a Basotho*, Morija: Sesuto Book Depot.

Martin, Minnie (1903), *Basutoland: Its Legends and Customs*, London: Nichols.

Martineau, John (1895), *The Life and Correspondence of the Right Hon. Sir Bartle Frere*, 2 vols., London: Murray.

Matthews, J.W. [1887] (1976), *Incwadi Yami or twenty years' personal experience in South Africa*, Johannesburg: Africana Book Society.

Miers, Sue (1971), 'Notes on the arms trade and Government policy in Southern Africa between 1870 and 1890', *Journal of African History*, xii, 4, 571-7.

The Mission Field. A Monthly Record of the proceedings of the Society for the Propagation of the Gospel at Home and Abroad (1868-84). London: G. Bell and Sons.

Moffat, Robert U. [1921] (1969), *John Smith Moffat, C.M.G. missionary: a memoir*, New York, Universities Press.

Mohapeloa, J. Makibinyane (1971), *Government by proxy: ten years of Cape Colony rule in Lesotho, 1871-1881*, Morija: Sesuto Book Depot.

Mohapeloa, J. Makibinyane (1965-6), 'The Essential Masupha', *Lesotho Notes and Records*, 5, 7-17.

Moodie, D.C. (1888), *History of the Battles and Adventures of the British, the Boers, and the Zulus, etc.*, Sydney, Melbourne and Adelaide: George Robertson.

Morris, D.R. (1966), *The Washing of the Spears: a history of the rise of the Zulu nation under Shaka and its fall in the Zulu war of 1879*, London: Jonathan Cape.

Moshoeshoe, Nehemiah Sekhonyana (1877), *The Queen v. Nehemiah Moshesh: statement made by Nehemiah when in prison, for the guidance of Counsel*, King William's Town: Hay Brothers.

Murray, Colin (1981), *Families Divided. The Impact of Migrant Labour in Lesotho*, Cambridge: Cambridge University Press.

Murray, Colin, and Sanders, Peter (2005), *Medicine Murder in Colonial Lesotho: the anatomy of a moral crisis*, Edinburgh: Edinburgh University Press.

Omer-Cooper, J.D., et al. (1971), *The making of modern Africa, 1800-1960*, London: Longman.

Orpen, Joseph Millerd (1879), *Our Relations with the Imperial Government, considered as a whole, in reference to the late despatch, and to Confederation*, Cape Town: William Foster.

Orpen, Joseph Millerd (1880), *Some principles of native government illustrated and the petition of the Basuto tribe regarding land, law, representation and disarmament, to the Cape Parliament considered*, Cape Town: Saul Solomon.

Orpen, Joseph Millerd [1908] (1964), *Reminiscences of life in South Africa from 1846 to the present day*, Cape Town, C. Struik.

Orpen, Neil (1967), *Prince Alfred's Guard 1856-1966*, Port Elizabeth: Prince Alfred's Guard, Drill Hall and Cape Town: Books of Africa.

Pollock, John (1993), *Gordon: The Man Behind the Legend*, London: Constable.

Poulter, Sebastian (1973-74), 'The place of the laws of Lerotholi in the legal system of Lesotho', *Lesotho: Notes and Records*, 10, 33-47.

Quarterly Paper of the Orange Free State Mission (from October 1875 *Quarterly Paper of the Bloemfontein Mission*) (1868-88).

Ranger, Terence (1983), 'The Invention of Tradition in Colonial Africa', in Hobsbawm, Eric, and Ranger, *The Invention of Tradition*, Cambridge: Cambridge University Press.

Roche, Aimé (1951), *Clartés Australes*, Lyon, France: Editions du Chalet.

Rosenberg, Scott, Weisfelder, Richard F., and Frisbie-Fulton, Michelle (2004), *Historical Dictionary of Lesotho, New Edition*, Lanham, Maryland, and Oxford: Scarecrow Press.

Rotberg, Robert I. (1988), *The Founder. Cecil Rhodes and the Pursuit of Power*, New York and Oxford: Oxford University Press.

Sanders, Peter (1975), *Moshoeshoe, Chief of the Sotho*, London: Heinemann.

Saunders, Christopher, and Derricourt, Robin, eds. (1974), *Beyond the Cape Frontier. Studies in the History of the Transkei and Ciskei*, London: Longman.

Schreuder, D.M. (1969), *Gladstone and Kruger. Liberal Government and Colonial 'Home Rule' 1880-85*, London: Routledge & Kegan Paul, and Toronto: University of Toronto Press.

Schreuder, D.M. [1980] (2009), *The Scramble for Southern Africa, 1877-1895. The politics of partition reappraised*. Cambridge: Cambridge University Press.

Scully, William Charles (1913), *Further reminiscences of a South African pioneer*, London: Fisher Unwin.

Shervinton, K. (1899), *The Shervintons, Solders of Fortune*, London: T. Fisher Unwin.

Smith, Edwin W. (1939), *The Mabilles of Basutoland*, London: Hodder and Stoughton.

Solomon, W.E. Gladstone (1948), *Saul Solomon 'The Member for Cape Town'*, Cape Town: Oxford University Press.

Streatfeild, F.N. (1911), *Reminiscences of an Old 'Un*, London: G. Bell and Sons.

Tavender, I.T. (1985), *Casualty Roll for the Zulu and Basuto Wars, South Africa 1877-79*, Polstead, Suffolk: J.B. Hayward & Son.

Taylor, Henry, ed. Peter Hadley (1972), *Doctor to Basuto, Boer and Briton, 1877-1906: memoirs of Dr. Henry Taylor*, Cape Town: David Philip.

Thompson, Leonard (1971), 'The subjection of the African chiefdoms, 1870-1898', in M. Wilson and L. Thompson (eds.) *Oxford History of South Africa*. Vol.2: 1870-1966, Oxford: Clarendon Press, 242-86.

Thompson, Leonard (1975), *Survival in Two Worlds: Moshoeshoe of Lesotho 1786-1870*, Oxford: Clarendon Press.

Theal, George McCall [1883] (1964) *Basutoland Records*, vols 1-3, Cape Town: Struik.

Theal, George McCall (2002), *Basutoland Records*, vols 4-6, Roma, Lesotho: Institute of Southern African Studies, National University of Lesotho.

Trollope, A. [1878] (1973), *South Africa*, Cape Town: Balkema.

Tylden, Geoffrey (1929), 'Chief Moorosi and his mountain stronghold', *The Star*, Johannesburg, 29 June.

Tylden, Geoffrey (1936), 'The Basutoland rebellion of 1880-1881', *Journal of the Society for Army Historical Research* (UK), 15, 98-107.

Tylden, Geoffrey (1938), 'Brabant in Basutoland, 1879, 1880, 1881', *The Springbok*, February 1938.

Tylden, Geoffrey (1939), 'Majorobelle', *Basutoland News*, 19 September 1939.

Tylden, Geoffrey (1942), 'The Capture of Morosi's Mountain, 1879', *Journal of the Society for Army Historical Research*, 21.

Tylden, Geoffrey (1944A), *Early days in Maseru*, Maseru: British Empire Servicemen's League.

Tylden, Geoffrey (1944B), 'Notes on The History of the Basutoland Mounted Police', *Basutoland News*, 18 January 1944.

Tylden, Geoffrey (1945), 'Moorosi's Mountain', *Libertas*, December 1945.

Tylden, Geoffrey (1950A), *The rise of the Basuto*, Cape Town: Juta.

Tylden, Geoffrey (1950B), 'The senior South African regular regiment, 1852-1950', *Africana Notes and News* (SA), 8, 1, 2-33.

Tylden, Geoffrey [1945] (1950C), *A History of Thaba Bosiu: 'A Mountain at Night'*, Maseru: Basutoland Branch of the South African Legion.

Tylden, Geoffrey (1952A), 'Three mountains: Thaba-Bosiu, Morosi's Mountain, Sekukuni's Mountain', *Africana Notes and News* (SA), 9, 2, March, 36-46.

Tylden, Geoffrey (1952B), 'A note on the 'Edwards Papers', Basutoland, June to September 1881', *Africana Notes and News* (SA), 9, 4, 133-4.

Tylden, Geoffrey (December 1957), 'Majorobello in uniform', *Africana Notes & News*, vol. 12, pt. 8, p. 277 and plate between p. 296 and p. 297.

Tylden, Geoffrey (December 1969), *Military History Journal*, vol. 1, no. 5, 'Basutoland Roll of Honour 1851-1881).

Uys, Ian S. (1973), *For valour: the history of southern Africa's Victoria Cross heroes*, Johannesburg: the author.

Vincent, John (ed. 2003), *The Diaries of Edward Henry Stanley, 15th Earl of Derby (1826-93) between 1878 and 1893*, Oxford: Leopard's Head Press.

Walker, E.A. [1936] (1963), *The Cambridge History of the British Empire, Vol.VIII: South Africa*, Cambridge: Cambridge University Press.

Walton, James (1958A), *Father of Kindness and Father of Horses: The Story of Frasers Limited*, Wepener, SA.

Walton, James (1958B), *Old Maseru*, Maseru: Basutoland Scientific Association.

Walton, James (1960), 'Villages of the Paramount Chiefs of Basutoland: II. Thaba Bosiu, the Mountain Fortress of Moshesh', *Lesotho: Basutoland Notes and Records*, 2, 11-19.

Webb, R.S. (1950), *Gazetteer for Basutoland* (Paarl: privately printed).

Widdicombe, John (1891), *Fourteen years in Basutoland*, London: Church Printing Co.

Widdicombe, John (1895), *In the Lesuto: a sketch of African mission life*, London: S.P.C.K.

Williams, Basil (1909), *Record of the Cape Mounted Riflemen*, London: Sir Joseph Causton and Sons Ltd.

Wilmot, Alexander (1897), *History of our own times in South Africa*, Cape Town: Juta, 3 vols. Vol. II: 58-88.

Wilmot, A. (1904), *The Life and Times of Sir Richard Southey*, London: S. Low, Marston and Co., Ltd.

Wilson, Monica, and Thompson, Leonard, *The Oxford history of South Africa. Vol.1: South Africa to 1870; vol.2: South Africa 1870-1966* (Oxford, 2 vols, 1969-71).

Woon, Harry Vernon (1909), *Twenty-five years soldiering in South Africa: a personal narrative*, London: Andrew Melrose.

Worger, William H. (1987), *South Africa's City of Diamonds. Mine Workers and Monopoly Capitalism in Kimberley, 1867-1895*, New Haven and London: Yale University Press.

Worsfold, B. (1923), *Sir Bartle Frere*, London: Thornton Butterworth Ltd.

Young, P.J. (1955), *Boot and saddle: a narrative record of the Cape Regiment, the British Cape Mounted Riflemen, the Frontier Armed Mounted Police, and Colonial Cape Mounted Riflemen*, Cape Town: Maskew Miller.

E UNPUBLISHED THESES

Benyon, J.A. (1968), 'Basutoland and the High Commission with particular reference to the years 1868-1884: The Changing Nature of the Imperial government's "Special Responsibility" for the Territory' (Oxford University, D.Phil.).

Bradlow, Edna (1966), 'The Cape Government's rule of Basutoland, 1871-1883' (M.A. Thesis, University of Cape Town, October).

Burman, S.B. (1973), 'Cape Policies Towards African Law in Cape Tribal Territories, 1872-1883' (Oxford University, D.Phil.).

Cassidy, Rita Mary (1967-68), 'Britain and Basutoland: a study of men and policies from the Gun War to the Anglo-Boer War' (Ph.D. Thesis, University of California).

Kimble, Judith (1978), 'Towards an Understanding of the Political Economy of Lesotho: The Origins of Commodity Production and Migrant Labour, 1830-c.1855' (M.A. Thesis, National University of Lesotho).

Saunders, C.C. (1964), 'The Cape Native Affairs Department and African Administration on the Eastern Frontier under the Molteno Ministry, 1872-1878' (Cape Town University, B.A. Hons.).

Saunders, C.C. (1972), 'The Annexation of the Transkeian Territories (1872-1895) with special reference to British and Cape Policy' (Oxford University, D.Phil.).

Van Niekerk, A.A.J. (1956), '*Die Gebeure wat gelei het tot die oorname van Basoetoland deur Brittanje (1878-1884)*' (M.A. Thesis, University of Stellenbosch).

Webber, P.E. (1967), 'The Church in Basutoland, 1833-1884' (Southampton University, M.A.).

F INTERVIEWS CONDUCTED BY ANTHONY ATMORE, 1965-6

Damane, Mosebi: Matsieng, 11, 14 February, 1965; 15-17 November 1965; 22 March 1966; 18 May 1966; 3 June 1966.

Goliathe: Potsane, Mohale's Hoek, 4 June 1966.

Kompi, Molungoa: Makeneng, 30 January 1966.

Lekhoba: Makeneng, 30 January 1966.

Lelosa: Qalo, 21 May 1966.

Letsie, Hopolang: Makeneng, 16 June 1966.

Maitin, Cely/Selly, 18 November 1965.

Majara, Leshoboro, 18 November 1965.

Masupha, Moorosane: Pilate, 22 May 1966.

Matete, 'Mamahao: Morija, 20 March 1966.

Molapo, 'Mako Moliboea: Hlotse, 26 November 1965.

Molapo, Motsarapane J.: Leribe, May 1966.

Moletsane, Abraham: Thabana-Morena, 7 May 1966.

Mota, 'Mantlama: Ha Ntlama, 23 April 1966.

Pinda, Stephen: Mafeteng, 7 October 1965, 22 November 1965.

Sebatana, Letsema: Kolo, 20 November 1965.

Sesoane, Likatana: Mokanametsong (Villa Maria), 21 January 1966.

G MAPS

1. Courtesy of Craig W. Hincks
2. Courtesy of Craig W. Hincks
3. C.2755 (1881), opp. p. 288
4. Courtesy of Craig W. Hincks

H ILLUSTRATIONS

Illustrations are supplied by Morija Museum & Archives, except as follows:

3. The author.
12. De Beers Archives.
13. Western Cape Archives and Records Service, photograph AG15251.
15 and 54. Photographs by Duggan-Cronin (1933), reproduced with the permission of the McGregor Museum, Kimberley.
21. With kind permission of Morena Jeremiah Moshesh.

25, 27, 28 and 60. Lagden (1909).
26. National Archives and Records Service of South Africa.
29, 50 and 51. National Library of South Africa.
30. www.clement-jones.com/ps06/ps06_177.htm (30 Nov 2010)
31, 34, 35, 36 and 38. Sandra Burman (1981).
32. Orpen (1964).
33. Moffat (1969).
37. Courtesy of Défap, Paris.
39 http://en.wikipedia.org.wiki/File:SirJohnGordonSprigg.jpg (30 Nov 2010)
40. http://en.wikipedia.org.wiki/Charles_George_Gordon (30 Nov 2010)
41. University of Cape Town Libraries.
46. Dove (1959).
47. Taylor (1972).
48. *United Services Gazette*, 5 November 1908.
49. The Kaffrarian Rifles Association.
52. Tylden (1950A), who obtained it from the *Journal of the Society for Army Historical Research*.
53 and 58. *Illustrated London News*, 4 and 11 December 1880 respectively.
55 and 59. Museum Africa, Johannesburg.
56. James Walton (1958B).
57. *The Graphic*, 5 February 1881.
61. *Vanity Fair*, 22 August 1901.

INDEX

A

Abel Matete, **illustration 24;** 99.
Aborigines Protection Society (APS), 83, 90, 96-7, 100-1, 103, 179, 251.
Advance Post, 33, 35, 88, 107, 109, 114, 201.
Afrikander Party, 252.
Aliwal North, 78, 110, 138, 177, 182, 183, 191, 192, 200, 280.
Aliwal North, Convention of, 2, 13, 18, 22, 25, 26, 30, 39, 242, 251.
Alwyn's Kop, 65.
Ammunition, Basotho's acquisition of, 54, 59, 109, 133, 139, 162, 170, 171, 173, 270; Cape supplies before Gun War, 67, 107, 108, 110; Cape supplies during Gun War, 143, 145, 148, 168, 170, 174; Jonathan Molapo, gift to, 241; Mhlonhlo, proposed gift to, 156; Moorosi's, 73, 74; OFS supplies, 13, 126; OFS supplying to Basotho, 109, 139, 170; Peace Preservation Act, 1; Sand River Convention and Bloemfontein Convention, 13, 126; shell exploding in Moorosi War, 75; Zulu's, 127.
Anglican Church, see Church of England.
Armstrong gun, 76, 126.
Artillery, see 'Guns, artillery'.
Artillery Troop, CMR, 74, 135. (See also Cape Field Artillery.)
Assegai/spear, 56, 72, 75, 79, 80, 84, 98, 106, 109, 127, 128, 129, 154, 159, 163, 266.
Atmore, Anthony, v, 65, 177, 289.
Austen, John, background and character, 33-4; Commission on Native Laws and Customs, member of, 49; conspiracy theory, 57, 58; court, 46; drought, report on, 120; Gun War and death, 110, 146, 164, 182, 201; on guns and disarmament, 59, 60, 88; Jonathan and Joel Molapo, opinion on, 133; land allocation generally, 41-2; land allocation in Quthing district, 96, 105; and Moorosi, 35, 64, 65, 66, 68-71, 75, 79, 145.
Ayliff, William, 67, 85, 90, 100, 192.
Azariele's Nek, 159, 160.

B

Bailie, Alexander, 201, 205, 207, 209, 210, 218-9, 220, 229, 235, 239, 241, 249.
Bakoena, 71-2, 133, 203.
Balimo (ancestral spirits), 2, 50, 139, 178, 248, 270-1.
Bamonaheng, 18.
Baphuthi, 20, 27, 29, 33, 35, 63, 64-80, 82, 83, 87, 95, 96, 97, 126, 127.
Barkly, Arthur (Mabekebeke), **illustration 36;** Gun War, 109, 110, 111, 116, 125, 139, 142-4, 154, 160, 167; Lerotholi, comment on, 104, 114; as Magistrate Berea, 34; as Magistrate Mafeteng, 35; opinion quoted, 95; resignation, 201.
Barkly, Fanny, **illustration 38;** 110.
Barkly, Sir Henry (Ramabekebeke), **illustration 26;** 16-7, 20, 30, 32, 34-5, 36, 39, 41-2.
Barolong, 263.
Basutoland Annexation Act, 16-7, 217, 222, 251.
Basutoland Disannexation Bill, 252.
Basutoland Progressive Association, 267.
Bataung, 20, 27, 29, 33, 41, 99, 104, 116, 126, 131, 132, 144, 154, 158, 162, 193, 211.
Batlokoa, 7, 33, 140, 156, 164, 182, 206.
Battle-axe, 106, 128-9, 144, 154, 163, 266.
Bayly, Col. 'Zach', **illustration 50**; 77, 78-80, 116, 135-6, 139-40, 142, 146, 148-50, 156-7, 158, 165, 166, 181.
Bechuanaland Protectorate, 6, 256.
Bell, Major Charles Harland (Majorobelo), **illustration 34;** and Austen, 33; background and character, 32; chiefs, comment on, 53; Commission on Native Laws and Customs, member of, 49; death, 201; Gun War 109, 110, 140, 150, 152, 166-74, 181, 184; on guns and disarmament, 55, 60, 88, 105, 106; Langalibalele, comment on, 46-7, 58; as Magistrate Leribe, 34-5, 42; and Molapo, 23, 45, 47, 57; Sprigg, meeting with, 94; Zulu messengers, arrest of, 82.
Bell, Charles (son of Major Bell), **illustration 35;** Gun War, 106-7, 109, 150, 168; on guns and disarmament, 88; as Resident Magistrate, Berea, 35, 47; as Resident Magistrate, Leribe, 201, 202, 203, 204, 208, 210.
Bellairs, W.G., 226, 229, 230.
Berea, battle of the, 7.
Berea, district, 20, 29, 33, 34, 35, 41-2, 45, 47, 106, 194, 202, 211, 238.
Berea, mission station, 109, 134, 259.
Berea, plateau, 148, 166.

Bereng, **illustration 11**; drink, 260; genealogy, ix; and George Moshoeshoe, 26, 205, 206, 212-3; Gun War and antecedents, 1, 2, 106, 108, 109, 111, 131-2, 148, 153, 160; hut tax, 221-2; and independence, 244, 246, 252; and Jonathan and Joel Molapo, 241, 249, 253; and Lerotholi, 264-5; and Masupha, 212-4, 234; Moorosi War, 72, 73.

Blenheim, battle of, 100.

Bloemfontein. 98, 263, 280.

Bloemfontein Convention, 13.

Blyth, Matthew, **illustration 31**; 60-1, 242-3, 245-7, 249, 250, 252-7, 258, 259, 261.

Boegner, Alfred, 245.

Bohali, marriage cattle, 38, 49, 50, 239.

Boleka, 158, 159, 181, 182, 183, 184, 186, 192.

Boundaries between chiefs, 20, 25, 39-42, 242, 248, 249, 262.

Bowker, James, **illustration 29**; on disarmament, 88-9, 95; as Governor's Agent, 52-3, 61-2, 64-5, 67-8; as High Commissioner's Agent, 30, 33, 39, 41, 65; refusing post of Governor's Agent, 196; Rolland, comment on 32; Select Committee, evidence to, 38.

Brabant, Col. E.Y., **illustration 49**; 76-8, 155-7, 160-5, 180, 183.

Bradlow, Edna, v.

Brand, President Jan Hendrik, 11, 12, 13, 36, 106, 126, 139, 169, 242, 260, 263-4.

Brandy, 69, 198, 217, 260, 264.

Bright, Under-Secretary for Native Affairs, 98.

Brookes, Edgar, 267.

Brownlee, Charles, 30, 42, 55, 156.

Brummage, Samuel, 107, 109.

Buchanan, D.D., 26.

Buffaloes, Jonathan Molapo's regiment, 128.

Burgher Law, 137.

Burghers, in Gun War, 135, 137, 138, 154, 160-3, 172-3, 181-2, 183.

Burghers, in Moorosi War, 76, 77, 78.

Burman, Sandra, v, 4, 33, 50, 65.

C

Caledon river (Mohokare), 13, 22, 27, 116, 132, 146, 150, 167, 168, 169, 172, 174, 237, 240, 248, 252, 258.

Cape Argus, 94, 96, 128, 139, 200, 243, 280.

Cape Dutch, 78, 139, 160, 161, 165, 172, 242.

Cape Field Artillery, 162, 196.

Cape police, 258.

Cape Mercury, 94.

Cape Mounted Rifles (CMR), and Major Bell, 32; in Gun War and antecedents, 112, 113, 114, 115, 116, 125, 127-30, 135-7, 139, 140, 142-50, 154-66, 173, 182; after Gun War, 196, 202, 225, 239, 241, 247; in Moorosi War, 70, 72, 74, 76-9.

Cape Mounted Yeomanry, 70, 72-8, 135, 137-8, 140, 153-8, 163.

Cape Times, 200, 280.

Cape Town, 26, 31, 35, 49, 69, 99, 104, 105, 108, 133, 138, 143, 166, 175, 181-2, 217, 224, 233, 236, 252, 255.

Cape Town Rangers, 181-2.

Carnarvon, Lord, 4, 83, 84, 85.

Carrington, Col. Fred, **illustration 51**; 116, 136, 139, 140, 142-3, 145, 153-66, 183.

Casalis, Dr. Eugène, **illustration 43**; 31, 120, 134, 159-60, 162, 187.

Casalis, Eugène, 19, 28, 47, 90, 221.

Casualties, overall, in Gun War, v; in Moorosi War, 80.

Cathcart, Sir George, 7.

Cetshwayo, 2, 58, 82, 84, 126, 127, 133.

Chalmers, W.B., 59, 60, 196.

Chamberlain, Joseph, 113-4.

Christianity and Christians, 22, 23, 24, 28, 38, 49-50, 52, 83, 134, 171, 217, 224, 232, 236, 256. See also individual missions and missionaries.

Church of England, 23, 28, 29, 120, 169, 196, 228, 258.

Clarke, Charles Mansfield, **illustration 48**; 113, 134-7, 139-40, 142, 145, 146, 152, 153, 154-7, 160, 165, 181-4, 186-7, 192, 217, 225.

Clarke, Marshal, **illustration 60**; 33, 201, 257, 258-65, 266-8.

Clerks, 32, 34, 35, 53, 64, 65, 70, 88, 167, 201, 219.

Clifford, General, 113.

Cochet, Irénée, **illustration 24**; 99.

Coillard, Christina, 233, 236.

Coillard, François, 22, 23, 96, 247, 248, 249.

Colesberg, 172-3.

Commissariat, 78, 133, 137, 231.

Commission on Native Laws and Customs, 49.

Index

Confederation, 4, 82, 83-6, 88, 102-3, 113, 134, 270.
Conquered Territory, 2, 5, 29, 117-8, 132.
Conspiracy, African against whites, 5, 34, 54, 57-9.
Cornet Spruit District, 20, 27, 29, 33, 35, 40, 59, 64, 205.
Cotton, Henry, 183.
Courts, chiefs', 36, 44-9, 51, 53, 259, 263, 265, 266, 267.
Courts, magistrates', 32, 44-9, 53, 57, 65, 66, 68, 115, 241-2, 259, 262, 263, 265, 269.
Crimean War, 113.
Cripps, G. St. V., 14.
Crisp, Canon, 120.
Cunynghame, General Sir Arthur, 24, 135, 137.
Currie, Walter, 11.
Customs duties, 251, 258.

D

Dalgety, Captain, 153.
Damane, Mosebi, 6, 59, 178.
Daniel, John, 15.
Daumas, François, 26.
Davies, Henry Lee, clerk and assistant magistrate under Griffith, 34, 35, 47, 48, 76, 87, 88, 106, 119, 120, 166; assistant magistrate under Orpen, 201, 202, 206-7, 208, 210.
De Kiewiet, C.W., 5, 117-121.
Delagoa Bay, 127.
Derby, Earl of, 251, 252, 254, 255, 256.
Desertion from Cape forces, 173, 182, 183, 196, 239.
Diamond Fields, 2, 3, 4, 18, 36, 37, 54-9, 61, 84, 87, 88, 109, 118, 126, 127, 135, 257.
Diamond Fields Horse (aka Kimberley Horse), 138, 153, 158, 168-9, 170, 171-3, 181, 184, 280.
Diamond Fields Native Contingent, 150.
Diamond News, 169, 280.
Dieterlen, Hermann, 96, 125, 162, 180, 210, 211.
Disarmament, see under guns.
Disraeli, Benjamin, 83, 223.
Districts, boundaries and sub-divisions, 20-1, 23, 29, 34, 35, 39-40, 41-2, 64.
'Ditlame', 70.
Doda, see Lehana.

Dormoy, Amos, 170.
Drakensberg, war below Drakensberg, 140, 152, 156, 161, 164, 176-7, 179, 181-2; other, 19, 26, 58, 60, 61, 206, 231, 239.
Dress, Basotho's, 22, 23, 24, 26, 37, 38, 67, 92.
Drought, 5-6, 61, 117, 118-21, 238, 257.
Drunkenness among Basotho, 69, 114-5, 131, 180, 198, 217, 227, 245, 260.
Drunkenness among white forces, 135, 136, 138, 169, 173, 174, 196.
Duke of Edinburgh's Own Volunteer Rifles, 138, 153, 158.
Duvoisin, Louis, 109, 260, 262, 263, 267.
Dyke, Hamilton, **illustration 44;** 87, 89, 94, 103, 125, 176, 178, 181, 185, 186, 226.

E

East London, 85. 208, 219.
'Eating up', 4-5, 44-5, 48, 53, 106, 107, 108, 115, 117, 177, 198, 244, 249, 264.
Edinburgh, 32.
Education and schools, of Austen and Rolland, 32, 33, 34; *bahlalefi*, 267; in Basutoland, 22, 28, 65, 85, 93, 217, 225, 258; of chiefs, 22, 24, 25, 26-7, 132-3; of Stanton and Laurence, 152, 169.
Egyptian Gendarmerie, 258.
Eldredge, Elizabeth, 5, 121, 130-1.
Ellenberger, Frédéric, **illustration 45**, 34, 64, 65, 67, 70, 97.
'Emigrant Tambookieland', 'Emigrant Tembuland', 119, 220.
Enfield rifles, 55, 59, 126.
Erasmus, Willem, 163, 270.
Expenditure on Eastern Frontier War, 1877-8, 127.
Expenditure on Gun War, 179.
Expenditure on Moorosi War, 81.

F

Fabius Cunctator, 261.
Faku, 26, 60.
Ferreira, Captain, 169-73, 181, 184.
Ficksburg, 109, 172, 173.
Fines in chiefs' courts, 36, 44, 65.
Fingoland, 251.
First City Volunteers, Graham's Town, 138, 155, 179.

Fobane, 132, 150, 166, 241, 249.
Fort Bell, **illustration 57**, 32, 150, 168.
Fort Gordon, 146, 148-9, 165, 166.
France, 26, 27, 183, 217.
Fraser brothers, 142, 144, 145.
Frere, Sir Bartle, **illustration 27**; appointment, 34; confederation, 4, 83-4, 88, 103; departure, 143; disarmament, 86, 88-91, 96, 97-8, 99-100, 101-2, 108, 113-4, 256, 266, 270; and Gordon, 223; Gun War expectations, 3, 134; Masupha, comment on, 24; Molteno, dismisses, 61, 85.
Froude, James Anthony, 84-5.
Fuller, Thomas, 15, 101.

G

Garcia, Arthur, 226, 230, 231, 232, 233.
Gcaleka, 2, 3, 61, 62, 66, 68, 72, 82, 83, 85, 86, 93, 96, 113, 126, 127, 134, 135, 148.
George (Tlali) Moshoeshoe, **illustration 21**; background and character, 25, 26**;** Cape government, supporting, 26; courts, 53; disarmament and guns, 56, 87, 93; education, 25, 26; genealogy, viii; Griffith, opinion on, 31; Gun War and antecedents, 3, 106, 113, 114, 117, 118, 125, 134, 148, 150, 195; his messenger, 235; and Moorosi, 66; move to the Queen's Mercy, 220; as police officer, 26, 35, 62, 87; post-war discussions and settlement, 195, 197, 205, 206-9; Tsekelo's petition, 62.
Germond, Paul, 120, 125.
Gladstone, William, 101, 113-4, 165, 179, 224, 251, 255, 256.
Gold mines, 268.
Gordon, General Charles George, **illustration 40**; 5, 165, 222, 223-37, 238, 242.
Grahamstown, 31.
Grahamstown Journal, 37, 280.
Grant, J.M., 74-5, 155, 183.
Granville, A.K., 78.
Granville, Lord, 264.
Grey, Sir George, 30.
Griffith, Charles Duncan, **illustration 30**; and Austen, 33-4, 69, 70, 146; background and character, 31-2; Basotho's laws and customs, 49-50; Basutoland for Basotho, 15; and Bell, 32; command on Eastern Frontier, 52, 61, 72, 148; Commission on losses, member of, 228, 240; comparisons with Blyth and Orpen, 201-2, 257; conspiracy theories, 54, 57-9; constitutional position, 16-7, 30, 98, 99; courts, 44-6; disarmament and guns, 1, 3, 54-8, 60, 61-3, 84, 86-9, 93-6, 97, 99, 102, 104, 105, 107-9, 270; drought, 119; 'foundation story', 12; Gordon, 225, 229; Gun War and antecedents, 110-5, 117, 125, 126, 130, 138, 139, 146, 148, 149, 150, 152, 167, 168; Langalibalele, 58; land, 39-44; *letsema*, 49; Letsie, 21, 31, 46, 99; Molapo, 23; Moorosi, 64, 65, 66, 68-76, 78, 93; Orange Free State, 84-5, 106; peace negotiations, 179-81, 185-7; police, 48-9; policy of undermining chiefs, 6, 30, 36, 51; post-war negotiations and warnings, 192, 197, 207, 208, 225; Quthing, 97, 101; resignation, 196-7; stray stock, 49; 'success', 38, 52, 268; Tsekelo's petition, 61-3, 82.
Griffith, Paramount Chief, 267.
Griqua, 2, 60, 140, 156.
Griqualand East, 60, 140, 156, 177, 200, 243, 251.
Griqualand West, 3, 4, 36, 54, 59, 83.
Gun War, 1-7, 18, 20, 21, 22, 24, 26, 28, 31, 34, 35, 45, 53, 56, 57, 61, 99, 116, 118, 120, 121, 123-88, 203, 208, 214, 240, 248, 249, 257, 259, 261, 264, 267, 269, 270, 271.
Guns, disarmament, 1, 3, 4, 86-91, 92-6, 98-101, 104-9, 114-5, 150, 178, 186-8, 193, 194, 195, 197, 219, 249; incorporation, effect on discussions, 269; Jonathan Molapo, given to 241, 247, 249; Langalibalele, 42, 58; Letsie's accident, 21; licensing (registration), 187, 188, 192, 193, 194, 196, 198, 216, 220; Natal's policy, 14-5, 41, 58, 59, 87, 93; Ngqika and Gcaleka, 127; Pedi, 61, 84, 127; police guns, 35; purchase of guns, 13, 54-61, 118, 139; retention of guns, 5, 266; Zulu's guns, 127. For use of guns, see accounts of Moorosi War and Gun War, *passim*. See also different types of gun, e.g. Sniders and Martini-Henry rifles.
Guns, artillery, in Seqiti War, 13, 126; in Moorosi War, 72, 74, 75, 76, 78, 80, 125; in Gun War, 125, 133, 135, 146, 148, 149, 153, 154, 155, 157, 158, 160, 162, 163, 164, 165, 169, 183, 196.

H

Haileybury school, 169.
Hannibal, 261.
Heliograph, 165.

Hermon, 157, 162, 210.

Herschel Reserve, 60, 72, 119, 138.

Hicks Beach, Sir Michael, 83, 100, 223.

High Commission Territories, 6.

Hlasoa, ix, 133, 150, 171, 203, 204, 218-9, 241, 247, 253, 255, 262.

Hlotse Heights, 6, 29, 32, 35, 40, 47, 57, 67, 88, 92, 106, 109, 110, 120, 133, 138, 139, 150, 152, 159, 166, 168, 169, 170, 171, 172, 181, 184, 192, 195, 196, 201, 205, 209, 216, 218, 219, 228, 229, 230, 231, 236, 240, 247, 248, 249, 260, 262.

Hlotse river, 150, 171, 247, 249.

Hlubi, 27-8, 40, 42, 46, 48, 58, 95, 106, 150, 152, 168, 170, 171, 248.

Hoffman, President Josias, 200.

Hofmeyr, Jan Hendrik, 191, 252.

Hook, David Blair, 138, 226, 230, 234-5.

Hope, Hamilton, 35, 64-8, 79, 156, 252.

Hope Town, 161.

Horses, *passim*, but see in particular Basotho's acquisition of horses and development of 'Basotho pony', 129; CMR horses, 137, 144, 183; Gun War, 4, 129, 144, 145, 146, 152, 187; *mafisa*, 47; *Mateketoa*'s claim for horses, 194, 195; Moorosi War, 72, 77; Pedi, 127; police horses, 35; theft, 68.

'Hottentots', 138, 184.

House of Assembly, Letsie's petition, 99; *Mateketoa*'s petition, 218, 220; Matthews, 220; Orpen, 101, 200-1; proceedings (debates etc.), 15, 96, 99-100, 101, 103, 105, 113, 188, 196, 214, 217, 218, 222, 252; Sauer, 177, 191; Select Committee, 88.

Housing, Basotho, 22, 23, 26, 37, 142, 248.

Hut tax, 20, 30, 36, 37, 41, 42, 47, 50, 51, 53, 62, 66, 93, 95, 97, 216, 218, 221, 222, 225, 227, 230, 231, 232, 234, 235, 238, 245, 249, 254, 264. See also under percentage.

I

Incorporation into South Africa, 266, 269.

India, 32, 83, 100, 258.

Indian ocean, 12.

Initiation schools, 24, 38, 49, 50, 95, 128.

Ireland, 100, 200, 242, 258.

Isandhlwana, 2, 5, 69, 82, 102, 109, 127, 184.

J

Jackman's Drift, 116, 168.

Jacob Moletsane, **illustration 24;** 99.

Jacottet, Edouard, 260. 261.

Jeremiah Jobo, 108.

Jobo (Lelosa), viii, 56, 241.

Joel Molapo, **illustration 16;** background and character, 132-3; Cape rule, approval of, 37; genealogy, ix; Gun War, 132, 140, 150, 166-8, 170-2, 183, 184; Jonathan, conflict with, 104, 126-7, 132-3, 150, 168, 201, 203-5, 207, 210, 212, 218-9, 229, 237, 239-42, 247-50, 253, 257, 258, 261-3, 264; and Makhoakhoa, 27; marriage, 19; and Masupha, 131, 132-3, 207, 210, 211-3, 228, 229, 234; Moorosi War, 72; peace overtures, 174-5, 177-80, 183, 184, 188; post-war discussions and settlement, 192, 193, 194, 195, 201, 203-5, 210, 216, 218-9, 221, 222, 223, 244, 254-5.

Jonathan Molapo, **illustration 15;** background and character, 132-3; disarmament, 56-7, 105, 106, 112; independence, longing for, 267; genealogy, ix; Gun War, 3, 118, 134, 139, 140, 150, 166-8, 170-1, 178, 184; Joel, conflict with, see under Joel; land allocation, 43; Langalibalele, 58-9; Letsie's petition, 95; and Makhoakhoa, 27; marriage, 19; and Masupha, 19, 112, 210-3, 228-9, 263, 265; Moorosi War, 71, 72; post-war discussions and settlement, 207, 209, 218-20, 244, 246, 254; regiment, 128.

Josefa Molapo, ix, 18, 19, 106, 132, 203, 219, 240, 257.

Josiah Letsie, 116.

Jousse, Théophile, 109, 222, 225.

K

Kaffrarian Watchman, 243.

Kat River Settlement, 138.

Keck, Daniel, 245.

Kei river, 85.

Kennan, Thomas, 78, 144-5, 260, 262.

Khartoum, 222, 236.

Khethisa, ix, 133, 150, 167, 170, 171, 172, 203, 204, 239, 247, 253, 255, 262.

Khoikhoi, 2.

Khomokhoana river, 229.

Khubelu Pass, 112.

Kimberley, 36, 54, 169
Kimberley Horse, see Diamond Fields Horse.
Kimberley, Lord, 101, 114, 179, 181, 215.
King Edward VII, 269.
King William's Town, 35, 70, 78, 80, 111, 139, 145, 156, 196, 224-5, 243, 280.
Knobkerrie, 56, 129.
Koali Makhobalo, 107, 117, 146, 148, 150.
Koali's Kopje, 146, 148.
Kok, Adam, 60, 140.
Kokstad, 111, 152.
Kolo, 109, 125, 157-8.
Kolonyama, 241.
Korokoro, 15, 71, 107, 109, 221, 264.
Kruger, Paul, 160, 165.
Kuili, 1.

L

Lagden, Godfrey, **illustration 61;** 27, 258, 259, 261-5, 266-9.
Laing's Nek, 165, 256.
Lances, 136.
Land allocation, 39-44, 269. See also 'Placing' of chiefs.
Landry's Horse, 184.
Langalibalele, 42, 46, 58, 59, 67, 93, 112, 201, 258.
Lashes, 48, 67, 265.
Laurence, Captain William Moorsom, 169-74, 184, 280.
Lebihan, François, 177.
Lefu Ramarothole, 164.
Legislative Council, 217, 219, 222, 252.
Lehana (Doda), 65-70, 79.
Leicester-Smyth, 255.
Lekhooa (pl. *Makhooa*), 6, 67, 92.
Lelingoana Maketekete, 33, 140, 156, 164, 182, 206.
Leloaleng Technical School, 65.
Leluma Posholi, viii, 244.
Lenkoane, 73.
Leonard, James, **illustration 41.**
Lepoqo Masupha, ix, 71, 94, 95, 108, 148, 149, 162, 166, 198, 247-8.
Lerato valley, 162.
Leribe, district, 20, 23, 27, 29, 32, 33, 35, 40, 46, 106, 165, 166, 184, 194, 201, 203, 204, 207, 211, 218, 220, 227, 228, 237, 240, 242, 249, 250, 257.
Leribe, magistracy (before move to Hlotse Heights), 32, 47, 55.

Leribe, mission station, 134, 170, 248.
Leribe, pass, 247-8.
Leribe, plateau, 171, 239.
Leribe, village, 12, 22, 93, 133, 168, 220, 248, 249.
Lerotholi, **illustration 8;** Cape rule, attitude to, 54, 59, 244, 252; disarmament, 1-2, 5, 56-7, 104, 105, 106, 108; drink, 114-5, 180, 260; Gun War and antecedents, 1, 109, 110, 111, 112, 114-6, 125, 131, 132, 140, 142-5, 146, 154-6, 158, 164, 165, 167, 177-8, 182, 183-4; genealogy, ix; imperial government, relations with, 258, 263; and Joel and Jonathan Molapo, 203, 241, 244, 249, 253, 262; land allocation, 40-1, 44; Maama, rivalry with, 132, 214, 264-5, 266; marriage, 19; Masupha, conflicts with, 5, 112, 198, 203, 204, 209-14, 227, 228, 231-6; 264-5, 266, 267; Moorosi War, 67, 71, 73; peace negotiations, 174-5, 176-8, 179-80, 185-8, 191; and Orpen, 201, 223, 238; post-war discussions and settlement, 192-5, 198, 204-14, 216, 221, 244, 246, 254; praise poems, 1-3, 11, 22, 38, 71, 133, 139, 164, 189, 270, 271; Seqiti War, 11, 130, 203; succession to Letsie, 18, 132, 203.
Lesaoana, see Ramanella.
Leselinyana, 23, 48, 52, 63, 89, 94, 96, 263, 280.
Leshoboro Majara, ix, 25, 106, 108, 112, 115, 131, 148, 198, 211, 212.
Leshoboro Majara (interviewee), 177.
Letlatsa's village, 186.
Letsema (pl. *matsema*), work-party, 49, 206.
Letsie, **illustration 5;** advisers, 28, 82, 87, 108; background and character, 20-2, 53; Blyth, attitude to, 243, 257; Blyth's view of Letsie, 246, 249, 252, 253, 257; Cape rule generally, 30, 55, 239; chieftainship, general, 19, 20, 25, 29, 40; Christianity and Mabille, 22, 28, 50, 96, 102; constitution, 36, 98; courts, 44-8; death, 264; disarmament and guns, 1-3, 5, 56, 61, 84, 88, 92-6, 98-100, 103, 104-6, 108, 116; drink, 217, 260; genealogy, viii, ix; and Griffith, 21, 31, 46, 99; Gun War and antecedents; 3, 117, 130, 144, 156, 271; imperial rule, 259, 263-4; incorporation, 269; and Joel and Jonathan Molapo, 132, 240-1, 247-9, 253, 257, 262; land allocation, 41-4; Lelingoana, 164; *letsema*, 49; marriage arrangements, 19; and Maama, 132; and Masupha, 24-5, 41-2, 111-3, 198, 203, 209-14, 215, 227-32, 235, 252-3, 263, 265, 267; and

Molapo, 20, 22-4, 28, 29, 104, 263; and Moorosi, 66-7, 70-4, 77, 83; negotiations to avoid war, 111-5; and Orpen, 201, 221, 223, 243; peace negotiations, 177-9, 181, 185, 188, 191; post-war discussions and settlement, 193-5, 198, 205-14, 215-8, 221, 222, 225, 227-32, 235, 240, 244-6, 252-4; Quthing, confiscation of 97; Seqiti War, 11, 130; stray stock, 49; succession to, 18, 25, 115, 132, 203, 240, 257; Tsekelo's petition, 61-2, 82.

Letsie II, 267.

Letsosa, Daniel, 40.

Letuka, 68-9, 71, 79.

Lichaba, 116.

Lifaqane, 7, 19, 20, 27, 64, 129.

Likhoele, 44, 115, 131, 133, 142, 143, 144, 154, 155-6.

Lineo, 214.

Liphiring, 142,143, 144, 145, 154.

Lobengula, 58.

Loch, Sir Henry, 266, 269.

M

Maama, **illustration 9**; background and character, 132; and CMR deserters, 239; disarmament, 132; drink, 260; education, 132; genealogy, ix; Gun War and antecedents, 2, 110, 131, 148, 149, 153, 160, 162-3, 177, 270, 271; imperial rule, 254-5; and Jonathan and Joel Molapo, 241, 249, 253; land allocation, 43; Lerotholi, rivalry with, 132, 214, 264-5, 266; marriage, 132; and Moorosi, 71; peace negotiations, 177-9; post-war discussions and settlement, 212-3, 221, 234, 244, 246; praise poems, 6, 7, 71, 92, 132, 149, 163-4, 178, 214, 270, 271; regiment, 128.

Mabelete (sing. *Lebelete*), aka rebels, origin of name, 3. For other references, *passim*.

Mabille, Adèle, 21, 28, 217.

Mabille, Adolphe, **illustration 42;** 14, 21, 22, 28, 83, 89, 95, 96, 98, 102, 195, 216, 217, 221, 226, 227, 246, 258.

Maboloka (aka Makoaisberg), 155.

Maclear, 156.

Maeder, François, 52, 104, 129, 162.

Mafeteng, v, 34, 35, 46, 57, 59, 64, 74, 104, 109, 110-1, 114, 115, 116, 131, 139, 142, 144-6, 149, 152-62, 164, 165-6, 167, 168, 170, 172, 176, 181, 192, 195, 199, 201, 207, 209, 216, 220, 226, 260.

Mafeteng district, 34, 35, 194, 205, 222.

Mafisa, 19, 23, 38, 47.

Maikela, 66-7.

Maitin, C.J., 65, 70, 88, 176.

Maize, 18, 38, 119, 120, 133, 172, 177.

Majara, viii, ix, 19, 25, 131, 211, 264.

Majuba, 165, 183, 256.

Makhabane, viii, 19, 25.

Makhoakhoa, 27, 193.

Makoae, 182.

Makoaisberg, see Maboloka.

Makosholo, Filibert, 48.

Makotoko, Nathanael, **illustration 24;** 24, 56, 99, 168, 171, 229.

Maloti, 11, 18, 42, 72, 73, 109, 120, 130, 133, 162, 164, 176, 201, 206.

Mangoaela, Z.D., 6.

Mapeshoane Posholi, viii, 108, 112.

Mapoteng, 25.

Marlborough, Duke of, 100.

Martini-Henry rifles, 126, 127, 136, 157, 161, 162, 169, 170, 241.

Martins Masupha, 148.

Maseru, **illustration 56; sketch map 147;** 1, 26, 34, 35, 38, 39, 40, 47, 48, 49, 66, 71, 72, 77, 87, 88, 92, 93, 105, 106, 110, 114, 115, 116, 119, 120, 131, 132, 139, 142, 145, 146-50, 154, 156, 158, 159, 160, 165, 166, 167, 168, 170, 181, 183, 184, 186, 192, 195, 196, 197, 201, 207, 209, 219, 220, 221, 228, 230, 231, 232, 233, 238, 239, 243, 244, 258.

Maseru sub-district, 34, 35, 202, 206.

Masite, 109, 125, 131, 183, 185.

Masitise, 64, 97, 134, 199.

Massyn's Farm, 153.

Masupha, **illustration 7**; background and character, 24-5; and Barkly, Arthur, 34; Cape government, approval of, 59; Christianity, 24, 50; 'conspiracy', 59; courts, 45, 47, 53, 252; death, 265; defeat in 1898, v, 264-5, 266; disarmament and guns, 55, 88, 94, 95-6, 102, 104, 105, 106, 108, 109, 219; drink, 198, 245, 260; genealogy, viii, ix; and General Gordon, 224, 225-36, 238; Gun War and antecedents, 2, 5, 6, 24, 45, 107, 109, 110, 111-3, 114-5, 125, 131, 132, 133, 139-40, 146,

148, 149, 150, 158, 162, 165, 166, 171, 176, 178, 183; hut tax, 51, 95, 222; imperial rule, 261, 262-3, 264; and Jonathan, 112, 133, 150, 253; land, 25, 26, 40, 41-2, 43, 222; *letsema*, 49; and Letsie, 20, 22, 25, 29, 41-2, 106, 111-3, 114-5, 193, 209, 210-1, 213-4, 215, 257; marriage arrangements, 19, 133; Moorosi, 71; newspapers, 102; peace negotiations, 177, 178, 179, 180, 181, 188; post-war settlement and discussions, 192-5, 197, 198-9, 201-8, 209-14, 215, 216, 218, 219, 220, 221-2, 223, 241, 244, 245-50, 252, 253, 254-7, 258, 259, 267, 270; Ramanella, conflicts with, 25, 40, 260, 262, 264; Seqiti War, 24, 130; succession to Letsie, 25; Tsekelo's petition, 62; and Tokonya, 28, 40, 106, 109, 110, 150, 171.

Matatiele, 26, 50, 176, 206, 212.

Matebele (sing. Letebele), 58.

'Matebele' (sing. 'Letebele', name given to Hlubi and also term of abuse), 27-8. 167, 195, 203.

Mateketoa (sing. *Leteketoa*) aka loyalists, disarmament, 93, 104-8; Gun War and antecedents, 26, 56, 110-2, 114-6, 118, 125, 134, 138, 140, 142, 146, 148, 150, 152, 158, 162, 165, 166, 168, 169-71, 177, 178; origin of name, 3; post-war discussions and settlement; 52, 179, 186, 187, 188, 192, 194-5, 197, 198, 201-10, 212-3, 216, 217-21, 224, 228, 229, 238-9, 241, 244-7, 249, 252, 263, 270.

Matela, 27, 193.

Mathebe, 183.

'Mathlelebe', 14.

Matsieng, **illustration 1;** 1, 20, 28, 158, 160, 162, 178, 179, 184, 198, 201, 240.

Matthews, Dr. J.W., 220.

Mauritius, 223.

Medicine, 80, 164, 167.

Merriman, John, **illustration 41;** 38, 101, 102, 126, 191, 223, 225, 226, 235, 242, 250, 251-3, 256, 267.

Mfengu ('Fingoes'), 2, 27, 28, 34, 61, 72, 73, 76, 77, 79, 83, 86, 87, 138, 149.

Mhlonhlo, 156, 176, 252.

Migrant labour, in the Cape generally, 29; at the Diamond Fields, 36-7, 54-8, 109; general, 117-8, 119; on gold mines, 268; in the Orange Free State, 29, 109; on railways, 3, 37, 55-7.

Millet, 18, 66, 119, 120, 133, 247.

Milner, Sir Alfred, 265, 266.

Missionaries, references to PEMS missionaries generally, Basotho customs, 49-50; 'Basutoland for Basutos', 15; Cape government, support for, 28, 38, 52; Marshal Clarke, support for, 258; courts, comment on, 47; disarmament and guns, 3, 59, 89-90, 91, 96, 97, 98, 101-2, 107, 125, 128, 195, 202; drought, 119-20, 121; and Frere, 83; and Griffith, 31, 89-90; Gun War, 159, 182, 195; imperial rule, comment on, 260; and Letsie, 22; and Maama, 132; malcontents, comment on, 54; and Masupha, 24; and Molapo, 22; peace initiative, 177, 178, 179, 181, 185-6; *pitso*s, attending, 92, 246, 254; post-war settlement, 195; Quthing, confiscation of, 97; and Sauer, 191. See also individual missionaries.

'Mamosa, 239.

'Masenate, vii, 18, 240.

Modderpoort, 228.

Moffat, John Smith, **illustration 33;** 238, 239, 245.

Moffat, Robert, 238.

Mofoka's Nek, 234.

Mohale, viii, 25, 33, 42, 48, 64, 132, 158.

Mohale's Hoek, 29, 33, 35, 46, 64, 67, 106, 107, 110, 111, 114, 120, 142, 145, 153, 154, 176, 199, 201, 210, 216, 222, 239.

Mohapeloa, J.M., v.

Mohapi Letsie, 239.

Mohlomi, 19.

Mohlongoafatše, 37.

Moiketsi Masupha, ix, 265.

Moiketsi Moletsane, 211, 213.

Mojela, **illustrations 12 and 24;** ix, 99, 153, 205, 211, 213, 244, 246, 253, 260.

Mokhachane, viii, 1, 2, 271.

Mokhahlane, Jan, 167.

'Mokhale', 185.

Mokhokhung, 42.

Mokhotlong district, 206.

Molapo, **illustration 6**; advisers, 24, 56, 99, 171, 229; background and character, 22-4; and Bell, 35, 42, 47; Cape rule generally, 53, 55; Christianity, 23, 50; courts, 45, 57; death, 105; dispute over succession and estate, see under Jonathan and Joel; genealogy, viii, ix; guns and disarmament, 55-7, 92, 93, 95, 104, 105; houses, 23, 248; Langalibalele, 42, 46-7, 58; *letsema*, 49; and Letsie, 20, 23-4, 28, 29, 104, 263; Makhoakhoa, 27; marriages, 19; and Masupha, 25, 40; placing of Jonathan and Joel, 132; police, 28, 57; and Moorosi, 71; and Ramanella, 25, 40; Seqiti War, 11, 22, 130; succession to Letsie, 18, 115, 240; Tsekelo's petition, 62; wealth, 23.

Moleko, 202-3.

Moletsane, **illustration 17;** 20, 27, 29, 33, 41, 99, 104, 116, 125, 131, 132, 144, 154, 155, 193, 211.

Moletsane, Jacob, **illustration 24;** 99.

Moliboea Molapo, ix, 239.

Molomo Mohale, **illustration 23;** viii, 210, 211, 244.

Molteno, John, 30, 61, 85, 191.

Moorosi, **illustration 18;** and Austen, 33, 64, 65, 66, 68-71, 75, 79; disarmament, 70, 77, 88, 89; and Hope, 35, 64-8, 79, 156; Moorosi War and confiscation of Quthing, 2-3, 4, 5, 27, 34, 63, 64-81, 83, 87, 88, 89, 91, 93, 94, 96, 97, 100, 111, 120, 125, 127, 128, 132, 135, 136, 137-8, 146, 206; semi-independence, 20, 27, 29, 97; Seqiti War, 27.

Mopeli, viii, 11, 25, 130.

Morija, **illustration 2;** 28, 67, 70, 98, 114, 120, 131, 159-60, 162, 179, 180, 183, 186, 192, 194, 201, 216, 220, 226, 227, 228, 230-4, 236, 243, 244, 258.

Morisse, James, 90.

Moroka, 263.

Moshoeshoe, **illustration 4;** as ancestral spirit, 1, 2, 50, 60, 271; annexation of Basutoland, 11-5, 101, 253, 254; Baphuthi, 64, 97; Barolong, 263; *boikokobetso*, 175; and Casalis, 28; death, 30, 240; disarmament, 14-5; Faku's cession of land, 26, 60; genealogy, viii; George Moshoeshoe, 26; government, nature of, 19-20, 27, 29, 193, 267; hut tax, 62; land allocation, 39, 44; Letsie, comparison with, 21-2; Letsie's marriage arrangements, 243; magistrates, 13-4; military system, 128-9; policy towards whites, 2, 21, 36, 52, 254, 268, 269; Molapo, 24; Orpen, 113, 200; Senekal's War, 129-30; Seqiti War, 11-3, 126, 130; succession arrangements, 18, 25, 115, 240; Thaba-Bosiu, 111, 129; Tsekelo, 26; Zulu, 82.

Motšoene, ix, 18, 25, 240, 247, 257, 264.

Mount Carmel, 236.

Mount Moorosi, **illustration 52;** 27, 64-81 (*passim*), 94, 100, 125, 135, 136.

Mpiti, ix, 132.

Mpoba, 95.

Mpondo, 26, 60.

Mpondomise, 139, 156, 176, 252.

Murder, 44, 48, 60, 156, 231, 245, 249, 252, 253, 259.

Muskets, 126, 129, 266.

Muzzle-loaders, 127, 241.

N

Natal, 12, 13-5, 22, 26, 42, 58, 59, 83-5, 87, 93, 118, 127, 138, 152, 256, 258.

Native Affairs, Department of, 16, 30, 67, 85, 98, 100, 177, 191.

'Native levies' or 'native contingents' in Gun War, 135, 138-9, 143, 148, 150, 153, 154, 162, 165, 168, 170, 172, 195, 196.

'Native levies' or 'native contingents' in Moorosi War, including Basotho, 67, 68, 71-3, 75, 76, 77, 79, 80.

Nehemiah (Sekhonyana) Moshoeshoe, **illustration 19;** accused of incitement to rebellion, 60-1, 200, 243; background and character, 25-6; confederation, 84; evidence on wishes of chiefs and people, 244, 247; genealogy, viii; Gun War and antecedents, 1, 56, 112, 117, 118, 148, 150; land, 42-3; Matatiele, 25-6; Quthing, move to, 220; regiment, 128.

Nettelton, Captain, 201 226, 231, 235.

Newspapers, colonial. See under press.

Ngqika, 2, 3, 61, 62, 66, 68, 82, 83, 85, 86, 93, 96, 113, 126, 127, 134, 135, 148.

Nguni, 7, 27-8, 64.

Nkuebe, **illustration 13;** ix, 108, 132, 153, 212, 214, 221, 234, 239, 252, 263.

Nomansland, 26, 58.

Ntoa ea Lepatla-patla (Battle of Helter-Skelter Flight), 240.

Ntho, **illustration 24;** 14, 22, 27-8, 43-4, 46, 49, 71, 87, 99, 104, 107-8, 113, 116.

Nthoana, 1.

Ntsane Moshoeshoe, viii, 35, 62, 105, 114, 117, 118, 150, 207.

O

Orange Free State (OFS), acquisition of land, 13, 39,

132, 204; Aliwal North Convention, 30; Basotho living and working in OFS, 29, 37, 109; Basotho refugees, 29, 106, 108, 150, 170, 237, 240, 241, 242, 248, 249, 260; boundary questions, 33; brandy, 260; confederation, 83, 84, 85; danger for Basotho of war with OFS, 36, 55-6, 57, 89, 117, 215, 231, 244, 245, 251, 254, 255, 256, 264, 266, 268; fears of Basotho attack, 54, 60, 264; Gun War, providing arms and ammunition to Basotho, 109, 139, 170; Gun War, allowing passage to colonial troops, 139, 144, 145, 153, 165, 168, 170, 172; Gun War, rioting by Cape troops in OFS, 138, 169, 183; imperial government, 225; Moorosi War, 76; Mopeli, 11, 25; OFS official, 180; Orpen, 200; security of border, 251-2; Senekal's War, 7, 20, 129, 270; Seqiti War, 2, 7, 11-3, 14, 19, 20, 22-3, 26, 30, 34, 39, 126, 130, 132, 176, 187, 270; Thaba Nchu, 263-4; Tsekelo in police, 26;

Orange, river (Senqu), 27, 35, 57, 64, 67, 70, 71, 73, 76, 103, 146, 164.

Orange River Sovereignty, 7, 57, 84, 93, 200.

Orpen, Joseph Millerd, **illustration 32;** appointment as Governor's Agent, 196-7; background and character, 200-1; Blyth, comparison with, 257; campaign against him, 218-20; Clarke, comparison with, 259, 261-3, 265, 267; Gordon's intervention, 223-35, 238; Joel/Jonathan conflict, 241-2; Leshoboro, comment on, 25; Masupha, attempt to coerce, 209-14; Moshoeshoe, mission to, 200; policy after Gordon, 238-9; policy of 'expectation', 220-2; policy of 'ultimatum', 215-7; post-war discussions and settlement, 194, 198, 200-9; Quthing, motion on, 101; replaced, 242-3; Rolland, brother-in-law of, 32; Seqiti War, comment on, 126; Sprigg, mission with, 113-6, 117, 197.

P

Palmietfontein, 35, 66, 69, 70, 72, 73.

Paris, 32.

Paris Evangelical Missionary Society (PEMS), 15, 28, 47, 52, 59, 90, 96, 100, 134, 159, 221, 245, 251.

Peace Preservation Act, 1878, 1, 61, 83, 86, 88, 90, 95, 97-101, 220-1, 270.

Pedi, 2, 3, 57, 61, 69, 84, 94, 96, 126, 127-8, 258, 270.

Peete, Moshoeshoe's grandfather, 139, 271.

Peete Lesaoana, viii, 108, 148, 262.

Peka, 241.

Percentage of hut tax paid to chiefs, 20, 41-2, 47, 51, 53, 95.

Phahameng, 70.

Phoqoane, 161, 162.

Phuthiatsana river (district boundary), 211-2, 257.

Phuthiatsana river (near Thaba Bosiu), 131.

Piet (Pita) Mokolokolo, 207, 208, 245, 254.

'Placing' (of chiefs), 19, 20, 25, 27, 39, 43, 44, 69, 70, 72, 105, 118, 132, 203, 206, 221, 222, 239.

Ploughs and ploughing, 11, 18, 36, 37, 42, 43, 50, 56, 112, 118, 194, 197, 202-3, 204, 206, 207, 240.

Police, Basutoland, **illustration 59;** Bell's police, 35; chiefs' attitude towards 28, 45, 48, 57; chiefs, employed as policemen, 26, 27, 35, 62, 87, 239; Derby's proposal, 251; establishment of Basutoland Native Police, 35; Gordon's proposal, 232; Gun War and antecedents, 106, 107, 109, 110, 113, 116, 138, 140, 142, 143, 144, 146, 148, 149, 150, 152, 158, 162, 166, 167, 170, 208, 219; under imperial rule, 259; post-war position, 196, 247; in Quthing, 65, 67, 69, 70; reluctance to join, 28, 45; Scanlen's proposal for new force, 225, 228; Sprigg's proposal, 93; Zulu, employment of, 28, 45, 48.

Police, Frontier Armed and Mounted, 11, 30, 31, 33, 35, 47, 135.

Police, white, 69, 72, 135, 258.

Polygamy, 19, 22, 38, 49-50.

Popolosi Mopheti, 193.

Population, 18-9, 27, 28, 37, 39, 54, 64, 88, 127, 129, 255.

Posholi, viii, 25, 33, 42, 132, 145, 158, 241.

Praise poems, 1, 2, 6-7, 9, 11, 22, 24, 33, 38, 71, 73, 92, 132, 133, 139, 145, 149, 163-4, 167-8, 178, 182, 189, 195, 203, 214, 270-1

Press, colonial, 54, 76, 96, 102, 154, 157, 181, 202, 208, 213, 218, 219, 222, 225, 243, 261, 280. See also individual newspapers.

Prince Alfred's Guard, 138, 153, 158.

Prison and prisoners, 27, 48, 68, 69-70, 80, 125, 135, 150, 243.

Prisoners in war, 78, 79, 162, 176, 177, 180.

Prophets and prophetesses, 50, 60, 115, 249.

Q

Qalabane, 133, 153-4, 155.

Qalo, 132, 204, 240.

Qiloane, 41-2.

Qoaling, 146, 148.

Queen Victoria, 2, 11, 12, 14, 16, 17, 20, 26, 29, 35, 39, 40, 43, 50, 53, 55, 56, 60, 62, 63, 71, 87, 92, 95, 97-101, 104, 112, 115, 125, 159, 175, 180, 193, 197, 200, 220, 222, 229, 234, 242, 244, 246, 251, 254, 255, 256, 257, 260.

The Queen's Mercy, 220.

Queenstown, 200.

Quthing, magistracy and district, 4, 27, 35, 64, 65, 69, 70, 80, 81, 88, 92, 96-7, 99, 101, 104, 105, 110, 117, 118, 120, 121, 142, 146, 164, 180, 185, 195, 201, 206, 207, 208, 210, 212, 215, 216, 220-1, 239, 252, 257, 258, 263.

Quthing, river, 73, 78.

R

Railway construction, 3, 37, 55, 56-7.

Rainfall, 112, 119, 120, 133, 134, 159, 162, 163, 164, 167, 172, 174, 182, 183, 196, 233, 234, 239. See also drought.

Raisa, 65-6.

Raliemere's, 162.

Ramabilikoe Matete, **illustration 24;** 22, 82, 87, 99, 104-5, 164.

Ramabilikoe's village, 164.

'Ramahopu', 185.

Ramakha, aka Setenane, 270.

Ramanella, aka Lesaoana, attitude to Cape rule after Gun War, 244, 246, 250; attitude to imperial government, 254, 255, 258; disarmament, 108; drink, 260; 'eating up', 45, 53; genealogy, viii; Gun War and antecedents, 111, 115, 131-2, 133, 148, 150, 166, 167, 168, 171, 183, 184; and Jonathan and Joel Molapo, 241, 247, 249, 253; land allocation, 43; loss of land, 25; marriage arrangements, 19; Masupha, conflicts with, 25, 40, 260, 262, 264; Molapo, conflicts with, 25, 40-1; peace negotiations, 179-80; post-war discussions and settlement, 198, 204, 210-2, 241; Zulu messengers, 82.

Reeds, 40-1, 43.

Regulations, Robinson's, 259, 263.

Regulations, Scanlen's, 245-6, 250, 252.

Regulations, Wodehouse's and Barkly's, 30, 39, 44, 50, 62.

Reserves, Government, 40, 43, 62, 205, 207.

Revolvers, 106, 116, 136, 154, 173.

Rhodes, Cecil, **illustration 41;** 228, 229.

Rifles, 13, 55, 59, 67-8, 79, 110, 116, 126, 127, 129, 136, 143, 148, 154, 157, 158, 160, 161, 162, 165, 167, 173, 174, 188, 266.

Roads (significant references only), 31, 38, 65, 72, 93, 111, 133, 143, 162, 164, 169, 174, 182, 183, 225.

Robben Island, 112, 115, 195.

Robinson, Sir Hercules, **illustration 28**; appointment as Governor and High Commissioner, 113, 178-9; award, making of, 184-8, 191; award, cancellation of, 216-7; award, compliance with, 194, 196, 198, 203, 207, 208-9, 210-6, 227; Marshal Clarke, opinion of, 268; imperial rule, 259, 261, 264, 267; peace negotiations 179-81; policy, change of, 242; transfer of Basutoland to imperial government, 251-2, 255;

Rolland, Elise, 200.

Rolland, Emile, **illustration 37**; appointment as Assistant Commissioner, 32, 34; appointment as superintendent of schools, 34; background and character, 32; Commission on Native Laws and Customs, member of, 49; courts, 45, 46, 48; disarmament and guns, 56, 59, 89; 'eating up', 48, 53; Gordon's view of, 235; Griffith, acting for, 32, 61, 66-7; land allocation, 40, 41, 43; and Moorosi and Hope, 66, 68, 70-1; opinions on chiefs, chieftainship, etc., 21, 23, 28, 29, 37, 38, 43, 52, 57-8, 118, 134, 221, 222; and Orpen, 114-5, 200, 210, 211, 218; Orpen, acting for, 217, 220; Surmon, opinion on, 201-2; Tsekelo's petition, 62.

Rolland, Samuel, 32.

Roma, 29, 177.

Roman Catholics, 28-9, 132, 177, 196.

Royal Artillery, 169.

S

Saint John's, 251.

Samuel Lehulere, 263.

San, 64.

Sand River Convention, 13.
Sandile, 62.
Sarili, 61, 62.
Sauer, J.W., **illustration 41;** 177, 191-9, 203-11, 213, 216, 217-8, 220-1, 223, 226-37, 239, 240-5, 247, 250, 257.
Scanlen, Thomas, **illustration 41;** 5, 191, 192, 197, 199, 214, 216, 217-8, 223, 225-6, 233-4, 236, 243-5, 247, 250, 261.
Schermbrucker, Commandant, **illustration 59;** 113, 148-9, 208, 219, 224.
Sebapala river, 73.
Sebothoane, 167, 184, 248.
Seeiso, **illustration 10**; ix, 2, 132, 149, 153, 179, 205, 212, 213, 214, 243, 255, 260.
Seetsa Molapo, 150.
Sekake Molomo, 48.
Sekese, Azariel, 23, 24, 52, 149.
Sekhukhune, 2, 61, 80, 84, 94, 126, 127.
Selebalo Moshoeshoe, 42, 106.
Select Committee into affairs of Basutoland, 217, 224.
Select Committee into causes of Moorosi War, 88.
Senate, ix, 18, 19, 240, 248, 257.
Senekal's War, 129. 130.
Senekane Masupha, ix, 158, 162, 231.
Sepechele's, 162, 173, 270.
Seqiti War, 13, 14, 21, 22, 23, 24, 25, 27, 29, 34, 37, 38, 41, 64, 126, 130, 131, 132, 133, 176, 187, 200, 256.
Seshope Lesaoana, 241.
Setaka Ranthako, 164.
Setha Matete, 22, 71, 246.
Sethabathaba, 182,193.
Seychelles, 224.
Shepstone, Theophilus, 61, 84, 102, 126, 139, 258.
Shervinton, Captain C.R. St. Leger, 143, 144, 162, 163, 164, 183.
Shields, 127, 128.
Siloe, 104, 162, 194.
Simon's Bay, 83.
Smallpox, 257, 259.
Smith, Sir Harry, 57.
Smith Posholi, 108.
Sniders, 48, 126, 127, 136-7, 138, 152, 157, 241.
Sofonia (Pii) Moshoeshoe, **illustration 20;** background and character, 25-6; disarmament, 56, 57, 87, 93, 105; evidence on wishes of people and chiefs, 52, 244, 245; genealogy, viii; Gun War and antecedents, 3, 112, 114, 117, 118, 134, 148, 150; house, 26; land, 43, 44, 118; Moorosi War, 66; police inspector, 26, 35; post-war settlement, 207; Tsekelo's petition, 62.
South African Republic (SAR), 61, 83, 84, 127, 139, 258. See also Transvaal.
Southey, Colonel, 76, 145.
Southey, Richard, 15, 38, 59, 235.
Spear, see assegai.
Sprenger, Lieutenant, 79, 80.
Sprigg, Gordon, **illustration 39**; appointment as Prime Minister, 61; confederation, 4, 85, 103; disarmament and policy of 'vigour', 4, 61, 62, 81, 83, 85-8, 90-1, 92-5, 96-7, 98-100, 107, 108, 117, 121, 134; 191, 219, 256, 266, 270; Frere, opinion of, 103; Gun War and antecedents, 3, 102, 105, 106-8, 111, 113-6, 117, 125-6, 128, 134, 137-9, 142-3, 146, 148, 153, 177, 178, 179, 182, 184, 200, 224; hut tax, 93, 97, 238; Moorosi War and confiscation of Quthing, 69-70, 72, 77-8, 81, 91, 96-7, 100, 101; opposition, leader of, 191, 196, 207, 215, 218; resignation, 188; response to peace overtures, 179-81, 185, 186, 188, 191; Scanlen, comparison with, 191, 192, 261; Tsekelo, moved by, 27.
Stanton, John, 152, 169, 172.
Stanton's Light Horse, 138, 152, 166, 169, 172, 173.
Stenson, E.W., 120.
Stock theft, 27, 36, 48, 68, 119, 225.
Stockenstrom Rifle Volunteers, 138.
Strahan, Sir George, 113, 175, 178.
Stray stock, 49.
Surmon, Captain, 74-5.
Surmon, William, Acting High Commissioner's Agent, 30; appointment to Advance Post, 33; appointment to Mafeteng, 34; appointment to Mohale's Hoek, 35; background and character, 33; brother to Captain Surmon, 74; Commission on Native Laws and Customs, member of, 49; courts, 45; drink, report on, 260; Gordon's view of, 235; Gun War and antecedents, 106, 107, 110, 111, 145, 153; harvest, report on 119; land allocation, 40; post-war discussions and settlement, 194, 201-2, 205, 210, 211, 245.
Swazi, 2, 6, 84, 127, 128.

T

Tainton, 76.
Taiping rebellion, 223.
Tarka division, 182.
Tax collectors, 26, 27.
Taylor, Dr. Henry, **illustration 47;** 6, 23, 32, 40, 67-8, 92, 133, 150, 152, 169, 171, 172, 173, 174, 201, 219, 228, 236.
Tele river, 35, 65, 70, 71, 73.
Teyateyaneng, 262.
Thaba Nchu, 263-4.
Thaba-Bosiu, **illustration 3;** 11-2, 13, 19, 24, 25, 29, 41-2, 59, 60, 105, 109, 111-3, 114, 115, 125, 129, 130, 131, 195, 198, 210-3, 215, 231-5, 236, 245.
Thaba-Bosiu District, 20, 31-2, 33, 34, 35, 40, 41-2, 43, 106, 194, 202, 205, 206.
Thaba-Bosiu mission station, 109, 134, 195, 231.
Thabana-Morena, 120, 134.
Thaba-Tšoeu, 159. 162.
Thebe Masupha, ix, 231, 235.
Theko, **illustration 14;** ix, 131-2, 148, 179, 213, 253, 255, 260, 265.
Thembu, 27, 33, 61, 64, 79, 86, 87, 140, 146, 156, 176, 219.
Thembuland (Tembuland) 219, 251.
Theunissen, Commandant, 172-3.
Tokonya, 28, 40, 106, 109, 110, 150, 152, 168, 170, 171, 248.
Trade in arms and ammunition, 13, 55, 60, 90, 109, 126, 127, 139, 170.
Trade generally, 36-7, 38, 83, 119, 146, 168, 238, 251, 256, 268.
Traders in Basutoland, 25, 32, 37, 70, 71, 90-1, 92, 94, 104-5, 107, 109, 142, 146, 188, 192, 194, 209, 217, 220, 254.
Trafalgar, Battle of, 169.
Transkei, 2, 6, 66, 68, 156, 177. 201, 242, 256.
Transvaal, 2, 5, 54, 69, 80, 87, 94, 102, 118, 128, 139, 160, 161, 163, 165, 169, 183, 196, 258.
Transvaal Horse, 169, 170, 171-2, 173, 181, 184.
Trower, Richard, 148, 149.
Tsakholo, 157.
Tsate, 84, 128.
Tsekelo Moshoeshoe, **illustration 22;** background and character, 25, 26-7; on confederation, 84, 88; on 'conspiracy', 57; on constitutional issue, 16; courts, 45; disarmament and guns, 55, 56, 88, 93, 105; education, 25, 26; genealogy, viii; Gun War and antecedents, 3, 113, 114, 117, 118, 148, 150; petition, 49, 61-2; as a policeman, 23, 35, 61; stock thief, 27, 48; on powers of chiefs, 53.
Tšepinare Letsie, 213, 260.
Tšepinare Moroka, 263.
Tsikoane, 150, 166, 167, 170, 247, 249, 257, 262.
Tšita Mofoka, 15, 50, 56, 244.
Tšita's Nek, 159.
Tsolo, 156.
Tswana, 2.
Tweefontein, battle of, aka Battle of the Swords, 164.
Tyali, 146.
Tylden, Major Geoffrey, v, 80.

U

Umtata, 156, 176.
Upington, Thomas, 86, 90, 93, 99, 215, 217, 218, 252.

V

'Vigour', policy of, see under Sprigg.
Volunteer Act, 138.
Volunteers, in Gun War, 89, 110, 116, 128, 129, 135, 136, 137-40, 144-9, 152-5, 157, 158, 161, 165, 169, 173, 181, 182, 183, 184; in Seqiti War, 14; in event of war with Orange Free State following abandonment, 256. See also individual corps.
Vultures (Maama's regiment), 128, 214.

W

Wagons, 11, 22, 36, 37, 38, 56, 65, 71, 110, 142, 144, 153-4, 155, 157, 164, 170, 172, 174, 198, 212, 217, 241.
Wardmasters, 39-40.
Wavell, Colonel, 183.
Wepener, 109, 110, 125, 143, 145, 153, 160, 162.
Wesleyans, 15, 33, 80, 183.
Western Levies, 182.
Westley-Richards rifles, 126, 127, 136, 160.
Wheat, 18, 38, 119, 120.
Widdicombe, Canon John, **illustration 46;** 23, 168, 171, 174, 184, 196, 201, 229, 236, 240, 247, 248,

260, 263.
Winchester repeaters, 160.
Witchcraft, 11, 44.
Wittebergen Native Reserve, 33.
Witzieshoek, 11, 25.
Wodehouse, Sir Philip, **illustration 25;** annexation of Basutoland, 2, 12-7, 64, 97, 130, 256; and Austen, 33; 'Basutoland for the Basutos', 4, 15, 97, 101; districts, establishment of, 20; and George and Tsekelo, 26; land, 22; and Letsie, 22; and Molapo, 22-3, and Nehemiah, 26; policy, 30.
Wodehouse Border Guard, 79.
Wolseley, Sir Garnet, 80, 84, 127, 128.
Women, becoming 'insubordinate', 50; killed in war, 249; labourers on Cape farms, 80; messages from ancestors, 50; prisoners, 150; refugees, 166, 248-9; supplying Basotho regiments, 133; war fever, 134; weeding and harvesting, 162.
Wool, 37, 50.
Woon, Harry Vernon, 'A Colonial Officer', 78, 135-6.
The World, the Flesh and the Devil, 146, 148, 165-6.

Y

Yeomanry, see Cape Mounted Yeomanry.

X

Xhosa, 2, 27, 82, 87, 270.

Z

Zanzibar, 83.
Zonnebloem, 132, 133.
Zulu, Basotho, compared with, 4, 126, 127, 128-9, 132, 133, 163; Basotho, relations with, 82; Marshal Clarke's appointment in Zululand, 258; drought, 118; Frere's view on, 84; Gun War, 138; and Langalibalele, 58; methods of warfare, 4, 127, 128-9; South African Republic, border dispute, 84; Zululand as possible refuge for Basotho, 12, 80; Zulu War, v, 2, 3, 5, 69, 87, 93, 96, 118, 126, 127, 133, 134, 169, 270.
'Zulu' in Basutoland, 27, 28, 45, 48.

OTHER PUBLICATIONS BY MORIJA MUSEUM & ARCHIVES

1. **D.F. Ellenberger** *Catalogue of the Masitise Archives* Edited by Beatrice Lasserre & David Ambrose, 175 by 245mm, 72p, (1987), Softcover ISBN 99911-793-0-5

2. **Thomas Arbousset** *Missionary Excursion into the Blue Mountains* Edited & translated from the French with an introduction & notes by D. Ambrose & A. Brutsch, 175 by 245mm, 219p, (1991), 14 illustrations, 12 maps & 2 sketch plans, Softcover, ISBN 99911-793-2-1 **Out of print**

3. **Eugene Casalis** *The Basutos, or Twenty Three Years in South Africa* Facsimile reprint of the 1861 edition, with an Introductory Essay and Index by Stephen J. Gill, 135 by 200 mm, [45] + xix + 355p + [17], (1992), 29 illustrations, Hardback, ISBN 99911-793-3-x

4. **D.F. Ellenberger & J.C. Macgregor** *History of the Basuto: Ancient & Modern* Facsimile reprint of the 1912 edition, with an Introductory Essay, Comprehensive Index and Large Pocket Map of Historical Place Names by Stephen J. Gill, 150 by 220mm, [55] + xxii + 394p + [37 + map], (1992), Hardback ISBN 99911-793-4-8

5. **David Ambrose** *Maseru: An Illustrated History* 175 by 250mm, 256p (1993), Over 130 illus with 17 maps & plans, Hardback, ISBN 99911-793-5-6

6. **S.J. Gill** *A Short History of Lesotho* Over 80 illustrations & maps, 147 by 210mm, xvi + 266p, (1993), Softcover ISBN 99911-793-6-4

7. **Robin Wells** *An Introduction to the Music of the Basotho* Over 60 musical examples, 152 by 222mm, vii + 338 pages, (1994), Softcover ISBN 99911-793-7-2 **Out of print**

8. **S.J. Gill** *A Guide to Morija* 148mm by 210mm, 36 pages, (1995), 23 illustrations and 2 maps, Softcover, ISBN 99911-793-8-0

9. **R. Fitter & M. Masoabi** *My Fun Book of Lesotho* 210 by 295mm, 72p, (1996)

10. **E.W. Smith** *The Mabilles of Basutoland* Facsimile reprint of 1939 edition (1996), 130 by 195mm, vi + 382p, Hardcover, ISBN 99911-793-9-9

11. **Martin Lelimo** *The Question of Lesotho's Conquered Territory: It's Time for an Answer* 148 by 210mm, x + 211, Softcover, ISBN 99911-632-0-4, (1998)

12. **Peter Sanders** *The Last of the Queen's Men: A Lesotho Experience* 148 by 218mm, 175 pages, Softcover, ISBN1 86814 353 8 (2000) (Published jointly with Wits University Press) **Out of print**

13. **Prof. J.M. Mohapeloa** *Tentative British Imperialism in Lesotho, 1884 – 1910* 160 by 215mm, xx + 437p, (2002)

14. **T. Makoa and A.L. Zwilling** *Shepherd Boy of the Maloti*, 148 by 210mm, 160 pages, (2005), Soft cover with colour illustrations, ISBN 99911-632-3-9

15. **Stephen Gill**, *The Story of Morija Museum & Archives: Pioneers in Heritage Management & Education in Lesotho*, 148 by 210mm, 108 pages (2005), Soft cover w/ many bl & w/colour illustrations, ISBN 99911-632-2-0

16. **Patrick Duncan**, *Sotho Laws & Customs*, 155 by 220mm, viii + 169 pages (2006, facsimile reprint of 1960 edition), Hardback, ISBN 99911-794-0-2

17. **Vernon B. Palmer** *The Roman-Dutch and Sesotho Law of Delict*, 148 by 210mm, 210 pages (2008, facsimile of 1970 ed.), Softcover, ISBN 99911-632-4-7

18. **Craig W. Hincks**, *Quest for Peace, An Ecumenical History of the Church in Lesotho*, 180 by 252mm, xx + 1084 pages [Heads of Churches & Christian Council of Lesotho], Hardcover, ISBN 978-999-110-8018

19. *Mekolokotoane Kerekeng ea Evangeli Lesotho / Jubilee Highlights 1833-2008*, ed. S.J. Gill et.al., 155 by 220mm, xx + 380 pages (2009), Hardcover, ISBN 978-999-11-794-1-4

For information on prices and ordering

Phone (+266) 2236-0324; Fax (+266) 2236-0308
E-mail   morijamuseum@leo.co.ls or sgill@morijafest.com

About the Author

Peter Sanders served as an administrative officer in Lesotho from 1961 to 1966, and his account of that experience was published in 2000 as *The Last of the Queen's Men*. With Mosebi Damane he wrote an edited translation of the praise poems of the Basotho chiefs (1974), and he also wrote a biography of Moshoeshoe (1975). His last publication, jointly with Colin Murray, was a detailed study of medicine murder in colonial Lesotho (2005).